SHELTER FROM THE STORM
THE STORY OF NEW ZEALAND'S BACKCOUNTRY HUTS

The original Routeburn Flats Hut, pictured early in the twentieth century.
PHOTO: S.T. PATERSON COLLECTION, HOCKEN LIBRARY, UNIVERSITY OF OTAGO, P05-014-394

SHELTER FROM THE STORM
THE STORY OF NEW ZEALAND'S BACKCOUNTRY HUTS

SHAUN BARNETT • ROB BROWN • GEOFF SPEARPOINT

craig potton publishing

Dedicated to Arnold Heine for his inspiration and vision; and to all those people who have built, maintained and continue to look after our backcountry huts.

Lee Stanton-Barnett, Kaweka Flats Biv, Kaweka Forest Park, Hawke's Bay, 2008.
PHOTO: SHAUN BARNETT/BLACK ROBIN PHOTOGRAPHY

First published in 2012 by Craig Potton Publishing
Updated and reprinted twice in 2013, and again in 2016

Craig Potton Publishing
98 Vickerman Street, PO Box 555, Nelson, New Zealand
www.craigpotton.co.nz

© Shaun Barnett, Rob Brown and Geoff Spearpoint
© Photographs: individual photographers

Edited by Susi Bailey
Designed by Robbie Burton
Maps by Geographx

ISBN 978 1 877517 70 9

Printed in China by Midas Printing International Ltd

This book is copyright. Apart from any fair dealing for the purposes of private study, research, criticism or review, as permitted under the Copyright Act, no part may be reproduced by any process without the permission of the publishers.

CONTENTS

PREFACE	7
MAPS	8
FOREWORD	10
INTRODUCTION	12

PASTORAL HUTS More than Tin and Timber — 28

Sutherlands Hut	42
Iron Whare	44
Old Manson Hut	46
Hideaway Biv	48
Shutes Hut	50
Ellis Hut	52
Riordans Hut	54
Meg Hut	56
Rangitata/Hakatere Mustering Huts	58
Beech Hut	62
Ida Railway Hut	64
Whariwharangi Hut	66
Avoca Homestead	68

MINING HUTS Refuge Among the Riches — 70

Bullendale Hut	80
Dynamo Hut	82
Asbestos Cottage	84
Cecil Kings Hut	87
Urquharts Hut	90
Glenorchy Scheelite-mining Huts	92
Waingaro Forks Hut	96

HUTS FOR TOURISM & CLIMBING The Mountains of Opportunity — 98

Old Waihohonu Hut	112
Earnslaw Hut	114
Mueller Hut	116
Godley Hut	119
Chancellor Hut	122
Almer Hut	125
Pioneer Hut	128
Flora Hut	132
Sign of the Packhorse	134
Cape Defiance Hut and Castle Rocks Hut	136
Locke Stream Hut	138
Red Hut	140

CLUB HUTS Forging an Identity in the Hills — 142

Field Hut	154
Kime Hut	157
Rangiwahia Hut	160
Powell Hut	162
Howletts Hut	165
Big Hut	168
Cone Hut	171
Aspiring Hut	174
St Winifred Hut	178
Waimakariri Falls Hut	180
Whangaehu Hut	182
Roaring Stag Lodge	184
Boulder Lake Hut, Adelaide Tarn Hut, Lonely Lake Hut	186
Mt Brown Hut	188
Cavalier Hunters Hut	190
Orongorongo Valley Huts	192

DEPARTMENT OF INTERNAL AFFAIRS HUTS Shelter on a Shoestring — 196
Historic Clark Hut — 204
Slaty Creek Hut — 206
Kiwi Hut and Museum Hut — 208
Rogers Hut — 212

NEW ZEALAND FOREST SERVICE HUTS The NZFS Takes Over — 214
West Coast Two-bunk Bivouacs — 228
West Coast Four-bunk Huts — 232
West Coast Six-bunk Huts — 236
Kaweka Forest Park NZFS Huts — 240
Bobs Hut — 242
Lake Sumner Forest Park NZFS Huts — 244
Sunrise Hut — 246
Ruahine Forest Park NZFS Huts — 248
Lower Gridiron Rock Shelter and Upper Gridiron Hut — 251

NATIONAL PARK BOARDS AND LANDS AND SURVEY HUTS Huts for the People — 254
Carrington Hut — 264
Blue Lake Hut, George Lyon Hut, John Tait Hut — 266
Mintaro Hut — 270
Lake Roe Hut — 273
Edwards Hut — 274
Gardiner Hut — 276
Top Forks Hut — 278
Shelter Rock Hut — 280

DEPARTMENT OF CONSERVATION HUTS New Huts, Old Responsibilities — 282
Leitch's Hut — 293
Syme Hut — 294
Zekes Hut — 297
Tarn Ridge Hut — 298
Brewster Hut — 300
Maungahuka Hut — 302
Woolshed Creek Hut — 304

HUTS AS MONUMENTS Memories in the Wilderness — 306
Colin Todd Hut — 310
Hunters Hut — 313
Barker Hut — 314
Esquilant Bivouac — 318
Park Morpeth Hut — 320
Manson-Nicholls Hut — 322

SCIENCE HUTS Research in the Mountains and Bush — 324
Ivory Lake Hut — 327
Cupola Hut — 330
Dominie Biv — 332
Caswell Sound Hut — 334

ENDNOTES — 336
SELECT BIBLIOGRAPHY — 348
ACKNOWLEDGEMENTS — 352
INDEX — 354

PREFACE

Readers might be surprised to find a 364-page book of stories about New Zealand backcountry huts. On the outside huts may seem to be just timber and tin, but through providing shelter, these simple structures act as a focal point for people in the backcountry. Unlike a peak, campsite or river valley, huts collect stories over time like a layered overcoat. The history of building the hut becomes enmeshed with the stories of people and adventures and place.

Selecting ninety huts to profile seemed at first an easy task; after all, this represents less than 10 per cent of the total public huts in the country. But as we compiled a list, we soon came to realise that every hut has its story and almost every hut has its fan – someone for whom it may be their most treasured retreat in the world. To help us narrow down our selection, we carefully chose huts that we felt best represented the full range of age and purpose, right from early farm huts to the latest Department of Conservation designs. These individual hut chapters are arranged in rough chronological order, placed in several sections representing distinct hut-building eras. The timescales spanned by the sections overlap, but together we hope they tell a reasonably coherent story of hut development in New Zealand, while allowing the stories of our selected huts to shine in the individual chapters.

The broad themes of these sections reflect each hut's purpose – who built it and why. Categories include huts built for farming, mining, tourism and climbing, deer-culling, outdoor clubs, scientific research and as monuments. Many huts, of course, were not originally intended to be huts: some were homes, workplaces or hideouts, but have since been retired from their original purpose to become backcountry huts. We decided early on not to feature many private huts, nor ones unavailable for overnight accommodation, but a few are so important from a historical perspective that we could not resist including them.

The tremendous support we have received while researching and writing this book reflects the great affection people have for backcountry huts. So many people shared stories and photographs, and helped with information, that we feel sure our efforts will be worthwhile. We've tried to adopt a thorough, rigorous approach to our research, while retaining a conversational story-telling text. Most facts are referenced through endnotes.

This book, we hope, serves as a monument to the extraordinary efforts of the New Zealanders who built these simple structures in our mountains as shelter from the storm. We've been building huts for over 200 years, and often we've taken them for granted, not recognising the enormous effort required to establish and maintain them. Tramper Elsie K. Morton expressed this during her 1950s visit to Douglas Rock Hut, on the West Coast's Copland Track:

> Of all the hundreds who during the coming years would find warmth and comfort at Douglas Rock Hut, how many, I wondered, would give a thought to the men who packed all the building material, the loads of iron and timber; glass for the windows, frames for the bunks; pots and pans, axes, saws, and even a grindstone for sharpening them, over nearly thirty miles of forest track, river-bed and boulders, up mountain slopes and down, everything having to be packed on the backs of men for the last six miles from Welcome Flat.[1]

Graham McCallum and Mavis Davidson at Douglas Rock Hut, Copland Track, in the 1960s.
PHOTO: MAVIS DAVIDSON COLLECTION, HOCKEN LIBRARY, UNIVERSITY OF OTAGO, MS-2985/373

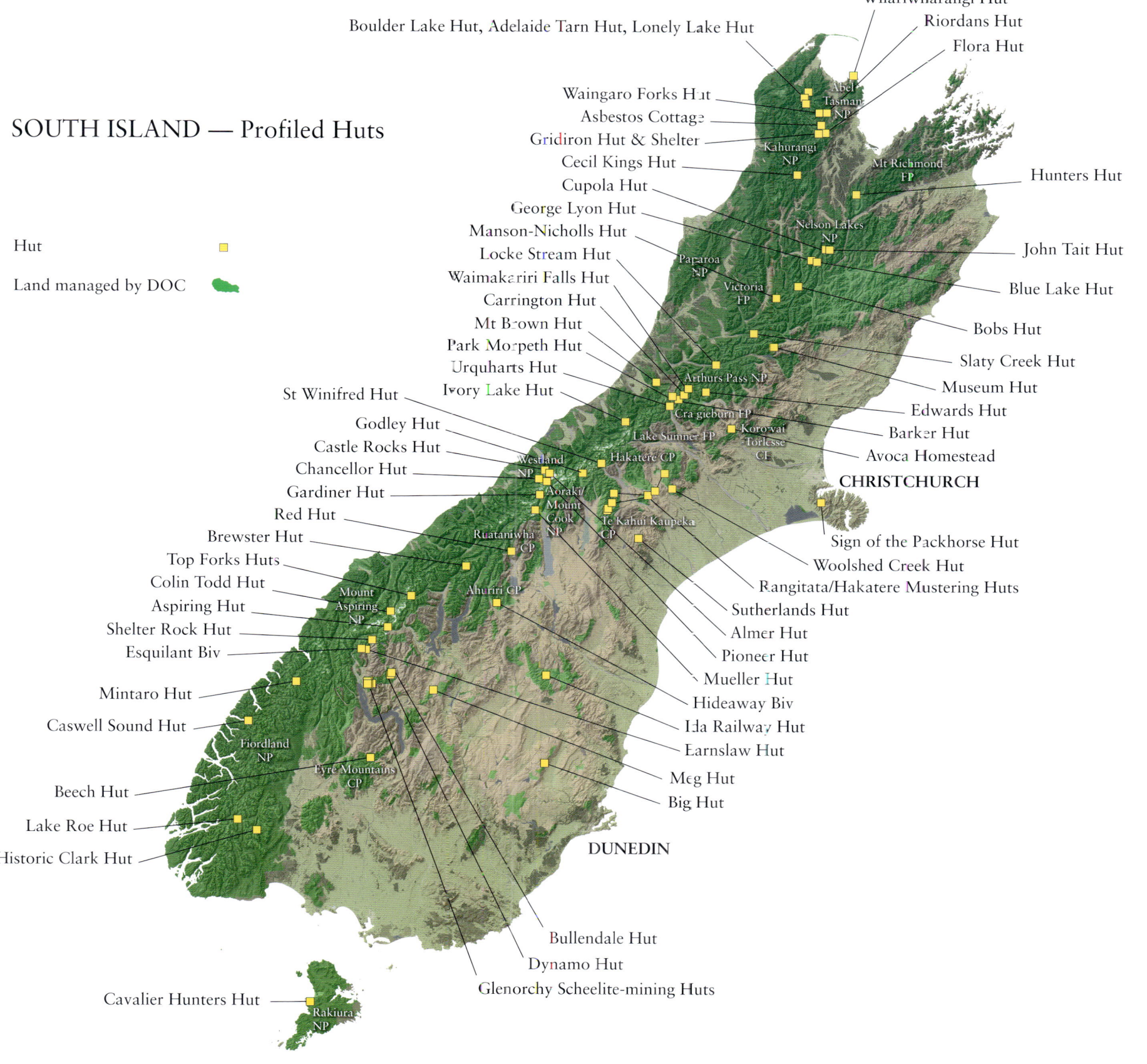

FOREWORD

In New Zealand we are lucky to have such a diversity of natural landscapes, and fortunate indeed that the people who have built our country over the years had the foresight to protect many of these wonderful places.

That foresight is also evident in the efforts made to provide ways for people to enjoy our unique natural heritage in a simple, egalitarian way. Nothing illustrates that better than the provision of backcountry huts. We owe it to future generations to pass this inheritance on for them to enjoy.

When I think of my own journeys into the New Zealand backcountry and mountains, I think of not just of the forests, tussocks, peaks and wildlife, but also of the wild weather and of the relief of reaching a backcountry hut at the end of a long day.

Also special are memories of people I have met and discussions I have had with others also out enjoying what is special about New Zealand. Our backcountry huts are places to meet, talk, and reflect. They have important cultural values – making them far more than mere refuges in the wilderness. They are places where people from all walks of life come together – usually humbled by the weather and landscape they have just been in. They are buildings that have always had an unfailing ability to get to the very core of what it means to be a New Zealander from the moment one walks in the door.

Our backcountry huts uplift our spirit. We feel better when we walk into them. The comradeship they engender makes an impact on us. For all these reasons and more, New Zealand's humble backcountry huts are a vital part of our country's cultural heritage.

Rt Hon. Helen Clark
Tramper, avid ski-tourer, Prime Minister 1999-2008

Nothing has more strength than dire necessity.

That observation captures in many ways the story behind the network of huts that are scattered across the backcountry of New Zealand. There was no grand plan but little by little the necessity of, for example, farming and mustering remote valleys and high mountain pastures saw huts both very basic and more enduring, of all shapes and descriptions find a home away from the eyes of those who only travelled the easy roads.

In other instances they emerged for the desire of others who, while trapped in cities for work, were driven to seek different experiences within nature's grand masterpiece, observing a scale of diversity and beauty that no mortal architect could design. These huts were, in the main, built by tramping clubs who – again driven by the necessity of having a safe place to rest before tomorrow's adventures – overcame the odds to make their contribution to those who seek to explore and enjoy the beauty of the backcountry. Others were built to permit more organised enjoyment of nature's beauty. All serve to enable us and our visitors to experience the emotional liberation of being in vast open spaces or viewing the grandeur of high mountain peaks.

The people who built huts and those who enjoy them are an important part of what makes New Zealand a special place. All societies have myths and the myths that emerge from the huts of New Zealand, the stories that are told and retold, are part of us, whether we have personally experienced the camaraderie of spending time in a hut or not, and they help explain our story.

We will all gain a slightly different insight as to who we are from reading *Shelter from the Storm*.

Rt Hon. Jim Bolger ONZ
Farmer and tramper, Prime Minister 1990-97

If I had to select one image that summed up tramping in New Zealand, it would be the basic hut. Beech leaves, an edelweiss flower or a rushing river might come close, but only the basic tramping hut is truly ubiquitous. Whether you are tramping in Northland, Stewart Island/Rakiura or anywhere in between, you are sure to encounter one.

This is no accident. Trampers and climbers have been building huts ever since they started heading to the hills. The extremes of weather that we all love in the New Zealand mountains make them a necessity, not a luxury. Huts are not just about the weather though. More than any other country in the world, New Zealand has developed a culture that prizes our mountains as a place for quiet enjoyment, rather than viewing them as a place to fear. Humans have created this culture over generations, with the hut at the heart of the interaction. Whether tucked against the bush edge on a river flat, high on an exposed tussock ridge, or anchored to the rock above a glacier, the hut forms the centrepiece of most trips. They are the place where modern-day legends are handed down, where friendships are forged and the fire to explore is kept burning.

The story of the Federated Mountain Clubs of New Zealand parallels the story of huts in New Zealand. Since 1931, the Federated Mountain Clubs have been at the forefront of advocacy for our wild places. Our member clubs have been at the forefront of building, maintaining and caring for our hut network.

We are delighted to contribute to this book. It is the least we can do to keep the stories alive.

Richard Davies
President, Federated Mountain Clubs of New Zealand

In 1987, the fledgling Department of Conservation inherited responsibility for managing a unique network of public backcountry huts that must surely be the most extensive and impressive in the world. DOC gladly shares this responsibility with enthusiastic and dedicated individuals and outdoor clubs throughout the country. DOC values their help, and that assistance will be even more desirable in the years ahead.

These huts belong to the people of New Zealand and outdoor New Zealanders love them. DOC, too, is committed to huts and many DOC staff value working on huts above all other tasks.

Over the years, DOC has done its best to listen to what people want for their huts and has developed 'service standards', committing itself to an ongoing inspection regime and a regular maintenance programme. DOC has worked with others to ensure a sensible and innovative approach is taken to designing new huts, to meeting the required legislation, and to managing risks to huts and people in them, including fire and geological hazards.

In the twenty-five years since DOC was established, a number of huts have come and gone (not always without controversy), but the backcountry hut network is still remarkably intact and in good heart. DOC is delighted to be able to contribute to the publication of a book dedicated to huts. It's a story that deserves to be told.

Brian Dobbie
Recreation and Historic Unit, Department of Conservation

INTRODUCTION

The Value of a Backcountry Hut

Mountain Hut
Rain eases down
Like a gentle strum
On the roof
All wet and dripping
In the forest
Snug and warm are we
In our mountain hideaway
Waiting the passing
Of the storm
Roaring fire
Licks blackened billy
Chasing damp from our socks
While we contemplate
Our next brew …
Simple delights
In a simple world

I wrote this poem in January 1993 during four storm-bound days in Pell Stream Hut, near Lewis Pass. I'd been surveying kiwi in the area with two companions, when a persistent nor'wester swept over the country. Not able to survey in the wet conditions, and unable to get down the flooded Pell Stream, we simply waited out the tempest at the hut.

Pell Stream Hut, a standard six-bunk Forest Service design built in 1961, eight years before I was born, was a bit rusty, a bit run down, but adequate enough for shelter. Rain fell with a relentlessness I've rarely witnessed for such an extended period, but to us it didn't matter much. Inside we played cards, read, slept, ate and generally enjoyed life at a slow, contemplative pace. For a few days, the simple shelter became our entire world, and by the time the storm passed and we could head out, I'd grown rather fond of the hut.

I started tramping in the mountains of Hawke's Bay during the mid-1980s.

McGregor Biv and the Waiohine Valley from near McGregor, Tararua Forest Park, Wairarapa, 2011. PHOTO: SHAUN BARNETT/BLACK ROBIN PHOTOGRAPHY

Back then, Kaweka Forest Park huts simply meant shelter to me, places to doss down for the night before trudging on. The four walls and a roof of huts allowed tramping without the need to lug a tent. The Kaweka Range boasted about thirty huts, mostly built by the Forest Service, which then still managed the area. Beyond that, I didn't give much more thought to huts than to the trash I tossed into the adjacent rubbish pits.

Twenty-five years on, I have an appreciation of huts that extends far beyond their value as shelters from the storm. Huts mean many things: destinations, incentives to get out into the hills, repositories of outdoor history and stories, and monuments to various styles of backcountry architecture, from the spartan to the elaborate.

Other countries also have hut networks, but there is probably nowhere else in the world with such an extensive collection of simple public huts as New Zealand. Australia has a good smattering of huts in Tasmania, Victoria and the Snowy Mountains, but the vast extent of the continent has very few. The European Alps and Norway's mountains also have large hut networks, but their huts are usually run more like hostels, with a permanent warden and often with food and bedding available.

In his book *A Tramper's Journey* (2004), Mark Pickering says that unlatching the door of a backcountry hut at the end of a day's tramping feels 'like a homecoming'.[1] I, too, love arriving at a backcountry hut. Imagine the scene: the hut lies on the far side of a clearing, a square orange shape. Behind it, slopes rise to open scree summits, while tongues of beech forest stretch down from spurs on either side. A small stream burbles its way through the clearing and past the hut.

By its colour and shape, the hut contrasts strongly with its surroundings. Yet at the same time, it's perfect in this landscape – its small size serving to better define the scale of the surrounding mountains. It forms a potent yet humble symbol of human endeavour in the otherwise natural setting.

Although I've never been here before, it's somehow familiar and reassuring. Hundreds of others like it exist in the backcountry, each one slightly different. The setting, the position and little design details all make each hut distinctive.

I stride across the clearing, shrubs brushing my gaiters, and reach the hut. I snip back the bolt and slip inside. The aroma of past fires filters into my nostrils,

Pell Stream Hut, Lewis Pass National Reserve, May 2008. PHOTO: GEOFF SPEARPOINT

First and foremost, people appreciate huts because New Zealand's climate is extremely tempestuous and frequently wet, particularly so in the mountains. The Cropp, a tributary of the West Coast's Whitcombe River, holds the record for the highest annual rainfall in New Zealand: 18 metres, making it one of the wettest places in the world.[2] It's not the only wet place in New Zealand though – Fiordland, Mt Taranaki and the Tararua Range also receive extraordinary amounts of rainfall. Even in the drier eastern mountains of the South Island, the weather can turn very nasty very quickly: the coldest parts of the country are up in the central Otago ranges. New Zealand's highly changeable climate increases the value of a hut immensely.

For some, the combination of poor weather and scenery on such a grand scale can seem forbidding, as tramper Elsie K. Morton found during a trip up Westland's Copland Valley in the 1950s:

> Almost terrifying in its utter loneliness and isolation was this high, remote valley, yet not so terrifying at a second glance, for there, just ahead, was a little wooden cottage with a wide, hospitable fireplace that bespoke warmth, good cheer – and the immediate promise of cups and cups of good, hot tea! Never was the site of a mountain hut more happily named than Welcome Flat.[3]

along with a slightly musty smell – no one has been here for a while. I shed my pack onto a bunk, open the window a fraction and haul out the burner for a brew. Then it's time to peruse the hut book. Who has been here before me? What adventures did they record?

Every hut has its own story, its own questions. Who built it? Why? How? Did anyone maintain it, or was it simply left to rot once its main purpose had faded? Who visited? What did they do here?

Shelter from the Storm

People go into the bush and mountains to tramp, hunt, fish and climb, or any number of other reasons, not necessarily just to stay in a hut. So why do huts captivate people so? Perhaps it's because they symbolise the wider experience of the outdoors: they provide a waypoint on a journey, a link with other trampers, a destination in their own right, a refuge where you can hang up your boots for a while and watch the weather.

For mountaineers, the shelter offered by huts is often not just a matter of comfort, but sometimes the difference between life and death. During the 1970s, renowned climber Bill Denz made a habit of establishing bold new routes, often in the coldest months of the year. He was the first to venture into the Hooker Valley of Mount Cook National Park in winter, where the original Empress Hut stood, dwarfed by the giant ice-festooned face of Mt Hicks. The hut may have been small and rough, but after a stormy descent from Mt Hicks in 1974, Denz found salvation there:

> We brave the sand-blasting wind to peer down the South Face, our next objective. Phil [Herron] is thrilled by its steepness and oppressive air. Our abseil down from the saddle, in darkness and blinding wind, is an eventful one, but soon we are at Empress Hut – that damp, cramped little shack, our haven away from it all, where we lie under a pile of heavy blankets and sip our fifth cup of tea.[4]

It's no exaggeration to claim that huts enabled the climbers of the 1970s to launch themselves up unclimbed faces once considered impossible. By staying in the huts, they didn't have to carry tents, and could use blankets in lieu of a sleeping bag.

People value huts as shelters, but that's not the whole story. Tents provide shelter too, but during a storm you can exist in a hut with a degree of comfort that is simply not possible in a tent. Mountaineer Paul Powell summed this up superbly:

> There's nothing so pleasant as preparing the meal in a back-country hut. You're relaxed and you know that for a few hours at least you're free from important decisions. Let it rain, thunder or snow. Provided the roof stays on the hut and the cooking-pots keep bubbling you don't worry. You don't care if the river floods or the wind blows itself inside out. The worse the weather, the more you revel in your temporary home. Like small boys safe from the bullies in a favourite hideout, you rejoice all the more.[5]

Tararua Tramping Club member John Gates also expressed this simple quality of huts in the 1961 club annual *Tararua*:

> Ignoring the purist who can bypass a hut even in bad weather for the philosophical comfort of a wet tent or melting snow cave, let us be human and admit that the rest of us would rather cross a welcoming threshold when the alternatives are rain, wind and cold as tempting bed companions.[6]

Although Gates enjoyed the shelter of a hut over a tent, he didn't want too much luxury. Writing during the 1960s, he always rated Cone Hut above its nearby alternative down the valley, Tauherenikau Hut: 'Cone, being smaller, darker, and further from the road, contrasts more with our homes and offices.'[7]

Huts then, are about shelter, but many trampers and hunters don't want them too flash. The outdoor experience provides a welcome contrast to our daily lives, and that's why so many people value simple, basic huts. That's not to say a rustic hut appeals to everyone. For many older trampers and family groups, there is no doubt that some of the modern, warm DOC huts serve a valuable purpose in enabling them to enjoy their experience more.

Huts also offer a destination for the curious. In her 1993 Masters thesis *Back-country Huts, More Than a Roof Over Your Head*, Lincoln University student Robin Quigg identified huts as a motivating factor for people to go into the mountains. As one tramper stated, 'If I know there is a hut there then I'd go there because it is like a stopping point drawing you in.'[8]

Huts as a Social Experience

Huts also provide the important social nucleus of the outdoor experience. Over the course of a tramp or hunt, people disperse over the track or mountainside but come together again at night within the confines of the hut. With people inside it, a hut develops a personality. John Gates recalled the tramping days of the 1950s in a crowded Tararua hut with everyone cooking, talking and singing: 'Te Matawai Hut is never quite the same as when chock-a-block with dripping, steaming trampers secretly cooking breakfast straight after tea in order to be first away for a "northern" [crossing]. Empty it is quite a lonely, chilly place.'[9]

Public huts, by their very nature – unlocked and open to all – encourage some degree of egalitarianism. In any hut, particularly the accessible ones on the Great Walks, large groups of trampers gather in the evening after a satisfying day's walk and rub shoulders with people from all branches of society. At night, after everyone dosses down in their sleeping bags, all must endure the rumbles of the snorer, the rustles of those reorganising their gear or the patter of rodents. The communal nature of sleeping in a hut is rather like staying on a marae; indeed, the term 'Maori bunks' is sometimes used for a sleeping platform.[10]

How Many Huts?

DOC has close to 1000 backcountry huts on its records: about 700 in the South Island and about 300 in the North Island. Tramper and hut enthusiast Mark Pickering reckons another 400 to 500 huts lie on pastoral lease stations in the South Island. The exact number of DOC huts changes from year to year, as high-country huts are added from tenure review, old huts become derelict, new ones get built, and some burn down or are washed away in floods. Fire is a persistent threat to huts, and on average one burns down every year.

After DOC, the New Zealand Alpine Club manages the next largest number of huts: seventeen, including base huts. The Canterbury Mountaineering Club, the Tararua Tramping Club and the New Zealand Deerstalkers' Association also have fine records of building and maintaining huts. A myriad of clubs have just one or two huts – Hawke's Bay's Heretaunga Tramping Club maintains the popular Howletts Hut in the Ruahines, while the Canterbury University Tramping Club manages Avoca Hut in Craigieburn Forest Park.

A surprising number of private huts are also secreted on conservation lands, some known only to those who built them, but others legally sanctioned. The fifty or so club ski huts at Iwikau Village on Mt Ruapehu are one example, and Caroline Hut, near Ball Pass, is another. Other locked club huts exist in the Waitakere Ranges, but by far the largest concentration occurs in the Orongorongo Valley in Wellington's Rimutaka Forest Park.

This egalitarianism has been a feature of huts since New Zealand's early colonial days, as Jock Phillips wrote in his 1996 book *A Man's Country?* Although 'major contrasts of wealth, power, and lifestyle' existed in colonial New Zealand, the backcountry provided a levelling effect:

> Yet when men left settled society and entered the frontier world of tents and huts, it became increasingly difficult to maintain the symbols of class distinction. 'Posh' clothes were an encumbrance or quickly became dirty; there was simply no chance of being served fine food or living in splendid style. The itinerancy and lack of specialisation of frontier labour broke down hierarchies within the working class.[11]

Phillips notes, for example, that Charles Money came from English upper-class origins, but in the Canterbury high country found himself among a wide variety of men. 'But in the men's hut, where Money preferred to mix, his social status counted for little. There his willingness to share a pipe around the fire was the level of expectation.'[12]

Early hut designs also reflected issues of gender and social etiquette. Many of the first climbing and tourism huts built in the Southern Alps during the late nineteenth and early twentieth centuries had separate quarters for men and women simply as a matter of privacy, in keeping with the social norms of the time. During the 1920s, however, tramping clubs often dispensed with this formality as it was simply too impractical to build huts that way.

Most clubs welcomed both men and women, but not all. For instance, the Canterbury Mountaineering Club (CMC) did not at first allow women to join as they felt that doing so might restrict not only men's activities but also their behaviour. While tongue-in-cheek, this comment by club stalwart Nui Robins reflected the views of some CMC members in the 1920s and 1930s:

> Twenty six people emerged with their impedimenta from the train at the Bealey corner and struggled as fast as riding breeches and ill-fitted puttees would allow up to Carrington [Hut] in order to get a bunk. Twenty five failed to arrive in time and had to bed down on the floor. That was not the worst. Two more people arrived – one a woman who despoiled the purity of our monastic organisation by entering the hut. Horrid thought, it appeared she might even stay the night. She didn't, thanks to her brother's kindly provision of a tent which he pitched for her just outside the adjective range of the hut.[13]

Today, the CMC has moved on, and includes women presidents and top female climbers in its ranks.

The early tramping, climbing and hunting clubs knew only too well the value of huts for shelter, as precious few existed during their early forays into

Trampers at Carrington Hut II, Arthur's Pass National Park, 1960s. PHOTO: RICK WATSON

mountain country. Clubs also soon learnt that building a club hut united members more than virtually any other activity. It created a different sort of camaraderie to tramping or hunting together; the shared purpose and sense of developing the backcountry ensured club members took deserved pride in their huts. Through hard toil and a great sense of accomplishment, hut building forged strong clubs and lasting friendships.

Cameron Hut in Canterbury's Hakatere Conservation Park provides an example of this extraordinary effort. CMC members built the hut over three weekends in 1953. On the first weekend, a group of six, led by Nui Robins, packed material up to the hut site, dumped their loads, then walked out for three hours, before repeating the procedure with fresh loads the next day. Another member of the hut-building party, J. Walton, described the weekend's efforts:

> The packers were well spread out and crosstrees of timber or iron could be seen floating up the river bed, bobbing along the flats and dumping themselves heavily when the human 'uprights' collapsed for a breather ... With shoulders sore, backs screaming, sunburn tingling and sweat constantly running into their eyes they scrambled on. Steep short climbs, traverses, slippery snow grass and large boulders were very nearly the last straw and the packers were very tired when they finally 'collapsed' at the site.[14]

While some packers performed such impressive feats to establish backcountry huts, they usually didn't do so out of any perverse sense of pain or pride. If alternative means of transport – packhorses or trucks – were available, people used them. After the Second World War, a number of huts were even built using ex-Army Bren gun carriers.[15]

Huts like Cameron remain as symbols that the mountains are not just empty scenery, but places of effort and activity, of human endeavour and enterprise. Hut building creates something for the common good, allowing people to gather and enjoy the bush and mountains.

A Refuge from Urban Life

For many people, huts are not just a refuge from mountain weather, but also a refuge from the commerce and busyness of our everyday lives. We go into the hills to escape from the pressures of urban life, retreating to an environment where the world is more natural and we can re-create ourselves. Huts are not essential to this need by any means; many people seek the remoteness and solitude of a wilderness camp. But for those without the skills or inclination to travel through untracked terrain, a hut provides a level of comfort.

Some people have even found huts to be a permanent refuge from society. Robert Long, also known as Beansprout, sought an alternative life – not away from people, but away from what he viewed as the evils of society – and wrote about it in his bestselling book *A Life on Gorge River* (2010). He began living in Gorge

Cameron Hut, built by the Canterbury Mountaineering Club, pictured in 1952.
PHOTO SUPPLIED BY RAY CHAPMAN

River Hut, an abandoned mining hut in remote south Westland, in 1980, and has even raised a family there with his wife, Catherine Stewart.

Yet others have sought refuge in huts for different reasons, even to escape the law, like suspected murderer James Ellis, who hid in the Ruahine hut that now bears his name. During the Second World War, the occasional deserting soldier also tried to evade authorities by hiding in huts. And at least one pair escaped to a mountain hut for love. The extraordinary Chaffeys of Asbestos Cottage lived in their prospecting hut for over three decades, after both escaped failed marriages.

Hut Diversity

Diversity is another important aspect of New Zealand huts, which reflect a range of designs and settings. A hut's style often speaks of the era in which it was built and the purpose for which it was used. Huts come in all shapes, sizes, colours and locations. Some are ugly; others are works of art. While a few bivs are so small you can only crawl into them, some of the large Great Walks huts sport flushing toilets and separate warden's quarters. Opinion on design and colour is, of course, varied. Some people love the classic orange of the old Forest Service huts, while others find green and brown a more acceptable backcountry tone. While opinions differ, everyone appreciates the diversity.

Some huts boast spectacular settings, which were chosen expressly for their ability to impress. For example, Cape Defiance Hut was built in 1913, during the early days of tourism, on the lower slopes of a bold headland jutting out into the Franz Josef Glacier. Elsie K. Morton was suitably awed by its location during her 1950s visit:

> A final scramble over the rough ice of the lateral moraine, a stiff climb up the shingly hillside, and we reached a little track leading up to a clearing in the bush, and to Defiance Hut, snugly set on a narrow ledge, with Mount Moltke rising dark and high above, and the frozen waves of the glacier plunging down into the valley below.[16]

Early huts were not usually salubrious. Some made up in character for what they lacked in comfort, but others fell well short. Glazebrook Hut, on Marlborough's Waihopai Station, failed to charm Wildlife Officer Ken Francis during the winter he spent there in the 1930s:

> Made of corrugated iron and unlined, it had an earth floor which froze if the fire went out for too long. The fireplace was huge and would take small logs, and there were bunks for three men, made of sacking, and the 'mattresses' were tussock grass. We added deerskins for additional warmth and soon got used to the smell. There was only one small window so, unless the door was open, the interior was rather dark. Water was drawn from the adjacent creek and manuka firewood from the hillside.[17]

Huts resulting from club efforts were not always works of architectural brilliance either. One bush poet described Heretaunga Tramping Club's Kiwi Saddle Hut (built in 1946) with this ditty:

This here shack must be about the roughest;
In the whole of the Kaweka Range,
Strictly designed for the toughest,
The architecture is rugged and strange.[18]

Many backcountry huts have expansive views, while yet others lie tucked away in tiny forest clearings. Whatever their location, these mostly simple shelters help to define New Zealand's outdoors, distinguishing it from other mountain areas of the world.

The Accumulation of Stories

Perhaps the least acknowledged quality of huts is their ability to act as a depository of backcountry knowledge and stories that might otherwise be lost. Older huts gather stories according to the changing use to which they have been put. They may, like Hideaway Biv (in Canterbury's Ahuriri Conservation Park), have begun as a mustering hut on a station, then been abandoned after sheep grazing became uneconomic, and finally became sufficiently venerable to attract the attention of DOC heritage specialists. Some of these huts feature the scrawled names of visitors etched with pencil or penknife onto their roof and walls, written before the idea of hut books became widespread.

Even historic huts are not simple museum pieces, but living structures that still have a function as shelter. Yet other huts become so strongly identified with a particular individual that their name is for ever associated with it. Other huts form monuments to those who have died: Fenella Hut in Kahurangi National Park and Colin Todd Hut in Mount Aspiring National Park are examples. Through the hut logbook, stories accumulate over time, providing a sense of ongoing community.

A Brief History of Huts

Huts as Home

Huts have served as shelter ever since Maori first stepped onto the shores of Aotearoa. Temporary whare served as seasonal bases for hunting and fishing expeditions to the coast and mountains. Maori used rock shelters or caves where they existed, and elsewhere made an art form of erecting temporary shelters

Huts as home: a man outside his canvas hut, probably Ohingaiti or Rangitikei.
PHOTO: EDWARD GEORGE CHILD, ALEXANDER TURNBULL LIBRARY, WELLINGTON, A G-32338-1/2

quickly and efficiently using whatever materials were on hand – tree bark and fern fronds served particularly well. Of more permanent huts, ethnographer Elsdon Best wrote this description:

> The term 'house' comes naturally to the point of the pen, but in many cases native habitations can only be described as 'huts'. The Maori strove to make his hut a warm retreat in winter on account of his lack of *kaka moe* (sleeping-garments), but comfort in other ways he never evolved; the native hut was a cheerless abode. The lack of a chimney meant that merely a small fire could be kept burning, and that the smoke from such fire was a source of great discomfort – or at least it would be to us.[19]

New Zealand's earliest European building was erected in the 1790s in Fiordland's Dusky Sound by sealers.[20] Later, European settlers often lived in huts

Hut Logbooks

Unlike tracks or bridges, huts hold a record of the visitors who pass through them in the form of hut logbooks, which include details of past trips, events, people and experiences. This informal record provides a sort of cultural history, particularly for lesser used huts, where logbooks may span a decade or more.

Hawke's Bay hunter and bush poet Lester Masters knew the value of hut logbooks for recording stories, and in the 1950s installed logbooks and holders in several Ruahine huts; the one for Ellis Hut featured two skulls on the cover. He neatly summed up their purpose with this ditty:

> Please write down brief what you have seen,
> Tell of the weather and the chase,
> The luck you've had, and where you've been,
> Then park the book safe in the case;
> So that maybe when some man's son
> Comes drifting in from off the spur,
> He'll read what you have seen and done
> When you were here in days that were.[21]

Palmerston North tramper Tony Gates continued this tradition with a beautifully etched logbook case for Howletts Hut, engraved with the Ruahine Tramping Club's logo by Fred Lemberg. Gates has also collected much poetry and quotes from Ruahine, Kaweka and Tararua hut logbooks, ranging from the sublime to the crude. There's nothing quite so enjoyable as arriving at a hut, perusing the contents of its logbook, and gleaning any amusing entries about past adventures and follies.

Hut logbooks on Stewart Island/Rakiura make frequent references – not usually complimentary – to mud. A Canadian tramper drew a picture of Yoda from *Star Wars* in one logbook and wrote, 'Worry NOT tired tramper, mud is friend of Jedi. It makes you strong in the mind. Hmmm … Yes!'

Sometimes there is even a broken dialogue between successive hut occupants. One of my personal favourites came from Middy Hut in Mt Richmond Forest Park. One disgruntled tramper made this plea: 'Please don't be an idiot. Don't leave your rubbish around this nice hut.' The next entry read: 'Ahhh, Grasshopper, so much Anger.'

Hut logbooks also provide useful information in the event of a search, as well as visitation statistics for hut managers. Unfortunately, a fair proportion of hut visitors do not sign logbooks, whether for reasons of avoiding hut fees, a dislike of records or simply forgetfulness. In the Nelson conservancy, DOC adds about 25 per cent on visitation stats to compensate for this shortfall.

Many early huts, notably mustering huts, often did not have logbooks, and instead visitors scrawled their names on the walls. Hideaway Biv and the Old Waihohonu Hut remain good examples of this, with graffiti preserved on both, inside and out.

Other huts had logbooks right from the outset. Archives New Zealand holds a copy of a logbook dating between 1914 and 1930 from Cape Defiance Hut, an early tourism hut on the West Coast built in 1913. Two members of the Beaglehole family visited the Franz Josef Glacier in 1917 and wrote in the Cape Defiance logbook, 'An entirely new and beautiful experience.'[22]

The Forest Service developed its own standard hut logbooks, dun in colour, during the 1970s, and DOC continued with its own green ones in the 1990s. These logbooks have become progressively more prescribed, with columns for specific details, and this certainly aids hut managers in recording information and statistics. But it does, to a certain degree, inhibit the creativity and free-flow that used to dominate logbooks.

Hut logbooks can be a rich source of informal backcountry history, but until recently there has been little consistency over preserving them after they become full. Some historic ones are held in museums, DOC offices, libraries and archives, but many have simply been thrown away. Bill Keir recently began a hut logbook inventory, which is accessible online.[23]

before they built more substantial homes, or erected huts in which to base themselves while employed in such occupations as bush felling and gum digging. Virtually none of these huts survive. The ongoing existence of a hut largely depends on use. A needed and used hut will persist; an abandoned one soon falls down and rots.

Farm Huts

The oldest existing huts in New Zealand were built for farming purposes during the early days of pastoral agriculture in the South Island. High-country farmers may have found pleasure in walking, but they didn't stroll simply for the fun of it. It was more a means to an end, as were the huts they built. Many used local stone, and the survival of these huts owes much to the durability of this material, along with their locations on the more easterly (drier) side of the Southern Alps.

Farm huts often served as accommodation for hunters employed by farmers to control wild dogs, rabbits or pigs, an example being the Iron Whare in the Kawekas. It's difficult to imagine now, but wild dogs – probably the progeny of Maori kuri and escaped Pakeha dogs – once roamed the mountains in menacing packs, and they found sheep an easy target. After rabbits reached plague proportions in the South Island, many farmers found it cheaper to employ rabbiters and house them in huts than to suffer the loss of grazing.

Mining and Road-building Huts

From the late 1850s onwards, gold prospectors also built ramshackle affairs from which they could toil over their pans and cradles, but very few from the earliest gold-mining period now survive. Most of those that still do exist, like Cecil Kings and Waingaro Forks huts (both in Kahurangi National Park), date from the 1930s, when the Depression spurred a brief flush of reworking old gold sites.

Road builders and men maintaining water races also lived in huts, some of which have survived. Jacks Hut, a one-time roadman's hut at Arthur's Pass, has in recent years been preserved beautifully, but it's more a museum piece than a backcountry hut. However, Blowfly Hut, once a roadman's hut on the West Coast's Haast–Paringa Track, serves as a public hut.

Huts for Tourism and Recreation

It's difficult to pinpoint which hut was the first erected purely for recreation. In 1882, English climber William Spotswood Green pioneered mountaineering in New Zealand with his attempt on Aoraki/Mt Cook. Green later urged New Zealanders to form their own alpine club so that they might devote 'the subscriptions to building a few huts in certain centres of [the] Southern Alps'.[24]

As the fledgling tourist industry grew in New Zealand, huts for recreation came onto the agenda. During the 1890s, the government paid for huts to be

The restored roadman's hut, Jacks Hut, Arthur's Pass National Park, Canterbury, 2004. Built in 1879, it is a rare example of a roadman's cottage. It served as a bach for the Butler family for many decades from 1923. SHAUN BARNETT/BLACK ROBIN PHOTOGRAPHY

built at Aoraki/Mount Cook and on the Milford Track, and many more were erected over the ensuing decades. Some of these huts have now been rebuilt several times. Pioneer Hut in Westland Tai Poutini National Park, for example, has had five incarnations spanning eighty years.

Club Huts

After the First World War there was renewed enthusiasm for outdoor pursuits. During the 1920s and 1930s, many tramping clubs formed in New Zealand, in addition to the already existing New Zealand Alpine Club, part of an international movement that saw interest in mountain walking flourish. Many members saw building a hut as a rite of passage for their club. The New Zealand Deerstalkers' Association (NZDA) was formed in 1937, and soon built its own huts too. Through the activities of clubs, huts in a wide range of designs and materials sprang up over the backcountry in a largely ad hoc fashion.

Before helicopters arrived in New Zealand, club members toiled to build these huts in ways that are now almost unimaginable. Even after planes began to be used for transporting material in the late 1940s, most clubs could not afford them and simply continued using traditional means: hard slog on foot.

To some extent a hut also served as a symbol of ownership, a way for a club to stamp its name on its patch. Neither clubs nor government agencies are immune to this desire. But overall, constructing public huts is a nice form of democracy, and most clubs were driven by an eagerness to do something for the greater good. Providing open huts, freely available to all-comers, also helped clubs to recruit new trampers.

Government Huts for Deer Cullers and National Parks

Coinciding with the golden age of clubs in New Zealand in the 1930s was the beginning of deer culling by the Department of Internal Affairs (DIA). One scientist described it as the 'biggest control campaign against large mammals ever undertaken in the world', and it lasted more than forty years.[25] Hut building was not a priority at first, but later on the DIA did build a significant number of huts and also pioneered the use of planes to air-drop materials.

Between the 1950s and 1970s, a great hut-building boom swept New Zealand, instigated by the New Zealand Forest Service (NZFS) when it took over deer control from the DIA in 1956. It was the NZFS that populated the backcountry with its now classic six- and four-bunk designs.

During the 1960s and 1970s, the Department of Lands and Survey, through the national park boards, augmented the number of facilities by building huts in the national parks it managed, which were often larger than the huts built by the NZFS. The impact of all these new huts on outdoor recreation, together with the construction of attendant tracks and bridges, was nothing short of transformational, and helped drive a second tramping boom in the 1970s.

After commercial helicopter hunting took over from ground culling in the late 1960s, the Forest Service – somewhat in rivalry with Lands and Survey – built larger huts too. Some, like the twenty-bunk Holdsworth Lodge, built near the road end in Tararua Forest Park, were aimed at school groups and signalled that the NZFS was now taking provision of recreation facilities very seriously.

The DOC Era

After Lands and Survey and the Forest Service were disbanded in 1987, the Department of Conservation (DOC) was formed, marking the first time a single body, rather than several, managed New Zealand's conservation lands – and huts. Unfortunately, DOC received only limited government funding at first, despite having even greater responsibilities than its parent departments. Consequently, some facilities – including huts – went through a period of neglect. As always, however, passionate DOC staff made do on shoestring budgets and undertook some superb maintenance work in many backcountry areas.

The changing nature of New Zealand's population, combined with the increasing numbers of tourists visiting the country, also had implications for backcountry huts. Up until the 1970s, the backcountry was still very much the domain of New Zealanders. During the 1980s, however, when cheap international flights became available, a growing tourist backpacker movement discovered New Zealand's tracks. The trickle of overseas visitors suddenly became a flood. Many enjoyed long stays in New Zealand, with huts providing the cheapest form of holiday accommodation possible. Recognising this trend early

Wilderness: A Backlash Against Huts

If any single measure exists of how successful the combined Forest Service and Lands and Survey hut-building programme was in changing the nature of the New Zealand backcountry, it is the counter-culture 'wilderness' movement that reached its crescendo in the early 1980s. Forest Service ranger Athol Geddes, whose team built nearly two dozen huts in the Tararuas between 1960 and the mid-1970s, recalled, 'Sometimes we copped a bit of flak from the tramping clubs. They said we were making the Tararuas too safe!'[26]

As early as the 1960s, some people within the Federated Mountain Clubs felt there was a very real danger that all these huts and tracks would erode the very wild and remote nature of the many mountainous parts of New Zealand's backcountry. Calls for the establishment of 'wilderness areas' culminated in a landmark 1981 conference hosted by FMC at Lake Rotoiti Lodge, Nelson Lakes. Participants included not only tramping and climbing club members, but policymakers, Forest Service and Lands and Survey managers, and politicians. Two years later, FMC's influential book *Wilderness Recreation in New Zealand* appeared, edited by articulate wilderness advocate Les Molloy. Molloy's early life was strongly shaped by trips to remote places like the Olivine Ice Plateau, and he firmly believed that New Zealand needed some places free from all human infrastructure, including huts, tracks and bridges. The book identified ten such areas, ranging from the Raukumara Range near East Cape to the Pegasus area of Stewart Island/Rakiura.

As early as the 1950s and 1960s, wilderness areas were established within Arthur's Pass and Tongariro national parks, but these were small and inadequate. In 1974, Lands and Survey had already responded to the call for larger wilderness areas by establishing two (the Glaisnock and Pembroke) in Fiordland National Park. After the FMC conference, the Forest Service responded positively with two more, the Raukumara and Tasman (Northwest Nelson), although these were not finally gazetted until 1988. Since then, six of the ten areas identified in the book have been gazetted as wilderness: places where trampers can meet nature purely on nature's terms, without even a track to lead them there.

Forest Service deer cullers G. Savage and H. Maunder in a hut, 1964.
PHOTO: JOHN JOHNS, NZFS COLLECTION, ARCHIVES NZ, WELLINGTON, M9756

Hut Fees

Many trampers believe the introduction of hut fees coincided with the formation of DOC in 1987. They have, however, been around for much longer; DOC merely initiated a consistent nationwide fee policy. Charging for the use of huts was not a new idea: tourist tracks like the Milford imposed fees right from their beginning in the late 1890s, and the same applied to the first huts established in the Aoraki/Mount Cook area.

In the early years of the Tararua Tramping Club in the 1920s and 1930s, it decided not to charge for the use of its huts, viewing this as a reciprocal arrangement with other clubs. However, during the Depression fees provided essential revenue for other huts. In 1930, for example, the Mt Balloon Scenic Reserve Board charged 1 shilling for Flora and Salisbury huts in Northwest Nelson,[27] and at the same time the cost of hut fees was a major point of contention in the Aoraki/Mount Cook area. During the 1940s, a 1-shilling fee also applied to the Port Levy Saddle Hut in Canterbury.

The New Zealand Alpine Club has charged overnight fees right from when it built its first hut in 1931. At the same time, the Mt Egmont Alpine Club charged modest fees for an overnight stay at Syme Hut. During the 1970s, Syme's fees rose to $1.25 for non-members and $1 for members, and included a 10¢ day-use charge.[28] Most tramping clubs, however, didn't charge fees, although sometimes club parties would deny access to private hunters, but only if the hut was full.

In the 1960s, national park boards charged modest fees for most huts in national parks, including Nelson Lakes and Abel Tasman. This was a small attempt at some cost recovery from the boards, which did not have the resources of the Forest Service. Geoff Spearpoint, who was working in national parks in the 1980s, remembers that charges were nominal when introduced, but escalated: 'Setting the fee was a bit arbitrary; there wasn't much alignment between costs and charges. During this time the $2 fee for Routeburn huts doubled to $4.'[29]

Forest Service huts were free, a fact not lost on either Lands and Survey or the fee-avoiding public. The working plan for Northwest Nelson Forest Park in 1965–70 clearly stated: 'No charge shall be made for use of any huts in the park, but donations may be accepted and used towards the upkeep of huts.'[30] However, by 1979 hut fees were accepted in principal by the Northwest Nelson State Forest Park Advisory Committee,[31] and were finally introduced to the park in July 1986, the year before DOC was formed.[32]

In 1989, DOC introduced the first nationwide hut fee system, based on hut standards: the more facilities, the higher the fee. A brief history of DOC published in 2007 recorded: 'The fee system for national park huts and DOC campgrounds was extended to forest park huts in 1989 and 1990, to general public outcry at having to pay $4 a night, and later grudging acceptance.'[33] The fee for a basic hut has since risen to $5.

Although some grumbled at the charges, and complained that they had already paid for huts through their taxes, no one could deny the enormous cost to DOC of maintaining such a large network. Later, an annual hut pass was introduced, to cover all but Alpine, Category 1 and Great Walks huts. Hut fees help offset maintenance costs, but by no means cover it. Compliance at many huts is often disappointingly low, except where resident hut wardens enforce payment.

Costs for staying in Great Walk huts rose steadily during the first years of the twenty-first century, to $51.10/night for the Milford Track in 2012. However, in 2008, after protests from Federated Mountain Clubs and others that the cost to families had become prohibitively high, DOC promptly abolished fees for under-eighteens.[37]

The NZAC's Murchison Hut, Aoraki/Mount Cook National Park, November 1977.
PHOTO: BRUCE POSTILL

on, DOC gave 'front country' areas more attention and developed the concept of Great Walks, making use of popular tracks like the Heaphy, Tongariro Northern Circuit, Milford, Routeburn, Lake Waikaremoana and Abel Tasman.

For a while the increasing use of huts, fuelled in part by the growing numbers of overseas tourists, created something of an arms race over hut size. The greater the use of huts, the more pressure to build ever-bigger designs. This perhaps culminated in the decision to build the Pinnacles Hut in Coromandel Forest Park in the early 1990s, which at eighty bunks remains New Zealand's largest hut. Crowded huts can be unpleasant, and DOC wanted to avoid criticism by catering for the increased demand. But larger and larger huts create their own catch-22, tending to attract even more people. Traditional New Zealand trampers tended to react negatively against the bigger huts, with not unjustified accusations that they were soulless and that taxpayer dollars were effectively being used to subsidise the tourist industry.

DOC has also had to contend with hut and fire regulations, which have imposed sometimes draconian standards that are suited more to urban situations than backcountry huts. Often DOC has been able to negotiate sensible decisions, such as the requirement for only those huts exceeding ten bunks to need a second fire exit. But Occupational Safety and Health regulations have sometimes added a layer of the ridiculous to this, occasionally provoking exasperated comments from trampers like Barry Dunnett, who on discovering a fire exit sign in a two-bunk hut wrote, 'Come on DOC! In some huts highlighting the fire exit is a useful safety feature, but in many smaller huts – especially bivs – they are totally redundant.'[35]

After a period of cutbacks, DOC gained additional funding for huts and tracks in 2002–03, which marked the beginning of a new era of hut building to DOC designs.

Hut Architecture

The words 'hut' and 'architecture' perhaps seem mutually exclusive. Indeed, many of New Zealand's oldest huts were put together without anything resembling a blueprint or plan. The style of architecture used in any one era was often simply dependent on the means available for transporting materials, and the type of materials readily to hand. For example, corrugated iron and timber were

Interior of Bealey Spur Hut, Arthur's Pass National Park, 1993. PHOTO: SHAUN BARNETT/BLACK ROBIN PHOTOGRAPHY

used without a great degree of architectural variation in many high-country stations, while stone served in other, treeless, parts of Otago and Canterbury. Although on a superficial level many of these huts do resemble one another, this is mostly the result of practicality, and to imply any master architectural plan is overstating the case.

Similarly, club huts built in the forested ranges of the North Island were often constructed using timber sawn on site. Fixed-wing planes used for air-drops could carry only limited lengths of materials, so huts were designed accordingly. Helicopters expanded the possibilities of using different materials, and over time have helped encourage the general drift towards larger huts.

Many New Zealand trampers have a clear preference for older-style huts, probably for several reasons: their simplicity, their small size, and the nostalgia associated with a bygone era. The more individualistic a hut, the more it speaks of its human character, of those who built it, maintained it and used it. For this reason, some despise larger, newer huts, and this opinion is not always confined to locals. On a visit in 2006, English hiker Stephen Pern made this comment in the NZFS-built Mid Waiohine Hut in Tararua Forest Park: 'At last – a proper

Hut Nuts

In recent years, a certain type of tramper has become obsessive enough about huts to 'collect' them. 'Hut baggers' will make strange and seemingly pointless deviations from their route just to visit an extra hut. They record their growing tallies, sometimes keeping photo albums of every hut they've visited, much as a twitcher might check bird observations from a list. The hut bagger places a higher value on the remotest huts, just as a twitcher does with a rare bird.

Hut bagging is not quite as eccentric or pointless as might be imagined. The number of huts visited does reflect a level of tramping experience. Marton's Rangitikei Tramping Club offers an annual prize for the member who has bagged the most huts. Other clubs, such as the Hutt Valley Tramping Club and Palmerston North Tramping and Mountaineering Club, run bagging competitions.

Self-confessed hut bagger Brian Dobbie, a keen tramper for thirty-five years, is DOC's national officer responsible for hut and track standards. He's visited more than 600 backcountry huts and says that to 'bag' a hut, a tramper must 'darken its door with [their] shadow'. The differences between huts interest him: 'I'm just intrigued by the decision to build a hut in a particular place, the way in which it is constructed, how it fits with the particular landscape … I love seeing huts with character, ones that have a little something extra.'[36]

Almost undoubtedly, the record for the most number of huts visited belongs to Christchurch tramper Mark Pickering, author of *Huts: Untold Stories from Back-country New Zealand* (2010). He has visited over 1150 backcountry huts, most of them on the public conservation estate but also a couple of hundred high-country mustering huts. In addition to mustering huts he particularly likes old Forest Service huts, but large modern huts leave him cold. He rates the Kepler Track's Luxmore Hut as New Zealand's ugliest.

Visiting so many huts led Pickering to write eloquently about them in *A Tramper's Journey* (2004): 'I confess to a deep affection for mountain

As one the least-visited huts in the country, the West Coast's Sir Robert Hut, photographed here in 1991, is something of a holy grail for hut baggers. In 2007, the hut book recorded the visits of just 61 people since 1983, an average of two to three people per year. The hut's popularity peaked in 1993, when eight people visited, one of them writing: 'Great hut! … maybe 1993 marks a revival in popularity.' It was a premature hope: the next entry came three years later. PHOTO: GEOFF SPEARPOINT

huts. They are durable and vulnerable, a bit like the people who use them I suppose. A few get blown to oblivion but most hang on in there, and even with years of neglect they can still manage to do the job they were set down on this earth for.'[37]

hut than smells like a hut and sounds like a hut – not a horrible barn like Mangahao Flats or Te Matawai which don't have anywhere to dry your clothes.'[38]

But rustic does not always equate to character or historic value. Old huts always have the added layer of history and stories that – by charming us – disguises their faults: cold, draughty, rodent-infested or dark. DOC managers have, over the past twenty-five years, tried to provide a range of facilities to suit differing needs, and this is reflected in the types of huts provided. The trend has largely been for more comfortable, better insulated and better lit huts, sometimes with sinks and running water – from a tap, not just a nearby stream.

Undoubtedly, the new DOC hut designs have been aimed at encouraging less experienced people to enjoy the hills by providing some degree of comfort, including double glazing and insulation. Soulless they may be, but practical and popular? Definitely. The reasons behind the appeal of a hut's design are as wide-ranging as the reasons why people enjoy the outdoors, and there is no doubt that many trampers much prefer a warm, dry, new hut. And over time, of course, these new huts will develop their own stories and personalities.

Throughout this book, we've tried to demonstrate the wonderful diversity of huts in New Zealand, and the fascinating history they represent. Retaining diversity across historic eras is important. Hut standards serve a necessary purpose, but if they are too regimental they stifle any design creativity. Somehow, regulation needs to make allowances for individual or regional designs, yet still maintain a basic standard to ensure low-maintenance, long-lasting huts.

The role of older huts in the story of our backcountry heritage is slowly becoming accepted – even celebrated. Indeed, DOC has in recent years identified many huts worthy of historic status, and many of the oldest huts have been assessed for their heritage value. DOC's Jackie Breen and Steve Bagley have been at the forefront of this effort, along with conservation architect Chris Cochran and historian Michael Kelly. Clubs have celebrated their huts in their journals, too, and since 2001 the Federated Mountain Clubs (FMC) has run regular 'Huts as Heritage' features in its quarterly *FMC Bulletin*. This growing interest in, and appreciation of, huts is extremely pleasing.

Though falling short of Buckingham Palace, these simple structures embody so many backcountry stories. Through the cycles of neglect and care huts also echo the wider political context. For ultimately, although on the surface they may seem to be just four walls and a roof, at their core huts are about people.

Perhaps no one has described the worth of huts better than mountaineer Paul Powell:

> It came to me what shelter means in the mountains. Huts, tents, shelter rocks, were more than stops along the way – places where men stayed to eat and sleep, leaving them to hunt deer, cross passes or cut transient steps up summit ice.

McCormack Hut at Luncheon Rock, Westland Tai Poutini National Park, about to be engulfed by the advancing Franz Josef Glacier, July 1985. The hut was dismantled and removed, and now forms part of other huts. PHOTO: BRUCE POSTILL

> Shelter in the hills meant more than cleaning a rifle, mapping the cross-country tramp, or resting for the climb. In huts or under bivvy rocks men were relaxed … By the fire they bragged like Norsemen, argued like Jesuits, sang like minstrels, and dreamed like poets … Such hospices were the beginning and the end of mountain life with the minutes of action sandwiched in between.[39]

SHAUN BARNETT

MORE THAN TIN AND TIMBER PASTORAL HUTS

The Romance of High-country Huts

For backcountry enthusiasts, it is hard to think of anything more romantic than a rustic corrugated-iron hut set beneath a backdrop of snowy mountains among the billowing tussocks of the high country.

For the farmers who built them, these huts were also more than just shelter during farm work and the annual muster. David McLeod, run holder at Cora Lynn Station between the 1930s and 1970s, summed up the feelings of many high-country farmers: 'My trips to Top Hut [Bealey Spur] were becoming melancholy now. The track unbearably beautiful and unspoilt; the horses and dogs and the whole procedure of an autumn muster unchanged and full of the deep romance it has always held for me.'[1]

Change, however, has also been a constant companion of high-country farming, and McLeod's nostalgia was somewhat tempered by the new generation:

> but each year widened the gap between me and the men who really do the job. They still talk of horse and dog and station and the men of the community but, horror of horrors, they bring transistor radios in their swags and drown with shrieking American cacophony the limpid drops of pure music which the mockies [bellbirds] let fall around the hut.[2]

Nobody quite knows how many huts associated with farming are spread throughout the New Zealand high country. A rough calculation can be made by estimating the number of stations and making an educated guess as to how many mustering huts there are on each. Historically, the South Island has had just over 300 high-country leasehold stations.[3] Most of these stations have between one and five mustering huts, giving a nationwide total of at least 300 to 400 huts. By adding a fudge factor for the huts on freehold farms, plus the remaining ones in the North Island, the total could be as high as 500 – possibly about one-third of all New Zealand's backcountry huts.

There were, of course, no standard designs for farming huts, but they roughly fall into three broad categories. The very first huts, built as early as

Bealey Spur Hut in 2010 (also known as Top Hut, it was built in 1925).
PHOTO: SHAUN BARNETT/BLACK ROBIN PHOTOGRAPHY

the 1860s and often made of stone, were associated with 'boundary keeping' on some of the vast high-country stations of the time. Some of these early runs in Otago and Canterbury covered more than 100,000 hectares and carried as many as 40,000 sheep. This made fencing the entire run largely impractical, so instead huts were established around the station perimeter for boundary keepers, shepherds who ensured the flock did not stray into the neighbour's run.

Rabbiting huts, built for men trying to keep the rabbit plagues under control, form a second distinct category. The largely self-inflicted problem of rabbits eventually required an entire government apparatus to rescue the high country from disaster, and farmers and the government spent millions of dollars killing the pests. Huts built specifically for rabbiting were often small, in most cases having the footprint of a tent. Once the rabbiting finished, farmers often found little use for these hut, and left them to fall down. Now rare, early rabbiting huts date back to the era when rabbit control simply meant one man, his gun and a dog.

The final broad group of huts, and by far the most numerous, are mustering huts. The larger high-country runs penetrated deep into the mountains, where sheep were left to graze in the summers. The autumn muster could take days, and the shepherds required shelter. Often simple corrugated-iron buildings, many of these mustering huts remain an integral part of New Zealand's high-country heritage. Despite the lack of a standard design, pretty much the same basic layout and construction was adopted by many farmers. Form follows function, and with five to six musterers, the owner/manager and a packie or cook, many of the huts had eight bunks spread around the inside walls, a simple table in the centre and an open fire at one end.

Many of the surviving mustering huts were built during the boom years of farming after the Second World War, although some are much older. Before this, smaller huts usually housed just a cook, packie and possibly the manager, leaving the mustering gangs to use tents. Most of these are in the South Island, but the North Island has its share too. Ngamatea Station, near Taihape, could in the 1970s claim to be the largest sheep station in the country. It mustered the southern Kaimanawa Mountains and western Kaweka Range, but was by no means the only large station in the vicinity.

In addition to these broad groups of huts, some farm homesteads have now

Blue Lake Hut in March 1994, Glenaray Station, Garvie Mountains, Southland. PHOTO: GEOFF SPEARPOINT

become part of the public hut network through changes in tenure. The Avoca Homestead, once the main house on the Avoca run, is in the Korowai/Torlesse Tussocklands Conservation Park. Further north, in Abel Tasman National Park, the historic Whariwharangi Hut dates back to a time when this area was farmed. Both of these buildings retain many of their original features, giving modern-day users an insight into the lives of early settlers in hard, often marginal farm country.

Seeking Land: the Beginnings of New Zealand High-country Farming

Understanding how high-country huts developed requires a broad overview of how New Zealand came to be settled, our farming history and, in particular, the history of merino sheep.

The Crown had acquired the bulk of the South Island high country exceedingly cheaply from the dominant South Island iwi, Ngai Tahu. How much of this land, mainly in the high country, came to be leased rather than sold fee-simple has complex origins that date back to the earliest days of the Wakefields' New Zealand Company settlement of the Canterbury Plains. Much of the farmland close to Christchurch had been sold in fee-simple title at the 'sufficient rate' of £3 per acre. The Wakefields hoped that pricing land this way would make their settlement venture pay for itself, leading to a 'civilised' society. They set prices at a level they hoped would discourage speculators – and the riff-raff. In Canterbury, the New Zealand Company administered these sales with the Canterbury Association, but the number of investors was not sufficient to keep it solvent. Eventually, in 1853, all but bankrupt, the company surrendered its Canterbury mandate.[4]

The Canterbury Association had anticipated difficulties, and started offering leasehold land in 1851. As the offers got cheaper, there was a fear that New Zealand would slip into the 'squatting' arrangement that had occurred in Australia. To head this off, New Zealand Governor George Grey set down nationwide regulations for pastoral leasing. The annual rental was based on the sheep numbers, and runs were let for fourteen-year terms.[5]

Grey's policy was aimed at encouraging people to invest in stock and improvements, and was intended to be affordable for the small farmer yet prevent speculation. In reality, the policy achieved only the first of these. Some got in quickly and transformed themselves from squatters into respectable run holders. The most notorious of these was George Duppa, who made a fortune from his Birch Hill Station in Marlborough's upper Wairau Valley, and later St Leonards near Culverden. A squatter from the early days of the New Zealand Company, Duppa pioneered a route from his station through the Molesworth country to the hills near Cheviot. Through persistence, he secured legitimate rights to this vast parcel of land, and after selling out in 1852 for the reported fortune of £150,000, he returned to his native Kent to a life of some luxury.[6]

By 1855, most of the Canterbury Plains had already been taken up by immigrant farmers. Some of these plains farmers did very well indeed in the first years of the settlement. Possibly the wealthiest sheep farmer of all was Robert Heaton Rhodes, estimated to be worth £521,241 when he died in 1884 – an enormous sum for the day and more than the value of the entire North Island provinces combined.[7] This was at a time when a head shepherd with dogs could earn £60–80 a year. Heaton Rhodes and his brother George owned most of the country inland from Timaru, a vast 60,700-hectare farm called Levels.

New arrivals were already exploring the harder high-country terrain closer to the Southern Alps. This land carried the risk of harsher weather and poorer soil quality, as well as being in the rain shadow of the mountains and so susceptible to dry years during westerly weather patterns. But the land here was cheap and readily available. A new arrival simply had to find a piece of vacant high-country land and apply to the Waste Lands Board for a run. At a cost of £1 per 1000 acres (400 hectares), a man with capital could lease land from the government and set about developing and stocking it.

Before registering a run, some spent time assessing the land's suitability for supporting merinos. Samuel Butler was one who spent a winter exploring the head of the Rangitata River. As a young twenty-four-year-old with a degree in classics, Butler came to New Zealand to escape a dysfunctional relationship with his father, and for his first winter camped in a small hut in Forest Creek, which he named the 'V' hut.

V-huts – what we would call today an A-frame – were a common design for the early settlers of Canterbury. Butler described their simplicity: 'The V hut is a fait accompli, if so small an undertaking can be spoken of in so dignified a manner. It consists of a small roof set upon the ground; it is a hut, all roof and no walls.'[8]

In June 1860, Butler built his little V-hut on a terrace above Forest Creek on the present-day Ben McLeod Station. His version of the hut was basic and constructed largely from wood cut from the nearby beech forest. It was barely comparable with the more solid V-huts he had seen on the Canterbury Plains and not always weatherproof:

> I had left the V hut warm and comfortable, and on my return found it very different. I fear we had not put enough thatch upon it, and the ten days' rain had proved too much for it. It was now neither air-tight nor water-tight; the floor, or rather the ground, was soaked and soppy with mud; the nice warm snow-grass on which I had lain so comfortably the night before I left, was muddy and wet; altogether, there being no fire inside, the place was as revolting-looking an affair as one would wish to see: coming wet and cold off a journey, we had hoped for better things. There was nothing for it but to make the best of it, so we had tea.[9]

By the end of the year Butler had purchased Mesopotamia and built a solid cottage on the run. While the rights to the run came cheap, stock was more expensive.

Stocking the Land: Merinos and Boundary-keepers

Stocking the high country required a breed of sheep that could manage the coarse fodder of tussock grasslands. The most suitable was the low-mainte-

Samuel Butler's Cottage, Mesopotamia Station, Rangitata Valley, Canterbury, circa 1870s.
PHOTO: SOUTH CANTERBURY MUSEUM TIMARU, P1933

nance, hardy merino, a breed originating in Spain. New Zealand's high-country story is essentially the story of merino sheep.

Captain James Cook had attempted to bring some merinos with him on his second and third voyages, but few survived the trip and those that did never established themselves. Missionary Samuel Marsden had a small flock in the Bay of Islands and was probably the first to export wool from New Zealand. In Canterbury and Otago, where the breed would thrive, it was William and John Deans and Johnny Jones, respectively, who first imported merinos.[10]

At the time of Canterbury's settlement, Australia already had a well-established flock of outback merinos. The fastest means of building up a New Zealand flock was to buy sheep from South Australia, where they were already experimenting with cross-breeding. The traditional Spanish merinos were thought to be a little on the small side for this part of the world, and were generally crossed with English breeds like the Lincoln and Leicester to bolster their size. To increase wool quality, New Zealand farmers also bred Australian merinos with the best stock from Europe. One example of this was the importation through Lyttelton of twelve ewes and two rams from the best German flocks on 5 February 1853.[11] Eventually, through careful breeding, New Zealand merinos became bigger and more robust than their Australian counterparts, were more resistant to footrot and had even finer wool.

In the early years, as the nation's merino flock was improved, the price per head escalated and provided run holders with a healthy income on top of the wool clip. In 1862, Samuel Butler at Mesopotamia offered to sell six tooth rams to his neighbour John Acland at Mt Peel for £2 per head.[12] Ewes were worth less – about 35 shillings a head – but either way, any animal with the potential to turn tussock into money commandeered a high price in colonial New Zealand.

PASTORAL HUTS 31

Polson's Hut was built in the 1860s on one of New Zealand's largest sheep runs; the vast Morven Hills Station. Today it is maintained and used by the owners of Shirlmar Station and pictured here in 2012. PHOTO: ROB BROWN

The speed at which merinos stocked the high country was astonishing. By 1869, an estimated 7 million sheep roamed the South Island, with a further 2 million in the North Island. New Zealand exported twice as much wool as South Africa, and while the quality of wool remained variable in the first ten years, by 1870 New Zealand-produced merino wool was regarded as the best in the world.

Before the 1870s, most of these merinos roamed the high-country grasslands, and a lack of cheap wire and fencing systems required boundary keepers. The risk of transmitting diseases like scab between flocks meant that boundary keeping was taken very seriously.

Keeping the boundary was a full-time job on the bigger high-country runs, with the shepherds and their dogs each patrolling a section of the station's perimeter from their huts. We don't know which of the remaining farm huts in New Zealand is the oldest, but in all likelihood it is one of the early boundary-keeping huts in Otago or Canterbury, dating back to the 1860s.

The life of a boundary keeper and his family was isolated and tough. Polson's Hut was on the original boundary of the huge Morven Hills Station and holds a tragic story.[13] In 1896, John Polson wife's found herself in premature labour during a severe winter when snow lay thickly around the hut. Ian Polson, their grandson, recalled their struggle to keep the twin babies alive:

No doctor, nurse or neighbour could be called and Grandfather Polson took the two babes on his knees and kept them warm by the fire, while Grandma attended to herself as best she could. But the cold and the prematurity of their birth plus the spartan conditions was too much for the twins and first one died and then the other.

The snow was too deep for the police to come from Cromwell to examine them and indeed it was scarcely possible to bury them for the ground was frozen hard and deep. After their death, their little bodies froze in the hut. They were eventually buried a quarter mile from the hut and a willow, either planted to commemorate the spot or there already, still grows robustly over the barely legible tombstone.[14]

Perhaps the greatest concentration of surviving boundary-keeping huts is found near Mt Peel Station, one of Canterbury's earliest high-country runs. In 1856, John Barton Arundel Acland and his friend and business partner Charles George Tripp established the huge station. Tripp and Acland, both Oxford-trained lawyers, came from upper-class English families. Together they abandoned their profession in their early thirties and travelled to New Zealand to seek a future in the new province of Canterbury. After spending a year gaining experience working on other runs, they applied for a lease of some 58,000 acres (23,000 hectares) of high-country land near Mt Peel.[15]

Both Tripp and Acland were devoted Anglicans and showed a strong sense of dedication and duty to their employees and the community. Boundary keeping may have been a tough, lonely life, but Tripp and Acland made every effort to ensure their shepherds had good accommodation.

In 1912, eight years after Acland died, sections of Mt Peel were subdivided off the high-country blocks to create a number of smaller runs. By that time, some of the property had fences and gorse hedges meaning boundary keeping had become a thing of the past. Tripp's Orari Gorge went through a similar down sizing and often blocks were subdivided off to pay death duties as the properties passed from one generation to the next. As a result the old boundary-keeping huts ended up on other stations like Ben McLeod Station, that was formally the western boundary of Mt Peel, and Blue Mountain Station to the southwest of Orari Gorge. Often built to last from local stone, most of these boundary-keeping huts are still there and serve as reminders of a time when a shepherd took care of his flock every day, not just during annual musters. They have a high heritage value for their unique role in New Zealand's high-country history.

Boom and Bust

Samuel Butler's arrival in Canterbury in the 1860s coincided with a literal race to register ownership of high-country runs. This rush for runs occurred as the economy boomed, partly due to the discovery of payable gold. Despite the egalitarian intent of Grey's leasing policy, most of the original Canterbury high-country runs were taken up by as few as twenty men.[16] With no restrictions on taking up multiple leases, these men saw opportunities and quickly took them, making an abject failure of the colonial attempt to encourage numerous small farms. After just a few years, many speculators sold their runs on. The short-term fourteen-year lease also encouraged overstocking and reckless pasture management, with little thought of the future.

Capital gains motivated Samuel Butler, who was quite open about his commitment to a quick buck. In the four years he owned Mesopotamia Station, Butler doubled his capital from £4000 to £8000, and he returned to England, goal achieved. In comparison, he earned just £69 in royalties from his famous bestselling book *Erewhon*.[17] Mesopotamia's next owner, William Parkerson, reputedly doubled his money too, but after just one year.[18]

Fabulous riches earned by the large estates of the Canterbury Plains farmers led to them being labelled 'wool barons' or 'wool kings'. Part of their huge success was due to their ability to diversify into crops and protect themselves against fluctuating wool prices. Many of these large estates cleared £5000–10,000 per year, sometimes more, and when the owners did come to sell their interest in the land, they usually got enough to guarantee a life of considerable luxury.

With the arrival of the economic downturn of the 1890s, the diversification of the Canterbury Plains farmers insulated them from financial difficulties. But it was an entirely different story in the high country. By the 1890s, many formerly profitable farms were sailing pretty close to the wind. Stocking with just merinos became progressively more difficult. Some of the remote high-country runs hadn't even had a chance to establish themselves properly, and the 'homesteads' on them were little more than huts, or at most small cottages. The grand station homestead was still the preserve of those lucky enough to have runs with some low country.

It was a tough life on these remote stations. In the 1870s, George McRae, a shepherd from Mesopotamia, took up the abandoned run of Erewhon and renamed it Stroneschrubie (meaning 'crooked nose') after a ridge that dominates the view. In some very tough years, he had to leave his wife in their hut for months at a time, with only a Bible for company, while he went off mustering. Some say this Scottish Highlands woman went ten years without seeing another member of her sex. However, her competence was admired, and by all accounts McRae's wife was, for twenty years, the real station manager. Eventually, however, the loneliness became too much, and a mental breakdown forced her to leave Stroneschrubie, never to return. McRae persisted through the bad times and eventually retired to Ashburton as a moderately wealthy man.[19]

Early run holders had to deal with a whole range of stock ailments, from scab to footrot. Sheep scab, caused by the virulent infestation of a tiny mange mite, was eventually eradicated through compulsory sheep dipping – the regular dunking of the flock in potent chemicals to kill the mites. Until the disease was wiped out in 1894, scab was a major problem, and the government came down hard on any farmer who did not adhere to the dipping rules.

McRae's Hut on Stroneschrubie (Erewhon) Station, Clyde Valley, Canterbury, 1961.
PHOTO: JOHN PASCOE COLLECTION, ALEXANDER TURNBULL LIBRARY, WELLINGTON, 1/4-044616-F

Random weather events added to economic pressures. Heavy winter snows were a reasonably regular occurrence in the high country, but the great snowfall of 1895 was particularly severe and wiped out some farmers' stock by a third or more. On Balmoral Station, for example, the snows decimated the 30,000-strong flock to just 3039 sheep.[20] That winter was the final straw for many. Even the cautious farmer John Acland at Mt Peel Station ended up on a financial knife edge, and his diaries reveal a growing anxiety about the future of high-country farming.

Declining terms of trade and commodity prices put yet more financial pressure on high-country farmers. The downward trend of wool prices, due to both competition from fibres like cotton and to a recovering Australian wool supply (after that country's disastrous 1860s droughts), became a particular problem.

A rush for profits in the boom years had also led many to overstock their properties with unsustainable levels of sheep. This overstocking, combined with the catastrophic increase in rabbit numbers and the ill-advised burning of tussock grasslands to promote fresh pasture, led to a decline in the environmental

Mustering hut, Macaulay Valley, Canterbury, circa 1950s. PHOTO: JOHN WILSON COLLECTION

health of the land, and a consequent drop in its carrying capacity. The high country never truly recovered from this, and never again witnessed such high merino numbers.

Despite the trials and challenges of the early run holders, many farmers remained committed to New Zealand. Of the 314 owners of large South Island runs in the latter part of the nineteenth century, only 19 per cent died outside New Zealand.[21]

Refrigeration, Land Tenure and the Break-up of the Great Estates

When the *Dunedin* left Port Chalmers in February 1882 with more than 4000 merino-Lincoln cross-breed carcasses on board packed in ice, it marked the world's first commercially successful export of frozen meat. New Zealand mutton now graced the tables of Britain. After refining the refrigeration method, New Zealand's fortunes turned around within a few short years. The new emphasis on meat rather than wool ended the dominance of merinos, as the Romney and its cross breeds yielded more mutton and lamb, while still producing coarse wool acceptable for commodities like carpets.

Broader changes in society also affected pastoralism. The gold rushes brought an influx of working-class immigrants to New Zealand, eventually causing a slow shift in the balance of political power. Far from the traditional image of a solitary miner working a claim, most diggers were in fact closely organised politically and often egalitarian in their views. Once work on the goldfields petered out, diggers wanted better prospects than serving the owners of the 'great estates'. Political pressure mounted for allowing smaller holdings that could support a working family.

The debate over land was intertwined with a debate about power. At the time, there was no universal franchise, and to be eligible to vote you needed to own or rent land of a certain value. The government policy to purchase the great estates went hand and hand with moving towards a universal franchise that was the right of every citizen. The 'great land debate' was, in fact, the 'great democracy debate'.

After provincial governments were abolished in favour of central government in 1876, the power of large South Island run holders, who had dominated provincial politics, diminished. The following year, the Land Act 1877 set up a new way of managing land sales nationally.

More political change came with the arrival of Richard Seddon, one-time West Coast gold miner. Seddon, a hero to the diggers and working class, cut his teeth in Westland politics and, after stepping into the premiership in 1893, set about championing the small farmer. Seddon dominated New Zealand politics for the next thirteen years until his death in 1906.

Seddon, along with Minister of Lands John McKenzie, revolutionised land policy. To provide working-class people an opportunity to own small farms, they began the messy business of breaking up the great estates. A former shepherd from Palmerston, McKenzie owned a small farm himself and became a champion of the so-called 'cockies'. Born in Scotland, he had seen the Scots evicted from their lands by wealthy English landlords clearing the Highlands for sheep. Both McKenzie and Seddon were determined that New Zealand would become a more egalitarian society, free from some of the class divisions they had experienced.

The government initially set its sights on the large estates of the lower country, and one of the first purchases was Cheviot Hills Station in North Canterbury. This 33,600-hectare property, owned by William 'Ready Money' Robinson, was one of the province's largest. The government bought the estate four years after Robinson's death and split it into hundreds of smaller farms. On the back of the boom in refrigerated exports, these smaller farms were profitable and arguably more efficient than the single large estate had been.[22]

One example of a high-country purchase was the 125,800-hectare Benmore Station. The Land Act 1892 meant no station could run more than 20,000 sheep. In 1916, the huge Benmore run was surrendered to the Crown and then split into several smaller runs. Hideaway Biv, one of several huts built during the Benmore era, became part of the new Quailburn Station. Other huts ended up on smaller runs too.

By this stage, government purchase of the great estates was actually almost a blessing for the owners. Ultimately, breaking up the large runs meant more farms, and it was on these smaller stations that the majority of the mustering huts still surviving in the high country today would be established.

Unfortunately for the new farmers, many of these divided-up runs were now in an advanced state of decline, thanks to rabbits. Stations like Benmore had felt the full impact of the rabbit plagues, and some of these degraded runs sold for as little as £140.[23] The new owners had a mountain to climb to make the farms profitable again. Many small station huts like Hideaway Biv were now serving two functions: mustering and rabbiting. To avoid financial ruin, nearly all high-country run holders had to spend heavily on controlling rabbits.

Rabbiters and their Huts

The introduction of rabbits to New Zealand as cheap food for the pot became an economic disaster for farming that broke some run holders, particularly in Otago and Marlborough, and pushed many others to the brink. Deliberately introduced in the 1830s, soon after Europeans began to settle New Zealand, rabbits took a while to become established, but once they reached the dry, fertile high country, their numbers exploded. Ten rabbits ate as much as one sheep, and as a result the merino flocks and stocking capacity of the high-country runs collapsed under the pressure.

Black Spur Hut, Marlborough, was built sometime in 1927-28 for shepherds, but was also used by rabbiters after the pest reached plague proportions in the Clarence Reserve. In the 1970s Alan Flint of Kaikoura substantially renovated it, and today DOC manages it as an historic hut. PHOTO: PAT BARRETT

Perhaps the most rabbit-infested run was Earnscleugh Station, near present-day Alexandra. Incredibly, despite the known problems caused by the pests, the Otago Acclimatisation Society released sixty rabbits near the station in 1866. In a spectacular lapse of judgement, the station's manager (and later owner) William Fraser encouraged the release.[24]

Just fourteen years later, rabbiters – armed with guns and dogs – killed an incredible 400,000 rabbits in a single year on Earnscleugh. In 1890, the station still carried 24,000 sheep, but by 1898 this had plummeted to just 234.[25] Fraser had sold the property in 1893 to the unfortunate W. S. Laidlaw, who walked off the land just a few years later, and the run reverted to the Crown. In 1902, Steven Spain took up the lease, but not for sheep. He set up a rabbit-canning factory and employed up to thirty-two rabbiters. Spain earned enough from selling rabbit meat and skins to build the impressive Earnscleugh Station homestead.[26]

It is hard now to understand fully just how much of a disaster rabbits became for what was then New Zealand's richest province. The gold rushes and healthy wool clips had made Central Otago an economic powerhouse for the new colony, but the rabbits threatened to eat that promise away. Between 1877 and 1884, farmers walked off seventy-five Otago runs, abandoning a total of 545,000 hectares.[27]

The government passed the first Rabbit Nuisance Act in 1867, just a year after the Otago Acclimatisation Society had released rabbits near Earnscleugh Station. It set up a system of 'rabbit inspectors', who had the power to order farmers to destroy rabbits on their farm. It also encouraged farmers to form collective rabbit boards, whereby each run holder contributed funds towards

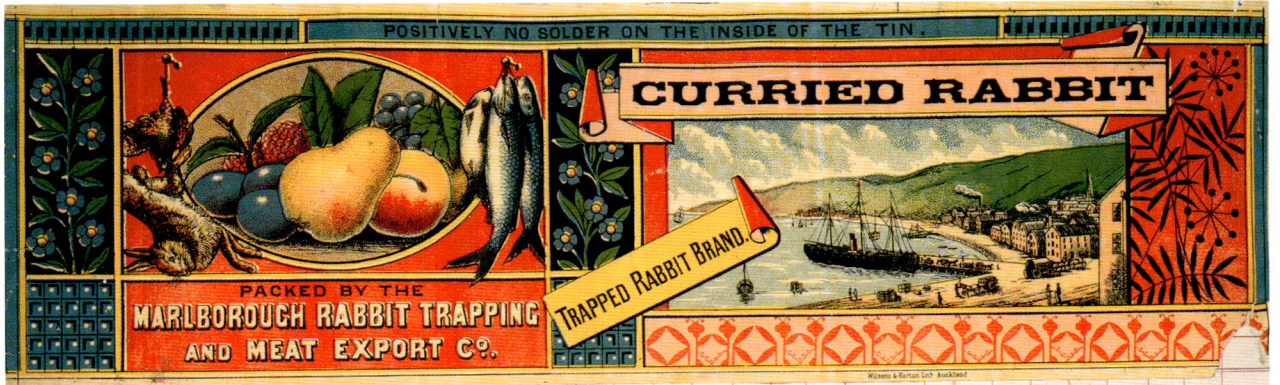

TOP Label from the Marlborough Rabbit Trapping and Meat Export Company, circa 1900.
PICTURE: ALEXANDER TURNBULL LIBRARY, WELLINGTON, EPH-F-MEAT-GEAR-130
BOTTOM Rabbiters outside their huts in Stony Creek, Southland. PHOTO: HOCKEN LIBRARY, UNIVERSITY OF OTAGO, C/N E2083/14

pest control. In a way, the rabbit plague in the nineteenth century had its parallel with the explosion in deer numbers in the twentieth century, and both pests were associated with periods of hut building.

The farmers and rabbiters understandably looked for ways to turn the pest into a commodity to help pay for its control – and rabbits became an industry. With few exceptions, rabbiters lived permanently on the station, in some cases in mustering huts but often housed in their own small huts. Surviving runs ended up employing as many as 140 rabbiters. With exports of 100 million rabbit skins in the 1880s, the wool presses were busy once again, but this time pressing the skins for export to European fashion houses.[28] In one year, 1893, New Zealand exported 17 million rabbit skins to Britain, but even this did little to control the numbers.

In retrospect, the commercialisation of rabbit culling led to some bizarre practices. In Central Otago, rabbiters had to pay up to £50 for the privilege of sole access to the most infested blocks.[29] Instead of pursuing a goal of returning sheep farming to its former glory, rabbiters became quite skilled at 'managing the numbers'. Indeed, rabbiters were sometimes making a lot more money than shepherds.

While the money was good, it was still hard, gory work. Peter Newton was on the Clarence Reserve in the 1920s and described the life of a rabbiter: 'For many years the Reserve kept eight rabbiters all the year round and the practice at one time was to pay them so much per skin … These were baled in the ordinary wool press and there must have been occasions on some of the badly infested properties when the bales of skins equalled the wool clip.'[30]

A good man could skin over eighty fat rabbits an hour, although he might manage as many as 200 when they were thin. Rabbiting in the high country was tough, especially as it was usually a winter job, as Newton recalled:

The dead rabbits had to be picked up before daylight on account of the hawks, dumped in heaps and then skinned (in ground frozen almost a foot deep) and then, in the light of the campfire and a candle or two, the skins were wired and fatted in the evening. Who could blame those chaps for playing up when they went down country?[31]

Bounties clearly weren't working, and by January 1937 rabbits still existed in plague proportions in Central Otago. North Island rabbiter Harry McLean remembered his first trip south: 'In the early morning in Alexandra it was common to see shop assistants, bank clerks, postmen, children and others biking back into town with rabbit carcasses hanging in bundles on their bicycles.'[32]

Despite the commercialisation of rabbiting, it was eventually recognised that the returns nowhere near matched those for wool and that 'farming' rabbits was not in the long-term interests of New Zealand. A better solution had to be found.

Even in the days of commercial recovery of rabbits, men had played around with pesticides, some of them fearfully poisonous. Strychnine and phosphorous were popular for a while, as was arsenic. In some places, people tried sealing up rabbit warrens and gassing them with cyanogas and carbon bisulphide. However, none of these measures provided long-term solutions.

Two changes after the Second World War ensured some progress with the rabbit problem. The first was the introduction of sodium monofluoroacetate, or 1080.[33] This proved to be extraordinarily efficient at killing introduced mammals and something of a silver bullet for controlling rabbits. Trials demonstrated its superiority to all other poisons being used at the time, and by the early 1950s aerial application of 1080-laced carrots laced became commonplace in the high country.

The second change was an amendment to the Rabbit Nuisance Act in 1947, which outlawed trade in rabbit meat. The Act also aimed at decommercialising the sale of rabbit skins by gradually phasing out the skin bounty, but allowed trade to limp on for another ten years until rabbiters drifted into other jobs. Following what was known as the 'killer' policy, the country's 100 or so rabbit control boards set about decimating rabbits as efficiently as possible using 1080.[34] The life of the rabbiters slowly disappeared, and with them went many of their huts. Often too small for use by mustering teams, most simply fell into ruin.

The Mustering Huts

In our age of instant communication and modern transport, it is hard to understand just how isolated some high-country runs were for much of their history. Mesopotamia, for example, didn't get full road access until the mid-1920s, and could easily be cut off by Forest Creek, which remained unbridged until the mid-1960s. For the first sixty years of the station's history, wool was often carted across the Rangitata to the Erewhon Road and then out to Mt Somers.[35]

Virtually nothing on the stations was mechanised and most farm jobs were done either on horse or on foot. Many of the high-country runs had some difficult terrain that was not suitable for horseback mustering, especially in the higher country prone to early snowfalls. Brabazon Ridge and Crooked Spur on Mesopotamia fitted this category, and by 1885 the station already had a rough hut on the ridge to accommodate mustering gangs. That year, the first muster in May was thwarted by heavy snow, while on the second attempt the hut burnt down. With no shelter, bad weather forced the shepherds out.[36]

By the end of the 1890s, many high-country farms were only just hanging on, but worse was to come. Continuing depressed wool prices and rabbit plagues meant the new century got off to a bad start. Many farmers were still financially shaky before the First World War, which had a devastating effect on manpower. The fit, healthy young men in the mustering teams were among the first to enlist. Eight signed up from the Mesopotamia mustering gang of 1915; only two came back.[37] In 1918, a devastating winter – almost as bad as that back in 1895 – signalled the start of thirty years of struggle for high-country sheep farmers.

But despite these hard times, run holders had to invest in their farm's infrastructure as best they could. Bealey Spur Hut, built in 1925 by Cora Lynn Station (now part of Arthur's Pass National Park), provides a good example of how improvements were made when times were tough. A frame cut from beech and corrugated-iron cladding was all that was needed to make a wonderfully durable mustering hut that has lasted over eighty-five years. The year it was built marked one of the few times when wool prices temporarily recovered during this period.

Hard times brought opportunities for some. With bleak prospects, only the really determined were attracted to the high country. At this time, a shepherd or shearer could aspire, through hard work, to eventually own a run.

During the Second World War, three terribly cold winters – in 1939, 1940 and 1945 – again knocked back flocks, and more men died in the violence of Europe. Even so, some hut building still took place. On Mesopotamia Station, manager Bob Buick, perhaps inspired by the Canterbury Mountaineering Club's wartime efforts up the nearby Havelock River (see p. 178), rebuilt Stone Hut in the remote block behind Crooked Spur.[38]

As Europe and Britain recovered from the war, commodity prices started to boom again for wool and lamb. Almost uniformly, people single out 1951 as the turning point for high-country farming, helped by a reduction in rabbit numbers through poisoning operations. Many of the mustering huts in existence today were either built during the 1950s or, in the case of older huts, given a much-needed makeover.[39]

At the very least, many of the old dirt floors in the tin huts were replaced with a concrete floor to make them a little more serviceable, and old problems with fireplaces were sorted out. Peter Newton remembered renovating some of the huts on Mt White Station in the 1950s:

OPPOSITE Musterer approaching Bayburn Hut, Minaret Station, Otago, 1962. PHOTO: DAVE OSMERS

ABOVE CLOCKWISE FROM TOP LEFT Inside a Walter Peak station hut; Kevin Lange reading inside Pykes Hut; Graeme Rive, Peter Presland, Peter Gazzard, Evan Waby and Kevin Lange outside Bells Hut on Minaret Station, autumn muster, 1962; cooking pots on the fire, Walter Peak Station hut, Otago.
PHOTOS: DAVE OSMERS

Forest Creek Hut, a stone boundary-keepers' hut on Ben McLeod Station, Rangitata Valley, pictured in the winter of 1995. Built in the 1860s, when this was part of Mt Peel Station, the two-room Forest Creek Hut is more substantial than many boundary-keepers' huts.
PHOTO: GEOFF SPEARPOINT

> When we rebuilt Pakety Hut we'd tried a new idea with the fireplace. Musterers' huts have just an open fire, with a corrugated iron chimney, and invariably the fireplace itself is anything from three to five feet deep – you could almost drive a horse and dray into them … Anyway we'd made Pakety fireplace just exactly two feet deep and it proved a complete success. We lined the back of the chimney with the side of an old 400 gallon iron tank and felt confident it would last for donkeys' years. Compared with the usual great caverns of fireplaces it was a simple matter to handle a heavy camp oven in it. Another advantage was that it threw out more heat – you could sit alongside the fire instead of being half a chain away. Those draughty old iron huts can be pretty cold in autumn and winter.[40]

In most cases hut history and records had become a living part of the tin and timber. For years, musterers fostered the tradition of signing their names on the outside of the hut – or sometimes on the beams inside. This 'graffiti' acted as a sort of hut logbook, recording everything from who was on the muster each season, to trampers and climbers passing by on their way to the higher peaks, and even locals on their honeymoon.

In renovating the old mustering huts, many farmers were conscious of preserving this history. With the Pakety Hut rebuild, Newton went to a great deal of trouble to salvage records of the station musters:

> The old Pakety Hut had the names of gangs dating as far back as 1912. That was well before my time on the hill, but it so happened that I had known practically every man in that 1912 gang. We now had to rebuild a hut there and although the old hut was half-buried … I remembered exactly which beam the 1912 gang's names had been written on, and I reckoned that if we had a fortnight I'd get that particular piece of timber out. It so happened that that piece was well buried; but we got it out, cleaned it, and found that the names were still discernible.[41]

Another significant change for post-war high-country farmers was the Land Act 1948. This extended the leasehold term from fourteen to thirty-three years and gave the leaseholder the automatic right of renewal in perpetuity when the term came to an end. It was an acknowledgement by the Crown that good stewardship of the land was closely linked to security of tenure, and it gave farmers confidence to invest for the long term.

Over the years, mechanisation has reduced the need for mustering huts – farmers can now round sheep up using helicopters and four-wheel-drives, making the week-long muster an increasingly rare event. However, some stations do still muster on horseback and on foot, with the huts playing an integral part of the working farm. Increasingly, station managers recognise the historic value of their huts too, although – as always – maintenance depends upon good export returns. Some farmers have expanded their horizons by restoring huts to serve as backcountry accommodation for tourism ventures. This is all part of a continuing search for diversification and sustainability in the challenging high country.

Farming Huts Today: Changing Use and Preserving Heritage

New Zealand has built a rich farming history that has largely reflected, at least from a European perspective, a young pioneer society at the end of the Earth. Some of this heritage has been lost over the years, as hastily built sheds have collapsed and sod huts have succumbed to weather and time. Fire has taken some of the grandest homesteads and changing land use has seen interesting buildings being demolished to make way for the new. But a surprising amount remains. One of the most appealing parts of this heritage is the mustering hut, a simple, no-nonsense structure made to provide a temporary home to the men who gathered sheep from the mountains for shearing.

As a group, high-country farmers are second only to the New Zealand Forest Service in the number of huts they have built, and for many years now they have run them in a public-spirited way – mostly leaving them unlocked for trampers and climbers heading for the mountains beyond. The generosity of this high-country tradition has been reciprocated, with most trampers leaving the huts clean and tidy, and perhaps also leaving a small note of thanks.

The tenure of high-country land, of who owns what, is something that New Zealand has struggled with over the entire history of European settlement. High-country land tenure and access have become hot topics in recent years, and good arguments can be made both for and against pastoral leaseholds versus fee-simple titles.

Over the years, modifications to the pastoral lease system have given farmers as much long-term security as possible, while stopping short of a fee-simple title – largely because of the enormous emotional attachment many New Zealanders have for the high country. At times, however, the sometimes acrimonious nature of the land debate has run a very real risk of driving a wedge between city and country, stifling genuine goodwill between farmers and those who seek to enjoy the high-country mountains. Sometimes you have to wonder whether a night in a mustering hut, bringing the interested parties together, would sort things out. Huts are great like that.

Today, there are just over 230 high-country leases left in the South Island, with more than sixty properties having gone through the government's tenure review process. Through this process, some of the higher summer grazing country with high conservation values has been voluntarily retired from grazing. Merino farming still remains the core of the remaining stations and is the key to their future, but is generally carried out on a much more sustainable basis than it has been in the past. The autumn muster still occurs on some of these stations, but on a smaller scale. The days of the great high-country musters have largely gone.

Much retired land now forms part of newly established high-country conservation parks, like Te Papanui in Central Otago, Korowai/Torlesse in the Waimakariri and Hakatere in the headwaters of the Rangitata. These conservation parks not only offer the chance to explore some incredible landscapes, but also provide an experience of one-time mustering country. A good number of mustering huts have come with the land, and are now managed by DOC. With the sheep and musterers gone, it is the huts that serve as the potent remnant of the farming heritage of these parks.

Dog Box Biv in 2005. Originally built in 1916 by Fairlight Station who had a lease to run sheep to the headwaters of Eyre Creek. Now part of Eyre Mountains/Taka Ra Haka Conservation Park and managed as an historic hut by DOC.
PHOTO: REBECCA REID, TELLTALE

Trampers, hunters and climbers staying in a former mustering hut sometimes feel a certain nostalgia for the high-country life, that huge part of New Zealand's history now so changed. In many places DOC has embraced this past by recording high-country stories on information panels inside the huts. Some run holders, too, have undertaken superb work on their own huts, telling their history and reminding us that these simple buildings are much more than just timber and tin.

ROB BROWN

Sutherlands Hut 1867 FOUR PEAKS STATION, CANTERBURY

Sutherlands Hut was built in the 1860s as accommodation for a boundary keeper on Charles Tripp's Orari Gorge Station. Along with Mt Peel Station, this was one of Canterbury's earliest high-country runs and the property covered some 27,500 hectares. In the early years of his partnership with John Acland (see p. 32),[1] Tripp lived at Mt Peel and the pair sublet the Orari run to Robert Smith, who had previously been the manager at Mt Peel in its first years. By the time Tripp and Acland married (to sisters Ellen and Emily Harper, in 1858 and 1860, respectively), they realised their business partnership would need to be amicably dissolved. In 1862, they tossed a coin to see how their land holdings would be split, with Acland taking Mt Peel and Tripp getting Orari Gorge. Tripp then moved with his wife to another run they had purchased at Mt Somers. Later that year, Tripp sold Orari Gorge for £25,000 and returned to England. Tripp's father had reputedly refused to believe his son had done well in the colony, and Charles Tripp recorded that his motivation for selling the station was 'to prove to my father what my property was worth'.[2]

On Tripp's return to New Zealand in 1866, he bought back Orari Gorge and moved there in September of that year, once the homestead had been built. While he was in England, Tripp had offered Devonshire man and expert stonemason James Radford a job. Radford accepted and emigrated to New Zealand, joining the Tripp family on the same ship for their return voyage.[3]

To provide accommodation for the boundary keepers and musterers on his many blocks, Tripp began a stone hut-building programme in 1866, part of a concerted effort to turn Orari Gorge into one of Canterbury's best stations. Throughout his life Tripp had a reputation as a generous man, often giving friends and family more than he could afford. He was certainly generous with the provision of accommodation on the station, eventually overseeing the construction of about nineteen huts.

One of the early stone huts Tripp got Radford to build cost him £33 and 6 shillings (not including thatching); a design for it, drawn by Tripp himself, appears in the Orari Gorge labour book now held at the Canterbury Museum in Christchurch. It is hard to say exactly when the hut was built, but the Orari Gorge labour book records that Radford and his assistant, John Hunt, were sent off to build a hut to this design in May 1867. They came back a month later, having presumably completed a hut – possibly Sutherlands. Each stone hut took about a month to complete and the labour book records that they built another at Hat Spur in November of that same year.[4]

Sutherlands Hut, situated beside the Mowbray River, was named after the first shepherd assigned to keep the boundary, and measures about 4.5 metres by 3 metres – a snug fit for six bunks. The door, just 1.5 metres high, must have caused headaches for taller men. The stonework of the walls reflects considerable skill. Throughout 1867 Radford continued to construct stone huts for Tripp on the station. Eventually, around six of the nineteen huts would be built

Sutherlands Hut with thatched roof, 1885.
PAINTING BY ELLA TRIPP, ORARI GORGE STATION COLLECTION

Sutherlands Hut in 2012. PHOTOS: ROB BROWN

out of stone. When a big snowstorm hit the region in August 1867, Radford was back at the homestead, working on other building projects around the homestead – mainly stone walls and a furnace for the blacksmith's shed. He left the station in 1868.[5]

After Tripp died in 1897, Orari Gorge Station continued under a partnership of his four sons, but was eventually split into smaller stations when the government purchased it in 1910 under its closer settlements policy. Two blocks were split off that year, with Saddle Peak Station getting the Waihi River Hut and Four Peaks Station inheriting Sutherlands Hut. In 1948, the Blue Mountain Block was also subdivided off Orari Gorge Station to pay the death duties for two of Jack Tripp's sons who had been killed in the war.[6] Blue Mountain Station ended up with Hat Spur, Totara Stream and Sandstone boundary huts. By this time, the stations were well fenced and no longer employed boundary keepers, although some of the huts were usefully sited for mustering and so continued to be used.

Four Peaks Station actively used Sutherlands Hut for mustering until the 1970s. At this stage the property ran Romney sheep rather than merinos, and the increasing use of four-wheel drives meant that musterers had no need to stay overnight in the Mowbray Valley. The hut fell into decline, and on a 2000 visit tramper Mark Pickering found it in poor condition and seemingly unused.[7]

In 2001, however, Steve and Jo McAtamney purchased most of Four Peaks Station to add to their nearby farm, and they immediately saw the potential of this special building. Over the next couple of years, they restored Sutherlands Hut to make it part of their Four Peaks High Country Track. The building had remained essentially sound, but the McAtamneys repaired the roof, relined the interior with Oregon timber, fitted six new bunks and rebuilt the chimney. At the same time, Steve poured concrete into the cavity between the inner and outer stone walls, considerably strengthening the building. This foresight ensured the hut came through the September 2010 Canterbury earthquake unscathed.

Together with Pleasant Gully Hut (built in 1900) and Devils Creek Hut (built in the 1930s), Sutherlands is one of the Four Peaks High Country Track's three huts. The station offers mountain-biking and walking options on the track, which can be booked through its website.[8] The walk, together with a night in Sutherlands Hut, offers a rare chance to experience the isolated existence of the early boundary keepers, in a hut little changed from when it was first built more than 140 years ago.

ROB BROWN

Iron Whare c.1870s KAWEKA FOREST PARK, HAWKE'S BAY

The evocatively named Iron Whare lies on a beech-covered ridge near the Kaweka Flats. One of the oldest huts in the country, and the most venerable in Hawke's Bay, the diminutive whare has strong links to the area's development through sheep farming.

In the latter half of the nineteenth century, wool was pivotal to the Hawke's Bay economy, with small empires built from the backs of sheep. Once graziers had stocked the easier low country, they pushed further and further inland, right up into the remote mountains of the Kaweka Range.

The government purchased some 20,200 hectares of the central and southern Kaweka Range from Maori in 1859, then began leasing it to farmers.[1] During the following decade, two large sheep stations were established there and began grazing sheep on the range's tussock tops. Mangawhare stocked the southern Kawekas, while in the east Hawkestone Station ran merinos, and later Romneys, onto the main range.[2]

The Hawkestone Stock Route (still visible near the whare) began at the station homestead at Puketitiri, traversed the Black Birch Range, then climbed up to the Kaweka Flats. Here, fenced and grassed paddocks provided sufficient feed to last two horses a week.[3]

John Frost Turner, the first Pakeha settler at Puketitiri, worked as a shepherd for the Hallet family when they took over Hawkestone Station in the 1870s, until he got his own land. With the help of others, Turner built the Iron Whare for the Hallets, most likely in the mid-1870s.[4] The original architecture comprised pole beech supports covered with a 'malthoid skin',[5] a dirt floor and sacking bunks. The existing totara slabs, hand-adzed from the surrounding bush, were added later to provide additional support and reinforcing. The original sod chimney no longer exists, and corrugated iron eventually replaced the malthoid roof.[6]

From Kaweka Flats, graziers drove sheep up Dicks Spur and across the main Kaweka Range to Kiwi Saddle. Typically, sheep were usually mustered just once a year for shearing.[7] Mist often wreaked havoc with the muster, and shepherds once lost 3000 sheep in the clouds until their exceptional dog, Toss, single-handedly rounded them up over the next two days, arriving at camp 'very weary and footsore'.[8]

Although small, the Iron Whare could accommodate four men – or five at a pinch, and once even twelve, crammed into it 'rather like sardines'.[9] It must have been welcome shelter at the relatively lofty altitude of about 1000 metres. Snow can fall here at any time of year, although in summer temperatures can be baking hot.

Hawkestone sheep numbers peaked at about 3500 wethers in 1890, by which time the station had taken over the whole Kaweka Range. But by then fires and overgrazing had already caused a rapid decline in the native vegetation. The rate of erosion accelerated and the fragile soils began to wash away, leaving bare patches of clay.[10] In 1882, Augustus Hamilton – teacher, scientist and, later, director of the Dominion Museum – visited the Iron Whare during a Hallett family muster, and recorded these observations:

> The Kawekas look very bare and as if the amount of denudation going on was much more than is usual even in New Zealand. The front range, here known as the 'Black Birch Range' seems to be rapidly losing all its vegetation, through the fires destroying the grasses and small shrubs. The wind then has full power over the soil and the rains wash everything into the valleys.[11]

During this time, wild pigs, dogs and cattle roamed the range, including some ferocious bulls, and hunters also used the Iron Whare. John Frost Turner wandered across the Kawekas on three-week shooting

Tramper Edna Ansell pictured beside the Iron Whare in 1956.
PHOTO: ALAN BERRY

stints, using home-made lead bullets fired from a muzzle-loaded rifle. Cattle meat supplemented his staple diet of oats, and skins served as bedding.[12]

Grazing became more and more uneconomic, not helped by a rabbit plague, and Hawkestone Station finally retired the range in 1905, after one final muster.[13] Burning continued, however, as grazing depended on encouraging the tussock to grow highly palatable new shoots, while keeping the inedible fern at bay. During the 1920s, Turner and his grandson John Graham Lewis spent weeks staying at the Iron Whare, not only hunting and shepherding, but also burning, using a kerosene-soaked pumice block stuck onto a length of No. 8 wire for the purpose: 'They poked the burning block under every tussock bush they passed, thus burning off large areas at a time.'[14]

Another settler, John 'Jack' Ball, made an attempt – possibly illegally – to graze the area in 1920. At his farm near Ball's Clearing, he had only enough grazing land for about twenty sheep. For companionship and help, Ball asked John Lewis, then thirteen years old, to stay with him at the Iron Whare. Lewis's daughter, Pam Turner, recalls his words:

> [He] was sent to the Iron Whare to await the arrival of 500 merino wethers coming over the Black Birch Track from Puketitiri. It took them two hours from when they first appeared, coming over the Black Birch, to walk past the whare doorway. My father's job was to head them south towards the Kaweka Flats … Of the 500 wethers, only three were recovered alive; the others simply disappeared without trace.[15]

Ball continued to look for his stray sheep without much luck (some persisted in the ranges as late as the 1950s, one of them perhaps the 'rogue' of Rogue Ridge). Earlier in life, Ball had lost an eye in a fencing accident, and responded by buying a one-eyed dog and horse.[16] On one occasion when he was out searching for sheep, the one-eyed horse misjudged the steep terrain. 'Ball was quite elderly then

The Iron Whare in April 2012. PHOTO: SHAUN BARNETT/BLACK ROBIN PHOTOGRAPHY

and on one of those trips he was riding the horse being led by Lewis when the horse lost its footing up Dicks Spur and went over the side. Just in time, Lewis managed to get a belay around a rock, saving the horse, and possibly its rider, from sure death.'[17]

During his last stay, Ball once almost burnt down the Iron Whare, after he left an unattended stew simmering on the fire. Lewis returned just in time to find 'flames coiling the surrounding malthoid'. Ball, then quite absent-minded, had wandered off, 'looking for those damned lost sheep'.[18]

After the 1920s, the Iron Whare ended its days as a base for musterers. Between the 1920s and 1960s, the occasional hunter, rabbiter or tramper used it sporadically, but construction of both Middle Hill Hut and Kaweka Flats Biv by the Forest Service in 1963 rendered the old whare obsolete for overnight accommodation.

By 1981, maps marked the Iron Whare as 'derelict'. But, recognising the hut's historic nature, the Forest Service undertook some restoration work later in the 1980s, replacing the corrugated-iron roof. DOC lists the hut as one of three archaeological sites in Kaweka Forest Park. In 1990, the old hut was fully restored and its entrance porch (a later addition) removed. More maintenance work occurred in 1993, 1998 and 2000.[19] Very recently, DOC cut away trees around the site, both to reduce the risk of them falling on the historic hut and to let in more light.

The two-bunk Iron Whare is found on a side track just north of Kaweka Flats Biv.

SHAUN BARNETT

Old Manson Hut 1957 KAWEKA FOREST PARK, HAWKE'S BAY

Like the Iron Whare, the Old Manson Hut owes it existence to the sheep-grazing era of the Kaweka Range.

Of the several sheep stations that had grazing on the Kaweka Range and surrounds during the late nineteenth and early twentieth centuries, only one has survived: Ngamatea Station, one of the few places in the North Island where the term 'high country' seems appropriate. Located in a great chunk of elevated land west of the Kaweka Ranges and south of the Kaimanawa Mountains, it comprises numerous flat tussock plateaux dissected by a number of substantial rivers. For a period after Molesworth Station converted to cattle during the early 1970s, Ngamatea could even lay claim to being the largest sheep run in the country.[1] One wit wrote of the station 'It's not a farm; it's a bloody province.'[2]

Not surprisingly for such a large area, the station required a number of huts to shelter musterers working in the remote backblocks. Between the 1930s and 1960s these were Golden Hills, Boyd, Kaimanawa (or Te Apunga), Mangamingi, Burglars, Hawkins, Log Cabin and Peters – and the Old Manson Hut.[3] Many of these huts no longer exist, and of the survivors, the Old Manson Hut remains the best preserved.

Situated on a grassy slope surrounded by manuka and beech forest, the hut lies about twenty minute's walk below a high ridge typical of the terrain in this western part of the Kaweka Range. Nearby is the Tapahiwhenua Stream, a tributary of the Ngaruroro River.

The shelter's precursor, the original Manson Hut, was probably built by David Lumsden, who leased this part of the Kawekas from the government between 1906 and 1920 and ran sheep from his base at Kuripapango. Beech pole framing supported cladding made entirely with malthoid. From photographs taken during the 1940s, it seems this hut occupied the same site as the newer NZFS hut, up on the ridge crest.

In his 1971 book *Sunrise on the Hills*, Christopher Lethbridge wrote of mustering on Ngamatea during the early 1950s and recalled that the Manson, so remote from the Ngamatea homestead, was considered the worst to muster. He described the hut as 'a little black malthoid shack beside a clump of shaggy beech trees'. However, he continued, 'the hut seemed like an oasis in a desert. We barely paused to notice the piles of debris left by several generations of vermin in the sack bunks.'[4]

Another musterer recalled, 'The Manson hut was the least like home. It leaked and the floor turned to mud; the boys wore their gumboots inside.'[5] Despite the sometimes damp interior, dry weather wasn't welcomed either, as it created another problem. Built on a steep hillside, the hut lay unusually far from a water source, and a series of steps led steeply down to the creek below. During a mustering stint, anyone venturing outside was given billies and told to bring them back full of water. One thirsty musterer burnt a message into a beam with a poker 'Was the bastard who built this hut man or camel?'[6]

Legendary hunter and yarn-teller Barry Crump recalled a deer-culling stint at the hut during the 1950s in his autobiography, writing, 'It was a view I never got tired of. The Kaimanawa and Kaweka Ranges, their sides streaked with great grey shingle-slides, and the cold green Ngaruroro crashing down through the gorge between them, three thousand feet below.' Of the hut, he wrote, 'The fireplace was big and smoky, no matter where the wind was blowing from. There was hardly any firewood at

Trampers Jason Roxburgh and Bruce Postill in the Old Manson Hut, 2011.
PHOTO: SHAUN BARNETT/BLACK ROBIN PHOTOGRAPHY

that altitude and the nearest water was a tiny trickle about three hundred feet down the side of the ridge that had to be bailed into a billy with a mug.'[7]

When Mavis Davidson and a Heretaunga Tramping Club party stayed in the original hut during 1957, she remarked, 'It is an old malthoid structure, soon to be replaced.'[8] Later that same year, a new hut – what is now known as the 'Old Manson Hut' – was built, at a site closer to water. By chewing out valuable sheep-grazing land, deer and rabbits had become an increasing menace, and so Ngamatea Station and the Hawke's Bay Rabbit Board combined resources for the hut project. Rabbiter Les D'Ott and Internal Affairs culler Jack Wire, both based at Ngamatea, built the hut.[9]

Like its predecessor, this hut also used beech poles with a malthoid roof, but the exterior walls were instead a split slab construction made from totara and probably also beech.[10] It had no piles, a dirt floor, and a large open fireplace with an exterior chimney. Materials from the original hut were possibly recycled. The new 'Old Manson Hut' served for more than two decades, but by the time the Manson tops became part of Kaweka Forest Park in the 1970s, Ngamatea had long ceased farming it. The poor grazing, bad erosion, rough country and isolation all made it marginal sheep country at best. When the Forest Service built one of their standard six-bunk huts in 1972, they placed it on the ridge crest above at the same site as the original Manson Hut. This time, the hut had a water tank!

Somehow, the Old Manson Hut survived for another two decades, but by the early 1990s the rotten roof left the interior exposed to rain. Conservation architect Chris Cochran examined the hut in December 1993 to evaluate its historic status. Cochran described Old Manson as 'an excellent example of bush carpentry' and noted that it is an unusual design even for a slab hut, with the slabs acting solely as exterior sheathing, rather than forming a structural part of the walls. As a result of Cochran's report, DOC staff undertook restoration work during 1995-6. Rotten slabs were replaced with freshly hewn totara, and the roof made watertight. Then, in 2008, a team led by Dave Heaps installed a new malthoid roof. In subsequent years, DOC teams also built a new corrugated-iron chimney, and put fresh sacking on the bunks.[11]

Old Manson Hut is also a good example of a hut intended for multiple purposes: rabbiters, deer cullers and musterers all used it. For modern-day trampers, a night in the hut provides an experience of a past era: dirt floor, smoky interior and all.[12]

SHAUN BARNETT

Old Manson Hut in December 2011. PHOTO: SHAUN BARNETT/BLACK ROBIN PHOTOGRAPHY

The Manson Country in Winter Time – Anon, from the original Manson Hut logbook, October 1941[13]

My Creditors have sent me here
To make a living shooting deer
How I'll do it I don't know
The place is cursed
with rocks and snow.

It nearly makes the squatters weep
It takes five acres to a sheep
And each year sees smaller flocks
For sheep don't thrive
on snow and rocks.

The weather could not be much worse
Tis under God's most bitter curse
The driving sleets cut like a sabre
Since God has leased this
To his neighbour.

Hideaway Biv c.1890 AHURIRI CONSERVATION PARK, CANTERBURY

'At present chief packer and bottle washer for greasy bloody musterers on Quailburn.' In December 1944, Clifford John Munro, then run holder of Otematata, Kurow, scrawled these words on the wall of the diminutive mustering hut he was camped in.[1]

Munro probably didn't expect his words would survive, nor the hut they were written in. Musterers then knew the hut as Camp Creek, after the nearby stream, and somehow it survived the decades, probably helped by its drier location east of the Main Divide. With the formation of Ahuriri Conservation Park in 2004, the hut became part of the public conservation estate, and also got its new moniker, the nicely appropriate 'Hideaway Biv'. Reaching the rustic hut, nestled behind a dome-shaped hill in the Ahuriri Valley, involves a two-hour tramp from Birchwood Road.

Built most likely in about 1890, this five-bunker is one of the older backcountry huts on the conservation estate. Conservation architect Chris Cochran described the hut's character: 'Despite its small size, its simple form and appearance befits the drama of its tussock, stream and rock-outcrop setting. It is a very good example of a back country hut, built by the men who were to use it, using some local materials, and consequently having a workmanlike, rustic and serviceable character.'[2]

It was one of several mustering huts built on Benmore Station, then one of the largest runs in Otago, with some 94,700 sheep grazing 125,800 hectares of leasehold land in 1898.[3] Nine huts, probably including Hideaway Biv, existed by 1892. Although generally small, they were appreciated; in the wet, any hut is better than a tent.

After Benmore was split into smaller runs in 1916, the hut became part of Quailburn Station.[4] Over the decades, dozens of those who sheltered within the hut's confines scribbled their names onto the exterior walls and roof. Clifford Munro's signature survived, along with that of Governor General Lord Bledisloe, written on the roof in 1931. However, the earliest decipherable name is Jack Wall's, who wrote it there in 1890, possibly not long after the hut first went up.[5]

Over the years, many high-country folk stayed at the hut, sometimes when conditions were anything but benign. Musterer Rob McLeod, who worked on Quailburn Station between 1953 and 1970, recalled a five-day stint pinned in the hut by snow with four others. Despite that, he said, 'I loved that type of country. It was terrific mustering country.'[6]

Not all names record farming folk: some note Lands and Survey staff, a government culler and even an escaped prisoner. While some huts have a good record of their history in their hut logbooks, more than a century of use is documented in Hideaway Biv's historic graffiti. DOC officer Kiersten McKinley painstakingly transcribed all the decipherable writing, and recorded it on a handsome panel installed in the hut during 2007.[7]

The interior of Hideaway Biv consists of beech-pole framing, with the cladding trusty corrugated iron. In mid-2005, DOC restored the former mustering hut tastefully with the help of contractors Clint O'Brien, Nick Taylor and Laurie Ruddenklau. The men laid a new clay-concrete floor (as late as the 1950s, musterers slept on tussock spread over a dirt floor), removed the open fireplace, replaced the netting on the bunks, and added the modern comfort of new mattresses.

The restoration team fashioned two rustic seats and a table that fit the hut's character perfectly. They also shaped a new wooden door, complete with a neat little metal latch, and fixed in some memorabilia – a pair of boots, an old milk-powder tin and a horseshoe. All in all, they made a fine job.

Set near a small rock cliff, the hut commands fine views of the surrounding mountains. One musterer didn't like the outcrop's proximity, fearing that an earthquake would collapse onto the tin hut and crush its occupants. He slept outside.[8]

The almost tangible sense of history at Hideaway Biv elicits a nostalgia for high-country life, of summer-bleached tussocks, frigid winters, persistent nor'westers, men and dogs, sheep and wool. Being there, you can still almost smell the lanolin.

SHAUN BARNETT

LEFT AND OPPOSITE Hideaway Biv, Ahuriri Conservation Park, March 2010. PHOTOS: SHAUN BARNETT/BLACK ROBIN PHOTOGRAPHY

Shutes Hut 1920 RUAHINE FOREST PARK, HAWKE'S BAY

There are few enough stone huts in New Zealand, but they are rare indeed in the North Island – Shutes Hut may, in fact, be the only one. Located beside a tributary of the Taruarau River in the northern Ruahine Range, the hut occupies a grassy clearing fringed by pine trees. Rabbiter Alex Shute built it early in 1920, and today it's the only rabbiting hut remaining in the range.[1]

If any backcountry character trod the fine line between madness and eccentricity, yet always stayed on the right side of it, Alex Shute did. He lived in his namesake hut, off and on, for more than twelve years, often shunning company or sometimes even feigning madness to scare off other would-be occupants. At other times, when he did have visitors, he ignored them and talked to his dogs instead.

Born in 1882, Alex Shute hailed from Timaru, where perhaps he learnt the stonemason's craft. Possibly the availability of local stone influenced his decision to build Shutes Hut using this material, but packhorses still had to heft in the heavy mortar and roof iron. The finished hut had rough-hewn bunks for four (made from kanuka slats), a concrete floor, a stone hearth and a gabled corrugated-iron roof. To Shute's credit, the hut stayed dry, and the chimney didn't smoke.[2]

Shute had built the hut with E. Smith for the owners of Big Hill Station, T.P. Vautier and J.T. Hewitt, who then ran about 1000 sheep on the nearby open tops. The northern Ruahine Range was marginal scrub-covered country for grazing at best, and when rabbits threatened to overrun the place, the need for a semi-permanent rabbiter was assured.[3] After completing the hut, Alex Shute became the resident Big Hill rabbiter. He first tackled the pests using poison baits, then a pack of dogs – all named after various spirits: Whisky, Port, Brandy and Gin.[4]

The clearing around the hut also bears testimony to Shute's efforts. He planted eucalypts and pines, and even established an orchard of apple, cherry, peach and plum trees. Shute once carried a stunted twenty-year-old pear tree from its original location near Ruahine Hut to his orchard, where it thrived.[5]

In the late 1930s, Big Hill Station abandoned the area, but Shute continued to visit and stay at the hut.[6] Rabbit skins provided some income, and Shute was self-sufficient for meat and fruit. But his fondness for alcohol must have drained his meagre finances.

Most of what is known about Alex Shute comes from the pen of Lester Masters, a Hawke's Bay hunter of the 1920s to 1950s, who recorded many yarns in his 1960 book, *Back Country Tales*. Masters knew Shute personally, and in one chapter relates something of the rabbiter's character: 'Alex was no man's mug. He was just a shrewd, sane man, living a lonely life, who gained amusement by trying and often succeeding, in fooling others, including myself, that he was nuts.'[7]

On one occasion a packman, new to the game, arrived at Shutes Hut with supplies on horseback. He found Shute, or more precisely just his bald head, sticking out of a nearby waterhole. The packman could get no word from Shute: 'No matter which side of the hole he stood, all Alex would do, was turn his head accordingly, and just keep staring fixedly at him.'[8] When the unnerved packie saddled up to flee, Shute raced after him, stark naked, saying he was just acting the goat. But the packie didn't come back. On another occasion a packie found Shute fighting with his coat, but when the station manager later questioned him about it, Shute claimed to have been simply hanging out his washing.[9]

Shute served during the First World War prior to his arrival in Hawke's Bay, where he worked as a shepherd for Big Hill before turning to rabbiting.[10] What drove him to lead his hermit-like existence? Avoiding the temptation of too much drink was one possible reason. Masters suggests this, in one of his poems, 'He would pull your leg, and he would drink your grog,' and also says Shute restricted access to money when on a spree in town.[11] Perhaps the horrors of what he experienced in the war led him to shun people. Who knows? After years of an often solitary existence, Shute died in 1948, and lies buried at the Napier cemetery.

Lester Masters knew the value of recording stories and route information, and during the 1950s installed hut logbooks in neat metal boxes at several Ruahine huts, a practice not yet in widespread use at the time. Fortunately, a copy of the original Shutes Hut logbook (1956–81) is still in the hut,

LEFT An illustration of Alex Shute from Lester Master's 1960 book *Back Country Tales*.
OPPOSITE Shutes Hut, April 2012 and the original Shutes Hut logbook case, donated by Lester Masters.
PHOTOS: SHAUN BARNETT/BLACK ROBIN PHOTOGRAPHY

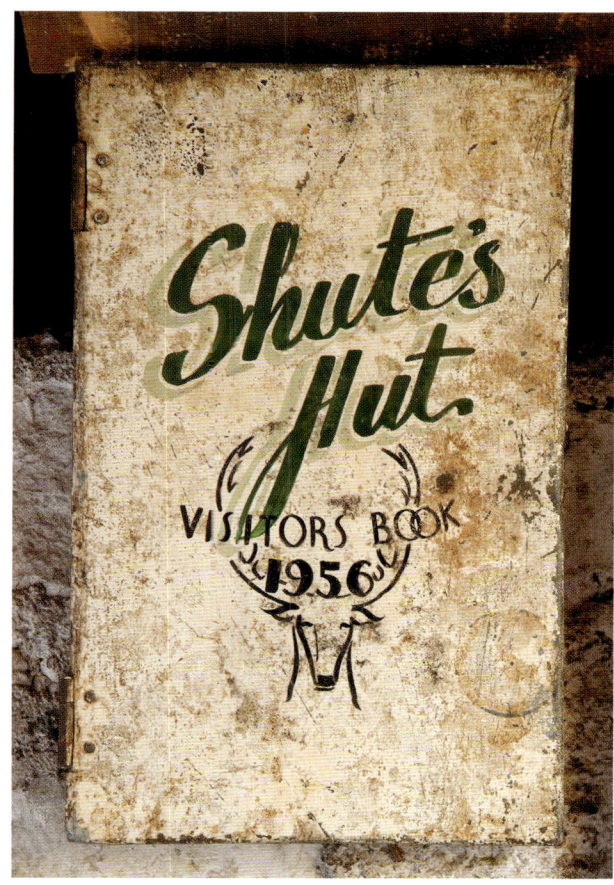

complementing the current large hardback tome begun in 1985 and still only half full. Very few huts have such a long and interesting record.¹²

In 1965, Forest Service personnel J. Hoy and Mike Barnett recorded their maintenance efforts in the hut book: 'Came from Nomans in the fog – oh my god! Came to try and fix the place up – what a job!; I measured here, I measured there; The materials are yet to come.'¹³

These days, Shutes remains in excellent condition, thanks to DOC and various individuals who have undertaken maintenance and restoration work at the hut, notably in 1994 and 2003.¹⁴ The logbook is full of praise for the hut, if not for the 'possum-sized' rats that occasionally plague it. One 2003 visitor, John Russell, reckoned that in over thirty years of roaming the backcountry he had never before 'seen such a charming hut'. He returned the following year to re-establish Shute's daffodil beds beside the hut.¹⁵ Russell also searched for remains of the orchard, but could find only one gooseberry bush. Another man, hunter Paul Sanderson, grew to love the hut, visiting often over a period of more than twenty years, and it was he who donated the huge 1985 logbook. He recorded delight at seeing the daffodils, writing, 'If old Alec could see them, from wherever he resides in the hereafter; I am sure he would have a grin a mile wide.' After Sanderson himself died in 2011, his family scattered his ashes near Shutes Hut.¹⁶

Shute's pine trees rise tall and majestic behind the hut, and there are still about forty of them, although DOC has cut some down to let in more light and reduce the risk of one falling on the historic stone hut, now over ninety years old.

SHAUN BARNETT

Alex
By Lester Masters (1956)

Old Alex is dead, his life now passed
His earthly days ended too fast
Leaving his hut, his home so loved
The grand old pines, towering above
The stranger who used his home once loved
Hoping, as I do, that they in turn
Will cherish and respect, not damage or burn
His wonderful home in the hills.

Ellis Hut 1884 RUAHINE FOREST PARK, HAWKE'S BAY

Historic Ellis Hut is a simple, square, two-room structure, with a corrugated-iron roof and a couple of sash windows. The oldest hut in the Ruahine Range, it owes its origins to sheep farming, but its name and notoriety to a suspected murderer. In 1904, police arrested James William Ellis at the hut in a dramatic event not unlike a scene from a cowboy film.

Ellis, also known by the alias John McKenzie, bore scars on his back from a lashing he'd endured as a punishment during his imprisonment for rape in the 1880s.[1] Despite departing prison early for good behaviour, Ellis found it hard to shake off his past. In 1903, he was working as a farmhand on the Wairarapa's Te Awaiti Station, cutting scrub with a gang headed by Leonard Collinson. Collinson taunted Ellis relentlessly about the scars and soon after had him dismissed for allegedly shooting station stags.[2]

Ellis suspected Collinson had dobbed him in, and – according to one source – swore revenge. 'Hold on till I see Collinson out back,' one witness claimed Ellis had said, 'I'll do for that bastard.'[3]

When Collinson was discovered dead on 26 February 1904, shot with a single bullet from a distance of about 250 metres, Ellis became the prime suspect. But by then, the crack shot was on the run, using his bushman's skills to evade authorities.[4] Newspapers ran dramatic headlines following the story.

After several months of searching for Ellis without success, sometimes following false leads, police heard of some petty thefts near a bushman's camp in Ormondville. Finally, a shepherd reported smoke rising from the chimney of Whitnell Hut, which was supposed to be unoccupied. Someone had recently stolen food from the nearby Wakarara Store, so the hunt was on.[5]

Two policemen, Detective Charles Broberg and Constable Willcocks, disguised as swagmen and accompanied by a local acting as guide, approached the hut furtively on 10 December 1904. Bush provided cover at first, but they faced the final 180 metres across open ground. Conscious that Ellis would be on edge, and also of his known ability as a marksman, Broberg decided to breach the hut from behind, where a gully in Dutch Creek provided some cover to approach its window-less southern aspect.[6]

Broberg reached the hut without being detected, and through a window spotted Ellis bending over the fire. Then he boldly stepped inside. Various versions of the arrest that followed suggest differing details, one claiming improbably (definitely the cowboy film version) that a shot was fired through the roof.[7] However, court evidence states that after Ellis made a move towards the door, lowering his rifle, Broberg tackled him and then, with the help of Willcocks and the guide, handcuffed him.[8]

The nation keenly followed the resulting murder trial, which was not without controversy. All evidence against Ellis was entirely circumstantial. The jury gave a guilty verdict but 'with a recommendation to mercy, on the ground of great provocation'. Nevertheless, Ellis was hanged on 8 February 1905, protesting his innocence right to the end.[9]

Those events ensured the hut subsequently became known as Murderer's or Ellis Hut. However, its previously name, Whitnell Hut, comes from shepherd Bill Whitnell, who lived for years at the hut while working at Poporangi Station. A remittance man, Whitnell was something of a character, and once had several fellow shepherds searching a 26-kilometre stretch of track for his missing false teeth, lost during a drunken ride home. Remarkably, they found them.[10]

The station, first established in 1856, was one of several large, high-country runs in the more mountainous parts of Hawke's Bay. It stretched from near the edge of the Wakarara Range to the tops of the Ruahine Range, and was never easy country to farm.[11]

The hut, built in 1884, has two rooms and a quality of workmanship that suggests it was probably an outstation – a building larger than the normal one-room mustering or hunting hut. The enormous size of Poporangi Station dictated more comfortable quarters that could serve as a permanent base for shepherds, as well as rabbiters and

hunters.[12] Two men, Bill Marsh and Jack Curtis, built the hut using pit-sawn timber and a corrugated-iron roof. They lined it with hand-dressed tongue-and-groove boards, which together with the rough-sawn exterior is a rare combination in a backcountry hut. Bill Whitnell lived in it for many years.[13]

Photos from the 1920s show quite open country surrounding the hut; today, the hut clearing is bordered by regenerating native forest on one side and the exotic pines of Gwavas Forest on the other. Access to the hut is easiest via Yeoman's Track, an old logging road that penetrates the forests in the Ruahine foothills and makes for a pleasant walk or mountain-bike ride.

Despite almost burning down once in 1935, when the wooden chimney framing caught fire, Ellis Hut remained in reasonable condition during the first half of the twentieth century, and even had its original china doorknob when a Heretaunga Tramping Club party visited in 1946. The Forest Service replaced the damaged chimney in the 1960s, but although deer cullers and trampers continued to use it, the hut became increasingly dilapidated.[14] In 1995, DOC staff undertook major restoration work of the hut as part of a workshop, removing graffiti, repiling the hut, replacing windows and recladding some of the walls with pine.

The information panel inside states that Ellis Hut 'has great significance as a rare example of a fully hand-worked early European timber building. It was built using old hand crafts once universal in western society but now extinct – hand rip-sawing, planing and moulding, and most significant, the hand worked tongue and groove lining.'

SHAUN BARNETT

OPPOSITE The 1904 wanted poster for suspected murderer James Ellis. ILLUSTRATION: THE DOMINION.
ABOVE Roy McGlasban checking sheep at Ellis Hut, Poporangi Station, circa 1926. The Forest Service later replaced the wooden-framed chimney visible here with a metal one. PHOTO: J. MCGLASBAN, COURTESY OF DOC.
LEFT Ellis Hut, February 2004. PHOTO: SHAUN BARNETT/BLACK ROBIN PHOTOGRAPHY

Riordans Hut 1926 KAHURANGI NATIONAL PARK

Despite the long tradition of high-country farming that continues in many parts of the South Island, notably Southland, Otago and Canterbury, many trampers might be surprised to learn just how extensive grazing once was in other mountainous parts of the country.

In Northwest Nelson, sheep once grazed the Wangapeka Valley and tops, the Gouland Downs, the Haupiri Range, the tops of the Arthur Range and the Matiri Plateau, the Douglas Range at Boulder Lake, the Cobb Valley, and the Tablelands. Farmers even ran cattle in the Leslie and Karamea valleys. Grazing continued in many areas, even after Northwest Nelson Forest Park was formed in 1965, under a licensing system administered by the Forest Service. However, grazing was largely phased out by the time DOC took over in 1987.[1]

Cyprian Brereton's book *No Roll of Drums* (1947) records the author's memories of days spent mustering the Lockett Range and Tablelands, and Gerard Hindmarsh's *Kahurangi Calling* (2010) details the lives of sheep farmers who worked the Haupiri and Boulder Lake areas. Despite quite extensive farming in the past, very few relics of this era remain in the park.

One exception is the three-bunk Riordans Hut. Set on a high, scrubby plateau inland from Takaka, the hut is reached after a strenuous ascent up the Kill Devil Track. These days, as you walk up the old gold-mining bridle track, it seems unfathomable that any of it was once suitable for sheep grazing. Precious little remains in the way of grass, the soils are thin, and vast stands of manuka cover much of the area. But this relatively recent regrowth has cloaked the land only since the late 1950s. During the early 1900s, pioneer farmers used fire to scorch the area's original vegetation, and once grass and grazing had become established, more blazes kept the scrub at bay.

Laurie and Fred Riordan built the hut in 1926 (with some material recycled from a shelter established five years earlier), using totara framing and mountain cedar slabs split on site for the cladding, then added a beech lean-to in the 1940s.[2] The hut served as a base from which they could muster the 2000 wethers they farmed on a government lease. Rather than spread grass seed by hand, the brothers reputedly sprinkled it onto the backs of the sheep for hoofed distribution.[3] During the Depression of the 1930s, the Riordans shared the hut with the occasional gold miner using it as a stopover on their way to Waingaro Forks. The brothers ran a sideline supplying these miners, using four packhorses to carry supplies in to Waingaro Forks for a reasonable profit.[4]

Farming such high, remote country would never be anything but marginal (grass cover peaked at about 30 per cent), but the Riordan brothers struggled on until the late 1950s, when they abandoned the area.[5] After that, Riordans Hut remained a rustic shelter for the few trampers and hunters that passed through.

In the 1970s, the hut had captivated Forest Service ranger Max Polglaze during the time he spent working in the Cobb Valley, and on a later visit in December 2000 he was saddened to see its increasingly dilapidated state. He recorded in the hut book: 'Five days of most excellent quiet time in & around this peaceful old cabin, fasting and listening for the small, still voice. Went and fetched the riding saddles from Skeet Creek one day … Rebuilt the disintegrating door one day – would dearly love to restore the whole hut.'[6]

At least one tramper agreed, writing in the hut book: 'Hey DOC, how about hiring Max to restore this hut? Both he and this hut are treasures not to be squandered.'[7]

Riordans Hut before restoration, circa late 1990s. PHOTO: DOC TAKAKA

Polglaze duly suggested the idea to DOC. Although the hut didn't fully meet priorities for restoration, DOC historian Steve Bagley from Nelson argued that the expenditure was warranted if trampers could use the hut.[8]

Between October and November 2003, Polglaze and DOC officer John Taylor (also an ex-Forest Service ranger) beautifully restored the hut, using a dead mountain cedar they milled on site. A long-handled adze made an authentic if arduous tool for splitting the cedar log into planks and shingles. By retaining the framing and rafters, and reusing any cedar slabs that were still in good condition, the two men retained as much of the original hut as possible – although the downward lean needed correction.[9]

Using stones and clay for mortar, the men rebuilt the chimney base, lugging the material from some distance away, and flattened old tar drums for the main chimney. The six-week project cost a modest $12,000.[10] On 15 November 2003, Polglaze wrote in the hut book: 'The job is done, the hut is repaired. On the whole, we think it turned out well.'[11]

Trampers who visited the hut after the restoration were enchanted. One wrote 'A great old hut of character has become a great new hut of character. Hopefully it will last another 75+ years. Wonderful to see some old Forest Service practicality Max & John.'[12]

Near the hut, remains of a six-wire fence serve as further reminders of the Riordans' farming era. Many of the silver pine and totara posts have withstood the vicissitudes of the mountain climate, although the battens have largely rotted away, and parts of the fence now lie on the ground.

In 2009, John Taylor undertook further restoration work at the hut with fellow DOC officer Joe Hambrook, who – fittingly – is a grandson of Laurie Riordan.

SHAUN BARNETT

CLOCKWISE FROM TOP LEFT Riordans Hut pictured in 2005 after its restoration. PHOTO: SHAUN BARNETT/BLACK ROBIN PHOTOGRAPHY Max Polglaze and John Taylor outside the restored hut in 2003. PHOTO: DOC TAKAEA Riordans Hut interior, 2005. PHOTO: SHAUN BARNETT/BLACK ROBIN PHOTOGRAPHY

Meg Hut c.1860s/1926 PISA CONSERVATION AREA, CENTRAL OTAGO

Huts have existed on the Pisa Range almost as far back as the 1850s, when the two original grazing runs were established to cover the high country between the Kawarau River and Lake Wanaka. The range initially comprised two Crown leases established in 1858 (one in the west and one in the east), but by 1860 both were combined as the Mt Pisa Station.[1] At this time the hinterland of Central Otago was considered an empty wilderness, but the Otago gold rush – just a few years away – would change the whole region from a remote pastoral backwater to a bustling land of opportunity.

Mt Pisa Station was initially owned by Robert Wilkin and Archibald Thompson, who sold it to Robert Andrew Loughnan and his cousin Ignatius Loughnan in 1867. David Howell joined Ignatius Loughnan in partnership in the early 1870s, and the two continued to run the property until 1924.[2] In 1882, when Mt Pisa Station was recorded at 82,044 acres (33,202 hectares),[3] calls from the government to break up such large estates resulted in the run being put up for auction. Such 'dummy' auctions were common at the time, and Howell and Loughnan outbid everyone for the entire block and simply continued as before.[4]

One of the earliest mustering huts in the Pisa Range, built in the 1860s, was a small stone building whose remains can be seen just behind the present Meg Hut. It was initially used by the station's cook and head shepherd during musters. Each March, the musterers brought the wethers down off the exposed tops and camped in tents near the hut, enduring the long, cold autumnal nights with the help of an outside fireplace. In the 300-hectare Meg Paddock, southwest of the hut, the sheep were eye-clipped before being turned out onto the warmer east faces of the Cardrona Valley. One of the early musterers, Jack Scurr, remembered that the whole process took six weeks, during which time the men were based at the camp.[5] The lack of firewood on these exposed tussock tops meant the musterers had to use peat for heating instead. They cut blocks of the fuel from the flats with a special L-shaped shovel, leaving them to dry under an iron shelter.

By 1907, some 35,000 merinos grazed the Pisa Range, a scale of sheep farming barely fathomable these days.[6] Despite such high sheep numbers, Mt Pisa Station went through some tough times, and the government purchased it in 1921 with the intention of splitting it into smaller farms for closer settlement.

The division into twelve blocks occurred in 1924.[7] In 1925, Robert (Bob) Lee took on the lease of the 2712-hectare Waiorau Station, which included a significant part of the Pisa Range tops. The following year, he replaced the original two-person stone hut with a corrugated-iron hut capable of housing six musterers. Bob Lee and his brother Edgar also planted a grove of exotic trees near the hut in 1926 to serve as firewood.[8] In 1958, Meg Hut was modified to its current size and was given a concrete floor, insulation and a modernised bunk layout. In 1964, Bob Lee sold the Waiorau lease to his son John.

In the early 1990s, Waiorau Station went through the tenure review process under the Land Act 1948. This enabled the owners to develop an extensive Nordic skiing snow park on the Pisa Range, as well as summer activities such as mountain biking and walking, while still farming the low country. As a result of these negotiations with the Crown, the Lees surrendered a good portion of the grazing lease, including a large part of the Pisa Range. This landscape became the core of the Pisa Conservation Area, which eventually expanded to 22,000 hectares after other leasehold blocks also went through tenure review.

The Pisa Conservation Area gives the public access to the spectacular tussock grasslands of this

range, and a visit to the eight-bunk Meg Hut is often part of that experience. One excellent route out from the hut passes over Tuohys Saddle and into the Roaring Meg catchment, and from there continues down to the Kawarau River.

The Lees kept ownership of Bob Lee Hut, at the western end of the Pisa Range, and on completion of the land exchange this was moved onto the freehold part of Waiorau Station and restored and updated; it now provides a key part of their back-country tourism business. A new hut, Meadow Lee, was also built by the Lees as part of this business.

ROB BROWN

Meg Hut, April 2010. PHOTO: ROB BROWN

Rangitata/Hakatere Mustering Huts c.1880s/1967
TE KAHUI KAUPEKA AND HAKATERE CONSERVATION PARKS, CANTERBURY

Farmers have grazed the high country of the Rangitata Valley since the late 1850s, mainly through the pastoral lease system. Over the history of grazing in this remote, tough country, sizes of sheep flocks have fluctuated greatly depending on economic and climate conditions. Before the 1960s, grazing occurred on a scale comparable to that on the largest Otago stations, with runs like Mt Possession carrying flocks of wethers that required mustering teams of ten or more men to round them up in the autumn. When bad weather hampered efforts, mustering on the highest stations like Mesopotamia could easily take weeks.

Some Rangitata stations once had boundaries that extended all the way to the crest of the Southern Alps, but much of this land has been progressively retired from grazing, most of it in the last decade. Some of this retired grazing land has been returned to Crown management and amalgamated into two conservation parks covering parts of the Rangitata headwaters: the Te Kahui Kaupeka and Hakatere.

Today, many of the remaining smaller stations, both freehold and leasehold, produce fine merino wool for firms specialising in high-quality garments, and several shepherds and dogs are still required for the musters. Grazing merinos in the Rangitata headwaters continues to be an integral part of the Canterbury high country, but many farmers have diversified to help provide more balance and sustainability to their operations.

Some of Canterbury's earliest high-country stations were located in the area. As a result, it has a rich heritage of mustering huts, some on the land that has been retired from grazing but many more on stations still in use. Only a few of the numerous farming huts in the Rangitata/Hakatere area are mentioned here; apart from Lake Emma Hut, all are on the Te Araroa Walkway – the walking track that extends the length of New Zealand.

Hakatere/Ashburton Te Araroa Trail Huts
In April 1857, just a year behind pastoral pioneers Charles Tripp and John Acland, Thomas Potts and his brothers-in-law Henry (Harry) Philips and Francis Leach explored the Ashburton Lakes area as far as Lake Heron in search of grazing country. Between them, Acland and Tripp had already taken up huge runs on both sides of the Rangitata, including what would become Mt Possession and Mt Somers stations. These added to their already extensive Mt Peel run south of the Rangitata.

Somewhat ironically given his fascination with wildlife, Potts had amassed a modest fortune as an investor in his family's small-arms manufacturing business in England. A man of wide interests, he took up the Hakatere run and was perhaps New Zealand's first farmer/conservationist. His regular writings for newspapers, as well his collected essays in the book *Out in the Open*,[1] expressed some of the earliest conservation ideals in the country, and

LEFT Hakatere Stone Cottage, May 2012. The cottage was built in 1862 for Thomas Pott's Hakatere Station. In September 2010, the Canterbury Earthquake damaged the hut's stonework slightly, which will be repaired in the planned restoration of this historic building. PHOTO: ROB BROWN
OPPOSITE Lake Emma Hut may date back as late as the 1860s, although the best current estimate suggests that the 1880s is more likely. Pictured here in 2012, the historic hut is now managed by DOC, and is no longer available for overnight accommodation. PHOTO: ROB BROWN

his 1878 article on 'national domains' fostered ideas that eventually led to New Zealand embracing the national parks concept.

Potts lived in his impressive mansion at Governors Bay on Banks Peninsula, while managers ran his 32,800-hectare Hakatere Station. After initially stocking the farm with cattle, he had converted to merino sheep by the 1860s. The manager's cottage at Hakatere, built in 1862, is now possibly the oldest stone building in the Rangitata/Hakatere area.[2] As its construction was coming to an end, a somewhat gruesome episode unfolded, demonstrating the harshness of winters here.

Jesson Davis, a young shepherd, left Mesopotamia one winter morning and crossed the Rangitata River before heading across towards the Hakatere. The further he went, the deeper the snow became, and by the time he made the safety of the Hakatere Stone Cottage he was more dead than alive. Jim Bradford, who was building the cottage, was in residence with another shepherd. They tried to rub some circulation back into Davis's legs, but when his boots and socks were cut off, the frost-bitten flesh came away to reveal the bones of his feet. By the morning, Davis, in excruciating pain, was rushed to Christchurch, where a doctor amputated his legs below the knee – without anaesthetic, of course. He survived the ordeal, however, and adapted to his shorter legs, eventually returning to farming.[3]

Further up the valley is another of the region's venerable huts, on the shores of Lake Emma. Its exact age remains unknown, but some type of hut possibly existed here as early as the 1860s. This area was originally part of Mt Possession Station, and one story is that George Lambie and his wife were based here before the stone hut at Hakatere was built.[4] This seems unlikely, and the earliest maps of the region, dating from before 1900,[5] don't show a hut here, but there is nothing unusual in that. A later 1918 map doesn't indicate a hut either, but Lake Emma Hut was definitely there by then. With Lake Emma we therefore have a hut that everyone knows is historic, but no one is sure quite just how historic.

The original hut cladding was slab and batten, fixed using square nails. A tack room, clad in corrugated iron, was added to the hut at a later date – probably in about 1900, as indicated by the trademark stamp on the iron.[6] The earliest signatures on Lake Emma Hut date from the 1890s, but confusingly these are on the door to the later tack room. One signature even dates back as far as 1886, but historians have treated this with caution given the date of the iron.[7] This is an example of just how hard it can be to date huts, which are sometimes a hotchpotch of recycled materials.

Its two rooms (one of which has a coal range) and the historical ground evidence of a vegetable garden, indicate that Lake Emma Hut was certainly used as a home at some stage, but its exact purpose has puzzled historians. Aspects of the hut design suggest a boundary-keeping hut, but its location has never been on any defined station boundary.

The hut's layout is not consistent with the classic mustering hut of the period either. Perhaps it was simply an outstation for shepherds, closer to their day-to-day work on the vast Mt Possession run, and used in a similar way to Ellis Hut in the Ruahines (see p. 52). However, its location just 7 kilometres from Hakatere Stone Cottage dampens that theory. Although reaching Lake Emma requires a side trip from the Te Araroa Track, a visit is well worthwhile for its history and location.

Another old hut site exists on the south branch of the Swin River, which drains the Taylor Range. An 1889 map held at the Canterbury Museum

CLOCKWISE FROM TOP LEFT Crooked Spur Hut; Stone Hut; Double Hut: all pictured in 2011. PHOTOS: ROB BROWN

indicates a hut at this location,[8] and by 1919 maps name the 'Double Huts'. The current Double Hut was probably built sometime between 1902 and 1906, possibly using material recycled from the earlier huts.[9] In the 1930s, a lean-to was added to enlarge the hut after Clent Hills was incorporated into Mt Somers Station. During the 1990s, the wall separating the lean-to and the main hut was knocked out to improve the bunk layout.[10]

Aside from Clent Hills Station musterers, trampers and climbers heading to Mt Taylor have used the hut. A couple of years before he climbed Mt Everest, a certain E. P. Hillary left his name scrawled into a discrete corner of the hut. Today, Double Hut is the first hut reached on the Te Araroa Trail after you cross from the Rakaia and drop off the Taylor Range into the Hakatere Basin.

Rangitata Te Araroa Trail Huts

Across the Harper Range on the southern side of the Rangitata is one of New Zealand's most famous stations – Mesopotamia. After the station went through the tenure review process in 2008, a number of its numerous mustering huts – some of which have an interesting history – were transferred to the public hut network.

Three of these huts are linked by the Te Araroa Trail, which heads up Bush Stream beside the Mesopotamia homestead area. The first to be reached is Crooked Spur Hut. A shelter was originally built at the foot of Crooked Spur to replace the Brabazon

Royal Hut in October 2011. PHOTO: ROB BROWN

Range Hut, which had burnt down in 1885.[11] In 1946–47, Malcolm Prouting rebuilt the hut on a tussock terrace higher up, which proved to be a sunnier site and was close to a much better holding area for mobs mustered off the tops near Brabazon Ridge.

Up over a small saddle from Crooked Spur, the landscape opens into a wide basin behind the Sinclair Range. As the trail curves into the headwaters of Bush Stream, trampers reach Stone Hut. This has always been a strategic site for a mustering hut, and people associated with Mesopotamia remembered a small, basic stone shelter near the current site from as early as the 1880s. Another stone hut was built close to the current hut in the early 1900s, but by all accounts it was pretty rough and not much loved.[12] The current Stone Hut was built in 1939 and is tucked under a slope on the western side of the Sinclair Range. The substantial structure once measured 7 metres by 4 metres, but after a 1967 winter avalanche demolished most of it, only the stone chimney and southern quarter remained. The following summer, the hut was rebuilt using corrugated iron and timber framing but incorporating the original impressive stone remnants.[13]

Further up, in an idyllic tussock basin, lies the eight-bunk Royal Hut, another mustering hut Initially known as 'New Hut', this was again built as part of Prouting's redevelopment of the station. After Prince Charles and Princess Anne visited the hut in 1971, it gained its 'Royal' moniker. Musterers from Lake Tekapo stations often shared the hut during the autumn months with Mesopotamia staff.

Situated just a couple of kilometres further up Bush Stream from Royal Hut is one of the oldest surviving mustering huts in the Rangitata – Richmond Hut. Signatures inside date back as far as 1896.[14] Although tiny, and with headroom and a door seemingly built for hobbits, it once provided welcome shelter for musterers nonetheless.

ROB BROWN

Beech Hut[1] c.1905 EYRE MOUNTAINS/TAKA RA HAKA CONSERVATION PARK, SOUTHLAND

Tucked in the head of the Mataura Valley and surrounded by the Eyre Mountains, Beech Hut has been variously known as Top Hut, Top Mataura Hut and Birch Hut. Beech was often referred to as birch in early New Zealand, and both trees belong to the same order, Fagales. However, all New Zealand beeches are part of the beech family (Fagaceae) and no natives belong to the birch family (Betulaceae), so birch is a misnomer.

A classic squat structure clad in corrugated iron, the hut has its door beside the open fireplace at one end and a sleeping bench across the back under a small window. With an earth floor, the hut is about as basic as they come. Packhorses would have brought the iron in, while local silver beech and mountain toatoa (celery pine) provided framing timber.

The upper Mataura was originally part of Glenquoich Sheep Station near Kingston. Owner William Cameron split the station in January 1862, and the upper Mataura ended up in a new run bought by Captain Howell of Riverton, who gave it the name Fairlight Station. Howell stayed in Riverton while a Mr and Mrs Daniel managed the property for him. According to George Hamilton, 'Most of the hands employed on the run came from the whaling station at Riverton, and were a mixture of all nations and colours.'[2] Cainard Station was later split off Fairlight, and in the mid-1870s the two runs were shearing a combined total of 78,000 sheep. But in 1878 a big snowstorm decimated the flocks, cutting numbers in half. This provides the background to Beech Hut being built for mustering in about 1905.

This is big country. Eyre Peak rises behind the hut to almost 2000 metres, with tussock growing much of the way up it. Sheep were spread out across the tops, and mustering was a five-day affair. A panel inside Beech Hut explains the station's autumn mustering technique. Up to nine men, each with their horse and dogs, would head up the Mataura Valley. After a night at Pig Gully Hut on the way, they all headed up to Beech Hut, where they split up. Three men and their dogs mustered over the ranges on foot, sweeping through the upper basins of Eyre Creek and down to Dog Box Hut. The others mustered the upper basins of the Mataura and returned to Beech Hut. On the fourth day, both parties converged again in the Mataura at Cowshed Hut. Together, they continued down with their 2500-odd sheep to stay the last night at Pig Gully Hut again.

After it stopped being used for mustering in the 1960s, Beech Hut deteriorated, and could easily have fallen into ruin.[3] However, in March 1989, a keen group of three volunteers – Dusty Coleman from Riversdale, Ken Lindsay from Invercargill and Gypsy Roth from the USA – set out to restore the hut over five days. DOC's Fergus Sutherland coordinated the project, while locals donated materials, including helicopter time. The trio did a great job, replacing rotten framing with the same local materials originally used to build the hut. Some of the original framing posts had been used as a kind of mustering logbook, with the names of mustering teams and events recorded in pencil dating as far back as the 1910s. These posts were saved during the restoration and incorporated into the walls. Nine names appear on one list from 1917, including 'W Cable ... A McCaughan ... F Padget ... P. Ryan Packer', but parts of the others are obscured. Underneath, 'Fall Muster Cainard 1919' heads another list of names.

Inside the hut, a panel records the 1989 restoration efforts in a slightly tongue-in-cheek style:

> This palatial abode was resurrected from the brink of imminent deterioration by a motley crew of novice conservationists. After 5 exciting days of intense planning, resourceful technique and skilled craftsmanship, this hut was transformed from its state of decay to its present condition of rugged splendour. Through torrential downpours, howling winds, spitting snow, plummeting temperatures and even a brief but orgasmic moment of brilliant sunshine these three persevered.[4]

Further restoration work occurred in 2002. Without these efforts, the hut would no doubt have succumbed to the harsh winters and collapsed, buried under a blanket of snow.

Like most of the people travelling to the hut, Becky and I drove in from Fairlight Railway Station along Cainard Road and crossed Robert Creek. The four-wheel-drive track leading up the Mataura Valley passes through Cainard run, on an easement negotiated by DOC for public access, passing through open tussock and matagouri country, scruffy and unadorned. Sheep graze in small groups, and cattle wander on the hill, but scatterings of beech forest remain in places too. A copse up one side valley has been given the wonderfully imaginative name 'Bowels of the Earth'. The mind boggles at what's up there. Further up the main valley is Cowshed Hut, another nicely restored farming gem managed by DOC.

Travel up the Mataura River above here is not difficult, and by the time we reached Beech Hut on a tussock and Spaniard flat, we had views of beech forest stretching appropriately across the valley. Most entries in the logbook tell of trampers and hunters up for a look before returning the same way, but others travel beyond, into the Lochy River and further corners of the little-visited Eyre Mountains.

GEOFF SPEARPOINT

Beech Hut, April 2012. PHOTO: GEOFF SPEARPOINT

Ida Railway Hut 1919/1980 MT IDA CONSERVATION AREA, CENTRAL OTAGO

As its name suggests, the Ida Railway Hut began life down in the Ida Valley on the Otago Central Railway line. Perhaps no other building has undergone such a remarkable journey to become a backcountry hut.

Opened in 1901, the Ida Valley Railway Station served for many years as the line's terminus before it was extended to Middlemarch. The original station building was identical in size to those remaining at Ranfurly and Middlemarch, but after it burnt down in 1919, the replacement was a much smaller standard design. The station served for almost sixty years until the line closed in 1978, when it seemed this fine piece of public service architecture would become redundant. However, farmer Laurie Inder got hold of the building, planning to use it to add to an already existing mustering hut near the Hawkdun Range.

This rather audacious plan involved hauling, pushing and manoeuvring the old station 800 metres up onto the Hawkdun Range, 200 metres along Walking Spur, then 200 metres up onto the vast plateau used by the Mt Ida Syndicate for summer grazing. The move took place in about 1980, when over a week two bulldozers dragged the old railway building 18 kilometres over a rough four-wheel-drive track to its new home at an altitude of 1500 metres. Things went almost without hitch until, just short of the new site, the building rolled, causing damage to the cladding. Inder repaired it with corrugated iron, but thankfully the rest of the building has remained authentic. It has since become known as Inder's Castle.[1]

The Ida Railway Hut now sits in its surreal tussock grassland setting, far from any train. During summer, the Mt Ida Syndicate grazes merinos on the plateau under a concession from DOC, and each autumn the men return to the hut for the muster. While the hut is now available to the public, musterers get preference between 7 January and 30 April.[2]

ROB BROWN

Inder's Castle
by 'Blue Jeans' (Ross McMillan)[3]
It perches on the mountain top miles from anywhere,
And prayers and sweat and God knows what else got it there;
Beyond the Poison barrel and the Stone Man and Swing bridge
Solid, squat, it braves the storms, anchored to the ridge.

Beyond the buster diggings, Sparrowhawk and Tailings Creek,
Beyond the Devil's Elbow, Lagoon Spur and Rocky Peak,
Beyond the Kyeburn and the Soldiers; past the last wire gate,
In the middle of the vastness of the Ancient Syndicate.

The troubleshooters for the gang they knew not when to quit;
Phil Jones and Ossie Phillips were the men who shifted it,
At times it seemed it must crash into the gorge below,
At times it seemed, forwards or back, there was no chance to go.

By creek and bluff and tussock face, through country hard on nerves,
They inched and winched and pinched it round the hairpins and the curves.
Around the switchbacks and the bends, a dozer front and back,
They moved it on and further out along the mountain track.

It takes the place of three huts now – and somehow that makes me sad –
When I think of Chimney Gully and the good times we had.
Wire Yards and Boundary huts are dead, the hill gangs come no more
To camp and boil their billies and sleep on earthen floor.

But yet I'm told (I think it's true) this fall from near and far,
From all around the South Island and where the North runs are,
Come shepherds, packers, hillmen in a sure and steady mob,
They've heard of Inder's Castle and they're looking for a job.

The neighbouring runs and stations though are thinking quite a bit,
There's nothing out on Glenshee Ranch could ever rival it.
And Yorky's Run and Allan Peaks and Shortlands too, I hear,
Will find it hard to get a gang to muster sheep this year.

LEFT AND OPPOSITE Ida Railway Hut, 2012. PHOTOS: ROB BROWN

Whariwharangi Hut 1898 ABEL TASMAN NATIONAL PARK

Some huts begin life with no intention of ever becoming huts. Whariwharangi Hut is one of these, having started out as a pioneer homestead. In the 1890s, settlers John and Edith Handcock leased 485 hectares of land from Maori at Whariwharangi Bay, on the Golden Bay side of Separation Point.

The coastal steamer *Lady Barkly*, captained by John Handcock's uncle, John Walker, delivered timber for the couple's proposed homestead. The materials were duly floated to the beach through the surf, and the house was completed in 1898.[1] With their children, the Handcocks farmed the area for about fifteen years, during which time the *Lady Barkly* continued to keep the family in contact with the wider world, ferrying supplies to them as necessary on its regular voyages past the bay. However, poor soil made the farming marginal, and the family supplemented their income with other ventures in the region, including bee keeping. The farm was transferred in about 1912 to George Manson, who last used the house as a homestead in 1926.

Then began the long transition from farmhouse to tramping hut in Abel Tasman National Park. Spirited conservationist Perrine Moncrieff first drove the idea of a national park for the area in 1937, after she was incensed about proposals to mill native forest at Totaranui. Her story is one of inspiration, and a testament to what one motivated individual can achieve, though of course others played prominent roles too. Moncrieff's efforts met official resistance at first, but she cleverly proposed the idea as a 300th anniversary of Dutch seaman Abel Tasman's first visit to New Zealand in 1642, and sought support from Dutch royalty. She later wrote, 'Thereafter all went smoothly, for the great government fish had risen to the beautiful Netherland fly and was safe in the landing net.'[2]

The park, New Zealand's fourth and its first coastal one, officially opened on 19 December 1942. Initially, however, the area around the Whariwharangi Homestead was not part of the park and continued to be farmed off and on until 1972. In the meantime, the deteriorating homestead served as a stockman's hut. Finally, in 1974, the Crockford family sold the land to the Abel Tasman National Park Board, and it was incorporated into the park in 1977.[3] Today, the track to the hut winds in from the Wainui road end through lush regenerating scrub. In the valley near the hut itself, it is hard to comprehend that the thriving overhead canopy of native shrubs and trees sheltering luxuriant ferns and mosses was failed farmland just forty years ago.

Before restoring the hut, park authorities were faced with a dilemma. Nearby, at Mutton Cove, another old homestead also provided an attractive option for conversion to a hut. In the end, however, the Mutton Cove homestead proved to be too dilapidated, and restoration efforts instead settled on Whariwharangi, even though it too was then described as 'derelict'.[4] The hut was wonderfully restored in 1980 to provide accommodation for park visitors, while keeping as much of its original character as possible. A steep staircase leads up to two dinky bedrooms, while downstairs offers more accommodation and a common room, with one old fireplace bricked up and another converted to take a wood-burner. A short track leading from this idyllic location to a sweeping beach of golden sands is backed by an ancient row of macrocarpa trees, part of the area's historical legacy and a great windbreak. Nearby, about twenty tent sites offer alternative accommodation to the hut.

In his book *A Tramper's Journey*, Mark Pickering recalls spending a night alone in the hut, when he was spooked by noises. Old huts, built by people long dead, can stir the imagination, and Pickering thought he could hear stealthy footsteps in the upstairs room. Not a little afraid, he turned the doorknob, only for a weka to streak past him.[5] Others, though, have been more certain the hut is haunted.[6] Despite the stories, the hut logbook is full of positive comments, like 'good hut, good place, good friends', 'lovely hut with history. Enjoyed the peace and quiet' and 'beautiful little cottage! We're so lucky!' What a great working historical legacy to have from those early days.

GEOFF SPEARPOINT

LEFT AND OPPOSITE Whariwharangi Hut, 2010.
PHOTOS: GEOFF SPEARPOINT

Avoca Homestead 1906 KOROWAI/TORLESSE TUSSOCKLANDS CONSERVATION PARK, CANTERBURY

The story of the Avoca Homestead, now a tastefully restored hut available for public use in the Korowai/Torlesse Tussocklands Conservation Park, is linked to the development of railways in New Zealand.

By 1875, the railways in Canterbury were more profitable than those in all the rest of the colony put together, earning profits exceeding £185,000 by transporting goods and people throughout the province. This success increased the desire to put a line through the Southern Alps to the West Coast to further the economic links between the two regions. By 1880, the rail line had reached as far as Springfield, but then the difficult construction work started – a complicated climb up through the mountains beside the Waimakariri River and on to Arthur's Pass. This would require numerous tunnels and viaducts, as well as a great deal of capital from the province's coffers.[1]

For the run holders on the southern bank of the Waimakariri River, the rail line would be a boon, greatly simplifying their transport problems in getting wool and sheep to Christchurch. However, it would take another twenty-six years of construction for the line to push from Springfield through the difficult landscape and up to one of the most isolated and marginal Canterbury high-country runs – Avoca.

Soon after the upper Waimakariri Basin was surveyed in the 1850s, farmers took up most of the easier runs. Charles and George Harper, two sons of Henry Harper, the first Bishop of Christchurch, leased the Avoca run in 1857.[2] The brothers called the station West End, and ran it from Christchurch, but the land offered only marginal grazing and hard work. With no farm buildings of any sort, sheep had to be driven to adjacent Craigieburn Station for shearing. Bullock teams sledged out the wool to the West Coast road on drays, carrying three bales at a time.

The Harper brothers sold the run in 1864 to Foster and Moore, but the big snow of July 1867[3] had a devastating effect on sheep farming in the area and this, combined with a dramatic fall in wool prices, forced them out in 1873 (this snow saw many Canterbury sheep farms pushed to the brink of financial collapse). The owners of Mt Torlesse Station then took over the lease, but the land was soon passed over to Craigieburn Station.[4]

The viability of the Avoca run as a stand-alone unit was improved in 1904 with the addition of some land on the south bank of Broken River. Two years later, the arrival of the railway at Avoca greatly improved the station's prospects. The run had a new owner by this time – H. G. Heath – and materials were brought in to build a station homestead. In 1906, Heath had a modest five-room dwelling constructed at Avoca, using rimu tongue-and-groove flooring and lining, corrugated-iron cladding, and kauri window and door fittings.

By 1917, the land was once again searching for owners. The northern part of the Avoca run was incorporated into Flock Hill Station (which itself had been carved off part of the original Craigieburn run) as the neighbouring run holders continued to pass this marginal grazing land between themselves. At the same time, coal was discovered in a small deposit in Broken River a few kilometres upstream from the homestead. After the establishment of the Mount Torlesse Collieries in 1918, 72,500 tonnes of coal was extracted and carted by a tramway to the Avoca railway station. Despite this promising start, a mine fire in 1924 signalled the beginning of the end for the venture. Fires continued to reduce profits, eventually forcing the mine to close in 1927.[5]

The burst of mining activity had little impact on the continued difficulties of farming such a rough piece of land. A simple woolshed, which still stands today, was built near the homestead in 1920 out of beech logs and corrugated iron. In the mid-1920s, the run was sold once again as a going concern, this time to Jack Kidd. He owned Avoca between 1926 and 1948, which was probably the run's most successful period.[6] On returning home from the First World War, Kidd had won a ballot farm near the Burkes Pass pub. Unfortunately, that run proved to be too close to the pub and he purchased Avoca for a change of lifestyle in a remote location, far away from licensed premises.[7] His family did not occupy the homestead for too long; when the coal mine was abandoned, they moved into the mine manager's house, which had been conveniently built near the Avoca train station (and is now used by Flock Hill Station).[8]

The run went through numerous owners in the years following the Second World War, and in 1987 it was taken over by Malcolm and Alana North of Christchurch. By the mid-1990s they were looking to dispose of the run, and DOC commissioned a report that looked into the feasibility of combining parts of the Torlesse Range that had been retired from grazing, Ben More Station, Avoca Station and the Adams Block into a new conservation park. In 1998, the tortured history of Avoca Station as a high-country run came to an end when the property was purchased by the Nature Heritage Fund and retired from grazing for good. In November 2001, the combined area of 22,000 hectares became the Korowai/Torlesse Tussocklands Conservation Park.

The old Avoca Homestead remained in excellent near-original condition, and DOC subsequently restored the building beautifully and made it available for overnight stays. By judicious use of interpretation panels in the hut, trampers can feel something of what it was like for a family to live in such an isolated part of the Canterbury high country. Impressive pine trees surround a large grassy field in front of the homestead, from which bellbirds sing

Avoca Homestead in 2009 PHOTO: ROB BROWN

to the steep hillsides above. Broken River rushes towards the Waimakariri, and every few hours a train clacks over the nearby Slovens Stream Viaduct, bypassing the station that history has long since left behind.

ROB BROWN

REFUGE AMONG THE RICHES MINING HUTS

In the Great Depression of the 1930s, George Davies left Wellington penniless and headed to the Howard Goldfield of the Upper Buller as part of the government's Gold Prospecting Subsidy Scheme. Later, with some other unemployed workmen, he moved to the Lyell Goldfield, lower down the Buller Valley, where they were assigned to the top plateau. He remained there until the Depression eased. In a National Radio interview during the early 1970s, Davies remembered arriving at the Lyell:

> Next day, after we got straightened out a bit, Big Mac says, 'Well we gotta build a hut.'
>
> 'What do you want a hut for?'
>
> 'Well,' he says, 'I been talking to the storekeeper, and you know, he tells me she snows here in the winter. You could get three or four feet of it, and if you don't get a hut you'll die. You want a hut and about five hundred tons of firewood.'
>
> 'Aw,' I said, 'that's hard to believe.'
>
> 'Well, that's what he said. Have a look around here. Can you see any tents?'
>
> He was right. There weren't any.
>
> So – all right, we'll build a hut. Well, we didn't know how to build a hut, so one bloke, he wrote it down on a bit of paper what we had to get. So many hundred poles, so many hundred slabs, so many lumps for the bottom and so many lumps for the top, and we started off.
>
> Well, I never worked so hard in my life. We must have cut thousands of poles. We brought 'em all down and stacked them all in nice heaps and we were proud of it. And we got the bloke over, and he had a look at them.
>
> 'Well, yes,' he said. 'About half of these are all right. The other half you can use for firewood.'
>
> 'What's wrong with them?'
>
> 'They are all curved.'
>
> So, he shows us – you go around the base of a tree and you look straight up from the bottom from several sides, and that way you can see if they are straight, or if they've got a curve on them.
>
> Well, we're away again, and we were weeks getting that stuff, but eventually we got it, and we built a good hut too.[1]

John Bennett's Hut at the Potter's No. 2 historic gold workings in 2012. Andrew Rees reputedly built this basic stone hut for John Bennett sometime in the 1920s. PHOTO: ROB BROWN

With nearly 40 per cent of working-age men without employment, the basics of shelter, food and warmth were part of a daily struggle that lasted for much of the 1930s. The Gold Prospecting Subsidy Scheme was one of the government's ideas to help relieve the unemployment misery. The subsidy was essentially a 'make-work' scheme, through which men were paid a small weekly allowance – a sort of minimum wage. In 1932 this amounted to 15 shillings for single men and 30 for those who were married. In return, miners were expected to pay 10 per cent of any gold earnings back to the government.[2] One miner wrote of the subsidy, 'I beg to inform you that it is a fair god-send; it gives a party a chance to get the dead work done to get a claim opened up.'[3]

To house miners working on this scheme, hundreds of rudimentary shelters and huts were built throughout New Zealand. By 1932, some 1400 subsidised men worked the goldfields scattered throughout the country, many in remote backcountry locations. Not surprisingly, given their historic wealth and how close they were to Dunedin, the Otago goldfields attracted the most prospectors, but the West Coast, Nelson and parts of the North Island also witnessed considerable activity.[4]

Many participants on the scheme – who might previously have been Wellington office workers – were ill-equipped and grossly underskilled for the hard life of a backblocks digger. In an attempt to bring inexperienced men quickly up to speed, the Mines Department even published a guide to the art of gold mining in 1933,[5] and in Dunedin the government employed a street demonstrator to show men how to pan for gold or use a cradle.[6]

Most men on the scheme lived away from their families, and sent home as much of their meagre earnings as they could. A few took their wives and families with them. Eric and Dora Perry lived in a log cabin at Maggie Creek in the Howard Goldfield during the Depression. They were married in 1936, spent their wedding night in a shed at Lake Rotoiti, and then proceeded to build their own log cabin to live in:

> First a tent was erected then trees felled and logs split and one room erected with a slab floor. Moss was collected and used to fill the gaps in the slab walls. A lot was scrounged from the derelict flea-ridden huts of previous miners. Panes of glass were retrieved, nails straightened and planks used from previous fluming.

Depression-era miner Don Harvey at his rough hut in Wakefield Gully, Golden Bay, 1939.
PHOTO: ALEXANDER TURNBULL LIBRARY, WELLINGTON, 1/2-050249-F

> Dora helped Eric as much as she could on his claim. She was the youngest woman on the field and it was frowned upon for women to work on a claim … Their daughter Joy was born in July 1937 and she spent much time hanging in a sugar bag hammock in the bush while her parents worked.
>
> The miners mostly lived off the land. They smoked fish and shot rabbits and if they got a deer or wild pig they shared the meat around. Piglets were cooked whole in the camp oven. Vegetables flourished in the gardens and Dora sometimes brought back currants and gooseberries from her riding trips to Tophouse.[7]

During the early years of the scheme, the government hoped that the gold would more than compensate for the cost of the subsidies. However, official returns for the whole of New Zealand only ever reached a maximum of 10,000 ounces per year.[8] The number of men on the subsidy peaked in 1933–34 at about 4000, by which time the Unemployment Board had spent £198,334 on the gold scheme. The *Ellesmere Guardian* reported enthusiastically that miners were recovering about £50,000 worth of gold per year, allowing some to pay back their subsidy. But of that return the government got back only 10 per cent, a fraction of its expenditure.[9]

However, the unemployment schemes also had an ulterior purpose. Like similar work schemes in the United States, those of New Zealand's United-Reform Government at the time aimed to keep unemployed men from being idle, preferably away from cities where they might band together. This government was an uneasy alliance between the two parties, with United's Gordon Coates, Minister of Works and of Finance, sympathetic to the unemployed, while others in the administration wanted to stamp out any drift towards socialism. The violent 1912 Waihi gold-miners' strike and the 1913 Wellington waterfront strike served as reminders of what a disgruntled workforce could unleash.[10] Riots in Auckland in 1932 demonstrated how high feelings ran amongst the unemployed, and stirred up further political unease.

Seemingly ignorant of the conditions confronting men on the Gold Prospecting Subsidy Scheme, the 1932 Unemployment Board report on relief gold mining was naively optimistic: 'The work, though hard, holds an unfailing interest for those engaging in it, while it has a sustaining effect on independence of spirit, and also gives opportunity for financial independence.'[11]

However, the reality of life on the Depression goldfields had more to do with hard, unrewarding slog. The election of New Zealand's first Labour Government in 1935 marked the arrival of change. Their introduction of social security in 1938, as well as more constructive public works schemes, helped relieve some of the misery caused by unemployment. By then, few men were left on the goldfields, and their huts lay abandoned. Huts remaining from this period often exude a kind of quiet, sombre air, with the echo of past hardship in every pore of the buildings.

A few Depression-era mining huts remain in lonely outposts of Kahurangi National Park. Two of the best include Cecil Kings Hut and Waingaro Forks Hut. Inland from Karamea, DOC also built a representation of a Depression-era mining hut in the Fenian Goldfield in 1999. Huts have a long history here, with an old slab hut being used by Irish miner John Adam back in the 1870s. In 1882, Adam died in his hut, aged forty-nine, but it survived until the 1930s and was probably used by other miners in the Depression. Another hut that survived in reasonable condition until the late 1990s was Taplins Hut, on the track to Mt Owen. Sadly, like so many others, it has now virtually melted into the forest.

History neglected. **LEFT** Taplins Hut, an old slab prospector's hut on the Mt Owen Track in Kahurangi National Park, photographed in 1993. PHOTO: CRAIG POTTON **RIGHT** The same hut 20 years later in 2012, collapsed and rotten. PHOTO: ANDY DENNIS

Further south, a scattering of Depression-era mining huts exists near traditional gold-mining towns like Reefton and Blackball. The Croesus–Moonlight Track in the southern Paparoa Range has three authentic examples: Garden Gully Hut, Top Hut and Meikles Hut. All preserve a feel for what life was like for the men working the goldfields here at the time. The Garden Gully Mine near Blackball had been worked before the First World War, but during the 1930s there was barely enough quartz to keep the stamper battery operating.

Many who went onto the Gold Prospecting Subsidy Scheme in the 1930s headed for Central Otago. Here, they reoccupied long-abandoned rock shelters, closing them off with rudimentary materials to form a crude hut, or built stone huts. It was into this grim reality that Fred Miller described taking his wife and young child: 'I was almost afraid to look at Peg's face … I knew it took all her courage to smile as she entered her new home, and as she unpacked and prepared a place in one corner for the child. I pretended I did not see the tear that splashed on to her hands.'[12] Depression-era mining was small scale and marginal – a long way from the heady early days of the New Zealand gold story, right in the heart of Central Otago.

The New Zealand Gold Rushes

In his book *Frontier New Zealand* (1992), writer Duncan Mackay describes the nineteenth-century gold miners as an army: 'Ambitious, practical and energetic, the gold diggers and their camp followers were a sprawling army which pushed relentlessly into new territory.'[13]

New Zealand's gold rushes followed quickly on the heels of rushes in California (1848) and Australia (1850s). A discovery in the Coromandel in 1852 resulted in the first sale of gold in New Zealand on 11 December.[14] But the first significant rush occurred in the Aorere Valley of Golden Bay in 1857, which led to the founding of Collingwood. The Aorere proved short-lived, however, compared with the much more substantial Otago and West Coast gold rushes of the 1860s.

A considerable proportion of the diggers who ended up on the New Zealand fields had worked in California or Australia over the previous decades. By the end of 1861, the first year of the Otago gold rush, some 23,000 hopeful diggers had arrived. In his gold-rush history *Diggers, Hatters and Whores* (2008), Stevan Eldred-Grigg noted their origins: 'English, Scottish, Irish,

MINING HUTS 73

A painting by J. B. C. Hoyte of diggers' huts, Hauraki, Coromandel, 1864-7.
ILLUSTRATION: ALEXANDER TURNBULL LIBRARY, WELLINGTON, A-234-012

German, Yankee and Southerner, together with lesser mobs of Italians, French, Scandinavians and a few born in the colonies.'[15] Tens of thousands more came later. Proportionately, gold attracted the largest wave of white immigrants ever to come to New Zealand, and also the first surge of Chinese settlers, many of whom mined harder and for longer than any other nationality.[16]

New Zealand would be the end of the line for many who had followed 'the colour' from America to Australia to this new colony near the bottom of the world. Despite later gold rushes in Queensland and South Africa, many miners chose to settle permanently in New Zealand. This 'clump' migration changed New Zealand society for good, having an effect in particular on the country's politics. The diggers would prove to be well organised politically and egalitarian in their outlook.

The gentrified farmers who had come to dominate South Island life complained at the arrival of this 'motley horde', genuinely believing it would upset their Arcadia. One observed: 'If N.Z. produces gold it will be the property of the refined quintessence and condensation of all the rascaldom of the world.'[17]

Their fears had some substance. The colonial government welcomed the diggers with open arms, and the passage of the Goldfields Act in 1858 gave the Crown wide-ranging powers to declare any area a goldfield, with compensation available for affected run holders. Not surprisingly, many hungry diggers saw the run holders' 'woolly pigs' as fair game.[18]

However, before long the more enterprising merchants and farmers worked out ways to participate in the riches being washed out of the country's alluvial riverbeds. Diggers desperately needed food, accommodation and transport, and the already established settlers could provide this at a tidy profit. Mining settlements were hastily erected, with some appearing almost overnight. Calico sufficed for a short period, but it was never good enough for the winter weather of Central Otago, and if the gold lasted, more substantial huts were required.

Maori also joined the immigrant diggers in limited numbers. Iwi had explored many, if not all, the South Island rivers in their search for pounamu and were aware of the glittering colour in some West Coast and Otago streams. However, the Crown decided to pre-empt all claims to gold and minerals in the colony, a move that was in direct conflict with the Treaty of Waitangi. From the first, the colonial government seemed nervous that the Crown claim, its unilateral issuing of mining permits, and its genuine attempts on the orderly administration of the goldfields, might breach the terms of the treaty. In the 1850s, Maori vastly outnumbered the new colony's 30,000 Pakeha settlers, and keeping the peace was seen as vital. This was more a problem in the North Island than in the South Island, where the Crown had – post-treaty – entered into purchase agreements for nearly the entire landmass. To avoid completely running roughshod over North Island Maori rights, the Crown negotiated various compensation claims. Eventually this was fixed at £1 per miner per year to work claims on Maori land. When the gold rush later gained momentum in places like the Coromandel, this proved a poor return for North Island Maori.[19]

Mining Eras

Gold mining in New Zealand broadly fell into three different categories. The first, and the one mostly associated with the rushes, was alluvial gold mining. This was comparatively cheap and simple, and could be accomplished by a solitary miner with as little as a pan and shovel. A digger 'washed' the gravel out of his pan, allowing the heavier gold to collect on the bottom. Usually, however, the pan was used for little more than prospecting, and once gold was struck diggers progressed to a cradle. Though more efficient, the cradle had to be operated manually by vibrating the handle for the small box and screen, while at the same time loading in fresh gravel with a shovel – a physically demanding task.

A digger willing to work hard could often earn a good living, and sometimes even strike it rich. Claims were named according to value. Those with an eye for good ground and a bit of luck might strike a 'homeward bounder' and indeed become rich. 'Wages' earned the digger a reasonable weekly income, while a 'tucker' claim provided only enough for food. A 'duffer claim' yielded hardly any gold, while a 'duffer rush' was a false alert.[20] Promoting a duffer rush could be hazardous to a digger's health – overseas, it was punishable by death, but in New Zealand more often resulted in a beating.

After the 'easy' gold on a field was won through alluvial mining, methods progressed to an industrial scale, whereby large amounts of water were used to sluice and screen alluvial deposits for waterborne gold. This type of mining, involving an army of diggers to construct water races, operate winding and pumping gear, work the screens and shovel tonnes of gravel, dominated the great gold rushes. In some cases, shafts were plunged 50 metres into alluvial deposits to access more material for sluicing. Most destructive of all was the process of hydraulic sluicing. This was essentially accelerated erosion of alluvial deposits on the side of gold-bearing rivers using high-pressure water jets. It had a devastating environmental effect on the adjacent waterways.

A second type of mining involved hard rock – quartz reefs – and required a whole new level of infrastructure and investment. By the 1870s, the great days of New Zealand's alluvial gold rush were over, and digger numbers fell to about 12,000.[21] Prospectors turned their attention to the mountains in search of the 'mother lode' – a term used by diggers to describe a seam of pure gold buried deep. More often, however, they found flakes of gold, locked hard into quartzite rock.

Mining quartz involved a lot more organisation, cost and effort than alluvial mining. Conglomerates and speculators invested in industrial-scale machinery and installed large stamper batteries, often run using water-driven Pelton wheels. They crushed the quartzite ore, enabling the gold to be separated from the pulverised rock via plush matting or mercury-coated copper tables. Later, separation techniques involved a quite sophisticated process using cyanide. Quartz miners constructed more permanent structures than diggers, and settled in for the medium haul. Diggers usually worked for themselves, but miners were employed on wages paid by companies who had the capital to invest in such risky ventures. Quartz mining took place in Otago, Coromandel, Nelson, Marlborough and the West Coast at various times after the 1870s and continues today.

The final type of mining used dredges to scour riverbeds. Mining dredges working the Clutha River as early as 1863 used a crude leather bag and iron

Gabriels Gully in 1862. PHOTO: BURTON BROTHERS, DUNEDIN, HOCKEN LIBRARY, UNIVERSITY OF OTAGO, NEGSHEET 85 SEE S/N E2911/33

pole to spoon the material out. Later, huge steam-driven contraptions hauled gravel out of the Clutha and Shotover rivers, and by 1900 as many as 228 dredges worked Otago and Southland rivers.[22] A dredge is still operating in the West Coast's Grey River today.

The Otago Gold Rush

On 4 June 1861, Gabriel Read made public his discovery of gold in the headwaters of the Tuapeka River in Central Otago. In just a few weeks, gold fever seized the inhabitants of Dunedin and Otago, and by the end of August more than 3000 men had gathered at the Tuapeka diggings.[23]

The early photograph (above) of Gabriels Gully shows how quickly the peaceful landscape was transformed. Surveyor John Turnbull Thomson described the scene to the *Otago Witness*: 'I was much astonished at the change that had taken place. The gully was studded with tents from one end to the

Chinese gold miners with Reverend Alexander Don, outside a sod hut at Tuapeka, Otago, circa 1900.
PHOTO: ALEXANDER TURNBULL LIBRARY, WELLINGTON 1/2-019148-F

other, and the surface, verdant with fine grass two months ago, was now gutted and ransacked in an extraordinary manner.'[24]

Miners had little respect for anything but gold. Trees, rapidly felled, found their way into campfires or makeshift shelters, and the gully, disfigured with stumps, become a 'nightmarish landscape'.[25] Read's gold discovery generated an unprecedented level of frenzy in New Zealand, one that was also destined to play out elsewhere.

By the following year, however, Gabriels Gully was already old news. In August 1862, American Horatio Hartley and his Irish mate from the Californian goldfields, Christopher Reilly, walked into the Dunedin Treasury to deposit 87 pounds of gold.[26] This was more than 1000 troy ounces and made them instant millionaires in today's terms.[27] They had been canny enough to work the Molyneux (Clutha) River for most of a particularly cold winter, when the low river levels caused by the freezing conditions exposed additional gravel beaches.

At first they were understandably cagey about the source of this fortune, but – prompted by a £2000 reward – divulged the location as upstream from the junction of the Manuherikia and Molyneux rivers (now underneath Lake Dunstan, not far from present-day Clyde). Within hours of this electrifying news, what became known as the Dunstan rush was in full swing. Although many diggers scarcely believed that such riches could come from the riverbed, hundreds of miners departed Gabriels Gully for the new rush. After proving to the other miners that this was no duffer rush, Hartley and Reilly disappeared from the scene shortly after. It is said Hartley died in California after a rich and long life, but no one knows for sure what became of Reilly.

The gold miners of Central Otago faced difficulties not encountered in most other regions. For a start, a lack of forests left timber in short supply for both building and firewood, as well as for the essentials of sluice boxes, flumes and pit props. Poor-quality lignite coal supplemented wood to provide for warmth and cooking, but timber remained highly prized.

Inflated prices of virtually everything the diggers needed also limited revenue to develop better accommodation. When the digging community – complete with banks, shops, theatres, liquor sellers, gambling dens, prostitutes and general stores – moved to a certain area, their entire economy went with them. This micro-economy created a bubble, whereby prices charged within it bore no relation to those in the rest of New Zealand. For example, timber at the Dunstan goldfields fetched fifty times the price of the same product in Dunedin, and cartage charges soared to £200 or even £300 per ton.[28] When suitable materials were available, essential community buildings usually took priority over miners' huts, and even then were kept to the smallest possible size.

For the most part, shelter took the form of temporary calico tent camps, as the diggers moved en masse to each new claim. Tents, however, provided poor refuge from the worst of Central Otago's winter weather.

In August 1863, a terrible snowstorm hit Central Otago. Bad weather persisted over the next month, trapping nearly 500 men in Campbells Gully on the Old Man Range, near the location of the present-day Potters Hut.[29] Many of these men were warned about the dangers of staying high on the ranges during the winter, but most feared losing their claim more than the cold.

The packers from the temporary service town called Chamounix, down near the Molyneux (Clutha) River, were unable to get through to help, and the trapped miners began to run out of food. Fearing starvation, some decided to make a break for it on 18 August, and, braving the blizzard, trudged off into the deep snow. In the white-out conditions, they could not locate the route down, and many were brought to a standstill with hypothermia. Initially it was feared that up to fifty miners had died, but the actual figure was closer to twelve or thirteen.[30]

All up, between 100 and 200 diggers died in the severe winter weather of 1863. Even the shelter of a hut was still no guarantee of safety from the cold or wet. During the same winter, five men found themselves trapped inside two small huts in the Nevis:

> In a little gully on the big range, nearly opposite Stuart's store, are two lone huts exposed to the full fury of the snow drift; in one of these huts were three diggers, in the other two; the inhabitants of the former finding their dwelling place enveloped in the snow, escaped by means of the chimney, and had to roll themselves down a steep declivity to escape. Of the two dwellers in the other hut, they saw nothing, and could not make them hear, and when taking a last look at the deserted dwelling, nothing more could be seen but a small portion of the top of the chimney, not bigger than a man's head.[31]

Pyramid Hut in the Arahura River, West Coast. This old miners' hut was used for many years between the wars by early tramping parties on the 'Three Passes' tramp. Jock Fisher recalled it was still being used in the 1950s by early deer cullers, but it was eventually superseded by Harman Hut. The hut remains are apparently still visible.
PHOTO: STAN CONWAY, NZAC COLLECTION, HOCKEN LIBRARY, UNIVERSITY OF OTAGO MS-1160/001

Earlier, in July, severe flooding had also affected Central Otago. On one night the Molyneux River rose 7 metres. In the headwaters of the Arrow River, a dam gave way and a wall of water swept down the valley, demolishing everything in its path.[32] Many huts and tents were swept away in the flood, and while most of their inhabitants escaped, some were not so lucky: an entire hut, filled with men, was washed into the Arrow River. The only survivor, George Pullen, described the scene:

> I was in bed with my three mates, when, in the middle of the night, we were awoke by a tremendous crash, we leapt out and rushed out of the hut; I found myself immediately struggling in the water and among logs of wood, and was an hour before crawling up into a place of safety. I could not see anything of my mates, but after a time heard groans. When daylight came, I went up the gully and found John Brown, one of the deceased, lying on his side, his legs covered with logs and stones, I could not extricate him. I went down to two men who live some way below, and they went to his assistance. He died on his way to the township.[33]

The men were all sawyers supplying timber for the newly established town on the Arrow River. The body of the second victim was found some distance from the hut, while a third man died after sand and debris completely buried him. They were far from the last miners to die on the Central Otago goldfields.

Although such incidents proved that huts gave no absolute guarantee of security, they certainly offered greater warmth, comfort and shelter than tents. Otago miners turned to the obvious abundant material for building their shelters — schist rock. Perhaps the longest-serving example of this type of schist mining hut was one built by Andrew Ree, one of the last of the old diggers. The remains of his stone hut still exist near the present-day Potters Hut on the Old Man Range. From 1873 to 1923, the hut provided Ree with solid shelter between spring and autumn each year, when he worked an old claim. After fifty

MINING HUTS 77

Hokitika, early in the West Coast gold rush, about 1865, showing a range of structures from canvas to wooden. PAINTING: T. O. HURT, ALEXANDER TURNBULL LIBRARY, WELLINGTON, E-501-F-002

years of mining at Potters, he retired to Timaru and died there in 1926, aged eighty-four.[34]

As the temporary nature of the rush passed, those that stayed put down roots. Throughout the Central Otago landscape small stone huts sprang up to house solitary miners working their claims. Many of these huts now lie in ruins, but a few have survived. Some of the most important of these are the stone huts inhabited by Chinese miners on the edge of Arrowtown. Archaeologist Neville Ritchie restored two in the 1980s, and they remain some of the best-preserved huts from New Zealand's early gold-rush era. Other huts built into the side of natural rock shelters in the Roxburgh Gorge near Doctor's Point have also been restored and rebuilt.

Some stone mining huts built during the Depression of the 1930s remain too. As on the West Coast and in Nelson, many old claims in Central Otago were revived through the government's Gold Prospecting Subsidy Scheme. A stone hut at Potters No. 2 claim dates from this period. (See photo on page 70.)

The West Coast

Gold transformed the South Island's West Coast from a relative wilderness, with a few hundred local Maori and a small number of Pakeha settlers in 1863, to a bustling district of thousands just three years later.[35]

As in Otago, West Coast diggers initially focused on the easily won alluvial gold washed down from the mountains and into the rivers. On the West Coast, the gold had even washed as far as the black-sand beaches. As the area exploded with mining activity, towns like Hokitika, Greymouth and Okarito sprang up and were soon surveyed.

Hokitika began life with Hudson and Price's store and a collection of a few calico tents late in 1864, but by the end of the following year 15,548 people had been recorded as having sailed into the unpredictable Hokitika 'harbour'.[36] About 40 per cent of these came from Australia, probably after abandoning the goldfields there. Not all diggers made it to the wharf though. Nothing perhaps illustrates the feverish pitch of the West Coast gold rush more than the number of shipwrecks on the beach and bar of the Hokitika River. Between March and December 1865, no fewer than twenty ships were completely wrecked coming into Hokitika and there were many other minor maritime mishaps.[37]

Those who could not afford the inflated prices of a boat passage came overland from Canterbury through Arthur's Pass, which had already replaced Harper Pass as the preferred route through the Southern Alps, or used other routes from Nelson. The phenomenal growth meant that by 1866 Hokitika had an estimated population of around 10,000, with 100 pubs and nine restaurants, making it one of the country's biggest towns.[38] That same year, miners sluiced a staggering £2,140,946 worth of gold out of the West Coast's rivers and beaches, meaning it had outstripped Otago in a very short time.[39]

Despite all the people pouring into Hokitika, most of the settlements were shantytowns, never constructed to last, and many soon descended into squalor. While Otago diggers had to deal with the extreme cold, on the West Coast they had to deal with rain and rats. In Otago, diggers suffered from frostbite, while on the West Coast outbreaks of diseases like typhoid were commonplace. One observer described the prevailing West Coast gold shanties as: 'of the usual bush accommodation house order of architecture – a simple but ingenious combination of the tent and the *whare*, which possesses the inestimable advantage of offering an irresistible rendezvous to all the sandflies in the neighbourhood, and admitting all the winds of heaven as well as the rain with delightful impartiality'.[40] When the diggers moved on to other claims, the regenerating forest quickly consumed most of their abandoned dwellings.

In 1870, rich veins of quartz were found in the forested ranges behind the little Inangahua Valley town of Reefton. This was one of a number of towns around New Zealand, including Thames, that was dubbed with the extravagant moniker of 'Quartzopolis'. In this case, the title was justified: between 1870 and 1951, as many as eighty-four separate mines operated around Reefton. A number of them were given names that reflected a combination of hope and reality – Wealth of Nations, Golden Lead and Keep it Dark.

While some mines in this area, like Kirwan's Reward Mine, were in service for only a short period (1900–06), others, like Big River, operated profitably

Miners' huts at Waiuta, Blackwater gold mine circa 1910.
PHOTO: WILLIAM ARCHER PRICE, ALEXANDER TURNBULL LIBRARY, WELLINGTON, 1/2-001741-G.

Garden Gully Hut, Croesus Track, West Coast, 2012. This was one of several Depression-era miners' huts near the Garden Gully stamping battery, restored by DOC in the 1990s.
PHOTO: ROB BROWN

between 1882 and 1942. Not far from Big River, Waiuta was similarly successful between 1906 and 1951.[41] In the case of Waiuta, shafts driven 1849 feet (564 metres) and 2881 feet (878 metres) into the ground had, by 1951, yielded more than 730,000 ounces (14,000 kilograms) of gold.

The Waiuta–Big River area is one of the few places on the West Coast where some gold-mining huts survive. Near Big River Hut, in Victoria Forest Park, is Rooney's Hut. The original hut was extended in about 1940 by attaching perhaps the oldest example of a single man's hut on the West Coast – once very common on the Reefton goldfields. Another important example at Waiuta is what is now the old police station in the historic settlement. This was originally a small two-roomed hut of similar design to the town's famous single-roomed red huts.[42]

Waiuta's population peaked in the 1930s at nearly 600. It continued as a functioning town until 1951, when the ventilation and pumping shaft for the Blackwater Mine collapsed. After facing steadily declining returns, this was the final straw for the mine's economic viability. Waiuta was abandoned, but a few of the buildings have fortuitously survived and have been preserved as an example of the quartzite gold-mining era.

The Golden Remains

The nature of gold mining throughout New Zealand's history – of quick exploitation followed by abandonment – has meant that most mining huts have not survived, unlike those associated with long-term activities such as farming, tramping, hunting and tourism. Although stone ruins are common enough in many parts of Otago, very few early mining huts have been preserved intact from the earliest gold-rush days. Some, like the Chinese miners' huts at Arrowtown, were restored as reminders of the New Zealand's mining history. The two huts at Bullendale in the Shotover Valley also provide modern-day visitors with an authentic experience of late nineteenth-century mining huts.

While most remaining mining huts are associated with gold, one or two huts were built for the recovery of other minerals. Asbestos Cottage (Kahurangi National Park) owes its name to asbestos prospectors working in the mountains behind Golden Bay, while the scheelite (tungsten) huts of Glenorchy are another example. The latter are all the more remarkable because they preserve an almost complete range of huts from a century of scheelite mining in Otago's Richardson Mountains.

Most of the mining huts that survive today date from the Depression of the 1930s rather than the original gold rushes. In their own way, these are just as precious, preserving a period of struggle and adversity in New Zealand's history.

ROB BROWN

Bullendale Hut c.1890 MT AURUM RECREATION RESERVE, OTAGO

Located in the upper Shotover Valley, Bullendale Hut is a relic of the great 1860s Otago gold rushes, an era that saw much frenzied development in the hinterland of this province.

During the early 1860s, the gold rush was in full swing near Queenstown, with prospecting activity concentrated on the Arrow, Shotover and Skippers catchments. By 1866, thirteen mining companies were working claims in the quartz lodes of mountainous terrain at the head of Skippers Creek. Most of these companies did little more than preliminary prospecting and by 1889 had been amalgamated by George Bullen, owner of the Phoenix Mining Company.[1]

For ten years the Phoenix Mine turned profits, despite the inevitable costs of servicing such a remote location. According to an 1896 census, the thriving community of Bullendale (also known as The Reefs) boasted 107 men and thirty-seven women.[2] Most buildings at Bullendale consisted of small huts – by one estimate there were as many as fifty buildings in total – but several service buildings also existed on the flats below the mine. During the boom years, Bullendale boasted a bakery, butchery, post office and hotel, and a hall that also doubled as a schoolhouse.

By the late 1890s, however, financial troubles plagued the mine as the workable lodes were exhausted. It finally ceased operation in May 1901, and Bullendale was virtually abandoned overnight, although the Mt Aurum Quartz Mining Company continued to work claims downstream.[3] The ghost town stood pretty much unchanged until the First World War, when a shortage of corrugated iron led to the dismantling of many structures.[4]

Today, little remains here but the rusting machinery of the gold workings and two small huts. One of these, Bullendale Hut, is in fairly good condition. Occupying a sunny face opposite the remains of the Phoenix stamping battery, it's a fairly typical example of a miner's hut, with beech-pole construction, corrugated-iron cladding, and a schist floor and hearth. The only hint the building is now managed by DOC is the provision of mattresses and a rainwater tank (many of the nearby streams are polluted with heavy metals from the gold workings). Exactly when the hut was built, or who lived here, remains unknown, but newspaper and hessian linings used for insulating the hut contained an 1896 edition of the *Otago Witness*.

By 1996, Bullendale Hut was starting to fail structurally, with the front wall leaning out from the roof, and DOC carried out some remedial strengthening. However, in January 1998 high winds flattened the hut completely.[5] DOC rebuilt the hut later that year, and did a remarkable job of retaining its historic character and fabric, using material salvaged from the original structure.[6] The hut's interior was originally split into two small rooms, but the dividing wall was removed during the rebuilding to ensure a more practical bunk layout. A second hut, downstream of Bullendale Hut and also in reasonable condition, reputedly belonged to Bullendale miner Robert Duncan.[7]

Bullendale remains an important historic site, and anyone visiting it could enjoy a full day wandering around the area, looking at the mining remains and imagining the town in its heyday. Over the years, fossickers and bottle hunters have given the site a thorough going over, but note that removal of any historical items is now prohibited under the Conservation Act 1987. Sadly, Bullendale is another historic hut site that is now potentially under threat from cuts to DOC funding.[8]

ROB BROWN

LEFT Bullendale miners' cottages, circa 1890s. Bullendale Hut, now the only remaining building, is visible just to the left of the tree in the centre.
PHOTO: LAKES DISTRICT MUSEUM & GALLERY, ARROWTOWN, EL0757
OPPOSITE Bullendale Hut, April 2010. PHOTO: ROB BROWN

Dynamo Hut 1917 MT AURUM RECREATION RESERVE, OTAGO

Dynamo Hut, situated in the headwaters of the Shotover Valley, must be one of the few huts in New Zealand to owe its existence to hydroelectric energy. While the hut was ostensibly built for mustering on Mt Aurum Station, the site itself is significant: New Zealand's first hydroelectric power scheme, commissioned in 1886, was located just 100 metres away. The hut was built later, in 1917, out of the remains of the scheme's generator shed and, along with the rusting remains of the generator itself, adds historical interest to the whole site.

During the 1880s, all of New Zealand's stamper batteries were driven by water wheels, but in the upper Shotover catchment the creeks regularly ran dry, causing work to grind to a halt. This problem led George Bullen, owner of Phoenix Mine, and the mine's manager, Fred Evans, to investigate the new technology of electrical power to drive the mine.

The plan involved the purchase of two Anglo-American Brush Electric Light Corporation arc dynamos, which were driven by two 6-foot (1.8-metre) Pelton wheels to harness the reliable water draining into the left branch of Skippers Creek. From here, the electricity was transmitted over Southberg Spur to the mine at Bullendale.[1] Unfortunately, this pioneering scheme used inefficient direct current (DC) technology, which resulted in large losses in power when the current was transmitted over any distance. In the case of the Dynamo Hut scheme, this translated into a 30 per cent loss over the relatively short 3-kilometre distance to the Bullendale Mine. The more efficient alternating current (AC) system did not come into widespread use for another ten years, after a lengthy, acrimonious and, at times, bizarre debate between Thomas Edison, who promoted the use of DC, and Nikola Tesla, inventor of the AC system.

Numerous other technical problems were discovered with the equipment – hardly surprising, given how little was known about electricity at the time. Balancing loads from the two generators proved difficult, and any imbalance tended to turn one dynamo into a motor and drive it backwards. Curiously, the combined power of the two dynamos produced only 15 amps: considerably less than their individual ratings of 10 amps each.[2]

Over the next two years, management solved these problems. One major improvement involved replacing the original cast-iron armatures with laminated iron units, and by 1888 the 40 amps generated could drive the full thirty-head stamper at Bullendale, as well as the compressor and stonebreaker.

Merinos were run in the vicinity of Mt Aurum before the gold rush, but the remoteness and rough terrain here always made farming a tough proposition. R.M. Patterson, who also owned Ayrburn Station near Arrowtown and West Dome in Southland, took over the run in 1916, employing fourteen-year-old Duncan Macnicol as one of his workers. The following year, Patterson had the five-bunk Dynamo Hut built, one of several huts constructed in these years from material salvaged from the abandoned gold-mining buildings. Macnicol recalled packing in flooring and iron from old buildings at Bullendale, and salvaging the rest of the timber from the dynamo generator shed. In 1919, Macnicol, now aged seventeen, became station manager.[3]

Duncan's younger brother Archie owned the run between 1940 and 1957,[4] but it was always marginal and was finally retired in 1982. Archie Macnicol also caught the gold-mining bug and worked a small three-stamp battery underneath Mt Aurum. This is still there today near his little hut, which he built out of water-race pipe painstakingly hammered flat.

After the station was retired, it became public conservation land and in 1986 was gazetted as the Mt Aurum Recreation Reserve – a century after the hydroelectric scheme had first begun. To commemorate the centenary, the New Zealand Electricity Department combined forces with the Department of Lands and Survey to reposition the hydro scheme's main components on a timber framework in their original context.[5] As some of oldest electrical motors in the world, they have international significance.

Also nearby is Dynamo Red Hut, built in the 1930s for Depression-era miners. There's still gold around today, as one visitor to Dynamo Hut recorded in the logbook on a 2010 visit: 'Fossicking – got a bit. Not saying where.'[6]

ROB BROWN

LEFT The Dynamo Shed shortly after it was built. PHOTO: LAKES DISTRICT MUSEUM & GALLERY, ARROWTOWN, EL 2352
OPPOSITE Dynamo Hut in April 2010. PHOTO: ROB BROWN

Asbestos Cottage 1897 KAHURANGI NATIONAL PARK

> Surely, New Zealand's history knows no stranger love affair than this, the true story of rock-like resolution and sorrow of the Exiles of Asbestos Cottage.
>
> – Jim Henderson,
> *The Exiles of Asbestos Cottage*[1]

Miners, rabbiters, roadworkers and men maintaining water races have all lived long years in backcountry huts, often leading a solitary existence for their jobs. Some sought the isolation; others endured it. Few huts, however, can claim to have been the home of lovers who exiled themselves to escape unhappy marriages. Between the years 1915 and 1951, Asbestos Cottage was the home of Henry and Annie Chaffey, and their extraordinary story is perhaps the most poignant of any in this book. Their life at Asbestos Cottage also offers an insight into the practicalities of a long-term backcountry existence.

In February 1914, thirty-five-year-old Annie Selina Fox arrived at Motueka. A week later, Henry Fox Chaffey, a wiry forty-four-year-old prospector, joined her and they headed into the backcountry.[2]

Both were tall and upright, and both were escaping previous lives: Henry, a divorce and possibly alcoholism; and Annie, a violent marriage.

Henry was well used to the demands of life in the hills, having prospected and packed for some years. But for Annie, a housewife from Timaru, life in a mountain hut would be a very different existence.

But adapt, she did. Whilst Henry made frequent excursions back to town for supplies, Annie remained in the mountains for almost forty years, extraordinarily coming out only twice: once for an illness that required a three-month stay in hospital; and the second, final time after Henry's death. Even after breaking her leg in 1938, she refused to budge; a doctor walked in from Takaka to set it.[3]

Henry and Annie initially lived in a hut at nearby Arthur Creek in the Leslie Valley, but after a couple of years they settled permanently in what became known as Asbestos Cottage.[4] Before the 1981 release of Jim Henderson's book *The Exiles of Asbestos Cottage*, surprisingly few written records existed about either of their lives – the basic facts of birth and death were known, but most of Chaffey's diaries and all of Annie's letters had been burnt or lost.[5]

To go into exile, Annie left her two teenage sons in Timaru. How she met Henry is not known, nor how he convinced her to seek refuge in the mountains.

Henry scraped together a living mostly by prospecting and mining. He loved the area around the Roaring Lion, and referred to the mountains on either side as the 'Super-Remarkables'.[6] He'd spend weeks there sometimes, and prospected an enormous area in the surrounding ranges. It was Henry who discovered an asbestos seam in the Takaka Valley in 1908, which he hoped to mine.

In 1919, Chaffey mined a promising 46 tons from his asbestos mine. No road existed into the Cobb before the 1940s, but after the road was bulldozed in to develop the Cobb Dam, the better access attracted interest from the Hume Pipe Company. They pushed a road to within 2 kilometres of the Asbestos Cottage, developed a mine, and by 1949 were producing more than 4 tons of asbestos per day. But good-quality asbestos never surfaced in great quantities, and after another few profitless years the company finally gave up.[7] Chaffey received a wage from the company for a while, but never made much from his discovery. It didn't matter overly, as the couple stayed largely self-sufficient – Henry shot pigs and goats for meat, and they tended a productive vegetable garden.

Before development of the road, access to the cottage was along the 20-kilometre pack track from the Graham Valley near Motueka, or an even longer one from Upper Takaka. Chaffey lugged supplies in on his back, never carrying less than 30 kilograms. When his swag was below the requisite weight, a storekeeper recalled that Chaffey added corned-beef tins for ballast.[8]

Once trampers met Chaffey on the track and were astounded by the weight of his pack: 57 kilograms. He replied, 'Oh, it's not bad now, but it was too heavy before. I had to put a twenty-five-pound [11-kilogram] bag of flour under a rock on the way.'[9] Perhaps to dull the pain of his shoulders, Chaffey often supped on a bottle of whisky, and locals claimed he got 'a good mileage to the bottle'.[10]

The couple needed lots of sugar, as Annie made pots and pots of raspberry, plum, peach, blackcurrant and gooseberry jam from the fruit bushes they

LEFT Henry and Annie Chaffey outside Asbestos Cottage, May 1936. PHOTO: MAC HARWOOD, COURTESY OF GERARD HINDMARSH, FROM *KAHURANGI CALLING*
OPPOSITE Asbestos Cottage in 2002.
PHOTO: SHAUN BARNETT/BLACK ROBIN PHOTOGRAPHY

managed to coax out of the thin soils. With Henry away prospecting, Annie endured the frightening 1929 Murchison earthquake alone, the jars smashing around her.

Life at Asbestos Cottage could be lonely for Annie, although a series of dogs provided company, and from the 1930s a battery-powered radio provided more. Occasional trampers, prospectors and musterers called in too, and Annie's hospitality became locally famous.

Guests to Asbestos Cottage remembered delicacies like cakes, biscuits and scones, as well as dinners of goat and weka stew. Despite the remoteness of their home, neither Henry nor Annie greeted their guests with rough appearances: Chaffey was always clean-shaven, and Annie covered from neck to toe in full Edwardian dress. One visitor remarked, 'I think they were determined to keep their social status, no matter how tough the environment.'[11]

Intending visitors were required to alert the Chaffeys of their approach. Over the years, a succession of signs graced the track, the simplest stating, 'Cooee for Chaffey'.[12] Guests had to wait patiently until Annie was ready. Inside, she served tea in cups, with saucers placed on doilies. Baking was nibbled delicately.

Chaffey's home brew, 'Asbestos Beer', was anything but delicate. One visitor recalled, 'I knew one alcoholic who would drink anything – except Chaffey's beer. He said it was much better to stay sober if that was all that was available.'[13]

While the Chaffeys became well known locally, the wider public remained largely ignorant of them until Henderson's book appeared. Henderson originally intended to devote just one chapter to the Chaffeys in a more general book on the area. But during his research, Henry and Annie somehow took over. Of them, he wrote: 'Durability ran through and reinforced this couple like steel girders.'[14] It must have done, for Henry had the alarming habit of sleeping with 'imperfect explosives under his armpits'.[15] While it would be easy to overly romanticise the couple's existence, they had a hard and often lonely life. One witness described their relationship as 'good natured bickering'.[16]

At Asbestos Cottage, days passed with Annie cooking, making her own soap and washing using water boiled over the fire. Henry gathered and cut firewood for the ever-hungry hearth and, aside from prospecting, wrote letters to politicians expressing his views. For twenty-eight years the couple kept weather records for the Meteorological Service and also witnessed many changes in the local wildlife. Henry lamented the extinction of saddlebacks, native thrushes and kokako in the area, and wrote a nature column for newspapers. Kea, weka, kaka and kiwi, however, did not escape the Chaffey billy, and Henry once ate a kakapo on the Tableland.

Asbestos Cottage itself was built of pit-sawn timber in 1897 by prospectors.[17] It has two rooms, a bedroom and a living area, which the Chaffeys made more comfortable with deerskin rugs on the floor. Pictures from mining journals and magazines papered the walls.[18] Around the door hung aromatic fresh green manuka branches. Annie cooked in a camp oven over a fire lit in the broad hearth.

The years passed. Visitors came and went. Henry prospected and wrote; Annie cooked, read and listened to the radio.

Ever strong, Chaffey was lugging a load on his back the day he died of a heart attack in the winter of 1951, aged eighty-three. After he failed to show up at home, Annie became worried. Searchers found his frozen body off the edge of the track. A hard life had at last taken its toll, and the old man of the mountains was gone.

A distraught Annie, in one bewildered moment, tried unsuccessfully to burn herself and Asbestos Cottage.[19] She was brought out of the mountains and spent some two months recovering in Takaka, before being taken to Timaru to live with her sister. But the combination of city life, electricity and too many people disturbed her. She was lost without Henry and her mountain home. On 14 July 1953, Annie took an overdose of sleeping pills and died in bed.

Asbestos Cottage slowly began to succumb to the elements, and would have quietly rotted away were it not for the efforts of Forest Service ranger Jack McBurney, who in 1967 arranged remedial work. The original malthoid thatch, well deteriorated, was replaced with iron to ensure the hut remained weather-tight.[20]

In 1997, Takaka builder Gregor Koolen oversaw a more extensive renovation with ex-Forest Service ranger Max Polglaze, both under contract to DOC. Koolen immersed himself in Henderson's book, trying to learn any details about the cottage that might help, before spending six weeks working on the hut, half of them alone. A helicopter ferried in materials for the restoration, which involved replacing the piles and rotten timber, and creating an inner chimney sleeve to ensure the fireplace could still be used, while retaining the original chimney exterior. The pair discovered the cottage was quite primitively built, with no studs, and boards nailed straight on the bearers. For a hut never intended to be anything more than a temporary shelter, it had survived a century remarkably well. Chaffey artefacts discovered included a rain gauge, a metal matchbox, prospectors' combing plates and blade shears.[21]

Many trampers who spend a night at Asbestos Cottage feel the presence of the Chaffeys – not in a haunted way, but in the sense of having slept somewhere steeped in history. Tramper Barbara Marshall, recalling one of the three nights she has spent in the four-bunk cottage, could 'vividly imagine Annie's long skirts rustling about the hut'.[22]

SHAUN BARNETT

Cecil Kings Hut 1935 KAHURANGI NATIONAL PARK

> Gold, gold, fine bright gold
> Tuapeka, Wangapeka, bright red gold.
> — Gold miners' song lyrics from the 1860s[1]

The Wangapeka Track owes its existence to gold. Miners discovered gold in the Blue, a tributary of the Wangapeka, in 1859, and by the 1870s a small town – with jail, courthouse and hotel – existed at Rolling River. Gold mining occurred throughout the valley, and was reflected in the names of some of its tributaries, like Nuggety Creek.[2] In 1862, surveyor John Rochfort blazed a trail up the Wangapeka and upper Karamea, and found a route through to Little Wanganui. But it took until 1899 before a benched pack track was largely complete.[3] The Wangapeka Track has been more or less in continual use ever since.

During the 1930s Depression, Cecil King worked a claim in the Wangapeka River, near the junction of the north and south branches. In September 1935, the thirty-two-year-old felled a large red beech tree, hand-adzed the timber, and used it to build a rustic hut to serve as a base – possibly with help from two others, Boyd and Hunter.[4] Beech-pole framing supported slab walls and a shingle roof; the wooden chimney sported a stone hearth. A small annexe served as storeroom and entrance to the main room.[5]

The Depression saw a resurgence in gold-mining activity nationwide, but Cecil King was not just an itinerant prospector. He returned to his hut to work gold almost every summer for the next forty-six years, at first taking leave from his job in Wellington to do so and later, after his retirement, spending longer periods there. Apart from a few years during the Second World War when his prospecting licence lapsed, King kept his mining claim current through the entire period.[6]

Many prospectors are happy to do nothing more than wash some gravel through a pan, but King was serious. He built fairly elaborate fluming, more than 300 metres long, to provide sluicing water for his claim.[7] Tailings around the hut remain visible even today.

Cecil King freely allowed others to use his hut during his absences, and was usually generous about sharing it even when he was in residence. One tramper recalled turning up at the hut to meet Cecil in 1979: 'We arrived mid afternoon that day and an elderly but fit, bearded man invited us in for a cup of tea by a crackling fire.'[8]

After the New Zealand Forest Service recut the overgrown track in the mid-1960s, the Wangapeka's popularity grew rapidly, prompting the department to build a new hut twenty minutes downstream in 1974. The new twenty-bunk Kings Creek Hut did not appeal to everyone (tramper Pete Lusk called it a 'cavernous' structure 'devoid of character, not a curve in it, painted like a hospital ward and a triumph of utilitarian design')[9] and many preferred the atmosphere of the old hut.

In 1973, Forest Service ranger Harry Ferris reported that King had been in residence at his hut for several prolonged periods:

> What the legal position of the hut is I am not sure but feel we have a moral obligation to leave Mr King be as long as he does not interfere with other people's enjoyment of the park. There has been only one complaint from a party who claimed Mr King would not allow them into the hut. All other people speak highly of his hospitality and feel he lends character to the area. Mr King has a fixation about hippies and long hair and I think this had a lot to do with his refusing entry to this party.[10]

Cecil King on the Wangapeka Track, 1975.
PHOTO: JOHN RHODES/WAIRARAPA VISUALS

To reduce the risk of fire – always a concern with historic huts – the Forest Service replaced the original wooden chimney with a new galvanised iron one in the 1970s.[11]

King probably earned only sufficient returns from gold to cover his expenses, but one gets the impression that mattered little to him. The delightful Wangapeka had seeped into his very skin, and after King died in June 1982, aged seventy-eight, his son Kevin scattered his ashes around the hut.

After King's death, no one actively maintained

MINING HUTS 87

the hut, and it began to deteriorate. As early as 1987, ex-Forest Service ranger Max Polglaze became concerned about the condition of the old hut. In 1990 he wrote to DOC:

> The old place is deserving of restoration; it is, quite simply, a shrine. The atmosphere at Cecil King's Hut is poignant, fragile and intense. Half an hour at the hut (or better still an overnight stay), just absorbing the feel of the place, is one of the major impressions of a Wangapeka Track walk. It provides a tangible link with the past, a reminder of an earlier and simpler life for which, it seems, many people yearn.[12]

Polglaze had his wish granted when DOC historian Steve Bagley employed him to restore the hut in the autumn of 1991. His main worry was finding suitable timber to replace rotten material. But soon after arriving on site, Polglaze found a recently fallen silver beech tree perfect for the job 'just fifty paces from the hut'.[13] In his diary he recorded:

> it looks like supplying everything the job needs, so wow!, how incredibly fortuitous. I mean it's been standing there over 3 centuries (no. of growth rings exceeds 300) and now, at this exactly right moment in history it falls in exactly the right manner so that the superb heartwood in its stem can be easily milled into planks to give an old hut … another lease of life. I call it an act of God.[14]

Over the next six weeks Polglaze worked hard, replacing rotten timber, correcting a lean in the old framing, repairing the bunks and fixing leaks in the roof.[15] He mostly worked alone, although Bagley came in to supervise and help at times, as did a friendly robin whenever Polglaze made bread in his camp oven.

King had planted a beech tree in the clearing as a replacement for the one he felled to build the hut. In 1991, the tree was big enough for Polglaze to use as an anchor to support the leaning hut while he worked on it.

Polglaze had met Cecil King briefly back in 1976. Of the restoration, Polglaze felt the old man would be 'quite chuffed'.[16]

SHAUN BARNETT

ABOVE LEFT Cecil King with his fluming, 1975.
PHOTO: JOHN RHODES/WAIRARAPA VISUALS
ABOVE Interior of Cecil Kings Hut in 1993. PHOTO: BRUCE POSTILL
OPPOSITE Cecil Kings Hut pictured in 1996.
PHOTO: STEVE BAKER/BLACK ROBIN PHOTOGRAPHY

Urquharts Hut 1933 CRAIGIEBURN FOREST PARK, CANTERBURY

Urquharts Hut was another by-product of government attempts to encourage mining during the 1930s Depression. Gold discovered in the Moa Stream tributary of the Wilberforce Valley in Canterbury in the 1870s precipitated a minor rush during the first half of 1880. A second rush in the upper Wilberforce followed in the latter half of the 1880s, with companies formed to mine quartz reefs as high as 1600 metres on the rugged slopes of Mt Harman. Ropes and stakes were sometimes required to access portals to the tunnels, and a quartz-crushing machine was even taken to the head of the river.[1]

However, all the effort and expense proved to be largely in vain, as not enough reliable gold was found to make it economic. Miners and syndicates continued to prospect the area through the turn of the century and beyond, using a variety of huts and buildings, including Dynamite Hut on Browning Pass itself (probably built in 1905) to store explosives.[2] On a 1921 crossing of Browning Pass, Bill Heinz noted this hut still had sticks of gelignite in it. As late as the 1950s and 1960s, trampers and climbers still used the old hut, but it no longer exists today. Heinz also noted a large machinery shed across the Wilberforce below the pass, but on a later visit in 1926 that had been buried by scree slides.[3]

The Wilberforce already had a long human history, beginning with Maori using Noti Raureka (Browning Pass) as a greenstone trail. In 1865, a benched track was built over the pass, part of an ambitious project to establish a road. Later in the 1860s, sheep were driven over the track and sold to hungry miners on the West Coast. Apart from irregular tramping parties, the occasional climber, and the activities of musterers from Glenthorne and Mt Algidus stations, the Wilberforce Valley experienced comparatively little activity for a spell after the 1880s gold rushes, until the 1930s Depression.

In March 1933, the Ashburton County Council sent an expedition of its unemployed men on gold-prospecting relief work up the Wilberforce from Glenthorne Station, paid for by the Unemployment Board. The party split into two groups: one to prospect and the other to build a base in the Wilberforce about 2 kilometres up from the Griffiths confluence.[4]

Rod Urquhart, former manager of Mt Algidus Station and a well-known figure in the Canterbury high country, led this second group of four men. The party used packhorses to carry the corrugated iron for the hut, but planned to frame it using timber from the bush. Like many of the earlier miners, they didn't have an easy time of it. Urquhart wrote, 'we had 8 days nor'west rain, an awful place for wet weather'.[5] Another in the party reckoned that building the hut was 'a bit of a job because we had to get the timber out of the bush, and up there it was all twisted'.[6]

Despite the difficulties, they found various ways to keep entertained: shooting deer for venison to supplement their mutton diet, and forming a camp band. Bill Bergman, aka 'Hokitika Bill', played the

Tramper Gaylene Wilkinson inside Urquharts Hut, winter 1987. PHOTO: GEOFF SPEARPOINT

violin 'pretty good' while Charlie Freeman squeezed an accordion.[7]

The men had another way to supplement their pantry and income. Bowing to pressure from farmers, who believed kea attacked sheep (rogue ones sometimes do), the government had placed a bounty on kea in 1890. In the 1930s, this amounted to 2 shillings and sixpence per beak. To put this in context, single men on the relief expedition earned 15 shillings per week, so six dead kea would double their weekly income.[8] Kea did not receive even partial protection until 1971, after an estimated 150,000 had been killed over the century before. Philip Temple called it the 'one of the worst cases of avicide in history', and despite full protection since 1986 the birds remain in decline today.[9]

The Wilberforce prospecting expedition was an eventful one. Conflict developed between the bosses of the two groups, and on top of that came dissatisfaction from the authorities. Public Works Department surveyor E.A. Gibson was sent to take full charge. Gibson moved the party to a camp in Moa Stream, but under Rod Urquhart work continued on the hut. Ultimately, however, the gold returns proved very disappointing.

By the end of May, with winter setting in, the expedition returned to Ashburton. The odd solitary prospector has probably since used the hut, but it never really served its intended purpose. That was left to generations of trampers, hunters and mountaineers, along with station staff mustering stock in the area.

Today, Urquharts Hut retains a real old backcountry hut feel, but perhaps more that of a mustering hut rather than a mining one. With an earth floor, sacking bunks, a frame of pole beech and a cladding of corrugated iron, it is perhaps a little rough by the standards of these days, but it still keeps out the rain – mostly. Harry Walker, writing in the 1948–49 issue of *Canterbury Mountaineer*, had this to say about Urquharts: 'Unlined and noted for the 6ft by half inch slabs of nor'west that squirt through every lap of the iron.'[10]

Urquharts Hut in February 2011. PHOTO: SHAUN BARNETT/BLACK ROBIN PHOTOGRAPHY

A more recent Christchurch Tramping Club party, approaching the hut in 2007, were told that a possum hunter was in residence. One member wrote:

> As the hut slept six we were confident of being able to share the accommodation, however when we arrived the hut was vacant. Vacant that is, except for the hundred or so possum pelts the hunter had hung up or laid on the bunks to dry … The tails were still attached to the pelts and hung down so that anyone walking around inside the hut had dead possum tails running through their hair.[11]

The last time I visited, it snowed, but the fire kept me warm. However, the lack of any real bush in the area means there isn't much around in the way of firewood.

Urquharts Hut is listed on DOC's National Register of Historic Sites and is now managed primarily for its historic value as a relict of Depression-era mining, with some recognition being given to its modest social, aesthetic and scientific values. Conservation architect Chris Cochran wrote of its 'workmanlike, rustic, and serviceable character'.[12] It's a reminder of past times and efforts, and of the folly of chasing imagined riches.

GEOFF SPEARPOINT

Glenorchy Scheelite Mining Huts WHAKAARI CONSERVATION AREA, CENTRAL OTAGO

Early gold miners in the Glenorchy region were annoyed to find a material called calcium tungstate, or scheelite, embedded in some quartz veins of the Richardson Mountains. This soft, heavy rock, thought to have little value, clogged up the riffles of their sluice boxes.

Scheelite is, in fact, an ore of tungsten, a hard metal with a very high melting point. The metal had limited commercial use until the late 1860s, when metallurgists produced a steel–tungsten alloy capable of withstanding great temperatures that was extremely useful for making machine tools and armaments. The associated demand for tungsten led to the development of several scheelite mines in the Buckler Burn catchment of Otago's Richardson Mountains. No less than seven huts associated with the main scheelite-mining eras remain in good condition today: McIntosh, Wallers, Heather Jock and McIntyre huts, which are open for overnight stays; and Jean, Boozer and Bonnie Jean huts, which serve as living museums.

Three shareholders of the Invincible Quartz Mining Company, formed to mine gold in the Rees Valley, were probably the first to discover a scheelite reef, on Mt Judah, in 1884. Shortly after their discovery, the Wakatipu Scheelite Company was formed, aiming to export tungsten to Germany.[1]

In the mid-1880s, the company succeeded in extracting at least 20 tons of scheelite by stripping out the easy veins. However, they encountered difficulties soon afterwards, not helped by the collapse of the German tungsten market, and went into liquidation.[2]

Little more scheelite mining happened until 1906, when a new enterprise, the Glenorchy Scheelite Company, began working the Mt Judah mines after renewed demand from Germany. The work was hard and sometimes dangerous, usually requiring deep underground shafts, and the area was isolated,[3] but that didn't stop others mining here too. Harry Birley, first to climb Mt Earnslaw (see p. 114), was one of a group of men who worked a claim high on nearby Mt Alaska.

On another mountain, north of Mt Alaska, William McIntosh discovered scheelite while sheep mustering in 1910. McIntosh started a company to mine the mountain now named after him, and sledged scheelite from this lode down an astonishing 1500 metres to the Glenorchy Battery for processing.

Shortly before the First World War, the Glenorchy Scheelite Company produced 63 tons of scheelite, valued at £6000. Although war stopped tungsten exports to Germany, demand from Britain for use in armaments almost doubled the price.[4] One of the surviving huts from this period is Jean Hut, lowest of those in the Bonnie Jean Valley, a tributary of the Buckler Burn that drains the northern slopes of Mt Judah. Clad in flattened tin drums, the hut makes use of rock weights hanging off the side to help fend off the full force of the nor'westerly winds.

LEFT Jean Hut in February 2012. **OPPOSITE** Heather Jock Hut in February 2012. PHOTOS: ROB BROWN

Processing plant at the end of the aerial ropeway in the 1950s. PHOTO: LYNNE WYLIE COLLECTION

Following the wartime peak in production in the Glenorchy scheelite fields, the industry collapsed in 1919 when the British government abruptly cancelled its contract. Returns had been declining anyway, with much of the more readily accessible ore already exhausted. All the mines were abandoned by 1921.[5]

The 1930s Depression attracted men back, however, and as many as forty miners worked the various fields. Harry Hopgood and John Craig biked all the way from Christchurch to find work. Hopgood married local girl Winnie Koch and eventually mined his own claim with her brother Gilbert.[6]

In 1937, the Wylie brothers (Bob, Dave and Jack) reopened the Heather Jock Mine, one of those originally worked during the First World War. They started the Heather Jock Syndicate and all had a long association with scheelite mining at Glenorchy, although none more so than Dave.[7] Accomplished as both a miner and manager, Dave Wylie ably filled both roles despite having lost his right arm below the elbow. Officially, he lost it when using explosives to enlarge a water race, but other stories tell of the arm being blown off during a fishing accident. 'Fishing' for trout using a plug of gelignite was a reasonably common practice by miners, particularly during the Depression. Dave's ability to use a jackhammer with just one arm left most of his workmates awestruck.[8]

The Wylie brothers worked the Heather Jock Mine through to the 1960s, and Dave's son John continued to work it until the very last days of scheelite mining at Glenorchy in 1977.[9] The best years for the Wylies at Heather Jock came in the Second World War, the Korean War and the Vietnam War. Predictably, the profitability of tungsten mining was always closely linked with war.

During the early days of the Second World War, the British government, strapped for cash as it fought Germany and Japan almost single-handedly, lowered the price it was prepared to pay for scheelite. This was bad timing for the miners, as producing the material was becoming ever more labour intensive – in 1941, some 145 tons of ore had to be processed to extract just 15 tons of concentrate – and some tension was created between the British and New Zealand governments.[10] However, after losing their supply of scheelite from Burma and China after the Japanese occupied these countries, the British recognised the scarcity of the mineral and doubled the price in 1942. For its part, the New Zealand government stepped in and bought the two major mines owned by the Glenorchy Scheelite Mining Company, including Mt Judah. Dave Wylie served as manager, and the government invested heavily in improvements to increase production. Aerial cableways and roads at some mines began negating the need for the laborious sledging. Scheelite production peaked at 128 tons of concentrate in 1944, and then dropped off dramatically as prices fell towards the end of the war.[11]

Bonnie Jean Hut, built near the entrance to the Bonnie Jean Mine in 1943, has been preserved by DOC in a manner that feels like the miners just left yesterday. It is a fitting memorial to New Zealand's scheelite mining efforts during the war.

Heather Jock Hut, originally built during the 1930s, is not at its original site. Tucked into a little crow's nest on a ridge running off Mt Alaska at 1300 metres, it's the highest hut of those in the

Dave Wylie (centre) outside Heather Jock Hut in the 1960s.
PHOTO: LYNNE WYLIE COLLECTION

Boozer Hut, 2012. PHOTO: ROB BROWN

Bonnie Jean catchment, and the only one of three now available for overnight stays. During the 1940s it was at an even more exposed site. Andy Paulin, one of four mining brothers, described his first night in the hut:

> About nine o'clock we could hear this particular gust coming up the hill, and when it struck the hut [the] three of us hit the floor at the same time. The door had blown open, a sheet of iron on the west side had worked loose, and all sorts of things were happening. Things were so bad in that hut that a decision was made to vacate the place … Jack and me, during the lulls, tried to nail the loose sheet of iron back in place, but it was pretty hopeless. We had no light of any kind, and the night was really black.[12]

After a harrowing escape in the dark, clinging to rocks and tussocks during gusts, they eventually reached the safety of the mine tunnel. Paulin continued:

> We sat around and yarned for a while then decided we might as well do some work. We had miners' lamps … That storm kept us pinned underground until five thirty the next morning, and when we returned to the hut the wreckage was just awful. A decision was made there and then to shift the hut to a site alongside the tunnel mouth.[13]

Opposite Heather Jock Hut, on the northern side of the Buckler Burn, are McIntosh Hut (dating from around 1915, when Mt McIntosh was first mined for scheelite) and McIntyre Hut (dating from much later, in the 1960s). McIntyre used to be a dilapidated shell until DOC restored it into a comfortable five-bunk hut in 2009.

Wallers Hut, built on a tributary of the Buckler Burn in the 1920s, was probably used only briefly for prospecting during the Depression, but got more use during the Second World War. Newspapers lining the walls for insulation date from this era. The corrugated-iron hut has pole framing, cut from the surrounding beech forest.

Other scheelite-mining huts in the area have been preserved for their historical interest. Boozer Hut, situated at the head of Bonnie Jean Creek, possibly started life as a shelter for miners working the nearby lode before the First World War. In the Depression years of the 1930s it was expanded into a hut and fitted out a little more comfortably; it was then that it was named after a scheelite miner notoriously fond of his grog.[14]

Aside from Boozer Hut, DOC has put a great deal of effort over the years into restoring the remaining Glenorchy scheelite huts, each with its own curious design and distinctive atmosphere. These important historical structures, some dating back 100 years, serve as testimony to the extraordinary efforts of the tungsten miners who worked the Richardson Mountains.

ROB BROWN

Waingaro Forks Hut c.1931 KAHURANGI NATIONAL PARK

Many miners have spent prolonged periods trying to wrest gold from the earth in the mountains of Northwest Nelson: prospectors worked the Waingaro in the 1850s, toiled on the Tablelands in the 1860s, and broke their backs in the Baton in the 1880s. For brief periods, tent communities arose in the most inhospitable of places. Waingaro Forks was one, a flat terrace above the gorged confluence of the Waingaro and Stanley rivers in what is now Kahurangi National Park.

Gold miners from the Collingwood diggings, New Zealand's first gold-rush site, prospected areas of Northwest Nelson in the late 1850s, and first found gold at Waingaro Forks around that time.[1] While never very profitable or large, the field was reported by one newspaper in 1885 as giving 'very favourable returns', with forty-four miners staking claims.[2]

By the twentieth century most of these goldfields were long abandoned, and the bush soon claimed any fleeting villages. However, during the 1930s Depression the government Gold Prospecting Subsidy Scheme encouraged unemployed men to return to many of Nelson's old mine sites.

Between 1929 and 1933, a band of about forty men reworked the Waingaro Forks area. Old water races still exist in the area, as do the remains of about a dozen huts.[3] One of these, Waingaro Forks Hut, was built by miners Les (Bang) Manson and his brother Choggy, probably in about 1931, using pit-sawn timber. The men cut 9- by 1-inch weatherboards for the cladding, and roofed the hut with timber shingles.[4] The Waingaro miners were supplied by farming brothers Laurie and Fred Riordan, who brought in goods by packhorse over the Kill Devil bridle track from Uruwhenua. Miners often used Riordans Hut on their way into Waingaro Forks (see p. 54).

Many of the 'miners' were actually office workers from cities like Wellington and Christchurch, and few had experience of backcountry living, let alone the demands of wresting gold from the gravels of frigid rivers. They had a tough, largely fruitless existence, often away from their families. Writer Jim Henderson summed it up sourly: 'exiled in banishment within their own country, scratching a haphazard living seeking gold … Not being *wanted* is the hell of unemployment.'[5]

Not all miners found their efforts wasted, however, as Henderson recorded: 'the winnings of a Maori family on the Flora Gold … helped them to take up a dairy farm in the north. Another paid his accumulated debts and bought his way into a butcher's shop, a third, similarly, with a garage in Australia.'[6]

Ultimately though, reworking the Waingaro was not a great success. Most of the miners had left by 1937, although one or two stalwarts persisted a while longer.[7] Any illusion that the miners of the previous century had not been thorough were totally dispelled.

Waingaro Forks Hut was the best of the remain-

DOC ranger Frankie Knowlson using a broad axe to hew timber for the hut's restoration, 2009. PHOTO: JOHN TAYLOR/DOC

ing diggers' huts when, in the late 1930s, Clive and Pete Petterson, along with Bill Brunning, patched it up with roof iron salvaged from other huts. In 1965, the Forest Service replaced the deteriorating shingle roof with some sawn timber framing and corrugated iron.[8]

At the time of DOC's 2003–04 Recreation Opportunities Review, Waingaro Forks Hut was earmarked for replacement – with only one small window, it had never been the most appealing overnight destination. However, a later assessment by DOC historian Steve Bagley recognised the four-bunk hut's worth, and he successfully argued for funds to restore it, along with Tin Hut on the old gold-mining trail.[9]

In 2009, DOC officers John Taylor, Joe Hambrook and Frankie Knowlson dismantled the old hut and then faithfully rebuilt it, with the addition of a second window and a skylight to make it lighter and more welcoming. Any timber that could be salvaged was treated and then reused, and rotten material was replaced with locally sourced wood. Taylor recorded:

> We also retained the original weatherboards although they have deteriorated and were covered over by iron several years earlier. As they were original fabric and contained records and dates of early visits in the form of graffiti on the inside, we decided to retain them and add an additional layer of sawn weatherboards over the top with batons providing an air gap in between.[10]

The men fitted a fire surround and chimney inside the original fireplace, and built a woodshed from poles and locally sourced split shingles, keeping the whole site authentic. They also grappled a huge rock slab from the river, eventually shifting it to the hut to serve as a hearthstone. Taylor reckoned, 'There is something special about these old huts, hand-hewn out of the bush and from the bush.'[11]

SHAUN BARNETT

ABOVE Tramper Louise Thornley pictured at Waingaro Forks Hut in February 2005, before its restoration. PHOTO: SHAUN BARNETT/BLACK ROBIN PHOTOGRAPHY
LEFT DOC ranger John Taylor putting the finishing touches on the restored Waingaro Forks Hut, May 2009. PHOTO: JOHN TAYLOR/DOC

No. 257. Mount Cook from Maltebrun.

THE MOUNTAINS OF OPPORTUNITY HUTS FOR TOURISM AND CLIMBING

New Zealand's early tourism huts are a curious mix of those built as public works, others constructed as part of private ventures and yet others that were erected as part of one man's dream. Very few were built without any government assistance; even early private tourism ventures seemed to rely on some form of public funding. From the late nineteenth century, the New Zealand government was keen to encourage tourists to New Zealand, as it rightly anticipated this could become a major source of overseas revenue. Indeed, when the government established the Department of Tourist and Health Resorts (Tourist Department) in 1901, this was the first example anywhere in the world of a national agency developed to advance the business of tourism.

Although building huts was only a small part of the government's overall endeavour to establish tourism, significant effort occurred in places like Aoraki/Mount Cook, Tongariro National Park, and on Fiordland's Milford Track. At Tongariro and Aoraki/Mount Cook, and in Westland, climbing and skiing huts were also established as interest in alpine sports grew during the first part of the twentieth century. Many of the earliest climbing huts were built in the days when the sport was largely a pursuit of the wealthy, who employed guides for everything from glacier excursions to ascents of the highest peaks.

Tourism in New Zealand traces its origins back to 1869, when Queen Victoria's second son, Prince Alfred, became the first member of the royal family to visit the colony. After ten years of instability through the 1860s with the New Zealand Wars, the new colony was now considered a 'safe' part of the British Empire and natural wonders like the Pink and White Terraces began to attract the world's wealthy. New Zealand was such a distant destination that only those who had the taste and means for adventure could afford both the money and the several months required to travel here. After the Suez Canal opened in 1869, negating the need to round the Cape of Good Hope, sea travel from Europe became quicker and safer.

For the next thirty years, New Zealand was considered a 'primitive' destination, undeveloped and without the grand accommodation of the northern hemisphere. It was strictly the preserve of those willing to 'rough it'. Investment in tourism at this time was mainly concentrated in two main attractions: the geothermal areas of Rotorua; and, on a much smaller scale, the alpine environment of Aoraki/Mount Cook.

Politicians like William Fox, an early champion of the national park idea, wanted to promote a tourism industry in New Zealand. While he had been inspired by his travels to the new national parks of the United States, other early proponents of tourism were enthused by the European idea of 'spa towns' and saw Rotorua as the obvious place to invest.

In 1881, the government passed the Thermal Springs Districts Act and purchased about 5000 acres (2000 hectares) of land, including all the best springs, which eventually became the city of Rotorua.[1] It then set about building a tourist town around the thermal attractions, but the venture received a significant setback when the Mt Tarawera eruption of June 1886 wiped out the famed Pink and White Terraces and alarmed potential investors. In an attempt to consolidate its investment in Rotorua, the government spent most of its tourism budget there until the turn of the century, culminating in the extravagant Bath House, built in 1908 at a cost of £40,000 – a significant sum for the day.[2]

While Rotorua's domination soaked up most of the government tourism subsidy in the early days, elsewhere small, humble huts began to play an important role in providing accommodation for visitors to New Zealand's scenic beauty spots.

In the South Island's mountains, tourism started on a much more modest scale, with such ventures as camping trips to view the Aoraki/Mount Cook glaciers in the early 1870s. However, completion of the first Hermitage in 1885 marked a new era, and the beginning of hotel-standard accommodation in the mountains. Built by artist Frank Huddleston, this simple cob and corrugated-iron building was initially used as a base for day trips onto the Mueller Glacier, where, in the days before glacial recession, the white ice flowed almost to the terminal moraine. Struggling to make a profit, Huddleston sold the venture to a private company, but stayed on as manager until 1893. The following year, the company folded, forcing a reluctant government to take over the venture.[3]

Despite the difficulty the Hermitage seemed to have in turning a profit, the surrounding alpine scenery did attract visitors, and it wasn't long before they demanded to see much more of the spectacular region. Having made the arduous journey to the hotel (the trip from Timaru took three days), many visitors

The first Malte Brun Hut in 1905, with Aoraki/Mt Cook above, and the Tasman Glacier on the right. PHOTO: THOMAS PRINGLE, ALEXANDER TURNBULL LIBRARY, WELLINGTON, 1/1-006958-G

Interior of the first Ball Hut in 1895, showing the curtain dividing the men's and women's quarters. PHOTO: JOSEPH KINSEY, ALEXANDER TURNBULL LIBRARY, WELLINGTON, PA1-Q-137-30-1

chose to stay for a considerable time at Aoraki/Mount Cook, exploring the local area, including the Tasman Glacier. The more adventurous embarked on overnight trips away from the Hermitage, led by guides such as Tom Fyfe and Jack Clarke (who with George Graham had been the first to climb Aoraki/Mt Cook in 1894).

As part of the Hermitage's expansion into the Tasman Valley, the government approved the building of two huts. In late 1890, a simple corrugated-iron hut, not dissimilar to an early mustering hut, was constructed near the junction of the Ball and Tasman glaciers. This, the first Ball Hut, was among the first backcountry huts constructed specifically for tourism in New Zealand.[4] Builder John Riddle of Fairlie oversaw its construction under the direction of the district surveyor, Noel Brodrick, and the governor, Lord Onslow, opened it in January 1891.[5] The main purpose of Ball Hut was to provide shelter for tourists coming to marvel at the towering white seracs of Hochstetter icefall, then an awe-inspiring sight. But it also served as a base for adventurous tourists wanting to explore the Tasman Glacier. And from 1892 onwards, guides also led more intrepid parties from the hut over Ball Pass and back to the Hermitage.[6] In keeping with the times, Ball Hut had two separate rooms for men and women (at first divided by a canvas curtain, but later replaced with a solid wall).[7]

A second hut was built in 1898 on a spectacular site high above the Tasman Glacier. This hut, on the western side of the Malte Brun Range, was initially named after Noel Brodrick, who had selected the site, but eventually became known as Malte Brun Hut. The same size as Ball Hut, it comprised two rooms, with four bunks in the women's room and six in the men's quarters. The hut's high location, well into the tussock and scree zone, meant guides had to carry wood for cooking and heating all the way from Ball Hut, a distance of some 9 kilometres over the glacier.[8]

Malte Brun Hut made it much easier for guides to escort their clients up easy peaks like Hochstetter Dome at the head of the Tasman Glacier, which previously had been tackled from the De la Beche Rock Biv. The hut was also well placed for those tackling the fine rock climbs on the Malte Brun Range. Blanche Baughan, an English tourist and poet who came to live in New Zealand, visited the Aoraki/Mount Cook region in about 1909. In her book *Snow Kings of the Southern Alps*, she wrote of Malte Brun Hut in the purple prose typical of the times:

> Here, at the right-hand side of the valley, upon a rocky shelf of the Malte Brun, there is perched, a few hundred feet above the glacier, another little Alpine hut. It is the merest scrap of a place, and its furnishing, though sufficient, is of the simplest – bunks and blankets, tinned stores, ice-axes, Alpenstocks and a kerosene stove made up the tale of its hardy comforts: – but its outlook is sublime. For, opposite its little platform – a coloured platform, scattered with reddish rocks, and carpeted with a silvery raoulia [vegetable sheep], and the thick and springy green of a little grass whose bright fringe edges its precipice and shines gaily out against the great white beyond, – there rises royally up from the curved causeway of the glacier, and sweeps away in uninterrupted whiteness

to the right and to the left, the long line of the very loftiest summits of these Alps: a company of kings, a congregation of princes.[9]

High praise for a hut's outlook indeed. Tourism huts had begun to populate the New Zealand backcountry.

The Milford Track and Fiordland Tourism

It was Blanche Baughan's writing that also helped to promote Fiordland's Milford Track, another area to which the government wanted to attract tourists. An article on the Milford by Baughan appeared in London's *The Spectator* magazine in 1908, resulting in its now famous byline, 'The Finest Walk in the World' – although it was the editor, not Baughan, who coined the title. In it, Baughan extolled the grandeur of the subalpine environment at Mackinnon Pass: 'The bare rocks, bare air, bare light, all give the place a look of nakedness that is almost destitution, an effect of freedom almost savage. Yet, at the same time, something else pervades it with a delicious intimate charm – its wealth of Alpine flowers.'[10]

Baughan's essays were music to the government's ear, and helped its efforts to trumpet the tourism possibilities of New Zealand abroad. It was the government who had offered a £50 reward for the first person to find an overland route to Milford Sound, a prize claimed by Scotsman Quintin Mackinnon back in October 1888. That year, Mackinnon led a track-cutting party up the Clinton River, and found the route over the pass now named after him into the Arthur Valley, where another Scotsman, Donald Sutherland, had already established tracks from the edge of Milford Sound.[11]

Sutherland and Mackinnon led work parties to fashion a track over the route from each end, aided by a government survey party, and built the first huts. The track opened over the 1888–89 summer, when forty people visited Sutherland Falls. The following season saw an increase to 100, and then in February 1890 the wife of artist Samuel Moreton became the first woman to traverse the whole track. These first walkers stayed in camps set up by Mackinnon at places like Pompolona (his name for griddle-fried scones) in the Clinton Valley, but had more solid accommodation at Sutherland's Beech Huts on the far side of the pass. Before he drowned in Lake Te Anau in 1892, Mackinnon built a basic hut to replace one of his camps, and more were built as the track developed. In 1890, the government had also built a basic hut at the mouth of the Clinton River, and this served until completion of the more elaborate Glade House in 1895–96.[12]

The government's new Tourist Department was given control of the Fiordland reserves when it was formed in 1901, and by October 1903 had purchased the Milford Track huts from the private operators who had previously run them. After taking over, the department recut the track, enlarged Glade House, lowered the guide fees and employed cooks for each of the huts.[13]

Track and hut work continued. One writer summed up the department's effort: 'A progressive policy of development instituted by the Government now assured the future of the track.'[14] This description of huts in the Clinton Valley in 1906 paints a picture:

A climbing and tourist party near the head of Lake Te Anau, Milford Track, in 1895, with Tom Fyfe standing at left.
PHOTO: BURTON BROTHERS, TE PAPA TONGAREWA, WELLINGTON, C.017344

Pompolona Hut in 1908, Milford Track, Fiordland.
PHOTO: MUIR AND MOODIE, ALEXANDER TURNBULL LIBRARY, WELLINGTON. REF: 1/2-021453-F.

McPherson Hut, circa 1920-30s, on the Grave-Talbot route, Darran Mountains, Fiordland.
PHOTO: ALEXANDER TURNBULL LIBRARY, WELLINGTON, PACOLL-6001-19

The huts are each about 14 by 12 [feet; 4.2 metres by 3.6 metres], built of wood, with a square corrugated iron chimney-place sitting out of the wall the door is in. Bunks are built round two sides, eight in all, and two deep. These bunks are most ingeniously fitted with spring mattresses of wire netting nailed to the frame, with a good kapok mattress on each, two pillows, and blankets galore.[15]

Three years later, another walker wrote, 'Compared with the early days the present accommodation is simply luxurious.'[16]

Despite these improvements, tourists tackling the track had to be fit and rather determined. Foul weather often made the route treacherous, particularly over Mackinnon Pass, and many tourists were unprepared for the rough conditions. One tramper recorded a difficult descent from the pass during a blizzard in March 1906: 'Every few yards there were pools we had to wade through, and the stones were all loose and very slippery so that on that narrow, winding, precipitous, and very rough track we were in momentary peril of being pitched headlong down the stony cliffs into the valley thousands of feet below.'[17]

For such trampers, arriving at Quintin Hut (which had by then replaced the Beech Huts) must have been a great relief. After seeing the Sutherland Falls, New Zealand's highest, some tourists turned back, although others carried on to Milford Sound down the Arthur Valley. At Milford Sound, Donald Sutherland and his wife provided welcome accommodation and meals, although Sutherland did not suffer fools, and often called city folk by the rather disparaging term 'Asphalters'. For trampers, an enjoyable stay spent appreciating the sights of Mitre Peak was, however, somewhat tempered by the certain knowledge that, unless they could afford an expensive boat journey out from Milford Sound, they had to retrace the 52-kilometre track back to Lake Te Anau.

After 1925, a few truly intrepid souls hired guides to take them up the Esperance River and over the exposed high-alpine route of Grave-Talbot Pass – a route pioneered by Fiordland explorers William Grave and Arthur Talbot in 1910–11. This mountaineering route climbed to the pass, traversed the flanks of Mt McPherson, descended Talbot Ladder to Homer Saddle, then ended in the headwaters of the Hollyford River. Even though the Tourist Department built huts in the Esperance (McPherson Hut) and Hollyford (McKenzie Hut) valleys, and cables were fixed over the most exposed parts, the route never proved popular – in 1932–33, for example, only thirteen trampers traversed it. The opening of the Homer Tunnel and Milford Road after the Second World War effectively made the route redundant and the huts were abandoned.[18]

Despite periods of closure, notably during both world wars, and constant work to combat avalanche and storm damage, the Milford Track continued to grow in popularity until it became the iconic track of New Zealand tramping. Figures show the steady increase: 300 in 1921–21; 420 in 1923–24; 1200 in 1948–49.[19]

In parallel with the government's development of the Milford Track was the establishment of a private tourist track linking Lake Manapouri with Doubtful Sound. In the 1890s, the Murrell family – who also served as guides on the Milford Track – took over the Grand View Lodge at Lake Manapouri. By 1899, the lodge boasted fourteen bedrooms as well as large dining and sitting rooms. Robert Murrell Jr was the driving force behind the idea of building a hut and track network from Lake Manapouri over Wilmot Pass to Deep Cove. A track was cut in 1900 and two huts built at either end, using a £300 government subsidy. For a spell, during the summer of 1906–07, the Doubtful Sound track's popularity even eclipsed that of the Milford Track, but lack of patronage during the First World War almost killed the scheme.

In the 1920s, Les Murrell, a member of the next generation of Murrells, reopened the track and in the 1930s even attempted to expand it into an ambitious circuit. This included a boat trip from Doubtful Sound to Bradshaw Sound, followed by a tramp back up the Camelot River, over Fowler Pass and down the Freeman Burn to Manapouri: a truly epic return route that – like the Grave-Talbot Pass – proved a little too rugged for most people. Freeman Burn Hut (built in the early 1930s) is a reminder of this almost forgotten venture.[20]

Tongariro National Park and the Main Trunk Railway

Back in 1901, the Department of Health and Tourist Resorts had first formed as a branch of the Railways Department, run by commercially minded Sir Joseph Ward, the Minister of Railways. The timing of investment in tourism was ripe, as steamships had reduced the time taken to get to New Zealand to about six weeks, and once here, tourists could enjoy train travel on the expanding number of railways, which provided a more civilised alternative to jolting, horse-drawn coaches.[21]

The main trunk railway finally penetrated the interior of the North Island in 1908, but not before the development of huts in the country's first national park, Tongariro. Soon after it formed, the Tourist Department built two huts in the park: Ketetahi Hut first, in 1901, and then Waihohonu Hut in 1903–04. Both served tourist parties travelling on horseback through to Tokaanu on Lake Taupo. These huts had only a very brief heyday, as development at Tongariro National Park shifted to the western side of Mt Ruapehu after completion of the railway. While the original Ketetahi has been replaced at least twice, the historic Old Waihohonu Hut remains perhaps the oldest surviving hut built for tourism in New Zealand.

The man leading the Tourist Department during the development at Tongariro was its first superintendent, Thomas Donne. Energetic and driven, Donne expanded the government's tourism infrastructure in many parts of the country for nearly a decade between 1901 and 1909. A keen hunter, he was also responsible for efforts to introduce game animals to the Southern Alps, notably chamois and thar, in the hope of attracting overseas game hunters. These introductions, added to trout and deer imports already established by the acclimatisation societies, were intended to turn New Zealand into a sporting paradise. Although New Zealand was thought by some to be at 'the wrong end of the world', Donne considered its scenery superior to Switzerland's and sought to make tourism a major part of the country's economy.[22]

In addition to investing in hotels in Rotorua, Waitomo, Te Aroha, Hanmer Springs and Aoraki/Mount Cook the Tourist Department also gained control over seventeen reserves, including the Aoraki Domain and Tasman Reserve at Aoraki/Mount Cook.

Hut Development at Aoraki/Mount Cook and Westland

When the Tourist Department first took over management of the Hermitage, it also inherited Ball and Malte Brun huts. However, tourism at Aoraki/Mount Cook still remained on a small scale. The department's 1902 report recorded that '28 people had visited Malte Brun Hut in the season and 50 had made use of Ball Hut'.[23] By the following year, numbers at Malte Brun had nearly trebled to eighty-two. Although these were hardly cracking figures, they weren't bad considering only 5233 international visitors came to New Zealand in 1903, mainly from Australia and the UK.[24]

The alpine region still lacked high climbing huts, but progress establishing these would prove difficult. By 1909, the Department of Tourist and Health Resorts had been absorbed into the Department of Commerce and Agriculture, and was now just a 'Tourist Division', ending Donne's reign and momentum, and ultimately hampering development at Aoraki/Mount Cook. Expanding guided activities to cater for a wider range of visitors, including climbers wanting to tackle the high peaks, required better infrastructure.[25]

Peter Graham, who had taken over as chief guide at the Hermitage from Jack Clarke in 1906, wanted to build a hut in the Hooker Valley, which would serve as accommodation on the planned track over Copland Pass to the West Coast. On the western side of the Southern Alps, Graham's elder brother Alex was developing his own guiding and tourism business at Franz Josef.

However, building Hooker Hut in 1909–11 proved to be 'a practical and bureaucratic nightmare' for Peter Graham. Climbing historian Graham Langton has unearthed more than seventy documents detailing the frustrating paper trail Peter Graham had to negotiate just to finalise the hut and get funding approval. The Tourist Division's director wanted a stone hut, something Graham considered impractical and too expensive. At the same time, Ball Hut also needed an extension, and a busy summer season precluded work, although materials for Hooker Hut were assembled and a bridle track established up the Hooker

LEFT Charlie Douglas's Lunch Hut near the Franz Josef Glacier terminal in 1929.
PHOTO: A. C. GRAHAM COLLECTION. MACMILLAN BROWN LIBRARY, UNIVERSITY OF CANTERBURY, 2141, ACCESSION NUMBER 1065/PHOTO 19459
RIGHT Thomas Edward Donne, the first General Manager for the Department of Tourism and Health Resorts, pictured in about 1910. PHOTO: ALEXANDER TURNBULL LIBRARY, WELLINGTON, 1/2-038683-F

Valley. Finally, after the winter of 1910, guides prepared to begin construction of Hooker Hut, only to find that an avalanche had wiped out a significant part of the track. After more track work, 'The guides manhandled the materials over the avalanche and horses did the rest of the carrying.'[26] Construction was prolonged too, interrupted by the demands of guiding tourists, and it wasn't until January 1911 that guides Jim Murphy and Darby Thomson completed the hut. Although based on a similar design to Ball and Malte Brun huts, Hooker Hut was longer, making it more comfortable.[27]

On the western side of the Southern Alps, private enterprise played an active role in establishing tourist facilities, including alpine huts, often in partnership with the government. The first tourist accommodation at Franz Josef was built in the late 1890s, and by 1909 the owner, Captain William 'Billy' Batson, had done well enough from his humble venture to erect a proper hotel. The first shelter built for tourists visiting the glaciers was located at the Franz Josef terminus in 1898. A prefabricated corrugated-iron building, it was assembled by renowned explorer Charlie Douglas and known as the 'Iron House'.[28] A shelter was also constructed in 1907 near Hende's viewing gallery beside the Franz Josef Glacier. This small hut is still in place today, serving as a shelter for day walkers on the Roberts Point Track.[29]

In 1911, Alex Graham bought the Franz Josef Glacier Hotel with his brother Jim and sister-in-law Rose, and between them they greatly expanded the venture.[30] To allow an overnight trip for tourists, Cape Defiance Hut was built in 1913 with financial help from the Tourist Division. The government also placed high priority on establishing a track between the Hermitage and the West Coast glaciers, with real progress made in the four years before the outbreak of war in 1914. Welcome Flat Hut was completed in November 1913, which along with the Douglas Rock Shelter and Hooker Hut created a full complement of shelters along the Copland Track.[31]

Above the Franz Josef Glacier, West Coast mountain guides also built a small shelter called Almer Biv, completed in 1914. The growing number of huts opened the possibility of guiding clients on a 'Grand Tour' over Copland Pass to the glaciers, up the Franz Josef Glacier to Almer Biv, then over Graham Saddle and back to the Tasman Glacier and the Hermitage, a challenging journey for both client and guides that usually lasted a week or more. For the first time the tourism operations on the east and west sides of Aoraki/Mount Cook began working together, cemented by the mountain skills of Peter and Alex Graham.

As early as 1903, the first Hermitage had begun to show its age and increasingly lacked the capacity to cope with the growing number of visitors. Com-

LEFT Tourists at the Hermitage in the 1920s. PHOTO: LESLIE HINGE COLLECTION, ALEXANDER TURNBULL LIBRARY, WELLINGTON, 1/4-016943-G.
RIGHT Men carrying timber up Haast Ridge for building King Memorial Hut in 1915.
PHOTO: M. E. EMMET COLLECTION, ALEXANDER TURNBULL LIBRARY, WELLINGTON 1/2-057095-F

plaints from some tourists reflected that they expected better quality accommodation too. During his time as head of the Tourist Department, Thomas Donne favoured an extension to solve the problem, which was built in 1906, but others in the department wanted an entirely new hotel. Planning for the new building began, but a lack of financial commitment delayed any concrete progress. Then, just before the First World War, a flood washed part of the first Hermitage off its piles, as if nature was signalling that its time was up. A second flood later that season undermined the new wing.[32]

Finally, in 1914, the new, much grander Hermitage was opened. Over the 1914–15 summer, a new hut, Mueller, was also built on the Sealy Range, in the hopes of catering for the new winter sport of alpine skiing. The short summer season meant many New Zealand hotels were largely left empty during the rest of the year, threatening their financial viability. Developing winter activities provided an obvious solution, but the ongoing war put a temporary halt to further skiing development. Nevertheless, despite the wartime limits on materials, a high bivouac was built on Haast Ridge during the war and another small hut (Sefton Bivvy) erected beneath Mt Sefton in 1917.

Climbers had used a bivvy rock on Haast Ridge since the early days of mountaineering in the area. By fashioning a ledge under the partial rock overhang, they could pitch a tent, which was usually left in place over summer. But its inadequacy for shelter in the often severe alpine environment was all too apparent, and calls for a bivouac came to fruition over the 1915–16 summer. It was built as a memorial to English climber Sydney King and his two guides, Darby Thomson and Jock Richmond, who were all overwhelmed by an avalanche after descending Aoraki/Mt Cook in 1914.[33] Contractors soon abandoned the job, however, even when offered the princely sum of £1 per day, leaving the guides the unenviable and difficult task of carrying lengths of timber and iron up the steep, unstable Haast Ridge – for only 30 shillings a week. King Memorial Hut, as the shelter was initially known, served as a climbing base for over thirty years until it was replaced by a new Haast Hut in 1948.[34]

Rodolph Wigley (centre) with his sons Harry (right) and Sandy (left) photographed in the 1930s during one of their early forays into aviation. PHOTO: GREEN & HAHN, HARRY WIGLEY COLLECTION, CANTERBURY MUSEUM, 1982.163.397

Ball Hut in the 1950s. PHOTO: JOHN WILSON COLLECTION

Rodolph Wigley: Private Enterprise Takes Over

After the First World War, government priorities changed and a more conservative approach to the development of tourism was adopted. Much of Donne's visionary tourism empire suffered pruning. Internal Affairs took over management of activities like sport fishing, and the government came under increasing pressure to divest itself of hotel management and let private enterprise in. Just then, a remarkable character emerged in the New Zealand tourism scene. If Thomas Donne was the public servant who had contributed so much to putting New Zealand on the map pre-war, then his private sector post-war equivalent was Rodolph Wigley. The son of a South Canterbury farmer, Wigley was fascinated with the evolving technologies of electricity and the motor car, and undertook the first automobile journey to the Hermitage in 1906. This launched Wigley's Mount Cook Motor Service (later the Mount Cook Tourist Company) and started a relationship with the Hermitage that would last almost until Wigley's death in 1946.[35]

After years of pressuring the government, Wigley finally secured the lease for the Hermitage in 1922, as well as that for the Aoraki Domain and the Tasman Reserve. This put New Zealand's premier alpine region in the hands of the entrepreneur's private tourism enterprise.

Wigley set about changing the Hermitage from being a preserve of the wealthy, to a place that catered for a much wider range of society. He offered different levels of accommodation, from basic to luxury, and dispensed with many of the more experienced and costly guides. Instead, he preferred to employ keen young student climbers and place them under the supervision of his chief guide. While this made guiding services available to a far greater proportion of society, Peter Graham, who by then had been chief guide at Aoraki/Mount Cook for more than fifteen years, strongly disagreed with this approach, believing that it could compromise the Hermitage's excellent safety record.[36] Not long after Wigley took over, Graham resigned and joined his brother Alex on the West Coast. Wigley soon replaced him with another outstanding chief guide, Vic Williams.[37]

Wigley also saw the potential of skiing to turn Aoraki/Mount Cook into a year-round destination and greatly expanded the government's initial experiments with this. Under Wigley's drive and direction, Ball Hut and the

Ball Glacier briefly became the centre of New Zealand skiing. For example, in August 1923 a party of thirty-three Aucklanders enjoying a holiday at the Hermitage enthused about 'the general comfort and rapidity of travel and complete absence of any inconvenience from cold'. Seventy guests occupied the Hermitage that weekend, after sixty-two had stayed the weekend before.[38]

However, the alpine environment took its toll on the basic facilities. The winter of 1925 proved particularly severe, and after repeated heavy snowfalls an avalanche wiped out the original Ball Hut. Work began immediately on a replacement at a safer site, closer to the end of Ball Ridge. Although initially a twenty-four-bunk hut (with two rooms of twelve bunks), Ball Hut II was progressively expanded during the 1930s, again to cater for the ever-increasing numbers of skiers that Wigley had encouraged to Aoraki/Mount Cook.

Wigley's timing for developing Aoraki/Mount Cook was good: his version of democratising outdoor adventure coincided with the formation of the first tramping clubs in the 1920s and 1930s, part of a worldwide movement that saw the increasing popularity of activities in the mountains. By the 1930s, the Railways Department started running innovative day 'excursions' to cater for New Zealanders' growing desire to visit the mountains. This was all part of a wider social change that saw citizens in the western world having more leisure time, which in turn drove a desire to participate in cheap recreational activities and lead a healthy lifestyle. Despite the financial difficulties of the Depression, even more people began walking, tramping and climbing through the 1930s.

From his success at the Hermitage, Wigley soon expanded his enterprise. In the late 1920s, he built The Chateau at Tongariro National Park, hoping not only to develop skiing here too, but also to expand his enterprise across both islands.[39] By 1928, his Mount Cook Tourist Company was publicly listed and included hotels in Auckland, Rotorua and Queenstown, as well as New Zealand's first rental car company. Wigley even began exploring the potential of aviation.[40] All this growth was built on the insight that there would be an expanding middle class, who could now easily reach Aoraki/Mount Cook with the convenience of the motor car and, perhaps one day, by aeroplane.

On the other side of the coin, Wigley found himself increasingly at odds with the growing number of trampers and climbers who felt that he had no right to charge for camping and access to New Zealand's highest mountains, and that it had been fundamentally wrong for the government to lease the reserves out to a private company. Wigley was perfectly within his rights as the lessee, but the privatisation of public reserves remained an affront to many New Zealanders.

In the 1930s, Wigley's relationship with New Zealand trampers and climbers became increasingly difficult. The New Zealand Alpine Club (NZAC), established in 1891, remains New Zealand's oldest outdoor club. Founder and influential president Arthur P. Harper was particularly concerned at private enterprise gaining control of public reserves. He had successfully lobbied the

NZAC members dismantling and burning De la Beche Memorial Hut in 1979.
PHOTO: DAVID BLUNT

government to set aside the Copland Valley and West Coast glaciers as a large scenic reserve in 1930, and soon sought to safeguard public access to Aoraki/Mount Cook.[41]

Clubs Build Public Huts

Tragedy struck in January 1930, when a party of four women, led by young twenty-year-old guide Edward Blomfield, died on the glacier between Ball and Malte Brun huts during a particularly sudden storm. The deaths of everyone in the party suggested that a fatal lightning strike may have played a role rather than simply exposure.[42]

Later that year, at the request of the victims' families, the NZAC raised £400 to build the De la Beche Memorial Hut on the western side of the Tasman Glacier, across from Malte Brun Hut.[43] Also in 1930, the NZAC made an agreement with Wigley's Mount Cook Tourist Company stating that the club would own the new De la Beche Hut within the reserve.[44] However, despite completion of the hut in 1931, the agreement was never officially signed and by 1933 A.P. Harper, who had negotiated the terms with the company for the NZAC, had come to the conclusion that Wigley had reneged on the deal. He was incensed, writing: 'The Hermitage district mountains have been reserved for all time as a National Domain, so that all should have access to them, and this Club cannot and will not stand by and tamely submit to be excluded from the very heart of the New Zealand Alps.'[45]

Hooker Hut, pictured shortly after it opened in 1910-11. Owing to glacier recession it had to be rebuilt in 1948 about 30 metres away from the edge of the increasingly unstable moraine wall. More subsidence of the ledge required a second relocation in 1963, and another in 1994.
PHOTO: HOCKEN LIBRARY, UNIVERSITY OF OTAGO, C/NE2217/24

The company harboured its own complaints against amateur climbers. Wigley felt irritated when climbers entered the reserve without signing in at the Hermitage and stayed in huts without paying. However, for many amateur climbers, the hut fees were prohibitive during these Depression years. Harper wrote, 'Today these huts, built by public money, and in one case [De la Beche Hut] by private subscription, have been handed over to a private company and climbers cannot use them except under prohibitive charges.'[46]

Although Wigley had some egalitarian ideals, he was first and foremost a businessman, and could not countenance clubs doing their own thing for free. Eventually, he struck a compromise with the NZAC, whereby its members could receive some discount on the hut fees, although this didn't entirely solve the problem as the price reflected fully stocked huts, whereas most amateur climbers preferred to carry in their own supplies.

Disgruntlement at the Aoraki/Mount Cook situation rumbled on. In 1931, Harper had encouraged tramping and climbing clubs to form their own collective, the Federated Mountain Clubs (FMC), in order to pressure the government into enforcing public rights to publicly owned land. Wigley's hard line at Aoraki/Mount Cook led the FMC to lobby the government, resulting in a veto on granting or renewing any more private leases as early as 1936. Eventually, the FMC's efforts helped drive national park status for Aoraki/Mount Cook.[47]

During November 1937, in an attempt to put the relationship back on a reasonable footing, Wigley, his lawyer and representatives of the Canterbury Mountaineering Club (CMC) and FMC met to hammer out a deal with climbers. They eventually agreed on hut fees of 25 shillings for Haast and Gardiner huts, 20 shillings for Malte Brun and Mueller huts, and 17 shillings and 6 pence for Ball Hut, reflecting the costs of stocking each of them. Importantly for amateur climbers, those willing to carry their own food paid the considerably lower flat rate of 6 shillings. The rates were initially set for two years, but ended up being extended right through the Second World War.[48]

As New Zealand dragged itself out of the Depression, tourist numbers peaked in 1938 with 20,000 overseas visitors, the majority from Australia. Just as things started looking up, war in Europe erupted, and New Zealand was once again embroiled in conflict. Naturally, the war severely reduced international arrivals, and with the introduction of petrol rationing, domestic travel declined sharply too.[49]

The commercial viability of the Mount Cook Tourist Company grew increasingly imperilled, and when its lease expired in 1944, the government did not renew it. Wigley was left with little option but to hand the Hermitage and the reserves back to the government. By 1952, New Zealand had a unified National Parks Act, with much FMC influence reflected in its wording. Fiordland and Aoraki/Mount Cook were the first two parks created under the new legislation, in 1952 and 1953, respectively.

Wigley died in 1946 after a short illness, aged just sixty-five, and sadly did not live to see his son Harry successfully rebuild the company. Harry Wigley refocused the business on its transport roots after the war, and pioneered glacier landings at Aoraki/Mount Cook with light aircraft. This later development required the invention of a retractable ski – a world first – which enabled aircraft to take off on wheels but land on skis. Eventually, Harry rebuilt the Mount Cook Group into a major road and aviation transport business with services throughout New Zealand.

On the West Coast, the Second World War also had a devastating effect on the Graham family's operation. After years of building up their business, they borrowed heavily in the 1930s to expand the hotel and install a hydroelectric scheme for Franz Josef. In 1939, they were fully booked and prospects looked good for this remote part of the world, far from the troubles of Europe. But the ongoing war sapped numbers of potential tourists and staff, forcing the Graham brothers, by now in their early sixties, to sell to the government in 1947. Disaster struck before completion of the sale, however, when a hotel wing burnt down, killing four female guests.[50]

Tourism After the Second World War

The end of the Second World War signalled a new era in tourism. Advances in aviation brought New Zealand closer to the rest of the world, and travel by ship through the Suez Canal reduced the sailing time from Europe to just three weeks. Domestic tourism grew also with greater car ownership, and – after 1945 – the forty-hour working week made a huge difference to people's free time.[51]

The 1950s saw another restructuring of the Tourist Department. The tourism side of the old department had already been incorporated in a larger Department of Industries, Commerce Tourism and Publicity, and the government once again found itself in possession of ten hotels. In 1956, these were separated out into the Tourist Hotel Corporation (THC), while the publicity side of the original tourism department was renamed the Tourist and Publicity Department.[52] THC took over control of the Milford Track, Chateau Tongariro and the Hermitage.

The post-war years were mixed times for Aoraki/Mount Cook. Legendary figures like Mick Bowie and Harry Ayres continued their association with the Hermitage and later Ayres became Chief Ranger for the new national park. Just a decade after the Fox Glacier conflagration, fire struck the eastern side of the Main Divide, when in 1957 the graceful old second Hermitage burnt down, marking something of the end of its golden age. The modernist building that replaced it was initially a controversial design, but over the years it has been progressively added to and forms the core building of the current Hermitage.

Harry Wigley was disappointed to find that the THC had little interest in fostering skiing to the pre-war extent extolled by the Mount Cook Tourist Company. During the 1930s, Ball Hut had expanded into a large, rambling edifice with over a hundred bunks and a diesel-driven rope tow on the Ball Glacier. However, by the late 1950s the glory days of the hut as a skiing base were largely over, resulting from a range of factors. First, the Ball Glacier began to retreat dramatically, leaving an increasingly unstable moraine wall near the hut. Second, commercial ski-fields were already being developed in more convenient places near centres of population like Queenstown and within easier reach of Christchurch. And finally, in the 1960s, Wigley's own ski-planes had opened up a whole new world of opportunity for skiing on places like the Tasman Glacier névé, and also provided fast access for climbers to new huts on the Grand Plateau and the upper Tasman Glacier.[53]

Wigley had foreseen the writing on the wall for Ball Glacier skiing, and instead sought to develop the Queenstown arm of his business, setting up New Zealand's first commercial ski-field at Coronet Peak in 1947.[54] By 1965, Ball Hut had ceased to be a ski destination, and the THC announced its intention to demolish it the following year.

Ball Hut received a temporary reprieve when the newly formed Alpine Guides Company used the hut in the late 1960s as their main base. However, maintenance became an increasing burden, and in the mid-1970s Ball Hut closed for good. The hut mysteriously burnt down while contractors were in the process of dismantling it in 1977, and this piece of New Zealand tourism history was lost for ever (although two subsequent shelters in the area, one built

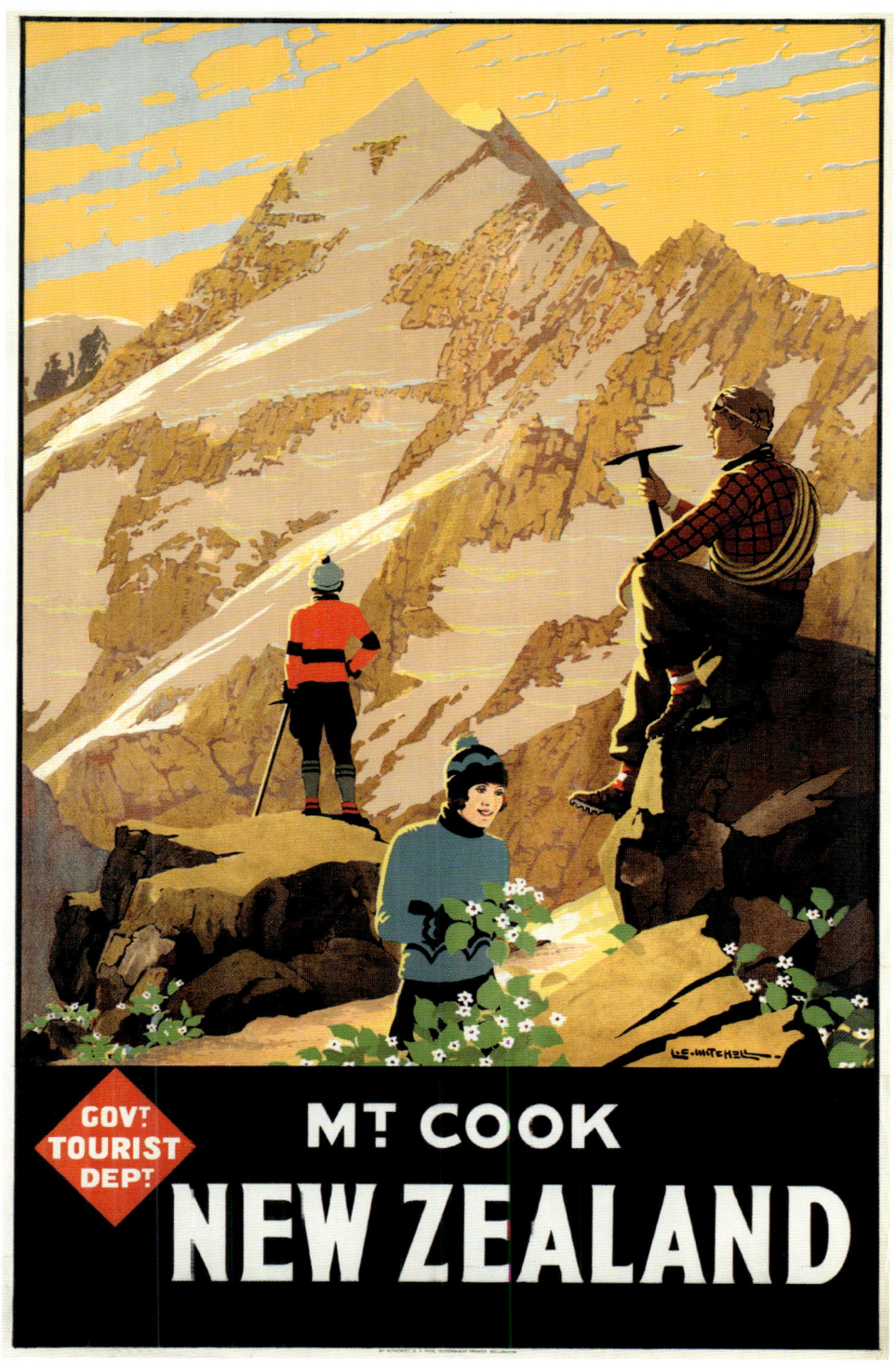

A Tourist Department poster promoting Mt Cook, c.1935, with artwork by Leonard Mitchell.
IMAGE COURTESY OF DAVE BAMFORD

HUTS FOR TOURISM AND CLIMBING 109

Sefton Biv in 2011. This historic hut, built in 1917, is now the oldest climbing hut in Aoraki/Mount Cook National Park still on its original site. DOC extensively restored the biv in 1999, replacing the corrugated iron, installing piles and building a wooden floor (the original floor was dirt). PHOTO: ROB BROWN

Here children first felt the magic of the mountains, aspirant mountaineers gained respect and understanding for the high hills and our clients from the cities planned adventures, reminisced or just talked to the keas.

To the last she was a grand old lady, wise and welcoming, but somewhat cranky in her ways. The jobs we hated most were sucking out the stove with an old vacuum cleaner, repairing diesel lines, lighting 'the monster' in a Nor-west wind to heat the water, digging out the old latrines or crawling under the floorboards to unfreeze water pipes with a blow torch.[56]

The original Malte Brun Hut had become obsolete too. A second, larger, Malte Brun Hut was built in 1929 by the Mount Cook Tourist Company for £1550. After heavy winter snowfalls had progressively pushed this hut out of alignment, it was completely rebuilt in 1949–50.[57] The building of Tasman Saddle Hut in 1963 drew some climbers away from Malte Brun Hut, and as the Tasman Glacier downwasted, the moraine wall edged closer to Malte Brun, creating progressively more difficult access to the hut. After losing much of its popularity, Malte Brun Hut II was dismantled in 1979. Although the iron was carted back to the village, most of the materials were simply burnt on site: a sad end to a hut that had served for so long. In 1986, a new hut – Beetham – was constructed in the nearby Beetham Valley and soon became popular, before an avalanche destroyed it in 1995.[58]

in 1978 and the other in 2011, have since carried the name Ball Hut).[55] Guide Gavin Wills summed up the thoughts of many who had stayed at Ball Hut over the years:

In her later years Ball Hut was a maintenance and logistical headache, a political football, and an embarrassment to local authorities. But with happy people warm inside her she never lost her sense of purpose and would resolutely lean against the storms that rattled stones against the roof, broke her windows and tore off sheets of iron.

For Alpine Guides she was a focus for clients and staff, a good base for the climbing school and a mountain refuge safe from storms and bureaucracy.

Throughout the 1970s and early 1980s, tourism promotion still echoed the inward focus that the Railways Department had encouraged in the 1930s, of urging New Zealanders to see their own country. Slogans like 'New Zealand is yours, go there now' and 'Don't leave home 'til you've seen the country' were the flavour of the day, particularly when the oil shock of the 1970s made overseas travel more expensive. In the 1980s, the government sold most of its tourism interests to private enterprise, just when New Zealand was on the cusp of a jet-age tourism boom, and mainly limited its involvement to international marketing through the New Zealand Tourism Board.[59] The THC huts on the Milford were also sold to private enterprise, while the high climbing huts had long been absorbed into the national park management, first under Lands and Survey and then the Department of Conservation.

Surviving Tourism and Climbing Huts

Today, there are few surviving original examples of the early tourism and climbing huts. Most, after being subjected to extreme mountain weather, have had to be rebuilt at some stage. Other tourism huts, like those on the Milford Track, have been progressively rebuilt or replaced as guided clients have demanded more and more luxury in the wilderness. One wonders what those early wealthy tourists would have made of the hot showers, individual rooms and three-course meals that the same walkers enjoy today on the private huts of the Routeburn, Milford and Hollyford tracks. Perhaps they would have enjoyed these luxuries, but perhaps too they would have had less of an adventure to talk about when they returned home.

Other huts from the early tourism and climbing era, although not original, have gone through several iterations but often serve the same function for which they were originally intended. For example, visiting the fifth Mueller Hut is still essentially the same experience as when the first version was built in 1914–15. The same can be said for Pioneer Hut, now in its fifth incarnation too, and still a critical base for climbers and skiers on the Fox Névé. The second Glade House still survives on the Milford Track as part of the guided walk, but is vastly modified. Most of the other huts on the track have been replaced by larger and more luxurious accommodation.

A few huts, however, survive in almost original condition, including Red, Locke Stream and Chancellor huts. Tongariro's Old Waihohonu Hut is probably the oldest original hut built for the age of tourism, while Red Hut and Sefton Biv are not too far behind in historical significance. Although the Old Waihohonu Hut is no longer available for overnight use, it forms an important reminder of the part huts played in establishing tourism in our mountains.

Since 1994, when floods washed away large sections of the track, Hooker Hut has remained intact but marooned and largely unvisited on its tussock ledge in the Hooker Valley. After much debate, DOC finally made a decision to dismantle the historic climbing shelter in 2012. No longer will families visit for a night to sit amongst the buttercups under the staggering south face of Aoraki/Mt Cook.

Huts, however, continue to play a significant role in tourism in the New Zealand backcountry. The existence of private tourism huts on public conservation land remains a vexed issue, and they are barely tolerated rather than openly embraced – particularly as the few that are allowed on places like the Milford, Hollyford and Routeburn tracks seem to now owe more to urban hotel design than any backcountry heritage.

In the early history of New Zealand tourism, huts were simply a means to an end and reflected the pioneer spirit of doing the best you could with limited resources. Those who visited early huts like Malte Brun really were embarking on adventurous trips. Today, a new generation of backpacker tourists are exploring the wider backcountry away from the 'icon' tracks and huts, and discovering interest and pleasure in more rudimentary, rustic huts. For some European travellers, a simple backcountry hut appeals precisely because it contrasts so strongly with the large hostel-like huts of their own Alps.

ROB BROWN AND SHAUN BARNETT

New Zealand's highest hut: Empress Hut, Aoraki/Mount Cook National Park, 1998.
PHOTO: SHAUN BARNETT/BLACK ROBIN PHOTOGRAPHY

Old Waihohonu Hut 1904 TONGARIRO NATIONAL PARK

> All will for many years think of [Waihohonu Hut] with affection as our little home for a little time in the Mountains of the North Island of New Zealand.
> – Ruapehu Ski Club souvenir diary, June 1915

Turoa and Whakapapa ski-fields sprawl over Mt Ruapehu's southern and western flanks, making it hard to imagine that once, a century ago, it was the mountain's eastern side that drew tourists and skiers.

Between the 1890s and 1908, Waihohonu was a staging post on a grand tourist route that took adventurous tourists through the heart of the North Island. After a paddleboat passage up the sinuous Whanganui River to Pipiriki, travellers embarked on a stagecoach trip across the Central Plateau and through the Rangipo Desert to reach Tokaanu, where a steamer ushered them across Lake Taupo. En route across the desert, they stopped at the staging post near the Waihohonu Stream, where horses were rested and billy tea brewed over a fire. This staging post was at first a basic camp, but later became a roadman's hut, described in an 1894 newspaper article as a 'slab whare in a natural clearing surrounded by towhai [silver beech] bush'.[1]

Horse-drawn carriage and group outside Waihohonu Hut, February 1910. PHOTO: GEORGE LESLIE ADKIN COLLECTION. ALEXANDER TURNBULL LIBRARY, WELLINGTON, PA1-O-003-105

While this sort of travel was adventurous enough, those wanting extra challenge could divert off the main route and take their horses over what is now part of the Tongariro Alpine Crossing and Northern Circuit, past Waihohonu and Ketetahi. Large cairns marked the route, some of which still exist, now covered in moss. With the route's growing popularity, the need for better accommodation became apparent. During the summer of 1903-04, the Department of Tourist and Health Resorts erected two huts on the route 'one on Mount Tongariro and one at the foot of Mount Ruapehu'. These became known as Ketetahi and Waihohonu.[2]

Pit-sawn totara sourced from Mt Pihanga provided framing for the building, while corrugated iron served as both cladding and a roof. Unusually for the times, however, thought was given to insulation – pumice sandwiched in the wall cavity. Situated beside a tongue of beech forest, the hut provided welcome refuge. Beyond, the prow of Ruapehu glistened with snow, or sulked behind cloud.

In those days of greater formality, the sexes were divided among the hut's two rooms: men enjoyed the larger space, with its open fireplace, while women were confined to the smaller, colder quarters. Bunks provided accommodation for about fourteen, although the tussock-stuffed hessian mattresses did not meet with approval from all.[3] The chimney, added in 1906, smoked 'abominably' – one skier, who spent several wet days beside the fire, subsequently recalled that he'd seen no smoke go up the chimney at all.[4] Consequently, most preferred to cook in a nearby shelter.[5] Skiers and trampers at the hut watched more distant smoke in 1909, when Ngauruhoe erupted.

Despite the rather primitive conditions, the popularity of the 'Grand Tourist Route' increased until 1908, when the main railway trunk line finally penetrated the interior. From then, Ruapehu's eastern side began to lose popularity, but not before Waihohonu became the base for the first ski expedition on Ruapehu.

In 1913, mountain enthusiasts Bill Mead and Bernard Drake imported skis from Switzerland – the first in the North Island. One newspaper article reported, 'In other lands these enormous "strides" are known as "skiis".'[6] In July of that year, the pair based themselves at Waihohonu Hut for a few days. They were impressed with the ease of ski travel on the snowy slopes, which would have been difficult to cross on foot, and soon gained enough confidence to make a ski tour around the nearby Tama Lakes and across to the Whakapapa Glacier. They posted a notice on the hut wall, inviting others to join the 'Ruapehu Ski Club'.[7]

For the next six years, Ruapehu Ski Club members used the Waihohonu Hut as their base. One 1915 party recorded:

> This was the first experience on Ski for five of the party, but all went merrily, tangle foot being fairly frequent at first, much to the amusement of those not involved in the tangle. It was soon found by the ladies that the limited skirts would not do, especially for what was termed the 'kick turn' and one lady was heard to say to another 'we are going to have a ripping time' and so they did. For thereafter the skirts were slit skirts – or may we say 'slit kilts'.[8]

The club grew, surviving the loss of members during the First World War, and Waihohonu became popular enough for plans to extend the hut's capacity by two more rooms. However, funds were instead directed to improving road access to

Whakapapa, which slowly developed as the centre of North Island skiing.

As early as 1911, Waihohonu Hut was used as a stopover for climbers embarking on traverses over Mts Ruapehu and Ngauruhoe from Rangataua to Ketetahi. An article in the *Wanganui Chronicle* advised that the traverse over Ruapehu to 'Waihohonu Government Hut' was 'a hard day, and most of the ladies require a rest day before proceeding'.[9] Not so the intrepid Jane Thomson, then in her fifties, whose party traversed Ruapehu from a bush camp above Rangataua to Waihohonu Hut in a single long day in 1911.[10]

Ronald Algie, secretary of the Ruapehu Ski Club, recalled visits to the hut from Waiouru in 1916–17. Entry to the hut at the time was, he remembered, from the '19 mile' road peg, and the 4 miles (6 kilometres) to Waihohonu 'almost trackless'. The hut was 'comfortable, while firewood and water were good and plentiful'.[11]

Waihohonu briefly became a mustering hut for shepherds grazing sheep in the area, and recreational use declined. Nevertheless, improvements to the hut in 1927 and 1928 by the Ruapehu Ski Club included a wooden floor and new bunks.[12] However by 1935 the Federated Mountain Clubs complained about the hut's 'unsatisfactory state of repair' and demanded the Tourist Department use the hut fees it received in 'large sums' to make amends.[13]

In the 1950s, the Department of Lands and Survey took over responsibility for the hut, and the growing number of trampers enjoying Tongariro National Park rediscovered the Waihohonu area.

After Lands and Survey built the 'new' Waihohonu Hut in 1968, a Lockwood construction on the other side of the Waihohonu Stream, the old hut was relegated to a museum piece. In 1995, however, it received a welcome make-over, when DOC and the Tongariro Natural History Society replaced rotten timber and repainted the cladding.[14] A small shelter nearby, installed during the hut's centenary year, houses good information panels about the hut's history.

For a brief period in 2010–12, three Waihohonu huts from each era remained: the historic 'old' hut, the 1968 Lockwood hut (due to be removed at the time of writing), and a brand-new, palatial twenty-seven-bunk hut built by DOC.

Old Waihohonu Hut provides modern-day trampers with a glimpse of a time past, when travellers braved long, rough journeys on horseback and riverboat, and when skiers were willing to cope with rudimentary gear and poor access. Over the years, many of these skiers carved or etched their names into the hut's woodwork, and signatures as early as 1918 still remain.

Although it had only a brief heyday between 1904 and 1908, the Old Waihohonu Hut remains significant as one of New Zealand's oldest surviving huts built for tourism.[15] Certainly it is Tongariro's most venerable building, and appropriately has a Category 1 listing with the Historic Places Trust.

SHAUN BARNETT

TOP Old Waihohonu Hut pictured in 2011.
BOTTOM Interior of the men's quarters in the Old Waihohonu Hut, 2011, showing Ruapehu Ski Club memorabilia.
PHOTOS: SHAUN BARNETT/BLACK ROBIN PHOTOGRAPHY

Earnslaw Hut c.1900/1920/1936 MOUNT ASPIRING NATIONAL PARK

The view up Lake Wakatipu to Mt Earnslaw has drawn praise since the earliest days of European settlement, when Alfred Duncan wrote: 'The water lay at our feet like a sheet of glass, broken only by two islands, and backed by the great snow-covered ranges which stand in vast array, with grand old Earnslaw towering over all and glistening in the morning sun.'[1]

An attempt was made to climb Mt Earnslaw in 1882, the same year that the Invincible Company began mining operations in the Rees. By this time, well-off but adventurous tourists, including governors general, were regularly visiting the head of Lake Wakatipu on excursions into what are still some of the world's most attractive mountains. Steamers, operated by a succession of companies, offered access to the lake head from the 1860s, with the government taking over this role in 1902. Their fourth steamer, the TSS *Earnslaw*, was built in 1912 and is still in use today.

Central to the mountaineering tourism that began to evolve was Harry Birley, son of the proprietor of Glenorchy's Mount Earnslaw Hotel. After participating in that initial climbing attempt, Harry subsequently succeeded in his quest for the summit of Mt Earnslaw in 1890 (solo), and went on to guide several further climbs of the mountain. But he was not alone, as various other hotels and guides offered similar opportunities.[2] The need for a base hut on the mountain soon became obvious.

To facilitate excursions to, and climbing on, Mt Earnslaw, local MP William Fraser obtained funds from the government for a track and hut around the turn of the century. County engineer J. Black surveyed a route up to Kea Basin, and J. Woodhead supervised a gang to construct a bridle path. The *Otago Witness* reported in March 1900: 'the bridle track zig-zags up the eastern flank of Mount Earnslaw, through a dense forest all the way. The timber line in Otago is fixed at 3200ft above sea level, and it is here where the shelter hut is now building.'[3] Located in a sheltered position on the lower edge of Kea Basin, the hut was called, appropriately enough, Earnslaw Hut. 'The track is a substantial piece of work, a great part of it being cut out of the rock, and it will be of permanent convenience.' By the time the bridle path was finished, horses could negotiate the whole route right to the door of the hut.[4]

By all accounts Earnslaw was a comfortable hut, patronised by locals, tourists and mountaineers alike. Guide James Wilson took Mr Aitken and his daughter, of Edengrove near Diamond Lake, up to the hut on the evening of 7 January 1903. An *Otago Witness* account of the trip reported, 'A swag of blankets and provisions had to be carried up through the bush, and candles used to light the path.' The party arrived at the hut just after midnight. 'The hut consists of two rooms, one for ladies and the other for gentlemen, and is provided with sleeping bunks.'[5]

After just four hours' sleep, the party set off for Mt Earnslaw, negotiating crevasses and cutting steps on the Birley Glacier. From some of the wider crevasses 'came the cracking, thunderous sound of the slowly travelling and breaking ice beneath and the sound of running water'.[6] They reached the summit at 3 p.m., reporting that the view from the peak was:

> magnificent beyond description, including the Western Ocean, endless snow ranges … From the sublime our travellers turned to inspect the curious mementoes deposited in a small loose stone structure thrown up for the purpose by the very few who had been there before them. These consisted of a nail, a staple, silver coins in bottles, buttons, a piece of turkey red cloth in a tin canister, and other articles of similar interest and value, including names on cards preserved in match boxes.[7]

The party then completed 'the round trip', climbing O'Leary Peak on their return. After re-

A tourist party at the first Earnslaw Hut, circa 1913. PHOTO: NZAC ARCHIVES, HOCKEN LIBRARY, UNIVERSITY OF OTAGO, MS-1164-2/83/7

turning to the hut by moonlight, they set off again early and arrived at the 'gates of Paradise' near Glenorchy the following morning.[8]

Kea Basin is a wonderful subalpine tussock amphitheatre, into which cascade waterfalls and, in winter, massive avalanches from the Birley Glacier above. These avalanches were the bane of Earnslaw Hut, and over subsequent decades it went through the proverbial nine lives, with several incarnations reflecting changing use.

In about 1920, wind from a large avalanche blew down the original hut, and the site was abandoned. However, Earnslaw Station staff salvaged materials and rebuilt the hut on a lower terrace, from where their shepherds could operate.[9] In this incarnation, Earnslaw Hut provided hospitality to many mountaineering parties throughout the 1920s and 1930s, many of whom developed a deep affection for it. Well furnished, it boasted 'cooking utensils, four bunks, an altogether abundant supply of blankets, two axes, a selection of mugs and plates, and, on occasions, may even run to a little tea and sugar. Being on [the] timber line, there is no dearth of firewood, and water is handy.' However, drawbacks included a lack of windows and a chimney that smoked when the door was open, so that 'an almost cimmerian blackness' usually prevailed. The hut's position, low down on the mountain, also made for a long climb up to the summit of Mt Earnslaw.[10]

Late in the spring of 1936, another avalanche raked past the hut and again blew it off its perch – leaving the debris to settle 60 metres below. Earnslaw Station's proprietors rebuilt it once more, this time tucking the hut in against a bluff where mature mountain beech trees offered shelter. It was expected to die there of old age, having been reduced by rough treatment from the elements to a crude two-bunk shelter with nail holes in the roof. The first Esquilant Bivouac, built in 1950 (see p. 318), reduced some of the pressure on the hut, and the rock bivvy in Kea Basin provided more shelter just a few hundred metres away. Earnslaw Hut

Earnslaw Hut in 1997. PHOTO: GEOFF SPEARPOINT

mouldered away, awaiting its next incarnation.

In the 1980s, the Varcoe family volunteered a week of their time each year to work on a project for Mount Aspiring National Park, and in May 1983 they were asked to restore the old hut. Garth was ideally suited to this sort of task, having supervised lighthouse maintenance around the country and worked for the Antarctic Division of the Department of Science and Industrial Research. Garth, Kath and their three children, aged eleven, nine and six, set to the old hut with a vengeance and completely refurbished it. Kath recalls:

> There were no bunks & no working fireplace in the hut so the first night we all slept huddled together on the floor … Over the next couple of weeks Garth jacked the hut up so it was level, rebuilt the chimney, built bunks from beech saplings & sacking, & put in a window. We only made 4 bunks so Russell slept sewn into a hammock made of a blanket.[11]

Today, DOC has taken over management of the little hut, recognising its historic significance and carrying out basic work to maintain it. The most recent work was completed in 2011,[12] the result being a wonderful old hut tucked under the forest – very basic, with two bunks and a fireplace. Climbers rushing by to conquer Mt Earnslaw hardly give it a look, but it still offers a great retreat, especially for hunters seeking chamois and deer.

GEOFF SPEARPOINT

Mueller Hut 1915/1950/1953/2003 AORAKI/MOUNT COOK NATIONAL PARK

Five different versions of Mueller Hut have graced the Sealy Range. Today's relatively new twenty-eight-bunk incarnation, built by DOC in 2003, is the most popular hut in Aoraki/Mount Cook National Park.

The first Mueller Hut, constructed over the summer of 1914–15, was primarily intended as a base for winter skiing on the Mueller Glacier. The Hermitage, at that stage run by the government, had been struggling for many years to make a profit – while a steady stream of tourists visited during summer, for much of the winter season it was essentially shut down. Starting the season earlier, in October, by encouraging tourists to try the developing sport of alpine skiing at Mueller Hut, looked a promising way to turn the resort's fortunes around.[1]

The first hut had a different location to that occupied by the current version, on a terrace 100 metres above the Mueller Glacier, between Mts Ollivier and Kitchener. Visitors walked up the track to Sealy Tarns and then attached sealskins to the base of their skis, which enabled them to 'skin' up onto the range and around to the hut. Once there, they could make short runs down the glacier, practising their stem Christie turns, before skinning back to the hut. Modern alpine skiing, a relatively recent progression of traditional Norwegian Telemark skiing, was still in its infancy at the time. Wooden hickory skis and loose leather straps holding boots in place did not allow much precision control, and these early skiers certainly had a healthy appetite for physical exercise and adventure.

One Auckland party of skiers reported on their exploits to the *Evening Post* in 1923: 'A group of twelve travelled on ski from The Hermitage, via Mueller Glacier, to Mueller Hut, a total distance of fourteen miles, and involving a climb of over 3000 feet. The run back down the middle of the glacier was something which all who made it state will not readily fade from their memories.'[2]

By the end of the Second World War, the first hut had deteriorated and was in need of replacement. With the Mueller Glacier wasting away, it was now also more than 150 metres above the white ice and its usefulness for skiing was declining. In February 1949, a Royal New Zealand Air Force Dakota aircraft dropped hut materials by parachute onto a new site on a ridge terrace near Mt Ollivier. Guides sledged the loads downhill to the terrace, riding the bundles and using ice axes to brake their runs.[3] These were the days before regimented workplace safety!

Bert Barley, in charge of the construction, completed the hut by April 1950. Unfortunately, a winter avalanche swept it all the way to the Mueller Glacier when it was barely four months old. Incredibly, the roof remained intact, with blankets still hanging from the rafters. Guides hauled the debris back up, and contrived a temporary four-bunk bivouac (the third hut) using the salvaged materials.

The design for the fourth Mueller Hut was the same as that of the 1950 Almer Hut (see p. 125). Guides chose a new site for it on the ridge, not far

LEFT The first Mueller Hut circa 1916.
PHOTO: FREDERICK GEORGE RADCLIFFE, ALEXANDER TURNBULL LIBRARY, WELLINGTON, 1/2-007570-G
OPPOSITE Mueller Hut V in 2010. PHOTO: ROB BROWN

The fourth Mueller Hut pictured at dusk with Mt Sefton beyond, 1992. PHOTO: SHAUN BARNETT/BLACK ROBIN PHOTOGRAPHY

from the current hut, which although more exposed was both safer and better suited to the purpose for which it was now being used: an exhilarating but easy overnight tramping trip from the village past Sealy Tarns onto the Sealy Range. By this time, the focus of skiing at Aoraki/Mount Cook had switched to Ball Hut.

Materials for the hut were air-dropped in late 1952, but things did not go as planned – a strong wind blew many of the bundles up to a kilometre from the site. These then had to be laboriously carried over rough terrain, which – combined with poor weather – meant completion of the hut was delayed until April 1953.[4]

By the late 1990s, it had become clear that the fourth Mueller Hut was coming to the end of its life. Battered by mountain weather for nearly fifty years, increasingly run down and under pressure from the growing number of backpackers visiting Aoraki/Mount Cook, the structure needed to be replaced. By this stage, the only other reasonably accessible tramping hut in the park, Hooker Hut, was cut off by glacial recession. DOC, however, could not afford to fund such an expensive capital project.

The Hermitage then stepped in with its own proposal to replace the hut with a private lodge that would cater for both backpackers and customers wanting more comfortable accommodation. That such a prime site could end up back in the hands of a private company – a return to the old days of the 1930s – was greeted with outrage from sectors of the New Zealand backcountry community. However, The Hermitage later withdrew the proposal when Sir Edmund Hillary was interviewed about the idea and made a strong statement against a private hut.

At around the same time, the government made more funding available to DOC for the maintenance and replacement of backcountry huts, which meant the department could fund a replacement public hut after all. The private proposal quietly faded away.

Sir Ed opened the new Mueller Hut in July 2003, on one of his last trips to Aoraki/Mount Cook National Park. The opening coincided with the fiftieth anniversary of the park, and also came just after the fiftieth anniversary of Hillary's May 1953 ascent of Mt Everest with Tenzing Norgay.

The new hut cost in excess of $400,000 and required 130 helicopter flights to transport all the materials on site – a stark example of the expense of building an alpine hut to modern standards. Mueller Hut V sits just below Mt Ollivier – the first mountain climbed by Hillary, aged twenty, which he described in his book *High Adventure*: 'I couldn't restrain myself any longer and scrambled quickly upwards. Next moment I was on the summit of my first mountain. I returned to The Hermitage after the happiest day I had ever spent.'[5]

The story of the new hut had a happy ending for the owners of The Hermitage, too. In many ways the debate over the Mueller Hut replacement was an opportunity for Hillary to rekindle his relationship with the resort, and the result of this was the Sir Edmund Hillary Alpine Centre, a worthy addition to the attractions in the park.

From Mueller Hut, trampers can admire the South Ridge of Aoraki/Mt Cook, first climbed by a party – again including Hillary – in 1948. It was renamed Hillary Ridge in 2011.

ROB BROWN

Godley Hut 1934 AORAKI/MOUNT COOK NATIONAL PARK

In the early 1920s, the New Zealand Alpine Club (NZAC) revived itself after a couple of decades of semi-dormancy, and soon grew in ability and confidence. Hut building became a priority, and after erecting De la Beche Hut on the Tasman Glacier in 1931, the club raised money to build another shelter in the area.

However, the NZAC faced difficulties from Rodolph Wigley and his private company. The 1935 *New Zealand Alpine Journal* reported: 'The Mount Cook District was naturally suggested, but in view of the acknowledged opposition of the Mt. Cook Tourist Company to amateur climbers entering its territory and climbing without employing its guides, it was considered useless to apply for the Company's permission to erect a Club hut.'[1]

In 1929, Wigley had tightened his grip on the Aoraki/Mount Cook region when he secured a lease from the government of the 18,000-acre (7000-hectare) Godley Reserve, which included the Godley, Maude, Grey and Classen glaciers. As a result, when the NZAC decided to build Godley Hut, they opted to ask the run holder of Lilybank Station, Reginald Malthus, for permission to situate it on his run. The station stretched from the head of Lake Tekapo right to the boundary of the Godley run, near the Godley Glacier. Malthus agreed with the Lands Department to sublet an acre of his run near the glacier terminus to the club. The NZAC had their Godley Hut site.[2]

Club member and architect Eric Miller designed the hut, while Simpson and Co. prepared the building materials free of charge. Fred Trott transported materials from Tekapo to Lilybank, and Malthus, using packhorses, took them up to Separation Stream. The contract for the actual hut construction was given to Kurt Suter, a noted alpine guide. By October 1934, Kurt was busy carrying the materials – 4.5 tons of them – 1.5 kilometres up from Separation Stream, which was the limit of the packhorses. Initially, a platform for the hut had to be built, and then the shelter itself.

The NZAC Wellington Section organised a club camp to the Godley area for Christmas 1934, drawing about thirty-five people from all over the country. By the time they began arriving, the hut was finished. Arthur P. Harper and George 'Guy' Mannering, both early mountaineers and ex-presidents of the club, officially opened Godley Hut on 24 December 1934, no doubt reminiscing about their first visit to the valley more than forty years earlier.

In its early days Godley Hut was reasonably well furnished, as many huts were at the time, boasting a kerosene cooker, Primus, pots, frying pans, a bucket and broom, several billies, cutlery and a spare ice axe donated by Otago climber Hugh F. Wright. Roland Ellis contributed pillows and mattresses.[3] Like many alpine huts, the structure was anchored with wires into concrete and stone foundations. The inside lining was (and still is) an unusual stippled form of iron sheeting. Although Suter did a great job, maintenance work was eventually needed. Ten years after the initial construction, on Anzac weekend 1944, a party of four went in to paint the hut, but poor weather hampered them and only the first coat was completed.[4]

The Godley Glacier has, in recent times, become one of the fastest receding glaciers in New Zealand, its rate of recession accelerated by a rapidly growing terminal lake. By the 1950s, this recession began affecting the hut. In January 1955, a massive flood cut into the gravel moraine on which the hut sat, undermining its foundations and leaving it teetering over a 60-metre cliff.[5] The NZAC Canterbury–Westland Section decided to save it.

NZAC member Allan Rattray on belay while removing cladding from Godley Hut in 1955, with the Godley River below. PHOTO: IVAN PICKENS

Luckily, two Land Rovers were available to transport members and tools to within 5 kilometres of the hut. After stripping off the corrugated-iron cladding, hut wall sections were moved complete, while the floor required excavation in four sections to the new site, 300 metres to the northeast.[6] Fortunately, little rot had infested the timber. Five weeks later, nails, paint, cement and replacement timber were taken up to supplement the temporary dump. At Easter, a determined party of seventeen headed up the Godley for the rebuild, assisted by

HUTS FOR TOURISM AND CLIMBING 119

NZAC members dismantling Godley Hut in 1955, Derrick Cook on right. PHOTO: IVAN PICKENS

the Dick family of Lilybank Station. Getting to the site wasn't easy. A northwesterly storm drove them back, and flooding forced most of the party to walk in from below Weka Hut. Somehow though, C.G. Buchanan managed to get further materials up to the hut site by driving his Land Rover across the river and back, which was rather enterprising.[7]

Work began in earnest on Easter Sunday, and by nightfall the roof was pitched and most of the loads were at the new site. By the Monday, with the roof finished and corrugated iron on the walls, the hut was weatherproof, and the last five members set off down the valley to the Land Rover. Darkness overtook them before they reached Weka Hut and they had some tricky river crossings as a consequence.

However, the welcome hospitality of an evening meal from Mrs Dick revived them and they made Christchurch by 4 a.m. the next morning.

Another work party of four completed a last Land Rover trip up to the site on Anzac weekend, building the bunks and finishing off other odd jobs. The number of bunks remained at eight, and the layout was essentially the same as the original hut.

The mid-1950s was an active time for NZAC hut building. In the year leading up to the Godley Hut relocation, other club sections were also busy building. The Wellington Section built Steffan Memorial Hut in the Murchison Valley, and the Southland Section built Moraine Creek Hut in the Darran Mountains.

In 2000, an engineering assessment precipitated thoughts of 'retiring' Godley Hut. Thankfully, the NZAC decided to improve the old hut instead. In 2004, new mattresses were installed and minor repairs carried out, and an agreement was signed between the Department of Conservation and the club for ongoing management, with meetings held by the two bodies twice a year to decide on work plan priorities. Locally, the South Canterbury Section of the NZAC, based in Timaru, looks after the hut.

Today, the hut sits on a quiet terrace amongst moss and gravel within the boundaries of Aoraki/Mount Cook National Park. It's a grand, raw place, with relatively few visitors. The glaciers have all down-wasted and crept behind lake barriers. Gone are the days of walking out of the hut and onto the Godley Glacier, but the increased difficulty of access serves only to make the hut more useful. There's also a certain beauty in the disintegrating barrenness of the place. Moraine walls constantly crumble, the cold grey waters of the lake ripple in the breeze and peaks of impossibly rotten rock discolour the snow. The hut serves as a haven for those traversing from Arthur's Pass to Aoraki/Mount Cook, winter wilderness skiers, climbers tackling Sealy Pass, and the occasional party attempting Mt D'Archiac or other nearby peaks. With significant historical values, it's a wonderful relic of a 1930s mountain hut, complete with many of the accoutrements of the time.

GEOFF SPEARPOINT

OPPOSITE Godley Hut in February 2011, with Peninsula Tramping Club member Kevin Hughes in the doorway.
PHOTO: GEOFF SPEARPOINT

Chancellor Hut 1931 WESTLAND TAI POUTINI NATIONAL PARK

Situated on a high, exposed shelf north of Fox Glacier, Chancellor Hut is one of the more remarkable buildings in the backcountry. For over eighty years this hut has survived the worst of the West Coast's wind, rain and snow, as well as periods of neglect and limited maintenance, to come through with much of its historic fabric intact.

The 1250-metre shelf beneath Chancellor Ridge provided access to the higher Fox Glacier névé for many years before the hut was built. By avoiding the upper Fox Glacier icefall, the shelf still offers the fastest route up to Pioneer Hut (see p. 128) and the higher peaks of the Main Divide. Not long after the First World War, Franz Josef guides Peter and Alex Graham suggested building a hut on Chancellor Shelf, but it took nearly ten years of correspondence and lobbying before the Department of Tourist and Health Resorts was convinced to fund the project. In June 1926, New Zealand Alpine Club president Arthur P. Harper also wrote to the government urging it to support the proposal, pledging £75 towards it.[1]

Chancellor Hut, like many other early climbing and tourism huts, was commissioned and funded by the Tourist Department and designed and built by the Public Works Department. In 1931, the Tourist Department also funded an almost identical hut in the Copland Valley – Douglas Rock Hut. Both huts adopted a similar design that had already been used for other alpine huts: Hooker, Almer (see p. 125) and Cape Defiance (see p. 136). After they were built, the Tourist Department planned to lease both Chancellor and Douglas Rock huts to the Graham brothers, who already held the leases for Almer, Welcome Flat and Cape Defiance huts.[2]

In November 1929, the Public Works Department in Greymouth contracted the supply of materials, prefabrication of the hut and its delivery to the Ross railhead to Timaru company D. W. Reece Ltd (Timber Colliery & Shipping Agents, Building Trades Merchants) for £155 and 10 shillings. Late in January 1930, the prefabricated hut duly arrived at Fox Glacier.

As the Grahams prepared to supervise the hut's construction, Rodolph Wigley of the Mount Cook Company, who then managed The Hermitage, made a late attempt to wrest the Chancellor Hut lease (and possibly also that for Douglas Rock Hut) from the Grahams. Wigley was in favour of the lease going to the Sullivan brothers, who had just built the Fox Glacier Hotel and naturally saw themselves in competition with the Grahams at Franz Josef. It is tempting to view Wigley's move as an effort to settle old scores with his former guide Peter Graham, who had left Wigley's employment after disagreements. But perhaps Wigley simply viewed the Chancellor lease as an opportunity to expand his empire over the Main Divide. Regardless, the government stuck to their plan and gave the lease to the Grahams.[3]

Peter Graham, accompanied by his young son Gar Graham, chose the hut site for Chancellor. It was a decision that has since proved to be perfectly inspired: sufficiently distant from Chancellor Ridge

LEFT Chancellor Hut in 1950. PHOTO: ASHLEY CUNNINGHAM
OPPOSITE Chancellor Hut in 2012, after its restoration by DOC. The chimney and fireplace were removed in 1972.
PHOTO: ROB BROWN

Interior detail of the congoleum lining. PHOTO: ROB BROWN

to avoid winter avalanches, and nicely positioned so as to avoid too much snow build-up during winters.

The Grahams tendered out the laborious load-carrying job to a collective of various guides working under Ron Wheeler of Waiho Saw Mills. For £2 and 12 shillings per 100 pounds (45 kilograms), they carted in 8900 pounds (4000 kilograms) of materials on their backs. The Public Works Department employed Charlie Jensen to supervise the hut's construction.[4] Some Public Works employees were asked to help out, but not all were keen. The Public Works storekeeper at Fox wrote this to his district supervisor in Greymouth:

> We have three men packing timber up the Glacier to the Chancellor Ridge Hut site who have on loan to them 2 picks, 1 mattock & 1 slasher. As they have the tools at the Hut site which is near the top of the Glacier I have taken their verbal assurance that the tools are alright. I should be pleased to receive your written approval of this, should such be the case, as I have been ordered by Eng. Asst. Wotten to proceed to Chancellor Ridge to check these tools on the spot. The journey to the Ridge is of a particularly arduous nature and fit only for an 'A' class man which unfortunately I am not. To me, the order, and the offensive manner in which it was issued, savours of pure vindictiveness and was not made in the interests of the Department.[5]

All the hut materials were on site by 12 December 1930, allowing completion of the hut by late January 1931. Chancellor Hut has a number of interesting construction details, not all of them immediately obvious. While it was clad in the vernacular material of the time – corrugated iron – the framing consists of imported Oregon, rather than native, timber. Over time, this light but strong timber has proven its durability. The superb workmanship in the framing displays proper joinery techniques, such as grooves cut into the wall plates to locate the wall studs, as well as roof trusses properly seated into the top wall plates. These techniques provide great strength, and the fourteen trusses in the pitched roof have ensured an exceptionally resilient building.

Chancellor Hut's layout still has its original separate rooms. The wall separating the women's quarters from the men's quarters also adds structural strength. The lining of patterned congoleum (a material similar to linoleum) provides limited but necessary insulation.[6] Douglas Rock Hut had a cheaper malthoid lining, and while Sefton Biv also used congoleum, Chancellor remains the country's only surviving alpine hut with this historic feature left intact.[7]

By 1972, when the run-down Chancellor Hut required serious attention, a team including Brian Ahern flew in to renovate the old hut. The team removed the fireplace, which, owing to a lack of wood at that altitude, had never been used – and this remains the only major change to the original hut. Fox Glacier guide and hotel owner Mick Sullivan remembered guides using the fireplace to store kerosene for their cookers.[8]

Over the next thirty years, the hut received sporadic maintenance. Then, in 2000, a DOC team re-piled it and replaced some bearers and joists (these were of native timber from the local mill rather than Oregon). DOC staff also improved drainage on the hut's south side.[9]

Between 2008 and 2009, Chancellor Hut underwent a major renovation, with a DOC team restoring it to its full former glory. As the slightly incongruous east-facing window (which had been put in when the chimney was removed in 1972) was not in keeping with the rest of the hut, the restoration team installed two small four-pane windows. Other windows and doors were repaired or replaced, and the entire hut was completely repainted. Over the years, kea had created all sorts of havoc by pulling out window putty, breaking into the hut, and generally amusing themselves through such antics as tearing the mattresses to bits. The hut posed an equal risk to the birds too – old lead roofing nails could easily poison a determined bird, so were replaced by steel ones. Kea continue to enjoy the shelf and the hut environs, adding to the whole experience of a stay at Chancellor Hut, and over time DOC staff have learnt new ways to make such structures kea-proof.

The Historic Places Trust lists Chancellor Hut as a Category 2 building, in recognition of its status as the oldest high-level hut (as opposed to bivvy) in the Southern Alps still on its original site.[10]

Today, heli-hikers from Fox Glacier are probably the most frequent visitors to Chancellor Hut, but the occasional hunter, climber and ski-tourer also stays. The hut serves as a welcome stopover for those en route to or from Pioneer Hut, as two ski-tourers commented in 1997:

> Out from Pioneer last night but forced to bivvy half an hour from the hut after following some crazy ski tracks in the dark that were a bit willy-nilly in their path to the hut. But all is not lost as the eggs are still intact so it looks like it's a good honest bit of a fry up for the boys before the whirly bird takes us away.[11]

ROB BROWN

Almer Biv 1914 & Almer Hut 1929/1950   WESTLAND TAI POUTINI NATIONAL PARK

In the early part of the twentieth century, two routes were commonly guided between Aoraki/Mount Cook and the West Coast glaciers. The first was the comparatively easy Copland Pass, on the Main Divide between the Hooker and Copland valleys. The second, Graham Saddle, involved far more snow and ice travel, and required parties to traverse both the Franz Josef and Tasman glaciers. Linking these two trips made possible a grand tour of the area's glacial wonders, beginning and ending at The Hermitage.

Guides and clients needed to travel light and fast to complete this rather challenging alpine circuit. To avoid carrying heavy tents, guides decided they needed a hut network to supplement natural shelters like the Douglas Rock Bivvy in the Copland. The first to be completed, in 1910–11, was Hooker Hut, in the Hooker Valley on the eastern side of the Copland Track. On the West Coast side, Cape Defiance Hut was built in 1913 on a terrace near the lower part of the Franz Josef Glacier to provide overnight accommodation for those on an extended visit to the glacier. However, this hut was too low down for those heading higher onto the Franz Josef névé. To break up the long day hike between Cape Defiance and the De la Beche Rock Bivvy on the other side of Graham Saddle, a small bivvy was therefore built the following year on a rocky knoll overlooking the Franz Josef Glacier. This simple tin shelter was 8 feet (2.5 metres) square and just 5 feet (1.5 metres) high. Rocks piled up around the sides protected the structure from the wind, leaving just the roof showing. The bivvy was named after the famous Swiss guide Christian Almer, who was active in the European Alps between the late 1850s and the 1880s – the so-called 'Golden Age of Alpinism'. Almer made first ascents of the Mönch and Eiger, among many other mountains.

For some years, local guide Frank Alack sought to replace Almer Bivvy with a larger, more comfortable hut on a stable terrace higher up. Alack was instrumental in lobbying chief guide Alex Graham for the larger hut, partly out of a desire for a better base for winter skiing. For a while his requests fell on deaf ears, but on one trip to the higher névé with Graham, Alack had to squeeze into the bivvy with five clients, leaving about 'fourteen inches per person'. As Alack recounts the story, he made sure that Graham got the worst spot on the stone floor. Graham had a terrible night's sleep, and in the morning Alack recalled that 'It took him some time to get his old joints pliable again.' Seizing the opportunity, Alack raised the idea of a new hut, and this time got a favourable response.[1]

In 1929, Alack set about organising funding

A climber at Almer Biv in 1929, with the Franz Josef Glacier below. PHOTO: J. MUNT, NATIONAL PUBLICITY STUDIOS, COURTESY OF DOC FRANZ JOSEF

HUTS FOR TOURISM AND CLIMBING 125

and materials for the hut, which was to be built to the standard Tourist Department design of the day – a floor area measuring 24 feet by 12 feet (7.3 metres by 3.7 metres), two rooms with twelve bunks in total (similar to Chancellor Hut on the Fox Glacier). However, Alack had a significant argument with guide Peter Graham over how to get the materials to the site.[2] Alack wanted to use sleds in the winter snow and an aerial ropeway system to raise the materials off the glacier, while Graham argued for transporting in the summer. In a clash between these two strong personalities, there was only going to be one winner, and that was the boss. In the summer of 1928–29, Peter Graham put guide Joe Fluerty in charge of getting the materials to the site. Some 11,110 pounds (5000 kilograms) of materials needed to be carted to the site in 200 loads.[3]

In these early days of the Depression, there was no shortage of people wanting to help carry these loads. However, many found the going too hard – most packers dropped their loads at the start of the ice, leaving the glacier guides to take over from there. Loads were scattered all over the place – even on the glacier, which threatened to engulf the materials.

Peter Graham went back to Alack, who had refused to have anything to do with the summer carry, and asked him to sort the mess out. Alack agreed, but only after he was persuaded to do so by Peter's more diplomatic brother, Alex. Alack and Fluerty established a system, and had to work their men like 'galley slaves' in a race against the ice. Alack recalled, 'With its insatiable appetite, the glacier was swallowing loads every day.' After working long hours for a few weeks, and with Fluerty and Alack sometimes carrying double loads, all the materials were finally in place.[4]

After such a slog assembling the materials on site, Alack found building the hut an easier part of the job. However, the opening presented its own drama. To gain publicity for the new hut, Alack

OPPOSITE The first Almer Hut photographed shortly after it was built. PHOTO: W. D. FRAZER, CANTERBURY MUSEUM, 1986.182.32

Almer Hut II in 2006. PHOTO: TOM HOPKINS/DOC

arranged for a professional photographer to capture a group staying there. Alack recalled, 'every bunk was taken, and we had no sooner settled in than a blizzard took possession of the locality. It kept up day after day. The hut was completely blocked in by snow. Influenza made its unwelcome appearance among the party, and to add to the trouble we ran out of food.' Eventually, the party was forced to descend in the fierce storm, and didn't make the safety of the hotel at Franz Josef until well after dark.[5]

One of those who packed supplies for tourists up to the hut in the 1930s was aspirant guide Harry Ayres, who learned his ice craft under Alack's tutelage. In turn, Ayres passed his knowledge on to Edmund Hillary.[6]

After the Second World War, the first hut began to show its age – its design wasn't really suited to the high alpine site, and couldn't cope with the weight of winter snows. It was replaced in 1950, and this time the materials were air-dropped using a fixed-wing aircraft.

The twelve-bunk 1950 hut remains in place today, and is the only air-dropped alpine hut of its era still in existence, giving it considerable historical significance. The building underwent a major restoration in 1992, which dealt with the problem of one room filling with snow, and then again in the mid-2000s. Appropriately, given its history, the hut is maintained by Franz Josef Glacier Guides in conjunction with DOC.[7]

ROB BROWN

Pioneer Biv 1933 & Pioneer Hut 1953/1965/1984/1999
WESTLAND TAI POUTINI NATIONAL PARK

High mountains are hard on huts – at Pioneer, for example, rockfalls and collapsing foundations have cut short the lives of two previous huts. For climbers, however, Pioneer remains a vital place for a hut, and over the years many organisations have been involved in maintaining a shelter here, from the Tourist Department, to private enterprise, the New Zealand Alpine Club (NZAC), Canterbury Mountaineering Club (CMC) contractors, Lands and Survey, and DOC. The current hut is the fourth, not counting the original bivvy.

Dr Ebenezer Teichelmann, Reverend Henry Newton and guide Peter Graham became the first recorded climbers to visit the upper Fox Glacier in 1903.[1] Substituting Peter for his brother Alex, Teichelmann and Newton returned in 1907, camped on the same exposed ledge on Pioneer Ridge at 2100 metres and made first ascents of Mts Douglas, Lendenfeld, Haast and Torres. 'Teichelmann's campsite' became the base for climbing at the head of the Fox for the next thirty years, under both Fox and Franz guides.

English climber Katie Gardiner visited New Zealand regularly in the 1920s, and with guides made many fine ascents. When Gardiner first ascended Aoraki/Mt Cook in 1924, she gazed on Mt Tasman and resolved to climb it. Her first attempt from the Fox Glacier with guide Frank Alack in 1929 proved unsuccessful.[2]

Gardiner planned a return in 1931, hoping that talk of building 'a small bivouac hut'[3] at Pioneer had come to fruition. Two years before, Peter Graham had floated the idea of shifting Almer Bivvy, made redundant by a new hut, to Pioneer Ridge – but it never happened. Instead, Frank Alack and Vic Williams tried twice to establish a camp in anticipation of Gardiner's 1931 climb, but 'the weather was so appalling that we finally gave up on the idea'.[4]

The following year, 1932, Gardiner asked Peter Graham at Franz to pack food and gear into Teichelmann's campsite. This they accomplished, but Gardiner did not make it to New Zealand that season. So guides Jack Cox, Joe Fluerty and Jack Pope took the opportunity of good conditions and, spurred on by their employer, made the first ascent of Tasman from the west – ahead of their Fox rivals. In doing so, Fluerty became the first Maori to climb the peak.[5]

Gardiner finally reached Teichelmann's campsite again in February 1933 with guides Vic Williams and Jack Pope, and English climber A.M. Binnie, for another attempt. If ever a storm underscored the need for a hut, the one they experienced was it. One tent blew down and one was 'nearly uprooted', and the group was forced to retreat into a crevasse, where they repitched a tent to provide shelter. Wind howled and snow flurried around them for nine days. Gardiner later wrote of her stormbound ordeal: 'Then it rained and we were in deadly fear of the overhanging lip of the schrund coming down and crushing us.'[6]

Frank Alack had made enthusiastic attempts to establish a hut at Pioneer as early as 1931, and gained financial support for the project from the Sullivan brothers, owners of the Fox Glacier Hotel, despite the onset of the Depression. Alack planned a small shelter measuring 3 metres by 2 metres, with a roof apex of 1.8 metres and side walls just 1 metre high.

Aspirant guide Harry Ayres was among those with the unenviable task of helping carry the bivouac materials up the Fox Glacier. After timber and sheet iron were cut to size at the hotel, Ayres and Alack transported them to the glacier terminus by packhorse. Then began a 'siege carry', manhandling the awkward loads up an 800-metre altitude gain to Chancellor Hut.[7] But then Alack went to work on a farm, and the materials languished on the Chancellor shelf for a year.[8]

By the time Alack returned in 1933, Arthur P. Harper had offered NZAC involvement. However, Alack regarded the already prefabricated bivvy as too small to share with the club. Harper, dis-

Junee Grey (Ashurst) at Pioneer Bivvy, February 1938. PHOTO: HARRY AYRES, HAP ASHURST COLLECTION, COURTESY OF GRAHAM LANGTON

gruntled by recent problems over the NZAC's De la Beche Hut (see p. 107), threatened to get Lands and Survey to block the bivouac by refusing a building permit. Alack stood his ground. In the end, the more diplomatic NZAC secretary, Jim Shanks, managed to get an arrangement whereby club members could apply for a concession to stay in the bivouac.[9]

Alack arranged for the materials to be carried from Chancellor to the new site at 2400 metres, a further 2 kilometres up Pioneer Ridge from Teichelmann's campsite. Alack chose one of the packers, Bert Cowan, to help build it. A fierce storm blew in after only one day. Intense cold made picking up nails easy – they stuck to fingers; but the last iron sheet was a nightmare to nail on and flapped like a 'mad, living thing'. With the bivvy barely closed in, Alack was reluctant to retreat to Chancellor Hut. He later wrote:

> Just then the hut was something alive to me, and it seemed unthinkable to leave it to the mercy of the howling gale. It was in my care, and I was willing to face any danger to protect it. I put it to Bert, and we decided to stay where we were. We nailed, we blocked, we anchored till we were too cold and too exhausted to move, and it was too dark to carry on, and all the while the blizzard was shaking everything that was dry and petrifying everything else.[10]

The men shivered through twenty-eight degrees of frost, wrapped only in blankets, and escaped three days later, with the Pioneer Bivvy largely completed.

Katie Gardiner returned in November 1933, and after cutting the official opening ribbon for the hut, went on to climb Mt Tasman successfully with Alack and Williams, her tenth attempt.[11] Pioneer Bivvy served well for many years, but its small size often proved inadequate, and the guides' priority of use created tensions with other climbers, as did the cost of staying at a stocked hut. The CMC applied to build another hut at Teichelmann's campsite in 1937. Lands and Survey approved the proposal in 1939, but the club decided not to proceed.[12]

By 1950 the bivvy was deteriorating, and the NZAC decided to replace it with a new wood and iron hut measuring about 3 metres by 4 metres on a nearby site. Some stonework was also planned. NZAC member Neil Hamilton (son of jetboat inventor Bill Hamilton) led the project, and managed to convince the Royal New Zealand Air Force

The first Pioneer Hut, with the roof of the original biv still visible. PHOTO: MAVIS DAVIDSON COLLECTION, HOCKEN LIBRARY, UNIVERSITY OF OTAGO, MS-2985/472

to drop the materials from a Bristol Freighter. Four attempts later, in mid-December 1952, the air-drop was successfully completed. The *New Zealand Alpine Journal* reported:

> The bundles of timber and iron, and sacks of cement and sand had to be manhandled out of the open door in the side of the aircraft. This work

HUTS FOR TOURISM AND CLIMBING 129

Pioneer Hut II on its spectacular location below the South Face of Mt Douglas, 1983.

Burning the remains of Pioneer Hut II on 22 April 1983, in preparation for building Pioneer Hut III. Westland National Park ranger Bruce Postill recalled that although Pioneer Hut II had a conventional construction, it was built like the proverbial 'brick shit house.' 'Almost every thing was doubled up, the floor, steel rods through the framing, and the iron screwed on every second corrugation.' When it came time to dismantle it, the very heavy hut was impossible to move with a helicopter and not viable to pull down, so after removing what was practical, the remains were burned on site. PHOTOS: BRUCE POSTILL

was made very difficult by the rapid dropping and bumping of the aircraft to say nothing of the terrific air pressure on the bundles of timber as they were pushed half out the door into the airstream. In order to get all the bundles out it was necessary to circle over the site for nearly an hour.[13]

A second drop followed in January 1953. Volunteers helped prepare the site, and dug three large snow caves in which to store supplies and sleep. Levelling the rock platform was a major undertaking, not helped by the fact that crowbars dropped from an Auster plane for the purpose had buried themselves up to 4 metres deep in the snow. Hans Bohny managed the blasting. In blizzard conditions at the end of January, the party headed back down, having prepared the site and stored materials and food nearby.

The actual hut building took place quite quickly. The NZAC contracted Stan Muirson, a builder and member of the CMC, to undertake the construction. He set off with four others in his De Soto car on 12 March, and a little over a week later returned to Christchurch with the hut erected and weatherproofed.[14]

From this, the first full-sized Pioneer Hut, a new generation explored and climbed the obvious ridges in the area. The old bivvy remained, too. Right from the start, however, doubt was expressed about the safety of the new hut, which was positioned beneath unstable rocks.

During the morning of 7 January 1963, when eight people were asleep in the hut, a violent storm blew in. Most likely, it was lightning that struck the ridge above, dislodging numerous rocks there. These smashed down through the old bivvy and toilet, and also crashed into the hut, killing Gilbert Murray, and leaving two others trapped and with serious injuries.[15]

For the second hut, the NZAC chose a site further up, at 2550 metres on the Mt Alack ridge. This time the club joined forces with the Westland National Park Board, and NZAC member Trevor Chinn was co-opted into running the project. Chinn would have fun riding the corrugated-iron sleds used to bring the materials down from the landing strip; and he also noted that gelignite was very strong stuff! Completed in 1965, the hut served for only five years before its slumping foundations became apparent. By 1982, a detailed inspection revealed that only six piles were carrying any load, and the hut was closed soon after. It was time for another replacement.

Built in 1984, Pioneer Hut III was a joint effort between the NZAC and Department of Lands and Survey. This time a site was chosen back on Pioneer Ridge, a short distance from the original biv. Alex Miller from Westland National Park oversaw the project. About 15 tonnes of rocks went into gabion baskets for the hut foundations. In late May, the three hut sections – made of polystyrene panels sandwiched between an aluminium casing – were flown in and fitted together. The insulated panels resembled the inside of a freezer storeroom, earning the hut the nickname of 'Fridge', but it was actually a comparatively warm hut considering its altitude and location.[16]

By the late 1980s, Pioneer Hut III was already suffering from the stress of unexpectedly high snow loadings. Bruce Postill was a Lands and Survey ranger at Westland National Park during the 1980s, and remembers: 'It was generally considered that the hut changed the wind flow, resulting in a bigger build up of snow. No one ever anticipated the loadings would be so great. The type of construction was not robust enough.'[17]

By 1998, plans were afoot for Pioneer Hut IV. Keeping with family tradition, Trevor Chinn's son Derek coordinated the construction the following

Pioneer Hut IV, pictured in 2005. PHOTO: ANTHONY STEVENSON/CAM MULVEY COLLECTION

year, which was a joint effort by DOC, the NZAC and the New Zealand Army. Royal New Zealand Engineers of the 3rd Field Squadron demolished the old hut, prefabricated the new one and assembled it, and several mountain guides helped out on site.[18]

As part of the project, the unsanitary and dodgy old long-drop was replaced with a modern containment system, enabling DOC to fly out waste rather than letting it fall into a crevasse below. One of the more challenging pitches climbed at Pioneer Hut III was always the rope-length on belay to the wildly spectacular loo – especially during howling storms.

Pioneer Hut IV continues to bewitch many of the people who stay here with its wild mountains, wide glaciers and spectacular sunsets. Climber Mike Browne perhaps best summed up the experience of climbing at Pioneer Hut: 'Pioneer's site was so spectacular that one tended to feel a bit superior to all those people down below. Those god-like feelings were usually crushed on stepping out the door.'[19]

GEOFF SPEARPOINT

Flora Hut 1928 KAHURANGI NATIONAL PARK

Flora Hut occupies a grassy clearing a short distance from Flora Saddle in Kahurangi National Park. Nearby, the Flora Stream bubbles away, home to blue duck, which sometimes whistle when trampers pass by.

The hut is an example of a shelter built for tourism. In 1923, long before the area became Kahurangi National Park, the government gazetted the Mt Balloon Scenic Reserve.[1] In the early part of the twentieth century, scenery preservation and tourism were inextricably linked. A number of reserves were established throughout the country, but they tended to be in spectacular terrain such as Fiordland, the Rotorua geothermal areas or the Westland glaciers, so it is curious that such a remote, comparatively little-known area in Northwest Nelson gained reserve status. Perhaps it isn't surprising then, that the main drive to establish the reserve and build huts came from a local enthusiast, Fred Gibbs. A Nelson teacher, Gibbs was a keen tramper and amateur botanist, and he became involved in the Scenic Preservation Society when it was established in 1894. Through the society he advocated successfully for reserves in Nelson's Maitai Valley and at Lake Rotoiti.[2]

Northwest Nelson was another area through which Gibbs loved to tramp, and in 1926 he established the Mt Balloon Hut Scenic Trust Board. Gibbs was elected president of the board, and duly obtained government funds to build huts in the area. A working bee of members, including Gibbs, first repaired the deteriorating Balloon Hut (a mining hut built in 1909), then in 1928 they turned their attention to establishing two additional huts: Salisbury and Flora.[3]

They decided to build Flora Hut at what was then known as Edwards Clearing, after a man who ran a store there during the mining days.[4] The grass clearing covered about 2 hectares – considerably larger than it is now. Flora Hut is unusually long, with two six-bunk rooms, separated by a large open-sided shed. This distinctive design is a relic from the days when men and women slept in separate rooms, for reasons of social etiquette. Horses were sometimes housed in what is now the woodshed. Salisbury Hut had the same design. The Mt Balloon Hut Scenic Board Trust also supplied frying pans, billies, a crosscut saw and an axe, but these were often stolen. They charged 1 shilling for maintenance to anyone using the hut.[5] Fred Gibbs himself marked many of the surrounding tracks with white discs.

Back then, access to the Flora Hut was on a bridle track from the Graham Valley, first established in the 1870s. Veteran tramper Arnold Heine recollects spending a night in the hut during the early 1940s: 'There was no road in the upper Graham, so we walked up the pack track to Flora Saddle and Flora Hut. The bunks were sheep netting and we gathered fern for mattresses. There was a lot of snow around and I only had a blanket, so we kept a fire going to stay warm.'[6]

Although largely rebuilt in 1972 by the New Zealand Forest Service, the twelve-bunk Flora Hut retained its original shape and character. In 1974, the NZFS improved the road to Flora car park and widened the Flora Track some distance past the hut using a bulldozer. Flora Hut was now an easy thirty-minute stroll from the car park and – like many other huts near road ends – consequently suffered from vandalism. Although the removal of the hut was mooted in 1986, the NZFS concluded, 'we shouldn't deprive ordinary people of the opportunity to take families to a hut which is easily reached by even little children in order that they might have a first, secure experience of the great outdoors'. Suggestions for a log cabin replacement using $1000 donated by author Jim Henderson never eventuated either.[7]

Unfortunately, the hut continued to be vandalised. Partly for that reason, and partly because several other huts and shelters exist nearby, DOC planned to replace it with a shelter following its 2003–04 Recreation Opportunities Review. At the time, the idea had public support, but a change in opinion became evident early in 2008, notably reported on in a *New Zealand Listener* article by Golden Bay local Gerard Hindmarsh.[8] Local tramping clubs and others also stated strongly that they valued the hut as a place for young children and older people to enjoy an overnight tramp.[9] Following further community consultation, DOC commendably reconsidered their decision, and announced in May 2008 that the historic hut would stay.[10]

A local community group called the Friends of Flora, founded in 2001, controls pests in the valley to help enhance birdlife. In May 2010, they reintroduced great spotted kiwi to the area, in partnership with DOC.[11] Their efforts can only add appeal to the hut and its environs.

SHAUN BARNETT

LEFT Flora Hut, 2005.
PHOTO: SHAUN BARNETT/BLACK ROBIN PHOTOGRAPHY
OPPOSITE Trampers at Flora Hut, Northwest Nelson, 1964.
PHOTO: BEN GIBBS

HUTS FOR TOURISM AND CLIMBING 133

Sign of the Packhorse Hut 1916 BANKS PENINSULA, CANTERBURY

During the First World War, a new hut and track network in Canterbury was started, with the idea of appealing to New Zealanders' desire to enjoy the outdoors, but one much closer to a city. Christchurch MP and conservationist Harry Ell had almost single-handedly fought for the protection of reserves along the crest of the city's Port Hills, but had a more ambitious scheme in mind: a series of 'tea houses' and huts situated along a splendid skyline walk between Christchurch and Akaroa. In the end, only four buildings were erected, one of which, the Sign of the Packhorse, remains a functional and well-used hut.

Ell began the Summit Road project in 1908 and continued with tireless determination until his death in 1934. The stalwart Cantabrian is now widely recognised as one of the early advocates of conservation in New Zealand, and a visionary champion of public access to our natural heritage.

Ell initially envisaged fifteen rest stops and shelters on the route to Akaroa as part of his grand plans. It is a testament to his single-mindedness that, while the world was bogged down in the trenches of war-torn Europe, he oversaw the building of the first three of these tea houses and even started a fourth. Today, all four remain as well-known buildings in the Port Hills landscape: Sign of the Bellbird, built in 1914, burnt down by arsonists in the Second World War and which is now a picnic shelter; Sign of the Packhorse, built in 1916; Sign of the Kiwi, built in 1917 and operated as a tea house until 2010, but now reduced to an information centre; and Sign of the Takahe, started in 1918 as a tram station and eventually completed in its present form – a virtual castle – in 1949.

Sign of the Packhorse is the only one of Ell's buildings still run as a public hut and open for overnight accommodation. Designed by well-known Christchurch architect Samuel Hurst-Seager, the hut was constructed from local volcanic stone. Hurst-Seager used a vernacular style that is a hallmark of his buildings in Christchurch, and the hut fits into the landscape in a reasonably sympathetic way. During construction, materials were delivered to the Parkinson homestead in Kaituna Valley and from there taken up to the pass using a sledge towed by a team of six bullocks. Initially called the Kaituna Saddle Rest House, the shelter was renamed Sign of the Packhorse by Ell in 1922.[1] The three other buildings were renamed at the same time and all have endured through the years despite the recent earthquakes.

By the start of the Second World War, the Packhorse hut was sadly neglected and suffering from vandalism. The Summit Road Trust folded in 1940 and the lease for the hut defaulted back to the Crown. The Youth Hostel Association (YHA) then took over the lease for three years, and in May 1940 members of the Christchurch Tramping Club (CTC) and YHA carried out extensive repairs and installed new bunks and windows. They also carried a coal range up to the hut and erected a fence around it to keep out cattle. Between them, the

Guests enjoying the tearooms at the Sign of the Kiwi, circa 1920. PHOTO: SAMUEL HEAD, ALEXANDER TURNBULL LIBRARY, WELLINGTON, 1/1-007550-G

Sign of the Packhorse Hut in 2010. PHOTO: ROB BROWN

YHA and CTC continued to maintain the hut for many years.[2]

In the late 1960s, a problem arose over the exact location of the hut relative to the scenic reserve. In his typical manner of forging ahead with his vision and leaving the details to later, Ell assumed that the building site for the Sign of the Packhorse was located on reserve land donated by William Gray. In fact, it was later discovered to lie on freehold land held by Cyril and Ivor Gray. In 1971, the Grays generously agreed to gift the 1434 square metre site and building to the adjacent scenic reserve.

During the 1960s and 1970s, the hut was maintained by local Governors Bay farmers Colin and Ben Faulkner, who were enthusiastic members of the Summit Road Society. During this time they marked and maintained many of the area's tracks, and in 1957 they constructed another hut, Monument Shelter, on the nearby Purau/Port Levy Saddle. The Faulkner brothers continued their personal commitment to the Packhorse and the tracks surrounding it into the 1990s, long after the scenic reserve, first managed by Lands and Survey, had been taken over by DOC.[3]

The building sustained minor damage in the 2011 Christchurch earthquakes, including losing part of the chimney, but it was easily repairable.

The Sign of the Packhorse has a spectacular view over Lyttelton Harbour, and offers accommodation in two rooms – one with four bunks and the other with six. It is a great place to sit in the evening light and contemplate the far-sighted vision of Harry Ell, a man to whom Cantabrians owe a great deal for the energy he put into protecting many reserves and public spaces on the Port Hills.

ROB BROWN

Cape Defiance Hut 1913 & Castle Rocks Hut 1974 WESTLAND TAI POUTINI NATIONAL PARK

Although younger than many other huts in the West Coast region, Castle Rocks Hut's history is irrevocably linked with the development of the Franz Josef Glacier for tourism and mountaineering.

Tourism started at Franz Josef Glacier in the early 1900s, when Captain Billy Batson built a small, rustic ponga cottage for accommodating adventurous tourists exploring the wild West Coast. About 1908, a more substantial hotel replaced the cottage, and Batson started guiding glacier trips and horse treks. The deterioration of his wife's health led Batson to sell the Franz Josef Hotel to Jim and Alex Graham in 1911 for £905. The brothers greatly expanded the operation in just a few short years, and the Graham family name became synonymous with mountain guiding, glacier guiding and tourism on the West Coast.[1]

At this time the government was taking an active part in developing tourism in New Zealand and had already funded the establishment of tracks to the glaciers. In late 1912, the Department of Tourist and Health Resorts granted £160 for the building of a hut at Cape Defiance, part of the way up the Franz Josef Glacier. The Grahams completed the two-room hut by 1913, according to the department's specified plans, on a terrace near Cape Defiance (using a similar design to the Hooker Hut). Under the deal with the department, the Grahams stocked and maintained the hut as part of their guiding business.[2]

The glacier's periodic surge and retreat according to the seasons was well known, but unfortunately the building of Cape Defiance Hut coincided with a more substantial and dramatic retreat of the ice. The shrinking glacier destabilised the terrace near Cape Defiance, and undermined the hut's foundations. Moving the hut in 1936 prolonged its life, but the glacier's ongoing retreat made access progressively more difficult.

Partly influenced by the changing nature of the Franz Josef Glacier, and partly by the economic restraints of the 1930s Depression, overnight glacier trips decreased in favour of day trips, and Cape Defiance Hut fell into disrepair. While the hut was intended mainly for glacier tourists, climbers also found it a useful staging post for climbing the Fritz Range en route to the Franz Josef névé and on to Pioneer Hut.

In the early 1970s, the Department of Lands and Survey decided to replace Cape Defiance Hut with a much smaller building on a spectacular site high on the Fritz Range. Surprisingly, Lands and Survey chose a standard Forest Service four-bunk S81 design, and it remains a rare example of an NZFS hut adopted by Lands and Survey in a national park.[3] The new Castle Rocks Hut was perched a good 500 metres higher than the old Cape Defiance Hut, and offered welcome refuge to hunters seeking Himalayan tahr and climbers heading to and from the higher peaks.

In 1978, the remains of Cape Defiance Hut were dismantled and rebuilt at the Franz Josef Visitor Centre to serve as a historic display of West Coast tourism. Along with Hooker Hut, it is one of the earliest surviving huts built for tourism in New Zealand.[4]

Castle Rocks Hut continues to attract climbers and skiers. The ski tour from the high névé down the Fritz Range to Castle Rocks Hut is regarded as one of the best in New Zealand. Guiding in the valley continues, and Franz Josef Glacier Guides contribute to the upkeep of the hut.

ROB BROWN

LEFT Jim and Alex Graham at Cape Defiance Hut shortly after it was built. PHOTO: A. C. GRAHAM COLLECTION, MACMILLAN BROWN LIBRARY, UNIVERSITY OF CANTERBURY, ACCESSION NUMBER 1065/PHOTO20229

OPPOSITE Castle Rocks Hut, high above the Franz Josef Glacier, 2002. PHOTO: ROB BROWN

HUTS FOR TOURISM AND CLIMBING 137

Locke Stream Hut 1940 ARTHUR'S PASS NATIONAL PARK

Locke Stream Hut is tucked in a small clearing on a forested flat not far from the bouldery headwaters of the Taramakau River. It and No. 3 Hut are the oldest remaining huts on the tramping route over Harper Pass, a track that has a long history as both a Maori pounamu trail and a gold-mining route.

Unlikely as it now seems, the New Zealand government once had visions for a state-sponsored commercial tramping route over Harper Pass. In the late 1930s, Labour minister Bill Parry headed the Department of Internal Affairs and set up its Physical Welfare Division. Parry, a large, enthusiastic man with a passion for outdoor sports, wanted to inspire the youth of New Zealand to take to the hills, get fit and enjoy nature.[1] In some ways, Parry's concern about the declining physical health of New Zealanders through urbanisation was a forerunner to modern-day worries about our increasingly sedentary and obese population.

While recognising that tramping clubs played a role in 'more ambitious, more arduous' trips, Parry believed that the government should provide tracks 'easing the degree of exertion' and 'increasing the comfort' at huts.[2] The Harper Pass track was the first attempt at doing so. Parry's vision was one where ordinary New Zealanders who did not belong to tramping clubs would pay modest fees to be guided over the track by trained division staff. He foresaw the need for something between the more upmarket (and expensive) huts of the Tourist Department's Milford Track, and the rougher routes and huts of tramping clubs.[3] In today's parlance, Parry was aiming for a 'front country' experience, an early policy that was later echoed by the Department of Conservation with its Great Walk tracks.

In the late 1930s and early 1940s, Internal Affairs engaged deer cullers to recut the Harper Pass track and built five large huts along the route.[4] Interestingly, they adopted the successful design used by the Tararua Tramping Club for its Waerenga Hut (in Wellington's Orongorongo Valley; see p. 194).[5]

The first hut, near Lake Taylor, was built in 1939. Unfortunately, the Second World War interrupted Parry's vision of large guided groups tramping over Harper Pass – although a party of forty Christchurch Tramping Club members made first use of the new track during the Easter of 1940, and felt it offered good value for money. Although they stayed at the Lake Taylor Hut, none of the other huts – including Locke Stream – had yet been completed.[6]

In the winter of 1940, bushman George Bolton and deer culler Harry Scott[7] occupied a sunless camp in the headwaters of the Taramakau River, and for two months hacked timber from the forest near Locke Stream. Imagine the agony of working a crosscut saw to fell totara and mountain cedar on a day when frost lay thickly over everything. Once enough trees had been felled, the pair adzed the logs into suitably shaped lengths of timber. Their handiwork is still evident in Locke Stream Hut today.[8]

Sam Burrows, a packman employed by Internal Affairs, oversaw the final building of the hut in the

Locke Stream Hut, December 1954. PHOTO: RON MACKIE

LEFT Locke Stream Hut, 2004. RIGHT No. 3 Hut, 2004. PHOTOS: SHAUN BARNETT/BLACK ROBIN PHOTOGRAPHY

spring of 1940.[9] In his book *Deer Hunter*, culler Joff Thomson recalls working on Locke Stream Hut:

> The material for the top hut was packed on to horses, but for a time the problem of packing eight-foot corrugated iron lengths was a ticklish one. However, after several experiments and the prospect of carrying them ourselves, we soon found a way. The timber for the top hut was cut from cedar in the neighbourhood and adzed by an old-timer who had been brought up to this type of work. Sam, as he was called, had spent the greater part of his life in the hills and through necessity had learnt to do just about everything, and to do it well. He was over seventy but was a valuable member of our party.[10]

The hut was completed in November, as was another at Tom's Creek (near the junction with the Otira), and two more huts on the eastern side of Harper Pass, at staged intervals in the Hurunui Valley. Initial suggestions for Maori names commemorating the pounamu heritage of the track unfortunately were not realised. Instead, the huts were named – with what tramping author Mark Pickering called 'splendid bureaucratic imagination' – Nos 1–5, although some later adopted the names of local features.[11] So No. 4 Hut got the moniker of Locke Stream Hut after the nearby tributary of the Taramakau. Edwin Lock had accompanied Leonard Harper during a crossing of Harper Pass in 1857, when they became the first Europeans to traverse the Southern Alps from coast to coast, but his name has since been misspelt 'Locke'.[12]

After the Second World War, Parry wanted Internal Affairs to expand the Harper Pass idea, and to organise a 'mountain track system so that whole families, including the mothers, can go out for an ideal holiday at suitable costs and in reasonable comfort'. He planned huts for the Kaitoke–Holdsworth Track in the Tararuas, but these did not eventuate.[13]

Although government-sponsored tramping was ultimately a failure, the track and hut infrastructure was not. After a period of disuse, quite large tramping club parties began to rediscover Harper Pass during the 1950s, and the area got a further boost in the 1970s when the Forest Service established Lake Sumner Forest Park. By the 1980s, the track was promoted in Lonely Planet's *Tramping in New Zealand* guide, ensuring an international profile.[14] With the official opening of Te Araroa Trail in 2011, which travels the length of New Zealand and uses the Harper Pass route, the track and huts are likely to receive even more use. Most trampers spend a night in Locke Stream Hut en route.

DOC restored Locke Stream Hut in 1993, using a donation from the estate of Arthur's Pass enthusiast Tom Beeston to pay for the work. The cladding, windows, fireplace and chimney were replaced and a removable veranda added.[15] No 3. Hut, on the east side of Harper Pass, is the only other original hut of the five still remaining on site. No. 5 Hut (located at Tom's Creek in the Taramakau Valley) burnt down in the 1950s; No. 1 Hut, originally located near Lake Taylor, was moved to the Lakes Station in 1994 to serve as a woolshed; and No. 2 Hut, near the head of Lake Sumner, burnt down in 1996.[16]

SHAUN BARNETT

Red Hut 1916 RUATANIWHA CONSERVATION PARK, CANTERBURY

Guide Frank Alack once described Rodolph Wigley as 'a dynamo of a man who was just as big in new ideas as he was in stature.'[1] A tourism pioneer and entrepreneur, Wigley had a genuine love of the outdoors, and in August 1923 he succeeded in making the first winter ascent of Aoraki/Mt Cook with guides Norman Murrell and Frank Milne.[2]

If any one project epitomises the drive and optimism of Wigley, Red Hut may well be it. Long before he took over The Hermitage in 1922, Wigley planned to take more adventurous clients up to the resort via the Hopkins Valley. From there they would cross over the Neumann Range into the Dobson Valley, and then head across Barron Saddle to the Mueller Glacier. It was certainly challenging, and Wigley hoped this venture would help expand his transport business into adventure tourism.

Such a demanding trans-alpine route required huts, and in 1916 Wigley extracted funding from the government to build the first hut in the Hopkins Valley on Huxley Gorge Station – Red Hut. Ultimately, however, it was the only hut completed.

While in hindsight Wigley's venture seems hopelessly misguided, the fact that he managed to convince the government to spend money on it in the middle of the First World War demonstrates his persuasive and forceful personality.

In keeping with tourist expectations of the day, Red Hut had two sleeping rooms – one for men and the other for women – and an open fireplace. The ceiling was match-lined, the floor tongue-and-groove boards, and the internal walls covered with malthoid. The exterior was clad in weatherboard and corrugated iron, all painted in what was once referred to as 'railway red'.

However, although Wigley built the hut and his tourism business grew, the alternative route to Aoraki/Mount Cook proved unsuccessful, and it's doubtful if any tourists actually did the whole trip.

Red Hut became part of Huxley Gorge Station, purchased by Wigley, his wife Jessie and one of their sons, Alexander (Sandy), in the 1930s.[3] The hut then took on another role as a musterers' base. By the 1930s, deer-culling operations had commenced in the Hopkins Valley under the Department of Internal Affairs, and when those operations passed to the Forest Service in 1956, Huxley Gorge Station handed Red Hut over too. Incidentally, Sandy Wigley also owned the adjoining Glen Lyon Station in the 1950s, which extends up the Dobson Valley.

During the 1960s, the Forest Service made some modifications to the hut, moving the fireplace, replacing several windows, and installing a sink and bench.[4] Essentially, however, the hut remained little modified until 2003, when DOC fully restored it using funds allocated for upgrading such facilities. Work included installing new windows and catches made in the original style, insulating the roof cavity and fitting a new log burner.

Red Hut now sits in Ruataniwha Conservation Park, formed in 2006. Backed by beech forest and grand mountains, the hut continues to get well used, although not perhaps in the manner in which Wigley originally intended.[5]

GEOFF SPEARPOINT

LEFT Red Hut, pictured shortly after construction, with Rodolph Wigley on the left.
PHOTO: HARRY WIGLEY COLLECTION, CANTERBURY MUSEUM, 1982.163.811
OPPOSITE Tramper Barbara Brown outside Red Hut in October 1996. PHOTO: GEOFF SPEARPOINT

HUTS FOR TOURISM AND CLIMBING 141

FORGING AN IDENTITY IN THE HILLS CLUB HUTS

> The objective of a Tramping Club is not only to arrange a programme of enjoyable outings in the bush and snow-country, but to create something that will be of a benefit to tramping in general, and our contribution to this end, as with most of our sister clubs, is a hut.
>
> – Ruahine Tramping Club report, 1938

Clubs began building huts in the backcountry from the 1920s onwards, as New Zealand communities developed a growing attachment to their local hills and mountains. Whether in nearby ranges or the Southern Alps, they took up the challenge of doing so with enthusiasm and ingenuity, pooling resources and creating their own connections to these places. Broadly speaking, outdoor clubs revolved around three different strands of activity: mountaineering (including skiing), tramping and hunting.

The Mountaineering Clubs

In the 1880s and 1890s, various affluent climbers from Europe began arriving in New Zealand with their guides to make first ascents of New Zealand's premier mountains. The class structure of these trips did not sit well with the more egalitarian young New Zealanders, who were themselves developing a passion for the same activities. To encourage participation and improve knowledge of mountaineering, Arthur P. Harper formed the New Zealand Alpine Club (NZAC) in 1891, with support from other pioneering climbers George Mannering and Malcolm Ross. Harper's father, Leonard, became the club's first president.

Back in 1857, Leonard Harper and companion Edwin Lock had made the first coast-to-coast crossing of the Southern Alps by Europeans.[1] Leonard belonged to one of Canterbury's more distinguished families, and his father was the Bishop of Canterbury. However, Leonard's later bankruptcy and embezzlement tarnished the family name, something that significantly affected A. P. Harper. Partly to escape this stigma, A.P. (as he was known) spent time surveying and exploring South Westland in the mid-1890s with Charlie Douglas.

Blue Range Hut, built by the Masterton Tramping Club in 1958, Tararua Forest Park, pictured in 2000. PHOTO: SHAUN BARNETT/BLACK ROBIN PHOTOGRAPHY

Although modelled on the English Alpine Club, the NZAC signalled a different approach in its first journal: 'The want of guides here will always tend to develop a different type of climber', with a more 'do it yourself approach'. The first ascent of Aoraki/Mt Cook in 1894 by three young working-class climbers, Jack Clarke, Tom Fyfe and George Graham, was proof of that. The NZAC also recognised hut building as a means to 'open out the more inaccessible parts to tourists and mountaineers'.[2]

However, by the turn of the century the club went into recess and wasn't revived until 1914. One of its first hut-building initiatives was De la Beche Hut in 1931, after the January 1930 tragedy on the Tasman Glacier (see p. 107), and by 1932 the Otago Section had built Cascade Hut in the Matukituki Valley.[3] In 1934, plans by the NZAC to build further huts in the Aoraki/Mount Cook area were thwarted by the Mount Cook Tourist Company, but the club did get permission to build Godley Hut on the edge of Lilybank Station in 1934 (see p. 119).[4] By 1939, NZAC President Roland Ellis was able to write:

> In the task of bringing climbing within the pocket of the average man, the Club has been engaged in the building of Huts, and has raised, by much hard work, the twelve or thirteen hundred odd pounds that now stands invested in the Godley, De la Beche, Hopkins (Elcho), Cascade, and Dart Huts. An unending battle has been fought to force down the financial barriers that barred access to the Mt Cook District, so that this, too, is now open to all.[5]

The club developed strong friendships with some high-country station owners. Reginald Malthus at Lilybank was one, and the Aspinall family in the Matukituki Valley another. In 1939, Jack Aspinall packed the materials for the Otago Section's French Ridge Bivouac up the valley, then generously donated most of his contract money back to the club.[6]

Jumboland Hut in the Wilkin Valley was next up in 1941, and in 1944 a hut in the head of the Murchison Glacier was planned.[7] Hut building continued apace, with Esquilant (1950) on Mt Earnslaw (see p. 318), Greenlaw and Crow huts in the Waimakariri, Liverpool in the West Matukituki, Pioneer on the Fox névé (see p. 128), Colin Todd Hut under Mt Aspiring/Tititea (see p. 310), a hut on Mt Ruapehu in 1951 (Auckland Section) and Moraine Creek Hut in the

Christchurch Tramping Club members outside Anti Crow Hut, Arthur's Pass National Park, early 1960s.
PHOTO: RICK WATSON

Darrans (Southland Section) in 1954. In the same year, the Wellington Section completed Steffan Memorial Hut in the Murchison Valley, and then in 1967 the Nelson Marlborough Section established Hopeless Hut at Nelson Lakes.

Just before the start of the Second World War, the NZAC began plans for the ambitious Aspiring Hut, and also discussed a base hut for Aoraki/Mount Cook. The magnificent stone Aspiring Hut was completed after the war in 1949, and the twenty-eight-bunk Unwin Hut was finished two years later. In 1965, the Southland Section completed a similar-scale project with Homer Hut in Fiordland's Darran Mountains. This replaced an earlier shelter, which had been built using materials from two dilapidated huts left over from the construction of the Homer Tunnel.[8]

Unstable mountain environs inevitably demanded much hut maintenance, and sometimes even a complete relocation (as in the case of Godley Hut).[9] But changes in national park management and the club's philosophy eventually reduced the need – and sometimes the desire – for building further new huts. From the 1950s onwards, national park boards increasingly saw the provision of facilities as their role, and ultimately some huts were transferred to park management.

This change caused tension between clubs and park management at times, but more recently, the NZAC has negotiated a useful co-management partnership with DOC. In Mount Aspiring National Park, for example, DOC took over day-to-day management of the club's huts in 1989, but the NZAC retained ownership. DOC could more easily collect hut fees, but agreed to direct these back into local hut maintenance rather than disperse it into DOC's general fund.[10] Today, the NZAC owns seventeen huts nationwide, including five base huts.

The Canterbury Mountaineering Club (CMC) began in 1925, largely through the drive of one young man, Gerard Carrington, who drew attention to the Waimakariri mountains by persuading the Department of Tourist and Health Resorts (Tourist Department) and Canterbury Progress League to run a trip into the valley. Initially formed as a tramping club, the CMC underwent successive constitution and name changes, eventually emerging as an all-male mountaineering club whose members soon developed a self-confident, independent attitude. When the NZAC invited the CMC to become a local branch, in 1931, the club declined, not willing to relinquish its already established identity.[11] At this stage, the NZAC had a hierarchical membership of associates and qualified full members, a distinction some saw as almost class division. John Pascoe, one of CMC's most famous members, later wrote of the club: 'As avant garde New Zealand climbers our alpine ideology was that of a club without qualifications for members.'[12] Pascoe disagreed with the CMC's men-only policy, which was eventually abandoned in the 1970s.

In 1928, the CMC completed its first hut, Carrington (see p. 264). Others followed in quick succession: Park Morpeth in 1931 (see p. 320) and Havelock in 1936 (the predecessor to St Winifred Hut). The club also adapted its building style to suit the needs of climbers, designing small, cost-effective bivvies that were less labour-intensive to construct, beginning with Eric Bivvy in the Havelock in 1937.[13] Other structures of this genre included Agnes Bivvy in the Clyde, which was built in 1939 but has since been destroyed.[14] Having constructed these as well as Banfield, Waimakariri Falls, Barker, Lyell, Edwards and Cameron huts, it's no wonder that CMC members today view the Southern Alps as part of their home.

As technology changed, means of transporting construction materials for huts changed too. The first Barker Hut, built in 1945, required forty-five CMC men to carry the materials in over three days. Nine years later, the club used a plane to fly in materials for Empress Hut at the head of the Hooker Glacier. And in 1980, a helicopter delivered supplies for the replacement Barker Hut.

In more recent times, the club rebuilt Kennedy Lodge at Arthur's Pass in 1987, and refurbished Wyn Irwin at Aoraki/Mount Cook in 1991, Lyell Hut in the Rakaia in 2002, St Winifred Hut in 2004 and Park Morpeth in 2006.[15] Altogether, the CMC has built twenty-six huts, many of them in isolated places, not to mention carrying out ongoing maintenance, reflecting almost ninety years of impressive effort. Currently, the club maintains eight huts and two lodges between Arthur's Pass and Aoraki/Mount Cook: a significant commitment for a membership of 400.

From the 1920s, other alpine clubs were also formed, including the Mt Egmont Alpine Club, Taranaki Alpine Club, Massey University Alpine Club and West Coast Alpine Club. Most of them also look after backcountry huts and lodges.

The Tramping Clubs

Tramping is embedded into New Zealand culture as much as No. 8 wire. Although people had been tramping for some time, it wasn't until the end of the First World War that New Zealanders fully embraced the outdoors through tramping clubs, as a more urban society sought to reconnect with the land.

The *New Collins Dictionary and Thesaurus* defines 'tramp' variously as 'to walk heavily … to wander about as a vagrant'. While the term 'tramp' carried negative connotations, the term 'tramping' was being used roughly in its modern context of hiking in newspaper articles from the 1860s onwards, coinciding with the gold rushes. Up until the early twentieth century, however, the term mostly lacked its recreational emphasis and was not in sufficiently widespread use for explorer Charlie Douglas to refer to it in a positive sense. After seeing an A.P. Harper photograph of himself in 1894, Douglas asked, 'Do you mean to say I have that general appearance? A Witch with a blanket on a tramp … well I suppose chemicals can't lie, I must be carefull [sic] to keep out of sight of the Police.'[16]

We do know that the term tramping was sufficiently recognised and respected by 1919 for MPs and other professional people to form the first tramping club, the Tararua Tramping Club, based in Wellington.[17] Their objectives were 'The encouragement of tramping, skiing, climbing, mountaineering, and camping in New Zealand, the fostering and developing generally of a greater love of the outdoors, the creation of an interest in the protection of the flora, fauna and natural features of our country.'[18] Within five years membership had grown to 265. Initially club members worked with tourism committees in Greytown and Otaki who had begun building huts and tracks in the local ranges in the

Field Hut in 2010. PHOTO: SHAUN BARNETT/BLACK ROBIN PHOTOGRAPHY

1890s, but by the 1930s those earlier committees had been wound up, and the club had firmly embarked on its own hut-building programme. In its first dozen years, the club erected six huts.[19]

Instead of paying for excursions guided by professionals, the trampers of the 1930s had developed their own amateur outdoor identity, along with the skills and confidence to run their own trips. And they thrived on it. The energy, enthusiasm, ability and goodwill expressed through the club bulletins of the 1920s and 1930s are nothing short of inspiring.[20] Members came from across the economic spectrum, but clubs had a strong egalitarian ethos and emphasis on keeping costs down. For the most part, tramping was then a youth movement. Through the challenges of the outdoors, young people found new abilities, fitness and pride. Some explored new places. Not only had they 'found themselves' – they were having a ball. Hut building became a natural extension to cutting tracks and improving access to the local ranges.

Right from the start, women played a major role in early tramping clubs, throwing off the shackles and social mores of the pre-First World War days. Most tramping clubs openly embraced this forward thinking. Women were actively involved in setting up clubs in the early 1920s, taking on key roles, serving on inaugural committees and leading club trips.

General society, however, did not always approve. Some citizens frowned upon the idea of young men and women spending nights together in the bush, so at first clubs carefully appointed chaperones on mixed trips. Many early huts had two rooms, to segregate the sexes, but as time went on, younger people

Tramping Clubs through the Regions

In Wellington, tramping clubs continued to evolve on the Tararua model. The Victoria University of Wellington Tramping Club was established in 1921 and the Hutt Valley Tramping Club in 1923, while further afield, the Levin Waiopehu Tramping Club began in 1927 and the Manawatu Tramping Club in about 1933. Together, they had built over a dozen huts by 1950. In the Wairarapa, a variety of clubs evolved from 1923 and built a further three or four huts.[22] Hut styles ranged from canvas-covered structures with corrugated-iron chimneys, to well-designed buildings of milled timber that was carried in for the purpose. In the 1950s, many of the above clubs extended their local ranges to include Mt Ruapehu and built huts up there too. Hut building was a very communal affair, and fellow clubs frequently supported one another in these projects.[23]

Not every club thrived. Some formed, built huts and then dwindled away, handing their huts on to a new club entity. The Paua Tramping Club, for example, formed by employees of the Shell Company in 1930, built a rough hut in the Orongorongo Valley near Wellington called the Biscuit Tin in 1932. When that became dilapidated, members erected the more substantial Paua Hut nearby in 1940.[24] But the club foundered in the 1960s, and in 1962 donated Paua Hut to the Wellington Tramping and Mountaineering Club (WT&MC), a newer club formed in 1947. WT&MC built or maintained several other huts as well, including Mountain

The camaraderie of hut life. Heretaunga Tramping Club members enjoy a cuppa at Kuripapango while preparing to build Kaweka Hut in 1936. PHOTO: HERETAUNGA TRAMPING CLUB COLLECTION, ALBUM 031

House, Walls Whare and Smiths Creek in the Tararuas. With the informal sense of humour that trampers enjoy, the WT&MC were nicknamed the 'Tongue and Meats' after a Wellington meat company with the same initials.

Further north, the Auckland Tramping Club formed in 1925, and built its first hut, Ngaro-Te-Kotare, in the Waitakeres in the late 1920s, when club membership was about 140. Its second hut, which members called Te Hapua, was built in the Hunua Ranges in the mid-1930s, and the third, a hut on Ruapehu in the late 1940s, served as a memorial to club members killed during the Second World War.[25]

Another Auckland group, the Alpine Sports Club, was formed in 1929. It soon inherited a dilapidated hut in the Waitakere Ranges behind Piha, which members repaired and then christened – with mischievous irony – 'Chateau

threw off restrictions in favour of practicality. In 1935, *NZ Truth* newspaper ran an article condemning the scandalous notion of women in shorts, but it didn't stop women adopting them.[21] Both men and women undertook difficult trips, and epics such as the so-called Sutch Search of 1933, where a mixed party struggled out of the Tararua Ranges two weeks late after fighting through gorges and traversing stormy mountaintops, only served to reinforce the equality of men and women in tramping circles.

The growth of tramping can be seen primarily as an urban development, with the main population centres leading the way. But regionally, clubs adopted slightly different practices for the types of trip they embarked on and the sort of hut projects they involved themselves in. This reflected not only the differing societies of each region, but also the demands of the local terrain.

Mosquito' after the Chateau Tongariro. In the mid-1930s, the club constructed the more substantial Waitakere Hut, still used today. Its third hut, the more basic Runnymead in the Hunua Ranges, now lies drowned under a reservoir. Club members also built huts on Ruapehu – one in 1950 and another in 1966. Current membership stands at about 500.[26]

The 400-strong Auckland University Tramping Club (AUTC), formed in 1932, owns a hut in the Waitakeres called Ongaruanuku, a cheeky amalgam of Maori words that roughly translates as 'belonging to the students'. AUTC members fashioned the hut out of an abandoned timber camp cookhouse in 1944. One member expressed the club's motivation to build a hut: 'We are fortunate in being able to use several excellent huts near Auckland, chiefly through the courtesy of kindred clubs outside the college, but we have nothing to offer in return. A hut of our own would do more than anything to ensure a really successful club spirit.'[27]

The Young Men's Christian Association (YMCA) was originally established in London in 1844 to provide inexpensive, safe accommodation for young men visiting the city. As the organisation expanded its geographical range, it also expanded its aims to include facilitating healthy outdoor travel and recreation for youths. The Christchurch branch of the YMCA was the first in New Zealand, and in the early 1930s a group at the branch, known as the Ramblers, tramped actively. However, the trampers formally split from the YMCA in 1932 after the popular Sunday walks affected church attendance to the extent that the hierarchy could no longer condone tramping under the YMCA banner. The trampers responded by forming both the Te Hapu Koa ('the Happy Family', later the Christchurch Tramping Club) and the Peninsula Tramping Club.[28]

Other clubs continued to form from YMCA roots for decades, such as the Napier Tramping Club in 1974. The provision of huts remained a common interest between the YMCA and tramping clubs, and some of the huts that Christchurch clubs helped maintain included the Sign of the Bellbird and Sign of the Packhorse on Banks Peninsula (see p. 134), and the Jim Adams Memorial Hut at Coopers Creek near Oxford.[29]

Better transport contributed to the explosion of tramping in the 1920s and 1930s, in particular a sympathetic railway network and the increased private ownership of cars. Many clubs hired trucks and spread the cost among participants to keep down expenses. During the Second World War, however, one club reported: 'The rationing of petrol to private cars has practically eliminated their use on official trips, but fortunately as yet no great difficulty has been experienced in arranging transport by lorry and public conveyance.'[30]

The popularity of tramping presented opportunities for the Railways Department, which actively courted trampers by arranging rail excursions to walking destinations. The December 1929 *New Zealand Railways Magazine* directed comments specifically at women walkers: 'Here are a few hints for the tramper, now summer is here and the "long white road", the knapsack, and the campfire

The Auckland Tramping Club's Ngaro-Te-Kotare Hut in the Waitakere Range, pictured at the opening on 17 March 1929. PHOTO: AUCKLAND TRAMPING CLUB COLLECTION

are calling us. Very few modern girls can resist a long day in the open, a jolly lunch miles from the "maddening crowd" and a limp home in the twilight.'[31]

In Canterbury, popular mystery train excursions ran to local tramping areas from about 1933 until the Second World War. Today, such rail trips may not appeal, but between-wars youths found them fun social events, with the added bonus of a challenging tramp. Aware of similar trends overseas aimed at encouraging physicality and health, the government supported these outdoor activities.

The Physical Welfare and Recreation Act 1937 resulted in the construction of a good track over Harper Pass, including five large huts (see p. 138), but the Second World War halted extensive plans for other parts of the country. In 1944, further plans were announced to 'make easy, well-defined tracks in interesting but safe country ... build accommodation huts ... and organize the mountain track system so that whole families, including the mothers, can go out for an ideal holiday at suitable cost and in reasonable comfort.'[32] This domestic focus contrasts strongly with the present one, which is aimed more at international tourists. Perhaps a greater local recreational focus would facilitate increased involvement in outdoor pursuits today too.

By 1940, Christchurch boasted at least five tramping clubs. One, the Wanderers, built Tom Cundell Hut on the Port Levy Saddle. It cost 1 shilling per night to stay in the hut and 'many great weekends were spent there until it

CLOCKWISE FROM TOP LEFT Levin Waiopehu Tramping Club carrying corrugated iron for Waiopehu Hut, Tararua Range, October 1927. PHOTO: GEORGE LESLIE ADKIN COLLECTION, ALEXANDER TURNBULL LIBRARY, WELLINGTON, PA1-F-006-284.
Nelson Tramping Club members at Balloon Hut, Northwest Nelson, 1935. PHOTO: NELSON TRAMPING CLUB COLLECTION.
Wanganui Tramping Club members carrying materials for building Mangaturuturu Hut, Tongariro National Park, March 1957. PHOTO: BRIAN CARTER, WANGANUI TRAMPING CLUB COLLECTION
Heretaunga Tramping Club members at Lawrence Hut, Kaweka Range, 1957. PHOTO: GRAEME HARE, HERETAUNGA TRAMPING CLUB COLLECTION

was demolished in the late 1960s'.³³ Canterbury University College Tramping Club, later called the Canterbury University Tramping Club, built Avoca Hut in 1947 (along with CMC members), and still maintains it with help from DOC.³⁴ Canterbury University students also helped carry materials up the Waimakariri in 1926 for the first Carrington Hut, and also built the first Ada Pass Hut in the St James area in 1955.³⁵ Further south, Dunedin trampers were active as early as August 1923, when a meeting formed the Otago Tramping Club (OTC). Club numbers swelled to 157 within the first year.

Given all this activity and enthusiasm, it's easy to assume that the membership of tramping clubs grew steadily, but records indicate wild fluctuations at times. For instance, OTC numbers dropped to almost half in 1926. A similar trend occurred in the Hutt Valley Tramping Club during its first few years, and the club almost folded. While one club noted in about 1930 that original members were 'abandoning mountaineering for less vigorous pursuits', another lamented in the same era that the younger generation were only too happy to use club facilities without joining or contributing.³⁶

For the most part, however, clubs thrived. The OTC soon began constructing huts too: Green Peak Hut in the Silver Peaks (1933) and Jubilee Hut (1951). Sadly, both suffered serious vandalism.³⁷ In 1938, a Green Peak Hut logbook entry demanded: 'Will the person who took door from the "Peaks Hut" kindly return same as he is known – to save further trouble.'³⁸

On a more successful note, the OTC bought Leaning Lodge in the Rock and Pillar Range from the Otago Ski Club in 1972, acquired 25 Mile Hut in the Rees (which had fallen into disrepair), and took over maintenance of Dart Hut from the NZAC in the early 1960s.³⁹ In 1971, the club morphed into the Otago Tramping and Mountaineering Club. Another major Dunedin club, the Otago University Tramping Club, probably began in the late 1920s and was certainly active by 1934. Some of its early members worked during their holidays on huts and tracks in the Hollyford Valley.⁴⁰

Although cities generated the largest clubs, many others formed throughout provincial New Zealand. Invercargill's first tramping club was established in 1926, but it didn't survive, and had no connection to the current Southland Tramping Club, formed twenty-one years later.⁴¹ Members of the more recent incarnation helped build Fiordland's Moraine Creek Hut in 1954.⁴²

At the top of the South Island, the Nelson Tramping Club was established in 1934 and built several huts, including John Tait Hut in Nelson Lakes (1951; see p. 266).⁴³ The Golden Bay Alpine and Tramping Club sprang up in 1960 and built three huts along the spine of the Douglas Range over the next decade or so.⁴⁴ The Waimea Tramping Club began only in 1973, but that didn't stop it adopting Kahurangi's Balloon Hut in 1992 when a DOC facility review proposed the cessation of its maintenance. In 1986, the Motueka Tramping Club built Flanagans Hut.⁴⁵

Formed in 1935, the Hastings-based Heretaunga Tramping Club built

Green Peak Hut, Silver Peaks, Dunedin, 1970s. PHOTO: GEOFF SPEARPOINT

Kaweka Hut the following year. Unfortunately, the hut burnt down in 2003, but the club still maintains three others.⁴⁶ Over on the other side of the North Island, sixteen-year-old Margaret Murch (now McGuire) began the Wanganui Tramping Club in 1952, and six years later the club built Mangaturuturu Hut on the slopes of Mt Ruapehu.⁴⁷

Hamilton's Waikato Tramping Club began hut building in 1954, four years after it formed, completing two huts in the Kaimai Ranges and a lodge on Ruapehu. Huts close to road ends have always been subject to vandalism, and sadly both the club's Kaimai huts proved to be no exception. One was burnt down in 1980 and the other in 2002.⁴⁸

Not all clubs saw hut building as a paramount priority. In the 1940s, one Auckland University Tramping Club member warned that a comfortable hut could stifle a club's adventurous spirit: 'on acquiring their own hut [tramping clubs] have tended to restrict their activities to country near to the hut, and eventually to merely the hut itself'.⁴⁹ Mostly, however, tramping clubs proved that exactly the opposite was true.

And even as it prepared to open its new Te Matawai Hut in 1932, the Manawatu Tramping Club warned that 'provision of such facilities may render a real disservice to tramping by attracting into a difficult and dangerous region the unwise, inexperienced or the merely foolish.'⁵⁰ However, it was instead the temptation of escaping the mountains during a terrible 1936 storm that resulted in tramper Ralph Wood dying from hypothermia after leaving the shelter of Te Matawai Hut. Clubs know that huts can, and do, save lives.⁵¹

The Deerstalking Clubs

Hunters, like trampers, often have a deep and clear attachment to their backcountry. Hunting already had a long history – one that included building camps, bivvies and huts – before the formation of the New Zealand Deerstalkers' Association (NZDA) in Invercargill in 1937, but this move marked a new level of organisation. Its creation was in no small part prompted by government deer-culling operations, begun by the Department of Internal Affairs in 1930. The NZDA sought to defend the interests of recreational hunters, which were clearly threatened when they were excluded from many hunting areas during the early days of culling.[52]

Dr Geoffrey Orbell, later famous for his rediscovery of the takahe in Fiordland's Murchison Mountains, became the NZDA's first president. Under a national umbrella, each area formed its own branch, culminating in the present total of fifty-one. Scattered widely throughout the country, the branches together now have a healthy membership of over 6000. The NZDA's mission statement clearly spells out its *raison d'être*: 'to retain, enhance and create opportunities for the enjoyment of legitimate recreational hunting and the sport of shooting, for the members of the Association'.[53]

The efforts of the NZDA remain perhaps the untold story of huts; many branches have built at least one hut or have responsibility for maintaining one or more. Many of the organisation's members served during the Second World War, so the NZDA went into temporary recess through these years, but it found new vigour in the post-war decades and began hut building with as much energy and drive as did the tramping clubs.[54]

Some snapshot examples: by 1977 local deerstalking branches had built at least four huts in the Tararuas;[55] in the South Island, the North Canterbury Branch, formed in 1949, built the Lewis Pass Hut in 1954 (later rebuilt in 1968 and named Palmer Lodge); in the wider Lewis area the branch also built the original Nina Hut in 1962, followed by Brass Monkey in 1971, Devils Den in 1973 and Tin Jug Hut in 1974, along with a couple of other bivvies closer to Christchurch. (Tin Jug replaced the older Stone Jug Hut.[56]) Many branches have joint management arrangements with DOC: the Bay of Plenty Branch maintains Mangamuka and Hurunui Huts in the Kaimai Ranges, while the Napier Branch helped build Te Puia Lodge and Makino Hut in the Kawekas.[57]

Since 1999, deerstalkers have also helped clean up makeshift hunting camps on Stewart Island/Rakiura by establishing thirteen huts through the Rakiura Hunter Camp Trust (see p. 190). The hunters also service bait stations to eradicate pests, making a substantial contribution towards conservation on the island. As the trust's website states, 'Everyone wins with this project. It is about hunters doing something positive for their sport.'[58]

Club Advocacy

Many outdoor clubs belong to Federated Mountain Clubs (FMC), a national organisation set up by A.P. Harper to advocate for the backcountry in 1931.[59] Harper understood the need for a national body to represent the interests of ordinary outdoor New Zealanders. Over the next eighty years, the federation's proactive campaigns and careful advocacy had considerable influence on the formation and management of national, forest (and now) conservation parks, backcountry institutions and huts. In 1932, a year after the FMC's formation, the organisation's first president, Fred Vosseler, expressed very clearly the connection outdoor people had developed with their country: 'We must guard closely the welfare of our National Parks and Reserves. These latter we should not regard as the property of our Ministers and our Government Departments, but that they belong to the people of today and tomorrow. We must fight for their protection if necessary.'[60]

In 1936, FMC proposed, among other things, a 'national authority' and local boards for each park, that commercial use be provided for but kept to a minimum, that the public have freedom of entry, and that native plants and animals be preserved and introduced species exterminated – all far-sighted proposals. This was reiterated in 1938, in a letter sent to the Minister of Lands, and at a meeting held in 1940. As Jane Thomson wrote in 1976, 'This short letter became an important document: as the first clearly presented statement of a possible policy for the administration of national parks'.[61] After four years of war, people were keen for a more positive future. Ron Cooper, of the Department of Lands and Survey, recommended a complete overhaul of the national

Members of the NZDA North Canterbury Branch building Brass Monkey Biv, Lewis Pass, 1971.
PHOTO: DAVE SAUNDERS

parks administration along the lines suggested, a move that ultimately led to the adoption of the National Parks Act in 1952.

Many of today's outdoor institutions had at least part of their genesis within FMC, including the Mountain Safety Council, the New Zealand Ski Association, Land Search and Rescue, the New Zealand Walkways Commission, the Wilderness policy, and even the Mountain Guides Association. Huts were also in FMC's sights – the organisation advocated nationally with the Forest Service and national park boards for clubs to be able to build huts. In 1949, Rod Syme from the Mt Egmont Alpine Club compiled a comprehensive list of public huts,[62] while the 1949 edition of the FMC's booklet *Safety in the Mountains* listed 120 huts, most of them owned by clubs.[63]

It is forgotten now, and to their credit the Forest Service generally didn't enforce it, but in the 1950s the public were required by law to have a permit even to enter a state forest, as the Forest Act 1949 clearly stated.[64] Clubs were also charged a firewood levy.[65] When the Forest Service began negotiating how to set up forest parks in the early 1950s, FMC lobbied for free public access and a say in the management through the forest park advisory committees.

With so much hut building going on, many trampers and climbers in the 1970s began to feel that New Zealand had become overpopulated with huts. They proposed the reverse of hut building – wilderness – recognising that some backcountry areas needed to be kept completely wild, free of huts and tracks. During the 1970s and 1980s, some clubs, through the FMC, became preoccupied with this vision. This was, in part, a direct reaction to the Forest Service hut-building programme. An article in the *New Zealand Alpine Journal* noted that in central Westland, '75 Forest Service huts … wilderness eliminated! … Further south … 12 Forest Service huts … wilderness diminishing!'[66] FMC identities like Arnold Heine and Les Molloy drove the idea nationally, but the movement enjoyed popular support throughout the tramping and climbing fraternity. An influential wilderness conference run by the FMC in 1981 ultimately culminated in an inter-departmental 'wilderness policy'. After its formation in 1987, DOC endorsed the policy, and most of the originally proposed wilderness areas have now been established.

Most clubs also supported policies to stop building new huts in national and forest parks, and instead only replace existing ones – a new hut going in meant an old hut had to come out. To this end, in 1972 the Victoria University of Wellington Tramping Club ran work parties to remove their club hut, Allaway Dickson Hut, in the Tararuas, partly because the Forest Service had just built a new hut called Tutuwai nearby, partly because of ongoing vandalism and partly because attitudes had changed so much that huts had come to be seen by some as unnecessary.[67] At the same time, many clubs – which had often had considerable pride in the tracks and huts they maintained – were effectively emasculated by the vastly superior resources that both the Forest Service and Lands and Survey brought to the backcountry. In this climate, many clubs reduced their

Tim Langrish and Ron Mackie at Anti Crow (Gizeh) Biv, Arthur's Pass National Park, June 1955. The cladding for this curious biv, built by the Canterbury Mountaineering Club, was fashioned using pressed metal ceiling panels. PHOTO: RON MACKIE

hut activities to just essential maintenance. Where hut replacement became necessary, collaborative arrangements developed between the club and the authorities. Sometimes clubs did most of the work, while in other instances club involvement was largely in name only.

Times continued to change. In the 1990s, as DOC struggled with the repercussions of the Cave Creek disaster and economic cutbacks, clubs became increasingly alarmed at declining hut maintenance. This was fuelled by the department's plans during the Recreational Opportunities Review in 2003–04 to actively remove many huts. It was one thing to lobby against new huts being put into pristine areas, but something else altogether to take out huts that had been around for decades and had come to be seen as part of our recreational heritage. Clubs, FMC and others advocated strongly for the huts to be retained, and an extended period of consultation began. DOC has done a great job of maintaining the hut infrastructure in recent years – in no small part due to a significant increase in funding made by the Labour–Alliance Government's 2002–03 budget.[68]

Recent Trends

In recent years, online technology has changed the way people network. Clubs are no different in this respect. Email and websites rule, but regular meetings and a trip syllabus keep most clubs active. Club membership today usually has an older demographic than in the past, reflecting a change in the age at which many now join, but that membership is also relatively stable. While in the 1970s heyday of outdoor clubs new members tended to be young and inexperienced, those joining today generally have previous tramping experience, and are seeking a community of outdoor friends. Widespread car ownership negates the need for many young people to join a club for transport, but the rising price of fuel may ultimately see this come full circle again.

Newer voluntary community organisations have built huts, such as the Hokitika-based group that built Mt Brown Hut in 2010, helped by members of the online outdoor community 'Permolat'. Permolat represents an interesting twist in the old club theme: it is an online 'club' with minimal rules, set up in response to the proposed outcomes of DOC's Recreation Opportunities Review in 2003–2004. The review proposed ceasing maintenance on a number of backcountry facilities, and removing others. Founder Andrew Buglass created the Permolat website to exchange information with others, to provide an inventory for each 'non-maintain' hut and to organise members to do the work themselves. Permolat (originally the trade name for rolls of red and white venetian blind material used by the NZFS to mark its tracks) has since signed 'maintain by community' agreements with DOC for various huts in Westland, including Scottys Biv and Mid Styx Hut.

The Rakiura Hunter Camp Trust, Permolat and Mt Brown examples strongly suggest that voluntary involvement with huts is moving once again to a more collaborative community-based approach. It's a way clubs and other groups can retain those huts DOC does not have the funds to maintain.

Hammer and Nails: Club Hut Building

Right from the start, club hut building was a very communal affair. Proposals went to committees, committees took proposals to meetings, and meetings went on all night. But at the end of it all, a hut usually resulted. Treasurers scoured club finances, leant on members who happened to work in companies that could offer materials, and encouraged donations. A site was selected and general club members began the physical work. Plans were drawn, and materials prepared. Between the 1920s and 1950s, materials were carried in on backs: framing timber, water tanks, cement and sheets of iron. In more accessible places, packhorses or even trucks provided an alternative to human mules, but backs remained the common, though not preferred, method. Major changes took place in the 1950s when planes were able to drop loads with varying accuracy to hut sites. Helicopters provided even better transport in the 1960s.

While early shelters were based on a frame of poles buried in the ground, most huts were established using standard construction techniques – piles and bearers or a concrete base. Design usually included a hinged door, a window and an open fireplace. Platform bunks increased the versatility of space and maximised the sleeping area. Some of the larger older club bush huts (like Field Hut) had mezzanine floors or a second storey as a sleeping space, covering half the hut. Huts usually had no mattresses, and individuals made their own arrangements for comfort.

Right from those earliest days, most club huts were covered with corrugated iron, a pragmatic choice eminently suited to the task, particularly at or above the bushline. Lower down in the valleys, slab huts made from timber hand-adzed on site were a practical alternative. A couple of club huts built this way were Cone Hut in the Tararuas and Baines Hut in the Orongorongo Valley.

Huts often became huge missions for clubs, draining people and their resources. But huts also enabled clubs to develop a connection with their mountain places, to have a home in the hills and to establish an identity with the land. Through their hut-building and maintenance programmes, clubs have also benefitted the wider community, providing shelter from the storm in all sorts of places.

Over several generations, outdoor clubs – particularly the stronger and more active ones – have evolved their own philosophy towards their home backcountry. Sometimes that philosophy doesn't mesh easily with a managing authority focused on service standards and tourism, where all recreation is carried out by 'visitors'.

Many of the huts built and managed by these clubs over the decades – now well bedded into the landscape – offer a cultural experience through their age and character that new buildings can't provide. In their context, they are absolutely in keeping with their purpose of shelter, and they remain part of a living history, a reflection of local backcountry culture in the bush and mountains.

GEOFF SPEARPOINT

NEXT PAGE Tararua Tramping Club members work on the second Tauherenikau Hut, Tararua Forest Park, June 1958, shortly before its opening. PHOTO: GREIG ROYLE

Field Hut 1924 TARARUA FOREST PARK, WAIRARAPA

Situated on the well-known Southern Crossing track, Field Hut has the distinction of being the country's oldest surviving hut purposely built for tramping. Erected in 1924 by the Tararua Tramping Club (TTC), the hut was completed in the earliest days of tramping club development in New Zealand. The club's care and effort over many decades has helped the hut to survive nearly ninety years of heavy use, ill-conceived plans to remove it and the rigours of Tararua weather.

Those visiting the hut soon observe its distinctive shape and character. A high-pitched roof houses an airy sleeping loft, with the somewhat more gloomy living area below. On the walls, large framed photographs display the hut's history.[1] One of these shows Fred Vosseler, sucking a pipe while staring at the fire embers when the hut was new. Another depicts Willie Field, the driving force behind establishing the hut. Vosseler and Field, already experienced trampers when they founded the Tararua Tramping Club in 1919, saw that tramping needed structure if it was to thrive. Through strength of numbers, a club could achieve what disparate individuals could not. Tramping clubs provided transport, bushcraft skills and the means to deal with the authorities that managed mountain lands.

While Vosseler provided practical leadership, Field drove the political and legal processes for developing the Southern Crossing track, which both men wanted accessible for public enjoyment. Field had earlier made efforts to establish the route through the Mt Hector Track committees in Otaki and Greytown. As MP for Otaki, he had influence in Wellington and knew how to get government support. As a tramper, he led the first party to travel the Southern Crossing route between Otaki and Greytown in 1912, and shrewdly engaged Otaki journalist Frank Penn to accompany the group. Penn's resulting 1920s booklet *Across the Tararuas and Beautiful Otaki* promoted the area's attractions.[2]

Despite interruptions, significant work on the track was completed through the First World War years, with funding from the Public Works and Tourist and Health Resorts departments. Huts were built too: Alpha (1915) and Top Tauherenikau (1917). Then in 1919, the Otaki Track committee erected a small slab hut called Te Moemoe near the farm–bush boundary about an hour from Otaki Forks.[3]

However, a hut near Table Top remained a high priority, particularly after the death of TTC member Harold Freeman on a club Southern Crossing trip in January 1922, and that of Esmond Kime later the same year (see p. 157). Field, this time in his role as TTC president, pushed for the construction of a hut in conjunction with the track committees; but funding proved problematic and war had sapped the ranks of young men capable of building such a structure.[4]

Instead, the TTC decided to tackle first a more manageable task – that of extending Alpha Hut – and commissioned master bushman Joe Gibbs for

The sawpit during the construction of Field Hut in 1924, Joe Gibbs at right. PHOTO: TARARUA TRAMPING CLUB COLLECTION

LEFT Willie Field. **MIDDLE** Fred Vosseler at Field Hut, 1920s. PHOTOS: TARARUA TRAMPING CLUB COLLECTION **RIGHT** Field Hut, 1930s. PHOTO: JOYCE NEILL, TARARUA TRAMPING CLUB COLLECTION

the job. Born in Murchison, where he learnt his bush skills, Gibbs had served in the Boer War and worked as a miner and axeman in North America. After returning to New Zealand, he worked on the Wellington wharves, but was most at home in the mountains. When he first visited the Tararuas, he said, 'That'll do me for a hunting ground all my life.'[5] With his partner Jack Fisk, Gibbs completed the Alpha Hut renovations in 1923, despite snowstorms late in the season.[6]

The following year, the TTC mustered funds to build Field Hut. The Public Works Department approved a design, and through Field's lobbying provided more than half the £430 cost of building the hut and improving the track. Field personally gave £100 towards the project as the government then matched such donations pound for pound.[7]

Gibbs and Fisk started work in the winter of 1924, widening and benching the track from Otaki Forks so that packhorses could negotiate it. They toiled for 161 days right through winter and spring, pit-sawing timber on site. One man hauled up on the blade, teeth rasping on the stubborn wood, while the other stood in the pit, aided by gravity in his job but cursed by it too when stinging sawdust fell in his eyes. Once the pair laboured for a whole day to produce only a few feet of timber. Whenever possible, Gibbs used durable totara.[8]

Fred Vosseler was one of the stoic pair who volunteered to lug a corrugated-iron water tank up to the hut – an awkward task that even the packhorses could not manage. Vosseler looks determined in the photograph that records the event, while his mate Billy Denton somehow manages to grin.[9]

The TTC officially opened the hut on 27 October 1924, boasting that it was 'the most elaborate and comfortable hut on the track'.[10] Measuring 7 metres by 4 metres, and with timber framing and iron cladding, it featured an upstairs loft capable of accommodating more than twenty trampers. Fittingly, it was named after Field.

Joe Gibbs went on to build Kime Hut and the second Tauherenikau Hut in 1930, and even at the age of seventy-two was sufficiently fit to complete the construction of a second Alpha Hut in 1951. By then he permanently occupied Tauherenikau Hut as a sort of informal hut warden, where he tended a garden, caught eels, ate possums and shot deer. Despite his isolated existence, Gibbs was no misanthrope, and thoroughly enjoyed the company of trampers and other hunters.

Field Hut 50th anniversary celebrations, 1974. PHOTO: BARRY DURRANT

In 1959, Tauherenikau Hut rocked with TTC partygoers celebrating his eightieth birthday; Gibbs sang and danced, and the icing on his cake read 'Born 1879, Still tramping'.[11] He stalked his last deer aged ninety, and died a few months later in Nelson.[12]

Over the decades, Field Hut underwent various alterations and modifications, including a new fireplace in 1945–46, and a new porch and water tanks in 1966. In 1974, the TTC celebrated the hut's fiftieth birthday in fine style, with about 150 people in attendance, and even baked a huge cake for the occasion.[13]

In 1982–83, the club undertook a substantial rebuild of Field Hut. Assisted by the Forest Service, Michael Bartlett led a TTC team that repiled much of the structure, replaced and extended the south wall, reroofed it, installed a wood burner and storage lock-up, and built the enclosed lean-to around the entranceway. Bartlett later commented: 'I feel sure that if this work was not done at that time Field Hut would have become derelict and unusable in the subsequent years.' A serious rat problem was also solved with poison and filling in the open rubbish pit.[14]

The TTC hoped this work would secure the hut's future, but in the mid-1990s the Department of Conservation earmarked Field for replacement with a shelter on nearby Table Top. There was outrage in the outdoors community, and naturally the TTC protested strongly, demanding that DOC consider the hut's historic status. Fortunately, subsequent assessment by conservation architect Chris Cochran recognised the hut's special place in the nation's tramping history and it was retained on site.[15]

DOC undertook significant work on the hut in 2003, which included fitting new piles, replacing a window casing with a 1924 design, strengthening the sleeping floor, and putting on a new roof. New fire regulations meant that any hut with a capacity of more than ten bunks had to have a fire escape, and DOC opted for a large wooden fire escape at the rear of the hut. Some TTC members felt unhappy about the expense and size of the fire escape, but at least the hut's front retains its historical charm.[16] The following year, during the hut's eightieth anniversary, the TTC installed a third information panel about Joe Gibbs.

The hut has changed hue a few times. In the late 1980s it was a red and green affair, but during the 2003 work the TTC opted for a more appealing tussock colour with a 'rata red' roof. Essentially it's the same shape and basic structure as the original. Now the Tararua Range's second-oldest hut after Sayers, it's also the only remaining original Southern Crossing hut.

Field Hut represents that golden era of the 1920s and 1930s, when outdoor clubs boomed. It also remains a tribute to Willie Field, one of the great men who drove the development of tramping in New Zealand, and the club he founded.

SHAUN BARNETT

Kime Hut 1930/1978 TARARUA FOREST PARK, WELLINGTON

The high above-bushline ridges of the Tararua Range, especially those near Mt Hector (1529 metres) on the Southern Crossing track, are dreadfully exposed places that suffer extreme wind and rain. They have claimed many lives through exposure, now known as hypothermia.

Climbing Mt Hector as part of the Southern Crossing track was a trip that gained early popularity in the first part of the twentieth century. Alpha Hut, built in 1915, provided shelter at the bushline on one side of the crossing, but the death of two trampers from hypothermia in quick succession in 1922 drove home the need for some sort of refuge on the long, exposed tops section.

The story of Esmond Kime, the second hypothermia victim,[1] is one of extraordinary survival, followed by tragedy. In June 1922, Kime had set out with Alan Bollons from Alpha Hut over the crossing, but after a few hours the pair began to falter when a strong southeasterly storm blew in. After Kime collapsed in the snow, Bollons returned to Alpha Hut to raise the alarm, but got into trouble himself after losing his way. A search party eventually found him down in the valley below Top Tauherenikau Hut.

Rescuers subsequently located Kime near the Beehives. By then he had survived five days and nights in the open, clad in wet clothing and blankets. Despite bad frostbite, Kime remained lucid and hopes for his survival ran high. After being given a swig of brandy, he was carried back to Alpha Hut. But in the shelter of the hut, fellow trampers administered what was standard treatment of the day – sitting him in front of the fire. At this time it was not known that rapid rewarming, plus alcohol, was the worst possible treatment for hypothermia. An hour later, Kime's condition deteriorated and he died. This tragedy, along with the earlier one, shook the fledgling Tararua Tramping Club (TTC) to its core.[2]

As a result of the two deaths, the club began building a shelter on the saddle between Field Peak and Mt Hector. Completed in September 1922, it soon became known as the Hector Dogbox, and although only about 4 square metres in size, it could accommodate eight people at a squeeze. A forerunner to the Forest Service bivs built in the Tararuas some forty years later, the Hector Dogbox proved to be too lightweight in construction, and a southerly gale literally blew it away in 1929.[3]

The loss of the Hector Dogbox precipitated the need for a replacement hut on the tops. In 1930, legendary Tararua bushman Joe Gibbs, then aged fifty-one, built Kime Hut for the TTC at a cost of £525.[4] He was helped by his seventeen-year-old nephew, Ralph Bawden, along with Bill Lyons and Wally Neill.[5]

The Hector Dogbox, 1928.
PHOTO: WALLY NEILL, TARARUA TRAMPING CLUB COLLECTION

Located in a more sheltered position than the Hector Dogbox, Kime Hut was built using standard backcountry methods of the day: hard yacker. Wally Neill later rated it as 'the most difficult hut building job ever undertaken in the Tararuas'. Packhorses carted materials up to the site, with some timber being pit-sawn back at Field Hut. But first Gibbs's team had to complete a major upgrade of the track to make it suitable for the horses. Early snow drove the workers back to Field Hut in April, but after thirteen weeks the shelter was finally completed. Officially opened on 1 June 1930, it was known as Kime Memorial Hut, in memory of Esmond Kime.

In the following years, a series of cold winters encouraged people to try skiing at Kime, and the hut even served as a base for annual inter-club ski competitions. In the enthusiastic spirit of the times, TTC members lugged skis up from Otaki Forks just for the pleasure of a few turns on slushy snow around the moderate slopes of the hut basin. And these were the days when everyone worked Saturday mornings until lunchtime.

In 1939, Jeff Gunn summed up the normal Tararua skiing experience in his diary: 'Left Fields Hut 9.10 p.m., arrived Kime Hut 3.40 a.m. Saturday. Felt completely done – severe cramp. Soft snow from Dennan onwards – waist deep mostly, armpit depth occasionally. What a night! Sunday. Snow and wind again. Tried my new skis for a couple of short runs then back to Fields and Forks.'[6]

By the mid-1940s, the harsh environment had already caused Kime Memorial Hut to deteriorate rapidly. It's design, based on Field Hut, never really suited the alpine environment and heavy winter snows. Despite its deficiencies, Kime Memorial was the only above-bushline hut ever built in New Zealand using horses and pit-sawn timber.[7]

In 1959, the TTC and Forest Service began

Wally Neill on left with skiers, Kime Hut, 1932. PHOTO: WALLY NEILL, TARARUA TRAMPING CLUB COLLECTION.

Kime Hut I, circa 1970s. PHOTO: GORDON ROBERTS

erecting a new hut, named after TTC founder Fred Vosseler, who had died that year. Slow progress delayed its completion until 1964. Meanwhile, the original Kime fell into further disrepair and, despite some maintenance efforts, turned into a derelict shell. Vosseler Hut, however, unfortunately proved too small for the growing numbers of trampers during the 1970s.[8]

In the mid-1970s, TTC members began planning a second Kime Hut. Prefabricated at the Petone Technical Institute, the hut was flown onto site in sections by helicopter, where Wally Neill – now forty-eight years older – again helped with the construction. On a typically wet and windy Tararua day, 100 people attended the opening on 16 April 1978.[9] The new hut cost $14,000.

Over the years, the twenty-bunk Kime Hut has developed a somewhat frigid reputation, with an ambient inside temperature often at least as cold as that outside (although minus the wind-chill factor). However, despite its deeply flawed design (every scrap of heat generated by burners and bodies escapes to the uselessly high ceiling) no one has questioned the importance of a hut on this part of the Southern Crossing, and Kime Hut II has remained popular. Having suffered thirty-four years of buffeting by the Tararua weather at its 1400-metre site, the hut will be replaced by DOC in 2013 with a similar-sized, modern hut at this important track junction.

Trampers, who know only too well how perilous the exposed Southern Crossing tops can be in the wrong conditions, will welcome a new and warmer Kime Hut III. The latest fatalities in the area occurred in July 2009, when Te Papa chief executive Seddon Bennington and his tramping partner, Marcella Jackson, tried to reach Kime Hut II in exceedingly bad weather. Just a kilometre from safety, they perished in deep snow and strong winds.[10] Sometimes, huts provide temptation to push on rather than turn back to the reliable shelter of the forest, and this sobering tragedy reminds trampers that anyone can misjudge Tararua weather.

ROB BROWN

NEXT PAGE Kime Hut II, June 2010.
PHOTO: SHAUN BARNETT/BLACK ROBIN PHOTOGRAPHY

Rangiwahia Hut c.1935/1967/1984 RUAHINE FOREST PARK, MANAWATU

Rangiwahia Hut occupies a fine position on the rolling tops of the Whanahuia Range, overlooking the farmland of the Rangitikei and distant Mt Ruapehu. While the current hut dates from 1984, this is only the latest incarnation, with the first dating back to the 1930s.

During the 1930s, skiing was becoming popular in New Zealand, but the Depression ensured few people could afford cars or petrol. While clubs hired trucks or buses for transport to share costs, the South Island's mountains remained out of reach to most in the North Island. Instead, members tried out their local ranges: those from Wellington and the Wairarapa skied the Tararua Ranges, while Palmerston North and Hawke's Bay skiers tried the Ruahine Range.

The Rangiwahia Ski Club was one of many outdoor recreation groups that formed in the Depression, and demonstrated admirable enterprise and energy. Established in 1935, the club – like many a good idea – was born over a pint at the Rangiwahia Hotel, then known as Heise's Hangout after the publican. It was the second official ski club formed in New Zealand, after the Ruapehu Ski Club.[1]

That same year, club members renovated a former mustering hut on the nearby Whanahuia Range, altering it into a T-shape to better serve as the base for their skiing. Members winched a bulldozer onto the tops to scrape a wide trail above the hut, and used an old Indian motorbike engine to power their rudimentary ski tow.[2]

In about 1938, during its heyday, the Rangiwahia Ski Club boasted some eighty members. For several years they enjoyed skiing around Rangiwahia Hut, until the Second World War sapped their ranks and the club began to founder.[3] Then, during the 1950s, Ruapehu's rapidly developing Whakapapa ski-field enticed skiers with its better facilities, easier access and more reliable snow. Rangiwahia Hut died away as a skiing destination after demolition of the rope tow in the 1960s, but the hut continued to attract trampers.

The current hut is the third or fourth Rangiwahia Hut, depending on how you count. The first was the basic shepherd's hut, built in the early 1930s. The second was the T-shaped modification of the Rangiwahia Ski Club, but this hut became dilapidated during the late 1950s, after the club's demise.[4]

In 1967, the newly formed Palmerston North Tramping and Mountaineering Club (PNTMC) rebuilt the hut, the third version, and maintained it for the next sixteen years. One of the tasks undertaken by the club was the installation of a wood stove. The Forest Service agreed to fly the stove in by helicopter, but inclement weather saw it dropped off on a knob a couple of kilometres away from the hut. PNTMC members located the stove on the snow-covered slopes of Mangahuia. Club president Lawson Pither recorded:

Ruahine Tramping Club skiers Boyd Tipling, Ken Tarr, and Beryl Harkness, at Rangiwahia Hut, 1939.
PHOTO: RUAHINE TRAMPING CLUB ARCHIVE, COURTESY OF TONY GATES

It was easy to fix the stove onto a sheet of galvanised iron, and with ropes on each corner – behold a sledge! To sledge it down to the hut, it was decided that the President (myself) would control proceedings from the sledge. The rope parties provided forward momentum and when required parties acted as brakes on the steep slopes. What developed was that the arranged load hurtled down hills at high speed, the President abandoned ship and the front rope party shot off to each side, out of the path of the juggernaut.[5]

Happily, the party eventually managed to manhandle the wayward stove to the hut for installation, although it always smoked badly and eventually had to be replaced.

Nothing can survive restructuring for ever, and despite the efforts of the club, the ageing Rangiwahia Hut finally had to be demolished in the summer of 1983–84. That same summer, the NZFS built the modern twelve-bunk hut.[6] In the 1990s, DOC installed gas heating and cooking rings.

The hut's popularity for both skiing and tramping can largely be attributed to the excellent benched track, which provides easy access onto the tops in as little as two hours. With its gradual gradient and wide nature, the track suited less experienced trampers and family groups, and when the snow lay low enough ski tourers could skin all the way from the car park. Disappointingly, an extensive slip in the late 1990s gouged out one section, requiring a steep detour. Happily, however, DOC has plans to rebench the track higher up.

In recent years skiing has enjoyed a comeback, with the advent of modern, lightweight ski-touring gear Palmerston North Tramping and Mountaineering Club members still frequent the hut, some on skis during winter, and know it fondly as 'Rangi'.

SHAUN BARNETT

TOP Rangiwahia Hut, 1990.
PHOTO: SHAUN BARNETT/BLACK ROBIN PHOTOGRAPHY.
BOTTOM Ruahine Tramping Club skiers at Rangiwahia Hut, circa late 1930s. PHOTO: RUAHINE TRAMPING CLUB COLLECTION, COURTESY OF TONY GATES

Powell Hut 1939/1981/2000 TARARUA FOREST PARK, WAIRARAPA

Tucked in a tussock alcove, this bushline hut looks out over the tops of gnarled silver beech trees. At night, the velvet sky twinkles, mirrored by a thousand lights scattered across the Wairarapa plains. It's a magical spot.

It's also on the route to Mt Holdsworth (1470 metres), making Powell one of the most visited huts in the Tararuas. Mt Holdsworth has been an attraction in its own right for over a century. In 1907, the Mt Holdsworth Club was formed, and its members cut a track and built a hut, Mountain House, part of the way up the peak at an altitude of 740 metres. One of the last sightings of huia had been made in the area a couple of years before. After the Mt Holdsworth Club went into limbo, Mountain House languished until the Hutt Valley Tramping Club (HVTC) took over maintenance in 1941. By then, a new hut had also been built at the bushline: Powell Hut. As club records show, skiing provided the major impetus to build it.[1]

In September 1923, in the first skiing trip in the Tararuas, a party of five trampers carried up and used two pairs of skis on the western side of the range, camping near what is today Kime Hut. By the mid-1930s, with Kime Hut built, regular winter ski trips were run, and the Wellington inter-club competition was held annually. But snow conditions, the long, weather-exposed access and the coldness of Kime Hut all kept people looking for alternatives. In 1937, Stan Davis, Fred Akhurst, L.J. Quinn and others investigated the slopes above Powell, and came away convinced that, with a new hut at the bushline, it would provide a better site for skiing and tramping. They set about convincing friends in the HVTC to back the plan.

This was the club's first hut, and they threw themselves behind the project with all the fervour of a new convert. In January 1939, under the heading 'Holdsworth Hut', the club newsletter recorded, 'Plans are at present being drawn up by our Architect, Mr Jim Bertinshaw, for a hut approximately 16ft by 24ft [roughly 5 metres by 7.5 metres] which it is hoped will provide ample accommodation for the needs of trampers and skiers in the Holdsworth area.'[2] On 4–5 February, a weekend work party of thirty men and women began preparing the site. Between then and Easter 1939, a further seven weekend work parties were organised, each with between thirty and forty helpers. Although the vast majority were HVTC club members, each weekend seemed to draw in a few outsiders, and altogether at least six other clubs assisted.

Of course, as was so often the case before planes and helicopters became the common means of transporting hut materials, most of the work involved manually hauling tools and materials to the site – 4 tons of it were lugged up 900 metres over a distance of about 5 kilometres. The weather didn't help at times either – the iron water tank, for example, was lugged up on the hottest weekend of the year. Load carrying went on weekend after weekend throughout February and March, until at last the

Hutt Valley Tramping Club members at the opening of Powell Hut, 14 May 1939. PHOTO: HUTT VALLEY TRAMPING CLUB COLLECTION, ALEXANDER TURNBULL LIBRARY, WELLINGTON, PA1-O-652-20

builders could begin erecting the framework. By Easter, the now closed-in hut had its first overnight occupants. After a little more internal work, preparing bunks and benches, the hut was ready.

Before a crowd of 120 – mainly HVTC members, but also folk from as far away as Hawke's Bay and Palmerston North – the hut was opened on the weekend of 14 May 1939. President Bill Wilson spoke, and the hut was officially named the Ian Powell Hut. The club newsletter reported that 'Joyce Webster, following the usual practice with Opening Ceremonies, presented a sweet smelling bouquet; Biddy with the old tin-snips cut the rope across the doorway – and the hut was populated.'[3]

A foundation member of the HVTC, Ian Powell spread his enthusiasm for the outdoors right across the fields of tramping, skiing and climbing. In 1934, he and Bert Mabin had climbed Aoraki/Mt Cook from Haast Hut in eleven hours, a record time that remained unsurpassed for many years. Powell also helped found the Heretaunga Tramping Club in the mid-1930s, and was the principal organiser behind the building of several huts, including Powell.[4]

On the club's first official winter visit in late July, twenty-seven club trampers arrived at the hut, only to find it already full; they crammed in, taking the total staying in the hut to fifty-three! That August, the club's newsletter noted: 'The popularity of Mt Holdsworth as a ski-ing ground has known no bounds. The hut, weekend after weekend, has been filled beyond capacity.'[5] In 1939, the Wellington Inter-club Ski Sports competition, which had previously been held annually at Kime Hut, was based at Powell. Plentiful snow made a real success of the event, and it was held there again the following year.[6] All the while, of course, the hut developed in popularity for tramping too.

In 1940, a porch was added and the hut painted: dark green walls and a red roof. Three years later, the club installed a little chip stove, with members of a local army attachment helping to carry parts of it up the hill. Another three years later in 1946, an oil drip heater was installed, but

Powell Hut I, early 1970s. PHOTO: GEOFF SPEARPOINT

the impracticalities of providing diesel reduced its value over time. An inside fireplace, added in 1961, attracted rubbish and vandalism, so was removed in 1977.[7] By mid-1978, the deteriorating hut prompted discussions between the club and the Forest Service about a replacement, and consequently an NZFS architect drew up plans for a twenty-four-bunk hut. A joint work party of eight from the club and the NZFS demolished the old hut in March 1981. They noted, 'it was obvious the hut would never have blown away. Purlins were wired to every other rafter and all rafters were wired over the ridge board. The rafter ends were wired down over the wall plate and onto the studs. At this point we sadly missed a pair of bolt cutters.'[8]

Lockwood got the building contract, but Forest Service carpenters finished off the interior. On 7 June 1981, Powell Hut II was opened, forty-two years after the first Powell had been completed. The Forest Service's Wellington District conservator, John Rockell, spoke in front of a crowd of sixty. The club had provided $5500 towards the total cost of $34,000.[9]

Powell Hut II served for eighteen years, at a time when the Tararuas enjoyed growing popularity. On most weekends the hut was well patronised, sometimes beyond capacity. It remained in prime condition throughout this time, but then disaster struck. On the night of 17 May 1999, observers in Masterton spotted a bonfire in the Tararuas, and soon the worst was confirmed.[10] The hut had burnt to the ground, possibly due to a downdraft blowing sparks out of the stove door and onto the wooden floor after the last party had left. A more sinister

Powell Hut III, 2000. PHOTO: SHAUN BARNETT/BLACK ROBIN PHOTOGRAPHY.

Powell Hut II, 1980s. PHOTO: GEOFF SPEARPOINT

event occurred a few weeks later, when the victim of a homicide was discovered nearby; there was probably no connection between the two, but speculation was rife for a while.

Rebuilding Powell Hut III was, once again, a collaborative effort, this time between the club and the Department of Conservation. HVTC's Ron Pynenburg designed a new thirty-two-bunk hut, and club work parties cleaned up the burnt site and dug drains; DOC, meanwhile, organised the bulk of the rebuild. Club members helped open Powell Hut III on 26 February 2000. While DOC collects the hut fees and carries out maintenance, the HVTC continues to have some involvement.

No story about Powell Hut would be complete without mention of Cedric the ghost. Cedric Wilson, a keen hunter who often based himself at the hut, went missing without trace on Mitre Peak in February 1945. Two of his friends went to Powell during the search, and, sensing his 'presence' in the hut, had a rather terrifying night.[11] A later party had a similar experience. John Rundle, in *The Tararua Book*, describes being spooked by 'something' following him down from Powell, even though the hut was empty and he was alone. Aged only sixteen at the time, Rundle was not then aware of Cedric, but later helped instigate a prank to further the ghost legend. In the late 1950s, Rundle and friend Don Millward were at Powell Hut when a group of Scouts set off up Mt Holdsworth. After dressing Millward in a white sleeping-bag liner, marked with skeletal ribs, they set about scaring the returning boys: 'Soon the scouts loomed out of the mist and Don did his act, drifting across the flat ridge in front of them to disappear over the steep edge leaving some satisfying yells and gasps. We made a rapid descent to the hut by another route ... The scouts arrived and we listened in amazement to the story of yet another appearance of Cedric.'[12]

GEOFF SPEARPOINT

Howletts Hut 1894/1940/1980 RUAHINE FOREST PARK, HAWKE'S BAY

Howletts hut's a lovely place
It's perched up in the sky,
And you can gaze out into space
And watch the clouds go by.

Four thousand feet's the altitude.
The hut is made of tin.
The shelter's only rough and rude
And rats walk out and in.
– 'Rest After Labour', by Never Again (1955)[1]

Howletts Hut occupies what is arguably the best tops location for a hut in the entire Ruahine Range. Set in a partially sheltered hollow, not far above the bushline, it affords fine views of Hawke's Bay and is nicely positioned to catch the early-morning sun. The hut owes its name to schoolteacher William F. Howlett.

When you look at a photograph of William Howlett, it's hard to imagine he left behind him a legacy of knowledge and interest in the Ruahine mountains. The Englishman, smartly dressed in a checked jacket and spotted tie, is upright and inscrutable, his dark goatee beard the only unkempt thing about his appearance. He doesn't look like a pioneering mountain man, yet this eccentric character was responsible for building the first hut on Daphne Ridge, a ledge of flattish terrain near the infamously serrated Sawtooth Ridge, and for undertaking the first forays into much of the surrounding terrain.

Howlett came to New Zealand in 1875 from Torquay, England, aged twenty-five, and eventually settled in Hawke's Bay in 1883. For several years he was the teacher at Makaretu School, situated near the foothills of the Ruahine Range, although remittance payments from England meant he didn't teach for the income alone. His unconventional attitudes earned him both praise and condemnation from the local community.[2]

Shortly after arriving at Makaretu, Howlett began exploring the Ruahine Range. He was keenly interested in the area's botany, but also realised its potential for recreation and made quite extensive tramps over the then untracked terrain of the Oroua, Pohangina and Waipawa headwaters. He even started a small 'alpine club', which had recreation and botany among its aims.[3]

By 1885 Howlett had established camps up the Tukituki, with the help of pupil Alfred Stenberg, and built a slab hut near a fork in the north branch (now occupied by the modern Daphne Hut). In the early 1890s, he then proceeded to build a second hut on what became known as Daphne Ridge, to serve as a base for his explorations.[4] Howlett employed a carpenter to adze slabs for the walls and cut shingles for the roof from locally growing mountain cedar, but he and Stenberg completed the construction themselves. The hut was finished by 1894.[5]

During the summer school holidays Howlett spent many weeks at the hut, which he called 'Daphne Hut' after the native daphne *Pimelea buxifolia* that proliferated in the central Ruahine Range.[6] Everyone else, however, knew it as Howletts Hut.[7] Howlett employed a friend to help carry in supplies, a man known as 'lame Petersen' because of his distinctive limp.

In 1902, Howlett took his twenty-one-year-old wife, Olive, up to the hut for their honeymoon – surely a most unconventional nuptial retreat for the times. Petersen helped carry the young bride over the fords, a task that Howlett – then aged fifty-two – might have struggled with.[8]

Howlett wrote many articles and letters for local newspapers (many under the heading 'Olla Podrida'), which are often tedious and pedantic, but occasionally amusing. However, through his willingness to supply plant specimens to professional botanists such as Leonard Cockayne and Thomas Kirk (Te Papa still holds some), Howlett earned a place as a pioneer botanist. Stenberg recalled that he had an extensive library and could name almost every plant in the Ruahine Range.[9] And through his writing and hut-building efforts, Howlett encouraged others to appreciate the values of the Ruahine Range long before it became popular for tramping. Even after he and Olive shifted away from Hawke's Bay, Howlett continued to use his hut for a few weeks each summer, until about 1906.[10]

Howletts Hut lasted until the 1930s, almost outliving its owner, who died in 1935. In 1937, members of the Palmerston North-based Ruahine Tramping Club decided to erect a new hut at the same site. One of their number recalled a Ruahine camp, when 'In the still of an erstwhile stormy night, there came to the befuddled brain of an erstwhile sober citizen an inane and myopic inspira-

Carrying hut material up Daphne Spur, 1940.
PHOTO: HERETAUNGA TRAMPING CLUB COLLECTION

Howletts Hut opening in 1940. PHOTO: HERETAUNGA TRAMPING CLUB COLLECTION, ALBUM 02 09 0311

tion which grew into a violent urge. It was to build a hut.'[11]

In 1938, Heretaunga Tramping Club members helped those from the Ruahine Tramping Club carry about 2.5 tons of materials up the Tukituki River to the base of Daphne Spur. Then in one supreme effort over Labour Weekend, both clubs formed a human chain to convey all the materials up the steep spur to the hut site. One member quipped: 'If you seek any details concerning the weight, portability, or general obstinacy of iron and timber, just consult a Ruahine work party.'[12] Anyone who has toiled up the lung-testing steepness of Daphne Spur will appreciate their efforts.

Construction began over Easter 1940, and proceeded rapidly in uncharacteristically good weather. One of the builders, Fred Lemberg, remembered, 'The greatest offenders at keeping us from work that day were sunshine, cameras, and a rustic chair.'[13] The completed hut was a simple square design with a gabled roof and corrugated-iron cladding. It boasted an open fire and a water tank, which was necessary because the small spring that had previously served as a water source had dried up, possibly as a result of the 1931 Hawke's Bay earthquake.[14]

Representatives of both clubs celebrated the hut's official opening together on 25 November 1940. In subsequent decades the hut sheltered all manner of people, including deer cullers, trampers, researchers and even climbers, who came during winter to test themselves on the steep, icy gullies of the Sawtooth Ridge. For a brief period during December 1948, the hut even served as a base for teams recovering the wreckage and bodies of the three crewmembers from an Oxford plane that crashed on a nearby slope in the upper Oroua headwaters.[15]

By the mid-1970s, however, the deteriorating hut required serious attention. After the Ruahine Tramping Club had folded in 1956, control of the hut was transferred to the Manawatu Tramping Club. Palmerston North, however, was not the most logical base from which to maintain the hut, and in 1978 this club handed it over to the Hastings-based Heretaunga Tramping Club, whose members embarked on a major rebuild in 1979–80. A potbelly stove replaced the open fire, and extra bunks were added in the attic.[16]

In subsequent decades the Heretaunga Tramping Club installed a new wood stove and windows, and also added a veranda. Howlett could little have envisioned that his well-chosen hut site would still be in use more than a century on.

SHAUN BARNETT

OPPOSITE Howletts Hut, July 2011.
PHOTO: SHAUN BARNETT/BLACK ROBIN PHOTOGRAPHY

Big Hut 1946 ROCK AND PILLAR CONSERVATION AREA, CENTRAL OTAGO

The first skiers in New Zealand were probably Norwegian miners who used skis to access the Serpentine diggings, 25 kilometres northwest of Otago's Rock and Pillar Range, during winters in the 1870s. But skiing for recreation did not gain popularity until the 1920s and 1930s.

A series of heavy snowfalls in Dunedin in July 1932 prompted a small group to form the Otago Ski Club. At their first meeting in August, they decided to establish a ski base.[1] The club wisely decided that, as the hills around Dunedin were unlikely to get consistent snow, the higher Rock and Pillar Range would be more suitable, especially as it was accessible via a convenient rail service between Dunedin and Middlemarch (part of which today forms the Otago Central Rail Trail). Run holder A. Mckinnon offered the use of an 1870s stone shearing hut at Glencreag Station, and this became the club's base (later known as Bottom Hut).

For the first few years, skiers breakfasted early at 4 a.m., then trudged a strenuous 1000 metres up onto the range with their heavy skis to practise a few turns on the rolling open tops. By the mid-1930s, however, club members had had enough of this and decided to construct a shelter on the range crest itself. In December 1936, work started on a 4-metre by 6-metre stone hut, built into the side of a large rock tor.[2] Club members used a block and tackle system to shift the larger stones. The shelter, known as Top Hut, was complete by the summer of 1937–38 and reportedly had room for twenty-eight people on the two platform bunks.[3] Scott Gilkison captured the chaos of hut life at the time in his book *Peaks, Packs and Mountain Tracks*:

> Daybreak. Slowly, very slowly, the first slender rays of light filter thinly through the one window. Gently fades the gloom, and in its place appears a picture of orderly chaos as the various objects vaguely assume their shape. Orderly, indeed, for the hut rules and regulations have been widely circulated and carefully followed; chaos too, for it could not be otherwise with such a mass of human bodies and personal gear within this limited space. By the window, the most clearly defined object in sight, a large table with its trim shelves and tins of food set the standard – 'a place for everything'. Beside it, on one side is the cooker which provides so many welcome hot drinks for parties arriving wet and cold, or late at night; on the other side, thirty pairs of skis are neatly stowed away in their wooden rack. The distant, dark side of the hut also becomes slowly visible, and is shown to be entirely filled with two great wooden shelves, on which are sardined together a mass of shapeless forms.[4]

Gilkison remembered that the end positions were the worst, where the sleeping person had only 'the cold, roughly unyielding wall of rock and clay' beside them.[5]

Heavy snowfalls in 1939 prompted some members to consider building a hut closer to Dunedin, but in the Second World War the club decided instead to build a replacement for Top Hut on the

Big Hut during construction 1945-6, with Top Hut to the left.
PHOTO: STUART BOYD COLLECTION, COURTESY OF BRUCE MASON

Rock and Pillar Range. Initial plans for a somewhat grand 140-bunk stone lodge were eventually downsized to a sixty-bunk version, designed in 1944 by club stalwart Norman Joel.[6]

Post-war shortages made it difficult to obtain materials for 'non-essential' projects. The club requested the release of 2 tons of corrugated iron for roofing and cladding from the Minister for Internal Affairs, who politely refused in September 1945: 'unfortunately stocks of galvanised [iron] in the country are at a very low ebb and the quantity which it is possible for the Government to import from overseas is inadequate by some thousands of tons per annum to meet normal requirements for repairs and maintenance'.[7] Undeterred, the club obtained enough roofing iron by 'devious means', but had to be content with cladding the walls in cheaper Pcilite asbestos-cement board.[8]

Work began just before Christmas 1945, with Harry Stevenson using an RD4 Caterpillar tractor and trailer to haul around 30 tons of material and equipment from the Bottom Hut straight up the east face of the range to Top Hut. Construction took place in January 1946, and the hut – dubbed Big Hut – was finished by Easter. Extensive cross-bracing ensured the building could withstand the fierce winds that sometimes sweep over the Otago block mountains. An oil-burning stove, carted from the Old Dunstan Road by John Turnbull on the back of a 1.5-ton truck, provided heating. On the steep descent afterwards, Turnbull, fearing his brakes would fail, dragged a slab of schist down behind the truck – work party members hitching a ride down were terrified enough to bail out halfway down.[9]

Loans raised from club members covered the £657 hut construction costs. Otago University Ski Club members received discounted rates at Big Hut, and in return established a portable rope tow – greatly appreciated by all.

After ten years, Big Hut's popularity declined as skiing shifted towards Queenstown and Coronet Peak – in 1947, Harry Wigley and Bill Hamilton installed the first rope tow at Coronet Peak.[10] Otago

Skiers at Leaning Lodge, 1960s, during the hut's heyday. PHOTO: DAVID PAULIN

Ski Club members moved with the times and built huts at Skippers Saddle, as well as Joel Lodge at Coronet Peak, still used today. Although stunningly located, Coronet Peak suffered in lean snow years before the advent of snowmaking, and in the 1950s a series of warm winters saw a drift of Otago Ski Club members back to the Rock and Pillar Range. However, the increasing sophistication of skiing techniques demanded steeper slopes, and the rolling tops near Big Hut were not as suitable for modern skiing.

So in 1958, club members decided to move an old Otago University Ski Club hut from Big Gully to the base of the skiable face in the steeper south-facing gully below Castle Rock.[11] This hut later became known as Leaning Lodge, after the ground under the foundations subsided and the floor developed a noticeable slope. A rope tow was eventually established up to the range crest. The Otago Ski Club put money and time into excavating a road up to Leaning Lodge from Lug Creek, and briefly contemplated moving Big Hut across to this field in 1960, but wisely decided this would waste valuable club resources.

In 1962, Harry Wigley imported and installed a chairlift on Coronet Peak. This was a revelation for South Island skiers and was effectively the death knell for any further skiing development in the Rock and Pillar Range. By the 1970s, the Otago Ski Club had abandoned both Leaning Lodge and Big Hut. The Otago Tramping Club purchased Leaning Lodge in 1972 for $100, and in 1980 the Otago

Big Hut in 2012. PHOTO: ROB BROWN

University Tramping Club (OUTC) bought Big Hut for $200.[12]

Unfortunately, both of these tramping clubs experienced difficulties in financing the maintenance of the shelters. In 1988, the OUTC sold Big Hut to the Otago Tramping and Mountaineering Club (OTMC) for $300. The hut was being passed around from club to club in search of someone with the will and time to restore it.

Despite the trend towards downhill skiing, many Otago people understood the value of the Rock and Pillar Range huts, which were useful for other activities like summer walking and botanising. A resurgence in cross-country skiing using lightweight Telemark skis or alpine touring skis also saw the huts being used again in winter.

During the Department of Conservation's 2003–04 Recreational Opportunities Review, staff at its Dunedin office proposed that both Leaning Lodge and Big Hut should be demolished, despite owning neither.[13] This prompted Bruce Mason and his brother Peter, along with John Langley, to begin talks with the OTMC about the future of the hut.

As a result, the trio formed the Rock and Pillar Hut Trust in 2003 and purchased the hut from OTMC for its book value (around $200). The hut needed considerable work, and after finalising a restoration plan, the trust got stuck in. Their efforts generated considerable community support and funding. Over the next few years, the trust – led by Bruce Mason and, latterly, Geoff McHardy, and assisted by many helpers who also had strong connections to the Otago Ski Club – restored Big Hut to its former glory.[14]

The hut was repiled and the floor levelled, and stone gabions were used to tie the structure down to its exposed site. The old exterior cladding was completely replaced using the material originally intended – corrugated iron, albeit of the more modern Colorsteel variety. Inside, the walls were relined and insulated, and the windows double-glazed to help keep the hut warm and dry – without heating, it's still cold (the diesel heater was removed long ago), but much less so than it was before the renovation. Solar lights help guard against the risk of fire from candles. Finally, a series of historical panels, researched, written and installed by Bruce Mason, add interest. These give a full interpretation of the scope of the Otago Ski Club's activities both here and further afield.

Leaning Lodge also has its own trust, again with close links to the OTMC and OUTC. Like Big Hut, it is set for a 'rebuild', but in this case little of the original hut may survive.[15]

The monumental effort by the members of the Rock and Pillar Trust to bring Big Hut back to life ensures the public can fully enjoy this part of the range. The original hut builders faced considerable hurdles, not least wartime shortages and difficult access. The trust had a different set of challenges, but set about work in much the same way as its predecessors – by setting a goal and then simply finding a way to make it happen. This spirit of commitment and effort has ebbed into every corner of Big Hut throughout its history, and is a familiar story for most backcountry huts that are treasured by their users.

ROB BROWN

Cone Hut 1945 TARARUA FOREST PARK, WAIRARAPA

One of the striking things about Cone Hut, which nestles under red beech trees in the upper Tauherenikau Valley, is the way it sits in harmony with the natural environment. Something about the scale, the slab construction and the way it blends in makes it, like Goldilocks' porridge, 'just right'. In the 1960s, Tararua Tramping Club (TTC) member John Gates wrote of Cone, 'Growing more directly out of the surrounding bush with totara slat walls, gnarled beech framing, and dry, sweet-smelling fern on its bunk, it reflects more closely its pleasant environment.'[1] Or, as Ian Baine commented, the hut 'retains a rather special character among huts in the Tararuas'.[2]

Although Cone Hut was built just after the Second World War, elements of it are much older. In fact, the 1936 Lands and Survey map of the Tararuas reveals that, surprisingly, six separate huts existed at that time in the Tauherenikau Valley, with another sited on Cone Saddle. The Greytown Track Committee built one of those huts, Top Tauherenikau Hut, in 1917 as part of a wider development scheme for the southern Tararua Ranges.[3] Nicknamed 'Honeymoon Cottage', its totara-pole frame was covered in malthoid and chicken wire, with a chimney of corrugated iron. By the late 1930s it was becoming derelict, and then in October 1945 a flood undercut a corner of the hut. Poles were salvaged before a further flood in December washed away what remained. Across the river, upstream on the true right, was the private Sherwoods Hut, but this was also derelict by the late 1930s.[4]

In about 1930, the Forest Service erected a small four-bunk slab hut just off Cone Saddle, called Cone Saddle Hut. Locked and intended primarily as a fire-watching station, it wasn't much of a success.[5] The back wall, hard against a bank as high as the roof, soon made the hut damp – so much so, in fact, that by 1938 the floor was covered in mud to a depth of 5 centimetres. Search and rescue teams used the hut intermittently as a base, and by 1934 the TTC had taken it over, but work parties failed to alleviate the dampness.

With the slow demise of these huts, the TTC considered building a new hut, but then the Second World War intervened. In 1944, however, a new club huts committee put Cone Hut first on its agenda. After gaining permission from the Forest Service to build the new hut, work began on gathering materials. A dozen studs from Top Tauherenikau Hut were salvaged, plus forty hand-adzed slabs, floor and ceiling plates, studs and a door from Cone Saddle Hut.

The hut site selected lay halfway along the Totara Flats–Kaitoke tramping route, and also provided access to Bull Mound. And: 'most important of all it should provide an excellent venue for those not so fit as an easy daytrip from Tauherenikau Hut'.[6]

Working parties, usually numbering about twenty people, built the hut over about six weekends between the end of June and mid-November 1945. And working parties they were, despite being entirely voluntary. The onerous tasks included car-

Cone Hut, pictured in the 1970s. PHOTO: GEOFF SPEARPOINT

rying 140 kilograms of cement, a roll of building paper, twenty-three sheets of iron, nearly 20 kilograms of nails, two windows in their frames and 30 metres of boxing timber – all from the road end. Nearly a tonne of shingle and sand was excavated from the river near the site and and carried up. Most of the carrying and building was done by TTC members, but members of other local clubs assisted too. The financial outlay of £29 5s 5d mostly went on hut materials.

In true club style, the hut was opened in front of seventy-three trampers on the evening of 9 March 1946, representing six different clubs. 'At half past seven the big blaze was started, a trifle feeble at first, but it soon outgrew Sports Meeting proportions. There was an air of celebration and jollification about; even I received a biscuit …We gave the place back to the moreporks and 'possums some time in the wee hours.'[7]

In the late 1940s, clubs maintained tracks throughout a wide area of the Tararua Range. Joint club meetings divided up track work between them. In 1946, for example, the TTC ran eleven official work parties and three further private ones. Apart from building the hut, members also worked on the Marchant Ridge, Tauherenikau and Bull Mound tracks, and on Field Hut.[8] Theirs was a busy time. Cone went on the list for future work parties.

Despite ongoing maintenance, Cone Hut slowly deteriorated over time. By the mid-1980s, the Forest Service, which had built nearby Tutuwai Hut in April 1972, wrote to the club asking what they planned to do with Cone. Although the Tararua Forest Park Management Plan 1977–87 specifically named Cone Hut for removal, the NZFS recognised the historic nature of its slab construction and supported restoration plans.[9] It also offered to make available a helicopter and other support. Meanwhile, the club began fundraising for the restoration. On the fortieth anniversary of the opening of the hut, thirty-five club members met at Cone to launch the project.

Bigger events intervened, with Forest Service expenditure on huts suspended during the year leading up to the formation of the Department of Conservation in April 1987. In the meantime, the TTC sought support from the Tararua Forest Park Advisory Committee. Sadly, the Forest Service, DOC and the Historic Places Trust appreciated the hut's value more than the club representatives on the committee. Discussions made little progress.

Finally, the TTC asked DOC to approach the Historic Places Trust for assistance, and they commissioned conservation architect Chris Cochran to report on Cone.[10] Cochran recognised the cultural value of the place and recommended restoration of the original hut. The TTC Huts and Tracks Committee accepted the proposal, and in 1988 drew up a plan of action.

Forward-thinking Derrick Field of DOC Masterton worked hard to facilitate the restoration. Michael Bartlett coordinated the project for the TTC and took a very careful planning approach.[11] The concrete fireplace slabs were made offsite by Keith Wood and flown in after misgivings about constructing them *in situ*. At the end of 1988, DOC flew the remaining materials in, and Willie Abel and other DOC workers cut some new hut slabs to replace rotting ones and had them flown in too. Through Christmas and New Year, Bartlett and several other club members began the restoration. By the time they went home on 5 January, new piles, bottom plates and top plates, and a new roof, had been installed. They estimated that a third of the work had been done.

How fantastic to have such wonderful collaboration for a hut restoration. A further five club working parties were run, each with about ten people. The fireplace and chimney were rebuilt, the exterior of the framework was lined with tanalised ply, more piles and plates at the front of the building were replaced, and timber preservative was used to future-proof the slabs, which were also replaced over the exterior ply to restore the historic look of the hut. Putting the slabs back took longer than expected. Greytown hunter Arthur Flowers, who regularly used the hut, also helped on the work parties.

The last major work party, in April 1989, replaced the door, and finished off the sleeping platform area. The total cost to the club was $5000, most of which was spent on building materials. Thirty-two people worked on the restoration, which took 167 work days, but on top of that Bartlett estimates he and Keith Wood spent another two months each on the project.

On 10–12 November 1989, sixty-two people gathered at Cone to celebrate the opening. TTC president Hugh Barr spoke, as did Derrick Field for DOC. Club members Alf Gollan and John Gates cut a cake made for the occasion. More than twenty years later, Cone Hut still offers good shelter and the ambience of an old slab hut in a peaceful forest setting.

GEOFF SPEARPOINT

Cone Hut in 2006.
PHOTO: SHAUN BARNETT/BLACK ROBIN PHOTOGRAPHY

Aspiring Hut 1949 MOUNT ASPIRING NATIONAL PARK

The West Matukituki Valley is the stuff of legend. Lush grass flats fringe stately red beech forest, and bluffs of slabby schist rise into a land of glaciers, culminating in Mt Aspiring/Tititea itself. By New Zealand standards, the valley offers easy walking, providing quick access to magnificent mountains. Not surprisingly, the area attracted mountaineers early on. Some went on to build a stone hut in the valley, the construction of which has become a bit of a legend in itself.

The Otago Section of the New Zealand Alpine Club was formed in Dunedin in 1931, and its members, full of drive and enthusiasm, soon decided to build a hut in the West Matukituki.[1] To raise the £100 needed, they held lantern slide talks and displays, then during Easter 1932, constructed Cascade Hut. Having bought two huts on the Waipori Dam site near Dunedin, members dismantled them for transporting to the Matukituki Valley. Beyond the road end, local farmers helped carry the building materials by packhorse to the hut site for a nominal charge. This began a long, deep friendship between successive generations of the Aspinall family, who owned Mount Aspiring Station, and the club.

Club journals note that, 'As the time occupied in the actual erection of the hut was only four days, it is evident that union hours were somewhat exceeded.' And 'at night work could be carried on outside by candlelight.'[2] The hut comprised two rooms, each with four bunks and a fireplace, connected to one another by a porch designed for packs and firewood. But some Otago Section members were already dreaming of something on an altogether different scale, and at the Cascade Camp of 1939 they proposed a new hut to serve as section headquarters.

Then the Second World War intervened, scattering club members far and wide, some never to return. But even overseas, Bob Craigie and others continued to discuss the headquarters idea at a leave camp in the Dolomites. By 1946, the hut committee of Craigie, Ernie Smith and Angus Black began fundraising and planning in earnest for a stone building to accommodate forty people. Black, who was also an architect, designed the building with a central lounge facing up the valley (with a view of Mt Aspiring/Tititea), flanked by bunkrooms and with a kitchen and smaller bunkroom at the rear. The project was ambitious for the lean years following the war, but donations – including one from the Minister of Internal Affairs – enabled a start to be made. The Section purchased two houses at Berwick, and soon demolished them for materials.

One of the biggest challenges involved transporting materials to the proposed site near Cascade Creek. Even moving 150 tons of rocks, gravel and sand from the nearby creek seemed impractical. Then Bruce Gillies offered his ten-wheeled GMC truck, 'which it was claimed could go anywhere, swim rivers, stand on its rear wheels, and pull itself out when it got into difficulties, all with five tons on board'.[3] Over the next few years it proved capable of all those feats. The first trip involved snowfall and a flat battery, but they reached Raspberry Creek and deposited their first 5-ton load. Given that the road petered out at Cameron Flat, this was a good effort, but still hours short of the proposed site. Others might have been daunted, but the Otago climbers seemed to relish the challenge.

Incised gullies in the Downs Creek fan, just beyond Raspberry Creek, prevented the truck from

Aspiring Hut during construction, late 1940s. PHOTO: NZAC COLLECTION, HOCKEN LIBRARY, UNIVERSITY OF OTAGO, C/NE2110/36

going any further. So Jack Gillespie organised and oversaw student gangs to build a road that became known as 'Gillespie Street'. Eventually, the driving time from Cameron Flat to the hut was trimmed to one-and-three-quarter hours, including four crossings of the West Matukituki River. The transport involved endless adventures: trucks stuck in the river, broken springs, a faulty generator, collapsed wheels, and many hours spent on repairs throughout cold nights with little sleep. At one stage they even had a brush with the law: 'a traffic inspector with a grouch at having to travel 150 miles on a holiday over vile roads in wretched weather on what appeared to be a "wild goose chase"; and a County Councillor, also with a grouch about the damage heavy transport did to roads and bridges' turned up. After checking documentation they left again.[4]

The load carrying and hut building took place between 1946 and 1949, mainly concentrated around Christmas and Easter working parties, the numbers of which frequently reached fifty people. Although men completed most of the work, women were both welcome and active participants on the work parties.

John 'Jack' Aspinall, the owner of Mount Aspiring Station who had helped at Cascade Hut, died in 1942.[5] His son John 'Jerry' Aspinall and wife Phyllis continued the close association with the club at Aspiring Hut, and later their son John and family followed in their footsteps. The Aspinalls helped in very material ways too. Mindful of the NZAC's problems during the 1930s over De la Beche Hut, the club sought to buy the Aspiring Hut site. With the Aspinall's generosity and Department of Lands and Survey consent, the club purchased 6 acres (2.4 hectares), which was surveyed by Arthur P. Harper.

The hut building itself began at Christmas 1946, with a work party of twenty-five overseen by Harper. A team of three horses bought by the club sledged 159 loads of rocks up from Cascade Creek for the foundations, with Harper laying the foundation stone on 31 December. The stonemason, G. Burghess, got cracking in the New Year and com-

Cascade Hut, Matukituki Valley, 2011. PHOTO: GEOFF SPEARPOINT

pleted the foundations in a week. The next big push came at Easter 1947, when two stonemasons and a concrete team raised the walls and put in the windowsills. Meanwhile, carpenters and others in the forty-seven-strong contingent erected interior framing and scaffolding for the masons. All the while, the GMC truck slogged back and forth, bringing loads, so that soon all the timber and much of the rest of the hut materials were on site.[6]

Dunedin is a long way from the Matukituki, yet on every available long weekend and holiday the drivers of the project forged up to work on the hut, taking all and sundry with them. One suspects section members were more or less press-ganged into helping. In late 1947, preparatory efforts were made for a full work effort over the Christmas break. But things didn't go well: the GMC truck broke down and the river flooded.

Under such circumstances most people would happily have given up and opted for an easy weekend instead, but not these guys. They gravelled the Cameron Flat road as rain began. Although loads eventually reached the hut, poor weather restricted building progress. In mid-December 1947, another group finished the outside stone walls. Christmas saw a party of seventeen erect the roof and partially close the hut in – again during difficult weather, which began with a thirty-six-hour downpour.

But the job wasn't finished yet, and fifty people returned for Easter 1948, 'with such a concentration of transport (despite petrol restrictions) as is seldom seen outside the Army'.[7] The hut was properly closed in for the winter and a cooking stove installed. The operation was drawing to a close. But not quite.

At Labour weekend they were back, crossing the West Matukituki and heading up to the hut in driving rain and snow. You have to admire their enthusiasm. This time, a generator and electric lights helped make work easier. Among other jobs, the porch was concreted, shelving and cupboards were built, and the interior was cleaned. The hut, which had cost £1600 and countless work hours, was now ready for use.[8] By the end of February 1949, more than 200 people had stayed there and the club began to work on other valley huts: repairing French Ridge Biv, and carrying materials to Pearl Flat for Arawhata Hut (later known as Liverpool Bivouac).

Aspiring Hut's official opening at Easter 1949 attracted more than a hundred people from around the country, including the National Film Unit fronted by cameraman Brian Brake.[9] Lousy weather at the start meant several vehicles got stuck.[10] Bob Craigie, convener of the huts committee and a major driving force in the whole project, handed the hut over to the club president Arch Wiren. Arthur P. Harper then declared the hut open. Among those present were Alex and Peter Graham, Kenneth Ross and Jerry Aspinall. After dinner everyone gathered around the fire recounting adventures.

Adventures sometimes end badly. Four years later, in January 1953, two people went missing near Cascade Saddle. Bob Craigie returned to Aspiring Hut, this time as a senior search officer, and helped deploy ground parties into the field. A Royal New Zealand Air Force Harvard began searching, with a friend of Craigie's on board: Chris Johnson. Johnson, a Second World War RAF veteran, was also a member of the NZAC, and had participated on almost all the Aspiring Hut work parties. When a semi-delirious Harvard pilot arrived at Aspiring Hut in ripped clothes, a recall signal was fired. Tragedy had struck: the plane had crashed in the headwaters of Rough Creek, and although Johnson survived the crash, he died before the searchers could get to him several hours later. In his book *Men Aspiring*, Johnson's friend Paul Powell described that night at Aspiring Hut:

> We lit the candles and sat around the windows and the bare trestle tables thinking. The stars came. There was an aura of pent up emotion, but we were too shy to break it. Then Bob Craigie came out of the bunkroom. He stood in the middle of the large room with the dignity that only a Scot can bring to his sorrow. The light showed the black stubble on his chin, and his shadow lay bent on the wall… 'Here's to Chris,' said Bob, leading us to the breaking point. We got up and drank in silence … We sat at the tables with tears running down our faces, but our voices lifted in song. We sang the songs Chris had sung in the RAF messes of the Western Desert, the ribald ditties of the Eighth Army, the bawdy ballads of the mountains. We sang hymns, we bellowed traditional lyrics … We sang until the strain had gone, and, our feelings released, we went to bed quietly at midnight.[11]

It was several days later before the searchers found the bodies of the original missing pair, deep in a ravine on the Cascade face, where they had fallen many days before.

There was no Mount Aspiring National Park then of course, but the NZAC's Otago Section

French Ridge Biv, 1980, with Arawhata Saddle to the left.
PHOTO: GEOFF SPEARPOINT

pushed to create that too. The club had already proposed an Otago National Park covering the Southern Alps in 1936, but the idea fell on deaf ears. In 1959, ten years after the hut was opened, they tried again with a submission to the National Parks Authority. Incredible though it now seems, the authority rejected the proposal, citing lack of public interest. Undeterred, club members and others spent a few years raising awareness, culminating in a Dunedin public meeting in 1964 that called for an Otago National Park.[12] This time, the National Parks Authority endorsed it, and Mount Aspiring National Park was gazetted in December 1964.

Aspiring Hut was always a valley base rather than one from which to climb, and so served a wide range of outdoor enthusiasts. During the mid-1970s, a slip threatened the hut. Gravel swept around the back door in storms, and the Otago Section was at sixes and sevens about what to do. Club member and geologist Graham Bishop suggested several options, and in the end a small stop-bank was built to divert the stream away from the hut.[13] It worked, but when I was hut warden in the summer of 1979–80, its success was far from certain. Today, the gravel around the hut is all grass again.

Wardens have been based at the hut intermittently over summer from the time it was built. One of them described the job, saying it involved cleaning the toilet and hut; maintaining the buildings; managing water, gas and firewood supplies; providing weather, track and other advice; tracing overdue people; dispensing first aid; collecting hut fees; writing up paperwork … and a whole lot more, especially facilitating the enjoyment and learning of those staying.[14] Once the national park formed, park board staff were very supportive of the wardens, as were the Aspinalls.

Times change. In 1989, the Otago Section decided that volunteer work parties couldn't keep up with the required maintenance. Discussions began with DOC, and a unique, far-sighted document, 'Management Agreement – Aspiring Huts', was drawn up. The hut remains under club ownership

Aspiring Hut, 2007. PHOTO: GEOFF SPEARPOINT

but DOC collects hut fees, which can be used only on facilities in the park. DOC carries out maintenance, and meets with the NZAC twice yearly.

Since then, DOC staff led by Paul Hellebrekers have carried out substantial maintenance work, built separate wardens' quarters, and installed a full septic tank and toilet block. In 1999, club members commemorated fifty years of Aspiring Hut with a memorable gathering of a hundred people. DCC staff and the Aspinall family celebrated with them.[15]

GEOFF SPEARPOINT

St Winifred Hut 1960   TE KAHUI KAUPEKA CONSERVATION PARK, CANTERBURY

Draining southeast off the Main Divide, the upper Havelock is a wide valley full of gravel, mossy flats and low scrub, dominated by rugged glaciated peaks. This is a land of arid speargrass, loose rocky outcrops of greywacke, dust storms and deep winter snow. Although St Winifred Hut wasn't built until 1960, its story really begins in the 1930s, when most of the surrounding mountains remained unknown, making them a magnet for the fledgling Canterbury Mountaineering Club (CMC).

In October 1935, the Erewhon Branch of the club decided to build a hut in the upper Havelock Valley at or above the Forbes confluence, to complete a chain of huts between Arthur's Pass and Aoraki/Mount Cook.[1] As in so many places, a friendship had developed between the mountaineers and the local run holder, J.S. Johnstone of Erewhon Station. The club's Jack Pattle and Johnstone combined forces to choose a hut site, but they felt restricted to building outside the state forest reserve, the boundary of which cut across the valley about a kilometre below the Forbes.

So Havelock Hut ended up about opposite Carneys Creek, on the Havelock's true left. The club raised the money (£26), bought the materials and organised transport. In October 1936, Johnstone loaded the materials onto a wagon at Erewhon and took them up to the site over three days: 'It was a rough journey over the Clyde and up the stony riverbed. Two or three times the load was dumped and the wagon dug out from mud and water.'[2] In November he built the hut. This match-lined (tongue-and-groove interior) six-bunk hut, with its stove and oven, served both musterers and mountaineers.

Despite being happy with their new hut, the CMC had already planned another shelter. In the same weekend that they opened Havelock Hut – Easter 1937 – they also built Eric Bivouac about 8 kilometres up the valley at the junction of Havelock River and Eric Stream.

Eric was a smaller affair, measuring about 2 metres by 3 metres. Some twenty-one club members and three packhorses managed by a station hand carried all the materials in on one hot day.[3] The following day, three carpenters built the hut, with just one hammer between them. A couple of willing helpers assisted, but the rest went climbing! This bivouac was a forerunner to several other light, relatively cheap (£6 in the case of Eric) bivouacs the club built in the region.[4] Others included Agnes (Clyde Valley) and Edwards (Arthur's Pass). For many years Eric remained a refuge from storms, but then river erosion caused by a New Year flood in 1948 threatened the shelter itself. The bivouac needed moving, and urgently.[5]

Tongue-and-groove flooring and match lining from unused supplies at Havelock Hut were salvaged, along with other scavenged bits and pieces. This time Malcolm Prouting from Mesopotamia Station helped. In February, six CMC members took four of Prouting's packhorses with loads up to the old bivouac site. At Easter 1948, they began rebuilding the hut 500 metres away, on a scrubby moraine mound called Agony Island, about 30 metres above the riverbed.

Building huts can be eventful. The team of thirteen worked away in atrocious conditions as the river flooded across the flats, making escape down the valley impossible. Jack Pattle recounted:

> We stuck to the hut and with numbed hands and soaked to the skin in driving wind and rain built our shelter against the unyielding forces … Holding roofing iron down and driving lead heads against a howling old man nor'wester has to be experienced to be fully appreciated. The roof was put on twice, first as a temporary shelter, and then later on, with a lull in the wind, it was torn off, the paper laid and the iron replaced and nailed.[6]

A long weekend in June saw the finishing touches completed: extra corrugated iron, a water tank and paint. This bivouac was safe, for the meantime. However, braided rivers can change course, and at various times the Havelock River channels switched sides around Agony Island.

Climber Jim Dennistoun named both Eric and St Winifred streams during his explorations in the Havelock Valley in 1908–10. The name Eric came partly from Dennistoun's companion Eric Harper (a cousin of Arthur P. Harper), but also derived from a character in a moralising book by F. W. Farrar, loathed by schoolchildren of the time. St Winifred made reference to another Farrar book.[7]

Which brings us to St Winifred Hut. In a kind of déjà vu, by 1960 the river threatened to dislodge

Eric Bivvy, Havelock Valley.
PHOTO: JOHN PASCOE, ALEXANDER TURNBULL LIBRARY, C5999

the twenty-four-year-old Havelock Hut. Before the river turned it into 'a fisherman's bach at the Rangitata River Mouth', the club dismantled the hut, and with the help of a borrowed ex-Army Quad truck moved the materials 8 kilometres up the valley near St Winifred Stream.[8] Members still had to lug a fair amount, with the loads of iron making the tramp an uncertain process: 'with creaking springs and sagging knees the lurching cavalcade began the slow journey upstream'.[9] One member found himself attached to the outside of a door 'but found that even without touching the handle it kept swinging open to place me on the inside'.[10] Others foundered when fording streams, but eventually the bulk of materials was assembled on site.

Easter 1960 saw most of St Winifred Hut built. One CMC member, Russ Kelly, muscled in the cast-iron stove on his back. Rain didn't help, but the carpenters – Alan Morgan, Jack Pattle, Arthur Dixon, Frank Morrison and Alan Kelly – were into it, and had the building virtually closed in before a storm chased them out. Morgan returned a couple of weekends later to finish the job with Tom Morton, in frigid conditions. To conserve warmth, Alan nailed his bed covers to the bunk. Tom commented, 'I will probably never see another person "untucking his bedclothes" in the morning with the aid of a hammer.'[11]

And so in 1960 the CMC finally ended up with a nine-bunk hut where they had probably envisaged having it in 1935. As part of a chain of huts in the central Southern Alps, St Winifred has offered welcome shelter to those attempting the traverse between Arthur's Pass and Aoraki/Mount Cook.

The hut got an extreme makeover in January 2004.[12] Flooded rivers caused problems for the maintenance team, but Laurie Prouting from Mesopotamia Station flew men and gear over swollen streams in his helicopter. The team installed a new chimney and fireproof lining, then added a new water tank and toilet. As they finished, rain started again. Pleasure at listening to the drumming on the freshly painted roof soon turned to anxiety as boulders knocked together in the nearby river, which resembled boiling mud. Getting out took time; like so many seemingly prosaic work parties, this one became quite an adventure.

With helicopter support from the Department of Conservation, CMC undertook further work on the hut in 2006, repiling it and remodelling the kitchen. This ensured St Winifred Hut will serve well into the future, representing a sustained effort by CMC over eighty years to provide refuges in this wild valley.[13]

GEOFF SPEARPOINT

St Winifred Hut, December 1990. PHOTO: GEOFF SPEARPOINT

Waimakariri Falls Biv 1944 & Hut 1962 ARTHUR'S PASS NATIONAL PARK

The Waimakariri River begins its journey to the sea high up on the western flanks of Mt Rolleston and flows down through a basin full of alpine plants, including the spectacular Mount Cook buttercup. Before the infant river plunges over an 80-metre cliff, it passes beneath a spectacular bluff of solid red rock, and on a nearby ledge sits Waimakariri Falls Hut. The small six-bunk hut occupies perhaps the most idyllic spot in Arthur's Pass National Park.

After the Canterbury Mountaineering Club (CMC) erected its first hut, Carrington, during 1928, the popularity of trips into the Waimakariri headwaters blossomed. Carrington Hut served well as a valley base hut, but was perhaps a bit too remote from the higher peaks to serve as the ideal climbing hut.

The New Zealand Alpine Club (NZAC) decided to built a hut near Waimakariri Falls during the Second World War. Club members packed materials for a small steel bivvy in to Carrington Hut, then during Easter 1943, a party of more than twenty lugged a load up to the site. Further work parties followed, until enough materials were assembled on site to build the bivvy in Easter 1944. NZAC stalwarts Neil Hamilton and Ian Powell oversaw construction of the bivouac, which was located close to the current hut site.[1]

While the climbing hut made a welcome addition to the park's recreational facilities, it was never a top priority for the NZAC. Furthermore, the NZAC presence in the CMC's traditional 'home patch' created some tension. Rivalry between the two clubs had existed for some decades, especially when NZAC women members stayed in the CMC huts like Carrington and Anti-Crow. Some members complained that the NZAC seemed to ignore the CMC's 'men only' rule.

Waimakariri Falls Bivvy often bulged at the seams during the holiday seasons, eventually precipitating the need for a proper sized hut. This time, CMC instigated the replacement hut, perhaps reasserting its traditional dominance in the valley. The CMC decided to adopt a design similar to that of Empress Hut, a high altitude hut built earlier by the club on the western side of Aoraki/Mt Cook. The design also bore a strong resemblance to the NZAC's Colin Todd Hut, at the base of Mt Aspiring/Tititea (see p. 310).

During the early 1960s, the club approached the Arthur's Pass National Park Board for funds to build the new hut. The board granted a subsidy on the condition that the park would retain ownership of the hut, while the CMC would be responsible for 'control and management'. Like all other CMC huts, the general public could openly use the hut too.

Waimakariri Falls Hut became the very first CMC hut built using materials flown onto site. The Forest Service arranged the flight in April 1961 as part of its burgeoning hut-building programme. In December, CMC members John Forsyth, Deryck Morse, K.C. Hall and G.E. Prior walked in to assemble the hut. Although they completed the hut

The original NZAC Wamakariri Falls steel biv, circa 1950s.
PHOTO: JOHN WILSON COLLECTION

The 1962-built CMC Waimakariri Falls Hut, pictured in 1997 before its most recent renovation. PHOTO: ROB BROWN

shell on this trip, another year passed before the hut was completed. The climbers of the 1960s appreciated this alpine haven, which served admirably for climbs of Mt Rolleston, Carrington Peak and Mt Armstrong. Trampers also stayed during trans-alpine trips over Waimakariri Col.

Tension arose in the mid-1970s between the CMC and the park board, when the latter unilaterally decided to replace CMC's Carrington Hut (see p. 264) with a park board hut, bringing the vexed issue of hut ownership to a head. If the board owned all the club's huts in the park, that left huts like Waimakariri Falls in some sort of maintenance limbo. The issue had not been fully resolved in 1987 when the Department of Conservation took over management of the park. Throughout the next decade, Waimakariri Falls Hut deteriorated. DOC would not fully commit to maintaining a hut at that site (partly because of the avalanche risk), while CMC was reluctant to commit money towards its upkeep until the ownership issue was resolved.[2]

Following a review of recreation facilities in 2004, DOC transferred ownership of the hut to CMC. DOC also accepted CMC's contention that years of uncertainty and neglect had rendered the hut a maintenance liability, and as a consequence agreed to upgrade it fully. In 2005, DOC staff installed a new floor and bunks, and at the same time double-glazed the windows and relined the hut to create a warmer, drier interior.[3]

Today, Waimakariri Falls Hut stands as the last of a classic 1960s six-bunk alpine hut design. The two other examples, Colin Todd and Empress huts, were replaced in the 1990s, leaving Waimakariri Falls the only one still on its original site.[4]

ROB BROWN

Whangaehu Hut 1964 TONGARIRO NATIONAL PARK

How many huts can claim to have been built only after some of the materials were lugged over the top of a volcano, and the highest mountain in the North Island at that? Situated at 2060 metres on the eastern slopes of Mt Ruapehu, Whangaehu Hut is the highest of all the North Island's huts. Its magnificent setting, on a ledge above bluffs in the upper Whangaehu Valley, offers views of Ringatoto and Pyramid Peak rising above, and the Kaimanawa and Ruahine ranges to the east. Indeed, one climber quipped, 'The hut is daringly sited; you have only to walk five yards in your sleep and you will have an unimpeded fall of about a hundred feet into the valley.'[1]

In the early 1960s, after several years of discussion, the Auckland Section of the New Zealand Alpine Club (NZAC) decided to build a hut on Ruapehu's comparatively undeveloped eastern flanks. Once the hut site was chosen, the club faced the practical considerations of the design, and getting materials onto site. The site was 370 kilometres from where members lived in Auckland, and work had to be carried out during weekends. As the club had only a modest £500 at its disposal, logistical challenges awaited.

Club member David Hoyle, an engineer, was the main driving force behind the project, and it was in his Mangere backyard that the hut was designed and prefabricated over the course of some nine weekends. Club members had examined other prefabricated designs, including the Silver Hut used on one of Edmund Hillary's Himalayan expeditions, but in the end adapted their own distinct model.[2]

Even before the design was finalised, a work party led by Hoyle established the site and foundations for the new hut in February 1963. Hoyle recorded:

> It must surely be the first time on record that a mountain has been traversed by a ton of cement, boxing, reinforcing steel, shovels, buckets, a 44-gallon drum, rope, and part of a roll of linoleum. The climbing techniques employed may make the purists shudder, but we did feel justified in making use of local resources and travelling by chairlift and 'snowbus' to the 8,000 ft. level. The descent of the Whangaehu Glacier was a partially controlled sledging avalanche carried out in thick fog and fantastic heat, the five participants vowing that they would thenceforth be unavailable for future work parties.[3]

Hoyle remembers, 'on our return to civilisation we found we were the last to hear of president Kennedy's assassination'. During subsequent weekends they made concrete for the foundation block using scoria and other aggregates available onsite, added to snow-melt and the cement.[4]

Plans to fly hut components onto site had to be scuttled, as Hoyle wryly remarked: 'It was unfortunate that our negotiations for an airlift broke down at the same time as the helicopter.' Helicopters were less capable and reliable in those days, and the club members instead lugged 2 tons of materials up to the hut site from Tukino over the course of four

Whangaehu Hut, 2010.
PHOTO: SHAUN BARNETT/BLACK ROBIN PHOTOGRAPHY

weekends in 1963. Fortunately, a six-wheel Dodge enabled them to drive materials over the Tukino road to within 3 kilometres of the site, but they still faced a stiff 500-metre climb over rough terrain. Wellington and Taranaki section members helped lug the 'back-breaking' loads. Heaviest of these were two roof sections, weighing 180 kilograms, each of which had to be carried by some twenty people.[5]

The timber framework, Hoyle noted, 'probably departs a good deal from normal carpentry'.[6] Given the site's high altitude and vulnerability to storms, the framework was double-sheathed with aluminium foil, lined with oiled hardwood, and insulated with fibreglass and polystyrene. By using industrial-strength aluminium cladding, Hoyle hoped the hut would be low maintenance, and would also resist corrosion from the sulphur dioxide regularly belched from the nearby Crater Lake.

Many alpine huts have wire stays, but such cables have the disadvantage of posing a hazard to those moving around the outside of the hut, and in any case still allow sufficient movement during storms that joints open and the framework can become stressed. Consequently, the club decided to secure the framework of Whangaehu Hut with angle iron instead, and fixed the whole structure to the large concrete foundation.

Hoyle, absent during the final build owing to family ties, warned the builders to enclose the hut fully before leaving the site. Unfortunately, the tireless workers could not quite completely close it in before having to retreat to Auckland. In December 1963, before they could return, a storm tested the hut. Later that month, club member Ivan Pickens found cladding ripped off the porch and one main wall, and the floor damaged by snow. In early 1964, club members undertook repairs, built a platform bunk with capacity for six, fitted a sink and cooking bench, installed mattresses and a water tank, and sealed the main roof. Amenities included kerosene lamps, Primuses, fuel and billies. The hut was almost finished.[7]

On Good Friday 1964, several NZAC climbing parties approached the hut for the opening. One member recorded:

> Some parties, perhaps unaware of the persuasive powers of the chief carpenter [Hoyle], toiled up to the hut in anticipation of a quick climb, only to spend the rest of the day wielding paint brushes or hammers. Others, more wary, pitched camp at lower altitudes, and it was only towards the end of the day that they ventured near the hut.[8]

During the night, a brief storm flattened several tents, and by morning some climbers were found sheltering in the hut. The opening day dawned mercifully fine, and not even the chief carpenter could keep the climbers from the slopes above the hut. By mid-afternoon, however, all assembled back at the hut for the opening.

Edmund Hillary, then the NZAC Auckland representative, arrived to open the hut officially. Section chairman Ivan Pickens praised the hut builders, then Hillary spoke, suggesting 'that while a climber should not become a perennial hut builder, one such project was a good thing'. After he performed a ceremonial unlocking of the door, tea was served.[9]

One climber, watching the distant car lights of those travelling the Desert Road, pitied the drivers as 'poor mortals who would never savour the cold sweet air of the mountains on a clear March night'.[10]

Generations of climbers have since enjoyed the sweet (or sometime sulphurous) air at Whangaehu, until finally the hut needed major renovations. In the autumn of 2011 and summer of 2012, NZAC members led by Richard Knott undertook the necessary work, replacing the cladding and windows, and thereby ensuring this spectacularly sited hut will serve for decades yet.[11]

SHAUN BARNETT

Ed Hillary's signature in Whangaehu Hut logbook, March 1964. IMAGE: NZAC RECORDS, WHANGAEHU HUT BOOK 1964-1980, HOCKEN LIBRARY, UNIVERSITY OF OTAGO MS-1164-3/54

Roaring Stag Lodge 1963/2005 TARARUA FOREST PARK, WAIRARAPA

The New Zealand Deerstalkers' Association (NZDA) has a fine tradition of hut building, contributing as much to this endeavour as tramping and alpine clubs. Under the NZDA national umbrella, many branches have built their own huts. Roaring Stag Lodge is one example.

In the late 1950s, the Wellington Branch of the NZDA decided to build a hut beside the Ruamahanga River in Tararua Forest Park, one of the few valleys of the park still without shelter. Member Hong Tse recorded their motives: 'No doubt the occasional derisive comment about "bludging hunters" from the odd tramping club member when in one of the mountain huts had its effect, but in the main it was the desire for a "home away from home" that fuelled the branch desire to have its own niche in the hills.'[1]

NZDA members lugged in 'second-hand' materials by hobnail express over the Bottles Corner Track (which followed a different route to the existing track) between 1959 and 1963. Progress was slow, with some work parties cancelled: an indication of the enormous effort then required to build a hut. The hut was largely completed by 1962, and was finally opened by NZDA life member Bill Cowan on Labour weekend 1963.[2]

Over the following decades the NZDA faithfully maintained the hut, but by the late 1980s it was showing its age. Roaring Stag Lodge often suffered rat infestations to the degree that one tramper recalled it had become known by the alternative moniker 'Squeaky Rat' Lodge.[3] It still provided rough shelter for trampers and hunters alike, but eventually in 2004 funds were made available through the Tararua–Aorangi Huts Committee for a replacement. Given increased building costs and much more stringent building and fire regulations, funding a new hut was beyond the resources of the Wellington Branch members, who instead entered into a partnership with the Department of Conservation.

In May 2004, NZDA member Tony Macklin and DOC's Derrick Field from Masterton flew into the Ruamahanga by helicopter to assess a new site, and came to the conclusion that the old site remained best. Wellington architect Ron Pynenburg designed the new Roaring Stag Lodge, while Macklin managed the whole project. Builder Evan Mardell, an NZDA member, was awarded the contract to build the new hut, and began work in April 2005. Using a helicopter, 400-kilogram pre-nailed loads were ferried onto site and building progressed rapidly, with the hut completed swiftly.[4] The hut features a plywood exterior, a comfortable covered veranda, and a red roof and window frames, designed to reflect the area's rata forest. The total cost was $140,000, met mostly by DOC, but with a financial contribution by the Wellington Branch.[5]

Sally Te Hana from the local iwi blessed the new hut during its opening on 6 August 2005, a fine day attended by fifty-three people. Among the crowd were several NZDA members who had built the original hut some forty-two years before, including Hong Tse. Tony Macklin wrote, 'For me to see grown men with tears in their eyes as they met

NZDA members constructing the fireplace for Roaring Stag Lodge, early 1960s. PHOTO: PETER PLIM, NZDA WELLINGTON SECTION, COURTESY OF TONY MACKLIN

Roaring Stag Lodge II, 2010. PHOTO: SHAUN BARNETT/BLACK ROBIN PHOTOGRAPHY

fellow hunters they had not seen for 30 years was quite something.'[6]

In his opening speech, Macklin made some interesting comparisons between the old and new huts. The old hut took four years to build, involved hundreds of work hours, had no building code and required one sheet of plans. The new hut took four weeks to build, the helicopter turn-around time for loads was 12 minutes, and the hut had a full building consent with the local council and required twenty-six pages of plans.[7] Times have changed how they get built, but not the appeal of a hut. Soon after the opening, the new lodge began to attract trampers and hunters in droves – one night, forty-two people shared the twelve bunks.

SHAUN BARNETT

Boulder Lake Hut 1961/1994, Adelaide Tarn Hut 1964, Lonely Lake Hut 1973
KAHURANGI NATIONAL PARK

> At Lonely Lake, in Summer-time,
> the Drunken Sailors loom
> above steep alpine meadows where
> the bulbinella bloom.
> – Poem from the Golden Bay Alpine and Tramping Club archives

These three diminutive huts stand as a tribute to the extraordinary efforts of a small group of mountain enthusiasts called the Golden Bay Alpine and Tramping Club. Although basic in the extreme, the three small shelters have served well for generations of trampers testing themselves on the challenging routes over the craggy Douglas Range.

On the Douglas Range, nasty notches separate toothed peaks, and over the Burgoo Valley the peaks are so precipitous they overhang in a few places. Not surprisingly, the mountains sport imaginative names like the Drunken Sailors, Dragons Teeth, Needle and Trident.

Back in the 1960s, when the vast mountainous corner of the upper South Island was known as Northwest Nelson, most of it comprised state forests managed by the Forest Service. A group of Golden Bay mountain enthusiasts wanted to build a hut on the Douglas Range at Boulder Lake, and sought permission from the Conservator of Forests. As the Forest Service didn't allow individuals to built huts on Crown land, locals Frank Soper and Keith Marshall decided to form the Golden Bay Alpine and Tramping Club in 1960. Marshall served as the club's first president.[1]

Late in 1960, the new club gained permission from the NZFS for the hut, and sprang into action. Early in January 1961, members reopened the Brown Cow Track, little used since the gold-mining days of the previous century. On 29 January, a local top-dressing pilot flew in bundles of framing timber, and club members assembled on site, ready for building. Club archives recall that 'light rain and fog all day Monday made working conditions unpleasant'. However, 'Work continued according to plan, so that by the end of the day the club's first hut, 8 feet by 7 feet [2.4 metres by 2.1 metres] and sheathed in aluminium was standing solidly by the waterfall at Suicide Creek.' The four bunks consisted of chain-mesh netting. Later in the year, trampers laboriously lugged in a small iron stove and material to build a chimney, finishing just in time to host a Nelson Tramping Club party visit on the first weekend of winter.[2]

Even as they erected the hut, club members decided to seek protection for the whole vast mountainous area of Northwest Nelson. While the hut provided shelter from the elements, a park would provide certainty that the whole area remained wild. Berna Soper, the club's first secretary, recalled that the ten original members 'consisted of botanists, geologists and photographers and could all see the beauty of the area. We loved the backcountry and wanted to preserve it somehow.'[3]

Backed by support from Forest & Bird and the Ornithological Society, the club urged the Forest Service to create a park. Club members hosted scientists from Wellington's Dominion Museum for a two-day stay at Boulder Lake Hut, and their survey of the area added credibility to the club's idea for a park.[4] To its credit, the Forest Service heeded the call, approved the idea in 1963, and established Northwest Nelson State Forest Park two years later. At over 377,000 hectares it was then the largest forest park in the country, and second only to Fiordland National Park in size.

Boulder Lake Hut served as a useful base from which to explore the area, but one shelter wasn't adequate for the whole Douglas Range. Club members decided to build two more, providing a chain of huts connecting the Aorere Valley with the Cobb Valley. They funded the project by helping the Forest Service recut the then overgrown Heaphy Track, part of the push to develop outdoor recreation in the new park.[5]

With momentum still strong, club members built Adelaide Tarn Hut (originally called Trident Hut) in 1964. Set on a ledge beside the tarn, the hut has the spectacular backdrop of the Dragons Teeth beyond. This tiny hut has bunk space for four (including one fold-down bunk), and an entrance so narrow you can't get in with your pack on. The last hut built by the club, the three-bunk Lonely Lake Hut, went up in 1973. It is slightly more salubrious than its two predecessors, with probably just enough room to swing a small cat.

In 1994, when the Department of Conservation built a larger eight-bunk hut at Boulder Lake, the old hut was retired after three decades of service. It survives still, tucked into the bush, a monument to a small club big in determination.

SHAUN BARNETT

CLOCKWISE FROM TOP LEFT Adelaide Tarn Hut, 1994. The original Boulder Lake Hut, pictured in 2006. PHOTOS: SHAUN BARNETT/BLACK ROBIN PHOTOGRAPHY Noe Herman and Darryn Pegram inside Lonely Lake Hut, 1996. PHOTO: DARRYN PEGRAM /BLACK ROBIN PHOTOGRAPHY Boulder Lake Hut, 2006. PHOTO: SHAUN BARNETT/BLACK ROBIN PHOTOGRAPHY

Mt Brown Hut 2010 NEWTON RANGE, WEST COAST

Located at the end of the Newton Range, Mt Brown offers spectacular views over Lake Kaniere and the Hokitika backcountry. The original Mt Brown Hut, built by the Forest Service in 1973, was poorly located below the bushline on the southwestern side of the mountain.[1] By the mid-1990s, this hut was in a sad state of repair and a Department of Conservation review of West Coast huts recommended its removal, which occurred in 2006.[2] A number of locals from the Kokatahi Tramping Group wanted to investigate options for a new hut at Mt Brown, and DOC was supportive of the idea. Julia Bradshaw and Eddie Newman were the driving force behind the group, and together with other locals formed the Mt Brown Hut Community Project Team.

In early 2010, DOC decided to replace the nearby four-bunk Lower Arahura Hut (built in the 1960s) with a newer six-bunk hut, and subsequently offered the older hut to the team. They set about dismantling the old hut, ready for flying the salvaged materials to Mt Brown. Unfortunately, some of the framing proved rotten, and most of the rest was not strong enough for the hut's new alpine location, in a tussock hollow on the mountain. In the end, just the flooring, roof and tin cladding from the old Lower Arahura Hut could be used.[3]

As the scale and cost of the hut rebuild grew, Newman and Bradshaw encouraged local businesses to support the project. More than thirty enthusiastic local sponsors donated everything from the helicopter transport to the Resene paints matching the original Forest Service orange. Other financial contributors included the Federated Mountain Clubs' Forest and Mountain Trust and a number of individuals.

By Easter 2010, the foundations and floor had been laid by volunteers, while others recut the overgrown Mt Brown tracks. During the first weeks of May, volunteers prefabricated the hut in the DOC Hokitika workshop and then flew the materials onto the site on 28 May. With such good planning and preparation, the final hut assembly took just three days. A month later, team members returned in crisp, clear weather to finish the windows, doors and cladding. The hut was now weatherproof for the coming winter.[4]

Over the next few months, volunteers finished the hut's interior, and constructed a veranda and deck. Altogether, thirty-five volunteers worked on the project, many of them from the online backcountry network Permolat, which has a number of agreements with DOC to manage some of the more remote huts in the Hokitika area.[5]

On 18 November 2010, inspectors from DOC and the Westland District Council visited the hut, and it was approved for public use. The hut has been built to withstand winds of up to 250 kilometres per hour, but has not proved quite so kea-proof. Non-lead flashings were used to prevent the local alpine parrot hooligans from poisoning themselves, but they have nevertheless developed a fondness for attacking the aluminium.[6]

Few places along the rugged western side of the Southern Alps offer trampers such easily accessible tops as Mt Brown, with its mountain-to-sea vistas. The superb position of the new hut is reflected in its growing popularity – more than 175 visits in its first six months. The hut even has its own Facebook page, which details the story of its construction and provides testimony to the effort and vision of a local community.[7]

ROB BROWN

Mt Brown Hut, 2010. PHOTO: ROB BROWN

CLUB HUTS 189

Cavalier Hunters Hut LATE 1980s/1996 RAKIURA NATIONAL PARK, STEWART ISLAND

Cavalier Hunters Hut, at Mason Bay on Stewart Island/Rakiura, started life as a tiny shelter erected by the Forest Service in the late 1980s, but over subsequent years hunters progressively enlarged it with makeshift tarpaulins until it became a rather ugly, rat-infested shack. On the weekend of the very first Super 12 rugby final in 1996, hunters Ray Philips, Neville Millar and John DeLury – all members of the Southland Branch of the New Zealand Deerstalkers' Association (NZDA) – flew in to the hut with the aim of making something decent out of it.

As well as paying for the materials themselves, the trio carried out the work of extending and renovating the old shanty into a four-bunk hut. They also replaced the old drum fire with a potbelly stove, and removed all the rubbish and tatty tarpaulins. Keen to not miss the historic rugby match, they had brought in an old black and white TV, which they powered with a car battery.[1] After a hard day's building, the reception proved sufficiently good to witness the Auckland Blues thrash the South African Natal Sharks 45–21 at Eden Park. The hut maintenance trip sparked off the idea of doing something about the other hunting camps on the island.

Ever since the introduction of whitetail deer to Stewart Island/Rakiura in 1905, hunters have journeyed across Foveaux Strait to set up camp and pursue this elusive North American game animal. As many as 3000 hunters visit the island every year, and over time they established semi-permanent camps in the most popular hunting blocks. Hunters brought with them all manner of cheap materials for building these shelters, and by the 1990s some of the camps, like Cavalier, had become untidy tarpaulin shacks, infested with vermin and littered with rubbish.

With Stewart Island/Rakiura headed for national park status in the late 1990s, everyone accepted that things had to change. The Southland Branch of the NZDA, including DeLury, Philips and Millar, got together with the Department of Conservation and local transport operators to come up with a better way of managing the hunting camps.

The resulting Rakiura Hunter Camp Trust, a charitable trust formed in 1999, set about raising funds to build simple, cheap huts. The initial trust fund received gifts from individuals and hunting

LEFT The new Martins Creek Hunters Hut, Mason Bay, 2011. **RIGHT** Homestead Hunters Hut, Mason Bay, 2008. PHOTOS: JOHN DELURY

clubs (mainly NZDA branches) of $26,000, plus a grant of $30,000 from the Southland Community Trust. A further $11,000 came from the Lotteries Community Grants and DOC put up $20,000.[2]

This seed money was used to buy materials to construct simple six-bunk huts. The trust's design was a 3.6-metre by 8-metre hut, clad in tanalised ply, and with a Colorsteel roof, a wood burner and a veranda. With volunteers to carry out the labour, the trust hoped to keep the costs of each hut to a minimum. Operators such as Ian Munroe, who then owned the Stewart Island Ferry Service, helped out with cheap transport to the hunting blocks, most of which are accessible by boat. The trust's first six huts cost an average of $8500 each.[3] Changes to the building code and hikes in building consent costs over the last ten years have raised the cost to around $26,000, but in today's terms this still represents a remarkably small outlay for a six-bunk hut.

The trust's first two huts, built with the help of the Stewart Island Lions Club, replaced camps in the southern Port Pegasus blocks, where the island's weather can be at its wildest. Since then, seven more huts have gone up, on Little Glory, Hapuatuna, Chew Tobacco, South West Arm, North Tikotatahi, Kellys and Abrahams Bay hunting blocks. The most recent huts replaced older ones at Martins Creek block (Mason Bay) and the upper Lords River/Tutaekawetoweto.

The Rakiura Hunter Camp Trust also established five huts outside the national park boundary on hunting blocks owned by the Rakiura Maori Land Trust (RMLT). The RMLT paid for these huts and retains ownership, but the NZDA again provided all the labour and carries out maintenance.

Although Cavalier Hunters Hut pre-dated the Rakiura Hunter Camp Trust's hut-building activities, it has since become managed and maintained by it, along with four others in the area. By building the huts, the trust has transformed the experience of hunting on Stewart Island/Rakiura over a very short time. It has raised more than $270,000 and built thirteen of the fifteen huts it originally envis-

Cavalier Hunters Hut in 2008. PHOTO: ROB BROWN

aged. According to the trustees' estimate, over 9500 voluntary hours have gone into their huts. Other NZDA branches such as Central Otago, Taranaki and Gore have also helped.[4]

Naturally, when hunters book a hunting block, they have first priority at the trust's huts, but at other times the general public can stay for a flat levy of $20. In the most proactive way possible, the trust has largely eliminated makeshift shelters that attracted rubbish and vermin, and replaced them with good, cheap huts. Their commendable work has enhanced the whole Stewart Island/Rakiura experience.

ROB BROWN

Orongorongo Valley Huts c.1910–2011 RIMUTAKA FOREST PARK, WELLINGTON

Wellington's Orongorongo Valley holds a special place in many people's hearts. Countless children have experienced their first night in a backcountry hut in this valley, which is the main artery running through the Rimutaka Range. Yet others have continued to enjoy staying in the valley in their later years, when the harder, less accessible tracks elsewhere are beyond them.

The Orongorongo undoubtedly boasts the highest concentration of huts in New Zealand, with more than fifty in an 8-kilometre stretch of the valley. Most of these are private huts, although in recent years an increasing number have become available to the public, albeit through a booking system.

Hut building in the valley began during the 1910s, soon after the Five Mile Track was recut. The oldest remaining hut in the valley, Baine-iti, has its origin in this era. Built by Jack Baine in 1916–17, it was a rough affair of manuka framing and canvas; not surprisingly, it did not last long and had to be rebuilt in 1919.[1] The third version, built in 1925, had flattened kerosene tins in place of canvas. Baine became the Wellington City Council ranger in the area when the valley became a water supply catchment in 1927, and his job was to keep people out of the headwaters. He rebuilt the hut in 1930, calling it 'Baines Hut Ranger Station'. Later, when the hut was taken over and maintained by Jack's son Ian, it was renamed Baine-iti. Historically, it's the most significant hut remaining in the valley.[2] Generously, the Baine family leave the hut open for public use; today, it is the only unlocked one in the valley.[3]

During the 1920s and 1930s, hut building picked up pace, with a dozen or more constructed in the 1920s alone. Many Wellingtonians sought to have a bush retreat, and, after gaining a permit from the Wellington City Council Water Board, could build their own hut in the lower valley. In this way, hut development in the Orongorongo Valley mirrored coastal bach building elsewhere in the country, such as occurred on Auckland's Rangitoto Island. During the Depression, some people even permanently escaped to the valley, where they could live inexpensively by hunting deer and pigs.

Many huts were built on the cheap, with recycled materials commonly used. In 1939, the HM Customs Department Tramping Club recorded a total cost of $1.75 for building their Tainui Hut – everything was scrounged or donated except for the nails.[4] During the early 1930s, there was even a shop – 'Turners Bush Store' – in the valley, operated by an enterprising young Wellington clerk, who sold soft drinks to thirsty trampers on the Five Mile Track. Mountaineer John Pascoe recorded that although some trampers despised this commercialisation of the bush, 'they were not loath to buy his wares if they ran out of tobacco or tucker'.[5]

During the Second World War, some huts suffered from a lack of use and maintenance, although in 1941–43 the Hutt Valley Tramping Club built

Baine-iti, oldest surviving hut in the Orongorongo Valley, in 2005. PHOTO: SHAUN BARNETT/BLACK ROBIN PHOTOGRAPHY

their Baines Hut (again named after Jack Baine). Two army sergeants even built a secret hut known as the 'Deserters Whare' in the off-limits catchment area of the upper valley to avoid being sent overseas.[6]

Pascoe spoke fondly of the Orongorongo and its huts in his 1952 book *Land Uplifted High*: 'Many of these huts have a story that began with dogged youth who swagged on aching shoulders heavy sheet iron, nails, cement, and other materials. The story sometimes continues with wild parties, orgies of gramophone noises, and the sinking of gigantic meals with raucous laughter.'[7] He also recorded that hut licences then cost £1 per year.

Huts were often family affairs, and many of the existing shelters in the valley remain in private ownership. One woman whose father built a hut here in the early 1970s recalled, 'All were built out of recycled materials and decked out with furnishing discarded from home.'[8] A large number of huts were even connected by an emergency phone line, which spanned a section of the valley.

Yet other huts were built by tramping clubs, including most of the large Wellington clubs: the Paua Tramping Club built Paua Hut in 1940 (now owned by the Wellington Tramping and Mountaineering Club); the Tararua Tramping Club built Waerenga Hut in 1933; and the Hutt Valley Tramping Club built Baines Hut in 1943. Unfortunately, damaging 2005 floods meant Waerenga had to be shifted and Baines Hut removed permanently.[9]

Huts were not always locked, but vandalism was a problem at times, notably in the early 1920s and after the Second World War, resulting in a need for greater security.[10] One tramper wrote: 'Those who build the huts state that they have no objection to anyone making use of the comforts provided, but it is an outrage on hospitality for visitors to remove and destroy the articles which have been placed there under such great difficulty.'[11]

Max Coolahan, a Wellington art teacher, was one character who made his mark on the Orongorongo. He built the valley's first A-frame hut in 1963, naming it Stag Park Country Lodge. He even fashioned a thirteen-hole golf course nearby, whose rules included 'Watch out for deer on the fairway' and 'Billiard shots are permissible on holes 11 and 12'. One tramper who played the course remembered, 'It was the wackiest golf course I ever played on. Crafted around tree stumps, river boulders and the abundant shingle of the valley, it was a remarkable achievement.'[12]

By the 1970s, the total number of huts in the valley peaked at seventy-four, although it has since declined to about fifty-five, with some lost to fire, some to neglect, and others removed after they failed to comply with new standards.[13] Those that have survived best are huts well used by generations of a single family, or by the collective efforts of a tramping club. Others fell apart for various reasons, as Pascoe recorded:

> [After] the partnerships of trampers or hunters split up with the disintegrating factors of marriage, transfer or war … the story ends with a hut gradually rotting, with holes rusting in the roof iron, and neglect lurking in every bunk. Finally the hut, once the pride of its owners, becomes a shack of curiosity to passing couples who prefer to make their bed on manuka or fern fronds on the grass flats.[14]

In 1972, the Orongorongo became part of the Rimutaka State Forest Park, but administration of the huts remained with the Wellington Regional

The Orongorongo Valley. PHOTO: SHAUN BARNETT/BLACK ROBIN PHOTOGRAPHY

The original Waerenga Hut, circa 1936. PHOTO: FRANK FITZGERALD, TARARUA TRAMPING CLUB COLLECTION

Water Board, which banned the building of new huts in 1973. In 1980, control of the water board land finally passed to the Forest Service, and in the mid-1980s some private huts were transferred over to the NZFS for public hire, a system that the Department of Conservation has continued since it took over in 1987. Although the NZFS did not condone private hut construction on public land, it did renew licences for private hut owners on a twenty-year basis.[15]

Another significant event was the establishment of the Orongorongo Club in 1978. This was largely a group of hut owners who decided to organise themselves to deal with authorities, and to socialise and help record some of the valley's history. The club produces a regular newsletter, the *Five Miler*, and also runs a number of events in the valley each year, including the annual Easter Moa Hunt for children.[16]

In 1988, DOC felt the ire of hut owners when it increased annual licence fees from $30 to $250 and introduced new compliance standards.[17] Understandably, many hut owners who had long family traditions of staying in the Orongorongo Valley felt angry at these changes. However, DOC remained in a difficult position – ultimately it had responsibility for managing conservation lands and the structures on them, and new building and fire regulations meant many of the huts were below legal requirements. The conundrum DOC faced was this: conservation lands are supposed to be accessible to all, and egalitarian in nature. But by the same token, DOC is charged with fostering recreation and conserving backcountry heritage, and there was little question that some private huts in the valley hold value with both these functions.

Eventually, a compromise was reached, whereby huts now have a sunset clause that expires in 2050, or upon the death of the licence holder, whichever comes first.[18] Four-wheel-drive access up the valley is permitted once a month for hut owners to carry out maintenance. The long-term future of the private huts remains uncertain, and the Orongorongo Club continues to advocate for transferability of ownership.

DOC huts open for public use at the time of writing include Jans Hut, Boar Inn and Raukawa Lodge. Oaks Hut, also managed by DOC, was removed in 2011. Demand for huts in the valley proved so great, that in 2010–11 DOC built three new huts. Two were replacements for older huts (Shamrock, which was renamed Papatahi, and Haurangi), and the third a large thirty-two-bunk hut called Turere Lodge.

Most of the DOC huts are extremely popular, and must be booked weeks or even months ahead, especially for weekends. Aside from providing the usual mattresses, water supply and heating, they also have cutlery, utensils and gas cooking facilities, making them ideal destinations for people with young families. The booking system also allows families to have a hut to themselves, so they don't have to worry that their children may disturb other hut occupants or vice versa.

With these facilities, the Orongorongo will remain a place where many people have their formative experiences of a night in the bush. For others, the valley is simply a second home. Wellington tramper Rebecca Mitchison expressed this sentiment:

> I recently spent six months working in Fiordland. Even in beautiful Fiordland I still missed the

CLOCKWISE FROM TOP LEFT Waerenga Hut II, pictured in 2011. DOC's new Haurangi Hut, built in 2010. Boar Inn, 2011.
PHOTOS: SHAUN BARNETT/BLACK ROBIN PHOTOGRAPHY

Orongorongo Valley. Every time I am tramping, the damp smell of the earth underfoot and the call of the grey warbler never fails to bring back memories … Although it may fall short of the kind of beauty that Fiordland holds, it is still home to me.[19]

SHAUN BARNETT

SHELTER ON A SHOESTRING DEPARTMENT OF INTERNAL AFFAIRS HUTS

The Deer Menace

One introduced animal has, perversely, had more impact on hut development in New Zealand than all the efforts of the Tourism Department and tramping, deerstalking and alpine clubs combined. The New Zealand Forest Service is famed for its deer-culling huts, but few people know about those built by the original deer cullers, who operated under the umbrella of the Department of Internal Affairs (DIA). These cullers worked through the Depression years and the Second World War, in an age before aircraft were widely available in New Zealand, which makes their hut-building efforts all the more remarkable.

Deer were supposed to be a prized game animal, a source of meat and trophies, and a creature to fill the empty forests of New Zealand. But, like many other exotics introduced to the fragile ecology of islands isolated from the world stage of evolution for 80 million years, deer had unintended and long-lasting impacts.

Red deer were first introduced from Scotland to the new colony in the 1860s. Enthusiastic acclimatisation societies made many hundreds of later liberations, until the animals were present throughout all the main mountains and forests of New Zealand – excepting some forested parts of Northland, Coromandel, Taranaki and Stewart Island/Rakiura.

Nor were the acclimatisation societies content to settle for an ungulate monoculture, but sought to establish a diverse menagerie of game animals. In the late nineteenth and early twentieth centuries, further introductions followed: sika deer (Japan), rusa and sambar (India), chamois (the European Alps), tahr (Himalaya), fallow deer (Western Europe), wapiti and whitetail (North America), and even moose (Canada). And these are just the successful liberations; failed attempts included mule deer, wildebeest, a South American deer, mountain zebra and two species of llama.[1]

These animals were at first protected while their populations established, but their numbers – particularly those of red deer and chamois – reached plague proportions after just a few decades. By the early twentieth century, farmers were complaining about deer competing with their sheep, foresters reported trouble with ring-barked exotic tree plantations, and the Native Bird Protection Society (later Forest & Bird) became concerned about the impact of deer on native forests. Deer were also implicated in accelerating erosion, a belief that persisted even long after research revealed a high degree of natural erosion in New Zealand mountains.

The Deer Control Section Begins

Acclimatisation societies were pressured into 'thinning' herds around high-country farms, but farmers soon demanded a more systematic approach. In May 1930, the government hosted a 'Deer Menace Conference' in Wellington, which brought together all interested parties in the hope of finding a solution. Any remaining protection for deer was finally removed. The Forest Service made a failed bid to gain responsibility for deer control, but ultimately the job for an extermination campaign fell to the multi-faceted Department of Internal Affairs.[2]

The Deer Control Section was born out of this decision, and the mammoth task of deer extermination was handed to Captain George Franklin Yerex, a veteran of the First World War. Unsurprisingly, 'Skipper' Yerex tackled the problem in military fashion, planning armed sweeps up the deer-infested valleys to drive the pest from the forests. This exciting period in New Zealand's history saw hundreds of young men living and working in the mountains, a wave of backcountry activity not witnessed since earlier generations of prospectors prowled the valleys and passes for gold. Although officially termed 'government shooters', these men came to be known by the more laconic term 'deer cullers'.[3]

In November 1930, deer cullers fired their first shots in Canterbury and Otago, areas chosen because of high-country farmers' concerns, but soon expanded their range to many other parts of the South Island. Targeted animals grew to include goats, tahr, chamois, wallaby and wild pigs. In the North Island, a DIA culling effort began in 1932 around Lake Waikaremoana, but it faltered. DIA operations in the North Island did not really get going properly until 1935, when cullers moved into the Tararua Range. Efforts expanded into the Urewera region and Kaimanawa, Kaweka, Ruahine and Haurangi ranges in 1937–38.[4]

A deer-culling career attracted many, but suited few. Most aspirants lasted only weeks. As scientist Graeme Caughley, who began his career as a culler, put it, 'The work is so demanding, physically and mentally, that it quickly selected

Trampers meet a DIA deer culler at the slab Frew Creek Hut, Whitcombe Valley, 1935.
PHOTO: O. M. PREBBLE

LEFT Captain George Franklin Yerex (left) on a hunting trip in the Wainuiomata area, Wellington, 1930, with P. Wilson and J. Drummond. PHOTO: NEW ZEALAND FOREST SERVICE. **RIGHT** Deer culler Joff Thomson (right, with unknown companion) hauling deerskins in about 1946. PHOTO: ALEXANDER TURNBULL LIBRARY, WELLINGTON, PA COLL-6348-11

a small group who were not as other men. Those that remained for any length of time were held as much by their preference for wild country as they were for financial reward.'[5]

DIA culler Rex Forrester, who worked during the 1940s, concurred, saying he often carried packs weighing 40 kilograms or more, but that the physical hardship was less than the mental strain: 'A man stuck out in the mountains for weeks on end, living rough, wearing ragged clothes, eating hard tucker, and sometimes wet through for weeks on end, begins to feel terribly alone and depressed. I've been at screaming point myself several times and I've seen some blokes crack up completely.'[6]

But for those who could handle it, deer culling was an attractive job – especially during the 1930s Depression, when many were out of work. A select few cullers served for years. One of Yerex's field officers, Ken Francis, recalled that the campaign against the deer became to cullers 'a holy war, a cause in which hardships were endured far beyond the call of duty'.[7]

Hunters have recorded this history well, perhaps most notably Joff Thomson in *Deer Hunter* (1952), Philip Holden in *New Zealand, Hunter's Paradise* (1985), Graeme Caughley in *The Deer Wars* (1983) and Ken Francis in *Wildlife Ranger* (1983). But it was Barry Crump who catapulted deer cullers most into the public's consciousness with his 1960 semi-fictionalised book *A Good Keen Man*. What Thomson had recorded faithfully, Crump pushed into the realm of myth. His book opened with a culler in a hut: 'Trevor trod heavily about the hut in unlaced boots building a fire and swinging the first tea billy of the day. While he waited for it to boil he stood in the hut doorway yawning misty breaths and watching the light sifting down the valley through the dark bush and across the open river-flats.'[8]

Given the tempestuous New Zealand climate, the exacting nature of the mountainous terrain, and not least the adaptability and resilience of red deer, Yerex's military sweep never really stood a chance – and was further curtailed by a lack of resources. The campaign began just a year into the 1930s Depression, and this restricted the deer cullers in several ways. First, they had to spend vast amounts of time recovering deerskins and carrying them out in order to offset some of their costs. Rex Forrester recalled the effort: 'Coming down with green skins … is one of the worst parts of pack-carrying. The load hangs low and heavy and going downhill with a heavy load is a jarring strain on the knees. Then when you have to duck to go under a log the pack catches and throws you on your back time after time.'[9]

Second, as far as accommodation was concerned, cullers had to make do with canvas when timber and iron would have been preferable. Initially, during the first years of the 1930s, the DIA did not intend to build huts, as their shooting operations were supposed to deal with the deer problem quickly. Furthermore, where they began operating, in the backblocks of Otago and Canterbury's high-country stations, mustering huts served the cullers well. Huts provided a certain level of comfort, where a man was his own king. Culler Joff Thomson expressed this when he wrote:

> Now isn't it grand to open the door of a back-country hut, sling your rifle on a bunk, light up a cigarette and lie back with your thoughts. Ah! No nagging wife or girl friend to pick holes in your manners. Dirty boots, mud on the floor, smelly socks, clothes strewn around and other various oddments in disorder, are your sole responsibility.[10]

DIA Tent Camps

As the DIA expanded its operations into the remotest – and often wettest – parts of the country, particularly Fiordland and the West Coast, little shelter existed except for the occasional rock overhang. In the hut-less valleys of the South Island, the DIA established 'tent camps', many of which soon became semi-permanent structures.

The larger tent camps were usually built in clearings where firewood and water were in good supply, and often used pole beech for framing. A wooden floor on the more elaborate ones was the exception; dirt was the norm. In the mid-1930s, DIA officer Ken Francis designed an advance base camp, suitable for two men:

> With a 2 × 2.5-metre floor space and a long 4-metre fly which extended well beyond the doorway, the new tent provided room for stores and equipment, and a sheltered fireplace. Sides could be laced on to provide additional shelter. The tent was very successful and in immediate demand, particularly as sod chimneys could be built safely at the end of the fly, making it very cosy.[11]

Francis also designed a lightweight 2-kilogram aluminium camp oven, replacing the 9-kilogram cast-iron version.[12]

Culler Maurice (Red) Fairhall described a tent camp:

TOP A hunters' tent camp, Camerons Flat, Otago, 1930.
PHOTO: ALEXANDER TURNBULL LIBRARY, WELLINGTON, PACOLL-6208-41
BOTTOM In 2014, Golden Bay DOC staff built a replica tent camp (pictured) to replace the last known intact Forest Service-era tent camp (which had become badly dilapidated) on the same site in the Cobb Valley. In 2016, Golden Bay Alpine & Tramping Club members, working with DOC, built a second replica tent camp, called the Soper Shelter, in the Stanley Valley, also in Kahurangi National Park. PHOTO: SHAUN BARNETT/BLACK ROBIN PHOTOGRAPHY

A deer culler makes a precarious single-rope crossing of the West Coast's Kokatahi River, circa 1950s. PHOTO: JOCK FISHER

When we camped we only had tent camps, no huts. Sometimes we might have an old musterer's hut but mostly we put up a camp which consisted of a tent 6 foot by 6 foot which we slept in, with a big fly over the top. It had laced galley sides and you built a wooden chimney at one end as big as you could. You stacked rocks and mud in there to protect the wood, but you always kept a bucket of water alongside because the chimney would regularly catch fire …

These fireplaces served the purpose. But to show how you treasured things, if you went somewhere further afield and in the long grass you found an old kerosene tin, or even a biscuit tin, you would flatten it and put it in your pack. You would take this treasure back to camp and nail it onto the chimney. Some of those chimneys were really elaborate …

You would go to endless trouble to build a decent bunk or a little table for your food. Some of those pieces of furniture were beautifully made, real works of art.[13]

While packhorses could be used to supply the more accessible valley camps, cullers working in rugged or heavily forested areas had to carry all their own food and equipment. Rex Forrester: 'The worst loads of the lot are tinned food and cases of ammunition. It is all dead weight with lumpy corners and it hangs heavy on your back.'[14]

This meant the cullers could shoot in remote locations for only limited periods – usually no more than a week – before having to head out for additional supplies. Efficiency was even less on the tops, where food supplies dwindled fast and rough weather often forced cullers to abandon fly camps. Before Ken Francis secured lightweight silk tents for fly camps, the only alpine tents available were extremely heavy ex-army canvas models weighing 80 kilograms.[15] No wonder many cullers opted instead to sleep wrapped in deer hides.

Cullers shot tens of thousands of deer, some of them tallying up fantastic numbers, but the deer persisted. In the latter part of the 1930s, as the DIA campaign wore on with no end in sight, the need for more permanent shelter became increasingly apparent. Canvas rotted and was more vulnerable to storms and accidental fire, and the occupants suffered during cold snaps, particularly after heavy snowfalls. In the South Island, our parrot equivalent of a vandal caused havoc, too, as Ken Francis recalled: 'Later we had trouble with keas ripping the ridges of our alpine tents in our absence and exposing our vital reserves of food to the weather. This was a serious problem which remained unsolved.'[16] Lilo mattresses provided another favourite target: kea loved to peck holes in them 'and watch the puff of talcum that came out'.[17]

Another frustration with tent camps was the necessity of dismantling them each winter: vermin, kea and other humans had no respect for food supplies left on site. Establishing huts would enable cullers to leave caches of stored supplies in locked cupboards.[18] Accordingly, in the late 1930s Yerex developed plans for using planes to air-drop materials to supply camps and build huts. But he was too far ahead of aviation technology – aircraft of the day were too deficient in both power and manoeuvrability to enable safe operation in rugged mountain country. No twin-engine planes then existed in New Zealand.

Hunters Need Huts

In 1938, Yerex reported on the establishment of two 'permanent bases', one near Lake Waikaremoana in Te Urewera, and the other at Woodrow, Stewart Island/Rakiura. At these bases, a field officer would supervise a ranger and hunters. In addition to deer culling, these staff would work to 'put in tracks, erect huts, overhaul equipment, etc. … with the idea of constantly improving communications as they go'.[19] Yerex intended more such bases for the Tararuas and Fiordland. In short, he planned a strategy that preceded the one adopted wholeheartedly by the Forest Service twenty years later.

The following year, at a 1939 DIA conference, Yerex responded to criticism about the remoter valleys not being effectively cleared of deer by outlining quite extensive hut-building plans:

> The remedy appears to be to build more huts, and to build them in the more remote places and we must have more tracks … And even in places like the Landsborough we must try to get horse up there. If we could put a horse track

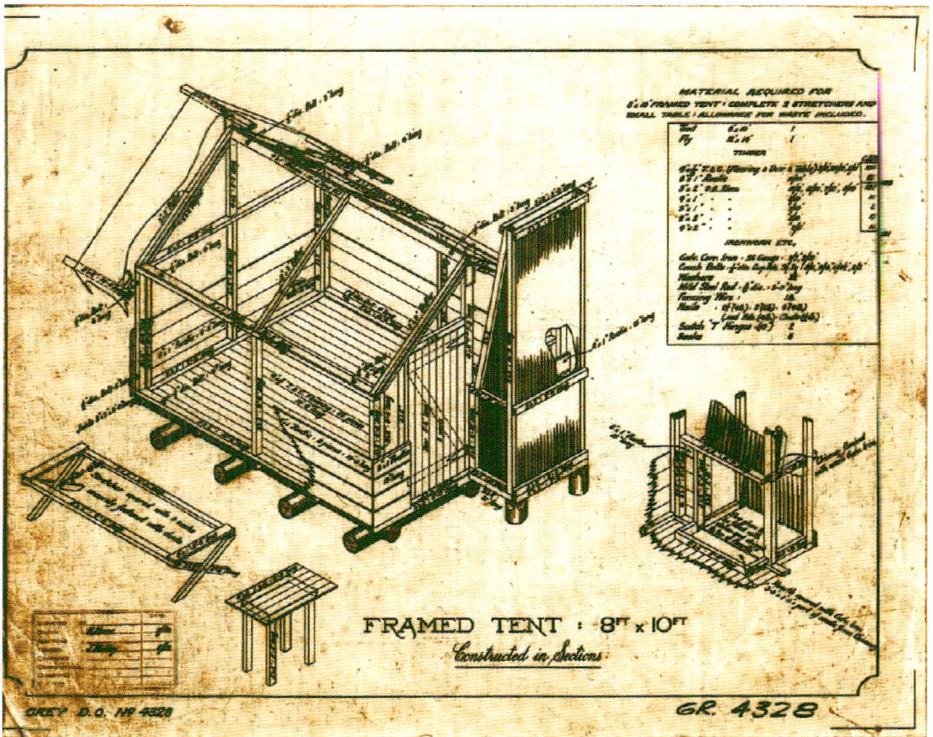

A 1930 architectural drawing for a Public Works Department 'tent frame hut'. These had wooden floors and framing, but a canvas roof. The DIA used this design in the Haast–Landsborough catchment during the 1940s, and it also served as a basic blueprint for later bivs and huts. ILLUSTRATION: COURTESY OF OPUS CONSULTANTS, GREYMOUTH

> over Harper's Bluff we could run our stores right up to the head of the valley … We do not want to make pack horse of our men. They will work better if they have less carrying to do.[20]

War and the First Deer-control Huts

Once again, however, financial constraints thwarted the DIA. Just as New Zealand began to pull out of the Depression at the end of the 1930s, the Second World War erupted, diminishing what could have become a much more widespread and intensive hut-building period in New Zealand's history. Nevertheless, despite the war, some construction did occur.

The DIA also collaborated with at least one tramping club to build a hut. In 1939, the department encouraged the Heretaunga Tramping Club to build a hut in the eastern Ruahine Range. The club agreed, chose a location in the Waikamaka River headwaters, and completed the hut over the summer of 1939–40 using £5 provide by the DIA for materials.[21]

In Fiordland, DIA cullers built several huts, of which now only two survive: the 1941 Clark Hut (now called Historic Clark Hut) in the Grebe Valley,

Rangers Hut, Landsborough Valley, pictured in 2007. This historic DIA base hut occupies a fine position downstream of Strutt Bluff. The first Rangers Hut was built in 1928 using a legacy left by a wealthy deerstalker, but by 1941 it had deteriorated and was replaced with two DIA 'tent frame huts' joined by a porch. PHOTO: CHRIS COCHRAN

and Rodgers Inlet Hut on Lake Monowai, a weatherboard hut also built in the 1940s.[22]

In 1941, the DIA also purchased 'tent frame huts' from the Public Works Department (PWD) and strategically relocated these at various places in the Haast–Landsborough and Makarora catchments. According to DOC historian Jackie Breen, these comprised the first real concerted government effort to build a network of culling huts. DIA Assistant Director Bert Vercoe described them: 'These huts are 8 × 10 with iron roofs, iron chimney, wooden floor and the sides boarded up half way or approximately 3 feet, the rest of the wall being 8 × 10 tents … These frames are all bolted and it would be an easy matter to take them down and shift them.'[23]

The first deer-culling huts were born. Only one original survives, in the Roaring Billy tributary of the Haast, albeit in a derelict state. Two more survive in the lower Landsborough Valley. Joined by a porch, they were constructed in 1941 as part of this first network of culling huts. Later attempts to preserve them saw corrugated iron nailed to the exterior. Known as Rangers Hut, it became an important base for cullers operating in the area. This historically significant hut combines elements of both road-making and deer-culling structures, and is now one of the oldest surviving huts built specifically for deer culling.[24]

The original Anderson Memorial Hut, with its unusual curved roof, pictured in the winter of 1977. Built using a Public Works Department design in 1946, it was the first deer-control hut in the Tararua Range, and lasted until 1979, when the Forest Service replaced it with the hut still in use today. PHOTO: GEOFF SPEARPOINT

Air-drops Take Off

After the Second World War, developments in aircraft technology opened up new possibilities for establishing huts. In 1946, the DIA undertook a highly successful supply air-drop in Marlborough for goat cullers, and now considered employing aircraft for hut building too. Yerex – promoted to Major after serving as head of the Forest and Jungle Warfare School at Mt Holdsworth – began to plan a network of huts in the Tararua Range. These huts, placed no more than eight hours' tramp apart, would not only house professional deer cullers, but hopefully also encourage recreational deerstalkers to help control deer.[25]

Before the war, private hunters had been prohibited from stalking in some areas, notably state forests, where government cullers were operating, so this marked an important shift in attitude. A tradition of allowing public access to huts built for government shooters began.[26]

Despite an offer of help from the Canterbury Mountaineering Club, which had considerable experience erecting backcountry huts, Yerex adopted his own approach. PWD architects designed a hut that could be air-dropped by pilots from the department's Aerodrome Services Branch. Plans developed for a nationwide network of between fifty and eighty huts.[27]

The first to be built was one near Mt Crawford on the main Tararua Range in January 1946. PWD pilot Oliver Anderson transported the materials in a Miles Gemini fixed-wing aircraft.[28] Wooden framing for the three-bunk hut was cut into sections no more than 1 metre long and 2.5 centimetres wide, which could be bundled into packages suitable for dropping from the aircraft by parachute. The *Evening Post* reported: 'In the first flights over the mountain neat parcels of stores swung pendulum-like beneath their tiny parachutes, to bounce finally, unharmed, on the snowgrass-covered plateau … Further trips were made while weather conditions permitted, for although baffling wind-currents from the rugged hillside could not deter the pilots, fog and mist on the "tops" made it impossible to land equipment.'[29]

War-surplus Royal New Zealand Air Force Dural aluminium sheets, used for the cladding and chimney, resulted in the curious curved roof.[30] Anderson died on a later flight in Fiordland (see p. 204), and in remembrance of him the hut became known as Anderson Memorial Hut.[31] The age of using aircraft to build huts had begun, and although marred by Anderson's death, continued to go from strength to strength. From 1948, smaller and more manoeuvrable planes such as the Beaver and Auster allowed air-drops in more demanding terrain.[32]

Air-drops were not only important for transporting materials to build huts; they also largely negated the onerous task of lugging in food and equipment. Rex Forrester recalled that packing in supplies before air-drops had sometimes taken weeks.[33] Joff Thomson recalled: 'When I think of those months of back-breaking toil packing in supplies to the valleys of the Makarora and the Haast, I envy the hunter of today. Not that he is entirely dependent on the plane, but there are few areas where his supplies cannot be dropped to him and that makes a world of difference.'[34] One disadvantage, however, was carrying out the parachutes, which made 'a big, bulky and heavy load, particularly if the chutes were wet'.[35]

Before the start of each summer, cullers still had to lug in all tent camps and equipment, plus sufficient food and ammunition to last until the first air-drop, an operation that took six to ten days. And at the end of the summer shooting season, the camps had to be dismantled and cleaned out of food and equipment for the winter.[36]

Huts would solve many of these inefficiencies. Somehow, however, Yerex's plans for more Tararua huts were stymied. Intentions for building a further twenty such huts in other parts of the country over the 1947–48 summer were not realised. Nevertheless, hut building had become an important objective of the DIA and it began to pick up pace, at least in some key regions.[37]

Regional Hut Developments

In the bush country of Te Urewera, DIA cullers constructed several huts in the early 1950s, seemingly to a more or less standard design. Where the forest could supply building materials, cullers used them, and often took the most durable timber available: heart totara. Practical though many cullers were, not all rated highly as builders. Of cullers wielding a hammer, Allan Farmer quipped, 'The best you could say about the results was that his second hut was better than his first and the third might end up much as it was supposed to be.'[38]

An exception was Rex Forrester, who knew enough about building to erect two huts that still stand today: Te Totara Hut (Te Urewera National Park) and Rogers Hut (Whirinaki Forest Park), both built in the winter of 1952. Although the cold and the short daylight hours must have been cursed, hut building usually occurred in winter, as this left the summer free for shooting deer.

The year 1955 saw significant hut-building activity. In Tararua Forest Park, both Bannister Basin and Dorset Ridge huts were built from air-dropped materials, while in Canterbury two three-bunk huts were constructed: Rokeby, on what is now the St James Walkway; and Jervois, on pastoral lease land.[39]

However, it was on the West Coast that DIA staff built the most huts. DOC historian Jackie Breen has documented huts built in the region during this period. Her figures for the years leading up the NZFS takeover in 1956 demonstrate considerable activity: one in 1949 (Prices Flat), one in 1950 (Nolans), two in 1951, five in 1952 (including Slaty Creek, Tutaekuri and Mud Flats), three in 1953, five in 1954 and four in 1955. Of these huts, most no longer exist, either because they did not last or because they were replaced by later huts. For example, the DIA built Mud Flats Hut in the Arahura in 1952, but in 1967 this was replaced with the existing hut.[40]

One of the oldest surviving DIA huts on the West Coast is the historic Prices Flat Hut in the rugged Whitcombe Valley. Constructed in 1949, it's a curious example of a slab hut built at a time when this primitive style of construction had become something of an anachronism.[41]

The Whitcombe River, named after explorer Henry Whitcombe, who drowned in the Taramakau River after becoming the first European through the valley in 1863, is typical of many West Coast valleys: heavily gorged, extremely wet, densely forested and hemmed in by rugged, glaciated mountains. If anywhere in New Zealand needed decent huts, it was here. Tracks had existed in the valley since explorer Charlie Douglas first cut them in 1906–07 for the New Zealand Geological Survey, which also established the first huts in the valley in about 1908. By the 1950s, however, these huts had deteriorated and cullers needed new shelter.[42]

Cullers Tom Lyes and Noel Bonnington built Prices Flat Hut in 1949. They used some material from one of the survey huts at Vincent Creek, but cut timber for the framing and cladding out of the surrounding bush. Significantly, though, other materials were air-dropped in – the first example of this occurring on the West Coast. Tools, nails, netting and malthoid (for the roof) survived being dropped onto a nearby shingle creek bed without a parachute. Although somewhat modified, the hut remains an historic example of West Coast DIA slab hut design.[43]

Slaty Creek Hut, situated in the Waiheke River, Ahaura Valley, is the other

Rob Brown at the historic Prices Flat Hut, Whitcombe Valley, 2001. First built by DIA cullers in 1949, the hut remains in roughly original condition, despite modifications (the NZFS laid a concrete floor in 1957). A 1983 restoration helped ensure its survival as an important example of West Coast DIA slab hut design. PHOTO: SHAUN BARNETT//BLACK ROBIN PHOTOGRAPHY

surviving example of slab construction on the West Coast. Completed in 1952, it is the last hut of its type built without aircraft assistance. The four-bunk hut, fashioned from slabs of locally felled red beech, had a malthoid and iron roof, with materials probably carried in by packhorse. Future West Coast huts were largely made from prefabricated materials air-dropped onto site.[44]

In fact, the West Coast would become the hotbed of hut development in New Zealand, one that contributed to the great explosion of huts built from the late 1950s until the early 1970s. But it was not the DIA that would build these huts; that role fell to the New Zealand Forest Service, which through intense political manoeuvring finally gained responsibility for deer control in 1956 – a role it had sought ever since the deer control campaign had begun more than twenty-five years earlier.

SHAUN BARNETT

Historic Clark Hut 1941 FIORDLAND NATIONAL PARK

Historic Clark Hut is located in the upper Grebe Valley, in eastern Fiordland. Although dark, the interior of the hut has considerable rustic charm, with beech-pole framing, sacking bunks and an open stone fireplace. Apart from a small cooking bench, that's about all there is to it. The original door was constructed from sawn rimu but has since been replaced, and the lean-to wood shed is a later addition too.

The structure is an example of a slab hut crafted from hand-adzed timber during the Department of Internal Affairs deer-culling era. The cladding is split beech, the floor wooden and the piles made from durable broadleaf timber. Fewer and fewer of these huts now survive, particularly in Fiordland, where in the 1970s the park board conducted a purge of deer-culling huts, demolishing most.[1] Clark Hut is the last split beech hut in Fiordland, and one of only two remaining deer-culling huts in the national park. Rodger Inlet Hut, on the shores of Lake Monowai, is the other.[2]

Internal Affairs culler Archie Clark built the hut in 1941, assisted by another culler, Allan Cookson. Clark was a builder by trade, which is probably one reason why the hut has survived so well. While the shelter is now most easily accessed using a side track from the popular Green Lake Track, which begins at Borland Road, this road did not exist in the 1940s. Clark and Cookson instead had a long approach from Lake Monowai. While they used local materials to build the beech-pole framing and slab cladding, other materials had to be transported in using a clinker-built whaleboat on Lake Monowai. Until an outboard motor was installed on the boat, the men used sail and oar to power it across the lake. From Boat Harbour at the lake-head, the men had to carry the materials over 9 kilometres of bush track to reach the hut site, the round trip taking an entire day.[3]

Soon after the pair built the hut, Archie Clark moved in to become the first resident culler. A skilled hunter, Clark developed a reputation as one of the most successful of all the cullers. Rex Forrester wrote in his book *Hunting in New Zealand*: 'One of the old-time government hunters, Archie Clark, averaged out at a bullet and a half for the many thousands of deer he shot through the years. There is no doubt that he must have been a crack shot, but I have heard fellers who knew him well say that he did it by expert stalking.'[4] Graeme Caughley, author of *The Deer Wars*, rated him among the finest dozen cullers of the DIA era.[5]

By 1947, another culler, appropriately named William Deer, witnessed the crash of a Percival Proctor plane in the nearby Jaquiery Stream. Deer marched out to get help, but no one survived.[6] The pilot, Oliver Anderson, was the same man who had, just a year before, pioneered the use of planes to build huts in the Tararua Range (see p. 202).

Archie Clark (left) and Bill Chisholm lead a team of cullers in the Grebe Valley, circa 1940s. PHOTO: LES PRACY

In the mid-1960s, Clark Hut took on a new function when a Forest Service 'Forest and Range Experiment Station' team based themselves there to carry out research on red deer. Headed by Graeme Caughley, the team included Nigel Prickett and Daryl Marshall, who hunted the Jaquiery and Florence valleys over the summer of 1966–67.[7]

By this time hunters had the advantage of regular food drops, delivered by air from fixed-wing planes. It certainly beat lugging in supplies on foot – at least if all went well. Meat hunter Jim Kane, also based at the hut that summer, had a rough introduction to the researchers. One day in October 1966 he found food parcels raining down near the hut. Legendary Southland pilot Bill Black had jettisoned his load a little too accurately, and Kane must have felt like he was being bombarded.

The second drop, in January 1967, was equally on target. Daryl Marshall recalled that Kane worked very hard hauling deer carcases out and often slept the sleep of the dead: 'Jim had three alarm clocks, two in billies to accentuate the noise, and even the combined racket of this raucous noise sometimes failed to wake him.'[8] Kane did wake up after hearing the roar of the Dominie, however, and was almost knocked over when a sack burst through the door, skidded over the floor and upended his camp oven of its contents. A second drop fell from the sky with equal impunity, when a load containing spuds and cans dented the roof.[9]

Clark Hut suffered more serious damage when another pilot scored a direct hit on the chimney with a box of ammunition. Legend has it that the chimney repairs used materials from the 1947 plane wreck.[10]

Basic maintenance ensured Clark Hut remained in reasonable condition through the following decades, but by the 1990s it needed more serious attention. In 1994, now recognising the hut had significant heritage value, DOC began remedial work. Annual maintenance and timber preservation work will hopefully ensure a long life for this rare and historic structure.[11]

SHAUN BARNETT

TOP AND BOTTOM Clark Hut, 2008.
PHOTOS: SHAUN BARNETT/BLACK ROBIN PHOTOGRAPHY

Slaty Creek Hut 1952 WAIHEKE VALLEY, WEST COAST

Government cullers began operations in Westland in the 1930s, but activity tapered off during the Second World War. Culling began again after E. R. Rye from the Department of Internal Affairs, Canterbury, overflew north and central Westland in 1947, reporting considerably increased deer numbers. The DIA built several huts between the Waiheke and Perth valleys on the West Coast around 1950. Today, these have particular historic significance, representing the switch from slab huts – built on site from local materials – to huts prefabricated off site. Slaty Creek Hut was one of the very last departmental huts cut from timber on site and built using technology and skills that were of a bygone era even by that stage.[1]

DIA hunters built the hut in the winter of 1952 from red beech trees felled nearby. The builders hand-hewed piles and structural beams from the heart timber. For the exterior cladding they cut slabs, and they lined the roof with chicken wire and malthoid paper, and covered it with flat sheet iron. The only window, made of Perspex, is probably original. Inside, timber for the bunks was hand-adzed too, with mesh wire between. Even the floor slabs comprise hand-adzed red beech.[2] It's quite a rustic affair.

In the same year, DIA staff built another hut, Tutaekuri Junction Hut, a few hours away at the fork of the Tutaekuri and Trent rivers. This was one of the first huts in Westland built from air-dropped materials, but in 2008 it was replaced by the Department of Conservation with a new six-bunk hut a kilometre up the Tutaekuri River.

Historically, the Waiheke Valley has provided access to Amuri Pass on the Main Divide, between the Lewis Valley to the east and the Ahaura and Grey rivers in the west. At an altitude of 993 metres, Amuri Pass offered an easy alternative to Harper Pass in the south and Lewis Pass in the north, and as a consequence a pack track was constructed over it during the 1860s gold-mining era. This gave the Waiheke some prominence, and another hut possibly existed there as late as the 1940s, built by a culler called 'Climo'.[3] However, this disappeared (it probably burnt down) and Slaty Creek Hut replaced it. It is easy now to think that culling and outdoor recreation have been the only activities in places like this, but as late as 1957 cattle mobs of several hundred were still being driven over Amuri Pass and down the Waiheke, where the drovers put Slaty Creek Hut to good use.[4]

A 1970s hunting guidebook stated that, like all huts in the Ahaura catchment, Slaty Creek was fully equipped with billies, camp ovens and axes.[5] By then, the Forest Service had assumed control of the hut.[6] However, by 1981 the Lake Sumner Forest Park map described the hut as 'derelict'.[7] At this stage, of course, the Forest Service had long developed its own style of huts, making the status of Slaty Creek Hut quite tenuous. Once their original function has diminished, older huts are often left to collapse, unappreciated. Sometimes, however, a new generation with fresh eyes gets inspired by the history these huts represent. Fortunately, Slaty Creek Hut was left to itself, rather than pulled down.

It is a credit to the durability of heart red beech timber that Slaty Creek Hut has lasted. However, when DOC began assessing its historical value in the mid-1990s, they found the hut in a sorry state. It was clearly important, but needed committed staff with a will to bring it back from the brink. Many DOC staff rallied around, and in April 2006 a plan was drawn up by conservation architect Chris Cochran and DOC historian Jackie Breen. By 19 May 2006, Dave Hawes, a Reefton builder, DOC worker Scotty and the rest of the team were able to write in the logbook: 'Hut restored. Still needs a bit of work. Hope you enjoy. Subfloor, roof and framing repaired. Hand split and hand adzed slabs for the exterior and floor repairs. Hand adzed timbers on the chimney and recycled tin from Tutaekuri Hut built in same era. Toilet and meat safe behind hut. Cheers, Nia Rowlands PM Historic.'[8]

When Rob Brown and I stayed in the hut in June 2011, it drizzled outside but we enjoyed the winter night, warmed by the fire in the ambience of a basic but nicely restored old slab hut.

GEOFF SPEARPOINT

LEFT Slaty Creek Hut, circa 1950s. PHOTO: HARRY BIMLER, COURTESY OF NZ DEER CULLERS, WWW.NZDEERCULLERS.ORG.NZ
OPPOSITE Slaty Creek Hut in 2011. PHOTO: GEOFF SPEARPOINT

Kiwi Hut 1937 and Museum Hut 1958 POPLARS STATION, CANTERBURY

The high country … life demands the best of men, women, and animals; it has a way of 'bringing out' character, as it brought out Dick Morris's.
– Robin Patterson, *A Sock in My Stew*[1]

Some huts are irrevocably linked with a backcountry personality. Kiwi Hut occupied a pleasant, sunny location near the junction of the Hope and Kiwi rivers not far from Lake Sumner, and for almost twenty years was the home of well-known deer culler Dick Morris. Museum Hut is its successor.

A culler, naturalist and radio personality, Morris was an unforgettable character who for much of his life lived in the Lake Sumner area. Born in Oxford, he first came to the Hope Valley in 1937, when he was in his thirties.

For a while in the early 1940s, Morris worked for Internal Affairs as a culler, when his rather lax attitude to personal hygiene earned him the nickname 'Dirty Dick'. It also meant other cullers refused to work with him. Major Yerex insisted upon a high standard of tidiness and cleanliness in his camps, and Morris did not meet the standard by a long shot. Undeterred, Morris went freelance, selling skins to earn a living, which was quite profitable during this period until prices slumped following the end of the Second World War. Around this time, he began his more or less continual occupation of Kiwi Hut, on Poplars Station.

Kiwi Hut was built from materials salvaged from roadmen's huts originally used by workers constructing the Lewis Pass highway in the 1930s. After the road was opened in 1937, Poplars Station staff bought several of these huts and dismantled them for their timber and iron. Station hand Charlie Wilks then used the materials to build two huts in the Hope Valley, one called Three Mile and the other Kiwi Hut.[2]

Morris, although married, rarely went into Christchurch to see his wife, and the union – unsurprisingly to everyone but Morris himself – eventually dissolved. He was no hermit though; he had an infectious delight in the natural world, and welcomed anyone who visited his neck of the woods. Forest Service scientist Ashley Cunningham was one of those who met Morris, and recalled:

> His camp was a bit odoriferous, and you had to spoon carefully in the condensed milk to avoid bringing out a dead fly. And Dick didn't seem to wash while in the field. But these drawbacks didn't seem to matter by comparison with his wonderful knowledge of the world around him. Dick Morris was a brilliant observer and quite eloquent. On his rare visits to Christchurch his radio broadcasts about the high country endeared him to thousands of Canterbury listeners.[3]

LEFT Dick Morris inside Kiwi Hut with Laffy, probably early 1950s. PHOTO: BILL DUKES, FROM *A SOCK IN MY STEW*
OPPOSITE Museum Hut, with the walnut tree planted by Dick Morris, photographed in 2004.
PHOTO: SHAUN BARNETT/BLACK ROBIN PHOTOGRAPHY

Musterer Bert Bunting recalled spending a few weeks with Morris at Kiwi Hut. He reckoned Morris's cooking tasted alright as long as you ignored the preparation methods. Most people usually made boiled pudding in a clean flour bag, but Bunting recalled: 'Well I saw Dick do this once, but he used a singlet knotted at each end – and it looked as though it hadn't been washed for a while. He boiled it in a billy. But the pudding was OK and the singlet came out clean … no worries at all.'[4]

Morris had a teasing sense of humour and liked to try out several tricks on visitors. When someone arrived at Kiwi Hut, he often asked if they wanted fish for dinner. If the answer was yes, he would grab his rod and head towards the river at speed. He would then return within minutes carrying a large trout, invariably impressing his guests. Little did they know that he had a small pond where he kept pre-caught trout for just such occasions.[5] Dick's constant companions were his dog, Laffy, and packhorse, Mixer. He taught them both to lie down and play dead, and he'd join them. Mixer got so used to hunting that Morris could shoot from horseback, and the packhorse knew to turn his head sideways to avoid the muzzle blast.[6] Mixer had a great capacity for carrying large loads, and Morris could even coax him onto the tops, where he was loaded up with deerskins.[7]

Another person who spent time with Morris during the 1950s was a young tramper called Robin Patterson, who later collected stories about the man in a wonderful book called *A Sock in My Stew*. The book not only celebrates the life of Morris, but other backcountry characters from the era.

In March 1957, Dick Morris died unexpectedly young, aged just fifty-four, from a stroke. In November that year, just months after his death, Kiwi Hut mysteriously burnt down.[8]

Canterbury Museum staff who knew Morris decided to build a replacement hut, known as Museum Hut, nearby in 1958. The Forest Service helped by transporting some materials in.[9] One of the museum staff, Rhys Griffiths, recalled the effort of carrying in materials from Poplars Station for the new hut: 'I've still got the scars. Looking back, I would say the worst thing to carry was glass because it was so heavy, and you had to be so careful with it: just a dead weight tied to your pack.' He added:

> Carrying the sheets of iron into a nor'west wind proved to be nigh impossible, too. The solution, we found, was to roll them up into bundles and carry them like that. I built the fireplace, basing it on the design of the one in Dick's hut: a raised hearth so that it was easier to reach, and the extra height helped send smoke up the chimney. It was a big chimney and we used it to smoke fish. We split them, rubbed in salt and brown sugar and left them in the chimney overnight … over embers on which green manuka logs had been placed. There was a tremendous labour that went into that hut which was matched eventually by our very great pleasure at moving into it.[10]

Poplars Station has since kept the seven-bunk Museum Hut open to the public when its staff are not using it. In 1978, Forest Service personnel added a sink, new windows and a water tank.[11] The hut provides an alternative to staying in the much larger Hope Kiwi Lodge in adjacent Lake Sumner Forest Park. A plaque outside commemorates Dick Morris, and across the valley is a small bush tarn named after him.

Even though Morris never saw Museum Hut, the place has something of his spirit. Outside, the walnut tree he planted still grows, paradise ducks continue to cry their melancholy calls, and the views over this delightful part of the Canterbury backcountry are much as Morris enjoyed them.

SHAUN BARNETT

TOP LEFT Dick Morris with kea featuring on the cover of *A Sock in My Stew*.
BOTTOM LEFT Dick Morris posing with bow and arrow, early 1950s. PHOTO: SHEILA CUNNINGHAM
OPPOSITE Geoff Spearpoint at Museum Hut, August 2004. PHOTO: SHAUN BARNETT/BLACK ROBIN PHOTOGRAPHY

Rogers Hut 1952 WHIRINAKI FOREST PARK, BAY OF PLENTY

Although the Department of Internal Affairs had been culling deer in Te Urewera since 1938, by the early 1950s the region remained a virtual wilderness, with only three huts in the whole of its vast forested extent. In the winter of 1952, plans were afoot to build four huts south of the Ruatahuna base, where no huts existed at all.[1]

During that winter, a DIA team led by culler Rex Forrester built the first of these huts, called Te Totara, in the Waiau Valley, in what is now Te Urewera National Park. Other cullers in the team included Bernie Chaney, Ron Christensen and Vic Nelson, and Jack Still served as packman. None had any previous hut-building experience, although during a stint of culling in the South Island, Forrester had learnt the art of hand-splitting timber in the manner in which early buildings were constructed by New Zealand's first European pioneers.[2]

After Te Totara was completed, the team began construction of a second hut – Rogers Hut. While one totara had provided sufficient timber for the Te Totara Hut, Forrester's team used matai studs and a red beech interior for Rogers Hut. By felling trees on site, construction costs were minimised and the lugging in of timber avoided.

Although the hut is sometimes called Te Wairoa Hut, the name Rogers Hut holds most sway. Rex Forrester named it after his son, who was born in Rotorua Hospital during its construction. Roger later recalled the effort undertaken by his father's team to built the hut: 'The old man and his three mates packhorsed all the materials from Ruatahuna, through White's Clearing to a bit of a shelter they set up on the saddle between the Waiau and Okahu valleys. But from there it was too steep for horses and they had to back-pack everything the rest of the way – windows, iron that was in rolls for the walls, axes, hammers and nails, the lot.'[3]

The building skills of cullers varied considerably, and it's a testimony to Forrester's ability that Rogers Hut and Te Totara have survived for more than half a century. The square design and slab interior of Rogers Hut contrast markedly to later huts built by the Forest Service.

Occupying a small grassy clearing near the junction of the Mangakahika and Moerangi streams, the bright orange hut has changed somewhat since the 1950s: the original flat iron roof has been replaced by corrugated iron, and tongue-and-groove wooden flooring replaces the original dirt floor.

By the mid-1990s, Rogers Hut required serious attention. It had a bad lean and some of the timber was rotten, and for a while there was even talk of demolition. However, Department of Conservation ranger Andy Blick and a local archaeologist managed to gain a reprieve for the hut by seeing to it that it was accorded historic status, and planned its restoration.

The 1995 restoration involved replacing some of the hut's original interior with fresh beech.

Deer culler Don Rush at Te Totara Hut, Waiau Valley, Te Urewera National Park, 1959. PHOTO: DON RUSH, COURTESY OF NZ DEER CULLERS, WWW.NZDEERCULLERS.ORG.NZ

LEFT Rex Forrester with six red deer, Mount Cook station, circa 1947. PHOTO: FROM *HUNTER FOR HIRE*, COURTESY OF ROGER FORRESTER. RIGHT Rogers Hut, 2005. PHOTO: SHAUN BARNETT/BLACK ROBIN PHOTOGRAPHY

Carpenter Eric Murray found an old beech log and used an Alaskan mill and adze to reshape replica slabs. According to Blick, the log was 'riddled with 303 bullets which didn't help the saw much'.[4] The team also built a veranda floor, and installed a water tank.[5]

Blick's finishing touch was a stained-glass window, inspired by the one at Fenella Hut (see p. 308). It was then that the hut's historic status proved to be a bit of a 'double-edged adze'.[6] The change got Blick into trouble with the archaeologist, but he reckoned the dark old hut needed a bit of light and cheer. This tension between practicality and authenticity is always a thorny issue at the heart of any restoration.[7]

Despite these modifications, the hut exudes much the same backcountry atmosphere it has since Forrester built it – especially when smoke creeps out the chimney and mist closes in on the surrounding canopy.

Forrester left culling to become a fisheries officer in Rotorua, then went on to forge a career as a well-known professional guide and author, writing hunting classics like *The Chopper Boys* (1983) and *The Helicopter Hunters* (1988). As a young hunter, Andy Blick had devoured these books and so it was a great honour for him to arrange a helicopter flight for Rex Forrester to look at the restored hut, along with his other ex-culling mates Alan Farmer and Russell Tulloch. Farmer quipped that the visit was the longest the friends had all lasted together without having an argument.[8]

Rex Forrester died in 2001, aged seventy-one. The following year, son Roger buried his father's ashes near the hut. For a man who spent so much of his life in the bush, there couldn't be a better resting place.

Rogers and Te Totara huts are among the few slab huts remaining in New Zealand from this era, and DOC have ear-marked them as historic animal control huts worthy of maintaining in near-original state. However, as the use it still receives by trampers and hunters testifies, the six-bunk Rogers Hut is no museum piece. Surely that would have pleased Rex Forrester.

SHAUN BARNETT

THE FOREST SERVICE TAKES OVER NEW ZEALAND FOREST SERVICE HUTS

> ... it was the New Zealand Forest Service that had the structure, the money, the clout and the will to scatter orange huts across the wilderness like Jaffas sent rolling through the landscape.
> – Mark Pickering, *Huts: Untold Stories of Back-country New Zealand* (2010)

By the mid-1950s, deer continued to persist in New Zealand despite the combined efforts of meat hunters, recreational deerstalkers and a sustained twenty-five-year culling programme by the Department of Internal Affairs. The word 'extermination' no longer peppered the department's annual reports, and it measured success largely in terms of numbers of deer shot – an increasingly meaningless figure. After its quarter-century deer-killing campaign, the DIA lost responsibility for deer control to the New Zealand Forest Service in 1956, a change that was to have far-reaching implications for hut development in New Zealand.

Ever since it lost its bid to control deer to the DIA in 1930, the NZFS had maintained that it was the logical choice to manage culling operations, for two main reasons. First, the NZFS managed many of the areas where deer were considered to be a problem. And second, the Forest Service was better resourced, with trained foresters and scientists who – it hoped – could research and understand the deer problem more thoroughly. The Forest Service argued that shooting deer was all very well, but were culling efforts focused in the right places? Deer, the NZFS believed, most needed controlling in the erosion-prone catchments of major towns and cities, and it had long advocated the policy 'Look after the catchments and the rivers will look after themselves'.[1] NZFS managers, notably Assistant Director Lindsay Poole (a botanist), firmly believed that control of wild animals preserved vegetation, thereby conserving soils and preventing erosion in key catchments.[2]

A new statute passed in 1956, the Noxious Animals Act, made the transfer to the NZFS official, and the takeover came on 1 April that year. Some of the DIA old hands saw this as the worst of April Fool's Day jokes. Mike Bennett, author of *The Venison Hunters* (1979), had a sour view of the change: 'It was not that the Old Firm had been exactly static over the years, but in the tradition of new brooms everywhere, dust had to fly and something had to happen to create the impression that something extra was being done. It was rather reminiscent of a supermarket chain taking over the village grocer's shop.'[3]

In one sense, little changed. Virtually the whole of the former DIA staff – including some fifteen field officers, 100 hunters and support staff – transferred en masse to the Forest Service. Yerex, soon to retire, stayed on at the DIA, and in his place Ron Fraser took charge of deer-culling operations.[4]

But in another sense, particularly with regard to huts and tracks, revolution was afoot. Not long after the NZFS took over deer culling, it embarked on the greatest hut-building programme ever undertaken in New Zealand and, possibly, the world. Mike Bennett summed it up: 'the Forest Service early took on a comprehensive campaign of hut building; contract carpenters were employed and larger parachutes were used for dropping off pre-cut timber. Later, the helicopter completely took over the role of the aerial packhorse.'[5]

Initially, however, NZFS hut design centred on fixed-wing plane transport. Jock Fisher was one of those who had worked for Internal Affairs and was transferred to the NZFS in 1956. He oversaw hut building for both outfits, and recalled:

> I always look back on the hut building as three eras: The Auster era where we dropped rolled up flat iron and four-foot lengths of framing timber from inside the plane. The Cessna era where we dropped rolled up iron and wing loads of six-foot lengths of timber from the wing racks. Then the Helicopter era where we carried in all components for huts.[6]

Initially, the use of fixed-wing planes had a disadvantage in that the length of any materials transported had to be limited to what could fit inside the fuselage. For this reason, the NZFS in Hawke's Bay experimented with a design using a bolt-together Dexion aluminium frame in the Kaweka Range. In 1957, it constructed two four-bunk Dexion huts: Makahu Saddle and Back Ridge. Jock Fisher recalled that Popeye Lucas, a major aviation figure in New Zealand who was heavily involved in air-drops, was the agent for Dexion, and so possibly influenced this decision.[7] Unfortunately, no extant records indicate how many Dexion huts were built, but the two surviving Kaweka huts are important examples of this brief flirtation with the framing.[8]

Mungo Hut, Hokitika catchment, West Coast, in 1991. PHOTO: GEOFF SPEARPOINT

TOP Bernie Coggan with packhorses at Jervois Hut, Canterbury 1956-7. PHOTO: JIM DAVIS
BOTTOM An NZFS airdrop in the Richmond Range, Nelson 1956. PHOTO: BEN GIBBS

Culler Ron Turner began to work for the NZFS under Jock Fisher in 1956, serving in both the West Coast and Nelson–Marlborough conservancies. He recalled:

The Forest Service, with its vastly different attitude towards the welfare of their shooters, started to improve operational standards, and I was part of that new hut building effort. This attitude is not surprising as most of the field officers were former shooters with the old Internal Affairs Department. The push for better huts was repeated in many of the backcountry valleys where shooting operations were carried out.[9]

Indeed, the regional hut-building efforts begun by DIA staff on the West Coast spawned a major development centre for NZFS hut design. At first, the Forest Service had a rather decentralised structure, meaning that regional conservancies often led the way in hut design.[10] Some of the earliest huts built by the NZFS were two-person bivouacs, as they solved the problem of accommodation on the tops. Ron Turner wrote:

Initially, on the West Coast, and after completion of the Wilkinson Hut [an early hut built in the Whitcombe Valley during 1957], we built some of the early bivouacs or 'bivvys' … Being in a snow zone meant the bivvys had to be water-and-moisture-proof and have a dry wooden floor for sleeping on. Food and ammunition would be dropped in by arrangement, also fuel for the kerosene stoves as there was no timber or alpine scrub nearby. These bivouacs may not have attracted a 'star rating', but when the weather suddenly turned foul they were just great.[11]

At first, these bivvies were very basic indeed, comprising not much more than a tent-shaped shell on piles, with a door at one end and a window at the other. In essence, the tent camp had evolved into a bivouac, with flat iron replacing canvas. The dimensions were essentially the same: 3 metres by 2 metres. In the late 1950s, this basic biv design changed rapidly, and by the 1960s bivs were more like small stand-up huts with bunks, and sometimes even boasted fireplaces and chimneys (see p. 228).

Helicopter Huts

While air-drops from fixed-wing planes enormously increased hut-building efficiency, helicopters ushered in a complete revolution. From mid-1950s onwards, commercial helicopters began to operate more widely in New Zealand. Although the first choppers were not particularly useful – culler Jack Lasenby called them 'unstable dragonflies' – helicopters rapidly ensured a transformation in hut design and building efficiency.[12]

With summer and autumn fully occupied by actual culling operations, winter and spring became the default hut-building and track-cutting seasons. In the spring of 1958, NZFS Nelson Conservancy building overseer Phil McConchie erected the first hut in New Zealand built using helicopter-transported materials.

Snow Corboy, the NZFS senior field officer in Nelson, engaged a Bell 47 helicopter to transport precut framing for four new huts in Northwest Nelson

Loading hut building materials, Styx Base Camp, Hokitika, May 1959. PHOTO: JOHN JOHNS, ARCHIVES NZ, M3264

Interior of Back Ridge Hut showing original Dexion framing, 2004. PHOTO: SHAUN BARNETT/BLACK ROBIN PHOTOGRAPHY

(now Kahurangi National Park): Mid Matiri, Luna, Kakapo and Karamea Bend. The huts were a basic four-bunk model, differing from the later NZFS standard S81 design, and another example of how regional offices led hut development before national standards came into force. Materials for all four huts were stacked at Karamea before being flown onto site by the Christchurch-based Braziers Air Works. To save flying costs, the helicopter was transported to Karamea by trailer, but this 'did more damage to the helicopter than the actual flying'.[13]

Ron Turner was employed to help McConchie, and recalled that all did not go smoothly with the first of the planned huts, Mid Matiri, in September 1958: 'There were two trainee hunters with me and my objective was to prepare a landing site for the helicopter, to ready a smoky fire to indicate both the landing zone and wind direction, and to clear the construction site. It rained, and rained, and kept on raining for days with low cloud.'[14]

After running out of food, Turner returned to the base hut at Murchison, only to be reprimanded by Snow Corboy for abandoning his post. Happily, Turner got to fly back in with the helicopter, although it remained cloudy, and he remembered having to 'wipe moisture from inside the Perspex bubble'. He continued:

> My flight was really exhilarating but noisy, lasting some 11 or 12 minutes. It was so easy compared to the wet, miserable hours of struggle and slippery rocks endured the previous day. The first load of timber and iron were placed on site, undamaged, with my pack.
>
> The particular method of construction of these huts called for the flooring to be put down extending to the outer edges of the building prior to erecting the walls. This was an effort to prohibit the entry of any rats, mice and possums, and to cut down on cold draughts. At the entrance end of the hut there was a covered-in area for firewood and a place to store our backpacks.
>
> A 'new' insulating material (sisalation) was provided and we actually

Luna Hut, Karamea valley, Northwest Nelson, January 1964. PHOTO: BEN GIBBS

Building Stone Creek Hut on the Wangapeka Track, Northwest Nelson, December 1962. PHOTO: BEN GIBBS

installed this sheeting back to front so that the silver side faced into the hut thus creating a better, lighter interior. This was a vast improvement from the rolls of dark malthoid sheeting or brown builder's paper used to line earlier huts which, while deflecting condensation from the under surfaces of the roof, made the interior dark. Overlapping joints of the flat metal exterior sheeting were sealed with ormonoid, a thick, black bituminous paint (which had a dual purpose of playing noughts and crosses on the chimneys).[15]

Swarms of insects often caused hardships for builders working on huts. Turner recalled, 'the sandflies were particularly thick at the hut sites, practically driving everybody mad. We must have killed at least 10,000 of them but about 40,000 came to their funeral.'[16]

In order to convince the NZFS head office that the £60 per hour cost of the helicopter was justified, Snow Corboy kept meticulous records of the hut-building exercise. His figures proved emphatically that helicopters were more efficient than a fixed-wing plane, in terms of both cost and time. There were other advantages, too, as Jock Fisher recorded: 'Huts could be precut by the NZFS carpenters at Golden Downs and landed safely on site, with no breakages, making it easier for unskilled hunters to erect.'[17]

Altogether, the NZFS experiment with helicopters was an unqualified success. In recognition of Phil McConchie's efforts, Mid Matiri Hut was later renamed after him. Although they have since been modified, McConchie and Kakapo are the only two surviving huts of the four built that momentous spring of 1958. Karamea Bend Hut has been replaced twice, and Luna Hut was flown out intact to a Tapawera farm when the Trevor Carter Hut replaced it in 2003.[18]

In the late 1950s and early 1960s, helicopters almost completely supplanted fixed-wing planes as the first choice for hut building. Helicopters allowed precision flying, with few lost or damaged loads. Later, longer lengths of timber could be carried on a strop slung beneath the machine, enabling efficient delivery of materials to even tiny bush clearings – something difficult to achieve with a fixed-wing aircraft, as parachutes often went astray in the forest. Helicopters ensured that the NZFS could embark on a grand hut-building programme at lower altitudes.

In the early 1960s, a second phase of hut building using helicopters got underway in the Nelson area, but this time the huts were mostly six-bunkers. The team involved, which included overseer Phil McConchie and carpenters Ray Osman, Graeme Coombes and Bob Sutherland, introduced new professionalism. Osman recalls that prefabricating materials back at base, such as cutting dwangs to the correct length, and scarfing corners and joints, enabled swifter construction in the field.[19] Among others, the huts they built included Speargrass, East Matakitaki, Sabine and Mole Tops in Nelson Lakes; Roebuck in the Richmond Range; Wheel Creek in the Victoria Range; and Pell Stream at Lewis Pass. In addition, base huts were built at road ends or places accessible via four-wheel-drive tracks; these included Mid Glenroy in Nelson Lakes, Branch River in Marlborough and Station Creek in the Maruia Valley.[20]

Employing trained carpenters, and working over summer, dramatically improved hut-building efficiency. In the 1961–62 season, for example, Osman completed an Awatere Valley hut, toilet and all, in just five days with fellow carpenter Bob Sutherland. Several factors helped: 'Long summer days, fine weather, good digging, and Bob under pressure from his fiancée to get back to town employment.'[21]

Ben Gibbs, who worked briefly for the NZFS as a labourer in the Nelson district, recalled building Stone Creek Hut on the Wangapeka Track in the 1960s. He says that eight days was the usual time needed to build a hut, depending on the site's suitability for digging holes for the piles and, of course, the weather. One of the builders usually spent a day hunting to ensure fresh camp meat.[22] Gibbs also recalls:

> [We] used to lay waste to acres of bush in those days – no regard for conservation values! – in order to clear a safe landing area for helicopters. Helicopter … pilots were still learning how to fly them safely in mountain areas. We NZFS hunters and track builders never managed to get a ride in a helicopter. We always had to walk into and out of the site, carrying all our own gear. We baked our own bread and cooked the meat we shot in camp ovens over the open fire.[23]

By this time the carpenters were using standard hut designs formulated in the NZFS head office.

Standard Hut Designs: The Classic NZFS S81 and SF70

In the late 1950s, engineers at the NZFS head office in Wellington adopted the best features of each regional design and combined them to create national standards. The chief architect of these designs was civil engineer Max Cone. By 1958–59, the NZFS had formalised standard designs for a two-bunk biv, a four-bunk hut (S81) and a six-bunk hut (SF70), with three-, five- and seven-bunk variations possible. The designs owed much to the work of Stan Fokerd on the West Coast, and also to the helicopter transportation methods developed by Snow Corboy in Nelson. Soon after, NZFS huts and bivs began to pepper other parts of New Zealand's backcountry.[24]

By the early 1960s, the NZFS hut-building machine had become highly efficient. Its hut building peaked in 1960, when, remarkably, more than sixty huts were erected,[25] and in 1961 a further fifty-five huts were built: twenty-five four-bunkers, seventeen six-bunkers and thirteen two-bunk bivs, equating to more than one per week.[26]

Despite this incredible efficiency, hut building did not always proceed smoothly. In the 1961–62 season, for example, the NZFS dropped materials

Trampers Elise Bryant and Clare O'Neill outside South Huxley Biv, Ruataniwha Conservation Park, 2005. PHOTO: ROB BROWN

onto a flat at Mokihinui Forks after accepting an offer by Westport deerstalkers to move them across the river to a site cleared in the forest for the hut. Disaster struck, however, when a flood swept everything downstream before they got there. Ray Osman recalled the strange sight of mattresses caught 3 metres up in dead tree spars.[27]

NZFS deer-culling huts were basic but comfortable, and usually well positioned near a water supply or provided with a water tank. Although perhaps not intended to last for decades, many of the basic SF70 six-bunk and S81 four-bunk huts have survived remarkably well – a testimony to their sound design. It is no exaggeration to say that they became *the* classic backcountry hut, and an icon of the New Zealand mountains.

In the 1960s, most major catchment areas controlled by the Forest Service got a fair smattering of huts, among them the Ruahine, Tararua, Kaweka and Aorangi ranges in the North Island, and large parts of the Southern Alps, Northwest Nelson, Eyre Mountains, Takitimu Range and the Marlborough mountains. Culling huts were also established on high-country leasehold land, such as at Poplars Station near Lake Sumner Forest Park. The West Coast's Hokitika catchment, flagged early on as a priority area for hut building, soon became so well endowed with huts that one ex-culler quipped, 'How can they possibly have a noxious animal problem in the Hokitika? Half the bloody watershed is under corrugated iron.'[28]

With responsibility for all wild animal operations, the Forest Service also built huts on lands not directly under its jurisdiction, including national parks managed by the Department of Lands and Survey. For example, it built the vast

Unknown Hut, Wilberforce Valley, Canterbury, built in 1961, pictured in 2011. PHOTO: SHAUN BARNETT/BLACK ROBIN PHOTOGRAPHY

There is a suspicion that the unspent portions of the generous annual budgets were burned off in one way by an almost ludicrous surfeit of huts in some areas.
… Orange-coloured huts with large black numbers painted on the roofs blossom every two hours along the river bottoms of some valleys, and on the tops practically every basin has its bivouac or home away from home. They were expensive and largely unnecessary.[30]

How did the NZFS cullers themselves view these huts? Some, like Bennett, thought them too salubrious and lamented the good old days of tent camps, but that was partly nostalgia. Others appreciated them fully. In his book *Pack and Rifle* (1986), NZFS deer culler Philip Holden recalled one 1960s Ruahine Range culling stint when he moved from the Big Hill tent camp to the newly built Ruahine Hut. The change was

sheer heaven … For Ruahine is the latest kind of Forest Service hut: they have six bunks for a start, and each one has a foam rubber mattress. There's also a verminproof food cupboard, a workbench, and several bins for perishables such as flour, butter, cheese and so on. These huts are spacious, very practical and damn comfortable to live in.[31]

majority of huts (more than 80 per cent) in Te Urewera National Park, plus several in Nelson Lakes National Park. In the 1960s and 1970s, Lands and Survey also began building many huts in national parks (see p. 255), but the magnitude of their efforts paled in comparison with that of the NZFS.

Statistics often blunt a good story, but not this one. Between the years 1957 and 1972, the prodigious NZFS machine built 644 huts, 36 shelters, 26 vehicle bridges, 142 footbridges, 22 cableways, 2900 kilometres of roads, 1400 kilometres of four-wheel-drive tracks and about 4000 kilometres of tramping tracks.[29] By the 1970s New Zealanders could boast perhaps the densest network of backcountry facilities in the world, and certainly the only one almost wholly constructed by a government.

In *The Venison Hunters*, Mike Bennett takes a rather jaundiced view of all this development (somewhat echoed by modern-day complaints against DOC's recent hut-building programme):

However, despite such innovations as foam-rubber mattresses to replace the old sack bunks or beds of fern leaves, the entire programme got out of hand.

Most hut food cupboards were regularly stocked by helicopter drops, and gone was the need to lug in supplies and dismantle tent camps for the winter. NZFS cullers could concentrate on their main task – killing deer. By the 1960s, the days of skinning deer were over, and cullers simply took tails as proof of their kills – which were then counted and destroyed by the field officer at the end of each culling stint.

Some thieving from huts by trampers or recreational hunters did occur. Jock Fisher recalls one such occasion when he was shooting in the West Coast's Whitcombe Valley:

[I] had picked up and stacked an air-drop in the Cave Camp, a party of CMC [Canterbury Mountaineering Club] came over the pass and scoffed the only two tins of fruit in the air-drop, which I had put aside for a Christmas treat. We normally did not get tinned fruit in an air-drop in those days. They left a bag of rice in its place. When they got to Prices Flat Hut they noted in the visitor's book their names and the comment 'looks like the Cave Camp has been hit by a grocer shop'. When I got to the hut, I added '… and it was not the self help'. At that time in NZ there were a number of stores called 'The Self Help'.[32]

NZFS deer culler Ted Smith at Neill Forks Hut, Tararua Ranges, Wairarapa circa 1969. Note the well-equipped hut, with tins for storing food and a large range of kitchen utensils, typical of a NZFS deer-culling hut – although *National Geographic* may not always have been standard reading material. PHOTO: PAUL GUSH

However, Fisher recalls that theft was the exception, not the norm, and generally relations in the backcountry were congenial:

> Cullers always had a reasonable outlook regarding trampers and mountaineers and never objected to a hungry man obtaining a feed in our camps … It was often good to meet and hear where they had been and what deer they had seen. And there was always a bit of outside news and world events that they could pass on, and for those sports-minded shooters how the All Blacks were faring in the latest test or how the cricket was going. Nobody had radios in those days.[33]

The Forest Service – to its credit – continued to allow free use of its huts by trampers and deerstalkers. Indeed, the NZFS had recreational use firmly on its agenda as early as 1961, the last year in which it built more four-bunkers than six-bunkers. Cullers usually worked in pairs, and so rarely needed more than four bunks – the fact that the NZFS six-bunkers became the most commonly built huts in 1962 shows how early the agency broadened its view of hut use.[34] Officially, members of the public needed a permit to enter state forests as late as 1965, but for decades the NZFS turned a blind eye to this.

By the end of the 1960s, deer-culling operations had become highly organ-

NZFS deer-cullers Herb Reihana and Kerry (surname unknown), Kuripapango, Hawke's Bay, Mt Kuripapango beyond, October 1966. PHOTO: BRIAN BURDON

ised. NZFS cullers had good tracks and bridges to get around on, and comfortable, well-stocked huts. Rex Forrester wrote in the 1960s that deer culling had become 'very civilized, with untold luxuries like mattresses, kerosene stoves and lamps in advance camps, which are now huts landed by helicopter instead of flytents; and even at the base camps electric stoves and showers'. He noted that shooting had changed from 'an affair of the individual against nature to a concentrated campaign organized like an army exercise … Today there are lots of blokes rushing round with forestry degrees, goatee beards and clipboards covered in figures.'[35]

Forrester's words were not dismissive; he was just commenting on how much had changed since his DIA days, adding: 'In areas like the Urewera Country, the Government has really got the deer down. Only a few years ago Allan Duncan killed 1,100 deer in six months in one Urewera district, but in 1962 it took six hunters as long to kill that many between them.'[36]

Venison Recovery

There is little doubt that the hut-building programme had a positive impact on the efficiency of backcountry animal control. Rather ironically, however, the great advantages of helicopters in transporting hut materials and supplies also made them ideal for shooting deer – so much so, in fact, that by the late 1960s and early 1970s helicopters made Forest Service ground cullers almost obsolete.

As early as 1964, John Henham shot deer from a helicopter piloted by Jack Eskew in the West Coast's Arawhata Valley, signalling an entirely new approach

NEW ZEALAND FOREST SERVICE HUTS 221

Cullers Jim Reed, Dave Down and Jim Warren at Crow Hut, Kawhatau Valley, Ruahine Range, 1966. NZFS huts were usually left unpainted for a short period after building. PHOTO: CHRIS SATHERLEY

to deer hunting.[37] By 1967, commercial venison-recovery helicopter operators began outgunning the foot sloggers. These dextrous machines could flush deer out of the most inaccessible places, surprising them by their sudden arrival and outmanoeuvring the animals with their speed. By the early 1970s, prices for wild venison soared, to the extent that dozens of commercial helicopter operators began to exploit the new bonanza. Many NZFS cullers jumped ship, lured by the better money and kerosene-fuelled adrenalin of a job that, though more dangerous, often got you home in time for tea.

At first these machines were used strictly for venison recovery, but as the market for deer meat expanded, entrepreneurial hunters developed techniques for capturing live deer to stock the country's burgeoning number of deer farms.

Perhaps unsurprisingly, the Forest Service responded slowly at first to these momentous changes, virtually ignoring them in its annual reports. As Graeme Caughley points out in *The Deer Wars*, the NZFS was very reluctant to admit that part of its *raison d'être* had been so quickly outgunned by private helicopters, and for not one dollar of taxpayer expense.[38]

Soon though, the NZFS recognised that the end of its ground-culling days were in sight, and in 1967 granted permits to private venison-recovery operators. On the West Coast the Forest Service also trialled aerial drops of 1080-laced carrots for deer control in the mid-1960s, and in August 1967 undertook its own aerial hunting trial. By 1971–72, the last ground culler on the Forest Service's books finished up on the West Coast, although in other areas, such as the Kawekas and Tararuas, ground cullers continued to operate as late as 1987. By then, however, the supreme effectiveness of aerial hunting had become undeniable.[39]

Huts continued to provide accommodation (and still do) for ground cullers shooting goats in places like Marlborough and the Richmond Range, as these animals were not targets for helicopter operators.

Parallel to the decline of deer culling was a changing understanding of the nature of erosion. Pioneer hunter Newton McConochie, whose hunting heyday was in the early 1900s, later became an influential member of the New Zealand Deerstalkers' Association. In his 1966 book *You'll Learn no Harm from the Hills*, he expressed a theory ahead of its time: 'There is the indisputable fact that erosion has been with us throughout the ages … May I suggest that erosion runs in cycles, varying in locality and time of activity?' McConochie reckoned that possums posed an even greater threat to native forests, and should be targeted rather than deer.[40]

Scientist Patrick Grant later proved emphatically that McConochie's ideas on erosion were correct. By comparing historic photographs with modern images of the Ruahine Range, he convincingly demonstrated than many slips were present long before introduced animals arrived in the range and had not grown significantly.[41] Erosion was more about natural cycles than browsing by deer. Deer were off the hook – at least concerning their contribution to erosion.

Forest Service research using deer exclosure plots, however, clearly demonstrated that deer dramatically depleted certain palatable plants, notably broadleaf, changing the natural composition of the understorey. But possums soon supplanted deer as the pest of most concern. The NZFS had begun aerial 1080 possum control on the West Coast in the late 1950s, and by the 1970s control of the pest became one of its major functions.

How much huts helped deer control seems, in hindsight, something of a moot point. At least part of the Forest Service's intention was to encourage private hunters into remote areas, and huts certainly helped achieve this goal. The NZFS continued to build huts, recognising their value for outdoor recreation. For trampers and other outdoor enthusiasts such as anglers, the impact of these huts was nothing short of transformational and set recreational patterns of use that persist to this day.[42]

Backcountry Boom

As tramper Mark Pickering points out in his 2004 book *A Tramper's Journey*, all the extensive new hut and track network, combined with accompanying well-sited bridges, contributed significantly to a tramping boom: 'For over 40 years the initials NZFS meant one thing to trampers: tracks and huts.'[43] All of a sudden, these facilities opened up vast areas of the bush and mountains to less experienced trampers. Huts negated the need to carry a tent, bridges avoided the problems of flooded rivers, and tracks offered easy, quick passage. Trampers could accomplish in a weekend trip what had taken their predecessors several days. In the 1970s, tramping clubs enjoyed a second golden age, and the NZFS huts and tracks played no small role in that surge of outdoor activity.

Pickering also reckoned the basic NZFS hut has probably never been bettered: 'There was nothing flash or clever about them, but they kept you dry through wet spring storms, were airy in summer and warm through winter. They did not intrude on the landscape, and were often positioned superbly well by men who knew the value of being close to water, firewood and views.'[44]

In the 1970s, the encouragement of outdoor recreation became an increasingly important role of the NZFS. As early as the 1920s, the Forest Service's first director, Leon MacIntosh Ellis, had stated: 'The rapidly increasing popularity of the national forest domain as a people's playground is being encouraged by the Service.'[45] By the 1950s, the NZFS had responded to demands from the public for better access to, and opportunities for recreation in, its state forests, developing the concept of 'state forest parks'. Tararua State Forest Park, established in 1954, was New Zealand's first, followed by Craigieburn State Forest Park, the first in the South Island, three years later. From the mid-1960s onwards, the state forest parks concept took off, with fifteen gazetted in the 1970s alone. The deer-culling huts and tracks neatly dovetailed with this development, and it is no accident that most state forest parks were formed in areas that previously had been a priority for deer culling.

Admittedly, forest park development was partly a reaction by the NZFS against proposals for national parks, which would have resulted in the agency losing land to its rival, the Department of Lands and Survey. But only the most cynical would dispute that the Forest Service increasingly encouraged outdoor recreation simply because this was a worthy public service. For example, in 1965, after responding to calls from the Golden Bay Alpine and Tramping Club to establish a park in Northwest Nelson, the NZFS recut the overgrown Heaphy and Wangapeka tracks, and established new, larger huts. The size of these huts undeniably indicated their sole function as facilities for outdoor recreation.[46]

The Forest Service also allowed clubs or other groups to build huts, subject to certain conditions, as this 1960s working plan for Northwest Nelson explained:

Forest Service ranger Max Polglaze greets trampers at Crow Hut, Karamea Valley, Northwest Nelson Forest Park, 1970s.
PHOTO: JOHN JOHNS, COURTESY OF MAX POLGLAZE

Hamilton Hut, Cass-Lagoon Track, Craigieburn Forest Park, Canterbury. One of the larger huts erected by the Forest Service, the 20-bunk hut, built in 1983, occupies a flat in the Hamilton Creek. PHOTO: SHAUN BARNETT/BLACK ROBIN PHOTOGRAPHY

Heaphy Hut, 2010. PHOTO: ROB BROWN

> Approved organisations wishing to build their own huts in the park may be allowed to do so, provided the site, design and materials are approved by the park administration and adequate provision is made for rubbish and sewage disposal. The huts shall be open to the public at all times. To assist with construction costs a 1 pound for 2 pound subsidy may be granted, but the maximum subsidy shall be 250 pounds.[47]

During the 1970s, the Forest Service continued to build an impressive number of huts, although its pace had slowed. For example, in 1976 it built four two-bunk bivs and ten six-bunk huts.[48] Hut building generally helped curry favour with the public too – an important consideration at this time, when the agency was facing increasing opposition to its native logging operations in places like Pureora, Whirinaki and the West Coast.

As outdoor recreation gained popularity, pressure on facilities created new issues, particularly rubbish, overcrowding and firewood use. At first, the Forest Service simply dug rubbish pits into which people threw all their refuse. When one filled up, rangers dug another. But not only were the pits unsightly, they also attracted rodents and even posed some degree of risk, as one NZFS ranger discovered during a night spent at Kings Creek Hut on the Wangapeka in 1976: 'our Senior E.F. [Environmental Forestry] Ranger took the opportunity to inspect and gauge the depth of the rubbish disposal hole by the unusual method of stepping into it in the dark. The depth was O.K. but the water level was rather high.'[49]

Rubbish pits were clearly unsustainable, and by the mid-1970s the Forest Service began considering alternative methods. Not long after the formation of the Department of Conservation in 1987, rubbish pits were abandoned in favour of a 'pack it out' policy that has succeeded in reducing rubbish to a large degree.[50]

As the popularity of huts on tracks like the Wangapeka and Heaphy increased, firewood became scarce, often resulting in damage to live trees by irresponsible trampers and hunters. The NZFS responded by supplying huts with firewood, cut from local trees at the beginning of the busy summer tramping season. In 1985, however, a revised indigenous forest policy meant public consultation had to occur before native trees were used for purposes such as firewood. For this reason the NZFS decided to investigate charging users for staying in huts to offset firewood costs, and to encourage trampers to carry their own portable cooking stoves and use the hut wood stoves only for essential heating.[51] Gas cookers offered another solution, and were trialled in several Heaphy Track huts in the mid-1970s.[52]

By the time DOC superseded the Forest Service in 1987, NZFS huts were a far cry from the shelters used by the early deer cullers. The agency had built large huts with more than twenty bunks, including Kings Creek Hut on Nelson's Wangapeka Track, Hope Kiwi Lodge in Canterbury's Lake Sumner Forest Park and Hamilton Hut in Craigieburn Forest Park. Others, like the Lockwood huts in the Kaimanawa Forest Park, boasted two bunkrooms and a central living area, joined by a covered veranda.

Overstayers were one measure of how good the huts had become. In 1982, the Northwest Nelson State Forest Park Advisory Committee received a com-

ABOVE Waipakihi Hut, a Lockwood design built by the NZFS in 1968, Kaimanawa Forest Park, pictured in 2009. Beginning in the 1960s, Lands and Survey used a Lockwood design for many huts in Tongariro National Park, and the NZFS followed suit in the Kaimanawas, ensuring the central North Island became (and still is) the Lockwood hut capital of New Zealand.

TOP RIGHT Kirwans Hut, Victoria Forest Park, West Coast, (pictured in 2006) is one of three huts designed by a Wellington architect for the NZFS during the mid-1980s; the other two are Big River (Victoria Forest Park) and Ces Clark (Croesus Track). With its many-paned windows, positioned to offer views of the Southern Alps to advantage, and its gabled roof, Kirwans is an example of a Forest Service hut with considerable aesthetic appeal.
PHOTOS: SHAUN BARNETT/BLACK ROBIN PHOTOGRAPHY

RIGHT Saxon Hut, Heaphy Track, 2010. PHOTO: JEANNINE TUFFIN

Mid Waiohine Hut, Tararua Forest Park, 2010. PHOTO: SHAUN BARNETT/BLACK ROBIN PHOTOGRAPHY

plaint from a 'Mr Cook', who felt he had been unfairly evicted from Trilobite Hut in the Cobb Valley by a Forest Service ranger after a stay of several months. Consequently, the committee recommended a maximum stay of seven nights when the hut was not occupied by other users, or a two-night maximum when others were in residence.[53]

In short, the NZFS had fully embraced outdoor recreation as one of its public services, and had attempted to provide a range of facilities to meet a diverse range of needs. Recognition of the role played by the Forest Service to foster recreation, particularly with its six-bunk huts, has been undervalued.

The Heritage Value of NZFS Huts

After the demise of the Forest Service in 1987, many of its deer-culling huts survived surprisingly well with only basic maintenance. During the 1990s, there was a trend in DOC to paint huts in more earthy colours, but recently this has been reversed, with bright orange making a colourful comeback. Makahu Saddle Hut (Kaweka Forest Park) and Makaretu Hut (Ruahine Forest Park) are shining examples of this switch. For many ex-NZFS huts a colour change back to orange has been the result of practical as well as historical reasons, as Southland tramper Robin McNeill opined about those in the Takitimu Range: 'As it would be darn hard to find the huts if they were painted green, orange is an enlightened choice.'[54]

DOC has made welcome improvements to many ex-NZFS huts. Good examples include those in Ruahine Forest Park, where a veranda was added to several, the layout changed to accommodate eight people on platform bunks, and skylights installed for extra light.

However, hut modifications are not always appropriate. To the heritage-conscious historian, some huts must survive in near-original condition. By 2006, a half-century had passed since the first NZFS huts had been built, and their heritage value needed fresh assessment. To this end, DOC employed Wellington historian Michael Kelly to research and write about deer-culling huts, the result being his informative 2007 publication *Wild Animal Control Huts: A National Heritage Identification Study*.

Crucially, Kelly identified key NZFS heritage huts, including Mid Waiohine (Tararua Forest Park), Top Maropea (Ruahine Forest Park) and Mt Fell Hut (Mt Richmond Forest Park). His report, together with the work of DOC historian Jackie Breen, has led to a renewed appreciation of these simple structures, the cullers who lived in them and their place in our history. As Kelly put it:

> the iconic status of the government hunter was inspired by the writing of Barry Crump and others. The role of the hut in all this is not often explicitly acknowledged but it certainly provided the 'settings' for the books. The hut was an ever-present stage or prop in such books. Some hunters remember particular huts with fondness, either for particular events, or for the scenery surrounding them, or the length of their association with them … Huts are therefore our abiding, tangible heritage of decades of wild animal control.[55]

SHAUN BARNETT

Construction of Top Olderog Biv, a B142 design, in 1971. PHOTOS: NZFS, COURTESY OF DOC HOKITIKA

NEW ZEALAND FOREST SERVICE HUTS 227

West Coast Two-bunk Bivouacs

Nowhere else in the country has such a concentration of two-bunk bivouacs as the West Coast. By the early 1950s, deer and possum browsing had led to the obvious destruction of forests in catchments like the Kokatahi, making them target areas for pest control. This, combined with the demanding geography and weather of the region, meant the central West Coast ranges became a real focus for hut building between the mid-1950s and early 1970s. The Hokitika catchment in particular ended up with a plethora of huts built over two decades of intense activity. For example, the relatively compact Toaroha Valley has been the site of at least eleven huts at one time or another, of which eight still survive – including three two-bunk bivs.

The particularly rugged Toaroha, Kokatahi, Whitcombe and Hokitika valleys bristle with gorges and dense forests, explaining the cullers' pragmatic preference for hunting the tops. When the NZFS took over deer-culling operations, it recognised a need for a high-level hut design, suitable for the tops, which could serve as a secure store for food and ammunition, and also as a shelter during bad weather. Two-person bivs evolved directly from this need.

Before the NZFS standardised its national hut designs in the late 1950s, a few conservancies developed their own ideas for huts, with the West Coast Conservancy leading the way. Indeed, the two-person bivouac, now one of the quintessential New Zealand backcountry hut designs, was first conceived in Hokitika.

Two-bunk bivouacs owe their shape and design to the earliest tent camps erected by the Department of Internal Affairs. In 1955, the last full year of deer control by the DIA, Stan Fokerd of NZFS Hokitika drew up some basic designs for what became known locally as the B49 Biv. At the same time, Fokerd was also working on a four-bunk 'river-level' hut.[1]

After the NZFS took over deer culling in 1956, this B49 design evolved to become known as the S86, and was later standardised nationally.[2] During this period of experimentation with hut design, field experience at a regional level played a hugely important role. National standards emerged only after practical field solutions were collated, rather than the usual top-down approach. This robust system resulted in good, practical hut designs that were fully supported by field staff. Over the ensuing decades, these simple designs have proven their resilience and practicality.

The first generation of two-bunk bivs featured a flat-iron cladding, wrapped around the entire frame, which could sometimes be prone to leaking through joints. Precut timber was packed flat, ready for flying to the chosen site. NZFS employee Jock Fisher remembers that when Stan Fokerd assembled the first prototype biv in the packing store at Hokitika, the cullers jokingly referred to it as 'Stan's chook house'.[3]

Forest Service staff built the first of these bivs in the Hokitika area in 1957, marking the first time

Tramper Andy Dennis at Frew Saddle Biv, February 2007.
PHOTO: ROB BROWN

Jumble Top Biv in 1958. PHOTO: RON TURNER

that bivs – or indeed any hut – were installed en masse using a standard design. Typically, it took just two days to assemble a biv on site. With just a wooden floor and no bunks, the bivs could house two men lying down and not much else. NZFS culler Ron Turner described them:

> The new high country bivouacs were designed to offer shelter to the shooters from bad weather and to minimise the load by not having to carry tents and food up the steep slopes … Measuring about 8 feet by 6 feet [2.4 metres by 1.8 metres], the bivouacs were designed to house two people and were equipped with two Lilos and a kerosene stove as they were well above the tree line and thus there was no firewood for cooking, or warmth. A wooden floor meant at least a dry spot on which to sleep.[4]

Surviving examples from this 1957 season include Frew Saddle Biv, the original Top Crawford Biv (recently relocated to a new site near the old Pinnacle Biv) and the Lower Olderog Biv. Of these three, Frew Saddle remains in the best condition and has added historical significance because it is also in its original location.

After materials were air-dropped onto site at Frew Saddle, Jock Fisher and Merv O'Reilly built the shell of the biv just before 'a storm broke all around us'. Fisher wrote: 'We lived and worked for the next two days in and on the Bivi while the storm, changing from driving rain to driving snow, raged around us.'[5]

After the biv was completed, Fisher had his doubts that it would last in the exposed location, and later commented, 'I'm surprised that Frew [Saddle] Biv has lasted so long. I did think it would have blown away which is why I dropped in iron standards to tie it down at the time.'[6]

Jumble Top, on the south side of the Toaroha, was another biv built in 1957, this time by a team of four NZFS deer cullers: Jock Fisher, Merv Ellwood, Ross Courtney and Ron Turner. Turner later recalled:

> One route to this site was the steep climb up from the river flats where the Cedar Flats Hut was located. We set up a tent camp between two tarns as this was the nearest sheltered place with water to the proposed bivouac site … During a later visit [to the completed hut], we found the marker pole had blown away and we had to dig the hard snow away from the front of the structure with our hands and sheath knives to open the door. This made me think of being trapped inside during a period of heavy snowfall and not being able to open the door [which opened outwards]. Fortunately, nothing remotely like this ever happened.[7]

At 1500 metres, Jumble Top was one of the highest bivs of this design – a little too high, as it turned out. By the 1970s, repeated heavy snowfalls had flattened it beyond use.[8]

In the following year, 1958, four more B49s were installed: Campbell, Whitehorn Spur, Pinnacle and Noisy. Of these, only Campbell Biv survives on site. An avalanche swept Noisy Biv off its foundations sometime in the 1980s, where it sat in the tussock for many years before finally being removed in 2006. Lack of maintenance meant Pinnacle Biv rotted beyond repair, and it was removed in 2011.[9]

The last iteration of these flat-iron bivs was Mikonui Spur and Scottys, both built in 1960. Culler Allan Farmer built Scottys Biv, which is now maintained by Permolat founder Andrew Buglass in a community management agreement with DOC.[10] Most bivs from this era have almost identical exteriors but vary somewhat inside. Some, like Frew Saddle and Top Crawford, were later fitted out with

CLOCKWISE FROM TOP LEFT Browning Biv and interior in 2002. PHOTOS: ROB BROWN. Mikonui Spur Biv in 2005. PHOTO: ANDREW BUGLASS. The old 1957 Top Crawford Biv was moved to this site in 2011 to become the 'new' Pinnacle Biv. PHOTO: ANDREW BARKER

two low bunks, while others, like Mikonui Spur, retain their original plain wooden floor.

In the early 1960s, a second-generation national standard biv, called the B55, was developed, with subtle but significant improvements on the original version: the small rear window became a louvre, allowing the luxury of ventilation; a proper corrugated-iron roof with eaves solved some of the leaking issues of the B49 (and also enabled the collection of rainwater); and all had two bunks. These small changes also significantly increased the bivs' durability.

Four outstanding examples of the B55 remain in the Hokitika area: Browning (1960), Newton (1962), Crystal (1964) and Adventure (1964). Five other B55 bivs were built but have not survived. In the late 1980s, DOC removed Knobby Ridge Biv, which ended up on farmland near the Inland Pack Track, where sharp-eyed Permolat members rediscovered it recently.[11] Sentry Biv, situated below Squall Peak in the Toaroha catchment, fell into disrepair and was consumed by the bush.[12] A storm destroyed the Whitcombe's Cat Creek Biv in 1974, and the original Top Toaroha Biv was replaced with a newer design in 1984. A fifth – Pfeifer Biv – was built on the Aicken Range west of Arthur's Pass and was later replaced by a new DOC biv in the late 2000s.

Most B55 bivs sported a two-hob kerosene burner, and in the case of Browning Biv, this remains today and still works. Between 1984 and 2004, scientist Mark Crompton of Hokitika studied snow retention on the Browning Range, and through his numerous visits to Browning Biv ensured the shelter was maintained in its original state.[13]

The final NZFS biv design was even more 'luxurious'. The B142 boasted greater headroom, and a larger side window replaced the smaller end window. Essentially, it was closer in design to a proper hut. Two out of three built to this design in the Hokitika area remain, both in excellent condition: Top Olderog (1971; see p. 227) and Gerhardt Spur

Gerhardt Spur Biv, October 2010. PHOTO: ANDREW BUGLASS

Biv (1972). DOC removed Rapid Creek Biv (1974) in the late 1980s.[14]

One variant on the B142 biv, the three-bunk B143, is known by only one example still in existence: Rocky Creek Biv (1974).[15] Toaroha Saddle Biv, built in 1984 at a cost of $2904 to replace the 1960s Top Toaroha Biv, marked the end of the NZFS Hokitika biv-building era.[16]

The two-bunk bivouacs of the Hokitika area exemplify how staff of one NZFS region pioneered a simple, robust design that was eventually adopted nationally. Today, the remaining bivs provide an almost complete collection, demonstrating the evolution of these simple wild animal-control shelters through three decades of development. In both a recreation and heritage sense, they are nationally important.

ROB BROWN

West Coast Four-bunk Huts

In 1957, the same year that the Forest Service began populating the West Coast backcountry with two-person alpine bivs, it also began designing and building simple four-bunk huts there. While the bivs were initially considered little more than a store for food and ammunition, the four-bunk huts were intended as valley bases from which to operate. In total, the NZFS built around 110 four-bunk huts throughout the country, with nearly a third of these on the West Coast. Most are in the central Southern Alps, inland from Hokitika.

Unlike the earlier deer-culling days of the Department of Internal Affairs, when materials had to be begged or borrowed, the NZFS takeover resulted in a 'whole new ball game'. Getting equipment and supplies was no problem now, and there were no real limits on flying time to 'get the job done'. Jock Fisher remembers this new world as a great time, 'although in retrospect we were probably small fry in the overall NZFS budget'.[1]

In Hokitika, Stan Fokerd had drawn up plans for the four-bunk hut in the last days of the DIA's animal-control programme. To go with the 'high-level' biv was the 'river-level' four-bunk hut, known locally as the B48. This design, in terms of both its appearance and basic layout, owed much to the five four-bunk huts that had already been built by Internal Affairs on the West Coast in the 1950s including Slaty Creek (see p. 206), Crawford Junction and Tutaekuri.[2]

Siting bigger huts in remote locations became possible thanks to the extra carrying capacity of aircraft such as the Cessna. This aeroplane could handle bigger payloads than the less powerful Auster used earlier in the 1950s, enabling longer lengths of timber to be strapped under the wings. In 1957, Cedar Flat in the Toaroha Valley was the first hut built using a Cessna air-drop. Jock Fisher witnessed the event:

> On the first load we flew in 8ft [2.4-metre] lengths of flooring timber. We made up bundles of nine bits of timber I think and wired them together with two pack saddle rings to hook them on the wing rack of the Cessna. The pilot Tex Smith experimented with them on the Hokitika airstrip and they worked OK. I went up to Cedar Flat the following day to receive the drop and report back on its success. Next afternoon the plane came up the valley with Stan Fokerd as observer. It flew up the valley turned around and came back down not far above the tree tops. One bundle came off the right hand wing and the other bundle on the left wing stayed put. The plane wobbled down the valley with the bundle still on the wing and Tex later told me that his worst moment was landing at Hokitika as he thought one ring might give way on the stuck load in the landing jolt and drop one end of the timber on the ground and flip the

Old Cedar Flat Hut, pictured in August 2008 after its restoration by DOC. PHOTO: ANDREW BARKER

Poet Hut, Hokitika valley, 2007. PHOTO: SHAUN BARNETT/BLACK ROBIN PHOTOGRAPHY

Frisco Hut, Hokitika Valley, 1978. PHOTO: GEOFF SPEARPOINT

plane. The bundle held tight on landing and we later discovered one of the rings had got twisted which is why it hadn't released. A couple of days later Tex and I went back up the Toaroha and dropped two bundles successfully.[3]

Although the air-drop supplied timber for the flooring and rafters, as well as roofing iron, the framing for Cedar Flat Hut was built using wood hewn from the surrounding forest. Dave Tiller led the building team and put his expertise with the adze to good use. While Cedar Flat Hut has been slightly modified over the years, with the addition of a porch, it remains the first B48 and was recently beautifully restored by DOC.

Towards the end of 1957, the NZFS erected three further B48 huts: Wilkinson, Poet and Serpentine. Timber for the framing was no longer hacked from the bush; instead, all three used materials precut at Granville, the NZFS workshop in the Grey Valley. Transportation by Cessna had largely negated the need for any laborious hand-adzing, although Julia Hut, built in the Taipo Valley in 1958, still had some framing cut from the forest. Now called Old Julia Hut, it was the last B48 built and remains in usable condition.

Cutting timber on site helped compensate for any materials lost during air-drops, which were not always perfect, thereby preventing any delays to the building project. However, as air-drop accuracy improved, all huts were built using fully precut materials. From 1958 onwards, helicopters helped further improve hut-building efficiency. The NZFS Nelson Conservancy experimented with chopper transportation that year when it built four four-bunk huts of its own design, including one on the West Coast side of Northwest Nelson: Kakapo Hut. It remains in good condition, and demonstrates the regional difference between Nelson and Hokitika four-bunk layout.

While the B48 marked a time when regional designs held sway, national standards were on their way. In October 1958, the NZFS head office produced the first standardised hut designs, heavily influenced by the developments in both the Nelson and West Coast conservancies.[4] The standard four-bunk S81 design incorporated a number of refinements, including slightly more room, additional windows and a small foyer for storing wet-weather gear and rifles. It also had a cupboard for storing food supplies, and sometimes a kerosene burner. The standard hut kit included a camp oven, several billies, an aluminium washbasin and a range of utensils.

Over a period of fourteen years, between 1958 and 1972, thirty-five four-bunk S81 huts were erected throughout the West Coast. By today's standards, this seems an astronomical number of huts for one area, but it needs to be viewed in the context of the NZFS's overall building programme. By the early 1980s, the NZFS on the West Coast

Dickie Spur Hut in 1993, with Mt Beaumont (left) and The Tusk (right) beyond. PHOTO: GEOFF SPEARPOINT

alone had more than 330 buildings on its books, ranging from backcountry huts to road-end bases and a collection of three-bedroom houses in milling towns like Harihari.[5]

Retaining good deer cullers had always been a problem owing to the tough nature of the work, and this was even truer for the wet, wild West Coast. The Forest Service recognised that good shelter not only improved the efficiency of animal-control operations, but also gave cullers a better standard of living. As culling operations proceeded from valley to valley, building huts kept pace.

Late in 1958, shortly after the standard design was approved, the West Coast's first S81 was built at Grassy Flats in the Styx Valley. Demonstrating the versatility and simplicity of the design, Grassy Flat Hut was later expanded to six bunks and, eventually, eight bunks in 1980, as the popularity of the Three Passes tramp grew. Recently, in 2005, DOC replaced it with a new ten-bunk hut.

In 1959, the NZFS began replacing the old tent camps at Boo Boo and Twins in the Kokatahi catchment with huts. The Boo Boo tent camp, used mainly for possum control, was a sophisticated affair with three bunks – one across each side and one along the back. Legend has it that eighty tins of raspberry jam – used for bait – were once stored under the end bunk.[6]

According to Jock Fisher, not all tent camp sites suited a new hut: 'Why they built huts at Boo Boo and Squid Creek beats me. When I shot the Kokatahi on contract both of these camps were of no use to me, but they were essential when I was on the possums. Possum control in the Kokatahi had ceased by then.'[7] The message from the field must have got through, because from the 1960s onwards huts were located in more strategic sites, making them useful long after the culling days were over.

Construction of four-bunk S81 huts was most intense between the years 1959 and 1963, when the NZFS built an average of five per year on the West Coast. Each year, the animal-control section ordered the appropriate materials from the production arm of the NZFS, and these were precut and packaged up ready for flying. After 1957, support for field operations became a full-time role within the NZFS, an important shift that also meant cullers no longer had to spend winters constructing huts; instead, full-time tradesmen were employed during the summers to build huts and bridges and cut tracks.

After 1963, installation of S81s slowed down to one or two per year. By now, recreational use of the hut network by both hunters and trampers precipitated a shift to the bigger six-bunk SF70 hut design. Huts were also lined after 1963, ensuring greater warmth, although none were insulated.

As huts became more popular with the public, the NZFS demonstrated creative solutions for catering to the increased use. Butler Junction Hut, installed in 1964, became popular with hunters, so the NZFS simply flew in another four-bunk hut and bolted it onto the original. Hey presto, it had an eight-bunk hut. The S81 design even proved resilient above the bushline. Dickie Spur (1968) and Healy Creek (1969) huts today remain excellently positioned for trans-alpine trips in the central West Coast.

Some S81 huts have been replaced or removed over the years. For example, Top Crawford and

Top Kokatahi huts (both built in 1959) have been relocated to better sites and rebuilt to the extent that they are now unrecognisable as S81s. Mid Trent Hut (1960), on the Trent–Elizabeth tramping route, was fully dismantled in 2007 to replace rotten timbers and then reassembled in near original condition – a significantly cheaper option than a total replacement. Materials from Lower Arahura Hut (1962) formed the basis of a new hut at Mt Brown, built in 2010 (see p. 188).

Some of the best examples of S81 huts on the West Coast still in place today include Mullins Basin (1960), Mungo (1962) and Townsend (1962). These huts, all in excellent condition, were originally unlined, and Mungo still has its original open fire. Perhaps the best, though, is the very last S81 built by the NZFS on the West Coast.[8] Scamper Torrent Hut (1971) occupies an idyllic alpine basin beneath Mt Durward above the Waitaha Valley, and attracts trampers and hunters who enjoy just this kind of remote West Coast location.

ROB BROWN

TOP Scamper Torrent Hut in 2010. PHOTO: GLENN JOHNSTON
BOTTOM Mullins Basin Hut in 2010. PHOTO: NICK GROVES

West Coast Six-bunk Huts

By the time the first Forest Service six-bunk hut was built on the West Coast, design experimentation at a regional level had largely ceased and been replaced by national standards. Everywhere the NZFS undertook deer control eventually got some of the now legendary SF70 six-bunk huts.

In the South Island, possibly the very first SF70 built was Bottom Gordons Hut, in the Leetham Valley. This was in the Raglan Range east of Dip Flat training camp, where the NZFS put prospective cullers through an intensive six-week course in bushcraft, survival skills, shooting and cooking on an open fire. Many prospective cullers going through this programme would have visited Bottom Gordons as part of their training.

The West Coast got its first SF70, Cropp Hut, in 1962, which was set in a basin high above the Whitcombe River. In the late 1970s, the Ministry of Works' Meteorological Division modified and insulated Cropp Hut to use it as a base for measuring rainfall and river flow.

Cropp Hut did not survive its mountain environment. In 1995, a huge storm hit the Southern Alps, causing widespread flooding, and the hut was washed off its piles. By the time it was discovered, the sodden insulation had rotted the framing.[1]

The same year Cropp Hut was built, Neave Hut was also installed in the Whitcombe catchment. Neave, strategically located near Whitcombe Pass, remains in excellent condition. Further north, on the western side of Arthur's Pass National Park, Otehake and Upper Deception huts were also built in 1962. Both remained in good condition, although in 2006 Coast to Coast legend Robin Judkins heard rumours that DOC planned to remove Upper Deception Hut. Reputedly, he told the powers that be that he would personally pay for an exact replica to be flown in.[2] Judkins' threat was enough, and the hut was never removed.

Between 1963 and 1967, the NZFS erected only seven more SF70 huts on the West Coast. Change was afoot. As early as 1958, the NZFS had experimented with using 1080-poisoned carrot drops to control possums, and this proved quite effective at killing deer. They also undertook trials with poison paste smeared on broadleaf trees (a deer favourite). The only voices of discontent were from cullers, who understandably thought these new experiments would put them out of a job.

In the mid-1960s, cullers operated under a combination of employment conditions, depending on the block. Cullers hunting difficult blocks were generally paid wages, while those on easier blocks were paid on a per tail commission basis. After achieving success in South Westland and Fiordland, the venison recovery industry began moving north. In August 1967, the NZFS issued its first two permits in central Westland, for the Taramakau and Waitaha catchments. Helicopter hire was about £50 per hour at the time, and on the West Coast up to 150 animals an hour could be shot from a chopper in

LEFT Rex Vink outside Neave Hut, Whitcombe Valley, in August 1964. PHOTO: RICK WATSON
OPPOSITE Tramper Elise Bryant at Smyth Hut, Wanganui Valley, 2001. PHOTO: SHAUN BARNETT/BLACK ROBIN PHOTOGRAPHY

NEW ZEALAND FOREST SERVICE HUTS 237

Shaun Barnett at Top Butler Hut, Whataroa valley, 1994. PHOTO: ROB BROWN

the right conditions. However, even this impressive kill rate paled into insignificance when compared with the much higher tallies near Haast, where bigger herds and slightly less challenging terrain paid better dividends.[3]

After watching the commercial operators, the West Coast NZFS ran its own helicopter hunting trial in 1968. Although its tallies were well down on those of the commercial operators, the Forest Service realised helicopter animal control showed some promise.[4]

After 1967, most huts built on the West Coast were SF70 six-bunkers. Despite the fact that they are now more than forty years old, many remain in good condition today, and still serve as welcome refuges for trampers and hunters visiting some of New Zealand's toughest mountain terrain. Of the thirty-three SF70 huts built on the West Coast, twenty were erected after 1968, reflecting the Forest Service's growing move towards providing for recreational hunting and tramping.

Most of the West Coast blocks were controlled by ground cullers for the last time over the summer of 1970–71, and the remainder during the 1971–72 season. All the huts were still provisioned for this season, but as some blocks were not shot, supplies and equipment remained inside, where they were enjoyed by trampers and climbers for some years to come.[5] As recently as the 1990s, trampers arriving at the remoter huts felt like they had walked into a living museum, with canned food still in the cupboards. Prices Basin Hut (an S81 built in 1962) was one good example.

By the end of the 1972 season, the last NZFS cullers on the West Coast received their final pay packet. For the men who had built, lived in and loved the SF70 huts, it was the end of an era that many of them still look back on as the best days of their lives.

Many huts received only a bare minimum of maintenance in the following years, and when the Department of Conservation was formed in 1987, it had even less money for huts and tracks. However, most of the huts survived this period of neglect, which came to an end when the Labour government of 1999–2002 committed reasonable funding to backcountry facilities. Throughout the next decade, the DOC West Coast Conservancy embarked on a comprehensive maintenance programme. Although a few huts were removed (such as Frew Hut, built in 1963, which was replaced in 2003 with a new twelve-bunk hut on a safer site at the junction of the increasingly popular Frew Saddle–Toaroha Saddle and Whitcombe Pass track), virtually all the SF70s were retained. Where DOC did not have funds for a particular hut Permolat often stepped in to help.

Many West Coast SF70 huts remain classics that today are sought after by hut baggers. Notable among them are Top Waitaha Hut (1968), Mid Robinson Hut (1969), Top Toaroha Hut (1971),[6] Top Butler Hut (1974) and Smyth Hut (1975). Smyth has the added bonus of hot pools nearby.

Construction of Roaring Billy Hut in 1978 marked the last time an SF70 was built on the West Coast. Situated in a remote tributary of the Haast River, South Westland, the hut is rarely visited today but still serves as a hunting base, or as a refuge for trampers crossing the Thomas Range to Thomas Hut (another SF70, built in 1971).

ROB BROWN

CLOCKWISE FROM TOP LEFT Mid Robinson Hut, Robinson Valley, Victoria Forest Park. 2010. PHOTO: GLENN JOHNSTON. Neave Hut, Whitcombe Valley, 2001. Top Waitaha Hut, Waitaha Valley, 1996. Mid Taipo Hut, Taipo Valley, Arthur's Pass National Park, 2007. PHOTOS: ROB BROWN.

Kaweka Forest Park NZFS Huts HAWKE'S BAY

It is difficult now for people to appreciate just how seriously the Forest Service took erosion during the middle part of the twentieth century. In fact, the agency considered the control of erosion as one of its foremost duties – and by browsing vegetation, deer were prime suspects of accelerating the problem. Deer culling became a priority in the mountain headwaters of rivers that were important to towns and cities downstream.[1]

As a catchment area for three major Hawke's Bay rivers (the Mohaka, Ngaruroro and Tutaekuri), the Kaweka Range was identified by the NZFS as a high priority for deer-control operations. Soon after taking over responsibility for deer control in 1956, the NZFS embarked on a comprehensive programme to establish a network of huts, tracks and bridges in the range.

Although a few tramping and mustering huts already existed in the Kawekas, most of these lay on the periphery of the main range.[2] The rest of the area remained essentially wilderness. Furthermore, as the old Hawkestone Stock Route was disused and overgrown, access from Puketitiri was difficult. In that momentous year of 1956, the NZFS approached the Heretaunga Tramping Club to help it locate a site on which to build a hut at Makahu Saddle. Club stalwart Norman Elder led a party, including Alan Berry, through scrub and beech forest over the old route to Makahu Saddle, encountering open bush and numerous deer trails. Berry remembered, 'As it turned out, we selected a site towards the southern side of the saddle but the Forest Service ended up by building the hut on the northern side, by the stream. That was probably a better site.'[3]

As helicopters were not yet in wide use, the NZFS decided to experiment with building huts using air-drops from fixed-wing planes. Lengths of timber made heavy and awkward loads, so the Forest Service opted to use a lightweight aluminium framing known as Dexion to build the hut. This came in suitable lengths for a planeload and could be bolted together on site.

Two Dexion huts were constructed in 1957: one at Makahu Saddle and the other at Back Ridge. Although the hut construction was successful, the uninsulated design proved cold, and deer cullers

LEFT Back Ridge Hut, 2004.
PHOTO: SHAUN BARNETT/BLACK ROBIN PHOTOGRAPHY
BOTTOM Trampers very quickly began using NZFS huts in the Kawekas. These Heretaunga Tramping Club members stayed at Makahu Saddle Hut in 1957, the same year it was built. PHOTO: GRAEME HARE, HERETAUNGA TRAMPING CLUB COLLECTION

were forced to stuff moss into the wall cavities to provide some semblance of warmth.[4]

Fixed-wing aircraft remained the primary means of transport when the four-bunk SF81 Ballard Hut was built in 1958, but timber framing replaced Dexion.[5] David Ballard, an ex-Royal New Zealand Air Force pilot, completed the air-drop, but was killed later that year in a topdressing accident.[6] Also in 1958, a two-bunk biv went up at Studholme Saddle, and the following year saw the construction of three more four-bunk S81 huts: Studholme Saddle, Lotkow and Mackintosh.

In 1959, Makino Hut became the first standard SF70 six-bunk timber-framed hut built in the Kawekas, using short timber lengths suitable for fitting into a plane. The Hawke's Bay section of the New Zealand Deerstalkers' Association helped with construction, and had a frustrating time when many of the loads were lost or damaged in the surrounding bush.[7]

In total, the NZFS built thirty-one huts and bivs in the Kawekas between 1957 and 1972, an average of two per year. In each of the years 1959, 1963 and 1966, four huts were completed.[8]

Although a few ground cullers continued to work in the Kawekas until as recently as the 1980s, helicopter venison recovery had largely taken over by the end of the 1960s. At this stage, however, the NZFS was taking outdoor recreation seriously and continued to build huts for that purpose. The twelve-bunk, three-room Tira Lodge is one example of a larger non-standard hut built in 1969 to satisfy the needs of recreational deerstalkers.

By the time Kaweka Forest Park was established in 1974, the range had a comprehensive network of tracks, and more than thirty-five huts and bivs.[9] Te Puia Lodge was the largest of these, at twenty bunks.[10]

SHAUN BARNETT

TOP Makino Hut, 2005.
BOTTOM Ballard Hut, 2012.
PHOTOS: SHAUN BARNETT/BLACK ROBIN PHOTOGRAPHY

NEW ZEALAND FOREST SERVICE HUTS 241

Bobs Hut 1958 NELSON LAKES NATIONAL PARK

Bobs Hut was among the first six-bunk SF70 huts built by the Forest Service in the South Island. It is set in a stunning location in the West Matakitaki Valley, part of an area added to Nelson Lakes National Park in 1980. This has always been a quieter corner of the park, although a steadily growing number of trampers now visit Bobs as part of a Lewis Pass–St Arnaud trip. This hut and another in the East Matakitaki remain among the most original and best-preserved SF70s dating from the late 1950s.

Driven by Snow Corby in the Nelson Conservancy office, hut building in the Nelson–Marlborough area went through an intensive phase in 1958. Jock Fisher transferred from Hokitika to Murchison in this year and, building on his West Coast experience, managed the programme under Snow to improve accommodation for cullers working in the Murchison area.[1] Shortly after the NZFS approved its standard hut designs in October 1958, staff selected the Matakitaki River West Branch as one of the first sites in the South Island for a six-bunk SF70. The other two SF70 huts built during the 1958–59 summer were Bottom Gordons and Barbers in Marlborough's Leatham Valley.[2]

Constructed towards the end of 1958, 'Forestry Hut 397' became known by the cullers as Top Matakitaki Hut, and was used by them in place of a rundown mining hut that previously existed here.[3] That much is known, but the hut's more recent moniker, Bobs, has uncertain origins. NZFS employee Ron Turner, who helped build the hut, certainly did not use the name, and asked recently, 'Who the heck is Bob?'[4] For some years, trampers arriving at the hut have also been bemused by a grave outside simply marked 'Bob'. Inside, old photos of the mysterious Bob look anything but authentic.[5] So to repeat Turner's question, just who the heck was Bob? Was he a gold miner?

George Fairweather Moonlight prospected the headwaters of the Matakitaki as early as the 1860s, and the lower valley was later mined extensively.[6] Mining huts existed along the West Branch probably from the start of the twentieth century, and today Bobs Hut contains mining relics recovered from the West Matakitaki flats. Remains of mining huts could also be seen at the junction of the East and West branches as recently as the 1970s.[7]

Gold miners working remote claims often lived and worked alone, and some died without being discovered for weeks or even months. So was Bob one of these miners, found dead and buried hastily?

Or perhaps one of the deer cullers' loyal canine companions answered to the name of Bob? Or was Bob simply a bit of NZFS humour – perhaps a Bob undertook hut maintenance in the 1970s? Some NZFS old-timer knows for sure, but the mystery remains.

Like many huts dating from this period, Bobs was built on a shoestring. When Allan Richards of the Department of Lands and Survey reclad the hut in the early 1980s, he found that some of the original cladding was made of old flattened kerosene tins.[8]

Over the summer of 1960–61, the Forest Service erected another SF70 six-bunker in the Matakitaki East Branch, replacing a Department of Internal Affairs culling hut dating from the early 1950s. Curiously, the old DIA hut was left in place, and it served as a woodshed right up until the late 1990s.

East Matakitaki Hut remains in near original condition, and DOC Nelson now manages it as a historic building so that its authenticity is retained. Bobs was modified in 1987 when the standard cupboard and wood store were enclosed to allow the number of bunks to be increased to eight. With their open fires and classic settings, both of these huts retain all the original ambience of the classic Forest Service SF70.

ROB BROWN

LEFT East Matakitaki Hut in 1994, with the old DIA hut just visible behind.
PHOTO: SHAUN BARNETT/BLACK ROBIN PHOTOGRAPHY
OPPOSITE Bobs Hut, 2001.
PHOTO: ROB BROWN

Lake Sumner Forest Park NZFS Huts CANTERBURY

After the Forest Service established Tararua State Forest Park as a successful model in 1954, its architect, Priestley Thomson, began to canvas other areas as possible candidates for 'forest park' status. In 1958, he engaged NZFS forester Ashley Cunningham to examine the Lake Sumner area, in the backcountry of North Canterbury, for its suitability. Cunningham spent several weeks in the region, based mainly at No. 2 Hut near the edge of the lake itself. His subsequent report recommended forest park status for Lake Sumner, but the political timing was not right. It was not until the 1970s, which turned out to be the great decade of forest park establishment, that Lake Sumner State Forest Park was officially gazetted.[1]

By then, the area had quite a decent infrastructure of huts and tracks. The Harper Pass route had been in use for centuries, with huts established along it in the late 1930s and 1940 (see p. 138). Mustering huts also existed in some valleys, including Cameron Hut, built in 1955.

In the 1960s, the NZFS began to build huts and bivs in the area. Altogether, eleven huts and bivs were erected over the course of the decade, and although the pace slowed somewhat, hut building continued into the 1970s.[2] The small two-bunk dog-box-style Harper Pass Biv, located in the headwaters of the Hurunui, served as a base for cullers working the nearby bush and tops. Set among prickly shield fern and ribbonwood, it is now used mainly as a lunch shelter for trampers passing through. It was almost lost in a flood in 1980, but was subsequently repositioned and repaired.[3] The two-bunk Lake Man Biv (1968) is a more substantial structure – you can stand up inside, and it even has an open fire.

Built in 1972, Three Mile Stream Hut (seven bunks) is a curious design peculiar to Lake Sumner Forest Park. With three rooms – two smaller bunkrooms on either side of a larger living area – the hut has a pleasing symmetry but is strikingly different to a standard NZFS hut. Built in the same year, Jollie Brook Hut is another example of the design.

If ever a hut exemplified the Forest Service's commitment to providing huts for recreation in the 1970s, the twenty-bunk Hope Kiwi Lodge is it. This large, multi-room hut is set in the idyllic grassy glades of the Kiwi Stream, and is corralled against grazing cattle and horses. It opened in 1974, the same year the NZFS established Lake Sumner Forest Park. Clearly, the NZFS envisaged large parties of trampers staying at the hut, and possibly horse trekkers too. These sorts of large huts demonstrated how the Forest Service stamped its mark on outdoor recreation, a move that made the less well funded Department of Lands and Survey nervous. While the hut now seems something of a white elephant – its size was rarely justified by its use – Hope Kiwi Lodge remains an interesting result of NZFS recreational policy and experimental hut design.

SHAUN BARNETT

LEFT Shaun Barnett at Harper Pass Biv, 2004. Built in 1964, the biv was renovated by DOC in 2003, and repainted in traditional NZFS orange. PHOTO: GEOFF SPEARPOINT
RIGHT Jollie Brook Hut, December 2008. After DOC refurbishment in 2003, one tramper commented in the hut book 'Congratulations DOC on the great work done on the hut without spoiling its genuine backcountry style.' PHOTO: SHAUN BARNETT/BLACK ROBIN PHOTOGRAPHY
OPPOSITE Hope Kiwi Lodge (pictured shortly after it opened), June 1974. PHOTO: JOHN JOHNS, NZFS COLLECTION, ARCHIVES NEW ZEALAND, WELLINGTON, M12,321

Sunrise Hut 1983 RUAHINE FOREST PARK, HAWKE'S BAY

Sunrise Hut occupies a fine position on the bush edge of the Ruahine Range, nestled among the stunted beech trees of Buttercup Hollow, with broad views over the Wakarara Range and the hill country of Hawke's Bay. As many trampers can testify, the hut is indeed a fine place to watch the sun slip above the horizon.

The twenty-two-bunk hut is undoubtedly the most popular hut in Ruahine Forest Park, and likely to remain so. A well-benched track ensures it is accessible to trampers of most abilities, including those with young families.

However, back in the 1930s, when Ian Powell was wandering the Ruahines, the track was a typically steep grunt. Powell, one of the most accomplished trampers and climbers of his generation, was a founder of the Heretaunga Tramping Club. On one occasion, while skiing in the winter of 1935, Powell discovered the crashed Tiger Moth of Hawke's Bay pilot Hamish Armstrong, who had disappeared two weeks before. Armstrong had survived the crash, but never made it out of the bush. The obvious saddle near Sunrise Hut is now named after him.[1]

Sunrise was not the first hut to occupy Buttercup Hollow. The original shelter here was probably just a basic structure built from punga logs, and was used by rabbiters in the late nineteenth century. A second hut was made from malthoid, and although its remains were still visible in the 1950s, it had long been superseded by then. Its replacement, Shut-eye Shack, was located in the bush about two-thirds of the way up to Buttercup Hollow, at a site now marked with an information panel.[2]

The Hawke's Bay Rabbit Board built Shut-eye shack in 1910–12 for rabbiters working the Ruahine Range.[3] According to one tale, it owed its name to a poor old packhorse, which collapsed after being coaxed up the steep ridge, encumbered with materials for the hut, and had to be despatched. It's a good story, but as Ashley Cunningham points out in *Hawke's Bay for the Happy Wanderer* (1993), the more likely explanation is that the name comes from the hut's chimney, which smoked 'incurably', making an eye-watering atmosphere for the occupants. Apparently, one man wrote the words 'Shut-eye Shack' on the hut wall using charcoal after a particularly smoky stay.[4]

The shack served as a base for searchers during the Armstrong search and continued to provide dubious shelter up until the mid-1960s. Its blackened interior did not invite much overnight use, however, despite repairs by the Heretaunga Tramping Club.[5]

In 1983 the Forest Service established another hut at Buttercup Hollow. Barrie Atkins, then in charge of the Gwavas area, received word that $50,000 had become suddenly available – if he could spend it in the next three weeks. Atkins quickly priced out two eight-bunk kitset wooden huts from Fraemohs Homes in Christchurch, valued at $25,000 each. While superficially similar to a Lockwood, these had a different design and did not creak with temperature fluctuations. Fraemohs transported the materials by rail to Waipawa, and those intended for Buttercup Hollow were flown onto site by helicopter. Forest Service staff including Vic Brosnan, Blue Wilkinson and Alan Lee built the hut.

Murry Bishop, Wally Romanes and Norman Elder at Shut-Eye Shack, 26 December 1954. PHOTO: ALAN BERRY

When completed in 1983, the new hut had platform bunks for eight, and a small cooking area. Although some favoured the name Buttercup Hut, Brosnan decided on the name Sunrise Hut. Shut-Eye Shack was pulled down the same year, having served for some seventy years. That same year the second Fraemohs hut was built in the Makarora valley. Materials were transported to site by truck after a bulldozer had forged a rough road up river. Named Barlow Hut, after a local settler family, it replaced the older NZFS Central Makarora Hut, which stood alongside for some years afterward.[6]

The original track to Buttercup Hollow followed the spine of the steep spur – a typically strenuous Ruahine ascent of some 700 metres, and one not suitable for less experienced trampers or family groups. Soon after the completion of Sunrise Hut, the Forest Service began a major realignment of the track, zigzagging a route at a more sedate gradient, with proper benching and drainage. The upgrade cost roughly $100,000, and was largely completed by the time DOC took over in 1987.[7] While some sneered as this 'tourist' trail, the improvements attracted a wider range of people. In October 1988, two Hastings men even managed to negotiate the track in wheelchairs, albeit with help from members of the Heretaunga Tramping Club.[8]

In the 1990s, Sunrise Hut began suffering from overuse, and often burst at the seams on busy weekends. Sensibly, DOC increased its capacity to twelve bunks by adding a second bunkroom, but even that lasted only so long. In April 2005, DOC completed a major extension and upgrade of the hut, increasing the number of bunks to twenty-two.[9] The new size and shape, together with a veranda, rendered the hut's original form almost unrecognisable.

Sunrise Hut's expansion to meet growing popularity has validated the Forest Service's decision to develop this fine site for recreation.

SHAUN BARNETT

TOP Sunrise Hut after its 2005 renovation and expansion by DOC. PHOTO: ROB BROWN
BOTTOM Sunrise Hut pictured in 1993, showing the original Fraemohs design. PHOTO: SHAUN BARNETT/BLACK ROBIN PHOTOGRAPHY

Ruahine Forest Park NZFS Huts HAWKE'S BAY AND RANGITIKEI

During the first half of the twentieth century, the Ruahine Range boasted a number of huts built for various purposes, including mustering, rabbiting, hunting and tramping. In his 1960 book *Backcountry Tales*, Hawke's Bay hunter Lester Masters recorded many stories about these huts, some of which had considerable character. Early huts included Bergesens, McIndoe, Herricks, Howletts, Matthews, Ellis, No Mans, Pohangina, Ruahine, Shutes, Shut-eye Shack, Stag's Head and Te Koau, the oldest of which was possibly Ruahine Hut, built in the early 1860s.[1]

From the 1930s, outdoors recreation clubs gained prominence in New Zealand and began building their own huts. In 1938, the Heretaunga Tramping Club helped the Ruahine Tramping Club build the second Howletts Hut, and in 1939–40 built its own Waikamaka Hut. The following year, the Ruahine Tramping Club also rebuilt a hut at Coppermine Creek out of the wreckage of a flood-ruined shelter.[2] Later in the decade, in 1948, Dannevirke hunter Bill Stanfield also built a small hut in the Tamaki River.[3]

However, up until the latter half of the twentieth century most of the range, particularly its more remote parts, remained devoid of huts. Of those that did exist, there was no systematic management, and the structures tended to become derelict once their original purpose had faded. Fires also took their toll, destroying many huts – sometimes when their wooden-framed chimneys caught fire. Others fell victim to the extensive bush blazes of 1946. Only tramping clubs kept a prolonged interest in maintaining huts.[4]

Things changed when the Forest Service assumed management of deer culling in 1956 and began to populate the range with a new generation of huts. They erected new huts at or near the locations of earlier huts, including No Mans, Ruahine, Herricks, Stanfield and Longview. And between the 1960s and 1980s, dozens of other standard four- and six-bunk designs were also built, along with a smattering of two-bunk bivs, in locations where previously no huts had existed at all. While they were primarily used by NZFS deer cullers, these new huts and bivs opened up the range for recreational hunters, as well as anglers and trampers.

One curious feature of the Ruahines was the long persistence of tent camps in the western side of the range. Even as late as the 1970s, cullers were still using tent camps at Wakelings, Unknown, Mokai Patea, Kelly Knight, Ohutu, Tupari, Maropea Forks and Iron Bark. NZFS culler James Jordan remembered a stint at the Wakelings tent camp in 1968 with fellow hunter Chris Satherley. The dilapidated tent camp was well past its use-by date when a vicious storm swept through, sending hail onto the cullers' sleeping bags through a gash in the canvas. The cullers woke to experience wind that 'blew the canvas like the sail of an America's Cup yacht'.[5] Gradually, however, huts replaced these camps too.

NZFS deer culler Chris Satherley at the Wakelings tent camp, 1966, replaced by Wakelings Hut in the 1970s. By the 1980s, huts had finally replaced most of the remaining tent camps. PHOTO: CHRIS SATHERLEY

Naturally, some huts became strongly associated with a particular deer-culling personality. Leon Kinvig was a young culler in the early 1950s. Forest Service scientist Ashley Cunningham remembered him as 'a slim, fair-headed young man whose closest possessions were his rifle and a 4-litre tin of Grey's tobacco'.[6] After Kinvig drowned, a hut in the mid-reaches of the Pohangina River was named after him. Kelly Knight is another Ruahine hut associated with a hunter.

Top Maropea Hut, one of the earliest NZFS huts built in the range (1958), remains largely in its original condition. The hut is a four-bunk SF40, and was one of the earliest of the few built to this design, although the lean-to entrance is atypical. It still has its original open fireplace (albeit modified to meet new fire regulations) and wire bunks – and not much else.[7] Aside from general maintenance, the only improvement made to the hut has been the addition of a new water tank. Top Maropea nestles just below the bushline in the headwaters of the Maropea River, not far from Armstrong Saddle, and the Department of Conservation has identified it as one of several deer-control huts that will be preserved according to its original design and materials.[8]

By 1960, hut construction in the Ruahine Range had reached a zenith. According to DOC's hut database, an astonishing thirteen huts or bivs were built in the Ruahines in that year alone.[9] Of this hut-building boom, Norman Elder wryly remarked in 1961: 'Search parties to find rumoured huts was fun while it lasted, but we'll soon have the lot pinpointed – and there isn't a great deal of room for more.'[10]

Toka Biv was probably one of the huts erected in that frenetic year of 1960. It's a classic example of the dog-box-style bivs scattered throughout the Kaweka and Ruahine ranges (others include Kylie, Tarn, Sparrowhawk and Taruarau). Located on the eastern side of the Ngamoko Range, with views over the Pohangina Valley and Hawke's Bay, it's accessible from the Knights Track.

By 1976, when Ruahine Forest Park was established, hut building had slowed somewhat but certainly not reached an end. Longview Hut, built in 1979, is unusual because of its steep, gabled roof (another example is Travers, or A-frame, Hut, further south in the range). This atypical design results from a time when the NZFS was experimenting with larger huts for recreational purposes. Longview replaced two previous huts in the area. The first of these was a hut at Pohangina Saddle, one of the windiest locations in the Ruahine Range, which served from the 1890s until 1946, when it burnt down; a rough shelter made from the ruins served for a while longer. In 1957, the NZFS built a replacement hut on the site, a four-bunker also called Pohangina Saddle. It was made of aluminium, which was then an experimental but expensive material for huts, and trampers often called the shiny hut 'Silver City'.[11] Sensibly, when the Forest Service combined forces with the Hawke's Bay Section of the New Zealand Deerstalkers' Association to build a replacement called Longview Hut in the late 1970s, they located it on a ledge on the lee side of the ridge, sheltered from the worst of the westerlies. Even so, tramping parties have been pinned there during high winds. In 1992, DOC extensively renovated Longview, and installed a gas heater and cooker.[12]

According to DOC's hut database, in 1980 the NZFS built an astonishing ten huts in the Ruahine Range, ensuring it had the largest number of huts and bivs of any national or forest park in the country. It even eclipsed Fiordland National Park in this respect, which is thirteen times its size.

Longview Hut, pictured in 2011. PHOTO: SHAUN BARNETT/BLACK ROBIN PHOTOGRAPHY

In the late 1990s and early 2000s, DOC tastefully modified many of the original NZFS huts in the Ruahine Range, usually by installing skylights, often by replacing open fireplaces with wood-burning stoves and sometimes by adding covered verandas. McKinnon Hut is one such example. Built in 1960, the hut is a standard six-bunker and one of the earlier SF70s established in the Ruahine Range. Situated on the edge of the bush in the northern Hikurangi Range, it offers commanding views of the Mokai Patea Range and Kawhatau Valley, and even distant Mt Ruapehu – when the weather permits. Despite modifications (a lining, wood stove and some aluminium joinery) it still retains the strong flavour of an NZFS hut in a grand location.[13]

While the Ruahine Range does not attract trampers to quite the same degree as the Tararuas, it remains a popular destination nevertheless. Every few years a tramping party attempts to traverse the length of the 90-kilometre range, and the fact that some succeed is due in no small part to the abundance of huts.

SHAUN BARNETT

TOP Trampers at McKinnon Hut, a little-modified NZFS SF70 six-bunker, pictured in 2007.
BOTTOM Chris Maclean at Toka Biv, Ngamoko Range, January 2011. PHOTOS: SHAUN BARNETT/BLACK ROBIN PHOTOGRAPHY

Lower Gridiron Rock Shelter 1978 and Upper Gridiron Hut 1980
KAHURANGI NATIONAL PARK

> In the vicinity of Gridiron Creek, giant blocks of [limestone] have, in ages past, fallen from the weathered edges of the parent formation higher up and tumbled into the Flora Valley. Of these, two in particular lent themselves (it seemed to me) to becoming dry rock shelters.
>
> – Max Polglaze[1]

Since the earliest humans arrived in New Zealand, rock shelters and caves have provided shelter. In the mountains, gravity – perhaps helped by an earthquake – periodically loosens large boulders, sending them crashing down until finally they lie at rest on the valley floor. Most are useless for shelter, but occasionally one comes to rest in such a way that the underlying space is sufficiently accessible and flat to make a dry refuge. Trampers and climbers call these shelters rock bivs. Some are reached by crawling through a cave-like entrance; others boast huge overhangs with expansive views. In the best rock bivs, resourceful trampers have often levelled sleeping benches, lining them with tussock or fern, and have even made shelves.

Schist boulders seem to have the characteristics most suitable for the creation of rock bivs, and there are well-established examples in places like the upper Arawhata and Forgotten valleys that provide refuge in the otherwise hut-less Olivine Wilderness Area of the Southern Alps. In other places, limestone forms a suitable substrate.

Undoubtedly, however, the best-developed rock bivs in the country lie in the Flora Valley of Kahurangi National Park. Lower Gridiron Shelter boasts tiered bunks and a cooking area, and even has a corrugated-iron roof extension to maximise the dry area beneath. Sadly, the swinging bucket seat that once hung from the roof is gone, and while still grand, the shelter no longer has all the bunk tiers either, nor the double bed with headboards.[2]

The nearby Upper Gridiron can more properly be called a backcountry hut, as it is literally a small hut with a limestone overhang for half of its roof. Light leaks in through a square Perspex window, etched with a forest scene featuring a kea. Outside, a swinging bench seat provides a comfortable place to contemplate your surrounds.

Both of these rock bivs owe their development to the efforts of Max Polglaze, a former Forest Service ranger. Polglaze stamped his mark on the area in the 1970s, when the NZFS managed it as the Northwest Nelson Forest Park.

When the Forest Service established the park in 1965, many of the area's tracks were overgrown, even famous ones like the Heaphy and Wangapeka. And so the agency began an extensive programme of cutting tracks, building new huts and promoting the recreational opportunities of the new park, which was officially gazetted in 1970.

Polglaze played an integral part in this development, and his name became almost synonymous with the park. A former deer culler, he displayed all the attributes of a first-rate ranger: practical, energetic, knowledgeable and able to work around the bureaucracy of head office. Well-known broadcaster Jim Henderson once called Polglaze a 'Wet Boot Man', a term that refers to the amount of time he spent in the field.[3] Polglaze had already spent some years carrying out track and hut work in the park by the time he was appointed ranger in the Cobb Valley in October 1959. Later, he shifted to the Graham Valley.[4]

Salisbury (or Dry) Rock had long been used as a shelter, first by musterers working the tops of the Tableland, and later by gold miners, hunters and trampers, but Polglaze was the first to realise the full potential of the limestone overhangs in the nearby Flora Valley. Polglaze recalls:

> No attempt had been made to make it more habitable, however, prior to 1975. It was at best a rough temporary camping spot for one or two people. Me and the boys did a bit of work on it from time to time. There was no master plan. It

Lower Gridiron Rock Shelter, 2004.
PHOTO: SHAUN BARNETT/BLACK ROBIN PHOTOGRAPHY

Upper Gridiron Hut, 2011. PHOTO: GEOFF SPEARPOINT

just kind of evolved – rock walling and back-filling to make levels; a fireplace here, a bunk or bunks there; a ladder up to another level and another three bunks; and then, finally, because it wasn't actually all that dry – a drip-stopping roof up there overhead along the lip of the rock to stop the rain from weeping down under the overhang and dripping off at random.

One of the great discoveries I'd made in times past was that a piece of one-inch galvanised pipe made a tight driving fit in a 33mm steel drill hole, and as you beat on this pipe with a 6 or 8lb hammer and drove it into the hole, the end would become peened and enlarged making a perfect head for what was in effect a giant nail. With these giant nails you could pin heavy timbers directly to rock – anywhere. Or lay out a row of pipes set into rock, from which other constructions could be fastened. The roof at the Lower Gridiron is fixed to framing timbers bolted to a line of such pipes, hammered into holes 30 feet [9 metres] up, drilled from a cage suspended on cables from the top of the rock 20 feet [6 metres] higher again. Looking up from below you can perhaps still see two names on the underside of the roof iron – Max Polglaze, Dave Shubart 1978.[5]

About this time Polglaze also discovered another, smaller limestone overhang nearby:

[It] was, I think it's fair to say, not known prior to 1977 when, looking up from the track one day at this outcrop and wondering 'What's up there?', I scrambled up to find a rather nice overhang formed by another giant erratic tumbledown block of stone. No flat ground or anything underneath except masses of goat droppings, the sun pouring in, and a bush-fringed view out over the valley.[6]

Polglaze decided to build the Upper Gridiron Hut as a base for staff – quite against NZFS head office regulations. 'This too just evolved without any deliberate plan. I put a zigzag track up to it and did a bit of levelling in August 1977, and we set up a tent camp to work out of in June 1978, because here, at around 2000 feet [600 metres], we could work on these Flora–Tablelands–Takaka Valley tracks in winter, resurfacing and so forth, when the country higher up was under snow.'[7]

In June 1980, Polglaze recycled materials from a dismantled possumers' hut to complete the Upper Gridiron Hut. When Forestry Service bosses later inspected his 'illegal' work, Polglaze offered to pull it down, but the order never came. 'They had to growl officially, but privately they liked it.' Polglaze later admitted to a journalist that building the huts 'was a bit naughty', but at least one generation of trampers have been thankful ever since.[8] Wayne Elia, one of Polglaze's workmates, etched the kea and native plants on the window.[9]

Both shelters take their name from nearby Gridiron Creek, itself christened during the mining era, when a grid of tracks was sometimes constructed in order to locate gold more easily.[10] Polglaze called it Gridiron Gulch, and even installed a slip-rail for those occasions when he used a packhorse.[11]

Polglaze did not last long after the Forest Service was absorbed into the Department of Conservation in 1987: the paperwork and lack of fieldwork stifled him beyond words. But he has continued to play an important role restoring huts, including Cecil Kings Hut (see p. 87), Asbestos Cottage (see p. 84) and Riordans Hut (see p. 54), and now lives in Central Otago. Both Gridiron shelters remain part of his legacy in what became Kahurangi National Park, and also form a salute to a style of ranger now sadly gone.

SHAUN BARNETT

OPPOSITE Ranger Max Polglaze seated on left at Lower Gridiron Rock shelter, circa late 1970s. PHOTO: JOHN JOHNS, NZFS COLLECTION, ARCHIVES NEW ZEALAND, WELLINGTON, M13315

HUTS FOR THE PEOPLE NATIONAL PARK BOARDS AND LANDS AND SURVEY HUTS

Origins of Lands and Survey

It was mainly in national parks, initially through the national park boards, that the Department of Lands and Survey played a major role in building and maintaining public huts. When the department was disestablished in 1987, New Zealand had eleven national parks: Abel Tasman, Arthur's Pass, Egmont, Fiordland, Mount Aspiring, Mount Cook, Nelson Lakes, Te Urewera, Tongariro, Westland and Whanganui. Understanding the role that Lands and Survey played in managing huts requires a look at the evolution of both the department and our national parks.

When, in 1876, New Zealand did away with provincial governments in favour of a more centralised system, one of the outcomes was the formation of the Department of Lands and Survey.[1] Its wide-ranging areas of responsibility included surveying, health and tourist resorts, immigration, Crown lands and roads; forests and agriculture were added ten years later. By 1896, Lands and Survey had 245 employees. From this one super-department came the Department of Agriculture (which split off in 1893), the Department of Tourist and Health Resorts (1901), Government Print (1901), Roads (formed in 1902, later becoming the Ministry of Works), the Department of Immigration (1913), and the State Forest Service (1919). Right from the start, Lands and Survey was progressive and development-oriented.

The first surveyor-general to be appointed was fifty-five-year-old John Turnbull Thomson, who after working in Singapore had spent ten years as chief surveyor for Otago, where he named Mt Aspiring.[2] His assistant in Otago, James McKerrow, later replaced him.

The Department of Lands and Survey was divided into land districts, each run by a commissioner of Crown lands. One of its first tasks was to complete a unified triangulation of the whole country to provide a sound basis for the mapping of New Zealand. In the pursuit of this survey, teams spent months staying in canvas tent camps. The camps were intended to be only temporary and in the main were dismantled when the surveyors moved on – hut building wasn't yet a priority. A little later, around the turn of the century, any government money allocated for huts was usually directed through the Tourist and Health Resorts or Roads departments.

Upper Travers Hut, Nelson Lakes National Park, 1962. PHOTO: BEN GIBBS

The First National Parks

The roots of our early national parks are both varied and interesting. In some ways their development mirrored that of the Department of Lands and Survey, with a hotchpotch of regional variations that were eventually unified under one central authority. Initially, each park required its own special legislation. For instance, when Horonuku Te Heuheu Tukino IV gifted 6508 acres (2634 hectares) of land covering the peaks of Tongariro, Ngauruhoe and Ruapehu to the Crown in 1887, it led to the adoption of the Tongariro National Park Act 1894, which vested powers for the park's administration with the governor. Park management trustees included the minister of lands (chairman), the surveyor-general, the director of the New Zealand Geological Survey, and, in the words of the act, 'Te Heu Heu the younger' and 'such other persons as the Governor shall appoint' under the Public Domains Act 1881. Tongariro was our first national park, and the fourth in the world.[3]

Egmont National Park came second. In 1875, the Taranaki Provincial Government created a forest reserve around Mt Taranaki (known then as Mt Egmont). The Egmont National Park Act 1900 also provided for governance by a board of ten members, with the commissioner of Crown lands being chairman. Executive support for the board came from the Department of Lands and Survey.

Officially, the third national park was Arthur's Pass. Commissioner of Crown lands for Westland, G.J. Roberts, in response to the surveyor-general's request for progress on native flora and fauna preservation in 1903, wrote, 'One area between the Otira and Bealey has been set apart for the purpose of a National Park'.[4] And a little later, 'To stop the pilfering of plants at Arthur's Pass, I would suggest that the drivers of the mail coaches be also made warders for that place.'[5] Arthur's Pass (1929) and Abel Tasman (1942) were both gazetted as national parks under the Public Reserves, Domains and National Parks Act 1928. They were managed by their own independent local park boards, which controlled each park's limited budget and had the power to instruct Lands and Survey on the management and services required.

Other important mountain areas were also set aside as reserves early in the twentieth century, but war and government apathy meant they did not achieve national park status for a long time. In 1905, most of Fiordland was protected

Whakapapaiti Hut, with Mt Ruapehu beyond, Tongariro National Park, 2008. PHOTO: SHAUN BARNETT/BLACK ROBIN PHOTOGRAPHY

as a 'national reserve' under the Scenery Preservation Act 1903. The reserve was managed by the Department of Tourist and Health Resorts. When this department was restructured in 1908, Fiordland returned to the control of Lands and Survey, still as a national reserve.

During the 1920s and 1930s, management of national parks was a relatively loose affair. Boards usually appointed a local as a custodian or warden on a part-time basis. Many of these worked hard to support their park, but sometimes their actions were misguided, such as the warden for Tongariro who actively introduced heather throughout the park over a ten-year period in around 1920. Any hut-building activity in national parks was usually accomplished by other groups, such as tramping clubs or the Tourist Department. For instance, the latter built huts on the George Sound Track in Fiordland.[6] The 1935 *Handbook of Arthur's Pass National Park* lists only two huts, both of them built by clubs, although the old schoolhouse had been procured by the park board for use as a public shelter.[7]

In 1919, when the Forest Service split off from Lands and Survey, responsibility for a significant portion of forested land went with it. National parks remained under the ambit of Lands and Survey, but were still directly controlled by local park boards. Adjoining forestry land was sometimes added to national parks after negotiations, but within the world of competing departmental policies the Forest Service later (in the 1950s) created its own system of state forest parks, with a more liberal multiple-use management concept.

The 1930s and 1940s were decades of increasing participation in outdoor recreation. Clubs were established throughout the country, and large groups regularly went into the hills on organised trips, such as railway excursions to Arthur's Pass, thereby putting pressure on park facilities.

Any backcountry land under the control of Lands and Survey that was not already reserved or suited to farming usually remained as 'unalienated Crown land' (UCL), later administered by the Land Settlement Board through the Land Act 1948. Generally, the Land Settlement Board wasn't interested in such places, and although hunters and others built huts on UCL areas, Lands and Survey was not involved.

The primary focus of Lands and Survey lay in developing and selling farmland, which became its economic arm, just as production forestry became the economic arm of the Forest Service. And just as environmental forestry was a poor cousin to production forestry, so national parks and reserves were poor cousins to farmland within the farm-focused Lands and Survey.

The National Parks Act 1952

Prior to the Second World War, the government recognised that the various national park acts needed unifying. Lands and Survey staff worked with organisations like the Federated Mountain Clubs to achieve this goal, and came up with the National Parks Act 1952, which was supported by both major parties in Parliament. The act consolidated all the varied and separate national park acts, and set up a national structure to overview the parks – the National Parks Authority. Under the authority, national park boards continued to manage the executive functions of each park, facilitated through Lands and Survey.

The twelve years following the passing of the new act witnessed a flurry of park development: Fiordland in 1952, Mount Cook in 1953, Te Urewera in 1954, Nelson Lakes in 1956, Westland in 1960 and Mount Aspiring in 1964. Whanganui was added in 1986, the year before the Department of Conservation was established.[8]

Doing a Lot With a Little – National Parks Staff and Huts

With the implementation of a national structure, parks now had the potential to expand their activities, including hut building, but better resourcing through Lands and Survey was slow to appear. Park board staff worked like Trojans to provide facilities, and their records are full of work efforts well beyond the ordinary. For instance, when Ray Cleland was appointed ranger at Arthur's Pass in 1950, he and his wife Connie moved into a corrugated-iron cottage with virtually no amenities,[9] and with no transport provided to manage the park. Track work, public relations, noxious-animal control, search and rescue, managing Lands and Survey rental houses in the area, raising money for a visitor's centre, building huts … there was so much to do and not much to do it with. In the early days, that was the story for most parks.

During the early 1950s, Cleland helped build five small huts in the Poulter and Hawdon valleys in cooperation with the Department of Internal Affairs as part of its animal-control activities. He salvaged materials from a demolished building and borrowed DIA horses, but a lack of money for horse feed restricted his ability to use the animals to transport materials – the park board simply didn't have the finance for it. The materials eventually got to their sites, either by packhorse or pack frame, but it took a long time.[10]

Outdoor clubs continued to grow and strengthen during the 1950s, and in many national parks the majority of public huts were either a legacy of the Tourist Department or clubs, which also maintained them. From the 1960s, this balance reversed, as parks consciously pushed higher building standards and a more professional approach to facilities. Outdoor people were spoilt for choice when the Forest Service sprinkled its deer-control huts everywhere, helping foster a second backcountry boom of younger people in the 1970s.

Free access to national parks was a guiding principle of the National Parks Act, but park boards could raise money through donations, which attracted a generous government subsidy. Consequently, where fees weren't charged for overnight stays in park huts, a donation was suggested. This changed over time to a specific hut fee, which although relatively meagre in the greater scheme of things was still an important source of revenue for parks. On the other hand, the well-funded NZFS chose not to charge for its huts, and the two conflicting systems caused some tension. From the beginning, the park boards and Lands and Survey were relatively conservative in the number of public huts they built compared to the Forest Service, partly due to a lack of resources (in 1979, the total expenditure for the ten national parks was just $2.5 million),[11] different needs and a different management philosophy. Instead, they tended to build larger huts, with twelve to twenty bunks, and many in Lands and Survey regarded their facilities as a cut above their rivals. When the Forest Service started building large, comfortable, high-quality huts itself in the new state forest parks from the late 1960s, this caused consternation among some Lands and Survey staff, who felt it challenged their recreational pre-eminence.

Mount Aspiring and Fiordland National Parks

Resourcing of national parks slowly improved, and by the 1960s several embarked on active hut-building programmes. Between 1963 and 1967, some thirteen huts went up in Fiordland in addition to those constructed along the Milford Track for freedom walkers. Many parks had also inherited old hunting huts, and in some cases the park board replaced these with their own, larger huts. In other cases they took over route and hut networks originally established by clubs.

As far as park staff were concerned, building huts to more professional standards heralded in the recreational future of national parks. Many of the new huts contrasted markedly from earlier structures, some of which pre-dated the formation of the parks. Although well designed and very welcome in bad weather, the new huts were, however, often very utilitarian, their abundance of space sometimes rendering them less evocative and homely. Perhaps the professional approach contributed to that. Yet at other times Lands and Survey huts did have that 'X' factor – Routeburn Falls Hut, built in 1967, is one such example.

In the 1970s, the cultural and historical value of the older huts got scant acknowledgement. Instead, park board rangers often felt these old structures conflicted with the pristine environment and should be removed or replaced with something more worthy of a national park. Consequently, some park staff were directed to burn down old huts and other historic buildings. In this purge, Fiordland lost all of its old culling huts, bar two.[12] Similar purges occurred in Mount Aspiring National Park, when staff flew into isolated valleys in the Olivine Range. During one such event, a television crew arrived and filmed a burning hut for a news story; the resulting public outcry embarrassed the staff and park board alike.[13]

When it was established in 1964, Mount Aspiring National Park became our tenth national park. Various huts in the park already existed, built by clubs, hunters, farmers, tourism interests and the NZFS. The first backcountry recreational hut built by the park board was the much-loved Routeburn Falls Hut in 1967.[14]

Ray Cleland had arrived in Wanaka as chief ranger in 1965, after successfully getting himself demoted from supervisor of national parks in Wellington, where a seven-year stint spent dealing with the bureaucracy had disagreed with him.[15] When another ranger, Mervyn Burke, arrived at Glenorchy in January 1967, the pair planned and built the Routeburn Falls Hut with assistance from students. Like many notable early park rangers, Burke, who had been chief ranger at Mount Cook National Park in the early 1960s, was a carpenter. Just as Fiordland staff developed their own hut styles, so too did those at Mount Aspiring. For instance, Fiordland huts often had communal sleeping platforms, while Aspiring park rangers preferred separate bunks for their huts.

Park huts replaced the old tourist hut at Routeburn Flats and the NZAC's Dart Hut. Others constructed included Daleys Flat Hut, and huts in the Wilkin,

Lands and Survey ranger Dick Ratcliff extending Routeburn Falls Hut, Mount Aspiring National Park, 1983. PHOTO: GEOFF SPEARPOINT

Siberia and Young valleys. In the mid-1970s, a bivvy went onto the tops near Mt Brewster. By 1980, the Mount Aspiring National Park Board owned nine huts, three of which were old NZFS deer-culling huts. In total, about twenty-five huts existed in the park.[16] In 1981, while senior ranger Brian Ahern was at Glenorchy, Shelter Rock Hut in the Rees Valley was built, replacing an old mustering hut. On more popular tracks – the precursors to Great Walks – hut wardens were introduced as early as 1960, and by the 1980s their presence was well established.

Aoraki/Mount Cook and Westland Tai Poutini National Parks

Aoraki/Mount Cook National Park was formed in 1953, and in 1959 its board inherited six mountain huts when the Tourist Hotel Corporation relinquished control of them.[17] A backlog of deferred maintenance awaited, and the park was simultaneously charged with reinstating mountain guiding. To carry this out, the government granted the board a special one-off lump sum of £7500. The park also took control of an old four-bunk Internal Affairs hut, Hunters Haven, at White Horse Hill, which could be rented out cheaply.[18] The area is now a major campground, with toilets and a shelter. Older tourism huts left a legacy of mattresses, blankets, stoves and fuel, as well as cooking and eating utensils, which continued to be supplied in new alpine huts. By 1962, the park board managed seven huts, while further huts were owned by clubs like the New Zealand Alpine Club, New Zealand Deerstalkers' Association and Canterbury Mountaineering Club.

In the 1970s and 1980s, building standards in the national parks continued to improve, and better concepts for alpine huts were discussed. Park carpenter Stuart King designed and largely built the circular Copland Shelter in 1972, based on laminated kahikatea hoops. Max Dorfliger finished it off. Ranger Mal Clarbrough designed Gardiner Hut (1976), which was built by Ken 'Digger' Joyce (see p. 276). Mal describes it as basically a grain silo on its side, utilising the strength of corrugated iron. At this time, park staff also studied at Lincoln College, and an engineering tutor, Ian Calvert, confirmed the strength of the design when his students ran wind tunnel tests. When Three Johns Hut blew away in 1977, the Gardiner design was also used to build Barron Saddle Hut in 1981.

Over in Westland Tai Poutini National Park, huts like Cape Defiance (see p. 136), Chancellor (see p. 112) and Pioneer (see p. 128) remained from the early tourism and climbing days, and Lands and Survey gradually took over maintenance of most of them. A ranger noted in the 1960s that, 'The THC [Tourist Hotel Corporation] had given up the reins for the region and tracks and huts were disappearing into a derelict state of neglect.'[19] By 1973, the park had assumed ownership of, or built, about ten huts – about the same number as at Aoraki/Mount Cook National Park.[20]

Other South Island National Parks

Further north, in Arthur's Pass National Park, straitened circumstances limited hut-building progress until the late 1960s. However, by 1971 park staff had built or acquired six roadside shelters (Greyneys, Klondyke, Hawdon, Andrews, Kelly and Summit), reflecting the importance the main road had on access to the park. They also managed Page Shelter in the Temple Basin ski area and seven backcountry national park huts.[21]

The park was also home to another twenty-five backcountry huts, owned by clubs, the Forest Service and farmers, bringing the total to nearly forty. As better funding flowed, building quality improved. Now, instead of cobbling together shelters using second-hand materials, staff built five new Lockwood huts with three or more rooms, capable of housing sixteen people or more.[22] In Arthur's Pass, as elsewhere, the park board became increasingly interested in owning other new huts, even those built by clubs. When the NZAC applied to build Crow Hut in 1958, the board gave permission only on the understanding that it would own the hut. In return, NZAC members retained controlling rights and had first preference on use.[23]

Nelson Lakes National Park, formed in 1956, had the usual park board management, serviced by Lands and Survey. George Lyon, one of the original board members, became the sole ranger for the park in 1959. He was one of only twenty-nine other rangers nationwide in the National Park Service at that time. The park had just one hut, the six-bunk John Tait in the Travers Valley, and two open shelters at the head of Lake Rotoiti, plus at least four old slab huts, most of them in poor condition.

Lands and Survey rangers John Ombler and Rob Young examine Barron Saddle Hut, ready to be flown onto site, 1981. PHOTO: BRUCE POSTILL

Trampers at Anne Hut, St James Walkway, Lewis Pass, 2002. PHOTO: GEOFF SPEARPOINT

Perhaps not surprisingly, for his first hut – the Sabine Forks Hut, built in 1959 – Lyon engaged help from the Forest Service, which by then was embarking on its great hut-building programme. The NZFS helped prefabricate materials for the hut to a modified NZFS design, with assistance from culler Percy Singer. Lyon and Singer based themselves in a Forest Service tent camp across the Sabine River during the build. Lyon remembered, 'There was a light fall [of snow] each night, about an inch, so imagine how invigorating it was to have to ford the river each morning!'[24]

By 1962 the park had six park huts, and this had further increased to sixteen by 1979, providing more than 200 bunks altogether.[25] Lyon was directly involved in the building of twelve of these, and one suspects that his wife, Jean, in a largely unpaid capacity, provided much support too.

Not all parks were equal – the big three were Tongariro, Mount Cook and Fiordland. Staff in more poorly-funded parks sometimes viewed expenditure in the big three as a little profligate. Lyon operated on a budget where every cent counted, and thought Lockwood huts were a 'complete waste of public money'. He made do with mattresses left over from hospital stock upgrades.[26]

National park rangers were a close-knit group who applied for jobs in different parks, and so often knew other rangers right around the country. They were resourceful, innovative, forward-thinking, strongly conservation-minded and immensely practical. They usually lived in isolated communities at a time when parks weren't automatically welcomed by some, and had the difficult and challenging role of explaining to locals a new way of thinking about the environment – often strongly at variance with the more traditional pioneering values of the community.

In 1964, Jim Hayter was appointed the first ranger to Abel Tasman National Park. Along with Jim Kilby, he built the first park board hut the following year, a three bunker at Anapai on the coast.[27] Over the next decade, his successors added substantially to the park's hut and track system, so that by the mid-1970s huts totalled about seven. By 1981 the dilapidated Whariwharangi Homestead had been restored by Nelson carpenter Graham Snadden and a team working under chief ranger Geoff Rennison (see p. 66).[28] In the mid-1980s, ranger Peter Fullerton designed the new Bark Bay and Awapoto huts. By 1984, there were ten park huts in Abel Tasman – much the same number as today.[29]

North Island National Parks

It was not until 1951, fully fifty-seven years after Tongariro National Park was created, that its first salaried ranger, carpenter Alex Salmon, was appointed.[30] Salmon had spent much of his life in the area, and had already built a public hut in the Whakapapaiti Valley, called Alex's Bivvy.[31] Although Tongariro was seen as a leader within the national park system, the number of huts built by its board was similar to that elsewhere. By 1969, the Tongariro National Park Board owned about eight public huts. By comparison, about fifty private club huts, used mainly for skiing, had been built, most of them at Iwikau Village.[32]

Daleys Flat Hut, Dart Valley, Mount Aspiring National Park, 1980. PHOTO: GEOFF SPEARPOINT

Dome Shelter, built in 1961 near the summit of Ruapehu, was the highest park hut in the country, at 2600 metres.[33] As in many parks at this time, building in Tongariro was a collaboration between park staff and volunteers, including Ohakune locals Peter and Rodney Winchcombe, the NZAC and Ruapehu Ski Club. During the 1960s, Lockwood-designed huts became popular in the park and were built at Whakapapaiti (1964), Waihohonu (1968), Rangipo (1968), Mangaehuehu (1969), Ketetahi (1968), Oturere (1970) and Mangatepopo (1974), all of which (apart from Waihohonu, which was replaced by DOC in 2010) remain, making the Central Plateau the Lockwood hut capital of New Zealand.[34]

Over in Egmont National Park, Gordon Atkinson was appointed its first chief ranger in 1943. Like Salmon he was also a carpenter, a skill shared by many rangers in the National Park Service and indicating the very practical nature of hut-building work in earlier decades. It also ensured that certain building standards were maintained.

Land added to national parks sometimes included a few exotic trees. In the early 1980s, a plantation of macrocarpas milled on Mt Taranaki provided timber for park signs, six mountain huts and the public shelter on Manganui ski-field. Like Tongariro National Park, Egmont caught the Lockwood bug too, with several of the huts built here in the 1970s adopting this design (Holly and Pouakai huts are examples of these, plus a number of other park buildings).

As national park staff became more capable and professional in their roles, tensions over management boundaries sometimes existed with the boards. The Egmont National Park Board seems to have excelled in this regard, and at one stage formed a subcommittee to select a colour scheme for a small picnic shelter. This wasn't the case everywhere though, as Wally Sander, Te Urewera National Park ranger during the 1960s, commented:

The Board of the day was as new to the park as I was and we spent a bit of time educating each other about the principles of managing a national park. They were a friendly practical group of members who gave me tremendous support and assistance, not just in terms of managing the park but also personally at times of need … It was pretty much a family affair.[35]

Limited funds continued to hamper park staff, who often had to make do with cast-offs from other departments. At Lake Waikaremoana in Te Urewera National Park, when the Wildlife Service's boat was condemned as unsafe in the early 1960s, they gave it to the park board for park staff to use.[36] And when the Ministry of Works replaced the decking on a road bridge, the old materials disappeared one night and later reappeared on park bridges and other facilities. Park staff also cadged gravel for track work from the ministry.[37]

Lack of funding is not a part of our park history that we tell overseas visitors. Often, however, the national parks were supported by a huge local and regional volunteer network – in Te Urewera help came from schools as far away as New Plymouth and Auckland. Wally Sander, who was employed as park ranger in 1963, recalled that locals provided twenty-two packhorses to transport Lockwood hut materials to remote sites for the park. The only capital funding available was a private £1000 donation and a government subsidy that the donation attracted. From this money, and with a great deal of cost cutting and clever planning, the Waikareiti, Waipaoa and Marauiti eighteen-bunk huts were built. A further seven park huts were built in Te Urewera through the decade, but the balance of the roughly sixty huts in the park were built by the NZFS.[38]

Although Whanganui National Park was gazetted only a year before Lands and Survey ceased to exist, the department built some recreational huts here also, notably along the Matemateaonga Walkway.

In the Lands and Survey era, the National Parks Authority clearly stipulated many aspects of building design. These were influenced by overseas park experience, particularly in the United States. The General Policy for National Parks 1983 states that: 'Buildings will be designed to harmonise with the natural landscape … An effort will be made to achieve a degree of unity of style in architecture within a park, and consideration will be given to construction materials and colour schemes which produce low-key building appearance.'[39]

The Forest Service, on the other hand, had given priority to hut visibility for safety reasons. Consequently, parks ended up with huts under Lands and Survey control the colour of mud, and those under the Forest Service bright orange. One might say that it was a case of too much policy on both sides.

In earlier days, park huts had open fireplaces. By the 1960s, these were being replaced by pot-belly stoves such as the 'Fatso' and 'Little Dorrit'. These stoves were designed to run on wood or coal, but did best on coal, which was delivered to some higher profile park huts. Although fuel efficiency was one of the reasons for the change, the pot-bellies were not particularly conservative on fuel themselves, and from the 1980s much more efficient wood burners began to replace them.

The Lockwood design Casey Hut, Arthur's Pass National Park, 2005. PHOTO: SHAUN BARNETT/BLACK ROBIN PHOTOGRAPHY

Beyond the National Parks: Other Lands and Survey Huts

Considerable 'unalienated Crown land' under Lands and Survey authority also existed on the West Coast of the South Island, particularly in the Southern Alps. Hut building there had been largely the preserve of the NZFS, but in 1984 Lands and Survey took a greater management interest in it. Neil Clifton of Lands and Survey had already carried out a major overview study of the region in 1981, *The Central Southern Alps Crown Land Management Strategy*,[40] mapping a way forward for its recreational use. And in the mid-1980s, the department went ahead and built two huts.

Ted Brennan remembers following the floor design of the old Mt Brown Hut (now gone) as an initial template for these two huts, one to be sited at Crawford Junction in the Kokatahi Valley and one at Julia in the Taipo Valley.[41] Both replaced older huts that had hand-hewn frames, the one at Julia having been built in 1958. The design of both new huts was identical, with a stove, veranda and split-level sleeping platforms. They were efficient and practical structures, with a reasonable amount of space. The huts were largely built on site, with only the roof trusses flown in intact.

The Forest Service was not supportive of these projects, given the prominent role it already had in building and maintaining huts and tracks in the area. Indeed, it had its own plans for hut replacement, and when Lands and Survey went ahead with the Crawford Junction and Julia huts, the hut the NZFS already in mind for one of the sites went south to Maori Saddle on the Haast–Paringa Cattle Track instead.

During the 1970s and 1980s, Lands and Survey also developed the St James Walkway in the Lewis Pass region, establishing new huts throughout. In part this was a response to the Forest Service's success with its Lake Sumner Forest Park hut and track system (see p. 244). Although cooperation existed in many

A Christchurch Tramping Club party at Alabaster Hut in the Pyke Valley in 1964–5, shortly after the hut had been built by Fiordland National Park staff. From the left are Brian Le Fevre, Rick Watson, Kieth Saunders, and Greta Vink.
PHOTO: REX VINK

places between the two departments, tensions also existed over recreational facilities and various environmental matters. Conflicting policies and obvious duplication inevitably led to questions as to how a cheaper and more unified approach could be achieved, both at an environmental and recreational level.

In 1980, a change to the National Park Act transferred executive functions from park boards directly to Lands and Survey, giving the department a more direct say in park management, including huts. Earlier, in 1969, employment of rangers had been transferred from the national park boards to Lands and Survey. By 1974, the year the Diploma of Parks and Recreation for rangers was introduced at Lincoln University, the number of rangers employed by the department had risen to seventy-eight. It says a lot for the international standing of New Zealand park rangers that in this same year the department agreed to a request from the Nepalese government to send a ranger to advise on the management of Nepal's first national park, the newly created Sagarmatha National Park around Mt Everest. Advice from Bing Lucas in the National Park Service set the pattern for future involvement, and Gordon Nicholls, accompanied by his wife Esther, took up the advisory role in 1975. Support and exchanges continued throughout the rest of the Lands and Survey era, with rangers posted to Peru, Australia and the Pacific Islands.

From Lands and Survey to DOC

By 1987, the number of rangers in the national parks and reserves service had risen to 110. However, in that year Lands and Survey, the Forest Service and the Wildlife Service (a branch of Internal Affairs) were all dissolved, and a new era was ushered in with the passing of the Conservation Act 1987. While most sections of these organisations were amalgamated to create the Department of Conservation, some parts of Lands and Survey went in other directions. For instance, the Honorary Geographic Board, set up to advise on place names in 1924, became the New Zealand Geographic Board in 1946, was incorporated into the Department of Survey and Land Information (DOSLI) in 1987, and now operates under its own act.

The legacy of Lands and Survey, the national park boards and the National Parks Authority is wide-ranging, and includes an internationally acclaimed park system, great conservation work, a professional ranger service, careful management plans and a well-established hut infrastructure. Many of the policies in place today in national parks, including those concerning huts, evolved under the park boards and Lands and Survey. At a practical level, Lands and Survey handed on a wonderful network of public huts, ranging from flash forty-bunk lodges through to basic but comfortable two-bunk affairs – all appreciated by outdoor people the length of the country.

GEOFF SPEARPOINT

One of the last huts built by Lands and Survey, Welcome Flat Hut is a bold, two-storey structure that was built in 1987 as a replacement for an old hut in the Copland Valley. The first Welcome Flat Hut had remained safe from avalanches since it was built in 1913, so Westland National Park ranger Bruce Postill decided to use the same sunny site for the new hut. However, disaster struck soon after, when a large rock avalanche came down one night in March 1987. Fortunately, all the hut occupants were sleeping in the top storey and none were injured. Postill arranged for a geologist to look for a better site, but he concluded that nowhere in the entire steep-sided valley was completely safe. DOC staff, who had by then taken over, orchestrated for the hut to be jacked up and shifted on metal tracks about 200 metres to its present location, where it has remained safe ever since.

ANTI-CLOCKWISE FROM TOP LEFT The rock avalanche that hit the new Welcome Flat Hut, pictured on 3 March 1987. An aerial view of Welcome Flat Hut site, 1986. Rolling Welcome Flat Hut onto its new site after the rock avalanche.
PHOTOS: BRUCE POSTILL

Carrington Hut 1928/1941/1975 ARTHUR'S PASS NATIONAL PARK

Carrington Hut's first logbook, started in March 1929, contains these words: 'to fulfil the purpose of Gerard Carrington, who loved the beauties of this part of the Southern Alps and conceived the thought of its use and erection and started the work practically single-handed'.[1] This tribute, from the Canterbury Mountaineering Club, acknowledged a remarkable young man, Gerard Carrington, who had been a driving force behind the hut and the formation of the club.

Carrington and Chris Fenwick were camped near the junction of the Waimakariri and White rivers in the mid-1920s when they decided on the idea for a hut. The site was a popular camping spot for CMC trips and an inspirational environment from which to launch exploratory trips to the higher peaks of Arthur's Pass. On his return home, the then eighteen-year-old Carrington set about raising money for the hut. After he wrote to the Department of Tourist and Health Resorts with a plea for the project, the government made a £50 grant towards the hut. Carrington and several companions began packing materials to the site in May 1926.[2]

That same year, on the return from a packing trip, Carrington and two friends decided to descend the Waimakariri River Gorge in a makeshift raft. After the raft overturned, Carrington and John Shannon drowned, while the third member of the party miraculously survived the swollen waters. Carrington was not yet twenty-one, and his death rocked the fledgling club. After nearly abandoning the hut project, the club rallied when members decided that finishing it would serve as a fitting memorial to Carrington.[3] Chris Fenwick organised a hut construction party for the summer of 1928–29, involving many of the early CMC stalwarts. Packhorses provided transport, and all went well until one animal got a fright, then bolted, dispersing its load over a large area of matagouri.[4]

Although Carrington Memorial Hut was opened in December 1928, it lacked bunks and still had a dirt floor. Despite these deficiencies, it became a focal point for further climbing and first ascents in the area, as well as opening up tramping trips such as the Three Pass route to the West Coast. CMC had already built a hut in the Wilberforce Valley – Park Morpeth (see p. 320) – and so it was now possible to complete a Three Pass trip to the West Coast without the need for a tent. A CMC climbing party at Easter 1929 built bunks in 'a real attempt to make the [Carrington] hut more comfortable'.[5]

Cedric Turner recalled his impressions of the hut from the 1930s:

> Outside it was as plain as Anne of Cleves, and inside it crammed into its small area just about all the mistakes it was possible to make in hut building but we loved it … The fireplace always smoked. Each end boasted a loft, used for everything from sleeping to providing a community centre for mice and there were 18 bunks in three tiers, the top one being lost in the gloom.[6]

In 1929, the mountains of Arthur's Pass were gazetted as New Zealand's third national park, mainly thanks to the campaigning of eminent Canterbury

The original CMC Carrington Memorial Hut, June 1933.
PHOTO: JOHN PASCOE COLLECTION, ALEXANDER TURNBULL LIBRARY, WELLINGTON 1/4-046806-F

botanist Dr Leonard Cockayne. In 1930, the CMC negotiated a lease of 5 acres (2 hectares) of park land that encompassed the hut site. This lease ran until a permit system was introduced with the National Parks Act 1952.

In the late 1930s, Gordon Buchanan reflected how Carrington Hut had embedded itself in the hearts of many early CMC members. Although Carrington was, he wrote, 'not the best of our huts … it brings back memories of packed bunks, a smoky atmosphere, a springless gramophone, a table packed with food, and companions now spread to the four corners of the world'. He also captured the awakening appeal of the mountains of Arthur's Pass felt by early members: 'In spite of all our ramblings the Waimak still attracts us with a charm of its own'. The area had inspired the formation of the club and became the main training ground for members. On the Waimakariri peaks, Buchanan concluded, 'we learned to love the hills and slowly master their difficulties'.[7]

The huge floods in February 1940 dramatically altered the course of the Waimakariri River and threatened to wash the hut away. Despite the wartime shortage of materials, the CMC decided to rebuild the hut on a nearby site in 1941. With so many members away on active service, it was left to mainly very young or old CMC members to complete the project.

Although salvaged materials from the old hut helped, the new hut required fresh timber, nails and cement. Jack Ede recalled the rebuild in his book *I've Lived Another Year* (2004). He and Andy Anderson tied about 120 pounds (55 kilograms) of timber onto their packs and struggled up the Waimak, able to progress in only twenty-minute bursts under their oppressive burdens. Another CMC member, Geoff Chisholm, carried in 50 pounds (23 kilograms) of nails, remarking that his load was 'horrible'. Ede offered to swap, but Chisholm 'looked at our exhausted condition and the wet timber, and made no further comment but moved up the riverbed'.[8] On another carry, rain meant that the cement bags had to be stowed in chimney pipes to keep them dry.

Finally, once materials were on site, the building could begin in earnest. Ede remembered CMC stalwart Nui Robins cooking eggs for breakfast one cold morning, with drips of snot falling from his hooked nose into the frying pan. There were few takers for fried eggs, causing Nui to comment, 'I'm surprised that the buggers can't be hungry.'[9]

Slowly, the rebuilt hut was enlarged over the next couple of years, with a cookhouse added and an additional bunkroom clad in 'artistic pressed steel'. Carrington Hut II served another generation of climbers and trampers, but by the early 1970s it was approaching the end of its life. CMC resolved to replace the hut as part of its fiftieth jubilee celebrations. Members approached the Arthur's Pass National Park Board with the proposal, but were surprised to be turned down. The park board had unilaterally decided to replace the old CMC hut with its own hut, thereby severing a historical link with the CMC that created bad feeling between the club and park managers for some time.[10]

At that stage, Lands and Survey had embarked on an extensive programme of installing huts and facilities in the national park. It was a time of better budgets, when the level of recreation facility improvement mirrored that of American national parks in the 1950s and 1960s. Added to that, tramping at Arthur's Pass peaked in the mid-1970s. Large groups were the norm, and easy rail access ensured the park became one of the most popular places for the ever-growing numbers of Christchurch trampers. The Arthur's Pass board had already authorised the building of four Lockwood huts in the park – Casey, Edwards, Goat Pass and Hawdon – and continued with this style for the new Carrington Hut. It was the last Lockwood hut built in the park.

Tragedy struck during the hut construction in 1975. Halfway through a day spent ferrying building materials to the hut site, helicopter pilot Tony Jones flew park worker Stan Scott to the Harman Pass tops so he could hunt deer for meat. But after picking Scott up later in the day, the chopper hit the Clough Cableway, killing both men. A ground party went in search of the missing helicopter, but failed to spot the crumpled wreck in the fading light. The following day, a Royal New Zealand Air Force Harvard plane, carrying on the search, almost ran out of power and turning space when it headed up the tight White River Valley.[11]

Today, when widespread car ownership allows people to range much more widely for their weekend tramping trips, the thirty-six-bunk Carrington Hut is rarely full. However, the Lockwood-style shelter still provides a useful night's accommodation for trampers and climbers setting off for the higher huts and mountains that so attracted early CMC members.

ROB BROWN

The Park Board-built Lockwood Carrington Hut, in 2000.
PHOTO: SHAUN BARNETT/BLACK ROBIN PHOTOGRAPHY

Blue Lake Hut 1970, George Lyon Hut 1973, John Tait Hut 1951/1978
NELSON LAKES NATIONAL PARK

> The 'purists' believe that no huts should be placed in a park – all should carry their own tents. I don't agree with this but rather believe … that if a hut site is properly managed, it is a means of giving people a chance to appreciate the park experience more fully.
>
> – George Lyon[1]

Many huts in Nelson Lakes National Park occupy grand locations: often set upon pleasant river flats, flanked by beech forest and with stately mountains visible in the valley beyond. John Tait Hut has just such a location in the Travers Valley, as does George Lyon Hut in the D'Urville Valley. Blue Lake Hut occupies an equally impressive site in the headwaters of the West Sabine Valley, near the exquisite lake after which it is named.

In 2005, George Lyon Hut, originally called Ella Hut, was appropriately renamed in honour of Lyon, chief ranger at Nelson Lakes National Park between 1959 and 1980. Lyon played a huge role in developing the park during the heyday of Lands and Survey, and altogether built twelve huts in the park.[2]

Lyon recalled the early years of the park being one of 'track cutting, building huts, maintaining and supervising motor camps … plus – I feel the most important aspect – public relations'.[3]

George Lyon (Ella) Hut and Blue Lake Hut

George Lyon and Blue Lake huts are the best remaining examples of the original Lyon standard design sixteen-bunk huts that once dominated the park in the 1970s and 1980s. John Tait, Lake Head and Angelus were other Lyon designs, but have either been substantially modified or replaced altogether by new Department of Conservation huts.

Lyon huts were designed with two eight-bunk rooms, each having a pot-belly coal-burning stove and gas cookers.[4] The double-room design meant that in winter, when the hut was not full, only one room needed to be heated, and in the busier summer season parties could separate themselves if desired. Rangers provided coal for the stoves.

Ranger Bruce Postill worked with Lyon at Nelson Lakes in the 1970s and remembers that Lyon prided himself on his frugal hut design, which he considered to be the cheapest in New Zealand.[5]

To save costs, Lyon used 50-millimetre by 50-millimetre studs instead of conventional framing timber, onto which he glued and nailed Bison Board (a 10 millimetre-thick particle board), which not only served as inside cladding but provided additional structural strength. The cost-conscious chief ranger considered insulation unnecessary, reckoning heat would escape out the windows anyway.

Postill says Lyon worked very hard, and expected the same of his staff, but never asked anyone to do anything he himself was not prepared to do.

George Lyon (formerly Ella) Hut, 2010. PHOTO: ROB BROWN

Lyon's advice to Postill was: 'When I tell you not to do something a certain way remember that I have already done it that way and it doesn't work.'[6]

In the late 1970s, after most of the park's huts had been established, Bruce Postill conducted a year-long survey, asking trampers if they would pay extra hut fees to keep the gas cookers. The result was a 90 per cent 'no'. As a result, park staff removed gas cookers from those huts that had them, and converted most into one-room huts with a single coal stove.

However, as Ella was a low-use hut with plenty of firewood available for two stoves, Lyon said, 'let's leave Ella Hut as is'.[7] It remains, fittingly, the most original Lyon design in the park.

Building a hut at Blue Lake was not without controversy. In the 1960s, the area was part of a proposed 'West Sabine Wilderness Area', which would have no huts or tracks. But by 1970 a track had been cut up the West Sabine, and Lyon's team had built Blue Lake Hut. Wilderness campaigner Les Molloy went to Blue Lake in the winter of 1962 with a tramping party, when the snow was so deep they had to camp in the branches of the beech trees. He felt a hut despoiled the area's remoteness, stating that this was a 'salutary lesson about the impending "back-country boom" in the New Zealand outdoors, and the dangers of making the experience of wilderness too easy'.[8] No doubt Lyon would have thought Molloy one of the 'purists'.

John Tait Hut

The current John Tait Hut is the second hut to occupy this site. The first hut was built by a tramping club, and the second by Lyon and his rangers. Then, during the 1990s, DOC substantially expanded and modified the hut, making it – at twenty-seven bunks – the second largest hut in the park. So, to some degree, John Tait represents an interesting example of three hut-building eras.

Long before Nelson Lakes National Park was formed in 1956, trampers and hunters were enjoying trips up the Travers Valley. John Tait was one of

Shaun Barnett at Blue Lake Hut, 1998. PHOTO: ROB BROWN

those making forays in the valley during the 1940s. Tait had come to New Zealand from Scotland as a teenager with his family, and by 1948 was teaching at Nelson College and serving as president of the Nelson Tramping Club. Although aged forty-seven at the time, he maintained good fitness and demonstrated considerable enthusiasm, prompting club members to give him the nickname 'The Moving Spirit'.[9]

After a 1948 climb of Mt Travers, John Tait foresaw the need for a hut in the valley, and set about enthusing club members to build one. The Rotoiti Scenic Board, which then controlled the area, gave permission for the club to build a hut but was unable to provide any funds.

Club captain Dave MacMorland drew up plans based on a Public Works Department hut and organised materials, before club members made a trial assembly in a Nelson backyard. Dismantled into colour-coded bundles, the hut was transported by truck and boat to the head of Lake Rotoiti. During the summer of 1950–51, load carrying up the Travers Valley began in earnest. In stages, the heavy bundles were carted up the 16 kilometres of valley track, with the chimney proving to be the most awkward load. John Tait himself carried this, wearing it like an oversize hat. His head poked out the top and, appropriately enough, smoke leaked out of the pipe in his mouth.[10]

With the weeks of arduous load carrying finally finished, a club working party completed the hut over the sunny Easter of 1951. The hut comprised

LEFT John Tait outside the original John Tait Hut in 1952. PHOTO: R. M. WEBBER, COURTESY OF DOC NELSON LAKES **RIGHT** Building John Tait Hut II, 1978, George Lyon on right. PHOTO: BRUCE POSTILL

Oregon pine framing, totara plates, cedar piles and aluminium sheeting. Construction costs totalled £250, including transport. Initially the hut had a dirt floor, inlaid with flat river stones, but George Lyon built a wooden one ten years later.[11]

The opening ceremony became a smoky, coughing affair as some wag had covered the chimney with a sack. Even without the sack, the chimney smoked badly for the next decade until the open fire was replaced with a wood burner.[12] The hut was named in honour of John Tait, who only reluctantly conceded the honour. This original six-bunker was located ten minutes' walk upstream of the present hut.

Bruce Postill was part of the team that pulled down the original John Tait Hut in 1978, replacing it with a new Lyon design. Prefabricated materials were flown in by Lama helicopter, and the new hut was built over a ten-day stint. Postill recalls:

> We started at first light (very cold on the fingers), would stop for dinner, then work on until it was too dark to see. I remember we would all just lay down in our sleeping bags and go to sleep straight away. There was no such thing as overtime!
>
> The hut was built in the way George built huts. We built a 'humpy' by nailing a section of timber between trees and leaning the roofing iron on this. We slept & ate under this. There was a bit of a crunch time when we needed the timber and iron for the hut – lucky it was not raining at that time.[13]

Lyon organised the food and would be cooking porridge 'before sun up'.[14] By now, the park had become popular enough to require small quarters for the hut warden. Postill recalled the last night of hut construction:

> George had walked out the day before. We were busy finishing off benches in one room … while some trampers were in the other room trying to sleep. As we were leaving early the next day, we had to finish that night. I remembered I had not fixed the bunk steps in the room where the trampers were … so went in with my torch and hammered these steps on whilst they lay in the bunks![15]

After persuasion from Postill, Lyon relented to using some insulation in the roof. It was the last hut Lyon built in the park, and he retired in 1980 after twenty-one years of service.[16]

SHAUN BARNETT

The DOC-modified, 27-bunk John Tait Hut, 2008.
PHOTO: ROB BROWN

Mintaro Hut 1889/1894/1966 FIORDLAND NATIONAL PARK

On day two of the Milford Track, 'freedom parties' using Department of Conservation facilities reach Mintaro Hut, tucked in at the head of the Clinton River under Mt Balloon and Mackinnon Pass. Nearby is a small bush-surrounded tarn, Lake Mintaro. Huts in the lake vicinity date back to 1889 with the surveyors' Fingerpost Hut, a simple wood-slab affair. That was a far cry from the serviced DOC hut standing here now. What are the histories that extend back beyond Fingerpost and lead forward to today?

As far back as the 1860s, Milford Sound's grandeur was recognised for its tourist potential. Donald Sutherland, after a life that included serving in various armies, gold mining, sealing and seafaring, settled in Milford in about 1880. He discovered the falls subsequently named after him, and took boat visitors to see them. Sutherland married Elizabeth Samuel in 1890, and 'the Mother of Milford' became an important player in the accommodation offered there.[1]

In 1888, the chief surveyor of Otago, C. W. Adams, sent a team to measure the falls, and another party, Quintin Mackinnon and Ernest Mitchell, up the Clinton Valley in the hope of finding a route across to Milford Sound. They found the Mackinnon Pass. On the return journey, Fred Muir accompanied Mackinnon, and they named Lake Mintaro. Why Mintaro? That was a puzzle for many years, but Milford Track enthusiast and hut warden Bill Anderson tracked it down in the late 1970s. Muir's full name was Fredrick Mintaro Bailey Muir, and the family had connections to the town in South Australia of that name. Whether the town's name came from Spanish or Aboriginal roots remains unclear.[2]

Lake Mintaro became a frequent stopping place on the track up to the pass. Initially, Fingerpost Hut, supplemented by tents, was the only shelter there for the guided parties, and it was pretty rough. After Edward Melland of Te Anau Downs Station made requests for better accommodation to the chief surveyor of Otago, Mintaro Hut was built in 1894.[3] Twelve years later, when Pompolona Hut was built further down the valley, its use was reduced to that of a shelter in which to brew a cuppa before tackling the pass. At this stage, of course, only guided parties walked the Milford.

Track Ownership

Right from early days, authority for the management of the Milford Track began to move in two different directions. On the one hand, all of Fiordland – including the Milford Track – was placed in a public reserve in 1905, and in 1952 that reserve became Fiordland National Park. On the other, in 1901 the Department of Tourist and Health Resorts took over all the services on the track and later, in 1955, it became the Tourist Hotel Corporation (THC).

One of the primary tenets of the National Parks Act (both the original 1952 version and the 1980 revision) is to guarantee free access to all, but exclusive control of Milford Track by THC contradicted that. Various outdoor groups wrote to the Tourist Department, and then the THC, requesting to walk the track independently, but they were turned down. One of these groups, the Otago Tramping Club, made its first request in 1947.

As an alternative option in 1952, and again in 1957, the National Parks Authority gave the Tourist Department permission to charge independent walkers 30 shillings per day, but the Tourist Department never allowed this. In 1964, things came to a head when a national kayaking group complained to the ombudsman.[4] The ombudsman sidestepped the issue, and the THC applied to have the track formally placed under its control. The Fiordland National Park Board acquiesced and agreed to vest full control of the Milford Track to the THC later in 1964 – for an initial period of five years. But the people the park board represented – the public – didn't appreciate control being given away to the THC. In fact, they got ratty about it. Led by the Otago Tramping Club, tramping clubs from Auckland to Southland, Federated Mountain Clubs, Forest & Bird and the Otago Section of the New Zealand Alpine Club opposed the move as contrary to the spirit of the National Park Act 1952, which it was.[5]

THC, on the other hand, understandably wanted to protect its investment and many years of track and hut maintenance. A public battle began to simmer.

At Easter 1965, about forty members of the Otago Tramping Club under John Armstrong publically declared their intention to freedom walk the Milford Track. The *Southland Times* reported,

> Mr Bowick [chairman of the Fiordland National Park Board] said a request for the party to make the trek was referred to the chief ranger of the park board and later to the board itself. The board referred the request to the hotel corporation, which replied that as far as it was concerned the track was closed for the season.[6]

But that wasn't quite that. A man from the Government Tourist Bureau in Dunedin also summoned John and told him in no uncertain terms that permission would not be granted for him to lead an independent tramping party on the Milford Track. 'It was against Government policy and it was against this and against that.' But as John also said, 'We were not going to ask permission of anyone, we were just going to go, which we considered to be our right.'[7]

John's wife, Robyn Armstrong, added, 'of course to do the trip we weren't able to make use of their facilities and that was fair enough, but we were trampers, we were capable of tramping on our own.'[8]

As planned, about forty trampers headed into the Milford Track by three different routes. Two parties approached the Clinton Valley, one from Lake Te Anau and the other over Dore Pass from the Eglinton Road, while the third party approached the track from Milford Sound via Sandfly Point and the Arthur Valley. The two Clinton parties crossed Mackinnon Pass and met up with the others, then all three parties headed out to Milford. Easter can be renowned for rain, and the Arthur River flooded, requiring quite a bit of ingenuity on the part of the trampers to get everyone safely over the river and down to Milford Sound.

Authorities weren't quite sure what to do about the protest walk. The chairman of the Fiordland National Park Board said, 'the party was exercising the right open to any member of the public to walk in the park where and when they liked.'[9]

Earlier in the year, 'The National Parks Authority had approached the corporation with proposals to allow experienced tramping parties, school parties, and so on to walk the track, using accommodation to be created by the park board.'[10] However, the directors of the THC refused.[11]

The National Parks Authority now stood its ground and,

> a letter from the authority chairman to the hotel corporation informed the corporation that, in view of the failure of negotiations, he intended to place before the authority the proposal that the Fiordland National Park Board resume full control of the track including responsibility for maintenance and that a per capita charge based on annual cost be made on all persons walking the track, whether in a corporation party or not.[12]

Ultimately, the 'freedom walkers' and the National

The first Mintaro Hut, 1914. PHOTO: EDGAR RICHARD WILLIAMS, ALEXANDER TURNBULL LIBRARY, WELLINGTON, PA11-148-02

Park Authority forced the reversal of the THC's track monopoly. The Fiordland National Park Board worked out arrangements with the THC to allow the walkers access to the track.

Freedom Walkers' Huts

During the summer of 1966–67, the Fiordland National Park Board built three huts, at Clinton Forks, Mintaro and Dumpling. All three followed a similar design, with the hut at Mintaro having a cooking and living area in the middle. Four bunkrooms, two off to the left and two to the right, catered for about twenty people. A coal range sat in the middle of the main room. These buildings were replaced from the 1980s on with today's more modern 40-bunk huts.

One wonders what the situation in the park might be today had it not been for the freedom walkers in the Otago Tramping Club and pressure from other groups. The park board had already signed away public rights to the corporation for an initial period of five years, and such arrangements are hard to reverse. Since then, the THC has been sold. The right of the public to walk the Milford Track on their own came about because New

Mintaro Hut, 2006. PHOTO: SHAUN BARNETT/BLACK ROBIN PHOTOGRAPHY

Zealanders chose to gazette Fiordland as a national park, and because concerned people then took a stand to ensure the freedoms that status guaranteed were honoured.

Largely oblivious to all this, I headed to Milford in the 1970s with some keen tramping friends to undertake a longer trip to the remote Light and Dark valleys, beginning from the Milford Track. When we sought boat transport to Sandfly Point from the manager of THC's Milford Hotel, the answer was no. However, after spending some time negotiating, he finally agreed to ferry us over. Normally the track is only walked one way, from Lake Te Anau to Milford. The first track walkers we met heading towards Milford told us we were going the wrong way. But we convinced a second party of track walkers that they were going the wrong way, so for a while people were walking in both directions!

In 2012, the five-day guided Milford Walk – including transport, food and accommodation – costs between $2000 and $3000, while hut fees for the four-day freedom walk total $153, with a further $200 for transport. Either way, guided or unguided, the Milford Track remains one of the finest walks in the world.

GEOFF SPEARPOINT

Lake Roe Hut 1968 FIORDLAND NATIONAL PARK

Except for the Milford and Hollyford tracks, and the routes to Doubtful Sound and George Sound, much of Fiordland was largely an untracked wilderness until the 1960s. When the national park, New Zealand's largest at 1.2 million hectares, was finally gazetted in 1952, attention turned to opening up more tracks for trampers to explore some of its vast extent.

In the 1960s, the Fiordland National Park Board also came under strong public pressure to open the Milford Track to non-commercial, or 'freedom', walkers (see previous chapter). To alleviate some of that pressure, the board moved to open up more tracks and provide public huts in less visited parts of Fiordland. One of those areas was the Dusky Track. These days, the track begins near the West Arm of Lake Manapouri, goes up the Spey Valley and then crosses Centre Pass into the Seaforth Valley, to terminate eventually at Dusky Sound. A through-route to Lake Hauroko branches off from Loch Maree, heading over the Pleasant Range and down the Hauroko Burn.

Back in the 1950s, only a rough track existed between the West Arm of Lake Manapouri and Dusky Sound. In the early 1960s, Pat and Len McConnell, park rangers based at Clifden, supervised borstal inmates in the recutting of this route to create a proper formed track. The track workers also established the route up onto the Pleasant Range and down to Lake Hauroko.[1]

At the same time, Murray Schofield, chief ranger for Fiordland National Park, established a design for a standard twelve-bunk hut that eventually spread throughout Fiordland's tracks. Lands and Survey staff built fifteen huts to this design, many in the late 1960s under Chief Ranger Harold Jacobs. The first of the twelve-bunkers went up in 1963 near the point where the Worsley Stream flows into Lake Te Anau. Over the next twelve years, others were built on the Hollyford Track for trampers, and at selected sites near Lakes Monowai, Manapouri and Te Anau to provide for recreational hunters and anglers.[2]

The first twelve-bunk hut on the Dusky Track was Halfway Hut on the Hauroko Burn, built in 1967. The following year saw the construction of Lake Roe Hut, and over ensuing years the Dusky Track eventually gained five more of these huts, including Loch Maree and Supper Cove. The last three, all built in 1975, were Upper Spey, Kintail and the replacement for Lake Hauroko (the original had accidentally burnt down the year before).[3]

All the twelve-bunk Dusky huts have been modified and upgraded over the years, but time has proved the original design was sound and practical.

As any tramper who has walked the Dusky Track can testify, the area's mud, rain and sandflies can form a substantial challenge, and the huts provide welcome respite from all three. Many have stunning locations, although that of Lake Roe Hut is arguably the very best – it sits on the aptly named Pleasant Range, whose open tussock tops are speckled with small tarns and larger lakes. Much of the range is just above the bushline, but the area around the hut dips to just under 900 metres and supports the odd patch of subalpine forest. The hut snuggles nicely into a small grove of gnarled beech trees at this altitude, just above Lake Laffy, and is perfectly situated to explore this incredible part of the Fiordland landscape.

ROB BROWN

Ken Tustin approaching Lake Roe Hut during the winter of 1999 PHOTO: ROB BROWN

Edwards Biv 1940 & Edwards Hut 1952/1969 ARTHUR'S PASS NATIONAL PARK

In 1940, in the midst of war, Canterbury Mountaineering Club recorded ninety-seven of its members overseas on active service. Those that remained continued to climb in the Canterbury mountains and even embarked on a few hut-building projects. That same year, they carried into the Edwards Valley a small bivvy modelled on a Nissen hut used by Allied forces in the hope that it would serve as a prototype for similar bivvies at key locations. Harry Walker was a key driver of the project, and basing costs on an estimated £5 per hut (plus any transport costs), he envisaged the club building up to six such shelters.[1]

With most of the eligible men away on service, it was left to the club's older and younger members to carry in the materials. One participant wrote up their efforts with some humour:

'A' picks up a load of 50 lbs, carries it 400 yards, drops it, rests 10 minutes, picks up a load of 40 lbs dropped by 'B', carries it 300 yards, drops it, rests 20 minutes, picks up a load of 30 lbs dropped by 'C', carries it 200 yards, drops it, rests 30 minutes, picks up a load of 20 lbs dropped by 'D', carries it 100 yards and collapses flat on his back. By this means and much going and coming by 'A's', 'C's', 'D's', 'E's' and some 'B's', the material makes a spasmodic approach to its destination, culminating in the case in question in a total collapse of everybody and everything at a spot about 800 yards short of the chosen site and from whence it was laboriously removed by Ivan Tucker and another whom modesty forbids me to name.[2]

In the end, this would be the only hut of this design. Instead, CMC opted to build future huts with a pitched roof, not too dissimilar to the design later adopted by the Forest Service for its two-bunk bivs. CMC would build two other 'experimental bivvies' in Arthur's Pass during the Second World War – Gizeh Biv, near the Anti Crow River, and the first Mingha Biv.[3]

In the 1950s, Arthur's Pass National Park was at last starting to receive sufficient funding from central government to allow some provision of public recreational facilities. Up to that time, the park had just a single ranger based at the village, and any existing huts had been built by Canterbury clubs.

Ray Cleland served as the chief (and only full-time) ranger from 1950 to 1958, and was the first park manager to have a budget worthy of a national park. In 1952, he decided to replace the original CMC Edwards Biv with a small four-bunk hut of a similar design to contemporary Department of Internal Affairs deer-control huts. A Bristol Freighter dropped materials for the second hut in the valley, then Cleland and ranger Hans Bohny assembled it.[4] The biv remained as overflow accommodation during this time, and was removed only when the third, current, Edwards Hut was built.

This first Edwards Hut lasted seventeen years, until 1969, when trampers Phillippa and John Fowles found it burnt down while on a trip to Tarn

CMC members at the original Edwards Bivvy, circa 1940s.
PHOTO: JOHN WILSON COLLECTION

The Lockwood design Edwards Hut, February 2012. PHOTO: SHAUN BARNETT/BLACK ROBIN PHOTOGRAPHY

Col. Although uncertain, the cause was most likely ashes blowing from the fire onto the timber floor.

The Arthur's Pass National Park Board decided to replace the hut with a new type of structure that was becoming popular at the time. The Lockwood building system, begun in Rotorua in 1953 by Dutch immigrants Joe La Grouw and Johannes Van Loghem, had agencies throughout the country by the 1960s. Pat O'Reagan had the franchise in Christchurch, and he offered to build a hut to head ranger Peter Croft's design. The first of these huts installed in the park was Casey Hut on the Casey Saddle–Binser Saddle Track. In 1969, the replacement Edwards Hut was installed, followed by Hawdon in 1971 and the new Carrington in 1975. All were built by Lockwood staff, with the assistance of National Park rangers John Charles and Chris Eden to build Edwards Hut, while John Charles, Tony Perrett and Chris Scott erected Hawdon and Carrington Huts.

Occupying a pleasant alpine location above the bush edge in the upper Edwards Valley, this latest Edwards Hut offers fine views of the Polar and Aicken ranges, as well as Falling Mountain. It's most often used by trampers completing the three-day Tarn Col trip, which connects the hut with the adjacent Hawdon Valley.

Hawdon Hut burnt down in June 2005, possibly also as a result of burning embers escaping from the fireplace. All the other Lockwood huts in the park are still in place today, proving the design has stood the test of time.

ROB BROWN

Gardiner Hut 1934/1976 AORAKI/MOUNT COOK NATIONAL PARK

The upper Hooker Valley, a wild area of big walls and broken ice, has drawn climbers since the 1880s. Three New Zealanders, Jack Clarke, Tom Fyfe and George Graham, used the Hooker Glacier for their approach during the first ascent of Aoraki/Mt Cook on Christmas Day 1894.

Climbers generally used one of two sites as a base for an attempt on the mountain: the Upper Cook Bivouac at the foot of Earle Ridge; and the Lower Cook Bivouac at Pudding Rock (also called Noeline Rock), where the Noeline Glacier feeds into the Hooker Glacier. A very active glacier, the Hooker was renowned – even back in the 1930s – for breaking up quickly through summer, making access or retreat difficult.[1] The upper Hooker wasn't a place to be trapped without shelter.

To provide a climbing base and somewhere to sit out storms for guides and their clients, the Mount Cook Tourist Company built a hut at the Lower Cook Bivouac site, 1750 metres above sea level, and named it after Katie Gardiner, a very accomplished English climber who spent many seasons climbing challenging new routes with a guide in the 1930s. The naming was very appropriate, as Gardiner knew only too well the value of shelter. In 1933, she was trapped with her friend A.M. Binnie and guides Vic Williams and Jack Pope at the head of the Fox Glacier by a major storm that forced them to abandon their camp and shelter in a crevasse (see p. 128). Nine days later, having had only meagre food rations to eat, they were able to descend. By then, Pope had already sworn never to climb again, and Gardiner had written out a will on the sixth day to say that, should they not survive, Pope and Williams' wives were to be cared for.[2]

Over two months during 1934, Vic Williams and his brother Percy, along with Mick Bowie and Felix Harvey, packed materials onto Pudding Rock for the new hut.[3] Arthur Leehy of Timaru built the hut, assisted by Vic Williams and Bowie. It soon inspired a lot of new climbing in the area.[4]

Measuring approximately 3 metres by 4 metres in area, the hut had a 1.8-metre stud. The walls and ceiling were match-lined, with malthoid between this and the iron cladding. Rocks were built up to the height of a metre around the hut, which was anchored by wires to big boulders. Facilities inside included three wire stretchers and mattresses, blankets, pillows, stores, a three-burner petrol stove, and cooking and eating utensils.[5]

The hut lasted well for decades, but by the 1970s it was getting old, musty and worn out. Forty years at Pudding Rock would weather anyone. An alternative barrel hut design had been tried at Copland Shelter in 1972, and it had worked well.[6] The new Gardiner Hut was, roughly, a grain silo on its side, and relied on the strength of corrugated iron and its barrel shape. This was though structurally quite different to Copland Shelter, and was designed by Mal Clarbrough, mountaineer and ranger in charge of hut maintenance and stocking under Chief Ranger Barrie Thomas.[7]

In the early 1970s, rangers were engaged in an

The original Gardiner Hut, early 1960s. PHOTO: MAVIS DAVIDSON, NZAC COLLECTION, HOCKEN LIBRARY, UNIVERSITY OF OTAGO, MS-2985/366

early version of the Parks and Recreation course at Lincoln College. While there, they found an ally in Ian Calvert, an Engineering tutor, who oversaw scale model wind tunnel tests on the barrel versus more conventional hut designs. The barrel proved very successful. A bigger version of the same design was also used to replace Three Johns Hut at Barron Saddle in 1981. Mal, Faye Kerr and Howard 'Twitty' Conway then went in to demolish the old Gardiner Hut and get the site ready.

The barrel was prepared at Aoraki/Mount Cook village, where Ken Joyce cut a hole in the end of the drum with a gas axe to create a door. Flying the barrel from the village up to the site wasn't plain sailing, however. Part of the way up, the helicopter nearly ran out of fuel and had to put the barrel down on the Hooker Glacier and return to refuel. Meanwhile, a foundation cradle was built at the site, and anchored down into the rocks. Eventually, the helicopter arrived and placed the barrel into the cradle. With the barrel on site, the building crew got stuck in, and within a week the hut was lined and tied down.[8] In the work team with builder Ken 'Digger' Joyce was painter John 'Cocker' Moore, while Ian 'Whit' Whitehouse and Carl 'Thomo' Thompson were involved in a host of ancillary work.[9] Like its predecessor, the new hut encouraged more climbing activity in the area.

The upper Hooker is in a 'no fly zone' for recreational users, leaving it relatively free of aircraft intrusion, and this is a particular attraction to the area for some. Although the Gardiner design was a success, not even barrel shapes could stop boulders crashing down and wrecking the hut during a rock avalanche in late winter 2014. The hut was removed early in 2015, and is now being privately restored by Jason Tweedie and friends.

GEOFF SPEARPOINT

TOP Flying in Gardiner Hut up the Hooker Glacier, 1976. PHOTO: IAN WHITEHOUSE
BOTTOM Gardiner Hut in place, 1976. PHOTO: BRUCE POSTILL

Top Forks Hut 1964/1976 MOUNT ASPIRING NATIONAL PARK

Lush grassy flats and walls of forest capped by ice on Mts Pollux and Castor make the panorama from Top Forks Hut as attractive and dramatic as anywhere in the country. 'Beautiful spot, best view yet,' comments an entry in the logbook.[1] At first glance, the two huts here seem a unique combination, a newer national park hut beside an old forestry hut. But the appearance of the older hut is deceptive, as it was built for mustering.

Like many huts, the original Top Forks rose from a succession of others in the valley. Robert Wilkin took up Wanaka Station in 1858, including the valley that bears his name. Donald 'Yankee Dan' Caudwell and his partner Alfred Neese built two huts in the valley for John Kerin, who leased land there in the 1890s.[2] One was a log hut with a wood-shingle roof, roughly opposite Wonderland Stream, and the other was Top Hut on Kerin Forks Flat (not to be confused with Top Forks Hut). By the 1880s, Caudwell even operated a sawmill in the Wilkin at Dans Flat, complete with a homestead and orchard.[3] National park status still lay eighty years into the future.

A run holder built another slab hut with a wood-shingle roof in Siberia Valley, and in 1941 the New Zealand Alpine Club erected its own hut at Jumboland. The club had considered Top Forks as a site, but decided against it for several reasons.[4] Jumboland Hut lasted until the early 1980s, when it was undermined by the river and removed.

Mt Albert Station held a grazing licence for flats in the Wilkin Valley and ran cattle on them up to the forks. In about 1964, John Quaife, who ran Mt Albert Station at that time, asked Alan Duncan to build a hut at Top Forks. This was the first hut built there. Using silver beech for timber, Duncan remembers it had flat-iron cladding and a corrugated-iron roof. Duncan hunted the area, and later became heavily involved in the deer industry, flying a helicopter from Makarora West. About 4 kilometres down from Top Forks Hut, another smaller (locked) hut lies tucked into the bush edge. Duncan built this one also, roughly around the same time. Another tiny hut he built in Siberia Valley has been removed.[5]

On my first trip to the valley in January 1976, I remember that old Top Forks Hut fondly, having come over Pearson Saddle and down to the hut in a rainstorm. My two companions and I were soaked, but the hut's occupants made room for us. Renowned philanthropic ophthalmologist Fred Hollows was amongst them, and he rigged up a hammock with a climbing rope in the rafters to make space. With the fire glowing, and a bit of encouragement, a myriad of stories tumbled out.

The formation of Mount Aspiring National Park in 1964 brought a watershed change to the style of huts in the area, and later in 1976 a new recreational hut was built beside that old hut at Top Forks. Chief ranger Ray Cleland designed this new ten-bunk hut, which was built by ranger John Trotter and Dick Barnett. Trotter remembers the roof truss design being particularly strong to withstand the expected snow loadings.[6]

In about 1986, major upgrades took place on both the old and new huts.[7] The old hut was stripped and largely rebuilt, while the new hut got a replacement roof and a veranda. Makarora ranger Paul Hellebrekers managed these operations, and

Jumboland Hut, Wilkin Valley, 1976. PHOTO: GEOFF SPEARPOINT

Top Forks Huts, January 2010, with Mt Pollux beyond. PHOTO: SHAUN BARNETT/BLACK ROBIN PHOTOGRAPHY

remembers that the chief ranger discouraged the additional expense of the veranda. But Makarora staff squirrelled away materials left over from other jobs and, believing in the value of the veranda, added it anyway. A month or two later, the chief ranger and his wife went up to stay in the hut and had a long weekend of wet weather. They said nothing when they came out, except to comment to the builders that the veranda was very useful![8] Today, both huts at Top Forks serve as a useful base for climbing and tramping in the upper Wilkin, or as a stopover for those attempting a crossing over Rabbit Pass to places beyond.

GEOFF SPEARPOINT

Shelter Rock Hut 1930s/1950s/1981   MOUNT ASPIRING NATIONAL PARK

The gentle Rees Valley has been farmed since the 1860s, and at one time stock even grazed the upper valley beyond the forest. Before any huts were built, an overhanging rock near the current hut provided shelter, but a creek now flows under this, making it unusable. The original Shelter Rock Hut was built on roughly the same grassy flat occupied by the current hut, and was there in the 1930s when W. Scott Gilkison made a 60-kilometre tramp to order replacement boots, missed a night's sleep, and then joined his climbing companions at Shelter Rock to continue with a first ascent of Cleft Peak.[1]

During the 1950s, a gale destroyed this original hut, and Rees Valley Station replaced it with a new four-bunk hut with an open fire in a slightly different location.[2] Situated in a small grassy basin at the bushline about fifteen minutes below the present hut on the true right, it occupied an idyllic spot on the old stock track. Although the area is notorious for its massive winter avalanches, the hut remained unscathed and simply deteriorated through lack of care.

When I first saw it in the mid-1970s, the hut was already an old shell, unpainted and scribbled over, the fireplace cluttered with rubbish and the chimney starting to decay. But it was still in use. The *coup de grâce* came after Mount Aspiring National Park staff finished building a new, third Shelter Rock Hut in 1981, up the valley on the true left of the Rees River, near the original 1930s hut site.

The Rees–Dart Huts

In the late 1970s, the Mount Aspiring National Park Board decided to encourage use of the Rees and Dart valleys as a tramping circuit, with replacement of the small, older huts at Shelter Rock and Dart as part of their strategy. The board's intention was to ease pressure on the Routeburn Track, but in that they weren't particularly successful.[3]

A track around the circuit already existed. Earlier, in the Depression of the 1930s, men in the No. 5 Unemployment Scheme had formed the track up the Dart Valley. The New Zealand Alpine Club raised money for Dart Hut, and timber was taken in, but the project stalled when work on the track was halted near the Whitbourn Junction.[4] The track was completed to Snowy Creek at a lower standard in 1936. Builder and alpine guide Kurt Suter (who had already constructed the NZAC's Godley Hut; see p. 119) built the hut for the club the following year.[5] This original eight-bunk structure was replaced with a much larger hut in 1979–80 by the park board, and this hut was replaced with an even bigger, thirty-two-bunk Department of Conservation Dart Hut early in 2003.

A third hut, Daleys Flat Hut, built in 1976 in the lower Dart Valley, completes the overnight shelter on the circuit.[6] It also replaced some earlier

shelter – Dredge Huts, ten minutes down the valley, which were originally built as accommodation for gold miners servicing a dredge across the river in about 1910. The dredge hardly got started when it hit boulders and jammed; its remains are still there, indicated by a couple of young beech trees out on the flat. In the 1940s the miners' huts were rebuilt into one hut by the Tourist Department. Dredge Hut was demolished after Daleys Flat Hut was built.

Merve Burke, Dick Ratcliff, Brian Ahern, Shona Maxwell and I built the third and current Shelter Rock Hut in 1981. Materials were taken up to Arthur Creek and loads flown from there to the hut site by helicopter pilot Rex Dovey on 24 April 1981. A 3-metre by 3-metre canvas tent provided a base from which we worked, and we cleared away vegetation before digging holes for the piles. Working together, we dwanged and cut and cooked, finally closing the hut in on about 10 May. Hut building has its highs and lows, often associated with the weather. We had our share of rain, and even one snowfall. When the weather did clear, wet surfaces froze and frost sparkled. Every now and then, we'd look around and think what a fantastic place it was to work. The completed building had a coal stove, twelve bunks and a sink.

Despite the new huts, use of the Routeburn didn't diminish. The new facilities did, however, attract more trampers to the Rees–Dart trip. Building a new, separate bunkroom in 1994 increased accommodation in the hut to its current capacity of twenty-two – an unusual approach, but one that has worked very well here.[7]

GEOFF SPEARPOINT

TOP Shaun Barnett at Shelter Rock Hut III, 1998.
PHOTO: ROB BROWN
RIGHT Shelter Rock Hut II, 1980.
PHOTO: GEOFF SPEARPOINT
OPPOSITE LEFT Dredge Hut, 1956, Dart Valley.
PHOTO: JOHN RUNDLE
OPPOSITE RIGHT Colin Todd at the NZAC's Dart Hut, Otago, circa 1947. PHOTO: BRIAN WILKINS

NEW HUTS, OLD RESPONSIBILITIES DEPARTMENT OF CONSERVATION HUTS

Origins

When the Department of Conservation came into being under the fourth Labour government on 1 April 1987, it inherited management responsibility for almost a third of the land area of New Zealand. Contained within that were our national parks, forest parks, reserves and other natural lands managed for water and soil conservation and recreation values. The recreation overlay had been built up over many generations through various departments, encouraged by mountaineers, trampers and hunters whose growing attachment to the land drove them to seek better protection for the environment and the recreation opportunities it provided. By the time DOC took over, many decades of recreation planning and consultation had already occurred with local users, and careful ten-year management plans in most parks were the norm.

The department also inherited about 1000 huts and a permanent staff of just over 1100. Although these huts had served widely differing purposes, by the time DOC formed, the primary function of virtually all of them was outdoor recreation.

The push to form DOC was multifaceted, coming from across the political spectrum. On one side, Forest Service timber policy had created a significant backlash from conservation groups like Native Forest Action Council, Forest & Bird and Federated Mountain Clubs. These groups were dissatisfied with the NZFS planting exotics in mountain lands, outraged at the extensive logging plans under the West Coast Beech Scheme, and openly fought felling operations occurring in the central North Island podocarp forests. On the other side, an equally strong push came from private forestry companies, seeking to break up the timber production part of the NZFS to allow greater market competition.[1]

Significant opposition to national park restrictions also existed, while some lobbied to rationalise what they saw as wasteful duplication by competing departments. Between the 1950s and 1980s, the Department of Lands and Survey took increasing control of national parks from national park boards, firmly identifying the department with the parks. However, behind the scenes they were breaking in new land for farms, where draining swamps and clearing native vegetation was the norm. These activities got significantly less public scrutiny than the NZFS's native timber logging, but also disturbed conservation groups and were another example of how muddled New Zealand's land management agencies had become.

As a consequence, there was common ground at both ends of the political spectrum for change. This coincided with the reforming Labour government coming to power in 1984, and led to the rationalisation many were after. To manage the new conservation lands, staff and resources were drawn from the environmental side of the NZFS, the National Parks and Reserves Division of Lands and Survey, and the much smaller Wildlife Service branch of the Department of Internal Affairs. Historic Places Trust was included for a time too.

Getting Started

The recreational role of the new department was almost included in its title, but in the end it simply became the Department of Conservation, often shortened to DOC. The first director-general, Ken Piddington, went out of his way to start afresh, putting aside the policies of the previous departments. But with little national structure in the early years, a certain amount of opportunism occurred amongst the eight DOC regions and thirty-four districts. In its first year, DOC was not well funded and overspent its budget by about 3 per cent. In response to that, the government reduced its funding by 3 per cent the following year.

Faced with such financial constraints, DOC restructured, shedding nearly 200 jobs. It also introduced universal hut fees in 1988, charging different amounts for various hut categories. Hut fees had long been charged in national parks, but within forest parks hut usage had been mostly free.[2] The changes to hut fees were controversial, but for regular outdoor people a yearly pass was introduced in October 1989.[3] At this stage DOC still had only a rough idea how many huts it had inherited nationally.

By October 1992, DOC indicated a clear new direction by rebranding seven high-use tracks as 'Great Walks', and added one more the following year. Huts on these flagship tracks would be maintained to a higher standard.[4]

OPPOSITE Maungahuka Hut, Tararua Forest Park, Wairarapa, 2010. PHOTO: ROB BROWN
RIGHT DOC's backcountry hut symbol. IMAGE: COURTESY OF DOC

CARTOON: COURTESY OF TOM SCOTT

Early on, Great Walks (except the Milford) still operated on a first-come, first-served basis, but in 1995 a booking system was introduced for Routeburn Track huts. At this time the ratio of New Zealanders to overseas tourists using the track had dwindled to three in ten.[5] As early as 1992, annual visitor numbers to New Zealand had topped a million. DOC rebranded itself with new colours in 1994, and began replacing all hut and track signs with the current yellow and green.[6]

Cave Creek Aftermath

In the 1987 changeover, DOC lost many of the Forest Service engineers who had overseen backcountry structures under national standards. Reasonable expertise from the original National Park Service remained, but skills were patchy, and DOC didn't really develop national standards. Regions operated within their own skill set, calling on local architects to design new structures. Those doing the building work in isolated places weren't necessarily trade qualified. This lack of oversight set the scene for Cave Creek, where a newly built viewing platform collapsed on 28 April 1995, killing thirteen students and a DOC staff member on the West Coast. This was a national tragedy and DOC was traumatised. At the commission of inquiry into the accident, Judge Noble concluded that inadequate departmental processes and systemic failure were the two major causes to be addressed. He also said:

No government organization can do its job without adequate resourcing. In my opinion, it is up to governments to ensure that departments charged with carrying out statutory functions for the benefit of the community are provided with sufficient resources to enable them to do so. Here, the evidence is clear that the Department of Conservation lacked and continues to lack those resources.[7]

The immediate consequence was the examination of 520 structures and the subsequent closure of sixty-five of these. Eighty engineers were employed over three years to write safety standards and design new or modified structures.[8] 'Closed' signs appeared on many backcountry structures as, understandably, DOC refocused on 'safe', meaning safe from departmental liability. In the hills, many people found themselves making risk assessments on the spot, having found a bridge intact but 'closed', and the alternative a much more risky ford of the river below.

Better emphasis on meeting building codes, fire regulations and health and safety in employment (as legislated by the 1992 act of that name) was required. DOC approached this through a process called quality conservation management (QCM) to ensure the establishment of clear operating procedures, appropriate standards and a systematic national approach. The standards for structures were developed in the late 1990s with engineers and the building industry.[9] At this time DOC spent about $53 million per year managing recreation on conservation lands, or about a third of its budget.

It is important to understand all these events in the context of DOC's ongoing hut management. Large numbers of remote backcountry huts had not been properly assessed, and DOC underfunding meant that many remained without maintenance. Deteriorating tracks, bridges and huts had not gone unnoticed in the outdoors community, creating a degree of alienation between the department and its core supporters. At this time DOC staff were busy getting basic systems and processes of asset management in place. They were also spending significant resources starting to inspect huts, gathering information which was then used to propose, for many, minimal or no maintenance, followed by removal. Outdoor New Zealanders the length of the country were frustrated by this process, knowing the department was underfunded, knowing only simple maintenance was required, but seeing staff fly to huts and leave only new signs on the walls to show for their visit.[10]

Establishing National Guidelines for Facilities

DOC's national survey to create an inventory of all structures and buildings on conservation land was carried out in 1996. Each structure was given an identifying numbered orange tag.[11] Then in 1999, after consultation with representatives from the outdoor community, DOC drew up and approved its hut service standards, binding itself to meet certain criteria. The standards, overseen by Brian Dobbie, DOC's senior Technical Support Officer for recreation, covered al unlocked backcountry recreation huts used for public accommodation and have contributed hugely to greater consistency of DOC facilities.

DOC created five hut categories: Great Walks, serviced, serviced – alpine huts, standard huts and basic huts. The categories are quite prescriptive. Hut size for new huts is limited to sixty bunks for Great Walks, thirty-five for serviced huts, twenty for standard huts and six in the basic category. Criteria of hut location, design, size, environment, sleeping facilities, cooking, heating, water supply and ablutions, toilets, lighting, safety facilities/notices, furniture/drying facilities, cleaning and wardens are all covered in detail. And you can swap chocolate bars for muesli with other people, but 'there shall be no sale of food or other products from the hut'.[12] This is an important distinction from standards overseas, such as in the European Alps, where huts often double up as small cafés or stores.

Generally, the standards offer clear and sensible operating procedures. Historic huts also have their own separate, prescriptive criteria. To help guide what hut standards it should provide, DOC uses the concept of differing 'visitor groups'.

Those attracted to Great Walks are termed 'backcountry comfort seekers', and as might be imagined, these folk are catered for with the highest standard of visitor facilities the department provides. DOC's priority here is a low-risk, comfortable experience – one aimed at families, overseas visitors, and occasional and first-time trampers.

The huts catering for users of the Great Walks are generally larger (lodges might be a better word), are reached on benched and well-signed tracks, and sometimes have flushing toilets. Spacious, architect-designed and often with gas for cooking (at least seasonally), they can lack the character and appeal some seek in a mountain hut. There's some irony that as standards increase to provide more urban-like comfort in the hills, the overall experience becomes more urban too. Despite that, these huts are popular and well liked. A warden will normally be in residence throughout the main season.

Serviced huts are similar in many ways to Great Walks huts, reflecting the fact that they cater for the same 'backcountry comfort seeker' visitor type. These huts usually provide heating, mattresses and clean water. Hand-washing sinks are provided, as are vented toilets, but toilet paper isn't. Neither are cook-

Highland Creek Hut, Motatapu Track, Otago, a new 10-bunker built by DOC in 2008, and pictured in 2010.
PHOTO: SHAUN BARNETT/BLACK ROBIN PHOTOGRAPHY

ing utensils. A hut warden will usually be in residence over the peak season, so long as revenue from hut use covers the associated cost.

Serviced alpine huts in Mount Aspiring, Aoraki/Mount Cook and Westland Tai Poutini national parks are in a subset of their own. They have more facilities (for example, radios) because they cater for a more specialist group. Wardens are not usually in residence. Climbers loosely fall into a 'backcountry adventurer' category.

Standard and basic huts serve as accommodation for 'backcountry adventurers', the group that best reflects trampers, hunters and other backcountry recreationalists. Many active outdoor New Zealanders fit into this category; they seek challenge but not extreme experiences in the hills. Standard and basic huts have bunks or sleeping platforms, a wood burner, usually a toilet and an outside water supply, with basic huts being maintained to the lowest safe standard – sometimes without mattresses. These are generally the smaller huts, with between two and six bunks.

The third visitor type, the 'remoteness seeker', looks for challenging adven-

Purity Hut, built by DOC in 2006, Ruahine Forest Park, Rangitikei. PHOTO: SHAUN BARNETT/BLACK ROBIN PHOTOGRAPHY

tures in more isolated country, often using huts and tracks just at the beginning and end of their trips. Sometimes these trips will be entirely on older remote and challenging hut and track networks, or sometimes in wilderness without any facilities. Basic huts may be an important highlight. The group includes hunters, trampers, trans-alpinists and climbers seeking difficult challenges to test their skills in the outdoors.

Complying with other Authorities

DOC cannot choose its own building standards, but must operate under government legislation and work with other government departments, including local bodies. The department has always had to consider the various building acts, as well as regulations governing fire evacuation procedures, but changes to those acts over time did not take account of backcountry huts. When DOC looked at what it needed to do to make its huts compliant after Cave Creek, it found itself in an impossible position. Where a new hut was being built, or where work on an existing hut required a building consent, the building code stipulated that a second means of exit from a building was required, along with smoke alarms, exit signage, emergency lighting, access and sanitary facilities for wheelchair users, a potable water supply and artificial lighting. Obviously, almost all huts were non-compliant.

To the credit of DOC and various other authorities, a national process began to seek practical solutions to these problems. One of these was for DOC to replace all mattresses in huts with fire-retardant ones. For its part, the Fire Service acknowledged that some expectations were impractical, such as requiring smoke alarms in small to medium-sized huts. The outcome was safer huts that DOC could maintain without going bankrupt. Without this co-operation to reach a compromise, many huts would have been removed, resulting in fewer shelters in extreme and isolated environments. That really would have led to tragedy.

DOC also worked with the Department of Building and Housing to come up with the Building (Building Code: Backcountry Huts) Amendment Regulations 2008. These allow the director-general some flexibility in applying the Building Act 1991 when building a new hut. Most huts do not now have to provide wheelchair access, smoke detectors, potable water or artificial lighting (all statutory requirements under the building code).

In addition, DOC has worked towards a framework for historical and cultural heritage conservation, useful in dealing with historic huts, and geological hazard assessment guidelines to assess the risk to huts from most natural events. In 2003, a comprehensive avalanche hazard assessment was carried out across the country where avalanche is a potential threat. Of forty-two huts identified as possibly under threat, about twenty-two were in some sort of avalanche danger. Some, like Whymper at the head of the Whataroa, have been moved to safer locations nearby.[13]

Fire remains the greatest danger to huts, and on average one per year burns down. Knowing this might ensure more sympathy among hut users over why a small DOC bivvy has a big, intrusive exit sign above its door – the requirement came from fire regulations, not DOC. And after Cave Creek, DOC has every reason to be as compliant as it can.

'Towards a Better Network of Visitor Facilities'

In 2002, as part of a process called 'Towards a Better Network of Visitor Facilities', DOC began its Recreational Opportunities Review (ROR) to examine the

Dunnies and Long-drops

Some have excellent views, some boast tinted windows and some enjoy fine surrounds. Others leak foul fumes, attract blowflies and have clammy seats. But hell, when you need one, a backcountry dunny is heaven indeed.

Most backcountry huts have an associated toilet, usually a good old long-drop – reminiscent of the days when most New Zealand houses had one. The traditional wood and iron long-drop has, in recent years, been increasingly displaced by the fibreglass Norski pit toilet. While not high on aesthetic value, these are cheap, easy to clean and light to transport, and the transparent roof lets in daylight.

Where the climate allows, DOC has introduced composting toilets, notably for some huts in Whirinaki Forest Park, Bay of Plenty. These have the significant advantage of managing waste on site, but require temperatures of around 4°C to work. Perhaps the earliest one was installed by 'sunny dunny' guru Tussock Chapman on the Routeburn Track in 1985. In 2000, Salisbury Lodge in Kahurangi National Park received an innovative composting toilet with a solar-powered unit that generates sufficient heat to allow it to function at the 1100-metre altitude.

Dealing with human waste is no one's favourite job. In the 1970s, one Forest Service officer tried to solve the problem of an overly full long-drop at Saxon Hut on the Heaphy Track using gelignite. He told a staff member who had his blasting ticket to: 'Get a bit of gelignite on a manuka stick, and poke it into the top of that pile. It'll just give it a wee shudder, and settle the whole lot down for another couple of months.' Despite doubts, the man did as instructed. The explosion, although muffled, proved more violent than expected, leaving not a single piece of the toilet intact.

Perhaps New Zealand's most spectacular backcountry dunny is that of Pioneer Hut, perched high on the Fox Glacier névé in Westland Tai Poutini National Park. The hut's toilet used to hang over the nearby cliff, and reaching it safely required the use of both crampons and an ice axe – gaining a grip on the sturdy door handle was always a relief. In those bad old days, you simply did your business into a blue plastic bag which, when full, was dropped down a crevasse in the glacier below. Fortunately, like those of many well-used huts, the new toilet at Pioneer now has a vault to contain waste, which is periodically flown out by helicopter for disposal in the Fox sewerage system.

Dealing with the pure volume of waste in popular areas like the Abel Tasman National Park and other Great Walks tracks has required more complicated and expensive measures. The Milford, Kepler and Routeburn huts produce, on average, around 40,000–50,000 kilograms of sewage per year with their flush toilet systems. At two Abel Tasman huts there are now septic tank systems, using solar-powered generators to pump effluent through a dispersal field. When full, the remaining sludge is transported out by barge.[14]

Chancellor Hut long-drop. PHOTO: NICK GROVES

future of all recreational facilities, including huts. With about 1000 huts and many more bridges and tracks on its books, this took some time, but by 2003 DOC released initial proposals and began public consultation. Under the Visitor Asset Management Programme (VAMP), huts and other facilities were grouped together in sites and given scores based on use, quality of the experience, and various other criteria. There was community agreement on many but, as could be expected, proposals to stop maintaining huts or even remove them were controversial. Spirited opposition to decisions on many huts surprised the department, which received more than 1500 written submissions on the proposals.[15]

DOC held open meetings to get community feedback, and as a result of this consultation changed some decisions when a good case was presented for retaining a particular hut. But once again, a lack of finance was the real nub of the problem. An insufficient budget had crippled DOC since its inception. Following Cave Creek, some additional funding had been provided by the governments of the day to set up proper asset management processes and to carry out some deferred maintenance on huts and other facilities, but it was Minister of Conservation Sandra Lee under Prime Minister Helen Clark in the Labour–Alliance government who achieved a more lasting solution. In 2002, she announced a $349 million increase over ten years, which considerably increased annual funding for huts, tracks and other facilities.

For the first time, DOC had sufficient resources to undertake more than shoestring maintenance, and could also embark on a new phase of hut replacement. DOC set about designing simple, cost-effective, national standard designs for four-, six-, ten- and twenty-bunk huts, making good use of common building materials to save wastage, and reducing the need for new sets of architectural designs for every hut, as had occurred until then. In June 2004, DOC invited a specialist group of outdoor users to examine the new designs.[16] This group suggested small improvements, and thought a two-bunk hut should be another option, but was generally impressed.

Architects Pynenburg and Collins drew up the new hut designs for DOC. Ron Pynenburg, an active tramper and long-time member of the Hutt Valley Tramping Club, had written his Bachelor of Architecture thesis on old huts in the Tararuas. He looked at classic backcountry designs and came up with a six-bunk model reflecting the best elements of the NZFS huts, so well known and loved throughout the country. It was an updated design, of course, and modified in subtle ways.

Pynenburg had previously been involved in baseline inspections of huts throughout the country, and had first-hand knowledge of what stood the test of time and where weak points existed. Newer building regulations and DOC voluntary codes dictated double-glazed windows. This has created a situation where many people now stay in new huts with higher insulating standards than their own homes, and some see this as a touch extravagant. But well-insulated huts require less heating, and they suffer less from damp and so save on maintenance in the long term. And they are far more pleasant to stay in.

Cosy two-bunk huts have long featured in isolated backcountry areas. Hunters love them and so do many trampers. Small enough to be flown into the hills pre-built and ready to bolt down on site, they are an economical way of providing overnight shelter in places that don't justify expenditure on larger huts. In regions with challenging terrain, such as the West Coast, huts like this serve a vital role; without these basic shelters travel would be particularly inhospitable and recreational use of such areas would decline.

DOC initially made no allowance for the two-bunk huts in their recreation planning. But outdoor enthusiasts pushed to get their value recognised. Their case was helped by taking John Ombler, DOC's Central Region general manager, and Ted Brennan, from the West Coast Tai Poutini Conservancy, on a tramping trip in 2003. Dripping wet from drizzle, the party arrived at the small but dry Mikonui Spur Bivouac and found welcome shelter. The experience helped Ombler steer his colleagues towards recognising the validity of these little huts for recreation. Now, upright two-bunk huts are included in the mix of options when a replacement is considered.

Having set up national hut standards and established new hut designs, DOC could progressively upgrade or replace facilities as required, and they had the money for it too. The 'Hut Procurement Manual for Backcountry Huts' sets

Pfeifer Biv, one of the new DOC two-bunk bivs, Arthur's Pass National Park, pictured in 2011.
PHOTO: GEOFF SPEARPOINT

out mandatory requirements for managers when replacing huts.[17] The figures before and after the department received their major funding increase speak for themselves: in the decade between 1988 and 1997, the department replaced just under thirty huts with new ones; of these, half had ten bunks or fewer and two-thirds were standard or basic huts. In the decade between 2002 and 2011, the department built almost 100 huts, most of them to replace existing ones.[18] About sixty had ten bunks or fewer, and about seventy were standard or basic huts. Only three Great Walks huts needed replacing in this period, with the balance being made up of serviced huts, including some alpine huts. In both decades virtually all other huts ranged between twelve and thirty bunks. An occasional hut distorts the figures – the 1994-built Pinnacles Hut in Coromandel Forest Park has eighty bunks, for example, but this is an exception.

Given the considerable angst amongst outdoor New Zealanders over DOC's initial proposals in the 1990s to reduce the hut network substantially, this new boom of huts has to be viewed as a great success. The larger serviced huts are considerably more expensive to build, but they are also DOC's primary revenue-generating huts as they are the most used, and serve an important role as DOC's tourism interface.

The geographic spread of new DOC huts between 2002 to 2011 shows about ten huts in Southland, fourteen in Otago, thirteen on the West Coast, fifteen in Canterbury, seventeen in Nelson/Marlborough, fifteen in Wellington, five in Wanganui, three in the East Coast/Bay of Plenty, and one each in Waikato, Auckland and Northland conservancies. This uneven spread reflects that most conservation land is in the South Island and that many of the new huts were built as replacements. The future will undoubtedly see new huts in new locations, but existing huts often ended up where they are for good reasons, which, together with their heritage value, needs recognition. However, as the majority of New Zealanders live in the top half of the North Island, DOC is quite justifiably likely to focus more effort in these areas in the future.

DOC Hut Building in the Regions

A snapshot look at DOC hut-building activity, while by no means representative or thorough, provides some overview of the scale of hut work the department is engaged in on a continuous basis. In the late 1980s and early 1990s, DOC built several huts in the Tararuas (Mitre Flats, Tarn Ridge and Mangahao Flats), as well as Syme (Mt Taranaki), Kelman (Aoraki/Mount Cook) and Colenso (Ruahine Forest Park) huts. Over the period, DOC huts also succumbed to fire and other disasters, such as when an avalanche destroyed Beetham Hut at Aoraki/Mount Cook in 1995.

Hut wardens began to make a regular appearance at many of the more popular, larger huts. In the 1990s, DOC recruited volunteer wardens for huts in the new Whanganui National Park. Serving a week at a time, they had separate quarters and were provided with basic supplies. In Canterbury, DOC conten-

DOC staff modifying the old NZFS Cedar Flats Hut in 2012 to expand its capacity to 12 bunks.
PHOTO: DOC HOKITIKA

tiously removed Lake Taylor Hut during a rationalisation of 'surplus' huts, despite public responses to a survey asking for it to be 'retained for shelter'. The hut's poor condition did not overly concern many survey respondents, and some said they felt quite 'attached' to it.[19]

At about the same time, DOC took a different approach in Nelson, when it worked with the Waimea Tramping Club to rebuild Balloon Hut and install information panels about the hut's history. When Kahurangi National Park was established a few years later, in 1996,

> The official party (including Prime Minister Jim Bolger) spent Saturday night in Balloon Hut which a few years ago was earmarked for possible removal. Thus a splendidly located hut was rescued by the sterling efforts of the Waimea Tramping Club who, in co-operation with DOC, have made this into one of the most pleasant of the 50 or so huts scattered through the new national park.[20]

Meanwhile, hut maintenance continued in all conservancies. In some regions, dedicated staff with a real interest in huts made subtle but significant improvements to older huts. One trend in the Ruahine Range was for adding skylights, platform bunks and a veranda to ex-NZFS huts, which made them brighter inside and increased the capacity from six to eight bunks. A team under DOC ranger Colin Giddy was particularly influential in this work. Remedial work in the western Ruahines carried out between 2002 and 2004 brought nearly all

Constructing the new Plateau Hut, Aoraki/Mount Cook National Park, 2005. PHOTO: DOC

the older huts up to a high standard. Typically, this included relining the inside, replacing piles, windows and frames, installing benches, repainting and replacing old fires.

With the new funding available in 2003–04, DOC Canterbury undertook deferred maintenance on fifteen huts and replaced Crow Hut in Arthur's Pass National Park. Several Tararua huts got major upgrades, and a new Waiopehu Hut was built as a joint effort between the Levin Waiopehu Tramping Club, the Tararua Aorangi Huts committee and DOC.[21] Around this time, DOC developed a split policy on the divide between the Wellington and Wairarapa sides of the Tararua Range. Under Wayne Boness, huts on the western side tended to be slightly more basic, while the more popular huts on the Wairarapa side under Derrick Field, like Powell and Jumbo, had gas cookers. This deliberate policy reflected slightly differing use patterns on either side of the range, and was a considered effort by DOC to provide an array of facilities across a spectrum.

Rangers Dave Grieve and Nico de Jong undertook deferred maintenance on eighteen huts in the Wanaka–Makarora area, completed in 2002. Some of this involved major work, including new floors, bunks, windows and benches, replacing rotten walls and a total repaint.[22]

From about 2003, hut building picked up pace. A new Greenstone Hut was built in 2003 on a better site, replacing Mid Greenstone and Slyburn huts. Down on Stewart Island/Rakiura, DOC and volunteers finished building Long Harry Hut in February 2003. Meanwhile, the old Forest Service hut there was flown to Doughboy Bay to replace an old hunting bivvy.

The old twenty-bunk Dart Hut, built in about 1980, was replaced with a thirty-two-bunk hut that same year, while in Kahurangi the new twelve-bunk Trevor Carter Hut replaced two older huts nearby, one of which was threatened by a rockfall. Frew Hut was replaced with a new ten-bunker in 2003 when it was discovered that moving the old hut to another site wasn't practical as its timbers were rotten. Likewise, in 2004 DOC largely rebuilt Carroll Hut in Arthur's Pass after discovering that its wall framing was rotten beyond repair.

Some of the largest projects DOC undertook were the replacement of ageing alpine huts in Aoraki/Mount Cook National Park. The 2003 replacement of Mueller Hut involved about 4000 work hours and a cost of around $470,000. The new twenty-eight bunker had a warden's quarters, LPG cooking in summer, a 6000-litre water tank, a two-pan toilet and a grey-water treatment facility.[23] In 2005, the new thirty-three-bunk Plateau Hut (with almost twice the floor area of the old hut) cost $770,000, of which the New Zealand Alpine Club contributed $49,500.[24]

On the West Coast, huts continued to receive remedial work and, in some cases, were replaced. Enthusiastic DOC staff, including regulars like Ted Brennan as well as office staff who didn't normally get out in the field, helped upgrade many isolated backcountry huts. I remember on one occasion arriving well after dark at the seldom-visited Boo Boo Hut in the Kokatahi catchment from up the valley. My surprise at seeing light in the hut window was eclipsed only by the startled surprise inside when I opened the door. Two DOC staff members, relaxing after carrying out remedial work on the hut, leapt up and scattered chairs everywhere. In 2005, Grassy Flat hut was replaced with a new standard design ten-bunker.

The Tararuas got new huts at Maungahuka, Elder and North Ohau in 2005, the latter largely built by a local section of the New Zealand Deerstalkers' Association with DOC help. A huge landslide almost wiped out Fiordland's Deas Cove Hut in August 2003, coming within 50 metres of it.[25] DOC replaced the hut in 2007, following on from the construction of new huts on the Hollyford Track at Lake Alabaster and Hokuri. In June 2009, Martins Bay Hut was doubled in size with the addition of a new bunkroom, the 40-plus tonnes of material required for the job having been ferried across Milford Sound by the fishing boat *Southern Legend*.[26]

Some of the first new two-bunk bivs went up in Arthur's Pass National Park in 2008. The four new huts included East Hawdon, Pfeifer, Sudden Valley and Poulter. After Hawdon Hut burnt down in 2005, a larger replacement was built further up the valley in 2007.

Once DOC was receiving sufficient funding from the government, maintenance and hut replacement around the country depended to a large extent on the passion and commitment of staff. While there was some variation, in general DOC staff grabbed the chance with enthusiasm. Happily, most feel equally as passionate about maintaining huts as many members of the public. Backcountry hut posters produced by some conservancies (Southland in 2006, West Coast in 2007 and Nelson/Marlborough in 2012) also reflect that enthusiasm. Hopefully, other conservancies will follow suit, so that every conservancy in the country has one.

Green Lake Hut, Fiordland National Park, pictured in 2008, two years after it was built by DOC.
PHOTO: SHAUN BARNETT/BLACK ROBIN PHOTOGRAPHY

Retaining a Diverse Range of Huts

Many of the best-loved backcountry huts we have in our hills are older, historic, small, cosy, unwardened, basic and often quirky. They have a freedom of the hills about them and offer an old hut experience of the highest quality.

Fortunately, DOC has a small band of dedicated hut historians responsible for restoring a considerable number of these older, and not so old, huts. They include Rachel Egerton (Southland), Jackie Breen (West Coast) and Steve Bagley (Nelson), who are sometimes aided by staff with specialised skills, like John Taylor in Golden Bay, who can still hand-adze timber. The aim of these historians is to maintain the integrity and atmosphere of the huts as living history; magnificent examples of their work include Riordans and Waingaro Forks huts (Kahurangi National Park; see pp. 54 and 96, respectively), Slaty Creek Hut (see p. 206) and the old Cedar Flats Hut (West Coast), and Cowshed Hut (Mataura Valley, Southland). These require special management, and to DOC's credit it has found ways to achieve this. Many basic recreational huts have significant cultural and historical values. For those who use them – hunters and adventurous trampers – such simple shelters provide the high-quality experience they are after.

What DOC has achieved in the last twenty-five years is a transformation from a hotchpotch of huts inherited from different departments with differing standards into a coherent national hut network that caters for a diverse range of recreation needs. Huts now meet required codes and have become a well-managed resource. When DOC was formed, there was no initial hut database and it took some time to establish just what the department was expected to manage. National hut designs have since been drawn up, allowing consistent quality that meets building and fire codes, and over 130 new huts have been built, usually replacing old ones. Yet along the way room has been found to maintain and keep many of our older huts too, some historic and some not, but all evocative and important in our backcountry. There are hut options to suit almost everyone. The efforts that have gone into maintenance and new hut building, especially over the last ten years, means that the hut network has probably never been in better shape.

There are minor niggles. Never have there been so many signs offering advice tacked and screwed up in and around huts as there are now. I counted over thirty separate signs just on the inside of a serviced hut recently; outside, there were several more. On the other hand, logbooks – such an important point of connection for many in the outdoor community – often seem to be replaced with sterile new ones when they are only half full, just at the point when they begin to provide an interesting evening read of others' adventures in the area. Such things lower the quality of the hut experience, especially at more remote huts. But overall, New Zealanders have a lot to thank DOC for, and can reflect on how much it has achieved for huts in less than thirty years, often under severe financial pressure.

Some see the locations of the different hut networks as being too far from population centres. I don't share that view. Several new huts have been built on Stewart Island/Rakiura that are popular. Other areas such as the West Coast are unique in terms of their forest and topography, and are particularly difficult to travel in; without the simple hut infrastructure that currently exists, many trampers would be excluded from travelling in the area. There, small huts on their current sites are totally appropriate. Places like the Tararuas and Ruahines also have hut networks, offering people the opportunity to be adventurous and plan their own trips without the need to be totally self-sufficient. The Old Ghost Road, an 80-kilometre multi-day cycleway currently under construction, runs from the Buller through to the Mokihinui, and four new huts have been built along it. It is isolated country but that won't stop the route becoming popular. Several of the Great Walks are as far from main population centres as can be, and they too are popular. However, there are no reasons why places in the upper North Island can't be carefully chosen to offer new hut-based tramping opportunities.

What is the future of huts under DOC management?

In 2010, DOC signalled a new direction with its 'Destination Management Framework' (DMF).[27] The implications for huts within this aren't really clear, but the focus is clearly oriented towards greater tourist and business involvement on our conservation lands. The DMF overview focuses on increasing use at accessible and popular sites, and developing others where there is similar potential. Huts on the Great Walks are assured, and the tourist 'icons' are too. But as the overview states, 'This will require a reduction of effort in low-priority areas'. Recognising the value of our unique backcountry huts clearly isn't so

assured, though certainly some will be maintained. These are the huts outdoor New Zealanders identify with the most, and many will measure the department's success on how they are managed. DOC is itself a work in progress, and where it goes will depend on what New Zealanders choose to value.

GEOFF SPEARPOINT

Cape Brett Hut, one of three lighthouse-keepers' huts that used to house families servicing the Cape Brett lighthouse, Northland. Restored by DOC in 1996, it is an example of an historic building modified to serve as a public hut.
PHOTO: SHAUN BARNETT/BLACK ROBIN PHOTOGRAPHY

Leitch's Hut 1994 WHAREORINO CONSERVATION AREA, KING COUNTRY

It's not often that a large forested region managed by the New Zealand Forest Service escaped without at least one hut being built. Prior to the 1990s, Whareorino Forest was one such area. Centred on the rugged Herangi Range, the extensive forest encompasses some 16,000 hectares, and boasts such biological curiosities as two species of native frog as well as the King Country's only mountain cedar and subalpine plants.

Although the Forest Service managed the area prior to 1987, deer had never spread into the forest, and that probably explains the lack of huts. Forest Service culling teams did scout the area to destroy mobs of goats, but these social animals were more easily controlled by periodic bursts of concentrated hunting, and so there was no need to build huts.

During the 1990s, after the Department of Conservation assumed management of the area, the need for some form of shelter in the area first arose. Whareorino became a high priority for possum control, and teams regularly monitored pest numbers after 1080 operations, as well as the health of the forest.

DOC decided to build a hut at Leitch's Clearing, roughly in the centre of the forest at the junction of several rivers. DOC staff from Te Kuiti dismantled an old homestead, known as Raspberry Hut, in nearby Tawarau Forest, and then used these materials to build a pleasantly roomy hut, with sixteen bunks in two rooms, a large living area and a welcoming veranda. The housing of staff working in the forest was only a small part of the hut's purpose: DOC also wanted to attract people to visit the underrated area.[1]

If the power of huts to attract people was ever in doubt, Leitch's Hut provides a ready answer. Prior to its completion in 1994, virtually no one but the occasional hunter ventured into the forest. Now, the hut attracts some hundreds of people annually, most of them trampers, many of them family groups, plus a few mountain bikers.[2]

The hut lies in a grassy clearing, and the track that leads to it follows an old route intended for a road that was never built. Surrounding macrocarpa trees provide shelter for the hut from breezes that sweep through the clearing, and also perches for the long-tailed bats that often emerge during twilight. These trees were planted by pioneer farmer Sam Leitch, who lived here for twenty years in a whare he built himself.

In 1902, Leitch was one of the first surveyors to visit Whareorino, an area long off limits to Pakeha after the tensions of the New Zealand wars. Believing it would become valuable property, he subsequently bought land around the clearing that now bears his name. It was supposed to become the hub of a busy crossroads, connecting routes from the inland towns of Mangaotaki and Mahoenui to Waikawau on the west coast. Once Leitch had bought the land, he planted the macrocarpas and an *Elaeagnus* hedge, built his whare and cut bush to make the clearing. This accomplished, he drove sheep up the Awakino River to raise on his land. Over the next twenty years, the pioneer farmer toiled to extend the clearing, leading a solitary life before becoming disillusioned when the roads never came. After he left, his whare succumbed to the elements in the 1950s.[3]

No doubt Leitch would have approved of the hut, and the fact that his clearing did finally become a destination, albeit for trampers, not vehicles. Perhaps his efforts were not in vain after all.

SHAUN BARNETT

Leitch's Hut at dusk, 1996.
PHOTO: SHAUN BARNETT/BLACK ROBIN PHOTOGRAPHY

Syme Hut 1930/1988 EGMONT NATIONAL PARK

Perched on the shoulder cone of Fanthams Peak beneath the imposing southern face of Mt Taranaki, and seemingly surrounded by a great arc of the Tasman Sea, Syme Hut occupies one of the most spectacular locations of any hut in New Zealand. Situated at an altitude of 1950 metres, Syme is also the North Island's second-highest hut after Whangaehu Hut on Mt Ruapehu (see p. 182). The hut, accessible after a steep ascent up the track from the Dawson Falls Visitor Centre, forms a convenient base for climbers tackling Mt Taranaki's southern slopes.

In summer conditions, the hut appears as a rectangular edifice above the moon-like surface of Rangitoto Flat, strewn with boulders ejected from past eruptions. During winter, rime ice often coats the hut thickly, sometimes requiring climbers to hack their way in using their ice axes. A 'stable door' entrance allows access through the top half of the door when snow still blocks the lower half – not just a convenience, but potentially a lifesaver.

While never as popular as the northern approach to Mt Taranaki, the route over Fanthams Peak has attracted climbers long before any hut existed there. In March 1887, plucky nineteen-year-old Fanny Fantham became the first woman to climb the cone now bearing her name.[1]

Such activity inevitably led to the formation of mountain clubs. First established was the Stratford Mountain Club in 1914, but war sapped its membership and soon killed the club. A rash of others formed in the late 1920s, led by the Hawera-based Mt Egmont Alpine Club in 1928. That club's formation was partly prompted by the death of two climbers the previous year, both masters from Wanganui Collegiate school. One man died as a result of a fall on Taranaki's southern slopes, and the other from hypothermia. Although two others on the same trip survived, the death from hypothermia highlighted the need for shelter high on the mountain.[2]

Soon afterwards, members of the newly minted Mt Egmont Alpine Club decided to build a hut on Fanthams Peak. The Egmont National Park Board provided funds for materials and building, while club members prepared the foundations and did the grunt work. This was no small task: those lugging materials faced an arduous 1040-metre climb up steep, unstable scoria slopes. Rod Syme, captain of the club and one of its founders, became a driving force behind the construction over the summer of 1929–30.

To maximise efficiency, the hut was prefabricated in the milder climes of Hawera, then dismantled for the big carry. Club members made some 150 trips, which took up most of the summer, before everything was assembled on site. In contrast, construction on 2–4 April lasted a mere three days. At the opening ceremony later that month, 300 people attended. Club archives recorded, 'The Club women who served tea for several hours were the hardest workers that day.' The National Publicity Studio even made a short film of the event. Fittingly, the hut was named after Rod Syme.[3]

Aside from establishing the club and building the hut, Rod Syme also played a major role in advancing outdoor recreation in New Zealand. He encouraged many people to climb Mt Taranaki, and his 'summit lunches' became legendary. Happy recipients enjoyed his cooked eggs, hot pork and beans, washed down with mugs of steaming cocoa.[4]

Among other achievements, Syme climbed Taranaki 227 times (he completed his last ascent at age seventy), pioneered a new ridge on Mt Tasman, edited the Mt Egmont Alpine Club journal for fifty years, served on the Egmont National Park Board, and was one of the main forces behind establishing the Federated Mountain Clubs in 1931.[5]

The two-room Syme Hut had bunks for ten, and the club kept it well stocked with fuel, cooking equipment and bedding. However, at one point so much ski gear cluttered the women's room that 'there was little room left for the "shes"', so a lean-to storeroom was added. Syme Hut received lots of use, especially at weekends.[6]

Unfortunately, the hut proved less resilient than its namesake. Mice and rats invaded the shelter, chewing blankets and mattresses, but poison dealt to them. More serious was the hut's site. Winter

LEFT AND OPPOSITE Syme Hut II pictured in the winter of 2001.
PHOTOS: SHAUN BARNETT/BLACK ROBIN PHOTOGRAPHY

snows often completely buried it – sometimes to a depth of 3 metres. In 1935, one party dug for two hours before they could get in. Rafters occasionally snapped, deformation gave the hut a permanent lean, and it required continual strengthening and repairs. The Second World War interrupted much club activity, with the hut closed during these years. Rebuilding occurred in 1953.

The club kept Syme Hut locked, at least until 1960, when the park board took control of it and left it open to the general public. Unfortunately, this resulted in a lack of maintenance, which, combined with vandalism, left the hut in very poor shape. Once again the club took over, and during 1967–69 undertook a second major rebuild.[7] The revamped hut served well, but by 1986 was again badly deformed and leaking, and considered beyond repair.[8] After negotiations with the Department of Lands and Survey to build a new hut, the club dismantled the old Syme Hut in 1987.

In the meantime, however, the Department of Conservation had superseded Lands and Survey. Happily, the fledgling department supported the new hut project. The Mt Egmont Alpine Club contributed plans, labour and more than $10,000 towards the project, while DOC took over responsibility for construction and ownership of the new hut. Mindful of past problems, the new twelve-bunk hut was located in a more elevated position where snowdrifts were less likely to cause damage. Built over the summer of 1987–88, it became one of the first huts completed by DOC.[9] The effort straddled both the centennial year of national parks and the sixtieth anniversary of the Mt Egmont Alpine Club.[10]

Rod Syme lived to help open the new hut, and died in 1994, aged ninety-four. He was a giant in stature, and achievements.

SHAUN BARNETT

TOP Mt Egmont Alpine Club members excavating the Syme Hut site, with Rod Syme on right, 1930.
BOTTOM Geoff McGlashan, Stan Phillips and Don Syme carry mattresses and blankets to Syme Hut, April 1930.
PHOTOS: MT EGMONT ALPINE CLUB COLLECTION

Zekes Hut 1960s/1990s/2007 HIHITAHI FOREST SANCTUARY, RANGITIKEI

The curiously named Zekes Hut occupies a small valley on the eastern slopes of Hihitahi, a small mountain in the heartland of the Rangitikei, near Taihape. While largely shunned by trampers, the area has long been popular with hunters.

Zeke Martin, a keen hunter from Turangi, built the original Zekes Hut in the 1960s just downstream from the site of the existing hut. As landowners restricted access to all but a privileged few, the hut was effectively a private one illegally built on public land – a not uncommon situation in many forested parts of the North Island.[1]

A tree fell through the hut, probably in the early 1990s, causing irreparable damage. The replacement Zekes Hut II was a three-bunker, constructed from totara split on site, and clad in corrugated iron. Hunters and Department of Conservation staff used the dirt-floored hut, but by the mid-2000s the walls had deteriorated badly.[2] With good access freshly negotiated over Maori land on the western side of the sanctuary, DOC decided to build a new hut on a nearby location, about 200 metres past the site of the second hut.[3]

Completed in August 2007, the new Zekes Hut – the only public hut in the sanctuary – is a cosy four-bunker. It is reached via a well-marked track beginning from a DOC car park on State Highway 1 near Taihape. After a steady climb through forest, the track bisects a small clearing on the summit of Hihitahi (1116 metres) and then descends into a valley, where the superb little hut sits above river forks in Kaitapu Stream. Well insulated, with double-glazed windows and a wood stove, the hut is warm even in winter, and despite its newness has character, perhaps because of its diminutive size.

The Hihitahi Forest Sanctuary is a remnant of a vast tract of pahautea, or mountain cedar (*Libocedrus bidwillii*), forests. These once covered some 300 square kilometres from near Waiouru to the northern Ruahine Range, forming dark canopies over large areas of hill and mountain country. Fires (predominantly lit by pre-European Maori but also later by Pakeha farmers) and, more recently, possums have sadly reduced these forests to fragments of their former range and splendour. Happily, recent possum control by DOC has started to reverse this decline in forest health.[4]

While DOC has concentrated mostly on building ten- and twenty-bunk huts around the country, Zekes proves that the department will also install less costly, smaller huts in locations where four bunks are all that's needed.

SHAUN BARNETT

Zekes Hut pictured in January 2008, six months after it was built by DOC. PHOTO: SHAUN BARNETT/BLACK ROBIN PHOTOGRAPHY

Tarn Ridge Hut 1961/1993   TARARUA FOREST PARK, WAIRARAPA

Soon after its formation in 1987, the Department of Conservation built a number of new huts in the Tararua Range, with Tarn Ridge Hut the fourth of these.[1] This replaced an earlier hut that, like Kime Hut (see p. 157), owed its existence to tragedy.

Tarn Ridge, a marvellously and uncharacteristically flat section of Tararua tops, provides enchanting travel during fine weather. When Carterton hunter Basil Ralph Blatchford struggled along here in 1959, however, conditions were anything but benign.

On Sunday, 29 March, forty-eight-year-old Blatchford left Te Matawai Hut to traverse the northern Tararuas to Dorset Hut. He had shared Te Matawai with a group of Scouts, who had come along the same tops. Their leader, Selwyn Pawson, warned of 'atrocious conditions', but Blatchford replied, 'I'll be all right, I've been doing it all my life.'[2]

Despite deteriorating weather, Blatchford almost made it. But about a kilometre north of the Tarn and Dorset ridge junction, the awful conditions exacted their full toll. Blatchford, perhaps after seeking shelter, collapsed from exhaustion, and sometime in the night succumbed to hypothermia.[3] He was thirty to forty minutes from the safety of Dorset Hut, then located near this junction.[4]

For several days, up to 130 searchers scoured the Tararua Ranges for Blatchford, finally locating his body on 5 April, about 10 metres below the ridge crest. Because of the remote location, he was buried on site at a mountain memorial service the following day. Blatchford's wife provided a flower wreath.[5]

Blatchford's death prompted the Wairarapa Section of the New Zealand Deerstalkers' Association to build a hut at the traditional camping area near Sentinel Rock on Tarn Ridge, 1.5 kilometres north of the present hut. The Forest Service flew the materials in by helicopter, and the NZDA finished the five-bunk hut at Easter 1961. Some knew the hut as Blatchford Memorial Hut, but the name Tarn Ridge Hut later became more commonly used.[6]

The hut served for the next thirty years, although it was never warm and suffered from mildew. No structure can survive the bleak conditions of the Tararua tops for ever, and by the late 1980s it had become musty, damp and unappealing. So much so, that tramper Chris Maclean once arrived at the hut to find another party had pitched their tent inside.

In the early 1990s, DOC's Derrick Field decided to replace the hut with a new one at a more strategic location near the junction of three ridges. Perched on a slope overlooking the Waingawa headwaters, the resulting spacious sixteen-bunker offers some of the best views in the range. Those staying at the hut often visit the nearby large wooden cross that still marks Blatchford's grave.

SHAUN BARNETT

OPPOSITE Tarn Ridge Hut II, 2000. PHOTO: ROB BROWN
LEFT The original Tarn Ridge Hut, pictured in 1988.
PHOTO: SHAUN BARNETT/BLACK ROBIN PHOTOGRAPHY

Brewster Biv 1976/1988 & Brewster Hut 2007   MOUNT ASPIRING NATIONAL PARK

Brewster Hut began life as an A-frame plywood bivvy in about 1976.[1] Some time around 1971, a tiny bivvy had been situated in Tiel Creek on the Makarora side of the Main Divide, and was used by Peter Child and Paddy Gordon during their attempts to rediscover the South Island kokako in the area. They used a taped recording of kokako calls to attract birds, but their search yielded no results. In the early 1970s, the ranger at Makarora played kokako tapes outside while working and one day found himself excitedly chasing a bird with the same call. It turned out to be a tui mimicking the recordings.[2] Although the history remains murky, it seems the original Brewster Biv may have been the Tiel Creek kokako biv, relocated to the site near Mt Brewster.

Situated in tussock at 1450 metres on the tops west of Haast Pass, the bivvy became a handy base for exploring the Brewster Glacier and climbing Mts Armstrong or Brewster. When the bivvy began to deteriorate, a team led by Makarora ranger Paul Hellebrekers designed and built a replacement in the summer of 1987–88. This second bivvy had two split-level bunks, and while more roomy than the original dog-box, was still pretty small. Brewster Bivvy II had some interesting features. Makarora helicopter pilot Larry Larrivee owned a yacht, and the boat's door was used as inspiration for the bivvy door, which had to be lifted up to open it.[3] Many parties enjoyed the comfort of the bivvy, but after twenty years in a subalpine environment it became run down.

By then, the Department of Conservation was well placed to rebuild a more substantial hut here, and acted accordingly. The design was loosely modelled on French Ridge Hut, although smaller and somewhat modified. Jones and Cooper from Gore built the hut in May 2007.[4] Following standard DOC policy, the old bivvy was removed once the new hut was in place. The replacement twelve-bunk serviced hut occupies a stunning spot, less than four hours' tramp up a ridge from the Haast Pass Highway.

GEOFF SPEARPOINT

LEFT Dean Nelson at Brewster Biv I, with Mt Brewster beyond, 1980. RIGHT Brewster Biv II, circa 1990s. PHOTOS: GEOFF SPEARPOINT OPPOSITE Brewster Hut in 2007, a few months after it was built. PHOTO: SHAUN BARNETT/BLACK ROBIN PHOTOGRAPHY

Maungahuka Hut 1962/2006 TARARUA FOREST PARK, WELLINGTON

Early in 1961, four men camped near a large tarn nestled on a terrace near the peak of Maungahuka on the main range of the Tararuas. Athol Geddes, Ted Smith and Noel Fraser worked for the Forest Service, and their companion was Wairarapa farmer and tramper John Welch. The men agreed that, with the large tarn (rare on this part of the range) and the excellent views, this would make a grand place for a hut. Located there, it would be roughly halfway between the already existing huts, Kime and Anderson Memorial, on the main range.[1]

The following year, Geddes oversaw the building of the first Maungahuka Hut for the NZFS. Geddes later recalled in 2004: 'Everyone said I was nuts, they said a hut wouldn't last five minutes there, but it's still there.'[2] The hut was a standard SF70 six-bunker and intended for use by NZFS cullers to control deer and goats in the area.

Maungahuka and Carkeek huts were the last two huts built in the range using fixed-wing air-drops. In January 1962, pilot Naylor Smith flew over the site in a Cessna equipped with bomb racks under each wing. The 1000-pound loads under each wing were released to parachute down as close to the site as possible.[3] The building team, which included Noel Fraser, Dick Hetherington, Simon Best and John Fischer, camped for days on the terrace during atrocious Tararua weather waiting for the air-drop,[4] and Geddes, back at base, suggested over the radio that they walk out. Fraser replied, 'If we come out now we'll never get to build this hut.'[5] Thanks to Fraser's persistence, the hut was completed, and served as a haven for hunters and trampers during the next thirty-five years.

After ground-based Tararua deer-culling operations ceased in 1987, management of the hut became a joint effort between the Wellington Tramping and Mountaineering Club and DOC.

I fondly remember my visit to this NZFS hut on my very first trip to the Tararuas. Three of us had tramped from the old Waitewaewae Hut for twelve hours through frigid mist and rain, and arrived at Maungahuka tired and chilled to the bone. The fireplace had been removed from the original design because of the obvious lack of firewood, but the leader of our party made a billy of hot lemon drink. It was the best thing I had ever tasted, and I felt huge relief that we had arrived at the shelter. The next day, we experienced more typical Tararua weather, and it seemed to take for ever to navigate our way over the tops before we escaped down to Field Hut and Otaki Forks. At the time it seemed a tough weekend trip, but I later learnt that this was normal if you wanted to consider yourself a real Tararua tramper.

Owing to the increasing popularity of the Tararua Peaks route, DOC decided to replace the hut in 2006. Contract builders Evan Mardell and James Coubrough took twenty-six days to erect the modern standard ten-bunk DOC design, and during this time experienced just six days of fine weather.[6] It was one of the very first of the new Pynenburg-designed DOC huts built in the country.

Unfortunately, the hut ventilation system didn't really suit the weather conditions so often experienced on the Tararua tops, and by allowing damp mist to waft inside, mould began to form on the ceiling and mattresses. DOC solved the problem by installing a cover over the door vent, and the hut is once again a comfortable refuge from Tararua weather.

ROB BROWN

LEFT The NZFS SF70 Maungahuka Hut, pictured in 1999.
PHOTO: SHAUN BARNETT/BLACK ROBIN PHOTOGRAPHY
OPPOSITE The new DOC Maungahuka Hut, pictured in the winter of 2006, shortly after it was built. PHOTO: WAYNE BONESS

Woolshed Creek Hut 1910/2006 MT SOMERS CONSERVATION AREA, CANTERBURY[1]

Quite possibly, a hut existed in Woolshed Creek as early as 1887. When Alfred Peache leased the original Mt Somers run, he left a cryptic note in his diaries about a simple 10-foot by 8-foot (3.4-metre by 2.4-metre) mustering hut he built there: 'It is a first rate hut in a most picturesque spot. Fireplace of stone and chimney of iron, the walls of split wood and the roof of thatch.'[2] Peache did not record an accurate location for this hut, but the 'picturesque spot' seems likely to have been near where the first recorded hut at Woolshed Creek was built in around 1910. This six-bunker, situated on the south side of the creek, was a typical mustering hut with an open fire at one end, although unusually it had weatherboard cladding. It was known as Mt Somers Hut.

In 1952, the hut had a major makeover when the weatherboard was replaced with the more durable, vernacular corrugated iron. For the next twenty-five years it continued to shelter men on their annual muster, as well as the occasional tramping club party.

In the late 1970s, this part of Mt Somers Station was retired from grazing and in 1983 the owner Bob Burnett sold the farm to Mark and Jo Acland. The hut remained in the ownership of the station, with the retired land passing over first to the control of the Forest Service,[3] then to Lands and Survey. With the formation of DOC in 1987, the area became conservation land.

In 1983, Mayfield farmer David Howden took some young farm exchange students to Mt Somers Hut for a night in a classic New Zealand mustering hut. Seeing how impressed they were with the landscape and environment at Woolshed Creek, he established the local Mt Somers Walkway Society that year with the aim of gazetting a walking track over Mt Somers Saddle to Sharplin Falls.[4] The Aclands, enthusiastic supporters of this idea, handed over management of Mt Somers Hut to the society, and in 1985, with help from the Rakaia Section of the New Zealand Deerstalkers' Association (of which Howden was a member), the society expanded the original hut to sixteen bunks. The walkway was formally opened in 1987.

In the mid-1980s, the society began fundraising for a second hut at Pinnacles, on the Sharplin Falls side of the track. Local businesses generously donated money and materials, and in 1989 the Royal New Zealand Air Force flew the prefabricated hut to its site in three sections. The following year, the society gifted the new nineteen-bunk Pinnacles Hut to DOC.[5]

In 1988, Mt Somers Hut received a much-loved addition. David Howden was back again that year on a trip with some students from Sweden. They commented that in a Nordic country the hut would have a sauna. So, after the trip, they reconvened at the Howden woolshed to build a sauna. The prefabricated log sauna room was transported to Woolshed Creek a few weeks later and assembled a couple of hundred metres from the hut.[6]

The perfectly serviceable sauna provided many years of enjoyable relaxation for trampers, until New Zealand entered the age of health and safety.

The original Woolshed Creek Hut, late 1990s.
PHOTO: NICK GROVES

David Howden PHOTO: WARREN JOWETT

The new Woolshed Creek Hut, January 2012. PHOTO: ROB BROWN

Sadly, in 2004 DOC instructed the society to remove the sauna. With the growing popularity of the Mt Somers Track, DOC decided to replace Mt Somers Hut at the same time – an ironic decision given that the sauna was partly the reason for the old hut's popularity.

DOC completed a new twenty-six-bunk hut in 2006, using one of its large standard designs, and renamed it Woolshed Creek Hut, with the support of the society. The well-insulated, warm hut provides an ideal place for young families to take their children on their first tramp. For many Canterbury kids, it's their first experience of staying in a hut. Perhaps the one disappointment (or, rather, lost opportunity) is the lack of any design feature paying homage to the huts and farming heritage that came before it.

The Mt Somers Walkway Society couldn't bear the thought of scrapping its old hut, which was so full of good memories and good times. So, again with the enthusiasm of David Howden driving them along, members stripped it out and took the original six-bunk shell down to Mt Somers village. Today, the Mt Somers Hut, fully restored, occupies a site next to the small Mt Somers Museum, which displays a variety of mustering and high-country memorabilia. The hut's reopening in April 2003 coincided with the opening of the new Acland Shelter, built on the south face of the Mt Somers Track.[7]

ROB BROWN

MEMORIES IN THE WILDERNESS HUTS AS MONUMENTS

People die in the mountains. Hypothermia, avalanches, landslides, drowning, falls and all manner of accidents resulting from misadventures have killed outdoor people – including some of the best – although the risks are probably no greater than driving a car.

It's hardly surprising then, that many huts have been built as memorials to lost adventurers. What could be more appropriate than a hut to commemorate someone who lost his or her life in the mountains? Several huts in this book were built as memorials: Kime Hut remembers Esmond Kime, who died of hypothermia in the Tararua Range; Park Morpeth is a memorial to two trampers who drowned in the Wilberforce; Hunters Hut commemorates two men who died in a flash flood in the Richmond Range; Colin Todd serves as a monument to a mountaineer killed in a motorcycle accident. The names of these huts provide an ongoing reminder of loved ones, but the huts themselves also serve as practical shelter, potentially warding off more deaths.

Huts are supposedly places of refuge and safety, a shelter where climbers and trampers can retreat from the storms and challenges of the mountain environment. How horrible then, when a hut becomes a tomb. And a memorial hut at that.

In January 1977, trampers Arnold and Jan Heine were at Marks Flat in the Landsborough Valley when a ferocious storm struck the Southern Alps. The Heines were holed up when the tempest reached its full fury, and remembered, 'We were in the head of the Clarke under the Bivvy Rock that night of the storm and it was a spectacular show, and rather daunting. We sat on the climbing ropes in case the rock got struck by lightning. All the waterfalls were flowing uphill, and the thunder was continuous. Pretty scary [even] where we were under a solid rock.'[1]

Just 40 kilometres from the Heines, as the kea flies, were four climbers belonging to the Wanganui Tramping Club, sheltering out the weather at Three Johns Hut. For them, the storm would prove fatal. Three Johns Hut occupied an exposed alpine location at about 2000 metres on the Sealy Range near the head of the Mueller Glacier in Aoraki/Mount Cook National Park. Inside the hut that night of 30 January were Fenella Druce, a twenty-five-year-old doctor, Craig Benge, also twenty-five and club president, and two nineteen-year-olds, Bill Bennett and Rob McLean.[2]

The party of four had successfully arrived at Three Johns Hut after a demanding trans-alpine trip up the Hopkins River, over the Neumann Range, and then up to Barron Saddle from the head of the Dobson. They must have been pleased to reach the shelter of Three Johns Hut, just as the storm began brewing. The foursome contacted the national park headquarters on the hut radio, saying they intended to walk out once the weather improved.[3]

Some time in the night, the four climbers realised that the storm was seriously undermining the hut's stability. The wire guy ropes buckled and screeched, then began snapping, thrashing like whips in the whirlwind of driving wind and rain. For Druce, Benge, Bennett and McLean there could have been no sleep. All four dressed and donned boots, ready for evacuation. But what chance would they have against the lashing gale if the hut itself could not survive? Eventually, the entire hut lifted off its foundations and was dashed down the nearby cliff. No one left inside stood a chance.[4] There's some evidence to suggest two of the party may have escaped the hut, perhaps just as it went over the cliff, as their bodies were located further away, not with the hut wreckage. But the savage storm was not through with them, and they died too, possibly from hypothermia.[5]

As the climbers had made no further contact by radio, concern for their safety grew. On 3 February, the storm eased somewhat, prompting Senior Ranger Lisle Irwin to send in two rangers, Max Clarbrough and Hugh Logan, to investigate. The pair reached Barron Saddle, only to find no hut. Logan, momentarily flummoxed, thought he'd lost his bearings, but after peering over the cliff edge, discovered the horrifying sight of the hut wreckage. As the storm worsened again, Logan and Clarbrough had to retreat, but a later team recovered the four bodies.[6]

Wanganui Tramping Club members were deeply shocked by the accident, and club activity almost ground to a halt during a period of mourning. The club's website states, 'All four of the young people being remembered had a deep love, enjoyment and respect for New Zealand outdoor life which they shared with so many others.'[7] In the following year, club members set up the Four Friends Memorial Trust to help fund worthy projects.

Trampers at Fenella Hut, Kahurangi National Park, 2011. PHOTO: GEOFF SPEARPOINT

Three Johns Hut, Aoraki/Mount Cook National Park, 1964. PHOTO: AAT VERVOORN

Fenella Druce was the daughter of prominent Wellington botanists Tony and Helen Druce, friends of the Heines, and members of the Wellington Botanical Society. Devastated by Fenella's death, the couple sought to find solace by doing something constructive. Through their Wellington Botanical Society connections, they raised funds for a hut in Northwest Nelson Forest Park (now Kahurangi National Park).

In March 1977, Tony Druce approached the Forest Service with the hut idea, and the agency approved it. He had spent many summers travelling around the tops of Northwest Nelson on botanical expeditions, which probably influenced his decision to choose a hut site in the park. Tony, with Fenella's brother Oliver, selected a site at the head of the Cobb Valley. Oliver Druce remembers, 'After a whole day wandering around that area we chose the current site with an eye to shelter, sun, setting, water supply, drainage and foundations (and firewood!).'[8]

Tony asked friends Nigel Oxley and Fiona Christeller to design the hut. The Forest Service supported the project by transporting the building materials to the site by helicopter, as well as supplying two carpenters who oversaw building of the foundations. A team of volunteers led by Nigel, Fiona and Tony, many of whom were also members of the Wellington Botanical Society, completed all the framing and timber structure, interior and exterior lining, roofing and window work.[9] With their wide range of expertise, they also undertook painting, staining, woodturning and stonework, while Tony, among other jobs, engineered the water supply to the composting toilet. The team also laboured extensively on intricate rock and slate work surrounding the hut and on all the paths leading around it. Oliver Druce remembers, 'Throughout the construction of the hut care was taken to preserve most of the trees and plants closely surrounding the hut and it is this I think that gives it its special character.'[10] Tony, his family and friends continued to visit Fenella for many years to carry out regular maintenance, with time also for reflection and stories.[11]

The hut, completed in 1978, occupies a peaceful location under Mt Xenicus. You might see kea winging among the crags, or at the nearby tarn – superb for swimming – see rock wren flitting among the boulder jumbles. Located on the bush edge, Fenella Hut has both the shelter of the forest and the nearby openness of the subalpine tops that so appeal to trampers and botanists alike. There's a stained-glass window in the loo, a welcoming veranda and hand-crafted furniture. The design speaks of attention to detail, of affection, of tribute. It's a fitting memorial to Fenella Druce, a young woman whose life was cut short before she could fulfil the promising tramping and medical career ahead of her.

In horrible irony, the Three Johns Hut itself had been built as a memorial to three Australian climbers killed in an earlier accident. An avalanche on the Linda Glacier overwhelmed John Hammond, John Young and John Vidulich after their ascent of Aoraki/Mt Cook in 1955. Members of the Canterbury Mountaineering Club, who built Three Johns Hut in 1959, became increasingly concerned about its extremely exposed location as early as the 1960s. Winds from both the north and south constantly tore at the hut, which consequently required endless maintenance. One climber, trapped there for a week, wrote: 'One would lie back in bed cuddling the blankets when the deadly silence of such calms hushed the hut, listening to the approach of the next gust wondering how many more the hut could stand before disintegrating.'[12] The club proposed building a new hut at a more sheltered location to the Mount Cook National

Park Board, but in the end the existing structure was strengthened instead.[13]

The Three Johns Hut tragedy did have other positive outcomes, as it forced designers to look more closely at the engineering requirements of alpine huts. Mount Cook Park Board staff who built a replacement eight-bunk hut in 1981 carefully located it in a more sheltered site, and its barrel shape was designed specifically to withstand severe storms. There was some dilemma about what to call it. What do you name a memorial hut that killed four people? One mountaineer who'd helped recover the bodies questioned, 'Maybe it's bad luck remembering the dead when naming huts.'[14] In the end, it became Barron Saddle Hut.

In the thirty-five years since the Three Johns Hut accident, no one else has died through the structural failure of a hut, although one deer culler came close. In May 1980, the NZFS six-bunk Angle Knob Hut in Tararua Forest Park was picked up by a storm and thrown over the forest canopy like Dorothy's house in the *Wizard of Oz*. It landed largely intact, but severely damaged, among the silver beech trees. The bunks are still sitting in the bush. Fortunately, the deer culler inside, Chris Jenkins, managed to escape after he became concerned at the increasingly violent winds. He spent the night in the long-drop, located in a more sheltered position below the bush edge. When the Forest Service replaced Angle Knob Hut with Jumbo Hut, they located it in a less exposed part of the Tararua tops.[15]

The first Neville Barker Memorial Hut, built in Arthur's Pass as a monument to a climber killed during the Second World War, was not quite up to the harsh alpine environment of its location either. Fortunately, however, its 1980 replacement certainly was. In 1995, climbers Ian and Paul Dawe sheltered in the hut as a storm struck. They recorded in the hut book:

Fenella Hut, Kahurangi National Park, 2011. PHOTO: GEOFF SPEARPOINT

> Gale force nor'westers have now become extreme gale force and it's raining and hailing even harder. All night it felt as though the hut was going to blow away, it's like you're sitting in a magnitude 7 earthquake for 24 hours. Even now the whole hut is lifting and shaking. I don't think we'll try for the summit today! … This hut is amazing, it would survive a nuclear holocaust. Top marks to the people who designed and built this hut … Time is 8:80 p.m. and we've just discovered the toilet has been blown over! The wind's changed to the south and with it came the most horrendously strong blasts of wind, easily over 250 km/hr.[16]

Barker Hut remains on site today, still serving as a shelter and still acting as a memorial to a climber who died in the chaos of wartime Europe. There's something deeply poignant about remembering the dead through building a shelter that, in turn, saves the lives of others.

SHAUN BARNETT

Colin Todd Hut 1960/1996 MOUNT ASPIRING NATIONAL PARK

The building of Colin Todd Hut must surely rate as one of the most determined, and ill-fated, stories of hut construction in New Zealand's history.

Although he was only twenty-eight when he died in a motorcycle accident in 1955, Colin Macdonald Todd was already one of the best-known climbers of the day. Inspired by both his father's and his own Olivine Range explorations, he went on to climb throughout the Southern Alps and then the Himalayas, making the first ascent of Baruntse (7161 metres) with Geoff Harrow on a Hillary-led expedition to Nepal in 1954.[1]

Following Todd's tragic death, an anonymous donation was given to the Otago Section of the New Zealand Alpine Club to build an alpine hut as a memorial. Plans were drawn up based on the Canterbury Mountaineering Club's Empress Hut design, and timber precut by the Brough brothers, carpenters and climbers.

Construction, however, did not proceed smoothly, and that the hut was ever completed is a story of considerable tenacity – four years of it, in fact, during which time the planned location was shifted 130 kilometres southwest along the Main Divide. Initially, Colin Todd Hut was to be sited in Westland National Park, at the head of Scott Creek on the Sierra Range above the Copland Valley.

A Royal New Zealand Air Force crew based at Taieri Airport was enlisted to help transport materials. On 29 November 1956, a Bristol Freighter loaded with 5000 pounds (2300 kilograms) of cargo took off, only to return still carrying the hut materials, having been beaten by the mist. The plane took off again on 16 December, but mist forced this second mission to abort too. Meanwhile, however, a hut-building party of twenty had left Aoraki/Mount Cook village and headed over Copland Pass towards the site to at least prepare foundations. They never made it either. Having crossed the pass, the climbers were beaten back from Scott Creek by bluffs and bad weather, and were forced to return to Aoraki/Mount Cook village via the Arthur's Pass road. In 1957, three further attempts were made to parachute the hut onto this site, but weather continued to intervene.

Then another problem arose. The RNZAF planned to close their base at Taieri, and future flights were limited. After some lateral thinking about an alternative site, the NZAC came up with the idea of Shipowner Ridge, on the slopes of Mt Aspiring/Tititea. Interestingly, an earlier proposal in 1950 to build a hut on the ridge had foundered through lack of funds. Changing the site of the Colin Todd Hut didn't initially bring any more success either.

Attempt number six, in January 1958, started in fine weather, but an hour later, by the time the Bristol Freighter lumbered up towards the Bonar Glacier, mist forced yet another retreat. Not only that, but the support team flown in by ski-plane then spent some very rough days camped out on the Bonar before they were able to retreat to the Matukituki Valley, empty-handed.

As the *New Zealand Alpine Journal* account of the saga comments, 'It became increasingly difficult to focus on the fact that the purpose of the exercise was to drop the hut, not just to send it for a height acclimatization trip. Another two trips followed.'[2] Mountaineers can be a persistent lot.

The second of these trips, in November 1958, was the eighth try overall, and this time the weather proved fine, the plane flew and the hut was dropped. But … it landed on the wrong site. Some of the loads were dropped on the Iso Glacier, but most ended up over 100 metres down the Therma Glacier, with a schrund threatening to cut them off. Two imperial tons (about 2000 kilograms) of equipment would need to be carried back up to the Shipowner and then down several hundred metres to the proposed hut site.

With the materials landed, getting a ground party on site became an urgent priority. However, what was planned as a one-day ski-plane trip by a party of three to secure and check the air-drop contributed the next saga. On landing, the plane slewed sideways and nose-dived, leaving its tail in the air.

LEFT Colin Todd on the Barun Expedition, Nepal, 1954.
PHOTO: BRIAN WILKINS
OPPOSITE Colin Todd Hut II, with Mt Aspiring/Tititea beyond, 2002. PHOTO: SHAUN BARNETT/BLACK ROBIN PHOTOGRAPHY

TOP LEFT Colin Todd Hut I, January 1976. PHOTO: GEOFF SPEARPOINT. **TOP RIGHT:** An RNZAF Iroquois flying in a section of Colin Todd Hut II, 1996. PHOTO ROB BROWN. **LEFT** Colin Knox outside Colin Todd Hut I, in August 1960. PHOTO: GRAEME WOODFIELD.

The occupants all walked out after two of the party had at least sighted the air-drop. The plane was repaired some days later and flown home.

Next, a party of four headed up to stack the materials on site, but limited time and manpower didn't allow them to complete much. Soon after, a larger party stubbornly hung on through several days of bad weather to carry all the loads up to the top of the Shipowner Ridge, where they could be safely stacked, but it wasn't until December 1959 that most of the loads were finally on site. Over the years, a cast of many dozens had been involved in building, packing, unpacking and supporting attempts to get the hut on site, but finally a crew of about ten finished building the hut over a few days in early January 1960 during a spell of fine weather. Construction itself was, in the end, simple; it was the delivery that had proved to be the problem.

By the 1990s, Colin Todd Hut had given over thirty years of magnificent shelter and it was time for a replacement. This plan was given impetus with a bequest from the late Leslie Corcoran for a high hut in the Otago Alps. DOC, the Lotteries Commission, NZAC members and many others also contributed. NZAC member Chas Tanner ably oversaw the project, and the RNZAF offered to fly the 700-kilogram sections of the hut to the site, this time by Iroquois helicopter. Stu Thorne at the Department of Conservation in Wanaka played a vital role in co-coordinating support, and DOC also supplied the hut builder, Dave Grieve. The hut was opened in January 1996.[3]

Colin Todd Hut owes its original existence to considerable perseverance and its second incarnation to a wonderfully forward-thinking agreement between the NZAC Otago Section and DOC. Although the NZAC owns the hut, DOC manages it, utilising locally generated funds from hut fees to carry out maintenance – including a major upgrade in 2010.

Colin Todd is a strong hut in a wonderful locations and as an alpine base it is worth every step of the walk in, whether from French Ridge, Bevan Col or somewhere else in the surrounding wilderness.

GEOFF SPEARPOINT

Hunters Hut 1997 MT RICHMOND FOREST PARK, NELSON

Huts are supposed to be havens; places where, after the rigours of a day outside, you can retreat to relative comfort and safety. Imagine, then, the horror of two hunters when a sudden flash flood engulfed their hut in 1995.

On the morning of 23 February that year, two Department of Conservation hunters, Russell Griebel and Bob Waldie, were at Bushedge Hut in Mt Richmond Forest Park. The pair had just completed a successful goat-culling operation in the nearby gorges of the upper Motueka River. Both men must have felt satisfied at a job well done, and – when the heavy rain increased – pleased that they had a roof overhead. During the night, the nearby swollen Motueka River Left Branch began to surge, but by then both men were probably asleep.

According to information collected by forecaster Erick Brenstrum in *The New Zealand Weather Book* (1998), heavy rainfall pummelled the Nelson–Marlborough region late on 22 February, greatly exacerbated by a wall of thunderstorms that developed behind the northerly front. As much as 40–55 millimetres fell in a single hour. The torrential rain caused flooding in Nelson and Blenheim, and over half a million dollars' worth of damage to roads. In the mountainous headwaters of the Motueka River, the excess water swelled the normally 30 centimetre-deep stream to a 5-metre torrent.[1]

At about 5 a.m., a massive wall of water and silt swept down the valley and engulfed Bushedge Hut, carrying everything away in its wake. Waldie and Griebel had no warning. The hut floor was washed 10 kilometres downstream, and a pack belonging to one of the hunters lodged 4 metres up a tree.[2]

Two days after the flood, Waldie's body was found 4 kilometres downstream, but Griebel's body wasn't located for another three years.[3] His dog, Freckles, was never found.[4]

A tramper who passed by a few weeks later wrote in the logbook of nearby Maitland Hut 'Was shocked to see the sad remains of Bushedge Hut. Just goes to show who has the final say…'.[5]

Bushedge Hut, originally called Top Motueka Hut, was a standard NZFS six-bunker built in November 1962 during a period of intense building activity in the Nelson–Marlborough region. It had survived many storms in the thirty-five years it stood on a small terrace above the river. In general, Forest Service huts were located on well-chosen sites, and no one could have anticipated such a freak weather event at this location.[6]

Colleagues of the two hunters decided the most fitting memorial would be a replacement hut. DOC staff opted to relocate the nearby Maitland Hut and upgrade it. The fine bush-edge site they chose, well above the river, overlooks the Porter Ridge and Inwood Lookout.

Completed in March 1997, the new eight-bunk Hunters Hut was opened on 5 April with a commemoration service for the two men. Forty people attended, many of them friends and family of Griebel and Waldie. A memorial plaque in the hut pays tribute to two dedicated hunters who lost their lives while on the job.[7]

SHAUN BARNETT

Hunters Hut in 2005.
PHOTO: SHAUN BARNETT/BLACK ROBIN PHOTOGRAPHY

Barker Hut 1945/1978 ARTHUR'S PASS NATIONAL PARK

In the brutal battle for Monte Cassino in Italy during the Second World War, a mine killed Lieutenant Neville Barker. He was thirty-two.[1] English-born, Barker had come to New Zealand as a teenager with his parents when they immigrated here in 1925. A stalwart of the Canterbury Mountaineering Club throughout the 1930s, Neville had regularly participated in club trips and made a notable ascent of Mt Murchison from Weka Stream. Shortly before enlisting in the Army, he helped build the club's hut near the Anti Crow River.[2] After his death, Barker's widowed mother, grief-stricken at the loss of her only son, offered to finance a high-altitude hut in his memory.

The CMC chose a site in the head of the White Valley, a tributary of the Waimakariri, where the hut could serve as a base for ascents of peaks like Mt Murchison, which at 2400 metres is the highest peak in Arthur's Pass National Park. Work began in 1945.

Because of wartime restrictions, no corrugated iron was officially available for such a frivolous project as building a mountain hut. However, Cedric Turner, one of the work party, later remembered that 'we had a few members who were keen students of Machiavelli and somehow enough material was assembled'.[3] There were plenty of buildings with iron from which 'a sheet here or there need not be missed'. As a result, the cladding of Barker Hut sported a colourful mixture of red, green, black and brand-new iron.

The main building team comprised Stan Muirson, Fred Hulston and Nui Robins, who were helped in assembling the hut by a small army of nearly forty other club members. The club had never built such a high climbing hut before (it was located at an altitude of just over 1500 metres), and transporting materials to the site proved something of a struggle. After the frame was prefabricated in Hulston's Christchurch workshop, it was disassembled and the materials sent by rail to Cass and, finally, by truck to Klondyke Corner. From there, packhorses carried the loads to Carrington Hut, before a mixture of young and old men portaged the materials up to the site. Judging from the photographs of these men – who were not of suitable age for war service – they handled the carry over 10 kilometres and an altitude gain of 650 metres remarkably well.

The building went up incredibly fast. Over Easter 1945 the materials were carted in, and after just two days a roof and some of the walls were in place, enabling the builders to move inside from their tents. By the next night they could sleep on bunks.

Although the war had taken its toll on CMC

CMC members lugging timber for the Barker Memorial Hut up the White Valley, 1945.
PHOTO: NUI ROBINS, JOHN WILSON COLLECTION

Barker Memorial Hut during construction and **(ABOVE)** completed, 1945.
PHOTOS: JOHN WILSON COLLECTION

HUTS AS MONUMENTS 315

membership, the post-war years saw renewed interest in the mountains. Trains provided easy transport from Christchurch, and large parties often trudged up the favoured 'Waimak' to earn their mountain skills. In 1946, the club recorded that eighty people made it to Carrington Hut for their Easter tramp, with many of them going beyond to stay at the new Neville Barker Memorial Hut.[4]

Disappointingly, the site chosen for this first Barker Hut caused endless maintenance headaches. While it was sheltered from the winds that swirl around the valley head, in winter it became something of a snow trap. By Labour Weekend in the first year of the hut's life, the club had to reposition it after winter snowfalls had shunted the structure off its piles. In 1948, the hut again 'slipped its moorings', this time due to high winds. And in August 1952, a party arrived to find the hut well buried and dug it out – only to find 'some clot had left the door half open'. They had a 'hell of a job' clearing the snow out.

By the late 1950s, the hut was very run down – indeed suspect and unsafe – and visitors were warned off staying there. Despite a complete makeover in 1961, problems remained. Then in 1968, a particularly heavy snowfall broke the central roof beam.

It became increasingly obvious that the hut was simply not suitable for its spectacular alpine site, and CMC prepared to replace it.[5] In the mid-1970s, Neville Barker's mother died and in her will gifted $2847 to the CMC, which served as seeding money for a new hut.[6]

The second hut, built in 1978, used a system of prefabricated 100 millimetre-thick metal-faced polystyrene panels held together with a camlock system. This same design had been employed at Scott Base by the New Zealand Antarctic programme. The basic hut assembled from these panels was bolted to an immensely strong triangular metal frame. This was the first, and only surviving, mountain hut built with this system.[7]

Royal New Zealand Air Force helicopters flew in the materials, losing just one load when a spinning strop forced the pilot to jettison it above Camp Spur. CMC selected a new, slightly more exposed site, which was near the first hut but less prone to snow build-up.

This second hut's design proved much better suited to the harsh alpine environment, and gave the club far fewer headaches. Fully insulated and with double-glazed windows, it warms up nicely when people are inside and Primuses are burning. A mountain radio and solar lighting add additional luxuries. The only weakness is the panel joints, which require regular sealing and painting to remain weatherproof. CMC continues to administer and maintain the ten-bunk hut, set in arguably the finest surroundings of Arthur's Pass National Park.[8]

ROB BROWN

BELOW A 1994 oil painting of Neville Barker Memorial Hut by Austen Deans. IMAGE: COURTESY OF PAUL DEANS, A. A. DEANS TRUST. ORIGINAL HELD BY CHRISTCHURCH ART GALLERY TE PUNA O WAIWHETU, PRESENTED BY JOHN H. WEBB, CHRISTCHURCH 1995.
OPPOSITE Climber Daryl Ball approaches Barker Hut II in 2000, with Mt Harper beyond.
PHOTO: SHAUN BARNETT/BLACK ROBIN PHOTOGRAPHY

Esquilant Bivouac 1950/1989 MOUNT ASPIRING NATIONAL PARK

Mt Earnslaw in the Forbes Mountains above Glenorchy has long been a destination for mountaineers, especially those in the Otago Section of the New Zealand Alpine Club. William Robert 'Bert' Esquilant was one of those, climbing the West Peak of Mt Earnslaw in 1941 at thirty-two years of age.[1] When Bert was killed climbing the Weisshorn in Switzerland five years later, he left a bequest of money 'for the erection of a high hut beyond the reach of trampers'. Many sites were considered, but in the end Wright Col was chosen for the climbing opportunities it provided, and the club set about planning to build.[2]

In the late 1940s, dropping hut materials by aeroplane was still in its infancy, especially in alpine environments. Despite a decision to fly materials to the hut site, the plane could only carry loads shorter than 1.5 metres, meaning some material had to be lugged up in the old-fashioned way. Over a wet Queen's Birthday weekend in 1950, seventeen load carriers suffered their way up to Earnslaw Hut and back again, staying in the four-bunk Twenty Five Mile Hut, which had a leaky roof and broken window.

The scheduled December air-drop did not occur until Christmas, when a team of sixteen, supervised by Bob Craigie, walked in carrying supplies, ready for building. On Christmas Day, well-known pilot Fred 'Popeye' Lucas flew low over Wright Col in his new Auster plane, and began dropping bundles, without parachutes, onto the snowy drop zone. However, the bulk of the 109 bundles were landed on Boxing Day. Altogether, 3264 pounds (1480 kilograms) were air-dropped, with a success rate of 85 per cent, while another 432 pounds (196 kilograms) of materials were carried up. On the last run, Lucas sneaked up in his Auster, roared over the heads of the unsuspecting club members, and dropped a sack of fresh vegetables from a height of about 10 metres. People scattered everywhere.[3]

Despite cold and windy weather – Paul Powell described one night inside while 'the hail beat its angry little fists against the roof' – the builders finished the hut by the night of 28 December. Inside, it measured 3.1 metres by 2.15 metres and slept eight, three on a raised sleeping bench and five on the floor. Esquilant Biv made a fine memorial to a mountaineer who had died on the other side of the world.[4]

However, that's only half the story. The NZAC Southland Section took over management of Esquilant from the Otago Section in the 1980s. Sadly, history repeated itself. On Labour weekend 1987, eighteen-year-old Darren Hawes, a bright and popular member of both the NZAC and Southland Tramping Club, died in a fall only a stone's throw from the bivvy. Just weeks before, he had reported to the committee that Esquilant needed maintenance, and had offered to lead a work party. After establishing a fund to remember Darren, the club chose to rebuild Esquilant Bivouac as a fitting memorial.[5]

Warren Herrick spearheaded the project; Murray Kokich designed the hut, while Ron McLeod and Hugh Rowe were the main builders. Ultimately, of course, it became a collaborative effort, involving a team of twenty-seven people on site during Easter 1989, reminiscent of the original work party. This time, however, helicopter pilot Dave Kershaw transported both materials and people to the site on Good Friday. By the end of Easter Sunday, the hut was essentially finished. It measured a roomier 3.6 metres by 2.2 metres, with an apex height of 2.4 metres.

A member of the original 1950 hut-building team, Owen Wynn, visited too. During construction, Darren's sister, Susan Hawes, laid his ice axe in the hut foundations. I suspect both Bert and Darren would be proud of the efforts made on their behalf. With both the old and new bivs still standing (the old one was later removed), Warren Herrick commented that: 'we could see two huts, one is a memorial to one, but the other one is one to two'.[6] Warren, too, has since passed on, and I am tempted to say it is now a memorial to three.

GEOFF SPEARPOINT

LEFT Paul Powell and Brian Wilkins at Esquilant Biv I in January 1951, just days after they had completed building it. PHOTO: BRIAN WILKINS
OPPOSITE Esquilant Biv II, February 2009, with Pluto Peak beyond. PHOTO: GEOFF SPEARPOINT

HUTS AS MONUMENTS 319

Park Morpeth Hut 1931 WILBERFORCE VALLEY, CANTERBURY

Memorial huts serve as one of the most lasting tributes of friends and family to those who have died in the mountains. Park Morpeth Hut is one of those huts. In January 1929, West Coast youths James Park and John Morpeth left Lake Kaniere to cross Browning Pass and descend the Wilberforce to Glenthorne Station.[1] This route, used extensively during the 1860s by miners and shepherds, had by the 1920s become an adventurous trip pursued mainly by trampers.

Park and Morpeth experienced a major storm, which raged on 10 January. A week later, they had still not arrived at Glenthorne, prompting fears about their safety. Musterers from Glenthorne and Algidus stations searched the Wilberforce, while a party of four Canterbury Mountaineering Club members scoured the terrain of the Three Pass tramp. Searchers also used a plane – a very innovative approach for the 1920s. The club party crossed from the Waimakariri to the upper Wilberforce, found notes from other searchers, then headed over Browning Pass and down the Arahura and Styx valleys. They found no sign of the missing trampers.

On 28 January, James Park's body was found below Mt Algidus Station, near the junction of the Wilberforce and Rakaia rivers. Several days earlier, a cape, towel and groundsheet were located near the Weka–Burnet confluence, suggesting the pair had drowned while fording Burnet Stream.

Money donated as a result of the tragedy precipitated plans for a hut in the upper Wilberforce. The only other shelter there – 'a large building containing a blacksmith shop and mining machinery', dating from gold-mining attempts in about 1906 – had by 1926 been completely buried under a massive scree slip.[2] A new hut seemed timely.

Urged on by Cuth Thornton, an early club member, the CMC raised more funds and coordinated the building project. They hired carpenter Larry Burrows (father of current club member Colin Burrows) and his brother William, who together had already built station huts in the lower Wilberforce.[3] In early 1931, they used a dray and then packhorses to take the materials up the Wilberforce, and built Park Morpeth Hut near its confluence with Cronin Stream.

Over subsequent decades, the hut sheltered many parties as the popularity of the Three Pass trip grew, but it needed sporadic maintenance. Work parties normally approached up the Wilberforce, but sometimes came from Arthur's Pass, carrying materials over two Main Divide passes: Harman (1321 metres) and Whitehorn (1753 metres). In 1952, one party followed this route to replace windows and renovate bunks at the hut. Two extra tramping parties arrived at about the same time as it started to rain, resulting in rather cramped working conditions, and the workers had to exit during a storm. At this stage, Park Morpeth Hut had sacking bunks and a dirt floor.

In September 1980, the Army helped with a major restoration.[4] Major Geoff Charles organised this through the Mutual Assistance Programme, designed in part to up-skill Fijian and Tongan soldiers. Flying in from Glenthorne by Iroquois helicopter with the materials, they set about pulling the hut to bits. Charles recorded:

> Much of the timber framing of the hut was rotten, and had to be replaced. We then tacked on new insulating foil, and over the next few days replaced the iron, put Perspex panels in the roof and repaired the chimney and bunks … The highlight of the work was the construction and siting of a monumental thunderbox, complete with a window on the side (a loo with a view!).[5]

The soldiers also laid a new concrete floor.[6] The work party then headed over Browning Pass, where they spent a night in their tent hammered by wind and snow, before exiting, in rain, to the West Coast. There is a theme developing here.

Major events can give backcountry locations a deep resonance for those involved: surviving a particular storm, discovering lifelong friendships or, like the genesis of Park Morpeth Hut, a tragic drowning. In January 1956, a party of three experienced and keen youths headed in from Lake Kaniere for a Three Pass trip during the school holidays.[7] Drizzly weather turned to rain, but they crossed Browning Pass and descended to the Wilberforce River. The party had been here once before, two months earlier, when they faced only a minor ford. But this time the Wilberforce was several metres across. The boys linked up, but the crossing went badly and sixteen-year-old Allan Clough drowned. Mountaineers in the CMC keenly felt the loss of their friend, and at Easter 1956 built a permanent cairn, both in Clough's memory and as a reminder of the dangers posed by mountain torrents.

One of Clough's companions, Brian Fineran, came back to Park Morpeth fifty years later as part of a CMC work party in 2006.[8] The team raised the hut on new bearers above the old concrete floor, and installed a new wooden floor. As they framed up the hut extension, the rain began. A hastily erected tarpaulin covered the exposed framing, and Fineran remembers that enough rain poured down to fill a 10-litre bucket overnight.

Although no doubt inconvenient at the time, the rain somehow seems appropriate. After all, rain and storms had brought about the tragedy that led to the hut's very existence in the first place. Park Morpeth Hut remains here in memory of it all, still providing shelter.

GEOFF SPEARPOINT

OPPOSITE Park Morpeth Hut, pictured in the 1990s, before its most recent renovation. PHOTO: GEOFF SPEARPOINT

Manson-Nicholls Memorial Hut 1976 LEWIS PASS NATIONAL RESERVE

Sometimes random events happen in the mountains. I remember having lunch in the forest by an isolated stream one day, when a truck-sized bank collapsed 10 metres away from me. One minute it was fine, sunny and quiet, and the next it was fine, sunny and quiet again, but a big area of stream bed was now covered in fresh clay and debris. I blinked, but it hadn't been my imagination, and the unexpected nature of the event shocked me.

Lake Daniell (or Daniells as it was known in the 1970s) is a tranquil place too. Surrounded by mature red, silver and mountain beech forest, it attracts anglers for its rainbow and brown trout. The jetty is a wonderful place to enjoy the breeze or reflections, depending on the weather. Only a few hours in from the Lewis Highway along a flat, gravelled track, where robins land at your feet, the lake has been popular for many years. So much so, in fact, that anglers built a simple corrugated-iron-roofed hut beside it, a few hundred metres along the western shore from the lake outlet. That was sometime in the 1950s.[1]

Easter 1974 was wet. In such weather Lake Daniells Hut would seem a pretty safe and comfortable bet, and four people were staying there. But sometimes random events have tragic consequences. A landslide came down behind the hut and engulfed it. Buried in mud, three people – Brian and Sharon Manson and Phillip Nicholls – died. Brian and Phillip were both members of the Christchurch Tramping Club, and Brian and Sharon were only recently married. It was a terrible way for a holiday weekend to finish.

A month later, at a CTC committee meeting in May 1974, club members – deeply affected by the loss of two of their number – decided to build a memorial hut to honour them. A combined field trip by the Lake Daniells Fishing Club (which owned the old hut), the CTC and the Department of Lands and Survey (which administered the reserve land around the lake) was held to decide on a new hut site. They chose a location at the south end of the lake, near fine shingle beaches a few hundred metres along from the outlet.[2]

Funding for the new hut came from donations, sports and recreation grants, and the insurance payout on the old hut. Lands and Survey contributed two-thirds of the helicopter bill, which totalled $1900. Added to that was the cost of the hut itself – another $5500. Even for the time, it was a remarkably low figure.

Clearing the new site began a year after the tragedy, with some of Brian's workmates from Rangiora helping out. What was left of the old hut was floated around the lake edge to become a temporary shelter during the building phase. Preparation of some of the building and supplies began in Christchurch, and six months later they were transported over the course of a weekend to Eric Timpson's farm near Springs Junction, where they were stored temporarily. The same weekend, the precut framing timber was collected from Reefton. Flying the hut materials up to Lake Daniells by helicopter took most of a weekend too – at 13 metres by 5.5 metres, the hut was a substantial one for its time.

The 'Lake Daniells Construction Company', as the builders called themselves, got stuck in, and by the end of 1975 the hut was closed in and partially

LEFT The original Lake Daniells Hut.
PHOTOGRAPHER AND DATE UNKNOWN
OPPOSITE Manson-Nicholls Memorial Hut, pictured in the 1980s. PHOTO: GEOFF SPEARPOINT

lined inside. Assistance came from many quarters, and several more work parties in February and March 1976 carried out additional internal work and finished the veranda. One of those involved, Gary Swarbrick, noted that, 'During the project there was never a shortage of "willing hands" from both within the two clubs and from other groups and individuals. Many returned time after time.'³ Preparation and construction of the hut absorbed more than 1600 work hours.

Two years after the tragedy, at Easter 1976, the hut was opened in grand style. Sharon's parents, Mr and Mrs Fitzgibbon, were helicoptered in, along with the food and kegs. Speeches outlined the history of the area and the hut, and the commissioner of Crown lands for Nelson declared it open. A plaque was dedicated to the three lives lost by Father Renwick, who had married Sharon and Brian.

The Department of Conservation now manages the serviced twenty-four-bunk hut, which has heating and mattresses. Since it opened, many thousands of people have enjoyed staying here – schoolchildren, anglers, hunters, trampers, tourists, those seeking a quiet weekend away in the hills and those seeking a place for a gourmet dinner. It is a place for everyone.

GEOFF SPEARPOINT

HUTS AS MONUMENTS

RESEARCH IN THE MOUNTAINS AND BUSH SCIENCE HUTS

Although they form only a small subset of huts, a surprising number of backcountry structures have been built specifically for use in scientific projects. Caswell Sound Hut (Fiordland National Park), Back Basin Hide (Craigieburn Forest Park), Dominie Biv (Kaweka Forest Park) and Cupola Hut (Nelson Lakes National Park) all served as shelter for scientists studying wild animals in the mid-twentieth century. Excepting Caswell Sound, all these huts had their origins with the Forest Service, which from the 1950s onwards established a significant number of study areas in the mountains to research forests and alpine ecosystems.

Beginning in 1959, Makahu Saddle in the Kaweka Range became a veritable hub of scientific work as the NZFS established its North Island Forest and Range Experimentation Station (FRES) at Napier, with Ashley Cunningham in charge. Dominie Biv was part of this hub, serving as a weather station. Jack Holloway ran the South Island equivalent at Rangiora. These stations were both successors to the huge National Forest Survey completed by the Forest Service in 1955. As a base for research, Holloway's team used a four-bunk hut, built in 1959 at Cave Stream headwaters in the Craigieburn Range. Landcare Research staff still use a hut named after Holloway in the area.[1]

Many huts had rainfall gauges, but only a few, like Dominie Biv, had more sophisticated meteorological equipment. Cropp Hut, in the Whitcombe Valley, provided important weather and rainfall records between 1962 and 1994. Yet other huts have served as shelter for scientists studying glaciers. Glaciologists at Ivory Lake used a modified NZFS-hut design as a base for their studies of the Ivory Glacier. In contrast, Graham Bishop and Jane Forsyth's A-frame hut was purpose-built for their research on the shrinking Dart Glacier between 1975 and 1987.[2]

Wellington's Orongorongo Valley has also been a centre of scientific efforts spanning decades, with several different huts serving as accommodation. Les Pracy, deer culler turned scientist, begun researching possums in 1946, at first working from a private hut called McGregor's Hut. In 1952, an 'Opossum Research Station' was built and subsequently run by a succession of government departments: first, Internal Affairs; second, the Forest Service; third, the Department of Science and Industrial Research (DSIR); and finally Landcare Research.[3] Between 1966 and 1990, part of the valley became the research area for probably the longest-term study of a forest ever conducted in New Zealand. Various huts in the valley served as accommodation for the researchers. The study generated at least eighty-five scientific papers, with a summary of the research collated by Robert Brockie in his 1992 book *A Living New Zealand Forest*.[4]

During the 1940s, Les Pracy also worked in the Aorangi Range in the Wairarapa, under scientist Ralph Kean, who was based at Pararaki Hut. One author described them as a balanced team: 'Ralph Kean the scholarly, careful scientist, and Les Pracy the energetic and experienced field worker.' They found that possums establish in dense, damp forest only with difficulty, but can more easily spread into deer- or goat-damaged bush.[5] Today, their old research hut in the Pararaki Valley has collapsed to just a shell, with only one wall standing. A more recent NZFS hut of the same name, built just downstream in 1964, has served as a science base too, with DSIR and then Landcare Research staff undertaking more possum studies there between 1980 and 2005.[6]

The Ecology Division of the DSIR also set up several research huts. Staff undertook studies of kaka and other birds in Nelson Lakes National Park, working out of a large base hut near Lake Rotoroa and a small hut on the nearby Mt Misery tops. In 1992, the DSIR became Landcare Research, which took over the Rotoroa hut. Landcare Research also has an A-frame hut in the Waihaha catchment of Pureora Forest Park, where among other projects scientists have studied the impact of aerial 1080 possum-control operations on deer.

The West Coast's Camp Creek Hut is one of the more salubrious huts built for scientific purpose, and once even boasted an outdoor bath-cum-shower linked to a wetback-fired hot-water cylinder. During the 1970s, Ian Payton – then a Forest Service botanist – set about studying subalpine scrub above Camp Creek on the western bush edge of the Kaimata Range, near Arthur's Pass. In 1975, he and others established a tent camp, but this proved inadequate lodging, especially in winter. The NZFS agreed to build a research hut in 1979, and planned to use a new upmarket model of their standard six-bunker. Head office contracted Canterbury building company Fraemohs to prepare interlocking materials for the hut.

Payton recalls that the hut took about five days to erect and 'fitted together like a jigsaw puzzle.' It was eventually expanded to have nine bunks, a full workshop, a meteorological station and the covered bath. The Forest Service

Ivory Lake Hut, with the Ivory Lake and Glacier beyond, 1989. PHOTO: GEOFF SPEARPOINT

flew in food and fuel supplies once a year, and for several weeks over summer and about once a month over winter, Camp Creek Hut served as a comfortable home for a range of scientists and field technicians. Payton researched possum impact on southern rata–kamahi forests in the area, as well as conducting studies of alpine tussock grasslands.[7]

Probably the largest group of science huts is located in Fiordland's Murchison Mountains. Between the late 1950s and mid-1970s, the Wildlife Service, Forest Service and Fiordland National Park Board collectively established some twenty-five huts and bivs in the region, which were initially used by deer cullers and Wildlife Service officers, and now provide lodgings for DOC biologists.[8] These 'biodiversity huts' are an eclectic mix of styles, ranging from two-bunk bivs to ordinary NZFS huts, but now with a few added comforts like an old armchair, a radio and, usually, a full complement of kitchen equipment. Some were named after their location, while others – like Wisely Hut – took the names of early takahe scientists. None of these biodiversity huts is available for public use, except for two on the western edge of the Special Takahe Area, and then on a seasonal permit basis only.[9]

A number of other huts have temporarily served as shelter for scientists over the years. Landcare Research scientists making long-term studies of rata and totara dieback at Crawford Forks in the West Coast's Kokatahi Valley stayed at Crawford Junction Hut. And in Lake Sumner Forest Park, Glenn Johnston remembers living at Jollie Brook Hut briefly in 1976 while carrying out experimental tree-planting in the high country here: 'The above job was the last I was on with the NZFS where pack horses were used. From then on it was 4×4 vehicles, helicopters & sometimes boats used to transport the heavy gear.'[10] During the 1960s, the Forest Service experimented heavily with using exotic trees for erosion control, notably in the Kawekas and at Craigieburn, and the work in the Jollie Brook catchment was part of this.

Over the last twenty years, the Department of Conservation has established a number of huts – often relocatable bivvies – specifically for ongoing monitoring and research. Such shelters are located in places like the Haast Range, Stewart Island/Rakiura, Kahurangi's Parapara Peak and Fiordland's Slaughter Burn.

If we expand the definition of science to include nature education, then places like Rotoiti Lodge at Nelson Lakes and another similar lodge in Craigieburn Forest Park must also count as places that have helped foster understanding of the natural world.

SHAUN BARNETT

Ornithologists Gordon Williams and Elwyn Welch outside Wisely Hut, Murchison Mountains, Fiordland, with takahe in the boxes, November 1958. PHOTO: PETER MORRISON, COURTESY OF DOC TE ANAU

Les Pracy at McGregors Hut, his first possum research station in the Orongorongo Valley, 1946. PHOTO: NZFS COLLECTION, ARCHIVES NZ, WELLINGTON, M11,395

Ivory Lake Hut[1] 1970 WAITAHA VALLEY, WEST COAST

At the end of the 1966–67 summer, young glaciologist Trevor Chinn flew around the Southern Alps looking for a specific feature – a suitable glacier to study. Spurring his study was the United Nations Educational, Scientific and Cultural Organisation (UNESCO), which in January 1965 began the International Hydrological Decade. UNESCO asked countries from around the world to make hydrological studies in the interests of increasing scientific knowledge. As an employee of the Water and Soil Division of the Ministry of Works (MOW), Chinn had been studying New Zealand's largest glacier – the Tasman – and became the obvious choice to hunt down the ideal 'representative glacier basin'.

Although scientists knew that the Little Ice Age, a cold period that started in the sixteenth century, had ended in the nineteenth century, resulting in glacial retreat, the phrase 'climate change' had not yet been coined. The study glacier, Chinn remembers, needed specific attributes: 'Reasonable year-round access, easy slopes to permit access over its entire length, a melt-water stream measuring site close below the glacier terminus with no underground water loss', as well as the potential for 'a good comfortable hut site'.

Prior to his 1967 flight, Chinn searched through photos and mountain publications to narrow down the list to a handful of possible glaciers. These included the Siege and Escape glaciers on the back of Mt Adams, the Victoria Glacier above Fox Glacier, the Brewster Glacier above Haast Pass, and the small 'ice puddle' at the head of the Waitaha Valley known as the Ivory Glacier.

In April 1968, Chinn led a party into the Waitaha Valley to inspect the tiny (0.8-square-kilometre) Ivory Glacier. No tracks existed in the Waitaha, and Chinn's only prior knowledge of the valley came from explorer Charlie Douglas, who in 1892 had described it thus: 'for grand scenery and difficulty getting to see it, this river very nearly holds first place in Westland'.[2]

After struggling up the heavily gorged valley, Chinn's group found themselves just short of Ivory Lake on 9 April. They were relieved to stumble upon the recently completed Forest Service Top Waitaha Hut, the first hut built in the valley, as a violent tempest was upon them: the same storm that led to the *Wahine* disaster.

Once the storm cleared, the party reached the Ivory Glacier and found it ideal for their study purposes. Over the next few years, the hydrology-glaciology team returned at three- to four-monthly intervals by helicopter to measure the annual gain and melt of the Ivory Glacier ice (the mass balance, measured using installed stake arrays), as well as recording the river flow and erecting a suitable climate station.

On the first trip in April 1969, they surveyed the glacier, installed the stake layout and measured stream flows. That July, the scientists endured a freezing tent camp, followed by a wet camp on snow and lake ice in September. During a three-day storm, their tent camp was slowly and surely

Ivory Lake Hut, 2008. PHOTO: MARK WATSON

flooded. A couple of days spent in soggy sleeping bags was sufficient motivation for the planning of a hut.

The MOW engaged the Forest Service to build an SF70 six-bunk forestry hut on a site offering views of the glacier and down the valley. Builder John Turton supervised laying the concrete foundations in February 1970, and during the April 1970 survey, hut materials were flown in. Curiously, the Forest Service delivered its bog-standard chimney and fireplace, taking no account of the fact that the alpine location offered no firewood.

While the MOW team measured up the glacier, the builders – Rodger Richards (carpenter) and Bruce Hassell (NZFS) – assembled a de luxe version of the hut, complete with insulation and plywood lining. With the chimney closed off and modified using a perspex sheet, it became a respectable kitchen alcove for the kerosene burner. The next big job was digging trenches to house wires connecting the meteorological instruments to the batteries stored at the hut. Burying the wires supposedly prevented chewing by the local population of about seven kea, but Chinn recalled that it only partially achieved its purpose.

In 1972, the team added a lean-to workshop for secure storage of the scientific equipment that included a purpose-built trapdoor to insert the long snow-depth poles. Shutters fitted to the hut windows helped prevent any potential glass breakage from bits of flying ice and rock.[3]

For three years, starting in 1972, a series of Masters students occupied the hut, carrying out microclimate and glacier research. In 1974, when there was no student, a friendly hermit called Sugra made the daily weather observations over the winter (Sugra still entertains visitors to Christchurch today with his juggling act on a unicycle). In August 1976, an armchair was flown in as part of the growing hut luxuries – it can still be enjoyed by visitors to Ivory Lake Hut today.

During the first few years of glacier work, teams could ski off the glacier terminus and across the lake ice to the hut for a hot brew. But as the years passed, the lake chewed away at the glacier until a calving ice cliff developed. As frontal access to the glacier grew more difficult, an aluminium dinghy and, later, two kayaks were necessary for access. The scientific mass balance work on the glacier finished in 1975, but the survey party returned again in 1986 to re-sound the growing lake to calculate the amount of sediment dropped by the glacier.

By the year 2000 the Ivory Glacier had retreated out of the lake to become a small apron of ice hanging on the headwall, and today it has all but disappeared. The lost glacier provides one of the most dramatic examples of recent glacial change in the Southern Alps. Work by New Zealand glaciologists continues, with annual flights to measure the snowlines and with similar glacier studies now carried out on the Brewster Glacier.

Over the ensuing years, the Department of Conservation has maintained Ivory Lake Hut, and it remains a coveted destination for trampers heading into this wild valley.

ROB BROWN

ABOVE Trevor Chinn in the 'Chair of Glaciology', 1976.
OPPOSITE An aerial shot showing Ivory Lake Hut, with the Ivory Lake and Glacier beyond, 2009. PHOTOS: TREVOR CHINN

Cupola Hut 1962 NELSON LAKES NATIONAL PARK

In the 1950s and 1960s, considerable conflict existed between various government departments about responsibility for controlling introduced wild animals. It was decided that more research was needed about deer, chamois and hare populations, and their impact on the ecology of mountain environments. To this end, in 1961–62, the Forest Service and Ecology Division of the Department of Science and Industrial Research chose Cupola Basin as the site for a joint study area.

Well-known Nelson pilot John Reid flew in materials for the hut in his Sikorsky helicopter in October 1962 and Forest Service personnel built it.[1] Although based on a standard NZFS six-bunk design, the hut was modified to have only four bunks plus a large boot room for storing scientific equipment. Extra insulation was required as the hut had no stove – smoke might have disturbed animals the scientists wanted to study. A small wind generator powered an electric light, and a telephone line enabled communication between the hut and a nearby hide built a few hundred metres away.[2]

Over a five-year period, DSIR and NZFS staff spent several months here studying chamois. Peter Bull managed the project, with NZFS staff including Les Batcheler, Chris Christie and Colin Clarke, and the DSIR team comprising Rowley Taylor, John Flux and Bill Magnusson.[3] The hut was designed both as the main accommodation base for researchers, but also as an observation site; its long, narrow windows suited this purpose well. One of the corner windows could be slid open, enabling the use of binoculars. During the study, a hunting ban was in place around Cupola Basin and part of the Travers Valley. Other research involved catching, marking and releasing grasshoppers.[4]

Tom Paterson, who during the 1960s worked for the NZFS, was recruited for the research. He recalls that Les Batcheler modified a Ramset nail gun, enabling it to fire tranquilliser darts into deer, so they could be identified and tagged for research:

> Our biggest problem was the drug that we used, which seemed to go off if not held at the correct temperature and it took quite some time to find this out. It would take 3–5 minutes for the drug to work and – believe you me – a deer can travel a long way in that time and tested our prowess in tracking, especially if they gained the bush edge. The down time was about 20 minutes for the deer, so really it was a matter of finding the animal quickly to tag, measure and take other information Les required.[5]

Paterson also remembers running down fawns to tag them:

> This could be achieved once the hind planted the fawn and started feeding away from it. The trick was to separate them and then the fawn seemed to lose some of its incentive … nevertheless some wild chases proceeded with uncontrollable downhill runs, waving large butterfly nets. Why someone didn't fall over a bluff I will never know. The amount of cuts and bruises was unbelievable and the night's entertainment was the tale of the day's chase.[6]

Deer were not the only animals to provide entertainment. John Flux recalled one occasion where a crafty kea managed to work open the sliding window, and caused havoc: '[It] tore into sacks of flour and cereals stored on a wire-netting shelf in the rafters, making a mess on the floor that was inches deep.'[7]

In the late 1970s, after the hut was no longer used for research, Lands and Survey rangers Bruce Postill and Peter Lowen flew to the site by helicopter with building materials in order to convert it to an eight-bunk tramping hut. Postill recalls: 'I remember it well because the snow was above the eaves. We had to tunnel in and were confined to working inside only. We lined walls, installed new bunks and a small coal-burning stove. We had planned to do some climbing as well but the weather was not good. Carried very heavy packs out with all our tools.'[8]

A snow avalanche destroyed the hide in the early 1980s,[9] but the piles are still visible in a small scrub-fringed clearing.

SHAUN BARNETT

LEFT Cupola Hut, 1981. PHOTO: BRUCE POSTILL
OPPOSITE Researcher Colin Clarke at Cupola Hut, 1960s.
PHOTO: JOHN JOHNS, NZFS COLLECTION, ARCHIVES NZ, WELLINGTON, M9347

SCIENCE HUTS 331

Dominie Biv 1968 KAWEKA FOREST PARK, HAWKE'S BAY

Of the many Forest Service bivouacs in Kaweka Forest Park, Dominie Biv is something of an anomaly. All the others (Studholme Saddle, Rocks Ahead, Manson, Kaweka Flats, Omarukokere, Black Birch and Back Ridge) are the classic dog-box style, built for deer cullers. In contrast, the upright Dominie Biv allows sufficient headroom for standing and, not surprisingly, has quite different origins to the others.

Beginning in 1959, the NZFS established a base at Makahu Saddle and over the following decades undertook a considerable amount of research in the Kaweka Range. Ashley Cunningham was the principal scientist, and initially operated out of the Makahu Saddle Hut (then known simply as Makahu Hut), built by the NZFS in 1957. But the deer-culling hut was rather small for sustained research, so in 1964 Cunningham oversaw construction of a larger hut (now called Makahu Chalet), near an area where a tree nursery had been established. The NZFS pushed a road through to Makahu Saddle in the mid-1960s, and then in 1968 the Ministry of Works built a base (now called Ngahere Lodge) for hydrological research.[1]

Dominie Biv was to become part of this complex of research buildings, but had already had a previous life in science on a different site. The biv was originally built in the early 1960s on the Blowhard in the southern Kaweka Range for scientist Mavis Davidson. A graduate of Victoria University, Davidson was one of a handful of women scientists employed by the Forest Service, and she used the tiny hut as a 'hide' for studying sika deer. At the hide Davidson worked two weeks on, two weeks off, using night-vision binoculars to observe the deer.[2]

As well as being a scientist, the remarkable Davidson was also a keen tramper, mountaineer and writer. In 1953, she led the first all-women ascent of Aoraki/Mt Cook, and a year later wrote a successful book, *The Mountains of New Zealand* with fellow climber Rod Hewitt.[3] Davidson remains best remembered, however, for her scientific achievements. She went on to become a world authority on sika deer, and in 1992 was awarded an OBE for her services to science.[4] Ashley Cunningham knew Davidson well:

> Women in those days were bank tellers or shop assistants until they married and became mothers. Mavis, however, was not an ordinary woman. She became, in many ways, a pioneer. She had opened a shop in Wellington, been a wartime army lieutenant, shot deer in the Tararuas, climbed many of the highest mountains in New Zealand, and gained a Master's degree in science.[5]

Davidson soon found the Blowhard locality unsatisfactory for her research, so shifted north to the Mangapapa and then to the Oamaru Valley (near the junction of the Kaweka and Kaimanawa forest parks). In 1968, the NZFS decided to shift her unused 'hide' up to a shoulder called Dominie Knob

Alan Wilburn and Peter Gannaway at Dominie Biv, 1968.
PHOTO: ASHLEY CUNNINGHAM, FRES COLLECTION, DOC WHANGANUI

on Makahu Spur, on the eastern flanks of the main Kaweka Range. This shoulder was named after an incident involving a De Havilland Dominie plane that occurred in 1961. Air-drops required precision flying, and accomplished pilot Tex Smith put the wind up crew member Charley Pearson, who was sure he saw the wingtip graze some *Dracophyllum* bushes on the knob.[6]

There, at an altitude of 1460 metres, Dominie Biv began a second life, still in science, as a meteorological station – one of the highest in the country. Although the instruments were automated, NZFS staff had to visit the hut every week to change charts. They did this for almost six years, building up knowledge of the weather in alpine environments.[7]

Early results revealed that the coldest month was July, with the monthly average just below −1°C. The hottest month, February, had a slightly more balmy average of 10°C.[8] In these days of automated weather stations, with data sent electronically back to warm offices, it's prudent to remember the efforts of researchers in places like Dominie Biv, who had to slog up the spur in all manner of weather.

Once its use as a weather station ended, Dominie Biv was retained on site by the NZFS. Ever since, the diminutive hut has provided refuge for trampers and hunters climbing up to Kaweka J, the highest point on the range.

SHAUN BARNETT

TOP Dominie Biv, April 2012.
PHOTO: SHAUN BARNETT/BLACK ROBIN PHOTOGRAPHY
BOTTOM Ken Tustin and Bernie Arnott reading the Dominie rain gauge in 1963.
PHOTO: ASHLEY CUNNINGHAM, FRES COLLECTION, DOC WHANGANUI

Caswell Sound Hut 1949 FIORDLAND NATIONAL PARK

Wapiti were released into Fiordland at George Sound in 1905 as part of the great New Zealand experiment with game animals. United States President Theodore Roosevelt – an avid hunter and outdoorsman himself – presented the eighteen animals as a gift to the New Zealand government. Only after the herd had established sufficiently to allow hunting was the initial protection of the animals removed in 1934.[1]

During the Second World War, Colonel John Howard, an American stationed in New Zealand, became interested in this herd and how they might have changed genetically from their American stock. Wapiti hybridisation with red deer in Fiordland also posed a question, as the two species are closely related. Howard, a member of the Harvard Museum of Comparative Zoology, proposed a combined study of wapiti between New Zealand and American scientists.

In 1947, Howard and a small team carried out reconnaissance trips and followed this up with a formal proposal to the New Zealand government for a larger-scale expedition. The Department of Internal Affairs made a £7000 grant for the study in 1948 – a very significant sum, amounting to about 10 per cent of the department's entire annual budget.[2] The following year, the expedition left to study the area between Caswell Sound and George Sound – the feral range of the wapiti herd.

Aside from tent camps, the field parties made use of Ministry of Works huts at George Sound (the main base), Lake Thomson and Lake Hankinson (all on what is now the George Sound Track). They also established a camp on the edge of Caswell Sound.

The expedition comprised as many as sixty people, and included the American scientific staff and New Zealand scientists from the departments of Internal Affairs, Scientific and Industrial Research and Lands and Survey, and the Dominion and Canterbury museums. Support staff came from both Internal Affairs and the Forest Service, with two photographers seconded from Internal Affairs and the prime minister's department. The major scientific expedition, the largest ever launched in New Zealand, involved 'Almost every field scientist of note' in the country.[3]

In addition to studying the wapiti, scientists examined the area's flora, fauna and geology, and carried out mapping surveys. Lindsay Poole, the expedition's deputy scientific leader, was a DSIR botanist who later went on to have a distinguished career with the NZFS.

Much of the party stayed in the area for four months between January and May 1949.[4] Poole edited a 100-page book summarising the expedition's major findings, published by the DSIR in 1951 and covering everything from climate to birdlife. Scientists observed some evidence of wapiti hybridisation with red deer, but comparisons with the American herd were not carried out. To preserve the purity of the wapiti herd, the scientists recommended culling red deer in the general area, and this formed the basis of the Fiordland wapiti herd management programme followed to this day.

Caswell Sound Hut was actually built at the end of the expedition, using left-over materials. Like many others before and after them, the expedition members were captivated by Fiordland's beauty and it seemed easier to leave something useful rather than cart the materials back out with them. The hut followed a fairly standard design for the times, including rimu framing, malthoid lining and corrugated-iron cladding. It not only provides shelter in a remote Fiordland sound, but remains as a historic symbol of significant peacetime scientific cooperation between two countries that had forged a close bond during the Second World War.

ROB BROWN

LEFT The DSIR-published results of the expedition, compiled by A. L. Poole, 1951.
OPPOSITE Caswell Sound Hut, 2007. PHOTO: GRANT TREMAIN, DOC

Endnotes

ABBREVIATIONS USED IN ENDNOTES

AJHR	Appendix to the Journal of House of Representatives. C3 covers forestry from 1920 to 1987
ANZ	Archives New Zealand
DIA	Department of Internal Affairs
DOC	Department of Conservation
DSIR	Department of Scientific and Industrial Reserach
NZAJ	*New Zealand Alpine Journal*, annual of the New Zealand Alpine Club
NZDA	NZDA
NZFS	New Zealand Forest Service

PREFACE

1. Elsie K. Morton, *A Tramper in South Westland*, 1951, p. 28.

INTRODUCTION

1. Mark Pickering, *A Tramper's Journey: Stories from the Back Country of New Zealand*, 2004, p. 128.
2. Carl Walrond, 'Natural environment – Climate', *Te Ara – The Encyclopedia of New Zealand* [website], 2009 (updated 3 March 2009), www.teara.govt.nz/en/natural-environment/3, accessed April 2012.
3. Elsie K. Morton, *A Tramper in South Westland*, 1951, p. 26.
4. Paul Maxim, *Bold Beyond Belief: Bill Denz, New Zealand's Mountain Warrior*, 2011, pp. 90–91.
5. Paul Powell, *Just Where Do You Think You've Been?*, 1970, p. 197.
6. John Gates, 'Building in the Hills and Mountains', *Tararua*, 1961, p. 30.
7. Ibid.
8. Robin Quigg, 'Back-country Huts, More Than a Roof Over Your Head: A Question of Values in Cultural Heritage Management', Masters thesis, 1993, p. 9.
9. Gates, 'Building in the Hills and Mountains', p. 31.
10. Tieke Kainga, on the Whanganui River, is a hut run on a marae-like basis by local iwi, with canoeists staying there in return for a koha.
11. Jock Phillips, *A Man's Country? The Image of the Pakeha Male – A History*, 1996, p. 30.
12. Ibid.
13. T.T. Robins, 'Some Reflections', *Canterbury Mountaineer* 5(19), 1949–50, pp. 71–73.
14. J. Walton, 'Cameron Hut', *Canterbury Mountaineer* 6(22), 1952–53, pp. 87–88.
15. The rebuilding of Banfield Memorial Hut is one example (see 'Banfield Memorial Hut Rebuild', *Canterbury Mountaineer* 5(19), 1949–50, pp. 64–66).
16. Morton, *A Tramper in South Westland*, p. 19.
17. Ken Francis, *Wildlife Ranger: My Years in the New Zealand Outdoors*, 1983, p. 55.
18. Harvey McCullough, 'Kiwi Saddle Hut', 1962, in Hans Willems, *North Island Back Country Huts*, 2004, p. 86.
19. Elsdon Best, *The Maori as He Was: A Brief Account of Life as it Was in Pre-European Days*, 1934, p. 225.
20. John Hall-Jones, *Fiordland Explored: An Illustrated History*, 1990, pp. 12–13.
21. Lester Masters, *Back Country Tales*, 1960, p. 52.
22. ANZ, Wellington, CAJF 20262 CH995/1 Defiance Hut Visitor Book 1914–1930, 9–10, accessible online at http://gallery.archives.govt.nz/v/christchurch/interesting+items+website/defiance+hut/Visitors+book+9-10.jpg.html.
23. Bill Keir, 'Hut Book Inventory', *FMC Bulletin*, March 2012, pp. 14, 44, accessible online at www.fmc.org.nz/wp-content/uploads/Circulars/HutLogBksBillKeir201112.pdf.
24. W.S. Green, *The High Alps of New Zealand*, 1883, pp. 287–88.
25. Graeme Caughley, *The Deer Wars: The Story of Deer in New Zealand*, 1983, inside front dust jacket.
26. John Rhodes, 'A Life in the Hills. Athol Geddes Talks to John Rhodes', *FMC Bulletin* May 2004, p. 29.
27. Mt Balloon Scenic Reserve board, [leaflet; Shaun Barnett's copy],1930.
28. R. Syme, 'Notes on Syme Hut', 9 February 1976, Mt Egmont Alpine Club archives, Hawera.
29. Geoff Spearpoint, pers. comm. with Shaun Barnett, April 2012.
30. *Working Plan Northwest Nelson Forest Park 1965–66 to 1969–70* [Shaun Barnett's copy], p. 39.
31. Northwest Nelson State Forest Park Advisory Committee, minutes [Shaun Barnett's copy], 13 September 1979, p. 7.
32. Ibid., p. 2.
33. 'A Rocky Start' in Bernie Napp (ed.), *A Short History of the Department of Conservation: 1987–2007* (online DOC publication), www.doc.govt.nz/publications/about-doc/a-short-history-of-doc/a-rocky-start, accessed February 2012.
34. 'Notice Board', *FMC Bulletin*, August 2008, p. 16.
35. 'Letters', *FMC Bulletin*, June 2008, p. 11.
36. Brian Dobbie, pers. comm. with Shaun Barnett, May 2005.
37. Pickering, *A Tramper's Journey*, p. 129.
38. Stephen Pern, Hastings, England, Mid Waiohine Hut logbook, 10 January 2006.
39. Powell, *Just Where Do You Think You've Been?*, inside dust jacket.

PASTORAL HUTS

More than Tin and Timber

1. David McLeod, *Down from the Tussock Ranges*, 1980, p. 248.
2. Ibid.
3. While the land of these leasehold properties is nominally owned by the Crown, the Land Act 1948 recognised that all the improvements belong to the farmer, and in acknowledgement of the practicalities of this, the terms of the lease are on a perpetual basis with an automatic right of renewal.
4. Roberta McIntyre, *Whose High Country? A History of the South Island High Country of New Zealand*, 2008, p. 88.
5. Ibid., p. 87.
6. Herbert Insull, 'Duppa, George', *Te Ara – The Encyclopaedia of New Zealand* [website], 2009 (updated 22 April 2009), www.teara.govt.nz/en/1966/duppa-george/1, accessed April 2012; Robert Peden, *Making Sheep Country: Mt Peel Station and the Transformation of the Tussock Lands*, 2011, p. 29.
7. Stevan Eldred-Grigg, *A New History of Canterbury*, 1982, p. 53.
8. Samuel Butler, *A First Year in Canterbury Settlement*, 1863, p. 69.
9. Ibid., p. 85.
10. Hugh Stringleman and Robert Peden, 'Sheep Farming – The Establishment Phase', *Te Ara – The Encyclopaedia of New Zealand* [website], 2009 (updated 1 March 2009), www.teara.govt.nz/en/sheep-farming/2, accessed 22 April 2012.
11. Johannes Anderson, *Jubilee History of South Canterbury*, 1916, p. 89.
12. Samuel Butler, letter to J.B.A. Acland, June 1862, quoted in Peter Maling, *Samuel Butler at Mesopotamia*, 1960, p. 57 (appendix).
13. Polsons Hut is now part of Shirlmar Station.
14. Philip Holden, *Station Country: Back-country Life in New Zealand*, 1993, p. 71.
15. After building up their flock and improving the grazing, Tripp and Acland dissolved their partnership amicably in 1862. Tripp took over the Orari Gorge part of the run, while Acland retained the area around Mt Peel. Eventually, after adding more leasehold land, Mt Peel Station grew to about 100,000 hectares, stretching all the way to Samuel Butler's Mesopotamia run at Forest Creek.
16. David Relph, *From Tussocks to Tourists: The Story of the Central Canterbury High Country*, 2007, p. 74.
17. James Belich, *Making Peoples*, 1996, p. 344.
18. William Vance, *Bush, Bullocks and Boulders: The Story of the Upper Ashburton*, 1973, p. 64.
19. L.G.D. Acland, *The Early Canterbury Runs*, 1975, p. 304.
20. Peden, *Making Sheep Country*, 2011, p. 217.
21. Stevan Eldred-Grigg, *A Southern Gentry*, 1980, p. 105.
22. McIntyre, *Whose High Country?* pp. 179–80.
23. 'Benmore Pastoral Runs, Result of Sale', *Evening Post*, 20 March 1916, p. 2.
24. William Fraser was elected to Parliament, served as Minister for Mines and was later knighted.
25. Peden, *Making Sheep Country*, 2011, p. 130.
26. www.earnscleughstation.co.nz/history.htm [website], accessed April 2012.
27. G. Norbury, 'Rabbits – Rabbits' Impact on Farming', *Te Ara – The Encyclopaedia of New Zealand* [website], 2009 (updated 1 March 2009), www.teara.govt.nz/en/rabbits/2, accessed April 2012.
28. Belich, *Making Peoples*, 1996, p. 344.
29. W.H. McLean, *Rabbits Galore!*, 1966, p. 54.
30. Peter Newton, *Big Country of the South Island*, 1973, pp. 101–02.
31. Ibid.
32. McLean, *Rabbits Galore!*, 1966. p. 54.
33. The active poison component of 1080, known from the African plant gifblaar (*Dichapetalum cymosum*) as far back as 1846, was first reproduced synthetically in 1946 (see McLean, *Rabbits Galore!*, 1966, p. 131).
34. The rabbit control boards carried on right through until 1989, when the government passed their pest-control function over to cash-strapped regional councils, which were barely funded to cope with the new responsibility (see Robert Peden, 'Rabbits – The Role of Government', *Te Ara – The Encyclopaedia of New Zealand* [website], 2009 (updated 1 March 2009), www.teara.govt.nz/en/rabbits/7, accessed April 2012).
35. Peter Newton, *Mesopotamia Station: A Survey of the First Hundred Years*, 1960, p. 32.
36. Ibid., p. 18.
37. Ibid., p. 24.
38. Ibid., p. 44.
39. Ibid., p. 51.
40. Peter Newton, *The Boss's Story*, 1966, pp. 126–27.
41. Ibid.

Sutherlands Hut

1. Tripp and Acland remained great friends for their entire lives, but were in a formal business partnership only between 1855 and 1862.
2. Charles Tripp, quoted in Mark Pickering, *Huts: Untold Stories from Back-country New Zealand*, 2010, p. 28.
3. Barbara Harper, *The Kettle on the Fuchsia: The Story of Orari Gorge*, 1967, p. 49.
4. Orari Station labour book, Canterbury Museum, Christchurch, referred to in Pickering, *Huts*, p. 29.
5. Harper, *The Kettle on the Fuchsia*, pp. 68–70.

6 Rosa Peacock, pers. comm. with Rob Brown, 18 May 2012.
7 Pickering, *Huts*, p. 23.
8 www.walkfourpeaks.co.nz.

Iron Whare

1 NZFS, *Kaweka State Forest Park* [map], 1:100,000, 1st edn, 1981.
2 Department of Conservation, *Kaweka Forest Park, Conservation Management Plan*, 1991, p. 5.
3 *Hawke Eye View* 12 [newsletter of DOC East Coast/Hawke's Bay Conservancy], June 1999, p. 3.
4 Pam Turner says the hut was most likely built in the early to mid-1870s, not late 1870s, as by then John Frost Turner was too busy managing his own farm, which was situated between Ball's Clearing and 'Ferny Ridge' in the Kaweka foothills (Pam Turner, email to Shaun Barnett, 22 March 2012).
5 Malthoid is a type of bitumen-coated paper, relatively light and easily carried (at least compared with corrugated iron), and was commonly used as roofing material for early huts.
6 Pam Turner, email to Shaun Barnett, 20 March 2012.
7 Miriam Macgregor, *Early Sheep Stations of Hawke's Bay*, 1970, p. 74.
8 Matthew Wright, *A History of Eastern Kaweka Ranges*, 1984, p. 43.
9 Ibid., p. 41.
10 Ibid., pp. 23, 41.
11 Iron Whare information panel.
12 Pam Turner, notes on Iron Whare written for Shaun Barnett, March 2012.
13 NZFS, *Kaweka State Forest Park*.
14 Turner, email to Shaun Barnett, 20 March 2012.
15 Turner, notes on Iron Whare.
16 Ashley Cunningham, *Hawke's Bay for the Happy Wanderer*, 1993, pp. 106–07.
17 Turner, email to Shaun Barnett, 20 March 2012.
18 Ibid.
19 Department of Conservation, *Kaweka Forest Park*, pp. 7–8; *Hawke Eye View* 12, p. 8; Turner, notes on Iron Whare.

Old Manson Hut

1 Christopher Lethbridge, *Sunrise on the Hills: A Musterer's Year on Ngamatea*, 1971, p. 15.
2 Hazel Riseborough, *Ngamatea: The Land and the People*, 2006, p. 88.
3 Ibid., map between pp. 88 and 89.
4 Lethbridge, *Sunrise on the Hills*, pp. 149–50.
5 Riseborough, *Ngamatea*, p. 110.
6 Ibid. p. 110.
7 Barry Crump, *The Life and Times of a Good Keen Man: An Autobiography*, 1992, p. 33.
8 Mavis M. Davidson, 'The Kaweka Range', *Tararua*, 1957, p. 16.
9 DOC records say that it was built in about 1946–50 (see *Hawke Eye View* [DOC East Coast/Hawke's Bay Conservancy newsletter] 12 June 1999, pp. 3–4) but Max Motley remembers still using the original hut during hunting trips with Jack Wire in the early 1950s, and reckons the existing Old Manson was built then too (Max Motley, letter to Shaun Barnett, 2 April 2012). Ken Tustin's tramping diary 1961–63 has a picture of the Old Manson Hut, with a caption stating 'built 1957', which seems a reliable date for the hut.
10 'Historic Manson Hut', DOC website, www.doc.govt.nz/conservation/historic/by-region/hawkes-bay/manson-hut, accessed April 2012.
11 Old Manson Hut information panel; 'Historic Manson Hut', DOC website.
12 Chris Cochran, *Old Manson's Hut Conservation Report*, 1994, pp. 2, 4.
13 Entry in Old Manson Hut logbook (the current whereabouts of the book are unknown).

Hideaway Biv

1 Hideaway Biv information panel.
2 Chris Cochran, *Hideaway Hut, Camp Creek, Ahuriri: Conservation Report*, 2006, p. 15.
3 Robert Pinney, *Early Northern Otago Runs*, 1981, pp. 44, 48.
4 Ibid., p. 56.
5 Hideaway Biv information panel.
6 Sally Rae, *Otago Daily Times*, 4–5 June 2005.
7 Cochran, *Hideaway Hut, Camp Creek, Ahuriri*, pp. 5, 31.
8 Rae, *Otago Daily Times*, 4–5 June 2005.

Shutes Hut

1 The original No Mans Hut was another, built in 1918 by the Hawke's Bay Rabbit Board (see Lester Masters, *Back Country Tales*, 1961, p. 71).
2 Mark Pickering, *Huts: Untold Stories from Back-country New Zealand*, 2010, p. 81; Matthew Wright, 'Early Huts of the Northeastern Ruahine and Central Wakarara Ranges' [unpublished NZFS report], 1986, p. 13; 'Historic Shutes Hut', DOC website, www.doc.govt.nz/conservation/historic/by-region/hawkes-bay/shutes-hut, accessed April 2012.
3 Masters, *Back Country Tales*, pp. 52, 63.
4 Ibid., pp. 51, 63.
5 Shutes Hut logbook 1956–81, p. 1. A copy of the logbook is in the hut but the whereabouts of the original is unknown.
6 Masters, *Back Country Tales*, p. 63.
7 Ibid., p. 44.
8 Ibid., pp. 45–46.
9 Ibid., pp. 46–47.
10 Pickering, *Huts*, p. 82.
11 Masters, *Back Country Tales*, pp. 44, 49.
12 Palmerston North tramper Tony Gates transcribed the original hut logbook.
13 J. Hoy and Mike Barnett, Shutes Hut logbook 1956–81, 27 January 1965.
14 Chris Cochran, *Shutes Hut, Ruahine Forest Park: Repair Survey*, 1997; Guy Natusch, *Shutes Hut Conservation Report*, 1992.
15 John Russell, Shutes Hut logbook 1985, 2 February 2003 and 14 June 2004.
16 Paul Sanderson, Shutes Hut logbook 1985, 6 November 2004; Carl Sanderson, Shutes Hut logbook 1985, 14 April 2012.

Ellis Hut

1 Lester Masters, *Back Country Tales*, 1961, p. 141.
2 Ibid., pp. 141–42.
3 Dudley Dyne, *Famous New Zealand Murders*, 1969, p. 128.
4 Masters, *Back Country Tales*, p. 142.
5 Ibid.
6 Matthew Wright, 'Early Huts of the Northeastern Ruahine and Central Wakarara Ranges' [unpublished NZFS report], 1986, p. 47.
7 Ibid., p. 47.
8 'Te Awaiti Murder Case', *Evening Post*, 11 February 1905, p. 9.
9 Dyne, *Famous New Zealand Murders*, pp. 135–36.
10 Masters, *Back Country Tales*, pp. 138–39.
11 Pam Bain, *Conservation of Ellis Hut: A Practical Workshop on Conservation Skills*, 2008, p. 7.
12 If Ellis Hut was indeed an outstation, it is a very rare surviving example. Lake Emma Hut is another.
13 Masters, *Back Country Tales*, p. 138.
14 Wright, 'Early Huts of the Northeastern Ruahine and Central Wakarara Ranges', p. 48.

Riordans Hut

1 *The Wangapeka Track, Kahurangi National Park* [DOC leaflet], 1997; Carol Dawber, *Bainham: A History*, 2000, pp. 182–83; Derek Shaw, *North West Nelson Tramping Guide*, 1991, pp. 45, 85; C.R. Brereton, *No Roll of Drums*, 1947, p. 125.
2 Gerard Hindmarsh, *Kahurangi Calling: Stories from the Backcountry of Northwest Nelson*, 2010, pp. 62–65.
3 Ibid.
4 Brandon Sparrow, 'Hard Work Sees Historic Hut Restored to Former Glory', *Nelson Evening Mail*, 3 January 2004, p. 15.
5 Hindmarsh, *Kahurangi Calling*, 2010, p. 62.
6 Max Polglaze, Riordans Hut logbook, 26–31 December 2000.
7 Kim Hastings, Riordans Hut logbook, 3 February 2003.
8 Sparrow, 'Hard Work Sees Historic Hut Restored to Former Glory', p. 15.
9 John Taylor and Max Polglaze, Riordans Hut logbook, October–November 2003.
10 Hindmarsh, *Kahurangi Calling*, 2010, p. 64.
11 Max Polglaze, Riordans Hut logbook, 15 November 2003.
12 Anonymous, Riordans Hut logbook, 18 February 2004.

Meg Hut

1 Land Information New Zealand, 'Mount Pisa Conservation Resource Report', p. 13, accessible online at www.linz.govt.nz/sites/default/files/docs/crownproperty/high-country-leases/leaselist/mt-pisa-con-res.pdf.
2 Katharine Watson, unpublished draft report for DOC Otago on pastoral and mining huts in the conservancy, 2012.
3 Land Information New Zealand, 'Mount Pisa Conservation Resource Report', p. 14.
4 Ibid.
5 Jack Scurr, pers. comm. with John Lee, passed on to Rob Brown, 16 April 2012.
6 Irvine Roxburgh, *Wanaka Story: A History of Wanaka, Hawea, Tarras and Surrounding Districts*, 1957, p. 260.
7 Ibid.
8 John Lee, pers. comm. with Rob Brown, 16 April 2012.

Rangitata/Hakatere Mustering Huts

1 Thomas Potts, *Out in the Open*, 1882.
2 Further south of the Rangitata, Orari Gorge Station has some historic wooden buildings that pre-date this.
3 A. Hewson, *Early Days in Ashburton Country*, 1996, p. 44.
4 Katharine Watson, 'Lake Emma Hut: Historic Place Active Management Appraisal' [unpublished report for DOC], August 2005, p. 7.
5 'Plan shewing [sic] pastoral runs in Canterbury N.Z.', CMU 19, Canterbury Museum, Christchurch (reprinted in Watson, 'Lake Emma Hut').
6 Watson, 'Lake Emma Hut', p. 23.
7 Ibid., p. 24.
8 'Plan shewing [sic] pastoral runs in Canterbury N.Z.' (reprinted in Watson, 'Lake Emma Hut').
9 Katharine Watson, 'Double Hut: Historic Place Active Management Appraisal' [unpublished report for DOC], August 2005, p. 14.
10 Ibid.
11 Peter Newton, *Mesopotamia Station: A Survey of the First Hundred Years*, 1960, p. 15.
12 Ibid., p. 44.
13 Gareth Wright, 'Mesopotamia Station Huts' [unpublished report for DOC], June 2009.
14 Mark Pickering, *Huts: Untold Stories from Back-country New Zealand*, 2010, p. 38.

Beech Hut

1 'Historic Beech Hut', DOC website, www.doc.govt.nz/conservation/historic/by-region/southland/southland/beech-hut, accessed April 2012.
2 G.A. Hamilton, *History of Northern Southland*, 1952, p. 76.
3 Helen McPhail, 'Beech Hut', *FMC Bulletin*, August 2006, p. 35.
4 Signed panel in the hut.

Ida Railway Hut

1 Laurie Inder, pers. comm. with Rob Brown, 16 April 2012.
2 'Ida Railway Hut', DOC website, www.doc.govt.nz/parks-and-recreation/places-to-stay/backcountry-huts-by-region/otago/central-otago/ida-railway-hut, accessed 10 March 2012.

3 Poem reprinted with kind permission from Blue Jeans (Ross McMillan).

Whariwharangi Hut
1 Whariwharangi Hut information panel.
2 Perrine Moncrieff, *People Came Later*, 1965, pp. 126, 129.
3 Dawn Smith, *Abel Tasman Area History*, 1997, p. 33.
4 Andy Dennis, *A Park for all Seasons: The Story of Abel Tasman National Park*, 1990, p. 26.
5 Mark Pickering, *A Tramper's Journey: Stories from the Back Country of New Zealand*, 2004, pp. 173–75.
6 Janet Huddleston, 'Whariwharangi Hut – A Quiet Escape in the Park', *Golden Bay Weekly*, 22 August 2003, p. 5.

Avoca Homestead
1 Robert Logan, *Waimakariri*, 2008, pp. 122–24.
2 L.G.D. Acland, *The Early Canterbury Runs*, 1975, p. 227.
3 Three metres of snow fell on Porters Pass (see Logan, *Waimakariri*, p. 99).
4 Acland, *The Early Canterbury Runs*, p. 227.
5 Logan, *Waimakariri*, 2008, p. 93.
6 Ibid.
7 David McLeod, *Many a Glorious Morning*, 1970, pp. 228–29.
8 Ibid., p. 228.

MINING HUTS
Refuge Among the Riches
1 Alwyn Owen and Jack Perkins, *Speaking for Ourselves: Echoes from New Zealand's Past*, from the Award Winning 'Spectrum' Radio Series, 1986, pp. 22–24.
2 'A Fair God-Send, Help to Gold Prospectors', *Evening Post*, 1 February 1932, p. 9.
3 Ibid.
4 Howard Keene, *Going for Gold: The Search for Riches in the Wilberforce Valley*, 1995, p. 92.
5 Mines Department New Zealand, *Fossicking and Prospecting for Gold*, Mining Leaflet No. 10, 1933 [reproduced 2011].
6 Dick Scott, *Inheritors of a Dream*, 1969, p. 142.
7 Dan Dungan (ed.), *Rotoiti Recollections*, 1999, pp. 93–97.
8 J.S. Murray and R.W. Murray, *Costly Gold: Clutha Riches and their Human Toll*, 1978, p. 53.
9 Keene, *Going for Gold*, p. 92; 'Winning of Gold', *Ellesmere Guardian*, 28 September 1934, p. 6.
10 Michael King, *The Penguin History of New Zealand*, 2003, p. 307.
11 Keene, *Going for Gold*, p. 92.
12 Frederick W.G. Miller, *There was Gold in the River*, 1946, p. 29.
13 Duncan Mackay, *Frontier New Zealand: The Search for Eldorado 1800–1920*, 1992, p. 36.
14 John Elder, *Goldseekers and Bushrangers in New Zealand*, 1930, p. 23.
15 Stevan Eldred-Grigg, *Diggers, Hatters and Whores: The Story of the New Zealand Gold Rushes*, 2008, p. 87.
16 Ibid.
17 Ibid., p. 39.
18 Ibid., p. 343.
19 Dr Robyn Anderson, *Goldmining Legislation and Policy*, 1996, p. 13.
20 Tony Nolan, *Gold, Gold, Gold: The Romantic World of Gold*, 1980, p. 106.
21 Eldred-Grigg, *Diggers, Hatters and Whores*, p. 205.
22 Carl Walrond, 'Gold and Gold Mining – Dredging', *Te Ara – The Encyclopaedia of New Zealand* [website], 2009 (updated 2 March 2009), www.teara.govt.nz/en/gold-and-gold-mining/8, accessed April 2012.
23 Elder, *Goldseekers and Bushrangers in New Zealand*, p. 71.
24 'Local Intelligence, Our Gold Fields', *Otago Witness*, 21 September 1861, p. 5.
25 Eldred-Grigg, *Diggers, Hatters and Whores*, p. 91.
26 Ibid., pp. 95–96.
27 The troy ounce is a unit of imperial measure used to gauge the weight of precious metals. One troy ounce is about 31 grams.
28 Murray and Murray, *Costly Gold*, p. 57.
29 'The Dunstan, Loss of Life from the Severity of the Weather', *Otago Daily Times*, 21 August 1863, p. 9.
30 John Hall-Jones, *Goldfields of Otago: An Illustrated History*, 2005, p. 50.
31 'The Dunstan, Continued Severity of the Weather', *Otago Daily Times*, 24 August 1863, p. 5.
32 Robert Gilkison, *Early Days in Central Otago*, 1930, p. 52.
33 'The Arrow, Frightful Casualties from Floods and Landslips', *Otago Daily Times*, 3 August 1863, p. 5.
34 Hall-Jones, *Goldfields of Otago*, p. 49.
35 Philip Ross May, *The West Coast Gold Rushes*, 1967, dust jacket.
36 Ibid., p. 125.
37 May, *The West Coast Gold Rushes*, p. 336.
38 Ibid., p. 351.
39 Elder, *Goldseekers and Bushrangers in New Zealand*, p. 23.
40 May, *The West Coast Gold Rushes*, p. 276.
41 Gerard Morris (ed.), *Waiuta, 1906–1951, the Gold Mine, the Town, the People*, 1986; Les Wright, *Big River Quartz Mine: A Worthwhile Speculation*, 1993.
42 Les Wright, pers. comm. with Rob Brown, April 2012.

Bullendale Hut
1 P.G. Petchey, *Gold and Electricity: Archaeological Survey of Bullendale, Otago*, 2006, pp. 7, 13.
2 Ibid., p. 17.
3 Ibid., p. 15.
4 Ibid., p. 18.
5 Ibid., p. 45.
6 *Otago Daily Times*, 29 May 1998, p. 3, quoted in Petchey, *Gold and Electricity*, p. 44.
7 Petchey, *Gold and Electricity*, p. 45.
8 John Edens, 'Otago Goldmining Relics at Risk', *Southland Times*, 27 April 2011, accessible online at www.stuff.co.nz/southland-times/news/4930336/Otago-goldmining-relics-at-risk.

Dynamo Hut
1 P.G. Petchey, *Gold and Electricity: Archaeological Survey of Bullendale, Otago*, 2006, p. 14.
2 Ibid., pp. 14–15, 39.
3 Mark Pickering, *Huts: Untold Stories from Back-country New Zealand*, 2010, pp. 266–70.
4 T. Macnicol, *Beyond the Skippers. Road*, 1965, p. 17.
5 Petchey, *Gold and Electricity*, p. 11.
6 Martin Douglas, Dynamo Hut logbook, 8 February 2010.

Asbestos Cottage
1 Jim Henderson, *The Exiles of Asbestos Cottage*, 1981, dust jacket.
2 Gerard Hindmarsh, *Kahurangi Calling: Stories from the Back Country of Northwest Nelson*, 2010, p. 116.
3 Henderson, *The Exiles of Asbestos Cottage*, pp. 36–38.
4 Ibid., pp. 17–18.
5 Ibid., pp. 22, 135.
6 Ibid., p. 110.
7 Ibid., pp. 103, 174–89.
8 Ibid., p. 98.
9 Ibid., p. 93.
10 Ibid., p. 164.
11 Ibid., p. 67.
12 Ibid., p. 23.
13 Ibid., p. 169.
14 Ibid., p. 26.
15 Ibid., p. 11.
16 Hindmarsh, *Kahurangi Calling*, p. 117.
17 'Historic Asbestos Cottage', DOC website, www.doc.govt.nz/conservation/historic/by-region/nelson-tasman/golden-bay/asbestos-cottage, accessed April 2012.
18 Ibid.
19 Henderson, *The Exiles of Asbestos Cottage*, p. 235.
20 Ibid., p. 55.
21 Don Grady, 'Lovers' Hideaway Restored with TLC', *Nelson Evening Mail*, 16 July 1997.
22 Shaun Barnett, 'Barbara Marshall – A Profile', *FMC Bulletin*, November 2008, p. 28.

Cecil Kings Hut
1 Various lyrics of the song existed; this version dates from 1861, when gold discoveries occurred at both Wangapeka (Nelson) and Tuapeka (Otago) (see http://folksong.org.nz/bright_fine_gold/brfigold1.html).
2 J.N.W. Newport, 'Goldfields in the Upper Motueka and Buller Valleys', *Nelson Historical Society Journal* 1(2), May 1957, pp. 8–10.
3 Derek Shaw, *North West Nelson Tramping Guide*, 1991, p. 50.
4 'Historic Cecil Kings Hut', DOC website, www.doc.govt.nz//conservation/historic/by-region/nelson-tasman/motueka/cecil-kings-hut, accessed April 2012.
5 Ibid.
6 Northwest Nelson State Forest Park Advisory Committee, minutes [Shaun Barnett's copy], 22 February 1973, p. 5.
7 Max Polglaze, 'Kings Hut Restoration', diary notes, May–June 1991, p. 5.
8 Dave Chowdhury, 'Kings Hut Takes on New Lease of Life', *Nelson Evening Mail*, 9 October 1991, p. 19.
9 Pete Lusk, 'Cecil Kings Hut', *FMC Bulletin*, March 2008, p. 19.
10 Northwest Nelson State Forest Park Advisory Committee, minutes [Shaun Barnett's copy], 22 February 1973, p. 5.
11 'Historic Cecil Kings Hut', DOC website.
12 Max Polglaze, letter to regional manager DOC, 26 October 1990.
13 Polglaze, 'Kings Hut Restoration', p. 3.
14 Ibid.
15 'Historic Cecil Kings Hut', DOC website.
16 Chowdhury, 'Kings Hut Takes on New Lease of Life', p. 19.

Urquharts Hut
1 Howard Keene, *Going for Gold: The Search for Riches in the Wilberforce Valley*, 1995, pp. 56–58.
2 Ibid., p. 87
3 Bill Heinz, 'An Early Crossing of Browning Pass', *Canterbury Mountaineer* Jubilee Edition, 1974–75, p. 52.
4 Keene, *Going for Gold*, p. 92.
5 Ibid., p. 94.
6 Ibid.
7 Ibid., p. 95.
8 Ibid., p. 92.
9 Philip Temple, *The Book of the Kea*, 1996, p. 68.
10 Harry Walker, 'The Wilberforce Valley', *Canterbury Mountaineer* 4(18), 1948–49, p. 287.
11 Andrew Tromans, '31 December 2006: 4 January 2007: Hokitika Saddle–Mungo Pass', Christchurch Tramping Club website, www.ctc.org.nz/index.php?option=com_tripreport&task=view&id=326, accessed April 2012.
12 Chris Cochran, *Urquharts Hut, Craigieburn Forest Park: Conservation Report*, 1999, p. 29.

Glenorchy Scheelite-mining Huts
1 Julia Bradshaw, *Miners in the Clouds: A Hundred Years of Scheelite Mining at Glenorchy*, 2007, p. 15.

2 Ibid., pp. 16–19.
3 Glenorchy remained isolated throughout the scheelite mining era – the road to the settlement was not completed until 1962, and before that it was accessible only by steamer from Queenstown.
4 Bradshaw, *Miners in the Clouds*, pp. 21–31.
5 Ibid., p. 35.
6 Ibid., p. 43.
7 Ibid., p. 42.
8 Ibid., p. 41.
9 Ibid., p. 86.
10 Ibid., p. 50.
11 Ibid., p. 65.
12 Ibid., p. 68.
13 Ibid., p. 69.
14 'Boozer Hut Put Back on Solid Foundations', *Otago Daily Times*, 9 July 2011, accessible online at www.odt.co.nz/news/queenstown-lakes/168368/boozer-hut-put-back-solid-foundations.

Waingaro Forks Hut
1 'First Discoveries of Gold in N.Z.', *Ohinemuri Gazette*, 19 September 1906, p. 2.
2 'Items of Interest', *Marlborough Express*, 1 August 1895, p. 4.
3 Hayley Gale, 'Links with Gold Rush Restored', *Nelson Mail*, 4 June 2009.
4 John Taylor (DOC Takaka), email to Shaun Barnett, 2 May 2011. Taylor says the source of his information was Clive Petterson, who first visited the hut in 1936, aged nineteen or twenty. Clive's father, Oscar Petterson, used to have a grazing lease in the Kill Devil–Waingaro area before the Riordan brothers.
5 Jim Henderson, *The Exiles of Asbestos Cottage*, 1981, p. 132.
6 Ibid., p. 111.
7 Gerard Hindmarsh, *Kahurangi Calling: Stories from the Back Country of Northwest Nelson*, 2010, p. 61.
8 Taylor, email to Shaun Barnett, 2 May 2011.
9 'Waingaro Forks Hut Restoration', DOC website, www.doc.org.nz/conservation/historic/docs-heritage-work/2010/waingaro-forks-hut-restoration, accessed April 2012.
10 Taylor, email to Shaun Barnett, 2 May 2011.
11 'Waingaro Forks Hut Restoration', DOC website.

HUTS FOR TOURISM AND CLIMBING
The Mountains of Opportunity
1 Margaret McClure, *The Wonder Country: Making New Zealand Tourism*, 2004, pp. 14–15.
2 Ibid., p. 37.
3 Lhian Gallagher, *A Feeling for Daylight: The Photographs of Jack Adamson*, 2010, pp. 19–20, 31.
4 The first huts on the Milford Track were built in 1888.
5 John Wilson and Junee Ashurst, 'Ball Hut – Shelter from the Storm', *NZAJ*, 1978, p. 95.
6 Graham Langton, *Summits and Shadows: Jack Clarke and New Zealand Mountaineering*, 2011, p. 75.
7 In 1903, the stone and dirt floor of Ball Hut was concreted over, giving the shelter a more permanent feel. The remains of the concrete floor can be seen near the current small hut, erected in 2011.
8 In 1902, head guide Jack Clarke tried to sow *Pinus sylvestris* and birch trees on the terraces, but the plantings were never a success (see Ian Whitehouse, 'Malte Brun Hut – A Tribute', *NZAJ*, 1979, p. 89).
9 B.E. Baughan, *Snow Kings of the Southern Alps*, 1910, p. 33.
10 Blanche Baughan, *Studies in New Zealand Scenery*, 1916, p. 23.
11 John Hall-Jones, *Fiordland Explored: An Illustrated History*, 1990, pp. 65–67.
12 William Anderson, *Milford Trails*, 1971, pp. 39–41, 50, 63–64.
13 McClure, *The Wonder Country*, p. 61.
14 Anderson, *Milford Trails*, p. 40.
15 Alys Lowth, 'The Milford Track in Snow and Sunshine', *Otago Witness*, 21 March 1906, p. 81.
16 Anderson, *Milford Trails*, p. 68.
17 Lowth, 'The Milford Track in Snow and Sunshine', p. 81.
18 Anita Crozier, *Beyond the Southern Lakes: The Explorations of W.G. Grave*, 2001, pp. 132–149; Anderson, *Milford Trails*, p. 72
19 Anderson, *Milford Trails*, pp. 70, 78.
20 Mark Pickering, *Huts: Untold Stories from Back-country New Zealand*, 2010, pp. 357–63.
21 McClure, *The Wonder Country*, pp. 25–27.
22 Ibid., p. 27.
23 'Mount Cook', *Ashburton Guardian*, 29 August 1902, p. 4.
24 Margaret McClure, 'Tourist Industry – Tourism Overview', *Te Ara – The Encyclopaedia of New Zealand* [website], 2010 (updated 26 November 2010), www.teara.govt.nz/en/tourist-industry/1, accessed 12 October 2011.
25 Graham Langton, 'The First Hooker Hut', *NZAJ*, 2004, p. 106.
26 Ibid., pp. 106–07.
27 Nan Bowie, *Mick Bowie: The Hermitage Years*, 1969, p. 175.
28 Langton, *Mr Explorer Douglas: John Pascoe's New Zealand Classic*, 2000, p. 199.
29 'Historic Hende's Hut', DOC website, www.doc.govt.nz/conservation/historic/by-region/west-coast/glaciers/hendes-hut, accessed 12 July 2011.
30 Alec Graham and Jim Wilson, *Uncle Alec and the Grahams of Franz Josef*, 1983, p. 131.
31 Jackie Breen, *Copland Track Heritage Assessment and Baseline Inspection Report*, 2007, pp. 12–15.
32 Langton, *Summits and Shadows*, pp. 91–93, 135.
33 Ibid., pp. 120, 214.
34 Bowie, *Mick Bowie*, pp. 179–80.
35 Gordon Ogilvie, 'Wigley, Rodolph Lysaght – Biography', *Dictionary of New Zealand Biography. Te Ara – The Encyclopaedia of New Zealand* [website], 2010 (updated 1 September 2010), www.teara.govt.nz/en/biographies/3w1/1, accessed 14 October 2011.
36 Guides Darby Thomson, Jock Richmond and their client Sydney King were the only fatalities in the twenty years of guiding activity at Aoraki/Mt Cook between 1894 and 1914 (see John Wilson, 'Mountaineering – Guided Climbing', *Te Ara – The Encyclopedia of New Zealand* [website], 2009 (updated 2 March 2009), www.teara.govt.nz/en/mountaineering/4).
37 Graham and Wilson, *Uncle Alec and the Grahams of Franz Josef*, p. 158.
38 'Local and General', *Evening Post*, 4 September 1923, p. 6.
39 Margaret McClure, 'Tourist Industry – Tourism in the Southern Alps', *Te Ara – The Encyclopedia of New Zealand*, 2010 (updated 5 March 2010), www.teara.govt.nz/en/tourist-industry/3, accessed 15 October 2011.
40 Ogilvie, 'Wigley, Rodolph Lysaght – Biography'.
41 Breen, *Copland Track Heritage Assessment and Baseline Inspection Report*, p. 19.
42 G.E. Mannering, 'The Disaster on the Tasman Glacier', *NZAJ* IV, 1928–31, pp. 125–26.
43 'De la Beche Refuge', *NZAJ* IV, 1928–31, p. 230.
44 Agreement held at the NZAC Archives, Hocken Library, Dunedin (access number MS-1164-2/43/17 'De la Beche Memorial Hut').
45 'Club and General Notes', *NZAJ* V, 1932–34, pp. 451–54.
46 'The First Twelve Months', *FMC Bulletin* 21, 1965, pp. 2–3.
47 A.R. Perry, 'Proceedings of the Federated Mountain Clubs of New Zealand', *NZAJ* VII, 1937–38, p. 166.
48 'Club and General Notes, Mt Cook Tariffs', *NZAJ* VII, 1937–38, p. 293.
49 McClure, 'Tourist Industry – Tourism in the Southern Alps'.
50 Graham and Wilson, *Uncle Alec and the Grahams of Franz Josef*, pp. 200, 205–07.
51 Paul Callister and Robert Didham, 'Workforce Composition – Hours of Work and Productivity', *Te Ara – the Encyclopedia of New Zealand*, 2010 (updated 14 April 2010), www.teara.govt.nz/en/workforce-composition/9, accessed April 2012.
52 Tourism New Zealand, *100 Years Pure Progress 1901–2001: 100 years of Tourism* [booklet], Tourism New Zealand, Wellington 2001, p. 11.
53 Wilson and Ashurst, 'Ball Hut – Shelter from the Storm', pp. 96–97.
54 Harry Wigley, *The Mount Cook Way: The First Fifty Years of the Mount Cook Company*, 1979, p. 90.
55 Wilson and Ashurst, 'Ball Hut – Shelter from the Storm', pp. 100–02.
56 Ibid., p. 102.
57 Whitehouse, 'Malte Brun Hut – A Tribute', pp. 88–93.
58 *Beetham Hut* [website], http://beethamhut.blogspot.com, accessed 12 February 2012.
59 McClure, *The Wonder Country*, pp. 239–82.

Old Waihohonu Hut
1 George Allen, 'Ruapehu', *Wanganui Chronicle*, 25 April 1894, p. 23.
2 AJHR 1904 H-2 p. 11; 'Tourists, Mountaineers and Skiers, the development of recreation in Tongariro National Park' by Graham Langton in Adlam, Tania (ed.) 2012. *Volcanic Taupo: Steaming ahead, New Zealand Genealogical Society Conference Proceedings*, held 1–3 June 2012, pp. 35–43. Some sources erroneously give the date for both huts as 1901.
3 Old Waihohonu Hut information panel.
4 'Inadequate Accommodation' [letter by 'Ski-runner'], *Wanganui Chronicle*, 18 January 1918, p. 7.
5 H.E.G., 'The Tongariro National Park', *Evening Post*, 26 June 1912, p. 17.
6 *Ngaruwahia Advocate*, July 1913, quoted in Karen Williams and Dave Bamford, *Skiing on the Volcano: Historical Images of Skiing on Mount Ruapehu*, 1987, p. 7.
7 William Mead, *Memories of a Mountain and a River*, 1979, pp. 14–15.
8 Ruapehu Ski Club souvenir diary, 1915, Ruapehu Ski Club archives, Auckland.
9 'Alpine Climbing in the Tongariro National Park', *Wanganui Chronicle*, 31 March 1911, p. 3.
10 Betty Moore and Graham Langton, *My Mountain Calls: Jane Thomson and her Mountain Adventures*, 1999, p. 51.
11 Information from Ruapehu Ski Club archives, emailed by Alan Graham to Shaun Barnett, 2 February 2011.
12 H.E.G., 'Tongariro Park, Meeting of Board', *Evening Post*, 5 September 1928, p. 11
13 'Mountain Clubs Committee Meeting', *Evening Post*, 20 April 1935, p. 5.
14 Old Waihohonu Hut information panel.
15 The Camphouse, Egmont National Park, is considerably older. Originally built as a military barracks in New Plymouth in 1852, it was possibly the first corrugated-iron building in New Zealand. It was moved to the slopes of Mt Taranaki in 1891 to serve as accommodation for tourists and climbers.

Earnslaw Hut
1 Alfred Duncan, *The Wakatipians*, 1964, p. 24.
2 Graham Langton, 'Harry Birley, the first working class climber', *Wilderness*, July 2002, pp. 4–6.
3 'Mount Earnslaw and the Rees Valley', *Otago Witness*, 1 March 1900, p. 63.
4 Ibid.
5 'Scaling Mount Earnslaw', *Otago Witness*, 18 March 1903, p. 45.
6 Ibid.
7 Ibid.
8 Ibid.
9 W.S. Gilkison and A.H. Hamilton, *Moir's Guide*, 1948, p. 17.
10 J.A. Sim, 'The First Ascent of Pluto Peak and an Unclimbed Peak on the Forbes Range now called Mt William', *NZAJ* 4(18), 1931, p. 192.
11 Kath Varcoe, pers. comm. with Geoff Spearpoint, 18 July 2010.

Mueller Hut
1 Nan Bowie, *Mick Bowie: The Hermitage Years*, 1969, p. 178.
2 'Local and General', *Evening Post*, 4 September 1923, p. 6.
3 Bowie, *Mick Bowie*, p. 178.
4 Ibid., p. 179.
5 Edmund Hillary, *High Adventure*, 1955, p. 16.

Godley Hut
1 'Club and General Notes, Godley Hut', *NZAJ* VI, 1935–36, p. 164.
2 Ibid.
3 Ibid., p. 25.
4 J.A. Sim, 'Club and General Notes, Godley Hut Maintenance', *NZAJ* 10(31), 1944, p. 195.
5 A.F. Shaw, 'Moving the Godley Hut', *NZAJ* 16(42), 1955, p. 203.
6 Ibid., p. 211.
7 Ibid.

Chancellor Hut
1 DOC Chancellor Hut Historic File: HHA-11-05-05 WCW-1, file letter, DOC Fox Glacier archives. It is not clear whether the government ever took up Harper's pledge.
2 Jackie Breen, *Copland Track Heritage Assessment and Baseline Inspection Report*, 2007, p. 19.
3 DOC Chancellor Hut Historic File: HHA-11-05-05 WCW-1; Tom Hopkins, pers. comm. with Mick Sullivan, related to Rob Brown via email, 27 March 2012.
4 DOC Chancellor Hut Historic File: HHA-11-05-05 WCW-1.
5 Ibid.
6 Congoleum, initially known as 'felt base', is made from paper saturated with bitumen.
7 *Chancellor Hut Conservation Plan*, DOC report, April 2001, p. 10.
8 Julia Bradshaw, pers. comm. with Mick Sullivan, related to Rob Brown via email, 23 March 2012.
9 Tom Hopkins, 'Chancellor Hut', *FMC Bulletin*, August 2003, p. 22.
10 Sefton Biv is arguably too small to be considered a 'hut' and has been upgraded rather than restored. Hooker Hut, about to be shifted to another site, was never considered a 'high-level hut'.
11 Rob Dunn and Brendon Haigh, Chancellor Hut logbook, 1 September 1997.

Almer Hut
1 Frank Alack, *Guide Aspiring*, 1963, p. 216.
2 Peter Graham had returned to the West Coast from Aoraki/Mount Cook in 1922.
3 Alack, *Guide Aspiring*, pp. 216–17.
4 Ibid., pp. 217–18.
5 Ibid., p. 220.
6 Jim Wilson, *Aorangi: The Story of Mount Cook*, 1968, pp. 167–68.
7 'Almer Hut', DOC website, www.doc.govt.nz/parks-and-recreation/places-to-stay/backcountry-huts-by-region/west-coast/glaciers/almer-hut, accessed April 2012.

Pioneer Hut
1 Bob McKerrow, *Ebenezer Teichelmann*, 2005, p. 137
2 Katie Gardiner, 'Tasman from the West', *NZAJ* 5(21), 1934, p. 289.
3 Ibid.
4 Ibid.
5 Graham Langton, 'Maori Guides of South Westland', *Wilderness*, April 2001, pp. 4–6.
6 Gardiner, 'Tasman from the West', p. 291.
7 Bruce Postill, email to Shaun Barnett, 24 May 2010.

8 Frank Alack, *Guide Aspiring*, 1963, p. 209.
9 Ibid., pp. 209–11.
10 Ibid., p. 213.
11 George Harris and Graeme Hasler, *The Mount Cook Alpine Region*, 1971, p. 40.
12 Dave Bamford, 'Eighty Years of High Living: The Story of the Pioneer Huts', *NZAJ*, 1984, pp. 116–17.
13 J.N. Hamilton, 'The Pioneer Hut', *NZAJ* 15(40), 1953, p. 252.
14 S. Muirson, 'Pioneer Hut Dreams Materialise', *Canterbury Mountaineer* 6(22), 1952–53, p. 55.
15 Bamford, 'Eighty Years of High Living', p. 119.
16 Bruce Postill, email to Shaun Barnett, 7 March 2012.
17 Ibid.
18 Tom Hopkins, 'Pioneer Hut Rebuild', *The Climber*, autumn 1999, p. 27.
19 Bamford, 'Eighty Years of High Living', p. 125.

Flora Hut
1 J.N.W. Newport, *Footprints Too: Further Glimpses into the History of the Nelson Province*, 1978, p. 150.
2 Shonadh Mann, *F.G. Gibbs: His Influence on the Social History of Nelson, 1890–1950*, 1977, pp. 53–59.
3 Waimea Tramping Club, *Balloon Hut* [booklet], 1996, p. 16; Newport, *Footprints Too*, p. 150; Mann, *F.G. Gibbs*, p. 60.
4 Newport, *Footprints Too*, p. 125.
5 *Mount Arthur District, Information for Would-be Visitors*, Mt Balloon Hut Scenic Trust Board [leaflet], 1930.
6 Shaun Barnett, 'Huts as Heritage, Flora Hut', *FMC Bulletin*, August 2008, p. 40.
7 Northwest Nelson State Forest Park Advisory Committee, minutes [Shaun Barnett's copy], 8 December 1986, p. 11.
8 Gerard Hindmarsh, 'What's up DOC?', *New Zealand Listener*, 10–16 May 2008, accessible online at www.listener.co.nz/current-affairs/ecologic/whats-up-doc-4.
9 Barnett, 'Huts as Heritage, Flora Hut', p. 40.
10 'Flora Hut to Stay Says DOC' [DOC press release], 6 May 2008, www.doc.govt.nz/about-doc/news/media-releases/2008/flora-hut-to-stay-says-doc, accessed April 2012.
11 Friends of Flora website, www.fof.org.nz, accessed April 2012.

Sign of the Packhorse Hut
1 Gordon Ogilvie, *The Port Hills of Christchurch*, 2009, p. 312.
2 Stella Woodham (ed.), *Christchurch Tramping Club Fiftieth Anniversary, 1932–1982*, 1982, p. 34.
3 Jennifer Loughton, *Fifty Years Along the Road: A History of the Summit Road Society Incorporated 1948–1998*, 1998, p. 92.

Cape Defiance Hut and Castle Rocks Hut
1 There were five Graham brothers. Jim lost part of a leg in a sawmilling accident, and was mainly involved in running the Franz Josef Hotel, while Alex ran the guiding operations. At this time, Peter was a famous chief guide at Aoraki/Mt Cook. David and John, the two eldest brothers, farmed (see Alec Graham and Jim Wilson, *Uncle Alec and the Grahams of Franz Josef*, 1983, pp. 124–31).
2 Graham and Wilson, *Uncle Alec and the Grahams of Franz Josef*, pp. 140–42.
3 Although in Te Urewera National Park the NZFS built more than thirty standard deer-culling huts in the 1950s and 1960s.
4 Archives New Zealand holds a copy of the hut's logbook, dating between 1914 and 1930, accessible online at http://gallery.archives.govt.nz/v/christchurch/interesting+items+website+defiance+hut.

Locke Stream Hut
1 Barry Gustafson, 'Parry, William Edward 1878–1952', *Dictionary of New Zealand Biography. Te Ara – The Encyclopaedia of New Zealand* [website], 2010 (updated 1 September 2010), www.teara.govt.nz/en/biographies/3p12/1, accessed April 2012.
2 'Call of Outdoors', *Evening Post*, 28 December 1944, p. 6.
3 Kirstie Ross, *Going Bush: New Zealanders and Nature in the Twentieth Century*, 2008, p. 88.
4 There were already existing huts in the Hurunui – Lake Sumner Hut, Springs Hut (near the hot springs) and Cameron Hut – but these were smaller station huts (see Jack McNair, *Shooting for the Skipper*, 1971, pp. 80–81).
5 B.D.A. Greig (ed.), *Tararua Story: Jubilee of a Mountain Club*, 1946, p. 20.
6 Stella Woodham (ed.), *Christchurch Tramping Club Fiftieth Anniversary, 1932–1982*, 1982, p. 27. The club was then known as Te Hapu Koa Tramping Club.
7 Probably the same Harry Scott killed in 1960 after an ascent of Aoraki/Mt Cook (see picture insert in Jonathan Scott, *Harry's Absence: Looking for my Father on the Mountain*, 1997).
8 Locke Stream Hut information panel.
9 Ibid.
10 Joff Thomson, *Deer Hunter: The Experiences of a New Zealand Stalker*, 1954, pp. 82–83.
11 Ross, *Going Bush*, p. 179; Mark Pickering, *A Tramper's Journey: Stories from the Back Country of New Zealand*, 2004, p. 59.
12 Geoff Chapple, *Te Araroa: A Walking Guide to New Zealand's Long Trail*, 2011, p. 197.
13 'Call of Outdoors', *Evening Post*, p. 6.
14 Steve Harrington, *A Hurunui History Trail: From the Peaks to Harper's Pass*, 1997, p. 18.
15 'Historic Locke Stream Hut', DOC website, www.doc.govt.nz/conservation/historic/by-region/west-coast/hokitika/locke-stream-hut, accessed April 2012.
16 'Historic Number Three Hut', DOC website, www.doc.govt.nz/conservation/historic/by-region/canterbury/north-canterbury-and-arthurs-pass/number-three-hut, accessed April 2012.

Red Hut
1 F. Alack, 'Radio Talks', *NZAJ* 49, 1962, p. 117.
2 Harry Wigley, *The Mount Cook Way: The First Fifty Years of the Mount Cook Company*, 1979, p. 60.
3 Gordon Ogilvie, 'Wigley, Rodolph Lysaght', *Dictionary of New Zealand Biography. Te Ara – The Encyclopedia of New Zealand* [website], 2010 (updated 1 September 2010), www.teara.govt.nz/en/biographies/3w13/1, accessed April 2012.
4 'Historic Red Hut', DOC website, www.doc.govt.nz/conservation/historic/by-region/canterbury/mackenzie-country-and-waitaki/red-hut, accessed April 2012.
5 David Barnes, 'Ruataniwha Conservation Park', *FMC Bulletin* 184, June 2011, pp. 34–39.

CLUB HUTS

Forging an Identity in the Hills
1 Lock's surname is incorrectly spelt on maps as 'Locke' (see Geoff Chapple, *Te Araroa: A Walking Guide to New Zealand's Long Trail*, 2011, p. 197).
2 G.E. Mannering, 'Editorial', *NZAJ* 1, 1892, pp. 9 and 13.
3 E. Miller, 'Proceedings of the Club and Sections: Report from the Otago Section', *NZAJ* 5(20), 1933, p. 283.
4 J.A. Sim (ed.), 'Club and General Notes', *NZAJ* 6(22), 1935, p. 164.
5 Roland Ellis, 'Presidential Welcome to the Ski Mountaineering Section', *NZAJ* 8(26), 1939, p. 104.
6 J.A. Sim, 'Camp Three', *NZAJ* 8(27), 1940, p. 160.
7 J.A. Sim (ed.), 'Club and General Notes', *NZAJ* 9(29), 1942, p. 196; B. Patterson and F. Gallas, 'A Murchison Holiday', *NZAJ* 10(31), 1944, p. 129.
8 J.D. Henderson, 'The New Homer Forks Hut', *NZAJ* 21(2), 1966, p. 309.

12 *Good as Gold* [DOC Otago Conservancy newsletter], March 2011, p. 1, accessible online at www.doc.govt.nz/upload/documents/about-doc/news/whats-new/good-as-gold-march-11.pdf.

9 A.F. Shaw, 'Moving Godley Hut', *NZAJ* 16(42), 1955, p. 211.
10 *Management Agreement Aspiring Huts*, agreement between DOC and NZAC, 1989.
11 D. Billing, 'The Canterbury Mountaineering Club', *Canterbury Mountaineer* 44, 1975, p. 10.
12 John Pascoe, letter to David Herron, 1958, quoted in *Canterbury Mountaineer* Jubilee Edition, 1974–75, p. 10.
13 Tom Beckett, *The Mountains of Erewhon*, 1978, p. 79.
14 A.G. Flower, 'The Clyde Bivouac', *Canterbury Mountaineer* 8, 1939, p. 82. Agnes Bivvy was situated 400 metres up Agnes Stream from the Clyde Junction on the true right; the iron remains of the shelter were still obvious in 2000.
15 Canterbury Mountaineering Club website, www.cmc.net.nz, accessed 2012.
16 C.E. Douglas, letter to A.P. Harper, 1894, quoted in John Pascoe, *Mr Explorer Douglas*, 1957, p. 186.
17 A few other tramping clubs had formed earlier, but none survived.
18 B.D.A Grieg (ed.), *Tararua Story: Jubilee of a Mountain Club*, 1946, p. 107.
19 Ibid., p. 18.
20 See, for example, club newsletters from the time: *Tararua Tramper, Hills and Valleys, Te Hapu Koa, Wanderlust*.
21 *NZ Truth* 3 July 1935, quoted in *Hutt Valley Tramping* 1973, p. 12.
22 N. Boniface, *50 Years of Masterton Tramping Club, 1957–2007*, 2007.
23 Grieg (ed.), *Tararua Story*, p. 19.
24 P. Barton, 'Simple Mountain Huts', in Dave Capper (ed.), *Impressions of a Tramping Club 1947–1968*, 1968 p. 41.
25 Beverley Meyer, 'Gemeinschaft in Hausknect, Community in Boots: A Study of the Auckland Tramping Club', 1987, pp. 12, 52.
26 Alpine Sports Club website, www.alpinesport.org.nz/club_profile.htm, accessed 2012.
27 Wayne Erb (ed.), *Auckland University Tramping Club, Jubilee History 1932–2007*, 2007, pp. 38–42, accessible online at www.autc.org.nz/sites/default/files/13-07-07%20Jubilee%20Magazine%20FINAL.pdf.
28 Stella Woodham (ed.), *Christchurch Tramping Club Fiftieth Anniversary, 1932–1982*, 1982 p. 10 ; Grant Hunter (ed.), *Peninsula Tramping Club Turns 75: 1932–2007*, 2007, p. 7.
29 Woodham (ed.), *Christchurch Tramping Club Fiftieth Anniversary, 1932–1982*, pp. 10, 26, 35.
30 Hutt Valley Tramping Club, 17th Annual Report, 1940, p. 2.
31 *New Zealand Railways*, 1 December 1929, quoted in *Hills and Valleys* [Hutt Valley Tramping Club newsletter], March 1959, p. 3.
32 'Call of Outdoors', *Evening Post*, 28 December 1944, p. 6.
33 Woodham (ed.), *Christchurch Tramping Club Fiftieth Anniversary, 1932–1982*, p. 26.
34 www.cutc.org.nz, Canterbury University Tramping Club website, accessed April 2012.
35 D. Billing, 'The Canterbury Mountaineering Club', *Canterbury Mountaineer* Jubilee Edition, 1974–75, p. 9; Ron Mackie, pers. comm. with Shaun Barnett, 2008.
36 *Hills and Valleys* [Hutt Valley Tramping Club newsletter], March 1953, p. 1.
37 R.J. Keen (ed.), *Outdoors 50th Anniversary Issue 1923–1973*, 1973, p. 29.
38 Ibid., p. 40.
39 Ibid., p. 19.
40 Kelvin Lloyd, *45 Years of Antics, Adventures and Escapades of the Otago University Tramping Club*, 2006, p. 19.
41 Gaffer, 'Looking Backward', in Southland Tramping Club, *Southland Tramping Club 25th Jubilee 1947–1972*, 1972, p. 7.
42 R. Stewart, 'Hut Notes', *NZAJ* 16(42), 1955, p. 209.
43 Margaret Verheul, 'Club Profile: Nelson Tramping Club', *FMC Bulletin*, August 2010, p. 19.
44 Shaun Barnett, 'Club Profile: Golden Bay Alpine and Tramping Club', *FMC Bulletin*, March 2011, p. 32.
45 Robert Woperis, 'Balloon Hut, Kahurangi National Park', *FMC Bulletin*, November 2010, p. 33; Ross Hall, 'Flanagans Hut, Kahurangi National Park', *FMC Bulletin*, November 2011, p. 45.
46 Lex Smith, 'Club Profile: Heretaunga Tramping Club', *FMC Bulletin*, June 2010, p. 40.
47 David Scoullar: 'Club Profile: Wanganui Tramping Club', *FMC Bulletin*, March 2007, p. 27.
48 John Wilson, 'Club Profile, Waikato Tramping Club', *FMC Bulletin*, November 2009, p. 19.
49 Erb (ed.), *Auckland University Tramping Club, Jubilee History 1932–2007*, 2007, p. 38.
50 'Opening up the Tararua Range's New Hut East of Levin', *Manawatu Times*, 22 August 1932.
51 Chris Maclean, *Tararua: The Story of a Mountain Range*, 1994, p. 34.
52 www.deerstalkers.org.nz, NZDA website, accessed April 2012.
53 'About the NZ Deerstalkers' Association', NZDA website, www.deerstalkers.org.nz/Site/About_Us/default.aspx, accessed April 2012.
54 Philip Holden, *New Zealand, Hunter's Paradise*, 1985, p. 81.
55 *Tararua State Forest Park Management Plan*, 1977–87, p. 68.
56 Dave Saunders, pers. comm. with Geoff Spearpoint, 2012.
57 www.nzdanapier.org.nz, NZDA Napier Section website, accessed 2012.
58 www.southlanddeerstalkers.org.nz, NZDA Southland Section website, accessed 2012.
59 Ray Burrell, *Fifty Years of Mountain Federation: Federated Mountain Clubs of New Zealand 1931–1981*, 1981, p. 7.
60 Ibid., p. 11
61 Jane Thomson, *Origins of the National Parks Act (1952)*, quoted in Burrell, *Fifty Years of Mountain Federation*, p. 83.
62 Burrell, *Fifty Years of Mountain Federation*, p. 20.
63 Ibid., p. 154; N.M. Thomson (ed.), *Safety in the Mountains*, 1949, p. 54.
64 Arnold Heine, 'Forest Parks in New Zealand: An Evolving Concept' [unpublished report], FMC archives, Wellington.
65 Levin Waiopehu Tramping Club, *Levin Waiopehu Tramping Club Golden Jubilee 1927–1977*, 1977, p. 11; Hutt Valley Tramping Club, 17th Annual Report, 1940.
66 Les Molloy, 'Wilderness Diminishing', *NZAJ* 29, 1976, p. 67.
67 T.S. Clarkson, 'The Fall of Allaway-Dickson Hut', *Heels* [annual of Victoria University of Wellington Tramping Club], 1972, p. 4.
68 'Budget Announcement – Recreation Facilities Funding' [DOC press release], May 2002, DOC, Wellington p. 1.

Field Hut
1 The photographs were installed by historian Chris Maclean in association with the Tararua Tramping Club in 1997.
2 Frank Penn, *Across the Tararuas and Beautiful Otaki*, 1920.
3 Ron Pynenburg, 'Huts of the Mount Hector Track' [B.Arch. thesis], 1981, Section 2, pp. 5–10; Hugh Barr, email to Shaun Barnett, 2 February 2012.
4 Pynenburg, 'Huts of the Mount Hector Track', Section 2, p. 20.
5 Jim Henderson (ed.), *Our Open Country*, 1971, p. 252; Hugh Barr, 'Field Hut Builder Honoured', *FMC Bulletin*, March 2005, p. 13.
6 Pynenburg, 'Huts of the Mount Hector Track', Section 2, p. 20.
7 Ibid., p. 21.
8 Henderson (ed.), *Our Open Country*, p. 252.
9 Geoff Spearpoint, *Waking to the Hills*, 1985, p. 7.
10 B.D.A. Greig, *Tararua Story: Jubilee of a Mountain Club*, 1946, p. 19.
11 Chris Maclean, *Tararua: The Story of a Mountain Range*, 1994, p. 218.
12 Pynenburg, 'Huts of the Mount Hector Track', Section 2, p. 20; Henderson (ed.), *Our Open Country*, pp. 253–54; Maclean, *Tararua*, p. 218.
13 Pynenburg, 'Huts of the Mount Hector Track', Section 3, p. 20; Wally Neill, 'Field Hut's Golden Jubilee', 1975, pp. 53–61; Barr, email to Shaun Barnett, 2 February 2012.
14 Michael Bartlett, email to Shaun Barnett, 15 February 2012.
15 Maclean, *Tararua*, p. 248–49; Barr, email to Shaun Barnett, 2 February 2012.

16 Wayne Boness (ex-DOC Waikanae Field Centre manager), email to Shaun Barnett, 22 December 2011; Barr, email to Shaun Barnett, 2 February 2012.

Kime Hut
1 The first death, in January 1922, was that of Harold Freeman (see p. 154).
2 Chris Maclean, *Tararua: The Story of a Mountain Range*, 1994, pp. 136–37; www.windy.gen.nz/index.php/archives/494 contains all relevant newspaper articles from the period.
3 Ron Pynenburg, 'Huts of the Mount Hector Track' [B.Arch. thesis], 1981, Section 1, p. 16; Wally Neill, 'Building the First Kime Hut 1930', *Tararua*, 1978, pp. 5–7.
4 Esmond Kime's father donated £50 towards this total, trustees of the Girdlestone Memorial Fund gave £25, and the remainder came from a government subsidy of £230 and funds from the TTC (see Neill, 'Building the First Kime Hut 1930', pp. 5–7).
5 Maclean, *Tararua*, p. 172.
6 Ibid., p. 176.
7 Pynenburg, 'Huts of the Mount Hector Track', Section 3, p. 13.
8 Ibid., pp. 14–16.
9 Maurice Perry and Ian Baine, 'Building the New Kime Hut', *Tararua*, 1977, pp. 8–11.
10 Kay Blundell and Tanya Katterns, 'Seddon Bennington's Chances of Survival in Ranges Slim – Experts', *Dominion Post*, 16 July 2009.

Rangiwahia Hut
1 Rangiwahia Hut information panel.
2 Ibid.
3 Ibid.
4 Terry Crippen, 'Huts as Heritage: Rangiwahia Hut', *FMC Bulletin*, June 2006, p. 23.
5 Lawson Pither, 'Life's Rich Tapestry: The Stove at Rangi Hut', late 1960s, reprinted in Palmerston North Tramping and Mountaineering Club newsletter, February 2011, pp. 5–6.
6 Crippen, 'Huts as Heritage', p. 23.

Powell Hut
1 Jane Forsyth, 'The Powell Hut Papers', *Hutt Valley Tramping* [Hutt Valley Tramping Club annual], 1980, p. 5
2 *Hills and Valleys* [newsletter of the Hutt Valley Tramping Club], January 1939, p. 4.
3 *Hills and Valleys*, August 1939, p. 2.
4 Trev Jones, 'Ian Powell' [obituary], *Hutt Valley Tramping*, 1993, p. 28.
5 *Hills and Valleys*, August 1939, p. 4.
6 P.L. Rundle, 'Ski Story', *Hutt Valley Tramping*, 1967 p. 36.
7 Forsyth, 'The Powell Hut Papers', p. 6.
8 Jane Forsyth, 'More Powell Hut Papers', *Hutt Valley Tramping*, 1981 p. 3.
9 Ibid., p. 4.
10 Gary Goldsworthy 'HVTC 1983–2003', *Hutt Valley Tramping*, 2002–03, p. 5.
11 Chris Maclean, *Tararua: The Story of a Mountain Range*, 1994, p. 224.
12 John Rundle, *The Tararua Book*, 1981, p. 46.

Howletts Hut
1 Never Again, 'Rest after Labour', *Beechleaves* [Manawatu Tramping and Skiing Club newsletter], March 1955.
2 J.F. Finclay, 'W.F. Howlett, Pioneer Ruahine Botanist', *Wellington Botanical Society Bulletin* 41, September 1981, pp. 35–37.
3 Ibid., p. 39.
4 Mark Pickering, *Huts: Untold Stories from Back-country New Zealand*, 2010, p. 313.

5 A. Stenberg, 'Some Reminiscences of Pioneering Days in the Ruahine Ranges', Ruahine Tramping Club report, 1938, p. 4.
6 Ibid.
7 Ashley Cunningham, *Hawke's Bay for the Happy Wanderer*, 1993, p. 162.
8 Pickering, *Huts*, p. 311.
9 Stenberg, 'Some Reminiscences of Pioneering Days in the Ruahine Ranges', pp. 3–4.
10 Matthew Wright, 'Early Huts of the Northeastern Ruahine and Central Wakarara Ranges' [unpublished NZFS report], 1986, p. 67; Ruahine Tramping Club report, 1938, p. 5.
11 Tony Gates, 'Little Hut On the Range', Horizons Regional Council newsletter, Palmerston North, 2001 p. 13.
12 'Timber and Tin in the Tuki Tuki', Ruahine Tramping Club report, 1938, p. 7.
13 Pickering, *Huts*, p. 317.
14 Wright, 'Early Huts of the Northeastern Ruahine and Central Wakarara Ranges', p. 66.
15 The plane that crashed was an RNZAF Oxford Airspeed 2127, with the loss of three lives (see Tony Gates, 'Oxford Plane Wreck', *Palmerston North Tramping and Mountaineering Club Newsletter*, October 2010, p. 5).
16 Wright, 'Early Huts of the Northeastern Ruahine and Central Wakarara Ranges', p. 68.

Big Hut
1 Stuart Boyd, *The First 50 Years: A History of the Otago Ski Club Inc.*, 1982, p. 1.
2 The remains of this hut are right next to Big Hut, and in the early years of Big Hut it served as a ski storeroom.
3 Boyd, *The First 50 Years*, p. 7.
4 W. Scott Gilkison, *Peaks, Packs and Mountain Tracks*, 1940, p. 83.
5 Ibid.
6 Boyd, *The First 50 Years*, p. 11.
7 Big Hut historical panel. Information courtesy of Rock and Pillar Hut Trust and Bruce Mason.
8 Ibid.
9 Boyd, *The First 50 Years*, p. 13.
10 Ibid., p. 14.
11 Ibid., p. 23.
12 Ibid., p. 48.
13 'Historic Ski Hut will be Retained' [Rock and Pillar Trust press release], 17 November 2003, accessible online at www.middlemarch.co.nz/big_hut/files/press_release.html.
14 'Big Hut Restoration', Rock and Pillar Trust website, http://middlemarch.larchgrove.co.nz/big_hut/files/progress.html, accessed May 2012.
15 David Barnes, pers. comm. with Rob Brown, 15 April 2012.

Cone Hut
1 John Gates, 'Building in the Hills and Mountains', *Tararua* 1961, p. 30.
2 Ian Baine, 'The Hut Builders', *Tararua* 1979, p. 50.
3 Chris Maclean, *John Pascoe*, 2003, p. 119.
4 Ron Pynenburg, 'Huts of the Mount Hector Track' [B.Arch. thesis], 1981, p. 22.
5 L.D. Bridge, 'We Build a New Hut', *Tararua Tramper*, May 1946, p. 4.
6 Ibid.
7 'Cone Hut Opening by A.T.', *Tararua Tramper*, May 1946, p. 8.
8 *Tararua Tramper* [newsletter of the Tararua Tramping Club], July 1946, p. 3.
9 'Tararua State Forest Park Management Plan, 1977–1987', NZFS, p. 59.
10 Michael Bartlett, 'Restoration of Cone Hut 1983–89', *Tararua* 1989, p. 40.
11 Ibid.

Aspiring Hut
1 'Alpine Club Notes', *NZAJ* 4(18), 1931, p. 229.
2 'Otago Section Notes', *NZAJ* 5(19), 1932, p. 117.
3 A.R. Craigie, 'The Aspiring Hut Campaign', *NZAJ* 12(34), 1947, p. 118.
4 A.R. Craigie, 'The Aspiring Hut Campaign Concluded', *NZAJ* 13(36), 1949, p. 117.
5 'John Aspinall' [obituary], *NZAJ* 9(29), 1942, p. 214.
6 Craigie, 'The Aspiring Hut Campaign', p. 118.
7 A.R. Craigie, 'The Aspiring Hut Campaign', *NZAJ* 12(35), 1948, p. 280.
8 Arthur Pearson, 'The Aspiring Hut Opened', *NZAC Bulletin* 9, July 1949, p. 10.
9 Brian Brake's 11-minute documentary, *Prelude to Aspiring* (1949), is a fascinating portrayal of the official hut opening; it is accessible online at www.nzonscreen.com/title/prelude-to-aspiring-1949.
10 Craigie, 'The Aspiring Hut Campaign Concluded', p. 119.
11 Paul Powell, *Men Aspiring*, 1967, p. 107.
12 New Zealand Alpine Club, *Aspiring Hut: 50 Years of Climbing and Adventure*, 1999, p. 11.
13 Ibid., p. 20.
14 Ibid., p. 13.
15 Rob Mitchell, 'Sunblest 50th Birthday Celebrations at Aspiring Hut', *The Climber* 30, summer 1999, p. 30.

St Winifred Hut
1 J.C. Pattle, 'The New Havelock Hut and Eric Bivouac', *Canterbury Mountaineer* 6, 1937, p. 18.
2 Ibid., p. 19.
3 Ibid.
4 Tom Beckett, *The Mountains of Erewhon*, 1978, p. 58.
5 J.C. Pattle, 'The New Eric Bivvy', *Canterbury Mountaineer* 4(17), 1948, p. 190.
6 Ibid., p. 191.
7 Beckett, *The Mountains of Erewhon*, p. 64.
8 T. Morton, 'The St Winifred Hut', *Canterbury Mountaineer* 8(29), 1960, p. 203.
9 Ibid., p. 205.
10 Ibid.
11 Ibid.
12 Robin Muirson, 'Extreme Makeover for Mountain Huts', *Canterbury Mountaineer* 2005, p. 77.
13 Owen Rees, 'St Winifreds Hut Refurbishment', *Canterbury Mountaineering Club News* 18(4), September–December 2006.

Waimakariri Falls Hut
1 John Wilson, 'The Steel Bivvy: A History of Waimakariri Falls Hut', *Canterbury Mountaineer* 64, 2007, p. 74.
2 Ibid., p. 75.
3 Ibid., p. 76.
4 After relocation to the Aoraki/Mount Cook Visitor Centre, the old Empress Hut was reassembled in 2008 and now forms part of a display on historic climbing huts.

Whangaehu Hut
1 M. Hutchinson, 'Whangaehu Hut: Climbs from Whangaehu', *New Zealand Alpine Club Bulletin* 43, June 1964, p. 8.
2 David Hoyle, 'Whangaehu Hut: Designing the Hut', *New Zealand Alpine Club Bulletin* 43, June 1964, pp. 2–3.
3 Ibid.
4 David Hoyle, email to Shaun Barnett, 27 March 2012.
5 David Hoyle, email to Shaun Barnett, 26 March 2012.
6 Hoyle, 'Whangaehu Hut: Designing the Hut', pp. 2–3; G.C., 'Whangaehu Hut: The Building of the Hut', *New Zealand Alpine Club Bulletin* 43, June 1964, p. 3.
7 Ibid.
8 G.C., 'Whangaehu Hut: The Building of the Hut', p. 5.
9 E.C.L., 'Whangaehu Hut: The Opening', *New Zealand Alpine Club Bulletin* 43, June 1964, p. 6.
10 Ibid., p. 5.
11 'Huts Update', *The Climber*, autumn 2012, p. 45.

Roaring Stag Lodge
1 Tony Macklin, 'Roaring Stag Lodge Rises Anew', *New Zealand Hunting and Wildlife*, summer 2006, pp. 41–42.
2 Ibid.
3 'Our Club', *Tararua Tramper* [newsletter of the Tararua Tramping Club] 83(5), June 2011, p. 13.
4 Macklin, 'Roaring Stag Lodge Rises Anew', pp. 41–42.
5 'Cosy New Roaring Stag Lodge', *Footprints* [DOC Wellington newsletter], 23 June 2005, p. 1.
6 Macklin, 'Roaring Stag Lodge Rises Anew', pp. 41–42.
7 Tony Macklin, speech notes for Roaring Stag Lodge opening, NZDA archive, Wellington.

Boulder Lake Hut, Adelaide Tarn Hut and Lonely Lake Hut
1 Janet Huddleston, 'Golden Bay's Tramping Club Marches On', *Golden Bay Weekly*, 18 July 2003, p. 5.
2 Frank Soper, notes and timeline, Golden Bay Alpine and Tramping Club archive.
3 Huddleston, 'Golden Bay's Tramping Club Marches On', p. 5.
4 Soper, notes and timeline, Golden Bay Alpine and Tramping Club archive.
5 Ibid.

Mt Brown Hut
1 Ted Brennan, email to Shaun Barnett, 27 February 2012.
2 'Mt Brown Hut', Permolat: Remote Huts Westland website, http://remotehuts.co.nz/huts/mt._brown_hut, accessed 4 June 2011.
3 Julia Bradshaw, information folder, Mt Brown Hut.
4 Ibid.
5 'FMC Supports New Mt Brown Hut', *FMC Bulletin*, March 2011, p. 17; http://remotehuts.co.nz, Permolat: Remote Huts Westland website, accessed 4 June 2011.
6 'Mt Brown Hut', Permolat: Remote Huts Westland website, accessed 4 June 2011.
7 www.facebook.com/mtbrownhut.

Cavalier Hunters Hut
1 John DeLury, pers. comm. with Rob Brown, 6 April 2012.
2 'Rakiura Hunter Camp Trust', NZDA Southland Section website, www.southlanddeerstalkers.org.nz/index.php?option=com_content&view=article&id=10&Itemid=12, accessed 4 April 2012.
3 John DeLury, pers. comm. with Rob Brown, 4 April 2012.
4 Ibid.

Orongorongo Valley Huts
1 Dates given for when the original Baine-iti hut was built are conflicting, but the hut information panel says it was constructed in 1915–
2 Chris Maclean, 'A History of the Orongorongo Valley' [typescript] 2012, p. 36.
3 Ross Kerr, *A Chronology of the Tararua and Rimutaka Ranges*, 20 p. 44; 'Huts in the Orongorongo Valley', *FMC Bulletin*, August 2 pp. 22, 24.
4 Euan Nicol and Jenny Nicol, *Tramping in North Island Forest P* 1991, p. 247.
5 John Pascoe, *Land Uplifted High*, 1952, p. 20.
6 Joanna Lane-Taylor, *The History of the Orongorongo Valley and Environs*, 1970, p. 46.
7 Pascoe, *Land Uplifted High*, p. 19.

8 Rebecca Mitchison, 'Home in the Orongorongo Valley', *Wilderness*, March 2007, pp. 14–15.
9 Waerenga Hut was moved in 2008, and Baines removed in 2010 (see Pat Tristram, 'Baines Hut: A Short History 1943–2010', *Hills and Valleys* [newsletter of the Hutt Valley Tramping Club] 63(5), June 2010, pp. 6–7).
10 Kerr, *A Chronology of the Tararua and Rimutaka Ranges*, p. 47.
11 'Wet and Weary Experiences in the Orongorongo Valley', *Evening Post*, 24 January 1922, p. 11.
12 Bob Stothart, 'Thirteen Holes in the Orongorongo', *Wilderness*, August 2002, p. 53.
13 Kerr, *A Chronology of the Tararua and Rimutaka Ranges*, p. 50.
14 Pascoe, *Land Uplifted High*, p. 20.
15 'Huts in the Orongorongo Valley', p. 24.
16 See the club's website: www.orongorongoclub.org.nz.
17 Kerr, *A Chronology of the Tararua and Rimutaka Ranges*, p. 53.
18 'Huts in the Orongorongo Valley', p. 24.
19 Mitchison, 'Home in the Orongorongo Valley', pp. 14–15.

DEPARTMENT OF INTERNAL AFFAIRS HUTS
Shelter on a Shoestring

1 Graeme Caughley, *The Deer Wars: The Story of Deer in New Zealand*, 1983, p. 2–3.
2 Ibid., p. 27.
3 Ibid., p. 35.
4 Peter McKelvey, *Steepland Forests: A Historical Perspective of Protection Forestry in New Zealand*, 1995, p. 95; Chris Maclean, *Tararua: The Story of a Mountain Range*, 1994, p. 182; Philip Holden, *New Zealand, Hunter's Paradise*, 1985, pp. 14–15.
5 Caughley, *The Deer Wars*, p. 25.
6 Rex Forrester and Neil Illingworth, *Hunter for Hire*, 1965, pp. 51, 59.
7 Ken Francis, *Wildlife Ranger: My Years in the New Zealand Outdoors*, 1983, p. 72.
8 Barry Crump, *A Good Keen Man*, 1960, p. 11.
9 Forrester and Illingworth, *Hunter for Hire*, p. 60.
10 Joff Thomson, *Deer Shooting Days*, 1964, p. 9.
11 Francis, *Wildlife Ranger*, pp. 93–94.
12 Ibid.
13 Robin Patterson, *A Sock in My Stew: Memories of Dick Morris and the Deer Cullers*, 1991, p. 11.
14 Forrester and Illingworth, *Hunter for Hire*, p. 60.
15 Francis, *Wildlife Ranger*, p. 73.
16 Ibid., p. 81.
17 Jock Fisher, email to Rob Brown, 18 June 2011.
18 Michael Kelly, *Wild Animal Control Huts: A National Heritage Identification Study*, 2007, p. 11.
19 Conference, 1939, HO IAD 48/26 Part 1 A.P. & Game Act – Deer Destruction – Conference of Field Staff, Head Office, ANZ, Wellington, 27/10/1937 to 30/9/1946, quoted in Chris Cochran and Jackie Breen, *Ranger's Hut, Landsborough, West Coast: Conservation Plan*, 2007, p. 7.
20 Ibid.
21 Matthew Wright, 'Early Huts of the Northeastern Ruahine and Central Wakarara Ranges' [unpublished NZFS report], 1986, pp. 62–63.
22 Kelly, *Wild Animal Control Huts*, p. 54.
23 Cochran and Breen, *Ranger's Hut, Landsborough, West Coast*, p. 12.
24 Ibid., pp. 7, 11–14, 31.
25 Ibid., p. 8
26 Kelly, *Wild Animal Control Huts*, p. 11.
27 Ibid., pp. 12–13.
28 J. Geddes, 'Anderson Hut', *Forestry News* XIV(1), January 1965, p. 27.
29 V.K., 'Air Transport for Mountain Country', *Evening Post*, February 1947, p. 10.
30 Maclean, *Tararua*, pp. 220–21.

32 Ross Galbreath, 1993. *Working for Wildlife: A History of the New Zealand Wildlife Service*, 1993, pp. 43–44.
33 Forrester and Illingworth, *Hunter for Hire*, pp. 53, 69.
34 Thomson, *Deer Shooting Days*, p. 24.
35 Ron Turner, email to Shaun Barnett, 10 July 2011.
36 Jock Fisher, email to Rob Brown, 18 June 2011.
37 Kelly, *Wild Animal Control Huts*, pp. 13–14.
38 Allan Farmer, *The Best Job Ever (a Life of Hunting)*, 1994, p. 106.
39 Galbreath, *Working for Wildlife*, p. 44; Athol Geddes, 'A Life in the Hills. Athol Geddes Talks to John Rhodes', *FMC Bulletin*, May 2004, p. 26; Kelly, *Wild Animal Control Huts*, p. 52.
40 Kelly, *Wild Animal Control Huts*, p. 14; Jackie Breen, 'Old Cedar Flat Hut Historic Assessment' [internal report for DOC Hokitika], September 2004, fig. 14, p. 8. Even after the NZFS took over on April 1956, it continued building some DIA-design huts until 1958, taking the total to twenty-eight on the West Coast (Jackie Breen, pers. comm. with Shaun Barnett, 23 March 2012).
41 Chris Cochran and Jackie Breen, *Slaty Creek Hut, Ahaura Catchment, West Coast: Conservation Plan*, 2006, p. 11.
42 'Winter Operations Hokitika Valley 1957', NZFS File F.S. 90/20 PRF:BMH, Hokitika, 5 November 1957, ANZ, Christchurch.
43 Cochran and Breen, *Slaty Creek Hut, Ahaura Catchment, West Coast*, p. 3; Kelly, *Wild Animal Control Huts*, p. 47; 'Historic Prices Flat Hut', DOC website, www.doc.govt.nz/conservation/historic/by-region/west-coast/hokitika/prices-flat-hut, accessed April 2012.
44 Cochran and Breen, *Slaty Creek Hut, Ahaura Catchment, West Coast*, p. 3; Kelly, *Wild Animal Control Huts*, p. iv.

Historic Clark Hut

1 Shaun Barnett and Rachel Egerton, 'Clark Hut, Fiordland National Park', *FMC Bulletin*, August 2009, p. 27
2 Ibid., pp. 26–27.
3 Ibid.
4 Rex Forrester and Neil Illingworth, *Hunting in New Zealand*, 1973, pp. 63–64.
5 Graeme Caughley, *The Deer Wars: The Story of Deer in New Zealand*, 1983, p. 26.
6 Barnett and Egerton, 'Clark Hut, Fiordland National Park', pp. 26–27.
7 Daryl Marshall, *Pikau and Rifle: Hunting Deer, Thar and Chamois in the Southern Alps, Fiordland, Stewart Island and Longwoods*, 2006, p. 43.
8 Ibid., p. 45
9 Barnett and Egerton, 'Clark Hut, Fiordland National Park', p. 27.
10 Ibid.
11 Ibid.

Slaty Creek Hut

1 Chris Cochran and Jackie Breen, *Slaty Creek Hut, Ahaura Catchment, West Coast: Conservation Plan*, 2006, p. 3.
2 Ibid., p. 9.
3 Robin Quigg, 'Back-country Huts, More Than a Roof Over Your Head: A Question of Values in Cultural Heritage Management' [Masters thesis], 1993, p. 107.
4 Clem Small, pers. comm. with Geoff Spearpoint, July 2011.
5 Lew Sutherland, *A Hunting and Tramping Guide to Westland*, 1970, p. 42.
6 Ibid.
7 NZFS, *Lake Sumner Forest Park Map*, 1:80,000, 1st edition, 1981.
8 Slaty Creek Hut logbook.

Kiwi Hut and Museum Hut

1 Robin S. Patterson, *A Sock in My Stew: Memories of Dick Morris and the Deer Cullers*, 1991, p. i.
2 Ibid., pp. 30–32.
3 Ashley Cunningham, 'Dick Morris of Lake Sumner', *FMC Bulletin*, June 2010, pp. 51–52.

4 Patterson, *A Sock in My Stew*, p. 72.
5 Ibid., p. 4.
6 Ibid., p. 5.
7 Ibid., p. 71.
8 Ibid., p. 281.
9 According to an information panel in Museum Hut written by Robin Patterson, the work party included George Brooklands, Bill Dukes, Jim Dukes, Rhys Griffiths and Jack Richards.
10 Patterson, *A Sock in My Stew*, p. 278.
11 Robin Patterson, information panel in Museum Hut.

Rogers Hut

1 Michael Kelly, *Te Urewera Slab Huts Conservation Report*, 1996, p. 7.
2 Ibid., p. 7; Chris Birt, 'Rex's Saga Ends Where it Began', *Daily Post*, 2002.
3 Birt, 'Rex's Saga Ends Where it Began'.
4 Ibid.
5 'Historic Rogers Hut', DOC website, www.doc.govt.nz/conservation/historic/by-region/bay-of-plenty/rogers-hut/, accessed November 2010. Later, a wood stove was installed, which superseded the original open fire.
6 Andy Blick, email to Shaun Barnett, 20 November 2010.
7 Ibid.
8 Ibid.

NEW ZEALAND FOREST SERVICE HUTS
The NZFS Takes Over

1 'Soil Conservation', AJHR C-3, 1950, p. 7
2 Ibid.
3 Mike Bennett, *The Venison Hunters*, 1979, p. 17.
4 Ross Galbreath, *Working for Wildlife: A History of the New Zealand Wildlife Service*, 1993, pp. 77–80; Peter McKelvey, *Steepland Forests: A Historical Perspective of Protection Forestry in New Zealand*, 1995, p. 98.
5 Bennett, *The Venison Hunters*, p. 17.
6 Jock Fisher, email to Rob Brown, 14 June 2011.
7 Jock Fisher, email to Shaun Barnett, 23 January 2012.
8 Michael Kelly, *Wild Animal Control Huts: A National Heritage Identification Study*, 2007, p. 42.
9 Ron Turner, 'Winter in the Hokitika 1957', accessible online at www.nzdeercullers.org.nz/LiteratureDetail.aspx?Titles=Winter%20in%20the%20Hokitika%201957.
10 Kelly, *Wild Animal Control Huts*, p. 30.
11 Turner, 'Winter in the Hokitika 1957'.
12 Jack Lasenby, *What Makes a Teacher?*, 2004, p. 28.
13 Jock Fisher, 'Huts Erected During My Time in Murchison 1958 to 1963' [unpublished notes held by Shaun Barnett].
14 Ron Turner, 'Hut Building in the Nelson–Marlborough Area', accessible online at www.nzdeercullers.org.nz/LiteratureDetail.aspx?Titles=Hut%20Building%20in%20the%20Nelson%20-%20Malborough%20area.
15 Ibid.
16 Ibid.
17 Fisher, 'Huts Erected During My Time in Murchison 1958 to 1963'.
18 Ron Turner and Harry Hancock, 'The Last Flight of Luna Hut', accessible online at www.nzdeercullers.org.nz/LiteratureDetail.aspx?Titles=The%20Last%20Flight%20of%20the%20Luna%20hut.
19 Ray Osman, email to Shaun Barnett, 23 February 2012.
20 Fisher, 'Huts Erected During My Time in Murchison 1958 to 1963'. A few of these huts remain, including East Matakitaki, Roebuck, Wheel Creek and Pell Stream. Others were replaced by later huts, or removed altogether.
21 Osman, email to Shaun Barnett, 23 February 2012.
22 Ben Gibbs, email to Shaun Barnett, 6 September 2011.
23 Ben Gibbs, letter to Shaun Barnett, January 2012.

24 Arnold Heine, 'SF70 6 Bunk Huts, the Classic Back-country Shelter', *FMC Bulletin*, April 2003, p. 20; Kelly, *Wild Animal Control Huts*, p. 31.
25 Kelly, *Wild Animal Control Huts*, p. 16.
26 Ibid., table on p. 32.
27 Osman, email to Shaun Barnett, 23 February 2012.
28 Bennett, *The Venison Hunters*, p. 18.
29 K.H. Miers, *Animal Control Policy on New Zealand Forest Land*, 1973, p. 19, quoted in McKelvey, *Steepland Forests*, p. 105.
30 Bennett, *The Venison Hunters*, pp. 17–18.
31 Philip Holden, *Pack and Rifle*, 1986, p. 74.
32 Jock Fisher, email to Shaun Barnett, 22 January 2012.
33 Ibid.
34 Kelly, *Wild Animal Control Huts*, graph on p. 32.
35 Rex Forrester and Neil Illingworth, *Hunter for Hire*, 1965, p. 53.
36 Ibid.
37 Fisher, email to Shaun Barnett, 22 January 2012.
38 Graeme Caughley, *The Deer Wars: The Story of Deer in New Zealand*, 1983, pp. 101–05.
39 Merv O'Reilly, NZFS report, 9 August 1967, DOC Hokitika archive.
40 Newton McConochie, *You'll Learn No Harm From the Hills*, 1966, pp. 172–74.
41 Patrick J. Grant, *Hawke's Bay: Forests of Yesteryear*, 1996.
42 Kelly, *Wild Animal Control Huts*, p. 17.
43 Pickering, *A Tramper's Journey: Stories from the Back Country of New Zealand*, 2004, p. 137.
44 Ibid., p. 141.
45 AJHR C-3, 1922, p. 7.
46 Although it was established in 1965, Northwest Nelson State Forest Park was not formally gazetted until 1970.
47 *Working Plan Northwest Nelson Forest Park 1965–66 to 1969–70* [Shaun Barnett's copy], p. 39.
48 Kelly, *Wild Animal Control Huts*, table on p. 32.
49 Northwest Nelson State Forest Park Advisory Committee, minutes [Shaun Barnett's copy], 6–7 May 1976, p. 8.
50 Northwest Nelson State Forest Park Advisory Committee, minutes [Shaun Barnett's copy], 21 November 1975, p. 2.
51 Northwest Nelson State Forest Park Advisory Committee, minutes [Shaun Barnett's copy], 21 June 1985, p. 9.
52 Northwest Nelson State Forest Park Advisory Committee, minutes [Shaun Barnett's copy], 26 February 1976, p. 2.
53 Northwest Nelson State Forest Park Advisory Committee, minutes [Shaun Barnett's copy], 17–18 November 1982, p. 4.
54 Robin McNeill, 'Uncle Jacko's Cookery Column', *FMC Bulletin*, August 2007, p. 45; Resene matched the old NZFS livery using their paint 'Sorbus'; *Footnotes* [newsletter of the DOC Wellington Conservancy], 25 June 2006, p. 5.
55 Kelly, *Wild Animal Control Huts*, p. 26.

West Coast Two-bunk Bivouacs

1 Jackie Breen, 'Old Cedar Flat Hut Historic Assessment' [internal report for DOC Hokitika], September 2004, pp. 1–4.
2 Michael Kelly, *Wild Animal Control Huts: A National Heritage Identification Study*, 2007, p. 30.
3 Jock Fisher, pers. comm. with Rob Brown, 11 March 2012.
4 Ron Turner, 'Winter in the Hokitika 1957', accessible online at www.nzdeercullers.org.nz/LiteratureDetail.aspx?Titles=Winter%20in%20 the%20Hokitika%201957.
5 'Winter Operations Hokitika Valley 1957', NZFS File F.S. 90/20 PRF:BMH, Hokitika 5 November 1957, held by ANZ, Christchurch.
6 Jock Fisher, pers. comm. with Rob Brown, 18 June 2011.
7 Turner, 'Winter in the Hokitika 1957'.
8 Fisher, pers. comm. with Rob Brown, 18 June 2011.
9 After finding Whitehorn Spur Biv in a dump, Permolat have restored it and hope to relocate it to a new site.
10 'Scottys Biv', Permolat website, www.remotehuts.co.nz/huts/scottys, accessed 8 March 2012.

11 Glenn Johnston, pers. comm. with Rob Brown, 10 March 2012.
12 'Archive of Huts Removed or Lost', Permolat website, www.remotehuts.co.nz/huts/archive, accessed 10 March 2012.
13 Mark Crompton was involved with snow retention studies in the Browning Range for various water and atmospheric agencies between 1986 and 2004.
14 'Archive of Huts Removed or Lost', Permolat website.
15 Kelly, *Wild Animal Control Huts*, p. 48. (Kelly gives the date as 1970, but it should be 1974.)
16 NZFS archives, DOC Hokitika.

West Coast Four-bunk Huts

1 Jock Fisher, pers. comm. with Rob Brown, 11 March 2012.
2 Jackie Breen, 'Old Cedar Flat Hut Historic Assessment' [internal report for DOC Hokitika], September 2004, p. 4.
3 Jock Fisher, pers. comm. with Rob Brown, 14 June 2011.
4 Breen, 'Old Cedar Flat Hut Historic Assessment', pp. 2–4.
5 1982 Forest Service building stock take, DOC archives, Greymouth.
6 Fisher, pers. comm. with Rob Brown, 11 March 2012.
7 Jock Fisher, pers. comm. with Rob Brown, 18 June 2011.
8 The Department of Lands and Survey built one S81, Castle Rocks Hut, in 1974.

West Coast Six-bunk Huts

1 'Archive of Remote Huts Removed or Lost', Permolat website, www.remotehuts.co.nz/huts/archive, accessed 20 Febraury 2012.
2 Robin Judkins, keynote speech to the Recreation Summit, Te Papa, 2006.
3 A.J. Collett, NZFS report on venison recovery permits for Taramakau and Waitaha, [n.d.], NZFS files, DOC archives, Hokitika.
4 Merv O'Reilly, 'Trial Helicopter Hunting, Hokitika Catchment', file note, 12 June 1968, NZFS files, DOC archives, Hokitika.
5 Glenn Johnston, pers. comm. with Rob Brown, 5 March 2012.
6 Top Toaroha Hut served in an area where cullers previously had only a rock shelter. Jock Fisher recalled that before the hut was built here there was just an old shelter at the Wren Creek hot spring and a dry rock shelter at the head of the valley that was on the true left near the stream that drains the eastern face of Mt Ross (Jock Fisher, pers. comm. with Rob Brown, 5 March 2012).

Kaweka Forest Park NZFS Huts

1 NZFS, minutes of meeting on deer control, head office, Wellington, 5–6 August 1958 [Shaun Barnett's photocopy].
2 These included Kaweka Hut (1936) and Kiwi Saddle Hut (1946), both built by the Heretaunga Tramping Club; and the Old Manson Hut (c. 1950s), the Iron Whare (c. 1870s) and Lawrence Hut (1954).
3 Alan Berry, 'Makahu Track Re-visited', *Pohokura* [Heretaunga Tramping Club newsletter] 229, January 2012, pp. 8–9; Alan Berry, email to Shaun Barnett, 9 February 2012.
4 Michael Kelly, *Wild Animal Control Huts: A National Heritage Identification Study*, 2007, p. 42.
5 Tony Gates, 'Ballard Hut', *FMC Bulletin*, May 2005, p. 20.
6 'ASN Wikibase Occurrence #63552', Aviation Safety Network website, http://aviation-safety.net/wikibase/wiki.php?id=63522, accessed March 2011.
7 February 2006, Makino Hut logbook.
8 NZFS, *Kaweka State Forest Park* [map], 1:100,000, 1st edn, 1981.
9 Ibid.
10 The original Te Puia Lodge, built in 1973, burnt down and was replaced by a second hut of similar design in 1975 (information from Te Puia Lodge logbook, February 2006).

Bobs Hut

1 Jock Fisher, pers. comm. with Rob Brown, 6 March 2012.
2 DOC hut database.

3 Peter Kemp (Nelson Lakes Shuttles), pers. comm. with Rob Brown, 25 September 2010.
4 Ron Turner, pers. comm. with Rob Brown, 19 June 2011.
5 Ibid.; Jock Fisher, email to Rob Brown, 14 June 2011.
6 Andy Dennis, *The Story of Nelson Lakes National Park*, 1984, pp. 94–96.
7 Kemp, pers. comm. with Brown, 25 September 2010.
8 Ibid.

Lake Sumner Forest Park NZFS Huts

1 Ashley Cunningham, 'Lake Sumner: The Making of a Forest Park', *FMC Bulletin*, August 2010, pp. 48–50.
2 NZFS, *A Guide to Lake Sumner Forest Park* [map], 1:100,000, 1st edition, 1982; DOC hut database.
3 Ron Mackie, pers. comm. with Shaun Barnett, 2009. Ron has a slide of the upturned biv taken in 1980.

Sunrise Hut

1 Ashley Cunningham, *Hawke's Bay for the Happy Wanderer*, 1993, p. 151.
2 Matthew Wright, 'Early Huts of the Northeastern Ruahine and Central Wakarara Ranges' [unpublished NZFS report], 1986, pp. 56–57.
3 Wright, 'Early Huts of the Northeastern Ruahine and Central Wakarara Ranges', p. 57.
4 Cunningham, *Hawke's Bay for the Happy Wanderer*, p. 151.
5 Wright, 'Early Huts of the Northeastern Ruahine and Central Wakarara Ranges', p. 62.
6 Barrie E. Atkins, letter to Shaun Barnett, 9 January 2013. The Forest Service also used a Fraemohs design for the research hut at Camp Creek on the West Coast, see p. 325.
7 Barrie E. Atkins, letter to Shaun Barnett, 9 January 2013.
8 Cunningham, *Hawke's Bay for the Happy Wanderer*, p. 151.
9 Sunrise Hut information panel.

Ruahine Forest Park NZFS Huts

1 Matthew Wright, 'Early Huts of the Northeastern Ruahine and Central Wakarara Ranges' [unpublished NZFS report], 1986, pp. 3–4, 17.
2 A.Z., 'The Rebuilding and Opening of Coppermine Hut, 1941', *Ruahine Rambler* [Ruahine Tramping Club newsletter], 1942, p. 2.
3 Ashley Cunningham, *Hawke's Bay for the Happy Wanderer*, 1993, p. 218.
4 Wright, 'Early Huts of the Northeastern Ruahine and Central Wakarara Ranges', pp. 3–4.
5 James Jordan, *At Home in the Hills*, 2002, pp. 106, 122–23; Chris Satherley, pers. comm. with Shaun Barnett, February 2012.
6 Cunningham, *Hawke's Bay for the Happy Wanderer*, p. 175.
7 Chris Cochran, *Top Maropea Hut: Maintenance Plan for the Department of Conservation*, 2009, p. 20.
8 Michael Kelly, *Wild Animal Control Huts: A National Heritage Identification Study*, 2007, p. 44.
9 These were Awatere, Cattle Creek, Kylie Biv, Herricks, Makaretu, McKinnon, Rockslide, Ruahine, Sentry Box, Sparrowhawk, Tarn Biv Taruarau Biv and Upper Makarora. No date is known for the construction of Toka Biv, but it probably took place in this year too.
10 *Pohokura* [Heretaunga Tramping Club newsletter] 87, April 1961, pp. 1–3, quoted in Wright, 'Early Huts of the Northeastern Ruahine and Central Wakarara Ranges', p. 4.
11 Wright, 'Early Huts of the Northeastern Ruahine and Central Wakarara Ranges', pp. 69–70.
12 Cunningham, *Hawke's Bay for the Happy Wanderer*, p. 164.
13 Kelly, *Wild Animal Control Huts*, p. 44.

Lower Gridiron Rock Shelter and Upper Gridiron Hut

1 Max Polglaze, letter to Shaun Barnett, May 2005.
2 These features are depicted in photos of the area taken in the [...] (see, for example, Jim Henderson and Bruce Foster, *Jim Hend[...] People*, 1986, p. 77).

3 Henderson and Foster, *Jim Henderson's People*, p. 75.
4 Polglaze, letter to Shaun Barnett, May 2005.
5 Ibid.
6 Ibid.
7 Max Polglaze, letter to Shaun Barnett, October 2010.
8 Dave Chowdhury, 'Autonomous Max Farewells His Labour of Love in the Bush', *Nelson Evening Mail*, 1988.
9 Polglaze, letter to Shaun Barnett, May 2005.
10 Ibid.
11 Polglaze, letter to Shaun Barnett, October 2010.

NATIONAL PARK BOARDS AND LANDS AND SURVEY HUTS
Huts for the People
1 Trish McCormack, *A History of Surveying and Mountaineering in South Westland*, 1988, p. 15.
2 John Hall-Jones, 'Thomson, John Turnbull', *Dictionary of New Zealand Biography, Te Ara – The Encyclopedia of New Zealand* [website], 2010 (updated 1 September 2010), www.TeAra.govt.nz/en/biographies/1t97/1, accessed 2011.
3 Tongariro National Park Act 1894, No. 55, p. 472.
4 'Forest Conservation: Reports by Commissioners of Crown Lands Dealing with the Preservation of Native Flora and Fauna', AJHR C-13B, 1903, pp. 23, 24.
5 Ibid., p. 24.
6 A.L. Poole (ed.), *New Zealand-American Fiordland Expedition*, 1951, p. 98.
7 R.S. Odell (ed.), *Handbook of the Arthur's Pass National Park: Its History, Tracks, Climbing Routes, Places Names, Geology, Botany*, 1935, p. 20.
8 David Thom, *Heritage: The Parks of the People*, 1987, pp. xvi–xix.
9 New Zealand National Parks and Reserves Rangers Archive [unpublished papers, collated by Geoff Rennison, Takaka], p. 18.
10 Ibid., p. 19.
11 Hugh Barr, 'National Parks', *FMC Bulletin* 62, June 1980, p. 4.
12 Rachel Egerton, 'Huts as Heritage: Clark Hut', *FMC Bulletin*, August 2009, pp. 26–27.
13 Anonymous, pers. comm. with Geoff Spearpoint, March 2012.
14 Mervyn Burke, diary; Dick Ratcliff (ed.), *Hut Wardens' Reunion* [booklet], 2004, p. 6.
15 John Purey-Cust, 'Ranger Who Could Turn His Hand to Anything: Raymond William Cleland 1920–2004', *New Zealand Journal of Forestry*, November 2004, p. 45.
16 Mt Aspiring National Park Board, *Draft Review Management Plan 1980*, 1980, Lands and Survey, Otago, accompanying map of huts.
17 W.P. Packard, 'The First Four Years', *NZAJ* 18(46), 1959, p. 156.
18 H.E. Connor (ed.), *Mt Cook National Park Handbook*, 1962, p. 54.
19 New Zealand National Parks and Reserves Rangers Archive, p. 223.
20 NZMS, *Mt Cook and Westland National Parks Map*, 180, 1:100,000 4th edn, 1973, Lands and Survey.
21 NZMS, *Arthur's Pass National Park* [map], 194, 1:80,000, 4th edn, 1971, Lands and Survey.
22 Andy Dennis, *Arthur's Pass National Park: The First Fifty Years 1929–1979*, 1979, p. 17.
23 W.B. Beaven, 'The Crow Hut', *NZAJ* 27(45), 1958, p. 449.
24 Dan Dungan (ed.), *Rotoiti Recollections*, 1999, p. 141.
25 NZMS, *Nelson Lakes National Park Map*, 164, 1:100,000, 2nd edition, 1962, Lands and Survey.
26 Bruce Postill, email to Shaun Barnett, 24 May 2010.
27 New Zealand National Parks and Reserves Rangers Archive, p. 8.
28 Ibid., p. 15.
29 NZMS, *Abel Tasman National Park Map*, 183, 1:80,000, 4th edition, 1984, Lands and Survey.
30 New Zealand National Parks and Reserves Rangers Archive, p. 154.
31 Ibid., p. 155.
32 NZMS, *Tongariro National Park Map*, 150, 1:80,000 3rd edition, 1969, Lands and Survey.
33 New Zealand National Parks and Reserves Rangers Archive, p. 157.
34 Relations in Tongariro National Park between NZFS and Lands and Survey, both based at Turangi, were good. At the same time that Lands and Survey adopted Lockwood huts at Tongariro, the NZFS did the same for huts in Kaimanawa Forest Park (Ray Goldring (ex-NZFS ranger), pers. comm. with Shaun Barnett, 2004).
35 New Zealand National Parks and Reserves Rangers Archive, p. 199.
36 Ibid., p. 195.
37 Ibid., p. 200.
38 Ibid.
39 National Parks Authority, *Buildings and Accommodation: General Policy for National Parks*, National Parks Authority, Wellington, 1983, p. 46.
40 Neil Clifton, *The Central Southern Alps Crown Land Management Strategy*, Lands and Survey, Hokitika 1981.
41 Ted Brennan, pers. comm. with Geoff Spearpoint, 22 September 2011.

Carrington Hut
1 Carrington Hut logbook, Canterbury Mountaineering Club archives.
2 John Wilson, 'Building a Hut, Builds a Club', *Canterbury Mountaineer* 63, 2004–05, p. 72.
3 Chris Maclean, *John Pascoe*, 2003, p. 33.
4 Gerald Nanson, 'Building the Original Carrington Hut', *Canterbury Mountaineer* Jubilee Edition, 1974–75, p. 36.
5 Stuart Meares, 'Easter Camp at Carrington Hut', *Canterbury Mountaineer* Jubilee Edition, 1974–75, p. 25.
6 Cedric Turner, 'Carrington Hut', *Canterbury Mountaineer* Jubilee Edition, 1974–75, p. 35.
7 Wilson, 'Building a Hut, Builds a Club', p. 76.
8 Jack Ede, *I've Lived Another Year: Adventure and Survival in the New Zealand Outdoors*, 2004, p. 282.
9 Ibid., p. 283.
10 Wilson, 'Building a Hut, Builds a Club', pp. 74–76.
11 John Charles, pers. comm. with Rob Brown, August 2010.

Blue Lake Hut, George Lyon Hut and John Tait Hut
1 Dan Dungan (ed.), *Rotoiti Recollections*, 1999, p. 149.
2 Tom Young, 'Ella Hut Becomes George Lyon Hut', *FMC Bulletin* March 2005, pp. 16–17.
3 Dungan (ed.), *Rotoiti Recollections*, p. 137.
4 Bruce Postill, email to Shaun Barnett, 24 May 2010.
5 Ibid.
6 Ibid.
7 Ibid.
8 Les Molloy and Craig Potton, *New Zealand's Wilderness Heritage*, 2007, p. 173.
9 Dungan (ed.), *Rotoiti Recollections*, pp. 49–50.
10 Ibid., p. 51.
11 Ibid., pp. 51–52; Bruce Postill, email to Shaun Barnett, 5 August 2010.
12 In an amazing feat of physical prowess, Lands and Survey ranger Tom Patterson carried this in on his back from Lake Rotoiti.
13 Postill, email to Shaun Barnett, 24 May 2010.
14 Ibid.
15 Ibid.
16 Ibid.

Mintaro Hut
1 Rebecca Reid, 'The Finest Walk in the World: An Historical Glimpse into a Century of Foot Travel on the Milford Track. Part 3' [interpretation document prepared for DOC, Milford Track huts], 1998, DOC Te Anau, p. 9.
2 William Anderson, *Mintaro: Milford Track*, 1978, p. 13.
3 Reid, 'The Finest Walk in the World: An Historical Glimpse into a Century of Foot Travel on the Milford Track. Part 2', p. 4.
4 Ibid., p. 4.
5 'The Milford Track', *FMC Bulletin* 20, November 1964, pp. 5–8.
6 *Southland Times*, 17 April 1917.
7 Rebecca Reid, interview with John and Robyn Armstrong in Dunedin, 24 April 1998, for DOC Te Anau.
8 Ibid.
9 *Southland Times*, 17 April 1917.
10 Ibid.
11 Ibid.
12 Ibid.

Lake Roe Hut
1 Ross Kerr (DOC Te Anau), pers. comm. with Rob Brown, 11 April 2012.
2 Ross Kerr (DOC Te Anau), pers. comm. with Rob Brown, 26 April 2012.
3 Ibid.

Edwards Hut
1 John Wilson, 'CMC Bivvies in the Arthur's Pass National Park', *Canterbury Mountaineer* 66, 2011, p. 72.
2 H. Walker, 'The Edwards Bivouac', *Canterbury Mountaineer* 10, 1941, pp. 40–41.
3 Wilson, 'CMC Bivvies in the Arthur's Pass National Park', p. 73.
4 John Charles, pers. comm. with Rob Brown, August 2010.
5 Ibid.; Tony Perrett, email to Craig Potton Publishing, 3 December 2014.

Gardiner Hut
1 A.F. Pearson, 'Further Climbs in the Hooker', *NZAJ* 6(22), 1935, p. 92.
2 Annette Walker and Michael Benn, 'Katie Gardiner: A Memoir', *NZAJ* 31, 1978, p. 111.
3 Photo caption, *NZAJ* 31, 1978, p. 108, quoted from an unpublished interview with Vic Williams by Nancy Cawley, 1977.
4 'Club and General Notes: Gardiner Hut-Upper Hooker Valley', *NZAJ* 6(22), 1935, p. 167.
5 Ibid., p. 166.
6 Barrie Thomas, transcript of taped interview, June 2008, New Zealand National Parks and Reserves Rangers Archive [unpublished papers, collated by Geoff Rennison, Takaka], p. 123.
7 Mal Clarbrough, 'Mountain (Barrel–Silo) Huts, Aoraki/Mt Cook National Park', unpublished document.
8 Ian Whitehouse, pers. comm. with Geoff Spearpoint, 27 April 2012.
9 Ian Whitehouse, pers. comm. with Geoff Spearpoint, 8 March 2012.

Top Forks Huts
1 Top Forks Hut logbook, 8 February 2009.
2 A local resident, 'Jumboland – Wilkin Valley', *NZAJ* 10(30), 1943, p. 197.
3 W.S. Gilkison and A.R Craigie, 'Wilkin Wanderings', *NZAJ* 10(29), 1942, p. 137.
4 'The Jumboland Hut', *NZAJ* 10(29), 1942, p. 197.
5 Alan Duncan, pers. comm. with Geoff Spearpoint, 22 April 2012.
6 John Trotter, pers. comm. with Geoff Spearpoint, March 2012.
7 Paul Hellebrekers, email to Geoff Spearpoint, 10 April 2012.
8 Paul Hellebrekers, pers. comm. with Geoff Spearpoint, 4 April 2012.

Shelter Rock Hut
1 W. Scott Gilkison, *Peaks, Packs and Mountain Tracks*, 1940, p. 35.
2 Peter Chandler (ed.), *Moir's Guide Book, Northern Section*, 1961, p. 11.
3 Mt Aspiring National Park Board, *Draft Review Management Plan 1980*, 1980, Lands and Survey, Otago, Appendix 11, Recommendation 5, p. 77.
4 'Club and General Notes', *NZAJ* 7(24), 1937, p. 121.
5 S.A. Wiren, 'Dart Headwaters', *NZAJ* 7(25), 1938, p. 224.
6 Richard Kennett, notes in Dick Ratcliff (ed.), *40 Years of Hut Wardening in the Mt Aspiring Area* [booklet written for hut wardens' reunion 2004], 2004, p. 13.
7 Richard Kennett, email to Geoff Spearpoint, 27 September 2010.

DEPARTMENT OF CONSERVATION HUTS
New Huts, Old Responsibilities
1. Michael Roche, *The History of New Zealand Forestry*, 1990, p. 373.
2. 'A Rocky Start' in Bernie Napp (ed.), *A Short History of the Department of Conservation: 1987–2007* (online DOC publication), www.doc.govt.nz/publications/about-doc/a-short-history-of-doc/a-rocky-start, accessed February 2012.
3. Hugh Barr, 'DOC Hut Fee Changes', *FMC Bulletin*, September 1989, p. 19.
4. Nigel Parrott, 'Great Walks', *FMC Bulletin* 111, October 1992, p. 20.
5. 'FMC Supports Routeburn Hut Booking System', *FMC Bulletin*, August 1995, p. 7.
6. 'A New Image' in Bernie Napp (ed.), *A Short History of the Department of Conservation: 1987–2007* (online DOC publication), www.doc.govt.nz/publications/about-doc/a-short-history-of-doc/a-new-image, February 2012.
7. Judge G.S. Noble, *Commission of Inquiry into the Collapse of a Viewing Platform at Cave Creek near Punakaiki on the West Coast*, Department of Internal Affairs, Wellington, 1995, p. 93.
8. 'Cave Creek and Afterwards', in Bernie Napp (ed.), *A Short History of the Department of Conservation: 1987–2007* (online DOC publication), www.doc.govt.nz/publications/about-doc/a-short-history-of-doc/cave-creek-and-afterwards, February 2012.
9. Alison Corich, 'What's Happening with Recreation Facilities', *FMC Bulletin*, March 1998, p. 23.
10. Robert Cross, 'New Year's Insanitary', *Dominion Post*, 24 January 2004.
11. Arnold Heine, 'DOC Structures Under Review', *FMC Bulletin*, August 1997, p. 7.
12. 'Hut Service Standards – 2004 Revision(1) QD code: VC/1199' [internal DOC document], p. 12.
13. John Henzell, 'Popular Huts Avalanche Death Traps', *The Press*, 16 August 2003, p. 1.
14. Adapted from articles by Shaun Barnett in *Wilderness* magazines.
15. Steve Sutton, 'Getting People Involved', *FMC Bulletin*, May 2004, p. 16.
16. Steve Sutton, email to Geoff Spearpoint, 1 June 2004.
17. 'Hut Procurement Manual for Backcountry Huts', DOC report DOCDM-417837, Wellington.
18. 'Huts Built by DOC', DOC spreadsheet DOCDM-929698, Wellington (this shows when and where DOC huts were built).
19. David Henson, 'The Lake Taylor Hut', *FMC Bulletin*, March 1995, p. 35.
20. Andy Dennis, 'Opening of Kahurangi National Park', *FMC Bulletin*, August 1996, p. 4; Waimea Tramping Club, *Balloon Hut* [booklet], 1996, pp. 19–23.
21. 'DOC Hut and Track News', *FMC Bulletin*, March 2002, p. 25.
22. Ibid., p. 31.
23. 'DOC Hut and Track News', *FMC Bulletin*, June 2003, p. 18.
24. 'Notice Board', *FMC Bulletin*, August 2005, p. 13.
25. Graham Hancox, 'Fiordland Earthquake', *FMC Bulletin*, November 2004, p. 24.
26. 'Martins Bay Hut Open Again After Renovations', *FMC Bulletin*, August 2009, p. 19.
27. 'DMF Overview', DOC report DOCDM-862311, Wellington, November 2011, cover.

Leitch's Hut
1. Ray Scrimgeour (DOC Te Kuiti Area Manager), pers. comm. with Shaun Barnett, November 2010.
2. Ray Scrimgeour, email to Shaun Barnett, November 2010.
3. *Whareorino Conservation Area* [brochure], DOC Te Kuiti, December 2007, p. 1, accessible online at http://csl.doc.govt.nz/upload/documents/parks-and-recreation/places-to-visit/waikato/whareorino.pdf.

Syme Hut
1. A.B. Scanlan, *Egmont: The Story of a Mountain*, 1961, pp. 61–63.
2. The Egmont National Park Board had built both Holly (1900) and Kahui (1903) huts earlier in the century, but no huts yet existed high on the mountain (see Scanlan, *Egmont*, 1961, p. 106).
3. 'Saga of Syme Hut', Mt Egmont Alpine Club archives, courtesy of Alan Kerrisk, Hawera.
4. Scanlan, *Egmont*, 1961, p. 105.
5. Ron Lambert, 'Syme, Roderick', *Dictionary of New Zealand Biography*. Te Ara – The Encyclopedia of New Zealand [website], 2010 (updated 1 September 2010), www.TeAra.govt.nz/en/biographies/4s59, accessed 31 March 2012.
6. 'Saga of Syme Hut', Mt Egmont Alpine Club archives.
7. R. Syme, 'Notes Supplied at Request of Mr Keith Anderson, Dawson Falls, for Use in Publicity Brochure', 9 February 1976, Mt Egmont Alpine Club archives, courtesy of Alan Kerrisk, Hawera; 'Saga of Syme Hut', Mt Egmont Alpine Club archives.
8. Syme Hut information panel.
9. Other huts built by DOC over the summer of 1987–88 were Kelman Hut (Aoraki/Mount Cook National Park) and Mitre Flats (opened in April 1988 in Tararua Forest Park).
10. 'New Syme Hut Opened', *FMC Bulletin*, June 1988, pp. 6–8.

Zekes Hut
1. Tim Gilbertson, File Note, PAR-07-05-6602, DOC Mangaweka Field Centre.
2. Alison Dorrian (DOC Mangaweka), email to Shaun Barnett, 1 November 2010.
3. 'Zekes Hut Track', DOC website, http://www.doc.govt.nz/parks-and-recreation/tracks-and-walks/central-north-island/turangi-taupo/zekes-hut-track, accessed April 2012.
4. Shaun Barnett, 'The Remote Ruahine', *Forest & Bird*, November 2004, pp. 12–15.

Tarn Ridge Hut
1. According to DOC's hut database, the first three huts built by the department in the Tararua Range were Mitre Flats (1988), followed by Waitewaewae (1991) and Mangahao Flats (1992).
2. Chris Maclean, *Tararua: The Story of a Mountain Range*, 1994, p. 242.
3. 'Body of Missing Deerstalker Found', *Wairarapa Times-Age*, 6 April 1959.
4. According to the Dorset Ridge Hut logbook, the original hut was built here in 1955, with a second erected in 1968 by the NZFS at its present location lower down Dorset Ridge. The Horowhenua Section of the NZDA undertook an extensive renovation of this NZFS hut in 2008.
5. 'Body of Missing Deerstalker Found', *Wairarapa Times-Age*, 6 April 1959; 'Deerstalker Buried in Tararuas', *Wairarapa Times-Age*, 9 April 1959; 'The Blatchford Search', *Tararua Tramper* [newsletter of the Tararua Tramping Club], July 1959, pp. 4–5.
6. Tararua Forest Park Advisory Committee, newsletter No. 9, February 1961, p. 1; John Rhodes, pers. comm. with Shaun Barnett, 20 April 2012.

Brewster Hut
1. John Ombler, pers. comm. with Geoff Spearpoint, March 2012.
2. Paddy Gordon, pers. comm. with Geoff Spearpoint, 22 April 2012.
3. Paul Hellebrekers, pers. comm. with Geoff Spearpoint, 4 April 2012.
4. Ibid.

Maungahuka Hut
1. Athol Geddes, 'Maungahuka Hut' [letter to editor], *FMC Bulletin*, August 2006, pp. 8–9.
2. Ibid.
3. John Rhodes, 'A Life in the Hills. Athol Geddes Talks to John Rhodes', *FMC Bulletin*, May 2004, p. 27.
4. John McCann email to Shaun Barnett, 30 October 2012.
5. Geddes, 'Maungahuka Hut', pp. 8–9.
6. 'New Huts Highlight Tararua's Assets' [DOC press release], 10 May 2006, accessible online at www.scoop.co.nz/stories/SC0605/S00025/new-huts-highlight-tararuas-assets.htm.

Woolshed Creek Hut
1. A current proposal aims to add the Mt Somers area to Hakatere Conservation Park.
2. Constance Grey, *Quiet with the Hills: The Life of Alfred Edward Peache of Mount Somers*, 1970, p. 43.
3. The retired part of the run was absorbed into forestry block 32, which included all the forests on the lower slopes of Mt Somers.
4. David Howden, pers. comm. with Rob Brown, 2 April 2012.
5. Ibid.
6. Ibid.
7. The Mt Somers Walkway officially became the Mt Somers Track in 2008.

HUTS AS MONUMENTS
Memories in the Wilderness
1. Arnold and Jan Heine, email to Shaun Barnett, 7 August 2009; Arnold and Jan Heine, email to Shaun Barnett, 23 April 2012.
2. 'History', Wanganui Tramping Club website, www.wanganuitrampingclub.org.nz/history, accessed 17 April 2012.
3. Paul Hersey, *High Misadventure: New Zealand Mountaineering Tragedies and Survival Stories*, 1990, p. 58.
4. Hersey, *High Misadventure*, pp. 57–60.
5. Carl Walrond, *Survive! Remarkable Tales from the New Zealand Outdoors*, 2008, p. 130.
6. Hersey, *High Misadventure*, p. 59.
7. 'History', Wanganui Tramping Club website.
8. Northwest Nelson State Forest Park Advisory Committee, minutes [Shaun Barnett's copy], 15–16 March 1977, p. 6. Oliver Druce, email to Shaun Barnett, 10 May 2012.
9. Druce, email to Shaun Barnett, 10 May 2012.
10. Ibid.
11. Heine, email to Shaun Barnett, 23 April 2012.
12. B.A. Fineran, 'Confinement at Three Johns', *Canterbury Mountaineer* 10(33), 1963–64, p. 26, quoted in Walrond, *Survive!*, pp. 130–31.
13. Hersey, *High Misadventure*, pp. 54–55.
14. Barry Briggs, 'Thee Johns Hut Plus Four', *Tramping and Mountaineering* [annual of the Wellington Tramping and Mountaineering Club], 1978, pp. 42–43, quoted in Walrond, *Survive!*, p. 130.
15. Shaun Barnett, 'Rest in Peace, Angle Knob Hut', *Wilderness*, December 2011, pp. 26–31.
16. Ian and Paul Dawe, Barker Hut logbook, 28 December 1995, recorded in Shaun Barnett, 'Tramping Diary 7 (November 1999–May 2001)', p. 46.

Colin Todd Hut
1. H.J. Harrington, 'Colin Todd' [obituary], *NZAJ* 16(42), 1955, p. 217.
2. B.F. Davidson and G.W. Goodyear, 'The Colin Todd Memorial Hut', *NZAJ* 18(47), 1960, p. 372.
3. Chas Tanner, 'The New Colin Todd Hut', *NZAJ* 1996, p. 85.

Hunters Hut
1. Erick Brenstrum, *The New Zealand Weather Book*, 1998.
2. Ibid., p. 51.
3. Ibid.
4. Hunters Hut information panel.
5. Daegal Braia, Maitland Hut logbook, 16 March 1995.
6. Ben Gibbs, letter to Shaun Barnett, January 2012.
7. 'Hunter's Memorial Hut', *Wilderness*, May 1997, p. 9.

Barker Hut
1 'Barker Memorial Cross', *Canterbury Mountaineer* 65, 2009, p. 74.
2 John Wilson, 'Barker Hut', *Canterbury Mountaineer* 64, 2007, p. 65.
3 Ibid.
4 Ibid., p. 67. The hut was originally called Neville Barker Memorial Hut, but this was later shortened to Barker Memorial Hut and then just Barker Hut.
5 Wilson, 'Barker Hut', p. 68.
6 Ibid., p. 65.
7 The only other hut built like this was the third Pioneer Hut.
8 'The Neville Barker Memorial Hut', Canterbury Mountaineering Club website, www.cmc.net.nz/huts/barker_hut, accessed 24 February 2012.

Esquilant Bivouac
1 A.R. Craigie, 'William Robert Esquilant [obituary]', *NZAJ* 12(34), 1947, p. 126.
2 A.R. Craigie, 'A High Hut – The Esquilant Bivouac', *NZAJ* 14(38), 1951, p. 106.
3 Paul Powell, *Just Where Do You Think You've Been?*, 1970, pp. 168–78.
4 Ibid., p. 178.
5 Warren Herrick, 'Esquilant Bivvy Reborn', *NZAJ* 42, 1989, pp. 125–28.
6 Ibid., p. 128.

Park Morpeth Hut
1 Brian Wyn Irwin, 'The Park-Morpeth Search, January 1929', *Canterbury Mountaineer* 44, 1975, p. 159.
2 Bill Heinz, 'An Early Crossing of Browning Pass', *Canterbury Mountaineer* 44, 1975, p. 52.
3 Colin Burrows, pers. comm. with Geoff Spearpoint, 16 March 2012.
4 Major Geoff Charles, 'Exercise Frozen Fijian', *Canterbury Mountaineer* 49, 1981, p. 72.
5 Ibid.
6 Brian Fineran, 'The Wilberforce', *Canterbury Mountaineer* 64, 2007, p. 47.
7 Ibid., p. 48.
8 Ibid., p. 50.

Manson-Nicholls Hut
1 Grant Hunter, 'Reflections at Lake Daniells', *Wilderness*, December 1999, p. 33.
2 Gary Swarbrick, 'Manson-Nicholls Memorial Hut', in Stella Woodham (ed.), *Christchurch Tramping Club Fiftieth Anniversary, 1932–1982*, p. 79.
3 Ibid., p. 80.

SCIENCE HUTS
Research in the Mountains and Bush
1 Peter McKelvey, *Steepland Forests: A Historical Perspective of Protection Forest in New Zealand*, 1995, pp. 46–47, 211.
2 Graham Bishop and Jane Forsyth, *Vanishing Ice: An Introduction to Glaciers Based on a Study of the Dart Glacier*, 1988.
3 Ross Kerr, *A Chronology of the Tararua and Rimutaka Ranges*, 2006, pp. 47–50.
4 Robert Brockie, *A Living New Zealand Forest*, 1992, p. 7.
5 McKelvey, *Steepland Forests*, p. 133.
6 Pararaki Hut information panel, Haurangi Forest Park.
7 Ian Payton (Landcare Research), pers. comm. with Shaun Barnett, 10 April 2012.
8 Michael Kelly, *Biodiversity Huts, Fiordland: Historic Heritage Assessment*, 2010, pp. 1–21.
9 These are Te Au and Robin Saddle huts. Junction Burn Hut is a public hut, not a biodiversity one, and so is freely accessible year-round (see 'Fiordland National Park Management Plan', DOC Invercargill, 2007, pp. 139–41).
10 Glenn Johnston, comment posted on 'Jollie Brook Hut', New Zealand Tramper website, http://tramper.co.nz/?5398, 9 August 2010, accessed 11 April 2012.

Ivory Lake Hut
1 This account of Ivory Lake Hut was condensed by Rob Brown from notes written by, and personal communication with, Trevor Chinn. While the hut was always known as Ivory Glacier Hut by the scientists, over the years it has become more commonly known as Ivory Lake Hut.
2 Douglas quote as related by Trevor Chinn.
3 At nearly 1400 metres, Ivory Lake Hut is probably the country's highest SF70, a design more suited for a maximum altitude of just above the bushline.

Cupola Hut
1 Dan Dungan, *Rotoiti Recollections*, 1999, p. 32.
2 John Flux, 'Cupola Hut', *FMC Bulletin*, November 2007, p. 20; Tom Paterson, letter to Shaun Barnett, 16 August 2010.
3 Flux, 'Cupola Hut', p. 20.
4 Paterson, letter to Shaun Barnett, 16 August 2010.
5 Ibid.
6 Ibid.
7 Flux, 'Cupola Hut', p. 20.
8 Bruce Postill, email to Shaun Barnett, 21 May 2010.
9 Probably in 1982 (Bruce Postill, email to Shaun Barnett, 26 August 2010).

Dominie Biv
1 Ashley Cunningham, letter to Shaun Barnett, 1 September 2010.
2 Ashley Cunningham, 'Mavis Davidson', *FMC Bulletin*, June 2009, p. 60.
3 Mavis Davidson and Rodney Hewitt, *The Mountains of New Zealand*, 1954.
4 Ashley Cunningham, *Hawke's Bay for the Happy Wanderer*, 1993, p. 99.
5 Cunningham, 'Mavis Davidson', p. 59.
6 Cunningham, letter to Shaun Barnett, 1 September 2010.
7 Cunningham, *Hawke's Bay for the Happy Wanderer*, p. 98.
8 A. Cunningham, *Headwaters of the Tutaekuri Catchment*, Forest Research Institute Technical Paper 62, 1974, p. 26.

Caswell Sound Hut
1 A.L. Poole (ed.), *New Zealand-American Fiordland Expedition*, 1951, p. 7.
2 Ross Galbreath, *Working for Wildlife: A History of the New Zealand Wildlife Service*, 1993, p. 68.
3 Ibid., p. 68.
4 Poole (ed.), *New Zealand-American Fiordland Expedition*, p. 10.

Select Bibliography

BOOKS AND REPORTS

Acland, L.G.D. 1975. *The Early Canterbury Runs*, 4th edition, Whitcoulls, Christchurch.

Adams, Grace. 1968. *Jack's Hut*, A.H. & A.W. Reed, Wellington.

Alack, Frank. 1963. *Guide Aspiring*, Oswald-Sealy, Auckland.

Anderson, Johannes C. 1916. *Jubilee History of South Canterbury*, Whitcombe & Tombs, Christchurch.

Anderson, Robyn. 1996. *Goldmining Legislation and Policy*. Rangahaua Whanui Report. Waitangi Tribunal, Wellington.

Anderson, William. 1971. *Milford Trails*, A.H. & A.W. Reed, Wellington.

Anderson, William. 1978. *Mintaro: Milford Track*, Craigs Printing, Invercargill.

Bain, Pam. 2008. *Conservation of Ellis Hut: A Practical Workshop on Conservation Skills*, 2nd edition, DOC, Napier.

Banwell, Bruce D. 1966. *Wapiti in New Zealand*, A.H. & A.W. Reed, Wellington.

Barnett, Shaun. 2008. *North Island Weekend Tramps*, 2nd edition, Craig Potton Publishing, Nelson.

Barnett, Shaun; Brown, Rob. 2010. *Classic Tramping in New Zealand*. Craig Potton Publishing, Nelson.

Bathgate, D.A. 1970. *Yesterday (Inanahi)*, Hart Printing House, Hastings.

Baughan, B.E. 1910. *Snow Kings of the Southern Alps*, Whitcombe & Tombs, Christchurch.

Baughan, Blanche Edith. 1916. *Studies in New Zealand Scenery*, Whitcombe & Tombs, Christchurch.

Beckett, Tom. 1978. *The Mountains of Erewhon*, A.H. & A.W. Reed, Wellington.

Belich, James. 1996. *Making Peoples*, Penguin, Auckland.

Bennett, Mike. 1979. *The Venison Hunters*, A.H. & A.W. Reed, Wellington.

Best, Elsdon. 1934. *The Maori as He Was: A Brief Account of Life as it Was in Pre-European Days*, Dominion Museum, Wellington.

Bird, Warren. 1998. *Viaducts Against the Sky: The Story of Port Craig*, Craigs Printing, Invercargill.

Bishop, Graham; Forsyth, Jane. 1988. *Vanishing Ice: An Introduction to Glaciers Based on a Study of the Dart Glacier*, John McIndoe and DSIR New Zealand Geological Survey, Dunedin.

Boniface, N. 2007. *50 Years of Masterton Tramping Club, 1957–2007*, Masterton Tramping Club, Masterton.

Bowie, Nan. 1969. *Mick Bowie: The Hermitage Years*, A.H. & A.W. Reed, Wellington.

Boyd, Stuart. 1982. *The First 50 Years: A History of the Otago Ski Club Inc.*, Otago Ski Club, Dunedin.

Bradshaw, Julia. 2007. *Miners in the Clouds: A Hundred Years of Scheelite Mining at Glenorchy*, Lakes District Museum, Arrowtown.

Breen, Jackie. 2004. *Old Cedar Flat Hut*, DOC, Hokitika.

Breen, Jackie. 2007. *Copland Track Heritage Assessment and Baseline Inspection Report*, DOC, Hokitika.

Brenstrum, Erick. 1998. *The New Zealand Weather Book*, Craig Potton Publishing, Nelson.

Brereton, C.R. 1947. *No Roll of Drums*, A.H. & A.W. Reed, Wellington.

Brockie, Robert. 1992. *A Living New Zealand Forest*, David Bateman, Auckland.

Burdon, Brian. 1993. *Of Mountains, Men and Deer*, Halcyon Press, Auckland.

Burrell, Ray. 1981. *Fifty Years of Mountain Federation: Federated Mountain Clubs of New Zealand 1931–1981*, Federated Mountain Clubs, Wellington.

Butler, Samuel. 1863. *A First Year in Canterbury Settlement*, Longman, Roberts & Green, London.

Capper, Dave (ed.). 1968. *Impressions of a Tramping Club 1947–1968*. Wellington Tramping and Mountaineering Club, Wellington.

Caughley, Graeme. 1983. *The Deer Wars: The Story of Deer in New Zealand*, Heinemann, Auckland.

Chandler, Peter (ed.). 1961 *Moir's Guide Book, Northern Section*, 2nd edition, New Zealand Alpine Club, Christchurch.

Chapple, Geoff. 2011. *Te Araroa: A Walking Guide to New Zealand's Long Trail*, Random House, Auckland.

Cochran, Chris. 1994. *Old Manson's Hut Conservation Report*, DOC, Hawke's Bay.

Cochran, Chris. 1999. *Bealey Spur Hut, Arthur's Pass National Park: Conservation Report*, DOC Canterbury Conservancy, Christchurch.

Cochran, Chris. 1999. *Urquharts Hut, Craigieburn Forest Park: Conservation Report*, DOC Canterbury Conservancy, Christchurch.

Cochran, Chris. 2006. *Hideaway Hut, Camp Creek, Ahuriri: Conservation Report*, DOC Canterbury Conservancy, Christchurch.

Cochran, Chris. 2009. *Top Maropea Hut: Maintenance Plan for the Department of Conservation*, DOC, Wanganui.

Cochran, Chris; Breen, Jackie. 2006. *Slaty Creek Hut, Ahaura Catchment, West Coast: Conservation Plan*, DOC Mawheranui Area Office, Greymouth.

Cochran, Chris; Breen, Jackie. 2007. *Ranger's Hut, Landsborough, West Coast: Conservation Plan*, DOC South Westland/Weheka Area Office, Fox Glacier.

Connor, H.E. (ed.). 1962. *Mt Cook National Park Handbook*, 3rd edition, Mt Cook National Park Board, Christchurch.

Crozier, Anita. 2001. *Beyond the Southern Lakes: The Explorations of W.G. Grave*, 2nd edition, Reed, Auckland.

Crump, Barry. 1960. *A Good Keen Man*, A.H. & A.W. Reed, Wellington.

Crump, Barry. 1992. *The Life and Times of a Good Keen Man: An Autobiography*, Hodder Moa Beckett, Auckland.

Cunningham, A. 1974. *Headwaters of the Tutaekuri Catchment*, Forest Research Institute Technical Paper 62, NZFS, Wellington.

Cunningham, Ashley. 1991. *Sheila, Happy Wanderer*, Ashley Cunningham, Napier.

Cunningham, Ashley. 1993. *Hawke's Bay for the Happy Wanderer*, 2nd edition, Ashley Cunningham, Napier.

Davidson, Mavis; Hewitt, Rodney. 1954. *The Mountains of New Zealand*, A.H. & A.W. Reed, Wellington.

Dawber, Carol. 2000. *Bainham: A History*, River Press, Picton.

Dennis, Andy. 1979. *Arthur's Pass National Park: The First Fifty Years 1929–1979*, Department of Lands and Survey/Arthur's Pass National Park Board, Christchurch.

Dennis, Andy. 1984. *The Story of Nelson Lakes National Park*, Department of Lands and Survey/Nelson Lakes National Park Board, Nelson.

Dennis, Andy. 1990. *A Park for all Seasons: The Story of Abel Tasman National Park*, DOC, Nelson.

Department of Conservation. 1991. *Kaweka Forest Park, Conservation Management Plan*, DOC, Napier.

Department of Conservation. 1997. *The Wangapeka Track, Kahurangi National Park*, DOC, Nelson.

Department of Conservation. 2001. *Chancellor Hut Conservation Plan*, DOC.

Department of Conservation. 2007. *Whareorino Conservation Area*, DOC Maniapoto Area Office, Te Kuiti.

Diggle, Lynton; Diggle, Edith; Gordon, Keith. 2007. *Shipwrecks of New Zealand: Over 200 Years of Disasters at Sea*, 8th edition, Hodder Moa, Auckland.

Duncan, Alfred. 1888 [reprinted 1964]. *The Wakatipians*, Lakes District Centennial Museum, Arrowtown.

Dungan, Dan (ed.). 1999. *Rotoiti Recollections*, 2nd edition, St Arnaud Community Association, St Arnaud.

Dyne, Dudley D. 1969. *Famous New Zealand Murders*, Collins, Auckland.

Ede, Jack. 2004. *I've Lived Another Year: Adventure and Survival in the New Zealand Outdoors*, Caxton Press, Christchurch.

Elder, John. 1930. *Goldseekers and Bushrangers in New Zealand*, Blackie & Son, Glasgow.

Eldred-Grigg, Stevan. 1980. *A Southern Gentry*. Heinemann Reed, Auckland.

Eldred-Grigg, Stevan. 1982. *A New History of Canterbury*. John McIndoe, Auckland.

Eldred-Grigg, Stevan. 2008. *Diggers, Hatters and Whores: The Story of the New Zealand Gold Rushes*, Random House, Auckland.

Erb, Wayne. 2007. *Auckland University Tramping Club, Jubilee History 1932–2007*, Auckland University Tramping Club, Auckland.

Farmer, Allan. 1994. *The Best Job Ever (a Life of Hunting)*, Halcyon Press, Auckland.

Forbes, Stan; McNab, Ian. 1986. *Alpine Sports: 55 Years of an Auckland Mountain Club 1929–1984*, Alpine Sports Club, Auckland.

Forrester, Rex; Illingworth, Neil. 1965. *Hunter for Hire*, A.H. & A.W. Reed, Wellington.

Forrester, Rex; Illingworth, Neil. 1973 (2nd edition). *Hunting in New Zealand*, A.H. & A.W. Reed, Wellington.

Francis, Ken. 1983. *Wildlife Ranger: My Years in the New Zealand Outdoors*, Whitcoulls, Christchurch.

Galbreath, Ross. 1993. *Working for Wildlife: A History of the New Zealand Wildlife Service*, Bridget Williams Books/Historical Branch, Department of Internal Affairs, Wellington.

Gallagher, Rhian. 2010. *A Feeling for Daylight: The Photographs of Jack Adamson*, South Canterbury Museum, Timaru.

Gallas, F.E. 1977. *Land Search and Rescue*, Federated Mountain Clubs of New Zealand, Wellington.

Gilkison, Robert. 1930. *Early Days in Central Otago*, Whitcombe & Tombs, Christchurch.

Gilkison, W. Scott. 1940 *Peaks, Packs and Mountain Tracks*, Whitcombe & Tombs, Auckland.

Gilkison, W. Scott. 1951. *Aspiring*, Whitcombe & Tombs, Christchurch.

Gilkison, W. Scott. 1957. *Earnslaw*, Whitcombe & Tombs, Christchurch.

Gilkison W. Scott; Hamilton, A.H. 1948. *Moir's Guide*, 2nd edition, New Zealand Alpine Club, Whitcombe & Tombs, Dunedin.

Graham, Alec; Wilson, Jim. 1983 *Uncle Alec and the Grahams of Franz Josef*, John McIndoe, Dunedin.

Graham, J.C. 1963. *Ruapehu: Tribute to a Mountain*, A.H. & A.W. Reed, Wellington.

Grant, Patrick J. 1996. *Hawke's Bay: Forests of Yesteryear*, Patrick Grant, Havelock North.

Green, W.S. 1883. *The High Alps of New Zealand*, MacMillan, London.

Greig, B.D.A. (ed.). 1946. *Tararua Story: Jubilee of a Mountain Club*, Tararua Tramping Club, Wellington.

Grey, Constance. 1970. *Quiet with the Hills: The Life of Alfred Edward Peache of Mount Somers*, Pegasus Press, Christchurch.

Halkett, John; Berg, Peter; Mackerel, Brian (eds). 1988. *Tree People: Forest Service Memoirs*, New Zealand Forestry Corporation/G.P. Publications, Wellington.

Hall-Jones, John. 1990. *Fiordland Explored: An Illustrated History*, Craigs Printing, Invercargill.

Hall-Jones, John. 2005. *Goldfields of Otago: An Illustrated History*, Craigs Printing, Invercargill.

Hamilton G.A. 1952. *History of Northern Southland*, Southland Times, Invercargill.

Harper, Barbara. 1967. *The Kettle on the Fuchsia: The Story of Orari Gorge*, A.H. & A.W. Reed, Wellington.

Harrington, Steve. 1997. *A Hurunui History Trail: From the Peaks to Harper's Pass*, Steve Harrington, Hawarden.

Harris, George; Hasler, Graeme. 1971. *The Mount Cook Alpine Region*, A.H. & A.W. Reed, Wellington.

Harte, G.W. 1956. *Mt Peel is a Hundred: The Story of the First High-country Sheep Station in Canterbury*, G.W. Herald Printing Works, Timaru.

Henderson, Jim (ed.). 1971. *Our Open Country*, A.H. & A.W. Reed, Wellington.

Henderson, Jim. 1981. *The Exiles of Asbestos Cottage*, Hodder & Stoughton, Auckland.

Henderson, Jim; Foster, Bruce. 1986. *Jim Henderson's People*, Reed Methuen, Auckland.

Hersey, Paul. 2009. *High Misadventure: New Zealand Mountaineering Tragedies and Survival Stories*, New Holland, Auckland.

Hewson, A. 1996. *Early Days in Ashburton Country*, Ashburton Museum and Historical Society Inc., Ashburton.

Hilary, Edmund. 1955. *High Adventure*, Hodder & Stoughton, London.

Hindmarsh, Gerard. 2010. *Kahurangi Calling: Stories from the Back Country of Northwest Nelson*, Craig Potton Publishing, Nelson.

Holden, Philip. 1985. *New Zealand, Hunter's Paradise*, Hodder & Stoughton, Auckland.

Holden, Philip. 1986. *Pack and Rifle*, Reed Methuen, Auckland.

Holden, Philip. 1987. *The Deerstalkers: A History of the New Zealand Deerstalkers' Association 1937–1987*, Hodder & Stoughton, Auckland.

Holden, Philip. 1993. *Station Country: Back-country life in New Zealand*, Hodder & Stoughton, Auckland.

Hunter, Grant. 1981. *The New Zealand Tramper's Handbook*, Reed, Auckland.

Hunter, Grant. 2007. *Coast to Coast: Who Was First?*, Fifth Camp, Christchurch.

Hunter, Grant (ed.). 2007. *Peninsula Tramping Club Turns 75: 1932–2007*, Peninsula Tramping Club, Christchurch.

Hunter, Kate. 2009. *Hunting: A New Zealand History*, Random House, Auckland.

Jordan, James. 2002. *At Home in the Hills*, Halcyon Press, Auckland.

Keen, R.J. (ed.). 1973. *Outdoors 50th Anniversary Issue 1923–1973*, Otago Tramping and Mountaineering Club, Dunedin.

Keene, Howard. 1995. *Going for Gold: The Search for Riches in the Wilberforce Valley*, DOC, Christchurch.

Kelly, Michael. 1996. *Te Urewera Slab Huts Conservation Report*, DOC East Coast and Bay of Plenty Conservancy, Rotorua.

Kelly, Michael. 2007. *Wild Animal Control Huts: A National Heritage Identification Study*, DOC, Wellington.

Kelly, 2010. *Biodiversity Huts, Fiordland: Historic Heritage Assessment*, DOC Southland Conservancy, Invercargill.

Kerr, Ross. 2002. *Seventy Five Years in the Hills: A History of the Levin-Waiopehu Tramping Club 1927 to 2002*, Levin-Waiopehu Tramping Club, Levin.

Kerr, Ross. 2006. *A Chronology of the Tararua and Rimutaka Ranges*, 5th edition, Ross Kerr Publishing, Levin.

King, Michael. 2003. *The Penguin History of New Zealand*, Penguin, Auckland.

Lane-Taylor, Joanna. 1970. *The History of the Orongorongo Valley and Environs*, Garratt Printing Co., Wellington.

Langton, Graham (ed.). 2000. *Mr Explorer Douglas: John Pascoe's New Zealand Classic*, Canterbury Univeristy Press, Christchurch.

Langton, Graham. 2011. *Summits and Shadows: Jack Clarke and New Zealand Mountaineering*, Steele Roberts, Wellington.

Lasenby, Jack. 2004. *What Makes a Teacher?*, Four Winds Press, Wellington.

Lethbridge, Christopher. 1971. *Sunrise on the Hills: A Musterer's Year on Ngamatea*, Hodder & Stoughton, Auckland.

Levin Waiopehu Tramping Club. 1977. *Levin Waiopehu Tramping Club Golden Jubilee 1927–1977*, Levin Waiopehu Tramping Club, Levin.

Lloyd, Kelvin (ed.). 2006. *45 Years of Antics, Adventures and Escapades of the Otago University Tramping Club*, Otago University Tramping Club, Dunedin.

Logan, Robert. 2008. *Waimakariri*, 2nd edition, Phillips & King, Christchurch.

Long, Robert. 2010. *A Life on Gorge River: New Zealand's Remotest Family*, Random House, Auckland.

Loughton, J. 1998. *Fifty Years Along the Road: A History of the Summit Road Society Incorporated 1948–1998*, Summit Road Society, Christchurch.

McClure, Margaret. 2004. *The Wonder Country: A History of Tourism in New Zealand*, Auckland University Press, Auckland.

McConochie, Newton. 1966. *You'll Learn No Harm From the Hills*, A.H. & A.W. Reed, Wellington.

McCormack, Trish. 1988. *A History of Surveying and Mountaineering in South Westland*, DOC, Hokitika.

Macgregor, Miriam. 1970. *Early Sheep Stations of Hawke's Bay*, A.H. & A.W. Reed, Wellington.

McIntyre, Roberta. 2008. *Whose High Country? A History of the South Island High Country of New Zealand*, Penguin, Auckland.

Mackay, Duncan. 1992. *Frontier New Zealand: The Search for Eldorado 1800–1920*, Harper Collins, Auckland.

McKelvey, Peter. 1995. *Steepland Forests: A Historical Perspective of Protection Forestry in New Zealand*, Canterbury University Press, Christchurch.

McKenzie, Doreen. 1973. *Road to Routeburn: The Story of Kinloch, Lake Wakatipu*, John McIndoe, Dunedin.

McKerrow, Bob. 2005. *Ebenezer Teichelmann*, Tara-India Research Press, New Delhi.

Maclean, Chris. 1994 *Tararua: The Story of a Mountain Range*, Whitcombe Press, Wellington.

Maclean, Chris. 2003 *John Pascoe*, Whitcombe Press/Craig Potton Publishing, Waikanae/Nelson.

McLean. W.H. 1966. *Rabbits Galore!*, A.H. & A.W. Reed, Wellington.

McLeod, David. 1970. *Many a Glorious Morning*, Whitcombe & Tombs, Christchurch.

McLeod, David. 1980. *Down from the Tussock Ranges*, Whitcoulls, Christchurch.

McNair, Jack. 1971. *Shooting for the Skipper*, A.H. & A.W. Reed, Wellington.

Macnicol, T. 1965. *Beyond the Skippers Road*, A.H. & A.W. Reed, Wellington.

Maling, Peter. 1960. *Samuel Butler at Mesopotamia*, National Historic Places Trust, Wellington.

Mann, Shonadh. 1977. *F.G. Gibbs: His Influence on the Social History of Nelson, 1890–1950*, Nelson Historical Society, Stoke, Nelson.

Marshall, Daryl. 2006. *Pikau and Rifle: Hunting Deer, Thar and Coamois in the Southern Alps, Fiordland, Stewart Island and Longwoods*, Halcyon Press, Auckland.

Masters, Lester. 1960. *Back Country Tales*, Hart Printing, Hastings.

Maxim, Paul. 2011. *Bold Beyond Belief: Bill Denz, New Zealand's Mountain Warrior*, Maxim Books, Wellington.

May, Philip Ross. 1967. *The West Coast Gold Rushes*, 2nd edition, Pegasus Press, Christchurch.

May, Philip Ross (ed.). 1975. *Miners and Militants: Politics in Westland*, University of Canterbury Press, Christchurch.

Mead, William P. 1979. *Memories of a Mountain and a River*, Wanganui Newspapers, Wanganui.

Miers, K.H. 1973 *Animal Control Policy on New Zealand Forest Land*, Tussock Grasslands and Mountain Lands Institute, Review No. 26, Lincoln College, Lincoln.

Miller, Frederick W.G. 1946. *There was Gold in the River*, A.H. & A.W. Reed, Wellington.

Mines Department New Zealand. 1933 [reprinted 2011]. *Fossicking and Prospecting for Gold*, Mining Leaflet No. 10, Dornie Publishing, Invercargill.

Molloy, Les (ed.). 1983. *Wilderness Recreation in New Zealand*, Federated Mountain Clubs, Wellington.

Molloy, Les; Potton, Craig. 2007. *New Zealand's Wilderness Heritage*, Craig Potton Publishing, Nelson.

Moncrieff, Perrine. 1965. *People Came Later*, R.W. Stiles & Co., Nelson.

Moore, Betty; Langton, Graham. 1999. *My Mountain Calls: Jane Thomson and her Mountain Adventures*, Betty Moore and Graham Langton, Waitati, Otago.

Morris, Gerard (ed.). 1986. *Waiuta, 1906–1951, the Gold Mine, the Town, the People*, Friends of Waiuta, Reefton.

Morton, Elsie K. 1950. *Fun in Fiordland*, J.E. Jenkins & Co., Auckland.

Morton, Elsie K. 1951. *A Tramper in South Westland*, J.E. Jenkins & Co., Auckland.

Murray J.S.; Murray R.W. 1978. *Costly Gold: Clutha Riches and their Human Toll*, A.H. & A.W. Reed, Wellington.

National Parks Authority. 1983. *Buildings and Accommodation: General Policy for National Parks*, National Parks Authority, Wellington.

Newport, J.N.W. 1978. *Footprints Too: Further Glimpses into the History of the Nelson Province*, Express Printing Works, Blenheim.

Newton, Peter. 1960. *Mesopotamia Station: A Survey of the First Hundred Years*, Timaru Herald, Timaru.

Newton, Peter. 1966. *The Boss's Story*, A.H. & A.W. Reed, Wellington.

Newton, Peter. 1973. *Big Country of the South Island*, A.H. & A.W. Reed, Wellington.

New Zealand Alpine Club. 1999. *Aspiring Hut: 50 Years of Climbing and Adventure*, New Zealand Alpine Club, Christchurch.

Nicol, Euan; Nicol, Jennie. 1991. *Tramping in North Island Forest Parks*, Reed, Auckland.

Noble, Judge G.S. 1995. *Commission of Inquiry into the Collapse of a Viewing Platform at Cave Creek near Punakaiki on the West Coast*, Department of Internal Affairs, Wellington.

Nolan, Iris. 2002. *Out of the Mountains*, 2nd edition, Reed, Auckland.

Nolan, Tony. 1961. *Bush Lore: A Handbook for Trampers, Shooters and Campers*, Whitcombe & Tombs, Christchurch.

Nolan, Tony. 1975. *New Zealand Camping and Tramping Handbook*, Paul Hamlyn, Auckland.

Nolan, Tony. 1980. *Gold, Gold, Gold: The Romantic World of Gold*, A.H. & A.W. Reed, Wellington.

Odell, R.S. (ed.). 1935. *Handbook of the Arthur's Pass National Park: Its History, Tracks, Climbing Routes, Places Names, Geology, Botany*, Arthur's Pass National Park Board, Christchurch.

Ogilvie, Gordon. 2009. *The Port Hills of Christchurch*, 2nd edition, Philips & King Publishers, Christchurch.

Owen, Alwyn; Perkins, Jack. 1986. *Speaking for Ourselves: Echoes from New Zealand's Past, from the Award Winning 'Spectrum' Radio Series*, Penguin, Auckland.

Palman, Alex. 2001. *Aoraki–Mt Cook, a Guide for Mountaineers*, New Zealand Alpine Club, Christchurch.

Palmer, Walter. 1976. *Public Use of the Orongorongo Valley, Wellington*, Information Series No. 113, DSIR, Wellington.

Pascoe, John. 1952. *Land Uplifted High*, Whitcombe & Tombs, Christchurch.

Pascoe, John. 1957. *Mr Explorer Douglas*, A.H & A.W. Reed, Wellington.

Patterson, Robin S. 1991. *A Sock in My Stew: Memories of Dick Morris and the Deer Cullers*, Robin Patterson, Christchurch.

Peden, Robert. 2011. *Making Sheep Country: Mt Peel Station and the Transformation of the Tussock Lands*, Auckland University Press, Auckland.

Penn, Frank. 1920. *Across the Tararuas and Beautiful Otaki*, Otaki Mail, Otaki.

Petchey, P.G. 2006. *Gold and Electricity: Archaeological Survey of Bullendale, Otago*, DOC, Wellington.

Phillips, Jock. 1996 *A Man's Country? The Image of the Pakeha Male – A History*, Penguin, Auckland.

Pickering, Mark. 2004. *A Tramper's Journey: Stories from the Back Country of New Zealand*, Craig Potton Publishing, Nelson.

Pickering, Mark. 2010. *Huts: Untold Stories from Back-country New Zealand*, Canterbury University Press, Christchurch.

Pinney, Robert. 1981. *Early Northern Otago Runs*, Collins, Auckland.

Poole, A.L. (ed.). 1951. *New Zealand-American Fiordland Expedition*, DSIR Bulletin 103, Wellington.

Potts, Thomas. 1882. *Out in the Open*, Lyttelton Times Co., Lyttelton.

Powell, Paul. 1967. *Men Aspiring*, A.H. & A.W. Reed, Wellington.

Powell, Paul. 1970. *Just Where Do You Think You've Been?*, A.H. & A.W. Reed, Wellington.

Reid, Rebecca, 2009. *Long Hilly Walking Track, Round Hill: A Self Guide for Te Araroa Southland Trust*, Te Araroa Southland Trust, Riverton.

Relph, David. 2007. *From Tussocks to Tourists: The Story of the Central Canterbury High Country*, Canterbury University Press, Christchurch.

Relph, David. 2010. *The Mackenzie Country: A Fine Plain Behind the Snowy Range*, David Ling Publishing, Auckland.

Rich, Margaret. 2004. *75 Years on Cockayne*, Mt Cheeseman Ski Club, Christchurch.

Riseborough, Hazel. 2006. *Ngamatea: The Land and the People*, Auckland University Press, Auckland.

Roberts, F.A. 1916. *My Forest Ways in New Zealand*, Heath Cranton, London.

Roche, Michael. 1990. *The History of New Zealand Forestry*, New Zealand Forestry Corporation/G.P. Books, Wellington.

Ross, Kirstie. 2008. *Going Bush: New Zealanders and Nature in the Twentieth Century*, Auckland University Press, Auckland.

Roxburgh, Irvine. 1957. *Wanaka Story: A History of Wanaka, Hawea, Tarras and Surrounding Districts*, Otago Centennial Historical Publications, Dunedin.

Rundle, John. 1981. *The Tararua Book*, Millwood Press, Wellington.

Rundle, John; Gordon, John. 1993. *Mountains of the South*, Random House, Auckland.

Scanlan, A.B. 1961. *Egmont: The Story of a Mountain*, A.H. & A.W. Reed, Wellington.

Scott, Dick. 1969. *Inheritors of a Dream*, A.H. & A.W. Reed, Wellington.

Scott, Jonathan. 1997. *Harry's Absence: Looking for my Father on the Mountain*, Victoria University Press, Wellington.

Shaw, Derek. 1991. *North West Nelson Tramping Guide*, Nikau Press, Nelson.

Sime, Ian (ed.). 1999. *Outdoors 1998: The 75th Anniversary Publication of the Otago Tramping and Mountaineering Club*, Otago Tramping and Mountaineering Club, Dunedin.

Sime, Ian (ed.). 2000. *Outdoors 2000: The Official Journal of the Otago Tramping and Mountaineering Club*, Otago Tramping and Mountaineering Club, Dunedin.

Smith, Dawn. 1997. *Abel Tasman Area History*, DOC, Nelson.

Smith, Barry. 2004. *Always a Little Further: Poems of Mountains and Valleys*, Barry Smith, Hamilton.

Southland Tramping Club. 1972. *Southland Tramping Club 25th Jubilee 1947-1972*, Southland Tramping Club, Invercargill.

Spearpoint, Geoff. 1985. *Waking to the Hills*, Reed Methuen, Auckland.

Sutherland, Lew. 1970. *A Hunting and Tramping Guide to Westland*, A.H. & A.W. Reed, Wellington.

Temple, Philip. 1977. *Ways to the Wilderness: Great New Zealand Walking Tracks*, Whitcoulls, Christchurch.

Temple, Philip. 1989. *The BP Guide to The Heaphy Track*, 4th edition, Penguin Books (NZ), Auckland.

Temple, Philip. 1996. *The Book of the Kea*, Hodder Moa Beckett, Auckland.

Thom, David. 1987. *Heritage: The Parks of the People*, Lansdowne Press, Auckland.

Thomson, Jane. 1952. *Origins of the National Parks Act*, Department of Lands and Survey, Wellington.

Thomson, Joff A. 1954. *Deer Hunter: The Experiences of a New Zealand Stalker*, 2nd edition, A.H. & A.W. Reed, Wellington.

Thomson, Joff A. 1964. *Deer Shooting Days*, A.H. & A.W. Reed, Wellington.

Thomson, N.M. 1949. *Safety in the Mountains*, Federated Mountain Clubs, Wellington.

Thornton, Geoffrey G. 1986. *The New Zealand Heritage of Farm Buildings*, Reed Methuen, Auckland.

Tourism New Zealand. 2001. *100 Years Pure Progress. 1901–2001 100 Years of Tourism*, Tourism New Zealand, Wellington.

Tustin, Ken. 1998. *A Wild Moose Chase*, Wild South Books, Dunedin.

Vance, William. 1973. *Bush, Bullocks and Boulders: The Story of the Upper Ashburton*, Alford Forest Bushside Springburn District Centenary Committee, Ashburton.

Walrond, Carl. 2008. *Survive! Remarkable Tales from the New Zealand Outdoors*, David Bateman, Auckland.

Wigley, Harry. 1979. *The Mount Cook Way: The First Fifty Years of the Mount Cook Company*, Collins, Auckland.

Willems, Hans. 2000. *South Island Back Country Huts*, Halcyon Press, Auckland.

Willems, Hans. 2004. *North Island Back Country Huts*, 2nd edition, Halcyon Press, Auckland.

Williams Karen; Bamford, Dave. 1987. *Skiing on the Volcano: Historical Images of Skiing on Mount Ruapehu*, Ruapehu Alpine Lifts/Tourism Resource Consultants, Wellington.

Wilson, G.B.; Ward, A.L. (eds). 1954. *Safety in the Mountains: A Handbook for Trampers, Deerstalkers, Skiers and Mountaineers*, Federated Mountain Clubs, Wellington.

Wilson, Jim. 1968. *Aorangi: The Story of Mount Cook*, Whitcombe & Tombs, Christchurch.

Woodham, Stella (ed.). 1982. *Christchurch Tramping Club Fiftieth Anniversary, 1932–1982*, Christchurch Tramping Club, Christchurch.

Wright, Les. 1993. *Big River Quartz Mine: A Worthwhile Speculation*, Friends of Waiuta, Reefton.

Yerex, David. 2001. *Deer: The New Zealand Story*, Canterbury University Press, Christchurch.

UNPUBLISHED DOCUMENTS

Breen, Jackie. 2004. 'Old Cedar Flat Hut Historic Assessment', internal report for DOC, Hokitika.

Cochran, Chris. 1997. 'Shutes Hut, Ruahine Forest Park: Repair Survey', internal report for DOC, Hawke's Bay.

Harsveldt, Patrick. 2010. 'Architecture of Isolation: Defining the New Zealand Backcountry Hut', MA thesis, University of Otago, Dunedin.

Maclean, Chris. 2012. 'A History of the Orongorongo Valley', unpublished manuscript.

Meyer, Beverley. 1987. 'Gemeinschaft in Hausknecht, Community in Boots: A Study of the Auckland Tramping Club', project prepared for the Community Work Certificate at Carrington Polytechnic, Auckland.

Meyer, Beverley. 1989. 'Stranger Upon the Upland Road, Recreation in the New Zealand Outdoors for the Uninitiated', paper submitted in partial fulfilment of a Diploma of Recreation and Sport, Auckland University of Technology, Auckland.

Natusch, Guy. 1992. *Shutes Hut Conservation Report*, Natusch Partnership, Napier.

Pynenburg, Ron. 1981. 'Huts of the Mount Hector Track', B.Arch. thesis, Victoria University, Wellington.

Quigg, Robin. 1993. 'Back-country Huts, More Than a Roof Over Your Head: A Question of Values in Cultural Heritage Management', Masters thesis, Lincoln University, Canterbury.

Wright, Matthew. 1984. 'A History of Eastern Kaweka Ranges', unpublished report for NZFS, Napier.

Wright, Matthew. 1985. 'The Early Sawmilling Industry in Hawke's Bay 1870–1950', unpublished NZFS report, Napier.

Wright, Matthew. 1986. 'Early Huts of the Northeastern Ruahine and Central Wakarara Ranges', unpublished NZFS report, Napier.

NEWSPAPERS AND JOURNALS

Ashburton Guardian
Canterbury Mountaineer
Daily Post (Rotorua)
Dominion Post
Ellesmere Guardian
Evening Post (Wellington)
FMC Bulletin
Footprints
Golden Bay Weekly
Good as Gold
Hawke Eye View
Heels
Hills and Valleys
Hutt Valley Tramping
Manawatu Times
Marlborough Express
Nelson Evening Mail
Nelson Historical Society Journal
Nelson Mail
New Zealand Alpine Journal
New Zealand Climber
New Zealand Farmers Weekly
New Zealand Hunting and Wildlife
New Zealand Journal of Forestry
New Zealand Listener
New Zealand Truth
Ngaruwahia Advocate
NZAC Bulletin
Ohinemuri Gazette
Otago Daily Times
Otago Witness
Pohokura
Ruahine Rambler
Southland Times
The Spectator
Tararua
Tararua Tramper
Tramping and Mountaineering
Wairarapa Times-Age
Wanganui Chronicle
Wellington Botanical Society Bulletin
Wilderness

WEBSITES

www.doc.govt.nz
Website of the Department of Conservation.

www.fmc.org.nz
Website of the Federated Mountain Clubs of New Zealand.

www.nzac.org.nz
Website of the New Zealand Alpine Club

www.remotehuts.co.nz
Website of Permolat, a voluntary group dedicated to maintaining West Coast huts.

www.teara.co.nz
Te Ara – The Encyclopaedia of New Zealand; it has some excellent sections on the bush, tramping and mountaineering.

www.tramper.co.nz
New Zealand Tramper website; it has numerous accounts and photographs of tramping trips, including huts.

Acknowledgements

At the start of this project we thought we were writing a book about huts. We soon realised that the human stories are what elevate huts above their status as simply shelter. What we actually produced became more a social history of backcountry New Zealand, told through the filter of huts. No single person – except perhaps New Zealand's finest historians – can claim to have the breadth of knowledge required to write authoritatively about such a range of subjects and span of history as we've covered, and we are indebted to the many people who have helped inform this project, commented on drafts and shared their expertise. Like building a hut, it has been a community effort.

We're also grateful to the many authors and historians who have written so well about hut-related subjects. Where possible, we've contacted living authors for permission to use quotes.

Shaun had the unenviable task of pulling all the text together from three authors, and he is grateful to Rob and Geoff for their forbearance with his pruning and editing.

This book would not have been possible without the generous financial support of the Department of Conservation (DOC), the Mountain and Forest Trust of the Federated Mountain Clubs (FMC), and the DOW Hall Publications Fund of the New Zealand Alpine Club (NZAC). Significant grants from these sponsors enabled the publishers to print such a large book at a modest retail price.

Our thanks go not only to these organisations, but also in particular to Kevin O'Connor and Brian Dobbie (DOC); Richard Davies (FMC); and Ollie Clifton and Sam Newton (NZAC).

Heartfelt thanks also go to former prime ministers Jim Bolger and Helen Clark, both trampers who have opened huts, supported conservation and championed national parks.

Department of Conservation
We owe a great deal of gratitude to the enormous support given to us by many DOC staff, both past and present. Staff generously gave information and photographs, read draft chapters, and provided encouragement; and all on top of their normal workloads of actually maintaining and preserving these wonderful huts. Thank you all.

Jackie Breen, DOC West Coast historian, has an extensive knowledge of backcountry hut history, and it is largely thanks to her help that we could present such detail about early animal control hut design. Jackie's work on such huts as Rangers, Slaty Creek and Cedar Flats helped us understand just how important the efforts of the Department of Internal Affairs were in creating a deer-culling hut network on the West Coast. Jackie also proofread the entire book, which was way beyond the call of duty.

Jim Staton, Shane Hall and Tom Hopkins all provided information about West Coast huts and commented on chapter drafts. Les Wright's extensive knowledge was also invaluable for the introduction to the mining huts section. Other DOC staff helped with various hut chapters, and thanks go to: Steve Bagley, Ted Brennan, Greg Carter, Warren Chippendale, Brian Dobbie, Alison Dorian, Rachel Egerton, Bill Fleury, Annette Grieve, Paul Hellebrekers, Sally Jones, Richard Kennett, Ross Kerr, Moira Lee, Katrina Lett, Greg Lind, Beth Masser, Kiersten McKinley, Dean Nelson, Martin Rodd, Alison Rothschild, Jason Roxburgh, Pat Sheridan, Shirley Slatter, Murray Thomas and Cornelia Vervoorn.

Derrick Field helped with the Tarn Ridge Hut chapter, and also with tracking down photographs from ex-cullers. John Taylor was extremely helpful with information and pictures for the Waingaro Forks and Riordan huts chapters. Pam Bain, Elizabeth Pischief and Pat Sheridan helped with Old Manson and Ellis huts.

Rebecca Reid of TellTale Limited has done a lot of historic and interpretative work on Southland huts, and was very generous with her time and support. Rebecca helped out with Beech Hut, Mintaro Hut and the photograph of Dog Box Biv.

New Zealand Forest Service
Ex-NZFS employees Jock Fisher, Ray Osman and Ron Turner have been immensely helpful, providing first-hand knowledge of the era when the Forest Service took over deer-culling operations. We are particularly grateful to Jock and Ron for allowing us to quote them so extensively in the essays on Department of Internal Affairs (DIA) and NZFS huts, and for checking chapter drafts.

Ex-NZFS ranger Max Polglaze was an invaluable source of information for several chapters: Riordans Hut, Asbestos Cottage, Cecil Kings Hut and the Gridiron rock shelters. Max also provided a full set of Northwest Nelson Forest Park Advisory Committee minutes, which gave extra detail on hut management.

Ashley Cunningham helped with the Dominie Biv, Museum Hut, and Kaweka and Ruahine NZFS huts chapters, as well as providing photographs and advice. Ashley continues to be an enduring source of knowledge on all things related to forests and mountains.

Merv O'Reilly, Ben Gibbs, Gordon Roberts and John von Tunzelman also provided insight into NZFS hut building, and supplied rare photographs of their working life. Glenn Johnston has been very helpful, through the Permolat group, providing information and photographs.

Department of Lands and Survey
Bruce Postill helped extensively with the Nelson Lakes and Pioneer huts chapters, and contributed many photographs. Bill Keir, a former member of the Mount Cook National Park Board, helped with the Colin Todd and Mueller huts chapters. For help with the Lands and Survey essay, sincere thanks goes to Geoff Rennison, Bruce Postill, Andy Dennis and Dave Bamford.

Geoff Rennison's oral histories with retired Lands and Survey staff were invaluable for this chapter, and we are grateful to the late Alex Miller for giving us his copy of this shortly before he passed away.

Clubs and individuals
For help, advice and support, we thank David Barnes, Julia Bradshaw, Harry Ferris, Sonia Frimmell, Jan and Arnold Heine, David Hoyle, Warren Jowett, Bill Keir, Paul Kilgour, Carl McKay, Margaret McMahon, Les Molloy, Colin Monteath, Max Motley, Peggy Munn, Tom Patterson, Lex Perriam, Ivan Pickens, Mark Pickering, John Rhodes, John Simpson, Kath Varcoe and Ian Whitehouse.

Steve Baker, Grant Barnett, Ted Brennan, Barb Brown, Dave Chowdhury, Fraser Crichton, Richard Davies, Andy Dennis, Tony Gates, Gavin, Sam and Daniel Harris, Robin McNeill, Chris Maclean, Shona Maxwell, Geoff Norman, John Ombler, Justin Palmer, Darryn Pegram, Jock Phillips, Bruce Postill, Rebecca Reid, Jason Roxburgh, Hugh van Noorden, Gaylene Wilkinson and Peter Wilson enthusiastically joined various hut-bagging missions.

Andy Blick, Chris Birt and Roger Forrester helped with the Rogers Hut chapter.

Alan Duncan, Paddy Gordon, Paul Hellebrekers, Kevin Lange, Alan Mark, Paul McGahan, John Ombler, Rhondda Osmers, Peter and Anne Presland and John Trotter all helped with huts in the Makarora area.

Thanks to Bernard Smith and Alan Graham of the Ruapehu Ski Club for their help with the Old Waihohonu Hut chapter. Alan Kerrisk, publicity officer with the Mt Egmont Alpine Club in Hawera, generously provided information and photographs for the Syme Hut chapter.

For permission to use quotes from their books or reports, we thank John and Robyn Armstrong, Mike Bennett, Brian Burdon, Chris Cochran, Paul Maxim, Jock Phillips and Mark Pickering.

Thanks to Peter Kemp of Nelson Lakes Shuttles for information about Bobs Hut.

Oliver Druce and Alison Druce kindly offered comments and information on the Huts as Monuments essay regarding Fenella Hut.

Andrew Buglass and members of the online network Permolat provided lots of responses to questions about NZFS huts. Trevor Chinn was the major source of information about Ivory Lake Hut.

Hugh Barr, Michael Bartlett, Brenda Neill and Alan Wright from the Tararua Tramping Club also offered tremendous support, notably Hugh with the Kime and Field hut chapters, and Michael with the Cone Hut chapter.

Alan Berry from Heretaunga Tramping Club provided much helpful information about, and photographs of, Ruahine and Kaweka huts. Pam Turner was an invaluable source of information about the Iron Whare.

Rebecca Mitchinson of the Orongorongo Club helped with the Orongorongo Valley huts chapter.

John Wilson, hut historian for the Canterbury Mountaineering Club (CMC), generously let us use his excellent articles on CMC huts, as well as some unpublished notes, as the basis for several chapters in the book.

Colin Burrows, also from the CMC, was very helpful with information about Park Morpeth Hut.

John and Phil Rundle from the Hutt Valley Tramping Club provided access to records and gave invaluable help sourcing information.

Tony Gates, collector of all things Ruahine, helped immeasurably with the Shutes, Howletts and Ruahine Forest Park NZFS huts chapters.

Graham Langton gave excellent historical scrutiny on a draft of the introduction to the tourism and climbing huts section, as well as providing historic photographs. Chris Maclean's advice on the Orongorongo Valley and Field huts chapters was invaluable, and Darryn Pegram did the same for the introduction to the DIA huts section. Brian Dobbie provided a helpful review of the NZFS huts essay.

Katharine Watson of Underground Overground Archaeology made available several unpublished reports on old mustering huts that are now managed by DOC, and we are grateful for her detailed research on these.

Tony Macklin from the New Zealand Deerstalkers' Association (NZDA) helped with both the Tarn Ridge Hut and Roaring Stag Lodge chapters, and also provided historic pictures of the building of Roaring Stag Lodge.

It would have been difficult to write the short, but magnificent, history of the Rakiura Hunter Camp Trust without the help of John DeLury.

Ian Payton helped with the introduction to the science huts section, notably with information about Camp Creek Hut.

Bruce Mason has done a significant amount of research on the ski huts on the Rock and Pillar Range, presented in Big Hut's impressive historical panels. Thanks to Bruce for providing invaluable information for the Big Hut chapter and for photographs from his collection.

Philip and Bob Todhunter of Lake Heron Station provided useful comments on the draft of the introductory essay to the Pastoral Huts section, and thanks also go to Steve and Jo McAtamney for their permission to include Sutherlands Hut in this section and their help with the chapter.

Several other high-country farmers generously allowed access to huts on their stations. Many thanks to Donald Aubrey of Ben McLeod Station, Roddy Brown of Blue Mountain Station and Rosa Peacock of Orari Gorge Station for permission to visit their historic huts, and especially to Rosa for sharing Orari Gorge's historical files.

Family
Shaun thanks his wife, Tania Stanton, and children, Tom, Lee and Lexi, for their tolerance and support during a very busy period researching and writing the book.

Rob will be for ever indebted to his partner, Jeannine Tuffin, who for the bulk of this project shouldered most of the load for raising their twins, Lily and Zara, all in the midst of ongoing earthquakes. He has also treasured the trips he has made to huts with his daughter Francesca.

Photographs and illustrations
Thanks go to Geoff Norman for help with scanning prints and Andrew Budd for scanning the transparencies. Many individuals, clubs, organisations and institutions provided photographs or pictures that significantly enriched the book's illustrations.

The following all provided access to their extensive photographic collections: Alexander Turnbull Library, Wellington; Archives New Zealand, Wellington; Hocken Library, Dunedin; Lakes District Centennial Museum, Arrowtown; Canterbury Museum, Christchurch; South Canterbury Museum, Timaru; Museum of New Zealand Te Papa Tongarewa, Wellington; and the MacMillan Brown Library, Canterbury University, Christchurch. Thanks also to Margaret D. Mort from Opus Consultants, Greymouth.

Steve Baker, Pat Barrett, Andrew Barker, Harry Bimler, David Blunt, Wayne Boness, Julia Bradshaw, Brian Burdon, Ray Chapman, Trevor Chinn, Chris Cochran, Ashley Cunningham, Jim Davis, Andy Dennis, Amanda Farrell, Derrick Field, Jock Fisher, Roger Forrester, Ben Gibbs, Paul Gush, Nick Groves, Graeme Hare, Glenn Johnston, Ralph Jorgensen, Warren Jowett, Ron Mackie, Tony Macklin, Peter Morrison, Cam Mulvey, Alasdair Nicoll, Ray Osman, Rhondda (and Dave) Osmers, Darryn Pegram, Bruce Postill, Don Rush, Chris Satherley, Dave Saunders, Ron Turner, Aat Vervoorn, Rex Vink, Ian Whitehouse, Brian Wilkins and Graeme Woodfield also all provided photographs.

Grateful thanks to Tom Scott for generously allowing us to use his cartoon.

Publishing and editing
Grateful thanks to Susi Bailey for her sterling and professional copy-editing skills. CPP Production Manager Alan Bridgland with Arnott Potter and Karen Jones managed production to a very high standard. Publisher Robbie Burton championed this project right from the start, gave us a free rein to produce a massive amount of material, and remained calm when we stretched deadlines – once by a year. Robbie's superb design has resulted in a handsome book. Thank you Robbie, and sorry we couldn't squeeze in a profile of Kea Hut.

Corrections
The authors are grateful to the following people who have provided corrections and updates since the initial printing in 2012: Barrie Atkins, David Harrington, John Hopkins, Graham Langton, Tony Perrett, Lew Shaw and John Wilson.

Index

Page numbers in **bold** refer to illustrations.

Abel Tasman National Park, 24, 25, 30, 66, **66**, **67**, 255, 258, 287
Abel, Willie, 172
acclimatisation societies, 197
Acland, John, 31, 32, 33, 42, 58
Acland, Mark and Jo, 304
Ada Pass Hut, 149
Adam, John, 72
Adams Block, 68
Adams, C.W., 270
Adelaide Tarn Hut, 186, **187**
Adventure Biv, 231
A-frame (Travers) Hut, 249
Agnes Bivouac, 144, 178
Agony Island, 178
Ahern, Brian, 124, 258, 281
Ahuriri Conservation Park, 19, 48, **49**
Aicken Range, 231
Akaroa, 134
Akhurst, Fred, 162
Alabaster Hut, **262**
Alack, Frank, 125, 127, 128–9, 140
Alex's Bivvy, 259
Algidus Station, 320
Algie, Ronald, 113
Allaway Dickson Hut, 151
Almer Biv/Hut, 104, 116, 122, 125, **125**, **126**, 127, **127**, 128
Almer, Christian, 125
Alpha Hut, 154–5, 157
Alpine Sports Club, 146–7
Amuri Pass, 206
Anderson, Andy, 265
Anderson, Bill, 270
Anderson Memorial Hut, 202, **202**, 302
Anderson, Oliver, 202, 204
Andrews Shelter, 258
Angelus Hut, 266
Angle Knob Hut, 309
angling, 14, 273, 322
Anne Hut, **259**
Ansell, Edna, **44**
Anti Crow (Gizeh) Biv, **151**, 274
Anti Crow Hut, **144**, 180, 314
Aoraki Domain, 103, 106, 108
Aoraki/Mt Cook, 21, **98**, 105, 107, 111, **117**, 118, 128, 140, 143, 144, 163, 276, 332
Aoraki/Mount Cook area (pre-national park), 24, 99–101, 103–5, 107–8, 119, 143
Aoraki/Mount Cook National Park, 14, 108, 109, 116–20, 145, 255, 258, 259, 276–7, 285, 290, 307
Aorangi Range, 219, 325
Aorere Valley, 73, 186
Arahura River and Valley, 77, 203, 221
Arawhata Hut, 176
Arawhata Valley, 251
architecture of huts, *see* building and design of huts
Armstrong, Hamish, 246
Armstrong, John, 270–1
Armstrong, Robyn, 271
Arnott, Bernie, **333**
Arrow River, 77, 80
Arrowtown, 78, 79

Arthur River and Valley, 271
Arthur's Pass, 68, 78, 120, 145, 178
Arthur's Pass National Park, 21, **28**, 37, 138–9, **144**, **151**, 180–1, **236**, 239, 255, 256, 257, 258, 264–5, 274–5, 291, 314–17
Arthur's Pass National Park Board, 180, 181, 258, 265
Asbestos Cottage, 18, 79, 84, **85**, 86, 252
Ashburton, 90, 91
Ashburton Lakes area, 58–60
Aspinall family, 174, 175, 177
Aspinall, John ('Jack'), 143, 175
Aspinall, John ('Jerry'), 175, 176
Aspiring Hut, 144, **174**, 174–7, **177**
Atkins, Barry, 246
Atkinson, Gordon, 260
Auckland, 72, 107, 182
Auckland Tramping Club, 146, 147
Auckland University Tramping Club (AUTC), 147, 149
avalanche hazard assessment, 286
Avoca Homestead, 15, 30, 68–9, **69**, 149
Awapoto Hut, 259
Awatere Valley, 219
Ayrburn Station, 82
Ayres, Harry, 109, 127, 128

Back Basin Hide, 325
Back Ridge Hut, 215, **217**
backcountry, changing nature of, 22, 25
backpackers, 22, 25
Bagley, Steve, 55, 88, 97, 291
Baine, Ian, 171, 192
Baine, Jack, 192, 193
Baine-iti, 192, **192**
Baines Hut, 152, 193
Ball, Daryl, **316**
Ball Glacier, 106–7, 109
Ball Hut, 100, **100**, 103, 106–7, 118
Ball Hut II, 107, 109–10
Ball, John ('Jack'), 45
Ballard, David, 241
Ballard Hut, 241, **241**
Balloon Hut, 132, **148**, 149, 289
Balmoral Station, 33
Banfield Hut, 144
Banks Peninsula, 134, 134–5, **135**
Bannister Basin Hut, 203
Barbers Hut, 242
Bark Bay Hut, 259
Barker Hut, 144, 145, 314, **314**, **315**, 316, **316**, 317
Barker, Neville, 314
Barley, Bert, 116
Barlow Hut, 247
Barnett, Dick, 278
Barnett, Mike, 51
Barr, Hugh, 172
Barron Saddle, 277
Barron Saddle Hut, 258, **259**, 309
Bartlett, Michael, 156, 172
Batcheler, Les, 330
Batson, William ('Billy'), 104, 136
Baughan, Blanche, 100
Bawden, Ralph, 157
Beaglehole family, 20
Bealey Spur Hut (Top Hut), **25**, **28**, 29, 37

Beansprout (Robert Long), 17–18
Beech Hut (Top Hut, Top Mataura Hut, Birch Hut), 62, **63**
Beech Huts (Mackinnon Pass), 101, 102
Beeston, Tom, 139
Beetham Hut, 110, 289
Ben McLeod Station, 32, **40**
Ben More Station, 68
Benge, Craig, 307
Benmore Station, 35, 48
Bennett, Bill, 307
Bennett, Mike, 215, 220
Bennington, Seddon, 158
Bergesens Hut, 248
Bergman, Bill ('Hokitika Bill'), 90–1
Bertinshaw, Jim, 162
Best, Elsdon, 19
Big Hill Station, 50
Big Hut, **168**, 168–70, **170**
Big River Hut, 79, 225
Big River Mine, 78–9
Binnie, A.M., 128, 276
Birch Hill Station, 30
Birley Glacier, 114, 115
Birley, Harry, 92, 114
Biscuit Tin Hut, 146
Bishop, Graham, 177, 325
Bishop, Murray, **246**
Bivvy Rock, 307
Black, Angus, 174
Black, J., 114
Black, Bill, 205
Black Ridge Hut, 240, **240**
Black Spur Hut, 35, **35**
Blackball, 73
Blackwater gold mine, **79**
Blatchford, Basil Ralph, 298
Bledisloe, Lord, 48
Blick, Andy, 212, 213
Blomfield, Edward, 107
Blowfly Hut, 21
Blue Lake Hut, 30, 266–7, **267**
Blue Mountain Station, 32, 43
Blue Range Hut, **142**
Blue River, 87
Boar Inn, 194, **194**
Bob Lee Hut, 57
Bobs Hut, 242, **243**
Bohny, Hans, 130, 274
Bollons, Alan, 157
Bolton, George, 138
Boness, Wayne, 290
Bonnie Jean Hut, 92, 94
Bonnie Jean Valley, 92, 95
Bonnington, Noel, 203
Boo Boo Hut, 290–1
Boo Boo tent camp, 234
Boozer Hut, 92, 95, **95**
Bottles Corner Track, 184
Bottom Gordons Hut, 236, 242
Boulder Lake, 54
Boulder Lake Hut, 186, **187**
boundary-keeping huts, 29, 32, 42, 43, 59
Bowie, Mick, 109, 276

354

Boyd Hut, 46
Brabazon Range Hut, 61
Brabazon Ridge, Mesopotamia Station, 37, 61
Bradford, Jim, 59
Bradshaw, Julia, 188
Brake, Brian, 176
Branch River Hut, 218
Brass Monkey Biv, 150, **150**
Braziers Air Works, 217
Breen, Jackie, 27, 201, 203, 206, 226, 291
Brennan, Ted, 261, 288
Brereton, Cyprian, *No Roll of Drums*, 54
Brewster Hut/Bivvy, 300, **300**, **301**
Broberg, Charles, 52
Brockie, Robert, *A Living New Zealand Forest*, 325
Brodrick, Noel, 100
Broken River, 68, 69
Brosnan, Vic, 246–7
Brown, Barbara, **141**
Brown Cow Track, 186
Brown Hut, 168
Brown, John, 77
Brown, Rob, 203
Browne, Mike, 131
Browning Biv, **230**, 231
Browning Pass (Noti Raureka), 90, 320
Brunning, Bill, 97
Bryant, Elise, **219**, **236**
Buchanan, C.G., 120
Buchanan, Gordon, 265
Buckler Burn catchment, 92, 95
Buglass, Andrew, 152, 229
Buick, Bob, 37
Building Act 1991, 286
Building (Building Code: Backcountry Huts) Amendment Regulations 2008, 286
building and design of huts, 17, 18–19, 25–7, 36; air drops from fixed-wing planes, 22, 25, 116, 118, 127, 129–30, 145, 152, 180, 186, 202, 203, 206, 215, 216, **216**, 232–3, 240, 241, 274, 302, 304, 310, 312, 318; alpine hut requirements, 258, 276–7, 309, 316; colour, 18, 188, 215, 220, 226, **244**, 261; congoleum lining, 124, **124**; helicopter use, 25, 62, 118, 145, 152, 158, 160, 179, 184, 185, 215–19, 217, 265, 268, 277, **277**, 281, 298, 308, 312, **312**, 316, 318, 322, 330; packhorse use, 17, 50, 62, 90, 119, 128, 152, 155, 157, 174, 178, 203, 212, 215, **216**, 260, 264, 314, 320; Public Works Department, 122, 124, 155, 201, **201**, 202, **202**, 267; six-bunk alpine hut design, 181; tongue and groove lining, 53; V huts, 31; *see also* club huts; Department of Conservation (DOC), and huts; Department of Conservation (DOC), hut restoration and maintenance; mining huts; mustering huts; New Zealand Forest Service huts, pastoral huts; tourism, and tourist and climbing huts; and also under Department of Internal Affairs and Department of Lands and Survey
Bull, Peter, 330
Bullen, George, 80, 82
Bullendale, 80, **80**, 82
Bullendale Hut, 79, 80, **80**, 81
Buller Valley, 71
Bunting, Bert, 210
Burghess, G., 175
Burglars Hut, 46
Burke, Mervyn, 257, 281
Burnett, Bob, 304

Burrows, Colin, 320
Burrows, Larry, 320
Burrows, Sam, 138–9
Burrows, William, 320
Bush Stream, 60, 61
Bushedge Hut, 313
Butler Junction Hut, 234
Butler, Samuel, 31, 32, 33; cottage, Mesopotamia Station, **31**
Buttercup Hollow, 246

Cable, W., 62
Cainard Station, 62
Cameron Hut, 17, **18**, 144, 244
Cameron, William, 62
Cameron's Flat, Otago, **199**
Camp Creek, 48, 325–6
Camp Creek Hut, 325–326
Campbell Biv, 229
Campbells Gully, 76
Canterbury, 25, 29, 30–1, 32–3, 147, 197, 199, 203; *see also* names of specific places
Canterbury Association, 30
Canterbury Mountaineering Club (CMC), 15, 17, 37, 108, 128, 129, 130, 144–5, 151, 178–9, 180–1, 202, 220, 258, 264–5, 274, 303, 314, **314**, **315**, 316, 320
Canterbury Museum, 210
Canterbury Progress League, 144
Canterbury University Tramping Club, 15, 149
Cape Brett Hut, 292, **292**
Cape Defiance Hut, 18, 20, 122, 125, 136, **136**, 258
car ownership, and outdoor recreation, 107, 108, 147, 152, 265
Caroline Hut, 15
Carrington, Gerard, **144**, 264
Carrington Hut, 17, 144, 145, 180, 181, **264**, 264–5, **265**, 275
Carroll Hut, 290
Cascade Hut, 143, 174, **175**
Casey Hut, **261**, 265, 275
Cass-Lagoon Track, **224**
Castle Rocks Hut, 136, **137**
Caswell Sound Hut, 325, **334**, **335**
Cat Creek Biv, 231
Caudwell, Donald 'Yankee Dan,' 278
Caughley, Graeme, 197–8, 204, 205, 222
Cavalier Hunters Hut, 190–1, **191**
Cave Creek tragedy, 151, 284, 286, 288
Cecil Kings Hut, 21, 72, 87–8, **88**, **89**, 252
Cedar Flats Hut, 229, **232**, 232–3, **289**, 291
Ces Clarke Hut, 225
Chaffey, Annie and Henry, 18, 84, **84**, 86
Chamonix, 77
Chancellor Hut, 111, 122, 122, **123**, 124, **124**, 127, 258, 287
Chaney, Bernie, 212
Chapman, Tussock, 287
Charles, Geoff, 320
Charles, John, 275
'Chateau Mosquito,' 146–7
Chateau Tongariro, 107, 109
Cheviot Hills Station, 35
Child, Peter, 300
Chinn, Derek, 131
Chinn, Trevor, 327–8, **328**
Chisholm, Bill, 204
Chisholm, Geoff, 265

Christchurch, 30, 59, 68, 94, 96, 109, 120, 134, 147, 208, 217, 316
Christchurch Tramping Club (CTC), 91, 134, 135, 138, **144**, 147, **262**, 322
Christeller, Fiona, 308
Christensen, Ron, 212
Christie, Chris, 330
Clarbrough, Mal, 307
Clarence Reserve, 35, 36–7
Clark, Archie, 204, **204**
Clark Hut (Historic Clark Hut), 201, **204**, 204–5, **205**
Clarke, Colin, 330, **331**
Clarke, Connie, 257
Clarke, Jack, 21, 100, 103, 143, 276
Cleft Peak, 280
Cleland, Connie, 257
Cleland, Ray, 257, 274, 278
Clent Hills Station, 60
Clifton, Neil, *The Central Southern Alps Crown Land Management Strategy*, 261
climbing huts, *see* mountaineering clubs; tourism, and tourist and climbing huts; and names of individual huts
Clinton Forks Hut, 271
Clinton River and Valley, 101–2, 270, 271
Clough, Allan, 320
club huts, 17, 18–19, 21–2, 25, 27, 107–8, 119–20, 143–95, 257; club advocacy, 150–1; deerstalking clubs, 150; hut-building, 152; mountaineering clubs, 143–5; recent trends, 151–2; *see also* tramping clubs; and names of individual clubs and huts
Clutha (Molyneux) River, 75, 76, 77
Clyde River and Valley, 178
coal mining, 68
Coates, Gordon, 72
Cobb Valley, 54, 84, 186, **199**, 226, 251, 308
Cochran, Chris, 27, 47, 48, 91, 156, 172, 206
Cockayne, Leonard, 165, 265
Coggan, Bernie, **216**
Coleman, Dusty, 62
Colenso Hut, 289
Colin Todd Hut, 19, 143, 180, 181, 307, 310, **311**, 312, **312**
Collingwood, 73, 96
Collinson, Leonard, 52
Cone Hut, 15, 152, **171**, 171–2, **173**
Cone, Max, 219
Cone Saddle Hut, 171
Conservation Act 1987, 262
conservation parks, 41; *see also* names of individual parks
Cook, James, 31
Cookson, Allan, 204
Coolahan, Max, 193
Coombes, Graeme, 218
Cooper, Ron, 150–1
Coopers Creek, 147
Copland Pass, 103, 104, 125, 310
Copland Shelter, 258, 276
Copland Track, 104, 125
Copland Valley, 14, 107, 122, 125, 263
Coppermine Creek, 248
Cora Lynn Station, 29, 37
Corboy, Snow, 216–17, 218, 219, 242
Corcoran, Leslie, 312
Coromandel, 73, **74**, 75, 197
Coromandel Forest Park, 25
Coronet Peak, 109, 169
Coubrough, James, 302
Courtney, Ross, 229

INDEX 355

Cow Hut, **223**
Cowan, Bert, 129
Cowan, Bill, 184
Cowshed Hut, 62, 291
Craig, John, 94
Craigie, Bob, 174, 176, 318
Craigieburn Forest Park, 15, 90–1, **91**, 223, **224**
Craigieburn Range, 325, 326
Craigieburn Station, 68
Crawford (Top Crawford) Hut, 235, **235**
Crawford Junction Hut, 232, 261, 326
Crockford family, 66
Croesus–Moonlight Track, 73
Croft, Peter, 275
Crompton, Mark, 231
Crooked Spur Hut, **60**, 60–1
Crooked Spur, Mesopotamia Station, 37
The Cropp, 14, 236
Cropp Hut, 236, 325
Crow Hut (Kawhatau Valley), **222**, 290
Crow Hut (Waimakariri), 143, 258
Crump, Barry, 46–7, 226; *A Good Keen Man,* 198
Crystal Biv, 231
Cunningham, Ashley, 208, 244, 249, 325, 332
Cunningham, Sheila, 246
Cupola Hut, 325, 330, **330**, **331**
Curtis, Jack, 53
Customs Department Tramping Club, 192

Daleys Flat Hut, 257, **260**
Daniel, Mr and Mrs, 62
Daphne Hut, 165
Daphne Ridge, Ruahine Range, 165, **165**, 166
Darran Mountains, 102, **102**, 120, 144
Dart Glacier, 325
Dart Hut, 43, 149, 257, 280, 290
Dart Valley, **280**, 280–1
Davidson, Mavis, **7**, 47, 332–3
Davies, George, 71
Davis, Jesson, 59
Davis, Stan, 162
Dawe, Ian and Paul, 309
De Jong, Nico, 290
De la Beche Memorial Hut, 107, **107**, 108, 119, 129, 143, 175
De la Beche Rock Biv, 100, 125
Deans, William and John, 31
Deas Cove Hut, 291
Deep Cove, 103
deer research, 330, 332, 334
Deer, William, 204
deer culling, 22, 140, 150, 196–203, 208, 215, 216, 219, **221**, 221–3, **222**, 240; helicopter use, 221–2, 236, 238, 241; huts, 22–3, 36, 47, 53, 138–9, 140, 200–14, 215–21, 222–3, 226, 228–31, 232–5, 236–9, 240–1, 242, 244, 248–9, 257, 274, 302, 309, 326; tent camps, 198, **199**, 199–200, 220, 228, 234, 248–9
deerstalking clubs, 17, 150, 190–1
Defiance Hut, 104
DeLury, John, 190
Dennis, Andy, **228**
Dennistoun, Jim, 178
Denton, Billy, 155
Denz, Bill, 14
Department of Conservation (DOC): animal control, 313; compliance with other authorities, 286; 'Destination Management Framework,' 292; funding, 22, 151, 238, 283, 284, 288, 289, 290, 291; grazing concessions, 64; and heritage, 19, 27, 41, 48, 291; national guidelines for facilities, 284–6; national parks management, 110; origins, 22, 262, 283; and public access, 62; quality conservation management (QCM), 284; Recreation Opportunities Review, 97, 132, 151, 152, 170, 286, 288; safety standards, 284; track maintenance, 247; visitation statistics, 20; Visitor Assessment Management Programme (VAMP), 288; visitor group classifications, 285–6; and wilderness areas, 151
Department of Conservation (DOC), and huts: categories, 285; co-management partnership with New Zealand Alpine Club, 144, 177, 312; co-management partnership with New Zealand Deerstalkers' Association, 150, 184, 190–1; fee policy, 24, 283; hut books, 190, 292; hut building, 15, 25–7, 116, 158, 164, 186, 188, 194, 220, 234, 280, 288, 289–91, 292, 293, 294, 296, 297, 298, 300, 302, 305; hut design and size, 15, 25–7, 285, 288, 292, 302, 305; number of huts, 15, 289; Permolat 'maintain by community' agreements, 152; private huts open for public hire, 194; removal and demolition, 231, 236, 284, 288, 289; replacement of huts, 118, 158, 188, 194, 206, 231, 234, 235, 238, 260, 266, 280, 288–9, 290, 291, 292, 296, 298, 300, 302, 305; representation gold mining hut, 72; retaining a diverse range of huts, 291–2; science research huts, 326, 328; two-bunk huts, 288, **288**, 291
Department of Conservation (DOC), hut restoration and maintenance, 284, 289–91, 292; club huts, 151, 156, 161, 172, 177, 179, 181, 289, 312, 322; deer cullers' huts, 47, 205, 206, 212–13, 226, **232**, 233, 238, 249–50; mining huts, 79, 80, 86, 88, 94, 95, **96**, 97, 97; mustering huts, 45, 47, 48, 51, 53, 55, 62, 68; national park huts, 267, **269**; New Zealand Forest Service huts, 247, **289**, 289–90; rabbiters' huts, 35, 47; tourist and climbing huts, 110, 113, 115, 118, 120, 124, 127, 128, 139, 140, 277
Department of Internal Affairs (DIA): deer control, 22, 140, 150, 197–200, 215; deer cullers' huts, 22, 47, 200–14, 232, 242, 257, 274; deer cullers' tent camps, 198, **199**, 199–200, 220, 228; and New Zealand–American Fiordland Expedition, 334; Physical Welfare Division, 138, 139; possum research, 325; tourism activities, 106; Wildlife Service, 260, 262, 283, 326
Department of Lands and Survey, 48, 82, 171, 175, 283; and club huts, 322; hut building programme, 22, 257–61, 262, 265, 266–7, 273, 296; huts in national parks, 22, 110, 113, 128, 129, 131, 136, 220, 255, 257–61, 262, 265, 266–7, 268–9, 273–81, 296; huts other than in national parks, 261–2; Lockwood huts, 258, 259, 260, 265, 266, 275; national park and reserve management, 135, 150–1, 219; and New Zealand–American Fiordland Expedition, 334; origins, 255; relations with New Zealand Forest Service, 22, 223, 261–2; and wilderness areas, 22
Department of Scientific and Industrial Research (DSIR), 325, 334; Ecology Division, 325, 330
Department of Survey and Land Information (DOSLI), 262
Department of Tourist and Health Resorts, 99, 103, 112, 122, 136, 144, 154, 255, 264, 270
Depression (1930s), 24, 107, 108, 127, 128, 136, 160, 192; deer culling, 197, 198; mining, 21, 54, 71, 72, 73, 78, 79, 82, 87, 90, 91, 94, 95, 96; track making, 280
'Deserters Whare,' 193
Devils Creek Hut, 43
Devils Den, 150
Dick family, 120
Dickie Spur Hut, 234–5
Dip Flat training camp, 236
Dixon, Arthur, 179
Dobbie, Brian, 26
Dog Box Biv, 41, **41**, 62
Dome Shelter, 260
Dominie Biv, 325, **332**, 332–3, **333**
Don, Alexander, **76**
Donne, Thomas, 103, **104**, 105, 106
Dorflinger, Max, 258, 276
Dorset Hut, 298
Dorset Ridge Hut, 203
D'Ott, Les, 47
Double Hut, 60, **60**
Doubtful Sound, 103
Doughboy Bay, 290

Douglas, Charlie, 104, 143, 145, 203, 327
Douglas Range, 54, 149, 186
Douglas Rock Hut, 7, **7**, 122, 124
Douglas Rock Shelter, 104, 125
Dovey, Rex, 281
Down, Dave, **222**
Drake, Bernard, 112
Dredge Hut, **280**, 281
Druce, Fenella, 307, 308
Druce, Oliver, 308
Druce, Tony and Helen, 308
Drummond, J., **198**
Dumpling Hut, 271
Duncan, Alan, 278
Duncan, Alfred, 114
Duncan, Allan, 221
Duncan, Robert, 80
Dunedin, 71, 75, 168, 175, 177
Dunnett, Barry, 25
Dunstan goldfields, 76
Duppa, George, 30
Dusky Sound, 19, **96**, 273
Dusky Track, 273
D.W. Reece Ltd., 122
Dynamite Hut, 90
Dynamo Hut, 82, **82**, **83**
Dynamo Red Hut, 82

Earnscleugh Station, 35
Earnslaw Hut, **114**, 114–15, **115**, 318
Earnslaw Station, 115
East Hawden Hut, 291
East Matakitaki Hut, 218, 242, **242**
Ede, Jack, 265
Eden, Chris, 275
Edwards Bivouac, 178, 274, **274**
Edwards Hut, 144, 274–5, **275**
egalitarianism, 15, 17
Egerton, Rachel, 291
Egmont National Park, 255, 260, 294, **295**, 296, **296**
Egmont National Park Board, 260, 294
Elder Hut, 291
Elder, Norman, **246**, 249
Eldred-Grigg, Stevan, *Diggers, Hatters and Whores,* 73–4
Elia, Wayne
Ell, Harry, 134, 135
Ella (George Lyon) Hut, **266**, 266–7
Ellis Hut, 18, 20, 52–3, **53**, 59, 248
Ellis, James William (alias John McKenzie), 18, 52, **52**
Ellis, Leon MacIntosh, 223
Ellis, Roland, 119, 143
Ellwood, Merv, 229
Empress Hut, 14, **111**, 145, 180, 181, 310
Erewhon (Stroneschrubie) Station, 33, **33**, 178
Eric Bivvy, 144, 178
erosion, 44, 75, 197, 215, 222, 240, 326
Eskew, Jack, 221
Esperance Valley, 102
Esquilant Bivouac, 115, 143, 318, **318**, **319**
Esquilant, William Robert ('Bert'), 318
Evans, Fred, 82
Eyre Mountains/Taka Ra Haka Conservation Park, **41**, 62, **63**, 219

Fairhall, Maurice (Red), 199–200
Fairlight Station, 41, 62
Fantham, Fanny, 294
Fanthams Peak, 294
farm huts, 21; *see also* pastoral huts
Farmer, Allan, 203, 213, 229

Faulkner, Colin and Ben, 135
Federated Mountain Clubs (FMC), 22, 24, 27, 108, 113, 150–1, 256, 270, 283, 294; Forest and Mountain Trust, 188; *Safety in the Mountains*, 151
fees, 24, 108, 113, 132, 144, 147, 257, 267, 272, 283
Fenella Hut, 19, 213, **306**, 307–8, **309**
Fenian Goldfield, 72
Fenwick, Chris, 264
Ferris, Harry, 87
Field, Derrick, 172, 184, 290, 298
Field Hut, **145**, 152, 172
Field, Willie, 154, **155**, 156
Fineran, Brian, 320
Fingerpost Hut, 270
Fiordland, 14, 101–3, 199, 200, 201, 236, 255–6, 257
Fiordland National Park, 22, 99, 108, 204, 249–50, 256, 257–8, 259, 270–3, 334–5
Fiordland National Park Board, 270, 271, 272, 326
fire regulations, 25, 156, 194, 284, 286
firewood, 56, 76, 113, 115, 151, 174, 177, 199, 217, 223, 224
Fisher, Jock, 77, 215, 218, 220–1, 228, 229, 232, 234, 242
Fisk, Jack, 155
Fitzgibbon, Mr and Mrs, 322
Five Mile Track, 192
Flanagans Hut, 149
Flint, Alan, 35
Flock Hill Station, 68
Flora Hut, 24, 132, **132**, **133**
Flora Valley, 251–2
Florence Valley, 205
Flowers, Arthur, 172
Flaherty, Joe, 127
Flux, John, 330
Fockerd, Stan, 219, 228, 232
Forest & Bird Protection Society, 186, 197, 270, 283
Forest Act 1949, 151
Forest and Jungle Warfare School, 202
Forest Creek, 37
Forest Creek Hut, 40, **40**
forest parks, 151, 244, 256, 257; see also names of individual parks
Forest Service, *see* New Zealand Forest Service
Forgotten Valley, 251
Forrester, Rex, 198, 200, 202, 203, 204, 212, 213, **213**, 221
Forrester, Roger, 212, 213
Forsyth, Jane, 325
Forsyth, John, 180
Four Friends Memorial Trust, 307
Four Peaks High Country Track, 43
Four Peaks Station, 43
Fowles, Phillippa and John, 274–5
Fox Glacier, **27**, 122, 124, 128, 276
Fox Glacier deer hut, 122, 124
Fox Glacier Hotel, 122, 124
Fox, William, 99
Fraemohs, 246-7, 325
Francis, Ken, 18, 198, 199, 200
Franz Josef Glacier, 18, 20, 104, 125, **125**, 136, **137**
Franz Josef Glacier Guides, 127, 136
Franz Josef (Glacier) Hotel, 104, 108, 127, 136
Franz Josef Visitor Centre, 136
Fraser, Noel, 302
Fraser, Ron, 215
Fraser, William, 35, 114
Freeman Burn Hut, 103
Freeman, Charlie, 91
Freeman, Harold, 154
French Ridge Biv, 143, 176, **176**, 300
Frew Hut, **196**, 238, 290
Frew Saddle Biv, **228**, 229
Friends of Flora, 132

Frisco Hut, **233**
Fritz Range, 136
Fullerton, Peter, 259
Fyfe, Tom, 100, **101**, 143, 276
Gabriels Gully, **75**, 75–6
Gannaway, Peter, **332**
Garden Gully Hut, 73, 79, **79**
Gardiner Hut, 108, 258, **276**, 276–7, **277**
Gardiner, Katie, 128, 129, 131, 276
Garvie Mountains, 30
Gates, John, 15, 171, 172
Gates, Tony, 20
Gazzard, Peter, **39**
Geddes, Athol, 22, 302
George Lyon (Ella) Hut, **266**, 266–7
George Sound, 334
George Sound Track, 256, 334
Gerhardt Spur Biv, 231, **232**
Gibbs, Ben, 219
Gibbs, Fred, 132
Gibbs, Joe, **154**, 154–6, 156, 157
Gibson, E.A., 91
Giddy, Colin, 289
Gilkison, Scott, 168, 280
Gillespie, Jack, 175
Gillies, Bruce, 174
Gizeh (Anti Crow) Biv, **151**, 274
Glade House, 101, 111
Glazebrook Hut, 18
Glen Lyon Station, 140
Glencreag Station, 168
Glenorchy, 79, 114, 257, 258
Glenorchy Scheelite Mining Company, 92, 94
Glenorchy scheelite mining huts, 92, **92**, **93**, 93–4, **94**
Glenquoich Sheep Station, 62
Glenthorne Station, 90, 320
Godley Glacier, 119, 120
Godley Hut, **119**, 119–20, **120**, **121**, 143, 144, 280
Godley Reserve, 119
gold mining, 21, 34, 71–4, 206; alluvial, 74–5, 78, 87, **88**, 90; Canterbury, 90, 320; dredges, 75; Nelson, 54, 71, 75, 78, 96, 242; Otago, 35, 56, 71, 73–4, **75**, 75–8, **76**, 79, 80, 82, 87, 281; quartz, 75, 78–9, 80, 82, 90; West Coast, 71, 72–3, 74, **75**, 78, 78–9, **79**, 90
Gold Prospecting Subsidy Scheme, 71–2, 73, 78, 96
Golden Bay Alpine and Tramping Club, 149, 186, 223
Golden Hills Hut, 46
Goldfields Act 1858, 74
Gollan, Alf, 172
Gordon, Paddy, 300
Gore, Henry, 75
Gorge River Hut, 17–18
government huts: for deer cullers, 22; for national parks, 22; for tourism and climbing, 99, 100–2, 103–4, 109–10, 112, 113, 138–9
Governors Bay, 59
graffiti, historic, 40, 48, 59, 60, 61, 62, 97
Graham, Alex, 104, 106, 108, 122, 124, 125, 127, 128, 136, 176
Graham, Gar, 122
Graham, George, 100, 143, 276
Graham, Jim, 104, 136, **136**
Graham, Peter, 103–4, 106, 108, 122, 124, 127, 128, 176
Graham Saddle, 125
Graham Valley, 84, 132, 252
Grand View Lodge, 103
Grant, Patrick, 222
Grassy Flat Hut, 234, 291
Grave, William, 102
Grave-Talbot Pass, 102, **102**
Gray, Cyril and Ivor, 135
Gray, William, 135

Great Walks huts and tracks, 15, 18, 24, 25, 138, 258, 283–4, 287, 289, 292; *see also* names of individual huts and tracks
Grebe Valley, 201, **204**, 204–5, **205**
Green Lake Hut, **291**
Green Lake Track, 204
Green Peak Hut, 149, **149**
Green, William Spotswood, 21
Greenlaw Hut, 143
Greenstone Hut, 290
Grey, George, 30, 32
Grey River, 75
Greymouth, 78, 122, 124
Greyneys Shelter, 258
Greytown, 145, 154
Greytown Track Committee, 171
Griebel, Russell, 313
Grieve, Dave, 290, 312
Griffiths, Rhys, 210
Gunn, Jeff, 157
Gwavas Forest, 53

Haast catchment, 201, 202, 238
Haast Hut, 105, 108, 163
Haast Pass, 300, **300**, **301**
Haast Ridge, 105, **105**
Haast–Paringa Cattle Track, 21, 261
Hakatere Conservation Park, 17, 41, 58
Hakatere Station, 58–9
Hakatere Stone Cottage, 58, **58**, 59
Halfway Hut, 273
Hall, K.C., 180
Hallet family, 44
Hambrook, Joe, 55, 97
Hamilton, Augustus, 44
Hamilton, Bill, 169
Hamilton, George, 62
Hamilton Hut, 224, **224**
Hamilton, Neil, 129, 180
Hammond, John, 308
Handcock, John and Edith, 66
Hanmer Springs, 103
Harihari, 234
Harkness, Beryl, **160**
Harman Hut, 77
Harman Pass, 320
Harper, Arthur P., 107, 108, 119, 128–9, 143, 145, 150, 175, 176, 178
Harper, Charles and George, 68
Harper, Ellen and Emily, 42
Harper, Eric, 178
Harper, Henry, 68
Harper, Leonard, 139, 143
Harper Pass, 78, 138, 139, 147, 243
Harper Pass Biv, 244, **244**
Harrow, Geoff, 310
Hartley, Horatio, 76
Harvey, Don, **72**
Harvey, Felix, 276
Hassell, Bruce, 328
Hat Spur Hut, 42, 43
Hauraki, Coromandel, **74**
Haurangi Hut, 194, **195**
Hauroko Burn, 273
Havelock Hut, 37, 144, 178, **178**, 179
Havelock River and Valley, 37, **178**, 178–9, **179**
Hawdon Hut, 275, 291
Hawdon Shelter, 258
Hawdon Valley, 257
Hawes, Darren, 318
Hawes, Dave, 206

INDEX 357

Hawes, Susan, 318
Hawke's Bay Rabbit Board, 47, 246
Hawkestone Station, 44–5
Hawkestone Stock Route, 44, 240
Hawkins Hut, 46
Hayter, Jim, 259
Healy Creek Hut, 234–5
Heaphy Hut, **224**
Heaphy Track, 25, 186, 223, 224
Heaps, Dave, 47
Heath, H.G., 68
Heather Jock Hut, 92, **93**, 94–5, **95**
Heather Jock Mine, 94
Hector Dogbox, 157
Heine, Arnold, 132, 151, 307
Heine, Jan, 307
Heinz, Bill, 90
Hellebrekers, Paul, 177, 278–9, 300
Henderson, Jim, 96, 132, 251; *The Exiles of Asbestos Cottage*, 84, 86
Henham, John, 221
Herangi Range, 293
Heretaunga Tramping Club, 15, 18–19, 47, 53, **146**, 149, 163, 201, 240, **240**, 246, 247, 248
Herman, Noel, **187**
Hermitage, 99–100, 103, 104–5, **105**, **106**, 107, 108, 109, 116, 118, 125
Herrick, Warren, 318
Herricks Hut, 248
Herron, Phil, 14
Hewitt, J.T., 50
Hewitt, Rod, 332
Hicks, Mt, 14
Hideaway Biv, 19, 20, 35, 48, **48**, **49**
high-country farming, 29–30; beginnings, 30–1; boom and bust, 32–4; farm huts today, 40–1, **41**; land tenure and break-up of great estates, 34–5, 40, 41, 56; mustering, 37–40; rabbits and rabbit control, 35–7; refrigeration, 34; stocking the land: merinos and boundary-keepers, 31–2
high-country huts, *see* pastoral huts
Highland Creek Hut, **285**
Hihitahi Forest Sanctuary, 297
hiking, *see* tramping
Hikurangi Range, 250
Hillary Ridge, Aoraki/Mt Cook, 118
Hillary, Sir Edmund, 60, 118, 127, 182, 183, 276, 310; signature, **183**
Hindmarsh, Gerald, 132; *Kahurangi Calling*, 54
Historic Clark Hut, 201, **204**, 204–5, **205**
historic huts, 19, 27, 29–30, 40–1, 285, 286, 292; *see also* names of individual huts
HM Customs Department Tramping Club, 192
Hochstetter Dome, 100
Hochstetter icefall, 100
Hokitika, 78, **78**, 188, 228, 232, 233
'Hokitika Bill' (Bill Bergman), 90–1
Hokitika catchment, **214**, 219, 228
Hokuri, 291
Holden, Philip: *New Zealand, Hunter's Paradise*, 198; *Pack and Rifle*, 220
Holdsworth Lodge, 22
Holloway Hut, 325
Holloway, Jack, 325
Hollows, Fred, 278
Holly Hut, 260
Hollyford River, 102
Hollyford Track, 111, 273, 291
Hollyford Valley, 149
Homer Hut, 144
Homestead Hunters Hut, **190**
Hooker Glacier, 111, 145, 276, 277, **277**
Hooker Hut, 103–4, **108**, 111, 118, 122, 125, 136
Hooker Valley, 14, 103–4, 111, 276

Hope Kiwi Lodge, 210, 224, 244, **245**
Hope Valley, 208, **209**, 210
Hopeless Hut, 144
Hopgood, Harry, 94
Hopkins (Elcho) Hut, 143
Hopkins Valley, 140, **140**, 141
Howard Goldfield, 71–2
Howard, John, 334
Howden, David, 304, 305, **305**
Howell, Captain, 62
Howlett, Olive, 165
Howlett, William F., 165
Howletts Hut, 15, 20, **165**, 165–6, **166**, **167**, 248
Hoy, J., 51
Hoyle, David, 182, 183
Huddleston, Frank, 99
Hughes, Kevin, **121**
Hulston, Fred, 314
Hume Pipe Company, 84
Hunt, John, 42
Hunters Haven Hut, 258
Hunters Hut, 307, 313, **313**
hunting, 17, 52–3, 136, 150, 155, 156, 172, 190–1, 202, 205, 215, 219, 223, 234, 238, 241, 248, 257, 273, 278, 285, 286, 288, 293, 297, 302, 322; *see also* deer culling; deerstalking clubs; venison recovery
Hunua Ranges, 146, 147
Hurst-Seager, Samuel, 134
Hurunui Hut, 150
Hurunui Valley, 139, 244
'hut baggers,' 26, 238
hut books, 20, **20**, 50–1, **51**, 62, 66, 82, 149, 206, 292; *see also* graffiti, historic
huts: backlash from wilderness movement, 22; brief history, 19–27; diversity, 18–19; fees, 24, 108, 113, 132, 144, 147, 257, 267, 272, 283; fire regulations, 25, 156, 194, 284, 286; government huts for deer cullers and national parks, 22, **23**; historic, 19, 27, 29–30, 40–1, 285, 286, 292; as homes, 17–18, 19, **19**, 21, 59; modern huts, 15, 26–7; numbers of huts, 15, 29, 289; as refuge from urban life, 17–18; road-building huts, 21, **21**; as shelter, 14–15, 19; as a social experience, 15–17; stories about backcountry, 19; toilets, 285, 287, **287**; *see also* building and design of huts; club huts; deer culling – huts; Department of Conservation (DOC), and huts; Department of Conservation (DOC), hut restoration and maintenance; farm huts; Great Walks huts; mining huts; mustering huts; New Zealand Forest Service huts; pastoral huts; private huts; ski huts; tourism, and tourist and climbing huts; also under Department of Internal Affairs and Department of Lands and Survey; and see names of individual huts
Hutt Valley Tramping Club, 26, 146, 149, **162**, 162–4, 192–3, 288
Huxley Gorge Station, 140
hydroelectric scheme, Mt Aurum, 82

Ian Powell Hut, *see* Powell Hut
Ida Railway Hut, 64, **64**, **65**
Inder, Laurie, 64
Invercargill Tramping Club, 149
Invincible Quartz Mining Company, 92
Iron Bark tent camp, 248
'Iron House,' Franz Josef Glacier, 104
Iron Whare, 21, **44**, 44–5, **45**
Irwin, Lisle, 307
Ivory Glacier, 325, **327**, 327–8, **329**
Ivory Lake Hut, **324**, 325, **327**, 327–8, **328**, **329**
Iwikau Village, Mt Ruapehu, 15, 259

Jacks Hut, 21, **21**
Jackson, Marcella, 158
Jacobs, Harold, 273
Jans Hut, 194

Jaquiery Valley, 205
Jean Hut, 92, **92**
Jenkins, Chris, 309
Jensen, Charlie, 124
Jervois Hut, 203, **216**
Jim Adams Memorial Hut, 147
Joel Lodge, 169
Joel, Norman, 169
John Bennett's Hut, **70**
John Tait Club, 149
John Tait Hut, 258, 266, 267–8, **268**, **269**
Johnson, Chris, 176
Johnstone, Glenn, 326
Johnstone, J.S., 178
Jollie Brook Hut, 244, **244**, 326
Jones, Johnny, 31
Jones, Tony, 265
Jordan, James, 248–9
Joyce, Ken ('Digger'), 277
Jubilee Hut, 149
Judkins, Robin, 236
Julia Hut, 233, 261
Jumble Top Biv, 229, **229**
Jumbo Hut, 290, 309
Jumboland Hut, 143, 278, **278**

Kahurangi National Park, 19, 21, 54–5, 72, **73**, 79, 84–9, 96–7, 132–3, 186–7, **199**, 216–17, 251–3, 289, 290; *see also* Northwest Nelson Forest Park
Kaimai Ranges, 149, 150
Kaimanawa Forest Park, 224, 225
Kaimanawa Ranges, 29, 46, 197
Kaimanawa (Te Apunga) Hut, 46
Kaimata Range, 325
Kaitoke–Holdsworth Track, 139
Kakapo Hut, 217, 218, 233
Kane, Jim, 205
Karamea, 217
Karamea Bend Hut, 217, 218
Karamea Valley, 54, 87
Kaweka Flats Biv, 45
Kaweka Forest Park, 13, **44**, 44–5, **45**, 46, 46–7, **47**, 226, 332–3; New Zealand Forest Service huts, **240**, 240–1, **241**, **332**, 332–3, **333**
Kaweka Hut, 146, 149
Kaweka Range, 13, 19, 20, 21, 29, 44, 46, 150, 197, 215, 219, 222, 240, 249, 325, 326
Kawhatau Valley, **222**
kea, 86, 91, 124, 188, 200, **210**, 328
Kea Basin, 114, 115
Kean, Ralph, 325
Keir, Bill, 20
Kelly, Alan, 179
Kelly Knight Hut, 249
Kelly Knight tent camp, 248
Kelly, Michael, 27; *Wild Animal Control Huts*, 226
Kelly, Russ, 179
Kelly Shelter, 258
Kelman Hut, 289
Kennedy Lodge, 145
Kepler Track, 26, 287
Kerin, John, 278
Kershaw, Dave, 318
Ketetahi Hut, 103, 112, 260
Kidd, Jack, 68
Kilby, Jim, 259
Kill Devil Track, 54, 96
Kime, Esmond, 154, 157, 307
Kime Hut, 155, **157**, 157–8, **158**, **159**, 162, 163, 302, 307
King, Cecil, **87**, 87–8, **88**

King Memorial Hut, 105, **105**
King, Sydney, 105
Kings Creek Hut, 87, 224
Kintail Hut, 273
Kinvig, Leon, 249
Kirk, Thomas, 165
Kirwans Hut, 225, **225**
Kirwan's Reward Mine, 78
Kiwi Hut, 208, **208**, 210
Kiwi Saddle Club, 18–19
Kiwi Stream, 244
Klondyke Shelter, 258
Knight, Kelly, 249
Knights Track, 249
Knobby Ridge Biv, 231
Knott, Richard, 183
Knowlson, Frankie, **96**, 97
Knox, Colin, **312**
Koch, Gilbert, 94
Koch, Winnie, 94
Kokatahi River and catchment, **200**, 228, 234, 261, 290, 326
Kokatahi Tramping Group, 188
Kokich, Murray, 318
Koolen, Greg, 86
Korowai/Torlesse Tussocklands Park, 30, 41, 68–9, **69**
Kuripapango, 46
Kyle Biv, 249

Labour Government: first, 72, 138; fourth, 283
Labour-Alliance Government, 151, 238, 288
Laidlaw, W.S., 35
Lake Alabaster, 291
Lake Daniells Hut, 322, **322**
Lake Emma Hut, 58, 59, **59**
Lake Hankinson, 334
Lake Hauroko Hut, 273
Lake Head Hut, 266
Lake Manapouri, 103, 273
Lake Mintaro, 270
Lake Monowai, 201, 204, 273
Lake Roe Hut, 273, **273**
Lake Rotoiti, 71, 132, 258, 267
Lake Sumner Forest Park, 139, 210, 224; New Zealand Forest Service huts, 244, **244**, **245**, 261, 326
Lake Taylor Hut, 138, 289
Lake Te Anau, 101, **101**, 102, 271, 273
Lake Tekapo, 119
Lake Thompson, 334
Lake Waikaremoana, 25, 197, 200, 260
Lake Wakatipu, 114
Lambie, George, 59
Land Act 1877, 34
Land Act 1892, 35
Land Act 1948, 40, 56
Land Search and Rescue, 151
Land Settlement Board, 256
Landcare Research, 325, 326
Landsborough Valley, 200, 201, **201**, 307
Lange, Kevin, **39**
Langley, John, 170
Langrish, Tim, **151**
Langton, Graham, 103
Larrivee, Larry, 300
Lasenby, Jack, 216
Le Fevre, Brian, **262**
Leach, Francis, 58
Leaning Lodge, 149, **169**, 169–70
Lee, Alan, 246
Lee, Edgar, 56

Lee, John, 56
Lee, Robert (Bob), 56
Lee, Sandra, 288
Leehy, Arthur, 276
Leetham Valley, 236
Leitch, Sam, 293
Leitch's Hut, 293, **293**
Lemberg, Fred, 20, 166
Lethbridge, Christopher, *Sunrise on the Hills*, 46
Levin Waiopehu Tramping Club, 146, **148**, 290
Lewis, John Graham, 45
Lewis Pass, 208, 218
Lewis Pass Hut, 150
Lewis Pass National Reserve, 322, **323**
Lewis Pass–St Arnaud tramp, 242
Lilybank Station, 119, 120, 143
Linda Glacier, 308
Lindsay, Ken, 62
Little Wanganui, 87
Liverpool Bivouac, 176
Liverpool Hut, 143
Loch Maree Hut, 273
Lock, Edwin, 139, 143
Locke Stream Hut, 111, **138**, 138–9, **139**
Lockwood hut designs: Department of Lands and Survey national park huts, 258, 259, 260, 265, 266, 275; New Zealand Forest Service huts, 163, 224, **225**, **225**, 246, **247**
Log Cabin Hut, 46
Logan, Hugh, 307
Lonely Lake Hut, 186, **187**
Long Harry Hut, 290
Long, Robert (Beansprout), 17–18
Longview Hut, 248, 249, **249**
Lotkow Hut, 241
Loughnan, Ignatius, 56
Loughnan, Robert Andrew, 56
Lowen, Peter, 330
Lower Arahura Hut, 188, 235
Lower Cook Bivouac, 276
Lower Gridiron Rock Shelter, **251**, 251–2, **252**
Lower Olderog Biv, 229
Lucas, Bing, 262
Lucas, Fred ('Popeye'), 215, 218
Lumsden, David, 46
Luna Hut, 217, 218, **218**
Lunch Hut, 104
Luncheon Rock, Westland National Park, 27
Lusk, Pete, 87
Luxmore Hut, 26
Lyell Goldfield, 71
Lyell Hut, 144, 145
Lyes, Tom, 203
Lyon, George, 258–9, 266–7, 268, **268**
Lyon, Jean, 259
Lyons, Bill, 157

Mabin, Bert, 163
McAtamney, Steve and Jo, 43
Macaulay Valley, **34**
McBurney, Jack, 86
McCallum, Graham, **7**
McCaughan, A., 62
McConchie (Mid Matiri) Hut, 217, 218
McConchie, Phil, 216, 217, 218
McConnell, Pat and Len, 273
McConochie, Newton, 222
McCormack Hut, 27
McGlashan, Geoff, **296**
McGregor Biv, **12**

McGregors Hut, 325, **326**
McHardy, Geoff, 170
McIndoe Hut, 248
McIntosh Hut, 92, 95
McIntosh, William, 92
McIntyre Hut, 92, 95
Mckay, Duncan, *Frontier New Zealand*, 73
McKenzie Hut, 102
McKenzie, John, 34–5
McKerrow, James, 255
Mackie, Ron, **151**
McKinley, Kiersten, 48
Mckinnon, A., 168
McKinnon Hut, 250, **250**
Mackinnon Pass, 101, 102, 270, 271
Mackinnon, Quintin, 101, 270
Mackintosh Hut, 241
Macklin, Tony, 184–5
Maclean, Chris, **250**, 299
McLean, Harry, 37
McLean, Rob, 307
McLeod, David, 29
McLeod, Rob, 48
McLeod, Ron, 318
MacMorland, Dave, 267
McNeill, Robin, 226
Macnicol, Archie, 82
Macnicol, Duncan, 82
McPherson Hut, 102, **102**
McRae, George, 33
Magnusson, Bill, 330
Main Trunk Railway, 103, 112
Maitland Hut, 313
Makahu Chalet, 332
Makahu Saddle, 325, 332
Makahu Saddle Hut, 213, 226, 240, **240**, 332
Makaretu Hut, 226
Makarora catchment, 201, 202, 278–9, 290, 300
Makino Hut, 150, 241, **241**
Malte Brun Hut, **98**, 100–1, 103, 107, 108, 111
Malte Brun Hut II, 110
Malte Brun Range, 100
Malthus, Reginald, 119, 143
Manawatu Tramping (and Ski) Club, 146, 149, 166
Mangaehuehu, 260
Mangahao Flats Hut, 26, 289
Mangahuia, 160
Mangamingi Hut, 46
Mangamuku Hut, 150
Manganui ski-field shelter, 260
Mangatepopo, 260
Mangaturuturu Hut, 148, 149
Mangawhare Station, 44
Mannering, George ('Guy'), 119, 143
Manson, Brian and Sharon, 322
Manson, George, 66
Manson Hut, 46–7
Manson, Les ('Bang') and Choggy, 96
Manson–Nicholls Memorial Hut, 322, **323**
Manuherikia River, 76
Maori: compensation for mining on Maori land, 74; gold mining, 74, 96; shelters, 19; trails, 90, 138, 139
'Maori bunks,' 15, 152
Maori Saddle Hut, 261
Marauiti Hut, 260
Mardell, Evan, 184, 302
Marlborough, 30, 35, 75, 202, 218, 219, 222; *see also* names of specific places
Marlborough Rabbit Trapping and Meat Export Company, **36**

Maropea Forks tent camp, 248
Maropea River, 249
Marsden, Samuel, 31
Marsh, Bill, 53
Marshall, Barbara, 86
Marshall, Daryl, 205
Marshall, Keith, 186
Martin, Zeke, 297
Martins Bay Hut, 291
Martin's Creek Hunters Hut, **190**
Maruia Valley, 218
Mason, Bruce and Peter, 170
Massey University Alpine Club, 145
Masters, Lester, 20, 50–1; 'Alex,' 51; *Back Country Tales,* 50, 248
Masterton Tramping Club, 143
Matai Valley, 132
Matakitaki Valley: East Branch, 242, **242**; West Branch, 242, **243**
Mataura Valley, 62, **63**
Matemateonga Walkway, 261
Matthews Hut, 248
Matukituki Valley, 143; West, 174–7
Maunder, H., **23**
Maungahuka Hut, **282**, 291, 302, **302**, **303**
Maxwell, Shona, 281
Mead, Bill, 112
Meadow Lee Hut, 57
Meg Hut, 56–7, **57**
Meikles Hut, 73
Melland, Edward, 270
memorial huts, **306**, 307–24
merino sheep, 30, 31–2, 33–4, 41, 44, 45, 56, 58, 64, 82
Mesopotamia Station, **31**, 33, 37, 58, 59, 60, 61, 178, 179
meteorological stations and records, 86, 236, 325, 328, 333, **333**
Mid Glenroy Hut, 218
Mid Greenstone Hut, 290
Mid Matiri (McConchie) Hut, 217, 218
Mid Robinson Hut, 238, **239**
Mid Styx Hut, 152
Mid Taipo Hut, **239**
Mid Trent Hut, 235
Mid Waiohine Hut, 25, 226, **226**
Middle Hill Hut, 45
Middy Hut, 20
Mikonui Spur Biv, 229, **230**, 288
Milford Sound, 101, 102, **3**
Milford Track, 21, 24, 25, 99, **101**, 101–3, **102**, 109, 110, 111, 257, 270, 287; freedom walkers' huts, 271–2; ownership, 270–1
Millar, Neville, 190
Miller, Alex, 131
Miller, Eric, 119
Miller, Fred and Peg, 73
Millward, Don, 164
Milne, Frank, 140
Minaret Station hut, **38**, **39**
Mingha Biv, 274
mining, 79, 84; scheelite, 92, 94, **94**; *see also* coal mining; gold mining; mining huts
mining huts, 21, 70–3, **72**, 74, 76, **76**, 77–8, **78**, **79**, 79–97, 142, 281; *see also* names of individual huts
Ministry of Works, 255, 260, 332, 334; Meteorological Division, 236; Water and Soil Division, 327; *see also* Public Works Department
Mintaro Hut, 270–1, **271**, **272**
Mitchell, Ernest, 270
Mitchison, Rebecca, 194–5
Mitre Flats Hut, 289
Mitre Peak, 102, 164
Moa Stream, 90, 91
Mokai Patea tent camp, 248
Mokihinui Forks, 219

Mole Tops Hut, 218
Molesworth Station, 46
Molloy, Les, 22, 151, 267
Molyneux (Clutha) River, 75, 76, 77
Moncrieff, Perrine, 66
Money, Charles, 17
Monument Shelter, 135
Moonlight, George Fairweather, 242
Moore, John ('Cocker'), 277
Moraine Creek Hut, 120, 143–4, 149
Moreton, Samuel, 101
Morgan, Alan, 179
Morpeth, John, 320
Morris, Dick, 208, **208**, 210, **210**
Morrison, Frank, 179
Morse, Deryck, 180
Morton, Elsie K., 7, 14, 18
Morven Hills Station, 32
Motatapu Track, **285**
Motueka River, 313
Motueka Tramping Club, 149
Mt Alack, 131, **131**
Mt Alaska, 92, 94
Mt Albert Station, 278
Mt Algidus Station, 90
Mt Harper, **317**
Mount Aspiring National Park, 19, 114–15, 144, 174–7, 256, 257–8, 278–81, 285, 300–1, 310–12, 318–19
Mount Aspiring National Park Board, 258, 280
Mount Aspiring Station, 174, 175
Mt Aspiring/Tititea, 143, 174, 255, 310, **311**, 312, **312**
Mt Aurum Quartz Mining Company, 80
Mt Aurum Recreation Reserve, 80, **81**, 82, **83**
Mt Aurum Station, 82
Mt Balloon Hut Scenic Trust Board, 131
Mt Balloon Scenic Reserve, 24, 132
Mt Brewster, 258
Mt Brown, 188, **188**, **189**
Mt Brown Hut, 152, 188, **188**, **189**, 261
Mt Brown Hut Community Project Team, 188
Mt Castor, 278
Mt Cook, *see* Aoraki/Mt Cook
Mount Cook Group, 108
Mount Cook Motor Service, 106
Mt Cook National Park, *see* Aoraki/Mt Cook National Park
Mount Cook Tourist Company, 106, 107, 108, 109, 110, 119, 122, 143, 276
Mt Douglas, 128, **130**
Mt Durwood, 235
Mt Earnslaw, 92, 114, 143, 318
Mount Earnslaw Hotel, 114
Mt Egmont Alpine Club, 24, 145, 151, 294, 296, **296**
Mt Fell Hut, 226
Mt Harman, 90
Mt Hector, 157
Mt Hector Track, 154
Mt Holdsworth, **162**, 162–4, **163**, **164**, 202
Mt Holdsworth Club, 162
Mt Ida Conservation Area, 64, **64**, **65**
Mt Judah, 92, 94
Mt McIntosh, 95
Mt McPherson, 102
Mt Misery, 325
Mt Murchison, 314
Mt Ngauruhoe, 112, 113, 255
Mt Ollivier, 116, 118
Mt Owen Track, 72, 73
Mt Peel Station, 31, 32, 33, **40**, 42, 58
Mt Pisa Station, 56
Mt Pollux, 278, **279**

Mt Possession Station, 58, 59
Mt Richmond Forest Park, 20, 226, 313, **313**
Mt Ruapehu, 15, 104, 112, 113, 143, 146, 147, 149, 255, **256**
Mt Sefton, **110**, **118**
Mt Somers Hut, 304, 305
Mt Somers Station, 42, 58, 60, 304
Mt Somers Track, **304**, 304–5, **305**
Mt Taranaki, 255, 260, 289, 294, **295**
Mt Tarawera, 99
Mt Tasman, 128, 129, 294
Mount Torlesse Collieries, 68
Mt Torlesse Station, 68
Mt White Station, 37, 40
Mountain Guides Association, 151
Mountain House, 146, 162
Mountain Safety Council, 151
mountaineering clubs, 17, 143–5; *see also* names of individual clubs and huts
Mud Flats Hut, 203
Mueller Glacier, 99, 116, 140, 307
Mueller Hut, 105, 107, 111, 116, **116**, **117**, 118, **118**, 290
Muir, Fred (Frederick Mintaro Bailey), 270
Muirson, Stan, 130, 314
Mullins Basin Hut, 235, **235**
Mungo Hut, **214**, 235
Munro, Clifford John, 48
Munroe, Ian, 191
Murch, Margaret (now McGuire), 149
Murchison, 155, 217, 242
Murchison Glacier, 143
Murchison Hut, **24**
Murchison Mountains, 150, 326
Murchison Valley, 120, 144
Murphy, Jim, 104
Murray, Eric, 140
Murray, Gilbert, 131
Murrell family, 103
Murrell, Norman, 140
Museum Hut, 208, **209**, 210, **211**
mustering huts, 20, 26, 29, **34**, 35, 36, 37, **38**, **39**, 40–69, 91, 113, 140, 199, 244, 248, 278, 304; musterers' tradition of signing names, 40, 59, 61, 62; *see also* names of individual huts
Mutton Cove homestead, 66

Napier Tramping Club, 147
National Film Unit, 176
National Park Service, 258, 260, 262, 284
national parks, 59, 99, 144, 150–1, 223, 255–6, 283; funding, 260, 274; hut design, 261, 273, 276–7; hut fees, 24; hut wardens, 18, 24, 177, 256, 258, 285, 289; huts, 22, 110, 219–20, 255, 256, 257–69, 271–81; management, 110, 256, 257, 258, 260, 262, 283; rangers, 109, 257, 258, 259, 260, 262, 266, 273, 274; volunteers, 177, 260–1, 289; *see also* names of individual national parks and huts
National Parks Act 1952, 108, 151, 256–7, 265, 270
National Parks Authority, 177, 261, 262, 270, 271
Nature Heritage Fund, 68
Neave Hut, 236, **236**, 239
Neese, Alfred, 278
Neill Forks Hut, **221**
Neill, Wally, 157, 158, **158**
Nelson, 71, 75, 78, 313; Northwest, 54, 96, 132, 186, 216–17, 219, 233
Nelson Lakes National Park, 24, 144, 149, 218, 220, 243, **254**, 255, 256, 258–9, 266–9, 325, 330–1
Nelson Tramping Club, **148**, 149, 186, 267–8
Nelson, Vic, 212
Neville Barker Memorial Hut, 309
New Zealand Alpine Club (NZAC), 15, 21, 24, 107, 108, 119, 120, 122, 128–30, 131, 143, 180, 258, 260, 278, 280, 290, 312; Auckland Section, 143, 182–3; Canterbury–Westland Section, 119–20;

co-management partnership with DOC, 144, 177, 312; Nelson–Marlborough Section, 144; Otago Section, 143, 174–6, 177, 270, 310, 318; South Canterbury Section, 120; Southland Section, 144, 318; Taranaki Section, 183; Wellington Section, 119, 120, 144, 183
New Zealand–American Fiordland Expedition, 334, **334**
New Zealand Army, 131
New Zealand Company, 30
New Zealand Deerstalkers' Association (NZDA), 15, 21, 150, 184, 258, 291; Hawke's Bay Branch, 241, 249; Rakaia Branch, 304; Southland Branch, 190; Wairarapa Branch, 198; Wellington Branch, 184–5
New Zealand Electricity Department, 82
New Zealand Forest Service, 215–16, 255; and club huts, 151, 172, 186; deer culling, 22, 140, 197, 203, 215, 219, 220–3, 228, 234, 236, 238, 240, 241, 242, 244, 248–9, 302; Forest and Range Experiment Station, 205, 325; forest parks, 151, 244, 256; grazing licensing, 54; hut building and maintenance, 13, 22, 45, 47, 51, 53, 86, 87, 97, 132, 140, 151, 156, 157, 160–1, 163, 171, 172, 180, 188, 190, 210; hut designs, 13, 18, 47, 87, 136; hut visibility, 261; National Forest Survey, 325; native logging operations, 224, 283; and New Zealand–American Fiordland Expedition, 334; possum control, 222, 228, 234, 236; possum research, 325; and private huts, 194; relations with Department of Lands and Survey, 261–2; timber policy and production, 283
New Zealand Forest Service huts: building programme, 215–16, 219–20, 224, 233–4, 241, 242, 249–50, 257, 259, 261; Dexion aluminium framing, 215, **217**, 240; free use, 24, 221, 257, 283; helicopter use in building, 215–19, **217**; heritage value, 226, **226**; hut books, 20; huts built by clubs and groups on Forest Service land, 223–4; Kaweka Forest Park huts, **240**, 240–1, **241**; Lake Sumner Forest Park huts, 244, **244**, **245**, 261; Lockwood designs, 163, 224, 225, **225**, 246, **247**; NZFS S81 and SF70 designs, 136, 217, **219**, 219–21, **220**, 233–5, 236, 238, **238**, 241, 242, **242**, **243**, 250, **250**, 302, **302**, 328; orange colour for visibility, 18, 188, 215, 220, 226, **244**, 261; recreational use, 223–4, 226, 234–5, 238, 241, 245, 246–7, 249–52, 257, 258; Ruahine Forest Park, 226, **246**, 246–7, **247**, **248**, 248–50, **249**, **250**; science research huts, 325–6, 328, 330–3; tent camps, 198, **199**, 199–200, 220, 228, 234, 248–9, 259; two-person bivouacs, 216, 219, **219**, 241, 249, **250**, 274; West Coast two-person bivouacs, **228**, 228–9, **229**, **230**, 231, **231**; West Coast four-bunk huts, **232**, 232–5, **233**, **234**, **235**; West Coast six-bunk huts, 236, **236**, **237**, 238, **238**, **239**; *see also* names of individual huts
New Zealand Geographic Board, 262
New Zealand Geological Survey, 203
New Zealand Ski Association, 151
New Zealand Tourism Board, 110
New Zealand Walkways Commission, 151
Newman, Eddie, 188
Newton Biv, 231
Newton, Henry, 128
Newton, Peter, 36–7, 40
Ngaere Lodge, 332
Ngai Tahu, 30
Nganatea Station, 29, 46, 47
Nganoko Range, 249
Ngaro-Te-Kotare Hut, 146, **147**
Ngaruroro River, 46, 240
Nicholls, Gordon and Esther, 262
Nicholls, Phillip, 322
Nina Hut, 150
No Mans Hut, 248
Noeline Glacier, 276
Noisy Biv, 229
Nolans Hut, 203
North, Malcolm and Alana, 68
North Ohau Hut, 291
Northwest Nelson Forest Park, 24, 54, 186, **223**, 223–5, 251, 308; *see also* Kahurangi National Park
Noti Raureka (Browning Pass), 90
Noxious Animals Act 1956, 215

Oaks Hut, 194
O'Brien, Clint, 48
Ohutu tent camp, 248
Okarito, 78
Old Carrington Hut, **16**
Old Cedar Flat (Cedar Flat) Hut, 229, **232**, 232–3
Old Ghost Road, 292
Old Julia Hut, 233
Old Man Range, 76, 77
Old Manson Hut, **46**, 46–7, **47**
Old Waihohonu Hut, 20, 103, 111, 112–13, **113**
Olderog Biv, **227**
O'Leary Peak, 114
Olivine Ice Plateau/Wilderness Area, 22, 251, 257
Ombler, John, 288
O'Neill, Clare, **219**
Ongaruanuku Hut, 147
Onslow, Lord, 100
Orari Gorge Station, 32, **42**, 42–3, **43**
Orbell, Geoffrey, 150
O'Regan, Pat, 275
O'Reilly, Merv, 229
Orongorongo Club, 194
Orongorongo Valley, 15, 146, 152, 192, 193, **193**, 325
Orongorongo Valley huts, 15, 146, 152, **192**, 192–5, **194**, **195**
Osman, Ray, 218, 219
Otago, 25, 29, 31, 32, 35, 75, 197, 199, 255, 289; Central, 14, 35, 36, 37, 41, 56, 73–4, 75–8, 79, 80, 82; *see also* names of specific places
Otago Acclimatisation Society, 35
Otago Central Rail Trail, 168
Otago Ski Club, 149, 168, 169, 170
Otago Tramping and Mountaineering Club, 149, 170
Otago Tramping Club (OTC), 149, 169–70, 270, 271
Otago University Ski Club, 169
Otago University Tramping Club, 149, 170
Otaki, 145, 154
Otaki Forks, 154, 155
Otehake Hut, 236
Oturere, 260
Oxley, Nigel, 308

packhorses, 17, 50, 62, 90, 96, 119, 128, 152, 155, 157, 174, 175, 200, 203, 210, 212, 215, **215**, 257, 260, 264, 314, 320
Padget, F., 62
Page Shelter, 258
Pakety Hut, 40
Palmer Lodge, 150
Palmerston North Tramping and Mountaineering Club, 26, 160–1
Paparoa Range, 73, 326
Papatahi Hut, 194
Pararaki Hut, 325
Park, James, 320
Park Morpeth Hut, 144, 145, 264, 307, 320, **321**
Parkerson, William, 33
Parry, Bill, 138
Pascoe, John, 144, 192; *Land Uplifted High*, 193
pastoral huts, 15, 21, 29–30; *see also* high-country farming; mustering huts; and names of individual huts
Paterson, Tom, 330
Patterson, R.M., 82
Patterson, Robin, *A Sock in My Stew*, 208, 210, **210**
Pattle, Jack, 178, 179
Paua Hut, 146, 193
Paua Tramping Club, 146, 193
Paulin, Andy, 95
Pawson, Selwyn, 298
Payton, Ian, 325–6
Peache, Alfred, 304
Pearson, Charley, 333

Pegram, Darryn, **187**
Pell Stream Hut, 13, **14**, 218
Peninsula Tramping Club, 120, 147
Penn, Frank, 154
Permolat, 152, 231, 238
Pern, Stephen, 25–6
Perry, Eric and Dora, 71–2
Peters Hut, 46
Petterson, Clive and Pete, 97
Pfeifer Biv, 231, **288**, 291
Philips, Henry (Harry), 53
Phillips, Jock, *A Man's Country*, 17
Phillips, Stan, **296**
Phoenix Mining Company, 80, 82
Physical Welfare and Recreation Act 1937, 147
Pickens, Ivan, 183
Pickering, Mark, 15, 26, 43; *Huts: Untold Stories of Back-country New Zealand*, 215; *A Tramper's Journey*, 13, 26, 66, 223
Piddington, Ken, 283
Pig Gully Hut, 62
Pinnacle Biv, 229, **230**
Pinnacles Hut, 25, 289, 304
Pioneer Bivvy/Hut, 21, 121, 122, 124, **128**, 128–31, **129**, **130**, **131**, 143, 258, 287
Pisa Conservation Area, 56, 56–7, **57**
Pisa Range, 56, 57
Pither, Lawson, 160–1
Plateau Hut, 290, **290**
Pleasant Gully Hut, 43
Pleasant Range, 273
poems: 'Alex' (Lester Masters), 51; ditty about hut books (Lester Masters), 20; from Golden Bay Alpine and Tramping Club archives, 186; 'Inder's Castle' ('Blue Jeans' (Ross McMillan)), 47; 'Rest After Labour' (Never Again), 165; 'The Manson Country in Winter Time' (Anon.), 47; 'Mountain Hut' (Shaun Barnett), 13
Poet Hut, 233, **233**
Pohangina Hut, 248
Pohangina River and Valley, 249
Polglaze, Max, 54–5, **55**, 86, 88, 223, 251–2, **253**
Polson, Ian, 32
Polson, John, 32
Polson's Hut, 32, **32**
Pompolona Hut, 101, **102**, 270
Poole, Lindsay, 215, 334
Pope, Jack, 128, 276
Poplars Station, 208, **209**, 210, 211
Poporangi Station, 52–3, **53**
Port Hills, 134, 135
Port Levy Saddle, 147
Port Levy Saddle Hut, 24
possum control and research, 222, 228, 234, 236, 293, 325, 326
Postill, Bruce, **46**, 130, 131, 263, 266, 267, 268, 330
Potters gold claims, 77, 78
Potters Hut, 76, 77
Potts, Thomas, 58–9
Pouakai Hut, 260
Poulter Biv, 291
Poulter Valley, 257
Powell Hut, **162**, 162–4, **163**, **164**, 290
Powell, Ian, 163, 180, 245
Powell, Paul, 15, 27, 318 *Men Aspiring*, 176, **318**
Pracy, Les, 325, **326**
Presland, Peter, **39**
Prices Flat Hut, 203, **203**, 220, 238
Prickett, Nigel, 205
Prior, G.E., 180
private huts, 15, 99, 106–8, 111, 165, 171, 192, 193, 194
Prouting, Laurie, 179
Prouting, Malcolm, 61, 178

public access, 62, 107, 134, 151, 194, 202, 221, 223, 270
Public Works Department, 91, 154; hut design and building, 122, 124, 155, 201, **201**, 202, **202**, 267; *see also* Ministry of Works
Pudding (Noeline) Rock, 276, **276**, **277**
Puketitiri, 44, 45
Pullen, George, 77
Pureora Forest Park, 224, 325
Purity Hut, **286**
Pynenburg and Collins, 288
Pynenburg, Ron, 164, 184, 288
Pyramid Hut, 77, **77**

Quaife, John, 278
Quailburn Station, 35, 48
Queenstown, 80, 107, 109, 169
Quigg, Robin, *Back-country Huts*, 15
Quinn, L.J., 162
Quintin Hut, 102

Rabbit Nuisance Act 1867, 35–6; amendment, 1947, 37
rabbiting huts, 21, 29, 35–7, **36**, 47, **49**, 50–1, **51**, 52, 246, 248
Radford, James, 42–3
Raglan Range, 236
rail transport, and outdoor recreation, 103, 107, 110, 112, 147, 168, 256, 265, 316
Railways Department, 103, 107, 110, 147; mystery train excursions, 147
rainfall, 14, 236
Rakiura Hunter Camp Trust, 150, 152, 190–1
Rakiura Maori Land Trust, 191
Ramblers, 147
Rangers Hut, Landsborough Valley, 201, **201**
Rangipo Hut, 260
Rangitata River and Valley, 31, **31**, 37, 41, 58, 59, 60–1
Rangitata/Hakatere mustering huts, **58**, 58–61, **59**, **60**, **61**
Rangitikei Tramping Club, 26
Rangitoto Island, 192
Rangiwahia Hut, **160**, 160–1, **161**
Rangiwahia Ski Club, 160
Rapid Creek Biv, 231
Ratcliffe, Dick, **258**, 281
Rattray, Allan, **119**
Raukawa Lodge, 194
Read, Gabriel, 75, 76
Red Hut, 111, 140, **140**, **141**
Ree, Andrew, 77–8
Reed, Jim, **222**
Reefton, 73, 78, 79
Rees Valley, 92, 258, 280–1, **281**
Rees Valley Station, 280
refrigeration, effect on farming, 34, 35
Reid, John, 330
Reihana, Herb, **221**
Reilly, Christopher, 76
Rennison, Geoff, 259
reserves, public, 255–6, 270
Rhodes, George, 31
Rhodes, Robert Heaton, 30–1
Richards, Allan, 242
Richards, Rodger, 328
Richardson Mountains, 79, 92, 95
Richmond Hut, 61
Richmond, Jock, 105
Richmond Range, **216**, 218, 222
Riddle, John, 100
Rimutaka Forest Park, 15, 193
Riordan, Laurie and Fred, 54, 96
Riordans Hut, **54**, 54–5, **55**, 96, 252, 291
Ritchie, Neville, 78
road-building huts, 21, **21**

Roaring Billy Hut, 238
Roaring Billy tributary, Haast, 201
Roaring Stag Lodge, **184**, 184–5, **185**
Roberts, G.J., 255
Roberts Point Track, 104
Robins, Nui, 17, 265, 314
Robinson, William 'Ready Money,' 35
Rochford, John, 87
Rock and Pillar Conservation Area, 149, **168**, 168–70, **169**, **170**
Rock and Pillar Hut Trust, 170
Rockell, John, 163
Rocky Creek Biv, 231
Rodgers Inlet Hut, 201, 204
Roebuck Creek Hut, 218
Rogers Hut, 203, 212–13, **213**
Rokeby Hut, 203
Rolling River, 87
Romanes, Wally, **246**
Rooney's Hut, 79
Ross, Kenneth, 176
Ross, Malcolm, 143
Roth, Gypsy, 62
Rotoiti Londge, 326
Rotoiti Scenic Board, 267
Rotorua, 99, 103, 107
Routeburn Falls Hut, 257, **258**
Routeburn Flats Hut, **2**, 258
Routeburn Track, 24, 25, 111, 280, 281, 284, 287
Rowe, Hugh, 318
Rowlands, Nia, 206
Roxburgh Gorge, 78
Roxburgh, Jason, **46**
Royal Forest & Bird Protection Society of New Zealand, 186, 197, 270, 283
Royal Hut, 61, **61**
Royal New Zealand Air Force, 116, 129, 176, 202, 241, 265, 304, 310, 316
Ruahine Forest Park, 50–1, **51**, 52–3, **53**, 160, 160–1, **161**, 165, 165–6, **166**, 167, 226, **246**, 246–7, **247**, **286**, 289; New Zealand Forest Service huts, 226, **246**, 246–7, **247**, 248, 248–50, **249**, **250**
Ruahine Hut, 248
Ruahine Range, 15, 18, 20, 50, 52, 201, 219, 222, 246, 248, 289–90, 292; deer culling, 197, 201, 220; skiing, **160**, 160–1, **161**
Ruahine Tramping Club, 20, **161**, 165–6, **166**, 248
Ruamahanga River, 184, **185**
Ruapehu Ski Club, 112, 113, 160, 260
Ruataniwha Conservation Park, 140, **140**, **141**, 219
rubbish disposal, 224
Ruddenklau, Laurie, 48
Rundle, John, *The Tararua Book*, 164
Runnymead Hut, 147
Rush, Don, **212**
Russell, John, 51

Sabine Forks Hut, 259
Sabine Hut, 218
Saddle Peak Station, 43
Sagarmatha National Park, Nepal, 262
St James Walkway, 203, 261
St Leonards Station, 30
St Winifred Hut, 144, 145, 178–9, **179**
Salisbury Hut, 24, 132, 287
Salisbury (or Dry) Rock, 251
Salmon, Alex, 259
Sander, Wally, 260
Sanderson, Paul, 51
Sandstone Hut, 43
Satherley, Chris, 248, **248**
Saunders, Keith, **262**

Savage, G., **23**
Saxon Hut, **225**, 287
Sayers Hut, 156
Scamper Torrent Hut, 235, **235**
Scenery Preservation Act 1903, 256
Scenic Preservation Society, 132
scheelite mining, 92, 94, **94**
Schofield, Murray, 273
science research huts, 324–35
Scott, Harry, 138
Scott, Stan, 265
Scottys Biv, 152, 229
Scurr, Jack, 56
Sealy Range, 105, 116, 118, 307
Sealy Tarns, 116, 118
Seddon, Richard, 34, 35
Sefton Biv, 105, **110**, 111, 124
Sentry Biv, 231
Serpentine Hut, 233
Shamrock Hut, 194
Shanks, Jim, 129
Shannon, John, 264
Shell Company, Paua Tramping Club, 146
Shelter Rock Hut, 258, 280–1, **281**
Sherwoods Hut, 171
Shirlmar Station, 32, **32**
Shotover River and Valley, 75, 79, 80, 82
Shute, Alex, 50, **50**
Shutes Hut, 50–1, **51**, 248
Shut-eye Shack, 246, **246**, 248
Siberia Valley, 258, 278
Sierra Range, 310
Sign of the Bellbird, 134, 147
Sign of the Kiwi, 134
Sign of the Packhorse, **134**, 134–5, **135**, 147
Sign of the Takahe, 134
Silver Peaks, 149
Sinclair Range, 61
Singer, Percy, 259
Sir Edmund Hillary Alpine Centre, 118
Sir Robert Hut, 26, **26**
ski huts, 15, 99, 106–7, 111, 112, 116, 118, 160–1, 168–70, 258, 259
skiing, 105, **106**, 106–7, 109, 112, 116, 118, 124, 136, 157, **158**, 160, 160–1, **161**, 162, 168–70, **169**
Skippers Creek, 80, 82
Skippers Saddle, 169
Slaty Creek Hut, 203, 206, **206**, **207**, 232, 291
Slaughter Burn, 326
Slyburn Hut, 290
Smith, E., 50
Smith, Ernie, 174
Smith, Naylor, 302
Smith, Robert, 42
Smith, Ted, **221**, 302
Smith, Tex, 333
Smiths Creek Hut, 146
Smyth Hut, **237**, 238
Snadden, Graeme, 259
Soper, Berna, 186
Soper, Frank, 186
South Huxley Biv, **219**
Southern Alps, 17, 21, 31, 58, 68, 78, 103, 143, 144, 176, 219, 236, 261
Southland, 54, 75, 82, 289; *see also* names of specific places
Southland Community Trust, 191
Southland Tramping Club, 318
Spain, Steven, 35
Sparrowhawk Biv, 249
Speargrass Hut, 218
Spearpoint, Geoff, 24

Springfield, 68
Squid Creek tent camp, 234
Stag Park Country Lodge, 193
Stags Head Hut, 248
Stanfield, Bill, 248
Stanfield Hut, 248
Station Creek Hut, 218
Steffan Memorial Hut, 120, 144
Stenberg, Alfred, 165
Stevenson, Harry, 169
Stewart, Catherine, 18
Stewart Island/Rakiura, 20, 150, 190–1, 197, 200, 290, 292, 326
Still, Jack, 212
Stone Creek Hut, **218**, 219
Stone Hut, 37, **60**
Stone Jug Hut, 150
Stony Creek, Southland, **36**
Stroneschrubie (Erewhon) Station, 33, **33**, 178
Studholme Saddle Biv, 241
Studholme Saddle Hut, 241
Styx Base Camp, Hokitika, **217**
Styx Valley, 234
Sudden Valley Biv, 291
Sullivan brothers, 122, 124, 128
Summit Road project, 134
Summit Road Society, 135
Summit Shelter, 258
Sunrise Hut, 246–7, **247**
Supper Cove Hut, 273
Sutch Search, 146
Suter, Kurt, 119, 280
Sutherland, Bob, 218, 219 Sutherland, Donald, 101, 102, 270
Sutherland, Elizabeth (née Samuel), 270
Sutherland Falls, 101, 102, 270
Sutherland, Fergus, 62
Sutherlands Hut, **42**, 42–3, **43**
Swarbrick, Gary, 322
Swin River, 59
Syme, Don, **296**
Syme Hut, 24, 289, 294, **294**, **295**, 296, **296**
Syme, Rod, 151, 294, 296, **296**

Tainui Hut, 192
Taipo Valley, 261
Tait, John, 267–8, **268**
Takaka, 84, 86
Takitimu Range, 219, 226
Talbot, Arthur, 102
Tamaki River, 248
Tanner, Chas, 312
Taplins Hut, 72, **73**
Taramakau River and catchment, 138, 139, 203, 236
Taranaki Alpine Club, 145
Taranaki, Mt, 14
Tararua Forest Park, 22, 25, **153**, 154–9, 162–4, 171–3, 184–5, 203, 223, **282**, 298–9, 302–3
Tararua Forest Park Management Plan, 172
Tararua Range, 14, 20, 22, 139, 146, **148**, **149**, 150, 151, 155, 219, 289, 290, 291, 292, 298; deer culling, 197, 200, 202, 203; skiing, 157, **158**, 160, 162; Southern Crossing, 154, 156, 157, 158
Tararua Tramping Club, 15, 24, 138, 145, **153**, 154–6, **156**, 157, 158, 171–2, 193; Huts and Tracks Committee, 172
Tararua–Aorangi Huts Committee, 184
Tarn Biv, 249
Tarn Ridge, 289, 298
Tarn Ridge Hut, **298**, **299**
Tarn, Ken, **160**
Tarurarau Biv, 249
Tasman Glacier, **98**, 100, 104, 107, 109, 110, 125, 143, 327

Tasman Reserve, 103, 106, 108
Tasman Saddle Hut, 110
Tasman Valley, 100
Tauherenikau Hut, 15, **153**, 155–6, 171
Tauherenikau Valley, 15, 152, **171**, 171–2, **173**
Taylor, John, 55, 97, **97**, 291
Taylor, Nick, 48
Taylor Range, 59, 60
Taylor, Rowley, 330
Te Anau Downs Station, 270
Te Apunga (Kaimanawa) Hut, 46
Te Araroa Walkway, 58–61, **59**
Te Aroha, 103
Te Awaiti Station, 52
Te Hana, Sally, 184
Te Hapua Hut, 146
Te Hapua Koa, 147
Te Heuheu Tukino IV, Horonuku, 255
Te Kahui Kaupeka Conservation Park, 58
Te Koau Hut, 248
Te Matawai Hut, 15, 26
Te Moemoe Hut, 154
Te Papanui Conservation Park, 41
Te Puia Lodge, 150, 241
Te Totara Hut, 203, 212, **212**, 213
Te Urewera National Park, 197, 202–3, 212, **212**, 220, 221, 255, 256, 260–1
Teichelmann, Ebenezer, 128, **129**
Temple Basin ski area, 258
Temple, Philip, 91
Thames, 78
Thermal Springs Districts Act 1881, 99
Thomas, Barrie, 258, 276
Thomas Hut, 238
Thompson, Archibald, 56
Thompson, Carl ('Thomo'), 277
Thomson, Darby, 104, 105
Thomson, Jane, 113, 159
Thomson, Joff, **198**, 202; *Deer Hunter*, 139, 198, 199
Thomson, John Turnbull, 75–5, 255
Thomson, Priestley, 244
Thorne, Stu, 312
Thornley, Louise, **97**
Thornton, Cuth, 320
Three Johns Hut, 258, 277, **307**, 308, **308**
Three Mile Hut, 208
Three Mile Stream Hut, 244
'Three Passes' tramp, 77, 234, 264, 321
Tiel Creek kokako biv, 300
Tiller, Dave, 233
Timaru, 78, 84, 86, 99, 120, 122
Timpson, Eric, 322
Tin Hut, 97
Tin Jug Hut, 150
Tipling, Boyd, **160**
Tira Lodge, 241
Toaroha Saddle Biv, 231
Toaroha Valley, 228, 229, **229**, 231, **232**, 232–3
Todd, Colin Macdonald, **280**, 310, **310**
toilets, 285, 287, **287**
Toka Biv, 249, **250**
Tokaanu, 103
Tom Cundell Hut, 147, 149
Tom's Creek Hut, 139
Tongariro, 255
Tongariro Alpine Crossing, 112
Tongariro National Park, 99, 103, 107, **112**, 112–13, **113**, 148, **182**, 182–3, 255, 256, **256**, 259–60
Tongariro Natural History Society, 113

Top Butler Hut, 238, **238**
Top Crawford Biv, 229, **230**
Top Crawford (Crawford) Hut, 234
Top Forks Hut, 278–9, **279**
Top Hut (Bealey Spur Hut), **25**, 28, 29, 37
Top Hut (Beech Hut), 62, **63**
Top Hut (Kerin Forks Flat), 278
Top Hut (on Croesus–Moonlight Track), 73
Top Hut (Rock and Pillar Range), 168, **169**
Top Kokatahi Hut, 235
Top Maropea Hut, 226, 249
Top Matakitaki Hut, 242
Top Motueka Hut, 313
Top Olderog Biv, 231
Top Tauherenikau Hut, 154, 157, 171
Top Toaroha Biv, 231
Top Toaroha Hut, 238
Top Waitaha Hut, 238, **239**, 327
Torlesse Range, 68
Totara Stream Hut, 43
Totaranui, 66
tourism, and tourist and climbing huts, 21, 22, 25, 40, 43, 56–7, 79, 99–101, 284, 285–6; after Second World War, 108–10; Aoraki/Mount Cook and West and, 103–5, 258, 276–7; clubs build public huts, 107–8; Milford Track and Fiordland tourism, 21, 24, 25, 99, **101**, 101–3, **102**, 270–2; Rodolph Wigley and private enterprise, **106**, 106–7; surviving huts, 111, 112–41; Tongariro and the Main Trunk Railway, 103
Tourist and Publicity Department, 109
Tourist Department, 99, 101, 102, 103, 105, 109, 112, 113, 122, 127, 128, 136, 144, 154, 255, 256, 257, 264, 270
Tourist Division, 103
Tourist Hotel Corporation (THC), 109, 110, 258, 270, 271, 272
Townsend Hut, 235
tramping, 13–14, 15–17, 79, 107, 113, 118, 132, 138, 139, 145, 154–8, 161, 163, 165–6, 171, 188, 256, 265, 267, 273–5, 280–1, 285, 286, 293, 298, 302, 304–5, 320, 322; and New Zealand Forest Service huts, **223**, 223–4, **224**, 225, 226, 238, 246–7, 248, 249–50; *see also* names of tramping tracks, eg. Milford Track
tramping clubs, 21–2, 107, 132, 138, 145–6, 193, 248, 256; regional, 146–7, **148**, **149**; *see also* names of individual clubs
Travers (A-frame) Hut, 249
Travers Valley, 258, 266, 267–8
Trent–Elizabeth tramping route, 235
Trevor Carter Hut, 218, 290
Trident Hut, 186
Trilobite Hut, 226
Tripp, Charles George, 32, 42, 43, 58
Trott, Fred, 119
Trotter, John, 278
Tse, Hong, 184
Tuapeka gold diggings, **75**, 75–6, **76**
Tukituki River, 165, 166
Tulloch, Russell, 213
Tupari tent camp, 248
Turere Lodge, 194
Turnbull, John, 169
Turner, Cedric, 264, 314
Turner, John Frost, 44–5
Turner, Pam, 45
Turner, Ron, 216, 217–18, 229, 242
'Turners Bush Store,' 192
Turton, John, 328
Tustin, Ken, **273**, **333**
Tutaekuri Hut, 203, 232
Tutaekuri Junction Hut, 206
Tutuwai Hut, 151, 172
Twenty-five (25) Mile Hut, 149, 318
Twins tent camp, 234

Unemployment Board, 72, 90
UNESCO International Hydrological Decade, 327
United-Reform Government, 72
Unknown Hut, **220**
Unknown tent camp, 248
Unwin Hut, 144
Upper Cook Bivouac, 276
Upper Deception Hut, 236
Upper Gridiron Hut, 251, 252, **252**
Upper Spey Hut, 273
Upper Travers Hut, **254**
Urewera region, 197, 202–3, 212, **212**, 220, 221, 255, 256, 260–1
Urquhart, Rod, 90, 91
Urquharts Hut, **90**, 90–1, **91**

V huts, 31
Varcoe family, 115
Vautier, T.P., 50
venison recovery, 221–3, 236, 238, 241, 278
Vercoe, Bert, 201
Victoria Forest Park, 79, 225, **225**, **239**
Victoria Range, 218
Victoria University of Wellington Tramping Club, 146, 151
Vidulich, John, 308
Vink, Greta, **262**
Vink, Rex, **236**
Vosseler, Fred, 150, 154, 155, **155**
Vosseler Hut, 158

Waerenga Hut, 138, 193, **194**, **195**
Waiheke Valley, Ahaura catchment, 203, 206, **206**, **207**
Waihi gold-miners' strike, 72
Waihi River Hut, 43
Waihohono Hut, 103, **112**, 112–13, 260
Waihopai Station, 18
Waikamaka Hut, 248
Waikamaka River, 201
Waikareiti Hut, 260
Waikato Tramping Club, 149
Waimakariri Falls Biv/Hut, 144, **180**, 180–1, **181**
Waimakariri mountains, 144, 314, **315**, 316, **316**, **317**
Waimakariri River and Valley, 41, 68, 69, 143, 144, 149, 180, 264, 265, 316
Waimea Tramping Club, 149, 289
Waingaro Forks, 54, 96
Waingaro Forks Hut, 21, 72, **96**, 96–7, **97**, 291
Waiohine Valley, Tararua Forest Park, **12**, 25
Waiopehu Hut, 148, 290
Waiorau Station, 56, 57
Waipahiki Hut, 225, **225**
Waipaoa Hut, 260
Wairarapa, 146
Waitaha Valley, **234**, 235, 236, **239**, **327**, 327–8, **328**, **329**
Waitakere Hut, 147
Waitakere Ranges, 15, 146–7
Waitomo, 103
Waiuta, Blackwater gold mine, 79, **79**
Wakatipu Scheelite Company, 92
Wakefield Gully, Golden Bay, **72**
Wakelings Hut, 248
Wakelings tent camp, **248**, 248–9
Waldie, Bob, 313
Walker, Harry, 91, 274
Wall, Jack, 48
Wallers Hut, 92, 95
Walls Whare, 146
Walter Peak Station hut, **39**
Walton, J., 17
Wanaka Station, 278

Wanaka–Makarora area, 290
Wanderers Tramping Club (Christchurch), 147, 149
Wanganui Tramping Club, **148**, 149, 307
Wanganui Valley, **237**
Wangapeka River and Valley, 54, 87
Wangapeka Track, 87–8, **88**, **89**, 218, 223, 224
war: First World War, 37, 50, 68, 80, 94, 102, 105, 112, 134, 140, 154, 294; Korean War, 94; New Zealand Wars, 99; Second World War, 17, 18, 37, 43, 87, 94, 95, 102, 108, 138, 146, 147, 150, 160, 168–9, 174, 192–3, 197, 201, 265, 274, 296, 309, 314, 334; Vietnam War, 94
Ward, Sir Joseph, 103
Warren, Jim, **222**
Watson, Rick, **262**
Wayby, Evan, **39**
Webster, Joyce, 163
Weka Hut, 120
Welch, Elwyn, **326**
Welch, John, 302
Welcome Flat, 9, 14
Welcome Flat Hut, 104, 122, 263, **263**
Wellington, 72, 87, 96, 146, 192
Wellington Botanical Society, 308
Wellington City Council Water Board, 192
Wellington Interclub Ski Sports competition, 163
Wellington Regional Water Board, 193–4
Wellington Tramping & Mountaineering Club (WT&MC; 'Tongue and Meats'), 146, 193, 302
West Coast, 34, 68, 99, 103, 104, 107, 108, 122, 136, 143, 188, 199, 203, 206, 216, 222, 261, 289, 290–1, 292; Department of Conservation two-bunk huts, **288**, **288**; Forest Service four-bunk huts, **232**, 232–5, **233**, **234**, **235**; Forest Service six-bunk huts, 236, **236**, **237**, 238, **238**, **239**; Forest Service two-bunk bivouacs, **228**, 228–9, **229**, **230**, 231, **231**; mining, 71, 73, 74, 75, 78–9, 90, 99; native logging operations, 224; *see also* names of specific places
West Coast Alpine Club, 145
West Coast Beech Scheme, 283
West Dome Station, 82
West End Station, 68
West Matakitaki Valley, 242, **243**
'West Sabine Wilderness Area,' 267
Westland National Park, 255, 256, 258
Westland National Park Board, 131
Westland Tai Poutini National Park, 21, **27**, 122–31, 136, **136**, 285, 310
Whakaari Conservation Area, 92, **92**, **93**, 94–5, **95**
Whakapapaiti Hut, **256**, 260
Whanahuia Range, 160
Whangaehu River, **182**, 182–3, 294
Whanganui National Park, 255, 256, 261, 289
Whareorino Forest, 293
Whariwharangi Hut, 30, 66, **66**, **67**, 259
Whataroa Valley, 286
Wheel Creek Hut, 218
Wheeler, Ron, 124
Whirinaki Forest Park, 203, **212**, 212–13, **213**, 224, 287
Whitcombe, Henry, 203
Whitcombe River and Valley, 14, 203, 220–1, 228, 231, 236, **239**, 325
White River and Valley, 265, 314, **314**, **315**, 316, **316**
Whitehorn Pass, 320
Whitehorn Spur Biv, 229
Whitehouse, Ian, 277
Whitnell, Bill, 52, 53
Whitnell Hut, 52–3
Whymper Hut, 286
Wigley, Alexander (Sandy), 140
Wigley, Harry, **106**, 108, 109, 169
Wigley, Jessie, 140
Wigley, Rodolph, **106**, 106–8, 119, 122, 140, **140**
Wilberforce Valley, 90–1, **91**, 220, 264, 276, **276**–7, **277**, 321, **321**

Wilburn, Alan, **332**
Wilderness Act, 151
wilderness areas, 22, 151, 267
Wilderness Recreation in New Zealand (FMC), 22
Wildlife Service, 260, 262, 283, 326
Wilkin, Robert, 56, 278
Wilkin Valley, 143, 257, **278**, 278–9, **279**
Wilkins, Brian, **318**
Wilkinson, Blue, 246
Wilkinson, Gaylene, **90**
Wilkinson Hut, 216, 233
Wilks, Charlie, 208
Willcocks, Constable, 52
Williams, Gordon, **326**
Williams, Percy, 276
Williams, Vic, 106, 128, 129, 276
Wills, Gavin, 110
Wilmot Pass, 103
Wilson, Bill, 163
Wilson, Cedric, 164
Wilson, James, 114
Wilson, P., **198**
Winchcombe, Peter and Rodney, 260
Wire, Jack, 47
Wiren, Arch, 176
Wisely Hut, 326, **326**
women: and Canterbury Mountaineering Club, 17, 180; separate quarters from men, 17, 100, **100**, 112, 124, 132, 140, 145–6; in tramping clubs, 145–6, 147
Wood, Keith, 172
Wood, Ralph, 149
Woodhead, J., 114
Woodrow, Stewart Island/Rakiura, 200
Woolshed Creek Hut, **304**, 304–5, **305**
Wright, Hugh F., 119
Wylie, Bob, Dave and Jack, 94, **95**
Wylie, John, 94
Wyn Irwin Hut, 145
Wynn, Owen, 318

Yeoman's Track, 53
Yerex, George Franklin, 197, 198, **198**, 200–1, 202, 208, 215
Young, John, 308
Young Men's Christian Association (YMCA), 147; Christchurch Branch, 147
Young South Valley, 258
Youth Hostel Association (YHA), 134–5

Zekes Hut, 297, **297**